National Intelligencer Newspaper Abstracts 1811-1813

Joan M. Dixon

HERITAGE BOOKS
2007

HERITAGE BOOKS
AN IMPRINT OF HERITAGE BOOKS, INC.

Books, CDs, and more—Worldwide

For our listing of thousands of titles see our website
at
www.HeritageBooks.com

Published 2007 by
HERITAGE BOOKS, INC.
Publishing Division
65 East Main Street
Westminster, Maryland 21157-5026

Copyright © 1997 Joan M. Dixon

All rights reserved. No part of this book may be reproduced or transmitted in any form or by any means, electronic or mechanical, including photocopying, recording or by any information storage and retrieval system without written permission from the author, except for the inclusion of brief quotations in a review.

International Standard Book Number: 978-0-7884-0658-2

TABLE OF CONTENTS

Preface v

National Intelligencer
   Washington, D C, 1811 1

National Intelligencer
   Washington, D C, 1812 98

Daily National Intelligencer
   Washington, D C, 1813 247

Index 326

Preface

National Intelligencer Newspaper Abstracts, 1811-1813
Joan M Dixon

Covering three years of information, this third volume in the series contains more abstracts from *The National Intelligencer* [formerly-*and Washington Advertiser*,] the first newspaper printed in Washington, D. C. Entries include advertisements, deaths, appointments by the president, legal notices, insolvent debtors, marriages, tax lists, miscellaneous notices, letters in the post office, military promotions, court cases, deaths by accident, postmaster appointments & opening of new post offices, impressed seamen lists, jurors, prisoners of war, skirmishes, Hse o/Rep-petitions & many others. The abstracts are a great aid to finding locations, ages or relationships of relatives in the Maryland, Washington and Virginia areas. People in the news of all locales are included. Items or events which might be a clue as to the location, age or relationship of an individual have been copied. The author has organized the material by year and date to make finding specific days easier. Surname and *land tract* index & a list of abbreviations is provided.

No attempt has been made to correct the spelling. Due to the length of some articles, it was necessary to present only the highlights of same; copy of the complete news item, letter, Chancery record, etc, is recommended.

Abbreviations:
abt-about	Eliza-Eliza
adj-adjoining	est-estate
appt-appointed	funer-funeral
A A Co-Anne Arundel Co [Md]	Michl-Michael
bet-between	Montg Co-Montgomery County
Calv Co-Calvert Co [Md]	mrd-married
cvlry-calvary	Md-Maryland
Co-Company/County	Nathl-Nathaniel
Cmder-Commander	oppo-opposite
Cmdor-Commodore	PG Co-Prince Georges Co [Md]
Danl-Daniel	prop-property/proprietor
D C-District of Columbia	prsnl est-personal est
decd-deceased	recd-received
dtd-dated	trust-trustee
dwlg-dwelling	v-vs/vie
Eliz-Elizabeth	Wash-Washington

| National Intelligencer |
| Published by Jos Gales jr |

1811

THU JAN 3, 1811
Mrd: Sam'l Sprigg, of PG Co, Md, to Miss Violetta Lansdale, of Wash, on Jan 1.

Died: Mrs Hellen, consort of Walter Hellen, of Wash, on Dec 31, 1810.

Orphans Crt of Wash Co, D C. Jan 3, 1811. Prsnl est of Matthew Brown, late of said city, dec'd. -Eliz Brown, admx.

Wash Polemick Soc meeting at Mr Findlay's Acad. -M St Clair Clarke, Pres Pro Temp, Robt Polk, Sec.

For London-the coppered ship, *Robt Burns*, Capt Thos Parson; passage only. -Jacob Morgan, Alexandria.

Orphans Crt of Dorchester Co, Md. Ltrs of adm on prsnl est of Lt John Trippe, late of U S N, dec'd. -Jas Kemp

In Chancery, Dec 22, 1810, State of Md. Wm H Pleasants, trustee of the will of Thos Pleasants. Ratify sale made by Wm H Pleasants in 1809 of 170 1/8 acs, cld *Brooke's Addition*, lying in A A Co & Montg Co, to Rich'd Green for $1700; also 89 acs to John Ellicott, part of *Brooke's Addition* & part of *Dickinson's Delight*, $1000; also 40 acs sold to Thos Davis for $500. -Test, Nichs Brewer, Reg Cur C.

SAT JAN 5, 1811
To be sold-hse, prop of John Vint, for tax due Wash City Corp. -Henry M Queen, coll 4th ward. To be sold-hse, sq 88, prop of Nicholas Voss, for tax due Wash City Corp. -H M Queen, coll 4th ward.

TUE JAN 8, 1811
Madame De Stael, authoress, having rec'd orders to quit France, & being permitted to make Cassel, Munich or the U S of America her future resid, chose the latter.

To be sold-hse in sq 929, prop of Jas Waugh, for tax due Wash City Corp. To be sold-hse in sq 906, prop of Electius Edelin's heirs, for tax due Wash City Corp. To be sold-hse in sq 381, prop of Notley Maddox, for tax due Wash City Corp. To be sold-hse in sq 907, prop of Philip Spalding, for tax due Wash City Corp. -H M Queen, coll 4th ward.

Notice-persons that have an acc't against him to bring them in for payment; those indebted will be waited on in a few days. -W S Nichols, Gtwn.

Wanted to hire-6 or 8 black boys to work in the rope walk; also black woman for hsework that can cook & wash & a girl ab't 14 yrs old. -Nathl H Heath.

Orphans crt of Wash Co, D C. Jan 5, 1811. Prsnl est of Jesse Baily, late of said city, dec'd. -Mary Baily, admx.

Collector's sale-The Wash Theatre, for tax due the Wash City Corp. -Ezl MacDaniel, coll 2nd ward.

Collector's sale-brick hse in sq 461, for tax due the Wash Corp by Crookshank's & Thompson heirs. -Ezl MacDaniel, coll.

To be sold-improvement in sq 875, lge brick hse, prop of Wm M Duncanson, for tax due Wash Corp. -H M Queen, Col-Ward 4.

Wm B Giles, re-elected Senator of U S, from Va.

Reward-$100 for Phil, also known as Dr Johnson, mulatto man, ab't 36 yrs of age. -Seth Smith, living in Jefferson Co, Va.

Ranaway-Henny, negro woman, ab't 50 yrs of age; bought her of a Mr Gregley on Capital Hill, 20 mos ago; he bought her from the est of Mr Geo Lee, dec'd, of Chas Co, Md. -Ann Kedglie

<u>Ladies with ltrs in Wash P O. Jan 1, 1811:</u>

Mrs Aleson	Miss Eliza Brown	Sarah B Adams
Dolly Bosfort	Ann Dorsey	Henrietta Brown
Mary Downing c/o John Lyons	Mrs Susan Essex	Eliz Earp
Miss Eliza Edmondson	Martha Gordon c/o John Mention	Matilda Hawkins
Madam Galezio	Henrietta Harrison	Mrs Harriot Jackson
Mrs Sarah Love	Mary Lowry	Sarah Miles
Susan Peed	Mrs Eliz Peltz	Miss Eliza Ramsay
Mrs Adela Shanon	Mrs Charity Smuthers	Miss Rosa Shanks
Mrs Ann Tilly	Hester Terpin	Mrs S Walker
Miss Nancy Wilson	Mrs Peggy Williams c/o Jas Johnson	
Mrs Ann Wimsett	Mrs Anne Walker	Mrs Mary White

THU JAN 10, 1811
For sale-small cargo of coal at the wharf south of the Navy Yd, on board the sloop *Mohawk*. -Apply to Wm Morrissett, on board.

Crct Crt of Wash Co., D C-Crt of Chancery. Conrad Dutteroe & Fred'k Wm Shriver, cmplnts, vs the heirs & reps of Andrew Kalderbach & others, dfndnts. Public auction at Ruth's Tavern, Gtwn, parts of lot 184, 183, 221 & half of lot 208, in *Beatty & Hawkins Addition to Gtwn*, with improvements, to satisfy creditors of Andrew Kaldenbach, dec'd. -Chas Glover, trust.

Meeting of the Wash Benevolent Soc of Young Men, Dec 12, Mr Geo Watterston-orator. -R Johnston, steward.

Sale of the right, title & int claim of Jas B Korkight in lot 24 sq 101 with improvements; suit of Jas Moore against said Korkight. -Wash Boyd, mrsh'l D C. [See Jan 17] Wash Co, D C.

I certify that Thos G Slye brought before me a stray bay mare. -Rich'd S Briscoe, Justice of the Peace.

Orphans crt of PG Co, Md. Ltrs of test on prsnl est of Baruch Duckett, late of PG Co, Md, dec'd. -Wm Bowie of Walter, exc.

Congress-Petition of Isaac Wayne, heir & exc of late Maj Genr'l Anthony Wayne, praying remission of sums found against the est of his fr. -Referred to committee.

John O'Connell, insolvent debtor, confined in Wash Co, D C, prison, for debt. -Wm Brent, clk.

Paragraphs on Banks by Erick Bollman, M D, just rec'd & for sale by Dan'l Rapine, Capt Hill; Orleans Term Reports of cases argued & determined in Sup Crt of Terr of Orleans; important decision by F X Martin, a Judge of that Court. Also a few copies of *The Magistrates Guide & Citizens Councillor*-a digest abstract of those laws of Md.

Note lost-Ross & Getty's note in favor of John Ross, for $500, dt'd Jan 1, 1811. -Ross & Getty, Gtwn.

SAT JAN 12, 1811
Despatches from Gov Claiborne state that Fulwar Skipwith, styling himself Govn'r of Fla, had avowed to resist the interposition of the United States. Skipwith & his forces are in the fort of Baton Rouge.

Meeting at Long's Htl, Capt Hill, mgrs to Generis's Balls: Chas W Goldsborough, Capt Hunt, Capt Fenwick, Silas Butler, Buller Cocke, Lt Williams, Lt Hanna, Wm Sanford.

Lost-jointed cane, cypered I T. -John Teackle.

Dan'l Adlington, insolvent debtor, confined in Wash Co, D C, prison, for debt. -Wm Brent, clk.

For sale-59 lots noted on Fenwick's map of Gtwn. -Tho S Lee.

Public sale at late resid of Walter Bowie, dec'd; horses & sheep. -Mary Bowie, admx; Wm Bowie of Walter, adm, PG Co-Md.

For sale-small casks of London wine. -Toppan Webster, nr W Mkt.

TUE JAN 15, 1811
Ration in small hospital at N Y, under the c/o Dr Sam'l R Marshall, surg-U S N;

has defrayed expenses for seamen, etc.

Died: on Jan 12, Vachel Stevens, late examiner-Genr'l of Western Shore of Md, age 58 yrs.

Hse o/Reps: Petition of Paul Beck & others of Phil, for imposition of duties on shot imported into the U S. -Referred to committee

State of Md-in Chancery, Jan 3, 1811. Dan'l Carrol of Hunting Ridge, Wash Van Bibber, Jos Heston, John Merryman, Caleb Merryman, John Mitchell, John Royer Champayne, Job Smith, Edw Pumphrey, Zebulon Hollinsworth, Wm Hammond, & Jonathan Munro, vs Chas Carroll of Carrollton, Nicholas Carroll, Dan'l Carroll of Duddington, Wm Smith, Isaac Van Bibber, *John Tasker Carter, *Geo Carter, Robt Mitchell & *Priscilla his wife, *Francis Tasker Jones, *Thos Ap Jones, *Eliz Jones, *Jane Jones, *Sarah Tekel Jones, Spencer Ball & *Betty Landon his wife, John Yates Chinn & *Sarah Fairfax his wife, *Harriot Lucy Maund, Robt Berkeley & *Julia his wife, *Sophia Carter, *Harriot Peck, *John Carter Peck, *Emanuel Peck & *Tasker Carter Quinlan. The Balt Co consisting of the dfndnts contracted to convey sundry tracts of land to the cmplnts; some have pd-the whole or part of said purchase money. Robt Carter, a mbr of said co, by his last will devised his int to dfndnts [*dfndnts named] & has since departed this life; severally reside in Va or elsewhere out of Md; Eliz Jones, Sarah Tekell Jones, Jane Jones, Harriot Peck, John Carter Peck, Emanuel Peck & Tasker Carter Quinlan, are severally infants of tender age. Bill is to obtain conveyances to cmplnts for lands so contracted to be sold to them. -Nich Brewer, Reg C C.

Congress-a bill for the relief of the heirs of the late brig Genr'l Anthony Wayne, read a 3d time & passed unanimously.

Post Ofc dept changes:
Eastham, Mass-Harding Knowles, vice Sam'l Freeman, rsgn'd;
Scarboro, Me-Abraham Millckin vice Wm Wood, rsgn'd;
Rutland, Vt-Wm D Smith, vice Dr Hooker, left the place;
New Holland, Pen-Sam'l Holl, vice Geo Thompson, rsgn'd;
Kaskaskia, Indiana Terr-Wm Arundell, vice Jas Finney, dismissed;
Mt Holley, Vert-Nath'l T Sprague, vice Miles Clark, dismissed;
Castleton, Vt-Sam'l Moulton, vice R C Mallary, rsgn'd;
Port Royal, Va-Newton Berryman, vice Jno Gray, mv'd away;
Harper's Ferry, Va-Roger Humphreys, vice T Beall, mv'd away;
Concord, Mass-John L Tuttle, vice Wm Parkman, rsgn'd;
Vienna, Md-Jas Horner, vice Edw H Blake, rsgn'd;
Blanford, Mass-Amos M Collins, vice Isaac Hardin, rsgn'd;
Waynesboro, Ga-Sam'l Sturgess, vice Hamilton Wynn, rsgn'd;
Church Hill, Md-Ed Robeson, vice J Watson, rsgn'd;
Piscataway, Md-David Koones, vice H B Berry, rsgn'd;
Jericho, Vt-Pliny Blackman, vice Wm Messenget, mv'd away;
Calland's store, Va-Jabez Smith, vice Sam'l Armistead, rsgn'd;
Chenango Point, N Y-Jacob McKenney, vice Robt Morrell, rsgn'd;

Chas City C H, Va-Wm Singleton, vice John Gregory, dec'd;
Colchester, Va-Peter Wagener, vice Wm Mellan, rsgn'd;
Lancaster C H, Va-Oliver Towles, vice Thos West, rsgn'd;
Hendersonville, Ten-Littleton Henderson, vice Rennet Henderson, rsgn'd;
Morrisville, Pen-Geo Lamning, vice Moses Wells, rsgn'd.
New Post ofcs est in Dec 1810:
Great Crossings, Scott Co, Ky-Mareen Duvall, postmaster:
Clover Dale, Botetourt Co, Va-Thos Evans;
Campbell's Mills, Abbeville dist, S C-Jas Cobb;
Liberty Hall, Morgan Co, Ga-Wm C Stokes;
Carlisle, Schoharie Co, N Y-Philip J Cromwell;
Boyd's, Newbury dist, S C-Archibald Boyd;
Mt Vernon, Oglethorpe Co, Ga-Thos Burdell;
Lyons, Ontario Co, N Y-Ezekiel Price;
Charleston, Worcester Co, Mass-Wm P Rider;
Southboro, Worcester Co, Mass-Peter Fay.
Offices discont'd:
Macfarlandsville, N C & Cressapsburg, Md.

THU JAN 17, 1811
Ltr rec'd from Wm Dickson, Reg of the land ofc at Nashville to sec of Treas-dt'd Jun 9, 1810: contained part of a ltr from Wm H Winston, clk of Co Crt of Madison, Miss; regarding persons purchasing land from Col Mich'l Harrison & not from the U S; the claim of Zachariah Cox, in said co, is making a considerable noise. Ltr from Wm Dixon, Reg of the land ofc at Nashville, to sec o/Treas, dt'd Jul 30, 1810: he encloses the returns for the month of June.

Congress-Petition of Eugene De Leitensdorfer, ntv of Tyrol, for compensation in land or money for svcs to Gen Eaton in Dern, as inspec Genr'l & Chief Engineer to America Army-referred.

Caution: persons take notice that lot 24 sq 101, advertised to be sold on the 19th by the mrsh'l of the dist, as prop of Jas B Korkright, was with many other lots in Wash, cnvyd by Benj Stoddert & Uriah Forrest to Jas Greenleaf, deed dt'd Sep 20, 1794; said lot & others were contracted to be sold to Walter Stewart, since dec'd; by deed dt'd May 13, 1796, Greenleaf cnvyd all his prop in Wash City to Robt Morris & John Nicholson-with some conditions; May 13, 1796-Morris & Nicholson had not yet pd for said lots; Jun 26, 1797, lots conveyed to Henry Pratt, Thos Willing Francis, John Miller jr, John Ashley & Jacob Baker, as trustees of an aggregate fund; W Stewart failed to pay for lots contracted. -Henry Pratt, Thos W Francis, John Miller jr, John Ashley, Jacob Baker, assigness of Morris & Nicholson & trustees of aggregate fund. John Miller jr, assignee of Jas Greenleaf under laws of Pa & U S. Wm Cranch, assignee of Jas Greenleaf & his trust, under law of Md, by their atty in fact. -Jas Greenleaf.

For sale-new brig, *Secretary Hamilton*. -John Tayloe.

Langdon Cheves, elected to Cong from S C, vice R Marion, rsgn'd.

SAT JAN 19, 1811
My wife, Sarah Armistead, has eloped from my bed & board. I will not pay any debts she may contract. -John Armistead.

In Chancery-Dec 18, 1810. Ratify sale made by Rich'd Watkins, trustee for rl est of Absalom Bedds, late of Montg Co, Md, dec'd; sold 205 acs in said co, $5.05 per ac; & 259 acs at $8 per ac. -Nichs Brewer, Reg Cur Can.

Collector's sale-brick hse in sq 502-3; do in sq 503 & 1 do in sq 504 [now in occupancy of Mr John Chalmers,] for taxes due by Messrs Pratt, Francis & others to Wash Corp. -Ezl MacDaniel, coll of ward 2

TUE JAN 22, 1811
Died: Mrs Cath Van Cortlandt, w/o Col Pierre Van Cortlandt & d/o Geo Clinton, VP of the U S; after an illness of svr'l wks, at Peekskill, on Jan 10.

Chain bridge-the breach of the Schuylkill bridge by a drove of cattle. Article written by Jas Findley, Union town, Pa.

Committed to Wash Co, D C, jail-Nancy Johnson, yellow woman, age ab't 21. -Cartwright Tippett, kpr of the jail.

THU JAN 24, 1811
Account of the purchase of sundry bills of exchange by John Stricker, Navy agent at Balt, dt'd between May 10, 1805 & Feb 21, 1807, amt'd to $256,000.

Wash Co, D C-In Chancery. Jas Stephens, Wm O'Neale, & Wm Doughty vs Ann Cook, adm & Thos Charles, & Sam'l Cook, heirs & reps of Chas Cook, dec'd. Ratify sale by Chas Glover, trustee appt'd, of west half of lot 18, sq 127, in Wash City for $770. -Wm Brent, clk.

Mrd: Wm Dudley Digges, of PG Co, Md, to Miss Norah Carroll, d/o Dan'l Carroll of Duddington, of Wash, on Jan 22, by Rev Mr Plunket.

Died: Mr Sam'l Duvall, in Fred'k co, Md, on Jan 17, srvyr of said county.

Jacob Leonard, watch maker, successor to Mr Geo W Riggs; new establishment on crnr of Jefferson & Bridge Sts, Gtwn.

Hse o/Reps: 1-Bill for relief of Lt Col Wm Beall, read twice & referred to committee. 2-Petition of Messrs Jas M'Culloch, Dan'l Ramsay & Laurie, colls of Port of Balt-increase in salary. 3-Pet of Dan'l Pettibone, praying to be employed in warming & ventilating the Reps hall-referred.

Congress-Petition of Moses Austin & John R Jones; they have been employed in working a mine in La, & praying assistance to enable them to prosecute their labors to advantage, viz a charter of incorporation to them-referred.

Geo M Bibb, is elected a Senator of the U S from Ky.

SAT JAN 26, 1811
Persons with claims against the est of Wm Augustine Washington, dec'd, are to exhibit same to Robt Beverley, exc of W A Washington, dec'd. -Gtwn, Columbia.

Elisha Hall, insolvent debtor, confined in Wash Co, D C, prison for debt. -Wm Brent, clk.

Appointments by the Pres of U S, confirmed by the Senate:
David Robinson-mrsh'l of dist of Vt;
Robt Habersham-com'r of loans for Ga;
Nehemiah Tilton of Dela-Reg of land ofc in Adams Co, Miss Terr;
Thos Freeman of Miss Terr-srvyr of U S south of Tenn;
Sam'l Mathews-srvyr & inspec of Rev for Port of Nixonton;
Wm Joyner-Coll of Port of Beaufort, S C;
Martin Duralde jr-mrsh'l of Orleans, vice, John M Fortier, rsgn'd;
Thos B Dorsey-atty of U S for Md, vice John Stephen, rsgn'd;
Sam'l Herrick-atty of U S for Ohio, vice Wm Creighton, rsgn'd;
Jona Smith-inspec for Port of Berevly, Mass;
Robt Butler-srvyr of Port of Smithfield, Va.
Renewed Commissions: Wm Hull-Gov of Mich Terr for 3 yrs;
Fred'k Bates-sec of La Terr for 4 yrs;
Thos G Thornton-mrsh'l of dist of Maine for 4 yrs;
Robt Cochran-mrshl of dist of S C for 4 yrs;
John Childress-mrshl for dist of West Tenn for 4 yrs;
Mich'l M'Cleary-mrshl of dist of New Hamp for 4 yrs;
Peter Curtenius-mrshl of dist of N Y-4 yrs.

Wanted-young man who has srv'd reg apprenticeship to tanning business & capable as a foreman. -Wm Cocking, Wash City.

TUE JAN 29, 1811
Hse o/Reps-relief of Geo Armroyd & Co-the drawback of duties on certain merchandise exported from Phil.

Sec of war is to settle the exterior line of the public land at West Point, N Y, now in dispute with Thos North, the adj proprietor.

Public sale by order of the Orphans Crt of Montg Co, Md. One moiety of a grist mill together with one moiety of two tracts; *Beall's Industry* & *Shaver is Shaved*-& dwl g hse; nr Thos Gittings; also svr'l negroes to be sold at late dwlg place of Jas W Perry. -Josiah Jones, Robt Jones, adms.

Partnership of Thos Baker & Elisha Riggs is dissolved by mutual consent; payments to Thos Baker, Gtwn.

Runaway-Maria, negro girl; says she is free & came from Charles-town, Va & her mthr lives on Mr Thos Hammon's place, nr that town. -Matthias Shaffner, shrf of Wash Co, Md.

Runaway-Will, negro man; says he is prop of Mr Rich'd Snowden, living in A A Co, Md. -John Ireland, shrf of Calvert Co, Md.

My wife, Nancy Morrow, hath eloped from my bed & board. I am determined to pay no debts of her contracting. -Patrick Kelly.

To be sold-hse in sq 907, prop of Philip Spalding, for tax due by the same to the Wash Corp. -Henry M Queen, coll-4th ward.

THU JAN 31, 1811
Congress-1-Petition of Dr Jas Smith, of Balt, he has procured vaccine matter & praying permission to disseminate it within the dist of Col, asking for comp that Cong may think proper. 2-Petition of Peter Casso, he had furnished troops of the U S whilst at Terre Au Boeuf-praying Governmental satisfaction.

Died: Dan'l Hylton, clk of the Privy Cncl of Va, on Jan 26.

Walter Swain of PG Co, Md; insolvent debtor. -Dan'l Clarke, Assoc Judge of the First Judicial dist.

Sam'l Hanson of Sam'l, Wash, Jan 28, 1811-Ltr regarding gross waste & mismanagement in the Navy Dept.

SAT FEB 2, 1811
Zerah Colbourn, born in Vt, age 6 yrs; arrv'd in Wash; possesses an extra-ordinary power of calculation; may be seen at Long's Hotel.

Public sale-order of Montg Co Crt; tract of land, 208 acs, where Mrs Verlinda Beall lives, late the prop of Mr Zephaniah Beall, dec'd. -Wm Duley, Dan'l Beall sr, Eden Beall, com'rs.

In Chancery, Jan 7, 1811. Overton Carr, Jona. B Carr, Sam'l Carr & Eleanor his wife, & Dabney Carr & Eliz his wife. vs, Geo Lowe, Sally Lowe, Lethe Greenwell, Jas Moore & Ann his wife, Mich'l Ranson Lowe & Winifred Drury. O Carr, fr of cmplnts, purch'd of Nichs Lowe, land in PG Co, Md; O Carr pd for same but died before obtaining a conveyance, leaving the cmplnts his heirs at law. Nichs Lowe is also dead, leaving the dfndnts his heirs at law. Jas & Ann Moore, & Mich'l Lowe & Ranson Lowe-reside in Wash D C. -Nichs Brewer, Reg C C.

TUE FEB 5, 1811
Pvt sale of hse & lot-on sq 378 on 10th St. -John McClelland.

For sale-mulatto boy, ab't 20 to 25 yrs of age, accustomed to take c/o horses. -Henry Pye, Cornwall's Neck, Chas Co, Md.

Order of Orphans Crt of PG Co, Md-sale of negro boy ab't 12 yrs of age, & horse colt, for benefit of the creditors of Colmore Duval, dec'd. -Chas Duvall, adm, d b n of C D, dec'd.

THU FEB 7, 1811
Supplement sale by auction-at hse of Mr Patrick Kelly, nr the canal on N J Ave, hsehld & kitchen furn. -Andrews & Jones, aucts.

Died: Alfred Madison, s/o Wm Madison, of Va & nphw of the Pres of the U S, in Phil, Jan 30.

Died: Mrs Sarah Gardiner, w/o Mr John Gardiner of Wash, on Feb 6, after severe illness. Funeral from her late dwlg-Pa Av.

Gentlemen of the Merchants & Traders of Phil Co & City, coming to Wash to present to Congress their ardent wishes for renewal of Charter of the Bank of the U S: Wm Newbold, Thos W Francis, Jacob Sperry, Thos P Cope, J S Lewis, Thos Leiper, Jos Grice, Sam'l Smith, Jacob Vogdes & Fred'k Foering.

Wm W Vernon, insolvent debtor, confined in Wash Co, D C, prison, for debt. -Wm Brent, clk.

Notice-those indebted to the est of Rich'd Beck, dec'd, are not to pay same to anyone but W S Nicholls, Gtwn.

For sale-land in Montg Co, Md, 530 acs, good dwlg hse. Mr Henry Robertson will show same; info from Walter Jones, or Benj G Orr, Wash.

SAT FEB 9, 1811
Jas Pleasants & F T Brooke, esqs, have been elected Judges of the Crt of Appeals of Va.

Mrd: Lt Robt D Wainwright of Marine Corps, to Miss Juliana B Scott, y/d/o late Gustavus Scott, of Wash, on Feb 7, by Rev A T M'Cormick.

For sale-a number of lots in Wash City; prop purch'd some yrs back by Benj Stoddert, of Wash, by a company of gentlemen in Norfolk: Thos Truxtun, Wm Plume, Moses Myers, Campbell & Wheeler, Wm Pennock, John Cowper, Thos Willock, Munford Beverley, Josiah Parker, Alex'r Wilson, Jas Taylor jr, Theo Armistead, Francis S Taylor, Dr J K Reed, Robt Taylor, John Granberry & Alex'r Maclure. -Luke Wheeler & John Cowper-trustees.

Meeting for election of Dirs of the Domestic Manufacture Co will be at the Crt hse. -John Macleod, agent, Alexandria.

For sale-403 1/2 acs nr St Clements Bay, St Mary's Co, Md. -Henry Allstan, agent, for Rich'd Lewellin, of Jffrsn C'y, Va.

Wm Gobright, insolvent debtor, confined in Wash Co, D C prison for debt. -Wm Brent, clk.

TUE FEB 12, 1811

In Chancery-Wash Co, D C. John G Ladd vs Amariah Frost. Bill is to foreclose a mortgage of half of lot 17 sq 634 in Wash City; given by A Frost to John G Ladd; dfndnt not found within his dist; cmplnt says that A Frost is not an inhabitant of D C. -Wm Brent, clk.

In Chancery-Wash Co, D C. John E Rigden vs Lucy Rigden & others. Ratify sale by Ninian Magruder, trustee, of lot 5 on High St, in Beatty & Hawkins add to Gtwn. -Wm Brent, clk, Wash Co, D C.

Edw Burrow's brought before me a stray cow. -Nichs Young, Jan 22

Hse o/Reps-1-Act for relief of Wm Mills: now imprisoned in Middlesex, Conn, shall be released & dischg'd from all claim & demand of U S. -J B Varnum, spkr of Hse o/Reps. 2-Act to change the name of Lewis Grant to Lewis Grant Davidson; enacted by the Sen & Hse o/Reps. Lewis Grant was devisee of Sam'l Davidson, late dec'd, both of Wash, D C.

Exchange for negroes-land where I live in Pr Wm Co, Va, 1800 acs & dwlg hse. -Wm Alexander

Mrd: Mr Robt Scott, of Ga, to Miss Susan R Madison, d/o Bishop Madison, Jan 31, by Rev John Bracken, in Williamsburg, Va.

Orphans Crt of PG Co, Md. Ltrs of adm on est of Sam'l Hepburn, dec'd; persons with claims to show same. -Gabr'l P Van Horn-adm.

D C to Wit. U S of America to Ezekiel McDaniel, greeting: where as Henry Pratt, Thos Willing Francis, John Mill jr, John Ashley & Jacob Baker, have exhibited their bill of cmplnt in Wash Co D C Crct Crt as a Crt of Chancery; E MacDaniel & all other persons are by authority enjoined from selling hse on sq 502, 3 hses on sq 503, hse on sq 504, Wash City, until further order of the Crt in the premises. -Wm Brent, Ck.

THU FEB 14, 1811

Hse o/Reps-Petition of David Cady, jr, of N Y State; in Rev war he rec'd a wound in svc of U S-sent to hosp in Albany & no attention was pd to him, taken to his own hse & attended by a surg at his own expence, for which he prays relief & an increase in pension. -Referred.

Lost-bet Wash & Fairfax Crt hse, a mortgage of Sam'l Daniel to me, for 100 acs of Hampshire land, a bond of Rich'd R Lee for $38, one of Alex'r Sterling for $30. Lodge same with John Mattox, at Fairfax Crt hse. -John M Gilmour.

SAT FEB 16, 1811
Town of Liberty, Dec 24, 1810. Ltr regarding land claims written by Squire Lee, srvyr in dist of West Fla in yrs 1806-07. Lee now has no interest in lands out of Miss Terr. Henry Baron has established an ofc in Urbana, Champaign Co, Ohio, to buying & selling land on commission, paying taxes, etc; he will practice as an atty at law.

TUE FEB 19, 1811
Wm Banks & Peter Watkins, negro men, committed to Fred'k Co, Md jail as runaways; Banks is ab't 22 & Watkins is ab't 28; they say they were free born & srv'd their time with Mr Sam'l Adams, nr Leonard town, St Mary's Co, Md. -Ezra Mantz-shrf.

Whereas I am ab't to visit prop which I have a claim & right to in Essex Co, Va; my enemies have reported that I am ab't to move & leave this place; my enemies may wish what I least intend. -Jas A Porter, City of Wash.

THU FEB 21, 1811
Mr Joshua B Bond's horse, *Bright Phoebus*, will stand at my farm nr Queen Anne, PG Co, Md at $26. -Isaac Duckett.

SAT FEB 23, 1811
Hse o/Reps-Petition of Ralph Eddowes, of Phil, praying relief for goods seized under authority of U S. -To lie on table.

Died: Mr Henry O Dyer, formerly a merchant in Gtwn, D C, on Feb 14, in Chas Co, Md.

Mrd: Benj Howard, Gov of La Terr, to Miss Mary Thompson Mason, d/o Stephen Thompson Mason, dec'd, on Feb 14, at seat of Mrs Mason in Loudon Co, Va.

TUE FEB 26, 1811
Wanted to barter-a lot in Wash City for a good horse & gig. -Henry Ryan, 10th St West nr Pa Av & the theatre.

Public sale-decree from High Crt of Chancery of Md; to pay sum of money due from Philip Fitzhugh, dec'd, to Isachar & Mahlon Scholfield; 3 tracts of land in PG Co, Md, *Gillead*-ab't 5 acs, part of *Hoskingson's Folly*, & another part of *Gillead*, 234 acs. -Jos L Scholfield, trustee.

Notice-to be sold, a negro boy & a chest of carpenter's tools, prop of the late Walter Adams, dec'd; sale at his hse, Navy Yd Hill. -Margret Adams, admx.

Orphans Crt of Wash Co, D C. Prsnl est of Tobias Bond, dec'd, late of said co. -Wm Bond, adm

For sale-mare & gig with harness. -Robt Elliott, Capitol Hill.

THU FEB 28, 1811
Post Ofc dept changes in Jan 1811:
Berry's Lick, Ky-Rich'd B Dallam, vice Jas Ratcliff, rsgn'd;
Annapolis, Md-John Munroe, vice Sam'l Green, dec'd;
Hartford, Md-Rebecca Nowland, vice Peregrine Nowland, dec'd;
Jas City, Va-Robt B Spillman, vice Dan'l James, rsgn'd;
Great Bridge, Va-Thos Bartee, vice J W Hunter, rsgn'd;
Sunbury, Ga-Davis Carter, vice Thos Nelme, rsgn'd;
Westminster, Vt-Aaron Wales, vice Phineas T Wales, rsgn'd;
Falmouth, Ky-Jos Wingate, vice W C Kennett, rsgn'd;
Willington, S Ca-Edmund Waddell vice John McCauley, rsgn'd;
Inglishville, Va-Andrew Perry, vice Mr Draper, mv'd away;
Buxton, Me-Sam'l Cutts, vice Thos Merrill, mv'd away.
New ofcs est in Jan 1811 & postmaster:
Rough Creek Chr, Charlotte Co, Va-Claiborne Barkesdale jr;
Hancock, Salem Co, NJ-Walker Beasley;
Greenwich, Cumberland Co, N_-Geo Bacon;
Readyville, Rutherford Co, Ten-Chas Ready;
Bradford, Essex Co, Mass-Wm Greenough jr;
Irwinton, Wilkinson Co, Ga-Dan'l S Pierce;
Sandbar, Wilkinson Co, Ga-Jonathan Sawyer;
Mt Zion, Henderson Co, Ky, James Latham;
Naples, Jefferson Co, N Y-Hinckley Stephens;
N Stonington, New London Co, Ct-Dan'l Parker;
Fouprille, Ontario Co, N Y-Wm N Luminis;
Easton, Bristol Co, Mass-Israel Alger;
Troy, Plymouth Co, Mass-Chas Pitman;
Wheatley's Mills, Morgan Co, Ga-Wilson Wheatley;
Beaver Dam, Dela Co, N Y-Thos Montgomery;
Elizabethtown, Essex Co, N Y- Benj D Pardy;
Potter's Mills, Centre Co, Pa-Jas Potter jr;
Kingwood, Monongalia Co, Va-John S Roberts;
Somers, West Chester Co, N Y-Milton F Cushing;
Merry Oaks, Buckingham Co, Va-David Evans;
Preston, New London Co, Con-Dan'l Briggs;
Lovel, Mo-Andrew Woodbury;
Ackworth, Cheshire Co, N H-Sam'l Slader;
Hancock, Vt-Reuben Lamb;
Williamsburg, Huntington Co, Pa-Wm H Harris;
North Norwick, Chanango Co, N Y-Pardon Morris;
Vosses, Montgomery Co, Va-Chas Lewis;
White Lake, Sullivan Co, N Y-John Lindley;
Charleston, Montgomery Co, N Y- As Lewis;
Florida, Montgomery Co, N Y-John Delameter;
Martin's Store, Nelson Co, Va-Hudson Martin;
Barnett's Tavern, Nelson Co, Va-Nathan Barnett;
Harrison's Tavern, Amherst Co, Va-Nicholas Harrison;
Hart's Store, Albemarle Co, Va-Andrew Hart;

Lyons, Nelson Co, Va-Peter Lyon;
Middle Hero, Grand Isle Co, Vt-Ephraim Beardsley;
Berlin, Fred'k Co, Md-Theodore Beall;
Smith's Stand, Fayette Co, Pa-Philip Smyth.
P O discont'd-Roxbury, Dela Co, N Y-Jan 1811.

Died: Maj Jos Eccleston, age 57 yrs, on Jan 13, at his seat in Amelia Co, Va; a patriot of the Rev & a Rpblcn.

Died: Hon Thos Rodney, a Judge of the Miss Terr; at his resid in Wash City on Dec 21; in battles of Princeton, Monmouth & Brandywine.

For sale-brown highland-stud horse; enquire of Cornelius W Vanranst, N Y, or to Fyler Dibblee, N E town, Dutchess Co, N Y.

Stray cattle came to me in Wash City, nr Gtwn. -Ignatius Lucas.

Runaway-Henry Short, mulatto man, ab't 30 yrs of age. -John Cord, shrf, Arundel Co, Annapolis, Md.

THU FEB 28, 1811
For sale-at late resid of Rich'd Mullikin, dec'd; parcel of negroes. -Ann Mullikin, admx; Horatio Beall, adm.

Sam'l Schany, living on Bladensburg Rd, brought before me 2 stray bay mares. -Thos Fenwick, J P, Wash Co, D C.

Orphans Crt of PG Co, Md. Prsnl est of Walter Bowie, late of said co, dec'd. -Wm Bowie of Walter, adm; Mary Bowie, admx.

Geo Watterson, atty at law, opened an ofc on Capitol Hill.

SAT MAR 2, 1811
Hse o/Reps-Act for the relief of Rich'd Tervin, Wm Coleman, Edwin Lewis, Sam'l Mims, Jos Wilson & the Baptist Chr at Salem Meeting Hse, Miss Terr; bill rejected in reserving a parcel of land of the U S for said Chr. -Jas Madison.

Sale by auction-of Gen Tureau's furn & chariot, at his present resid.
-Andrews & Jones, aucts, Wash.

For sale-negroes; conveyed by the late Thos Gantt, to John Duvall; at Robt Merrikin's Tavern, Nottingham. -Robt Bowie, Benj Oden, trusts, PG Co, Md.

Lost-certificates to Jean Louis Claparede Payia, of Geneva; dt'd Nov, 1793 & Jan 1811. -Jas Davidson.

For sale or rent-val tanner yd on Fayette & 4th Sts, Gtwn, now in occupation of Mr Staley. -R M Boyer, Gtwn.

For sale-ab't 1500 acs, PG Co, Md, part of tract cld *Aquasco*, with dwlg hse. -Stans Hoxton, intending to leave Md.

For sale-gig & harness. -Baum & Pritchard, Gtwn.

TUE MAR 5, 1811
Acts passed at 3d session of 11th Cong: 1-Act for relief of Geo Armroyd & Co. 2-Act to change the name of Lewis Grant to Lewis Grant Davidson. 3-relief of heirs of late Maj Gen Anthony Wayne. 4-relief of Peter Audrian. 5-relief of John MacNamara.

David Bailie Warden, appt'd by Pres of U S as Consul of U S to reside at Paris.

Public sale-order of Calvert Co, Md-Crt: land, prop of late John M'Dowell, dec'd; 100 acs at St Leonard's Crk with frame dwlg hse. -Thos Hellen, John Mackall, Wm D Taylor-com'rs.

Following gentlemen will receive subscriptions to a city library: [Wash]-John Hewitt, Jas Laurie, Sam'l H Smith, Wm James, Jas H Blake, Henry Herford, Robt Brent, Joel Barlow, Wm Cranch, John Law, Franklin Wharton, Thos Munroe, Jos Stretch; named *The Washington Library Company*.

Runaway-Jas, negro man, committed to the goal of Kent Co, Md; says he was sold by Mr Benj Massey, of this co, to Dr John Moore, of Tenn Co. -Edw Wilkins, shrf of Kent Co, Md.

Orphans Crt of Montg Co, Md-sale at late resid of Thos West, dec'd, all prsnl prop of said dec'd. -Evan Jones of Nathan, adm of same.

THU MAR 7, 1811
Hse o/Reps-Acts passed: 1-Comp for Geo W Erving as agent in receiving & paying awards of Brd of Commissioners, $22,392.67; 2-Expenditures made by Jas Simmons, late coll of Charleston, from Jan 1, 1799, to Dec 31, 1805, settlement of his acc't at the Treas, $9,379.03; 3-Bal due est of late Maj Genr'l Anthony Wayne, $5,870.34; 4-Mrsh'l of Maine authorised to discharge Nath'l F Fosdick from imprisonment, he shall convey all rl & prsnl est for use of the U S;
5-Pay of Capt to John Eugene Leitensdorfer, from Dec 15, 1804, to Jul 15, 1805, being the time he srv'd as adj & inspec in Egypt & a land warrant for 320 acs on public lands west of the Miss; 6-Peter Audrain-comp of $700, bal due for svc as clk to land comr's at Detroit, from Jul 1, 1807 to Jul 1, 1809.

Mrd: Jas M Varnum, s/o spkr of the Hse o/Reps, to Miss Mary Pease, niece of the Post Mstr Genr'l, on Mar 5, by Rev Mr Laurie.

Died: John Douglas, in England, age 86, Duke of Queensbury, Marquis of Durnfries, & Lord of Douglass. He had no issue.

Died: Maj Gen Sernamont, in Spain, before Cadiz, Cmder in Chief of the French Artillery.

SAT MAR 9, 1811
Appt'd by Pres of U S: 1-Geo Jefferson, of Va, to Consul at Lisbon; 2-Sam'l Hazard, of Mass, Cnsl at Archangel; 3-David Campbell, of Tenn, Judge in Miss Terr, v Judge Rodney, dec'd: 4-Edw Ward, mbr of Leg Cncl of Miss Terr, vice Jos Roberts, rsgn'd; 5-John Smith, of Pa, mrsh'l again for 4 yrs; 6-John H Peterson, srvyr & inspec of Rev for Petersburg & Richmond Ports; 7-Henry M Cooke, coll & inspec of rev of Beaufort, N C; 8-John Haile, of Va, coll & inspec for Tappahannock Port; 9-Jos Prentiss, srvyr & inspec of rev, Suffolk, Va, Port.

Horace H Edwards & Harvey Bestor are partners in the liquor & groc bus; adj Indian Queen Tavern, Pa Ave, Wash City.

Navy of the U S-*appointments confirmed by the Senate*: To Lt in Navy:
Augus C Ludlow	Fitzhenry Babbit	Wm Canter jr
Walcot Chauncey	John H Elton	Alex'r J Dallas
Edmund P Kennedy	Jesse Wilkinson	Joshua Watson
Horace Walpole		

Robt Greenleaf & John Williams-from Lts to Capts of Marines.
Wm S Bush & John M Gamble-from 2nd Lts to 1st Lts.
Wm Strong & John Urquhart to 2nd Lts of Marines.
J A Brereton, now Surg's Mate, to Surg in Navy.
Jas Page to be Surg in Navy.
Jos G Roberts & Walter New, to be Surgeon's mates.

Runaway-Minny, blk man, 18 yrs of age. -Chas Ewell, Milford, Pr Wm Co, Va.

Mrd: on Mar 5, Gen Thos Moore, mbr of Cong from S C, to Miss Mary Reagan, of Gtwn, by Rev David Wiley.

Mrd: Timothy Winn to Miss Rebecca Dulany, d/o Benj Dulany, on Mar 7, in Alexandria, by Rev Mr Gibson.

Died: on Mar 2, Robt Brent, age 52 yrs, at his resid in Chas Co, Md; hsbnd & fr. Remains are at Mt Carmel.

Orphans Crt of PG Co, Md. Prsnl est of Thos P Edelen, late of said co, dec'd. -Robt P Edelen, exc.

Good compositors wanted; for paper to be established cld-*Impartial Observer*, or *The Rights of Men*. -Gerard Banks, Va, Fredericksburg.

TUE MAR 12, 1811
Runaway-Will Clark, committed to A A Co, Md, jail; negro man; says he is prop of Capt Wm Mackey of Talbot Co, Md. -John Cord, shrf, Annapolis.

Died: recently, Robt Hare, at Germantown, Pa; formerly spkr of Hse o/Reps of Pa.

For sale or rent-frame hse on G St; now occupied by Dr Dinmore; possession Apr 1. -Francis Clark.

Sale of Sam'l Waters Beck entire stock of goods at his store in Gtwn; by deed of trust. -Jo Brewer, trustee.

Act-concerning invalid pensioners.

[Name-	rate per month	commencement date]:
Jas Trawbridge	$3.33	Feb 5, 1810
Sam'l Mears jr	$2.50	Dec 10, 1810
Ebenezer Brown	$5	Jan 3, 1811
Elisha Capron	$2.50	Jan 1, 1810
Wm Woodruff	$5	Oct 24, 1810
Levi Tuttle	$1.25	Jan 7, 1811
Nath'l Austin	$3.75	Apr 10, 1810
Isaac Vincent	$5	Mar 22, 1810
John Griggs	$2.50	Apr 7, 1810
Patrick Hart	$3	Aug 30, 1810
Wm Burke	$2.50	Oct 10, 1808
John Long	$2.50	Aug 17, 1810
Vincent Tapp	$2.50	Dec 6, 1810
Jas Batson	$3	Feb 13, 1811
John Brown	$2.50	Dec 1, 1810
Jas Campin	$13.33 1/3	Mar 25, 1809
Sam'l Wells	$3.75	Jul 22, 1807
Dan'l Mc Elduff	$13.33	Jul 21, 1811
Edw Miller	$5	May 3, 1809
Dan'l Fielding	$3.33	Sep 19, 1809

Persons with increase in pension:

John Lincoln	$3	Jun 15, 1810
Dan Culver	$5	Jun 10, 1810
Jos Whittemore	$10	May 12, 1809
Peter Hemmenway	$5	Mar 8, 1810
Benj Mastic	$5	May 11, 1809
Elisha Rice	$5	Mar 31, 1810
Wm Bailey	$2.50	Jul 3, 1810
Jared Knapp	$5	Nov 19, 1810
Solomon Reynolds	$5	Jan 16, 1811
Eleazar Hudson	$3.75	Feb 15, 1811
Job Bartram	$15	Oct 25, 1809
Geo Sheil	$5	Dec 19, 1810
Isaac Richards	$2.50	Mar 14, 1810
Jas Patton	$13.33	Mar 6, 1810
Robt Coddington	$5	Mar 6, 1810
Isaac Cotheall	$5	Mar 6, 1810
Seybert Odam	$5	Oct 27, 1810

To be placed on pension list:
John Calhoun $15   Feb 6, 1810
Benj Blackburn $5   Apr 1, 1810

Act for relief of John MacNamara-schn'r *Sally,* at Nassau, New Providence-was seized with her cargo, same released.

THU MAR 14, 1811
Gibraltar, Jan 7, 1811-ships detained: America schn'r *Ann Green,* Dan'l Green mstr, for Marseilles, stopped by British brig of war *Minorca;* brig *Edwin,* Jacob Endicott, from Salem for Marseilles, also detained on account of her destination.

Promotions in the Army by the Pres of the U S: [Jul 23, 1810]
Maj Alex'r Macomb, to Lt Col, vice Jared Mansfield, rsgn'd;
Capt Walker K Armistead, to Maj, vice Alex'r Macomb, promoted;
1st Lt Alden Partridge, to Capt, vice Walker K Armistead, promoted;
2nd Lt Jos G Totten, to 1st Lt, vice Alden Partridge, promoted;
Alex'r J Williams, cadet at Mltry acad to 2nd Lt in Corps of Eng.
Regt of Artl:
1st Lt Jas S Swearingen to Capt, vice Wm Cocks, dismissed;
2nd Lt John G Wyndham to 1st Lt, vice Jas S Swearingen, promoted, both Jan 29, 1811;
Thos J Beall, Jas Dalliba, Gustavus Loomis, Ezra Smith & Rich'd H Ashley, cadets, appt'd 2nd Lts.
1st Regt of infty:
Ormond March, Geo Ronan & Benj Field, cadets, appt'd Ensigns.
2nd Regt of infty:
2nd Lt Alex'r Brownson, prmt'd to 1st Lt, vice Wm C Mead, rsgnd Jan 1, 1810;
2nd Lt Sam'l Noah, to 1st Lt, vice John V DuForest, dec'd, Nov 6, 1810;
Ensign Perrin Willis, to 2nd Lt, vice Francis W Small, rsgn'd, Feb 13, 1810;
Hyppolite H Villard, John Bliss & Henry A Burchstead, cadets to Ensigns.
Regt of Light Dragoons: 1st Lt Seleck Osborn to Capt, vice Bille Williams, rsgn'd, Feb 20, 1811;
2nd Lt Elijah Boardman to 1st Lt, vice Alex'r S Lyle, rsgn'd, May 3, 1810;
2nd Lt John Hollingshead to 1st Lt, vice Selick Osborn, promoted.
Regt of Light Artl: [all 1810]
Capt Abraham Eustis to Maj, vice John Saunders, dec'd, Mar 15;
1st Lt Jas S M'Kelvey to Capt, vice Abraham Eustis-promoted, Mar 15;
1st Lt Jas Gibson to Capt, vice Alex'r S Brooks, rsgn'd, May 2;
1st Lt Wm Campbell to Capt, vice Solomon D Townsend, rsgn'd, May 30, 1810;
1st Lt Robt H M'Pherson to Capt, vice Nathan Esterbrook, rsgn'd, Jul 15, 1810;
2nd Lt Benj Branch to 1st Lt, vice Jas S M'Kelvey, promoted, Mar 15;
2nd Lt Geo W Melvin to 1st Lt, vice Henry Lenud, dec'd, Apr 17;
2nd Lt Thos L Butler to 1st Lt, vice Jas Gibson, promoted, May 2;
Marie V Bolsaubin, Adam Larrabee, Henry A Hobart, Thos Kitcham, Jas D Cobb & Armstrong Irvine, cadets, to 2nd Lts.

3d Regt of infty: Lt Col Wm D Beall of 5th Regt, to Col in 3d, vice Edw Pasteur, rsgn'd, Nov 30, 1810;
Capt Robt C Nicholas of 7th Regt to Maj in 3d, vice Homer V Milton, promoted, Sep 3, 1810;
1st Lt Robt B Moore to Capt, vice Jacob J Faust, rsgn'd, Sep 1, 1810;
1st Lt Duncan L Clinch to Capt, vice Mossman Houstoun, rsgn'd, Dec 31, 1810;
1st Lt Jas E Denking to Capt, vice Cadwallader Jones, rsgn'd, Feb 6, 1811;
2nd Lt Timothy Spann to 1st Lt, vice Robt B Moore, promoted, Sep 1, 1810;
2nd Lt Benj D Herriott to 1st Lt, vice Wm Johnson, rsgn'd, Dec 1, 1810;
2nd Lt Sam'l C Mabson to 1st Lt, vice Duncan L Clinch, prmt'd, Dec 31, 1810.

4th Regt of infty:
Capt Geo R C Floyd of 7th Regt, to Maj in 4th, vice Jas Miller, promoted, Nov 30, 1810;
1st Lt Wm Welsh to Capt-Jun 9, 1810;
2nd Lt John L Eastman to 1st Lt, vice Wm Welsh, promoted, Jun 9, 1810;
2nd Lt Benj Hill to 1st Lt, vice Minor Huntingdon, rsgn'd, Feb 20, 1811;
Ensign Geo Gooding to 2nd Lt, vice John L Eastman, promoted, Jun 9, 1810;
Ensign Josiah Bacon jr to 2nd Lt, vice Jonathan Simons, rsgn'd, Dec 1, 1810;
Ensign Parker Greenough to 2nd Lt, vice Benj Hill, promoted, Feb 20, 1810.

5th Regt of infty:
Lt Col Jos Constant of 6th Regt, to Col in 5th, vice John Whiting, dec'd, Sep 3, 1810;
Maj Jas Mill of 4th Regt to Lt Col in 5th, vice Wm D Beall, promoted, Nov 30, 1810;
1st Lt Geo M Brooke to Capt, vice Fayette Roane, rsgn'd, May 1;
1st Lt Rich'd Whartenby to Capt, vice Minrod Long, rsgn'd, May 3;
1st Lt Townsend Stith to Capt, vice Rich'd Dale, rsgn'd, Sep 30;
2nd Lt Jacob Hindman to 1st Lt, vice Geo M Brooke, promoted, May 1;
2nd Lt Washington Lee to 1st Lt, vice Rich'd Whartenby, promoted, May 3, 1810;
2nd Lt Wm King to 1st Lt, vice Townsend Stith, promoted, Sep 30;
Ensign Jos Owens to 2nd Lt, vice Jacob Hindman, promoted, May 1;
Ensign Edw L Lomax to 2nd Lt, vice Wash Lee, promoted, May 3.

6th Regt of infty: [all 1810]
Maj Homer V Milton of 3d Regt to Lt Col in 6th, vice Jos Constant, prmtd, Sep 3,
1st Lt Peter Muhlenburg to Capt, vice Wm P Bennett, rsgn'd, Oct 1,
2nd Lt Edw Webb to 1st Lt, vice Peter Muhlenburg, promoted, Oct 1,

7th Regt of infty: [all 1810]
1st Lt Enos Cutler to Capt, vice Robt C Nicholas, promoted, Sep 3;
1st Lt Zachary Taylor to Capt, vice G R C Floyd, promoted, Nov 30;
1st Lt Walter H Overton to Capt, vice Thos J Van Dyke, rsgn'd, Dec 3;
2nd Lt Jesse Jennings to 1st Lt, vice Elisha Edwards, rsgn'd, Aug 1;
2nd Lt Archibald Greer to 1st Lt, vice Enos Cutler, promoted, Sep 3;
2nd Lt Jeoffry Robertson to 1st Lt, vice Zachary Taylor, promoted, Nov 30, 1810;
2nd Lt Jas S Wade to 1st Lt, vice Walter H Overton, promoted, Dec 3,

Regt of Riflemen: [all 1810]
Capt Thos A Smith to Lt Col, vice Wm Duane, rsgn'd, Jul 31, 1810;
1st Lt Fielder Ridgeway to Capt, vice Thos A Smith, promoted, Jul 31;
2nd Lt Thos Ramsey to 1st Lt, vice Fielder Ridgeway, promoted, Jul 31;

2nd Lt Wm Smith to 1st Lt, vice Benj Champney, rsgn'd, Oct 1, 1810.

Wanted-300 piles & wharf ties, all of white oak. -Geo Blagden, nr the Navy Yd.

SAT MAR 16, 1811
For sale-233 acs in Calvert Co, Md, nr *Plumb Point*; with dwlg hse. -John M Heighe, Calvert Co, Md.

Thos Baker is opening in the hse formerly occupied by Wm McKenney, large assortment of spring goods.

National Museum now open in bldg formerly occupied by Mr G Stewart, portrait painter, on Pa Av; admission .25.

David Wiley was chosen mayor of Gtwn, a few days ago.

Wm Herbert was re-elected mayor of Alexandria, on Mar 8.

TUE MAR 19, 1811
Mrd: Capt Jas Barron to Miss Ann Davies, at Alexandria, Mar 14, by Rev Dr Muir, both of Alexandria.

Mrd: Mr Beale M Worthington to Miss Eliz R Rickets, on Mar 14, at the seat of John Worthington, nr Annapolis.

Orphans Crt of Wash Co, D C. Mar 18, 1811. Prsnl est of John Masters, late of said city, dec'd. -John Cannon, adm.

Sale at auction-at late dwlg nr Eastern Branch bridge, all prsnl prop of John Masters, dec'd.

Public sale-order of Montg Co, Md, Crt: the rl est of the late Thos Brook Beall, dec'd; 278 acs in Montg Co, ab't 4 miles from Leesburg, with dwlg hse. -Thos Fletchall, Basil Brooke, Chas H Crabb.

THU MAR 21, 1811
Mrd: Mr Lewis P W Balch, of Gtwn, to Miss Eliza E W Wever, d/o Mr Adam Wever, of Jefferson Co, Va, Mar 14, by Rev Mr Price.

For sale-stout young negro man. Mr Rich'd Young, living with Mr Pairo, F St, Wash City.

John Douglas intends to remove from Pa Av & has Liverpool ware, for sale.

Patent for sale-pendulum mill machine. -Jos Lefever, patentee, at his farm, Strasburg, Lr Co, Pa.

SAT MAR 23, 1811

Orphans Crt of PG Co, Md-with will annexed; ltrs of adm on est of Jos Messenger, of PG Co, dec'd. -Walter S Parker, adm, Piscataway. Sale of negroes, furn & stock of dec'd, followed.

To be sold-the establishment of the *Independent American* & all printing material. Terms apply to Mr A L Johncherez or to John Thomas 3d.

Sale of land-prop of Brig Genr'l John S Farley & Mrs Eliz Morson, part of Saura town, in N C; authority to Mr Wm Edw Broadnax of Brunswick-who has his hse for sale also. -G K Taylor, John Dunlop, attys for John S Farley & Mrs Eliz Morson.

Died: Jos Hughes, Mar 19-youth respected by all who knew him.

TUE MAR 26, 1811

Jeremiah Morrow, Rep in Cong from Ohio-declined re-elctn.

Wm H Cabell appt'd Judge of Crt of Appeals of Va, vice Jas Pleasants, rsgn'd.

E Oliver has rec'd spring & summer millinery. -Gtwn.

Post ofc changes in Feb 1811:
Pattonsburg, Va-Wm L Adams, vice Wm P Tebbs, rsgn'd;
Franconia, NH-John Punchard, vice Caleb Baker;
Charlotte Hall, Md-Dennis Donlevy, vice Jos Harrison, rsgn'd;
Broadallin, NJ-John Richards, vice Thos Bricknall, rsgn'd;
Sheldon, Vt-Epenetus H Wead, vice Sam'l Wead, rsgn'd;
Lancaster C Hse, So Ca-John Steward, vice Wm Howe;
Hawkesbill Mills, Va-Enos Mc Ray, vice Jas Headley, rsgn'd;
N W River Bridge, Va-Miles Brett, vice S Bright, dec'd;
Hungarytown, Va-Germany Stokes, vice Jno H Knight;
Strasburg, Pa-John Caldwell, vice Jas Whitehill, rsgn'd;
Ludlow, Vt-Nathan B Fletcher, vice Asa Fletcher, rsgn'd;
Jas City, Va-Benj Lewis, vice R B Spillman, rsgn'd;
Queen Anne, Md-Chas D Hodges, vice T Sparrow;
Hillsborough, No Ca-Wm Cain jr, vice Wm Lockart, rsgn'd;
Lebannon, Ohio-Dan'l F Reeder, vice M Ross, rsgn'd;
Salem, Ky-Sam'l C Haskins, vice Wm Ficklin, mv'd away;
Eddy Grove, Ky-Elijah G Galusha, vice Elisha Prince, mv'd away;
Kittanning, Pa-Robt Robertson jr, vice D Lawson, rsgn'd;
Woodsberry, Md-Brooke Baker, vice Jos Hedges, rsgn'd;
Winslow, Me-Hezekiah Stratton jr, vice N B Dingley;
Lovington, Va-R L Talliaferro, vice Chas Perrow, rsgn'd;
Jenkintown, Pa-Wm McCalla, vice C T Hallowell, rsgn'd;
Marshfield, Mass-Jabez Hatch, vice Isaac Paine, rsgn'd;
Wheelock, Vt-Thos E Edgarley, vice Chas Story, rsgn'd;
Quantico Mills, Md-Geo Malcomb, vice T Brady, mv'd away;

Ward's Bridge, N Y-Thos McNeall, vice Hugh Lindsey;
Chappel Hill, Md-Edmund Robinson, vice Jas Whatson, rsgn'd;
Newbern, N Ca-Green Bryan, vice Sam'l Gerock, rsgn'd;
Adams, N Y-David Perry, vice M Sterling, mv'd away;
Hector, N Y-Rich'd Smith, vice Grover Smith, rsgn'd;
Westborough, Mass-Nathan Fisher, vice John Sanborne, rsgn'd;
Pughtown, Pa-Matthew Law, vice David Townsend, mv'd away;
Richmond, Vt-Moors Russel, vice Isaac Glenson, rsgn'd;
Cross Keys, So Ca-Barrum Bobo, vice Geo Gordon, mv'd away;
Mt Pleasant, Pa-John Granger, vice Oliver Granger;
Big Lick, Va-Jas Echols, vice John Pate, rsgn'd;
White C Hse, Ten-Jacob A Lane, vice John M Garrick, dec'd;
Randolph, Vt-Wm Nutting, vice Sereno Wright, rsgn'd;
Chatham, Pa-Jas Monagan, vice Sam'l Harvey, rsgn'd;
Wayne C Hse, Ky-Anthony Dilrell, vice Joshua Oatts, rsgn'd;
Fryburg, Md-Judah Dana, vice J W Ripley, rsgn'd;
Pritchetts Store, Va-John G Rivers, vice Jas Pritchett, rsgn'd;
Pittston, Pa-Eleazer Carey, vice Nath'l Gradings, rsgn'd;
City Point, Va-John H Peterson, vice Andrew Torborn, dec'd;
Wheelock, Vt-Edw Tyfield, vice Chas Storey, mv'd away;
Bryan C Hse, Ga-Benj Burton, vice Jos Stillwell, rsgn'd;
Slate Creek Iron works, Ky-Andrew Bryan, vice P Davis, rsgn'd;
Norwalk, Ct-Wm M Betts, vice Wm Lockwood;
Beverley, Mass-Framham Plummer, vice John Lemon, rsgn'd;
Shelbyville, Ten-John Stone, vice B Bradford, rsgn'd;
Lawrenceburg, Ind Ter-Isaac Dunn, vice Jas Dill, rsgn'd;
White Horse Tavern, Pa-Jos Showalter, vice Edw Porter, mv'd away;
Lunenburg, Vt-Wm Gates, vice Sam'l Gates, rsgn'd.

Dewitt Clinton nominated by Rpblcns of N Y State, for ofc of Lt Gov, vice Mr Broome, dec'd.

Died: Mr Dennis Driscol, at Augusta, on Mar 10, late editor of the *Georgia Chronicle*.

New Post ofcs est in Feb 1811 & postmaster:
Sudlers Rds, Queen Anns Co, Md-John Kennedy;
Southerland, Orange Co, N Y-Roger Parmely;
Ragans, Baldwin Co, Ga-John Ragan;
Foxchace Tavern, Chester Co, Pa-Isaiah Fawkes;
St Michaels, Talbot Co, Md, re-est'd-R Harrington;
Baldwin, York Co, Me-Rich'd Fitch;
Phillipsburg, York Co, Me-Isaac Lane;
Sterling, Worcester Co, Mass-John Robbins;
Seaconk, Bristol Co, Mass-Phanuel Bishop jr;
Hyde Park, Orleans Co, Vt-Jos Matthews;
Wolcott, Orleans Co, Vt-Thos Taylor jr;
Derby, Orleans Co, Vt-Wm Howe;

Sidney Grove, Randolph Co, Ill Ter-B Stephenson;
Columbus C Hse, N C-Jas B White;
Cooper's Hill, Robertson Co, N C-Malcolm McNair;
McQueens Store, Robertson Co, N C-Jas McQueen;
Campsville, Spartanburg Co, S C-Jas Camp;
Haley's Bright, Greenville Co, Va-Allen A DeBerry;
Parkham's Store, Sussex Co, Va-Wm Parkham;
Rumford Acad, King Wm Co, Va-Rich'd Hill;
Pine Hill, York dist, S C-Hugh White;
Brookfield, Essex Co, N Y-Peter Denew;
Nine Bridges, Queen Anns Co, Md-Jas McGuire;
Chester, Hampshire Co, Mass-Harvey Bodortha;
Cresapsburg, Alleghany Co, Md, re-est'd-Wm Bruce;
New Phil, Tuscorora Co, Ohio-Jas Clarke;
Granville, Licking Co, Ohio-Timothy Rose;
Waterford, Worthington Co, Ohio-David Pardy;
Langford, Rock-Castle Co, Ky-Henry P Buford;
Skowheagan Falls, Somerset Co, Me-Jos Locke;
New Store, Buckingham Co, Va-Wm Thompson;
Pattonsburg, Bottetourt Co, Va, re-est'd-W L Adams;
Columbia Co, Ga-John Avery jr;
Clermont Co, Ohio-Wm Fees.
Post Ofcs discnt'd: Mahonsville, Ky; New Switzerland, Ohio; Canaan, Me; Black Lick, Pa.

Meeting of the Soc of the Sons of Erin; officers elected: Moses Young, Pres; Joshua Dawson, VP; Alex'r Kerr, Treas; Henry Whetcroft, sec; committee-Jas McClary, Jas D Barry, Alex Cochrane, Francis Clark, John Knapp. -Wash.

Died: Col Chas Little, on Mar 20, at Danby, Fairfax Co, Va, age 62 yrs; late Commandant of the Continental Regt of Militia of Va.

John Louis, negro, aged ab't 23 yrs, from St Domingo; says he belongs to Mr Delanot of Balt; committed to Fred'k co, Md, jail. -Ezra Mantz, shrf of Frederick Cty, Md.

THU MAR 28, 1811
Died: Col Jas Craufurd, on Feb 22, at N Y, formerly Govn'r of Bermuda.

Died: Mr Garret Barry, Mar 25, in Wash.

To be let-hse on 8th St nr the Navy Yd, lately occupied by Mr Shumway; also hse & store on L St, lately occupied by Mr Lewis Deblois. -Wm Cocking, 19th St W.

New Orleans, Feb 20. Disturbances in dist of St Helena; Mr Sam'l Baldwin, formerly a Lt in the U S M C, who resides in that dist, with a writ run a man through the body; Mr Baldwin was seized; he was an active friend of the conventionalists.

Auction sale-at hse formerly occupied by Wm Lovering, next dr to Mr Geo Miller's in F St-furniture & 2 cows. Virtue of a bill of sale from Lovering to Thos Hughes & Mich'l Dooling. -N L Queen & Co, aucts.

Public sale-decree of the Hon Chancellor of Md; at Montgomery Crt Hse, tracts of land cld: *Snowden's Second Additon to his Manor*, & *Snowden's Manor Enlarged*, formerly prop of Rich'd Snowden jr, dec'd; ab't 1400 acs. Lands were devised by said Rich'd Snowden to John Snowden, his bro, & Sam'l Thomas, his nphw; land not capable of division bet the heirs of said John Snowden & same of Rich'd Thomas, to whom the right of Sam'l Thomas descends, being his eldest bro & heir. Mr Wm Thomas will show same. -Gerard H Snowden, trustee.

Ranaway-Harry, negro man; raised in Chas Co by Capt Jamieson & then owned by Mr L Boon lvg on Eastern Branch; says he has a wife lvg with a Parson Davis. -C L Gantt, nr Bladensburg.

Orphans Crt of Wash Co, D C. Mar 13, 1811. Ltrs of adm on est of John Biot, late o/said co, dec'd. Claims to Jos Cassin. -Mary Biot, Jos Cassin, adms.

SAT MAR 30, 1811
Died: Mary Sutton, on Jan 22, of Bladen Co, N C, aged 116 yrs; ntv of Culpepper Co, Va, had 5 sons & 7 dghts-all now living, her descendants amount to 1492. At 52 her eye sight failed but returned again at 76 and continued until 98, it failed again. She has been at the births of 1121 chldrn. -W Caz

Monsr Serrurier, the New French Minister, has taken his residence at the seat of Joel Barlow, nr Wash.

John Johnson appt'd Chief Judge of first Judicial dist of Md, vice John M Gantt, dec'd; Jas Houston, Atty-Genr'l of Md, vice John Johnson, rsgn'd.

Thanks to all who have assisted in my attempt to do good; farther assistance, either in bks or money, may be sent to Mr Weightman's or Mr Rapine, bk-sellers in Wash, or to Mr J Friend, nr the Navy Yd, or to Mr Milligan in Gtwn. Public's most devoted, humble servant, T Osgood.

TUE APR 2, 1811
Mr Robt Fulton exhibited his system of torpedo war; in & near the city of N Y, from Sep 21 to Nov 1, 1810.

Dabney Carr, of Albemarle, appt'd by the Exec of Va, Judge of Genr'l Crt, vice Wm H Cabell, appt'd Judge of Crt of Appeals.

Cincinnati, Mar 9:-On Mar 1 the dwlg hse of John Cleves Symmes, on the Miami, nr the North Bend, was consumed by fire.

Coll of taxes for Wash City: ward 1-Jos Brumley; ward 2-Ez MacDaniel; ward 3-Zachariah Walker; ward 4-H M Queen.

For sale-land in Montgomery Co, Md; 249 3/4 acs; also tract cld *Crabbs Redoubt*, Montg Co. Apply to Dr Rich'd Orme, living nr the premises or to Chas H Crabb-Montg Crt Hse, Md.

Runaway-John Talbert, negro man ab't 25 yrs old; says he belongs to Mr Welden Brenton, Charlestown, Va. -Matthias Shaffner, shrf of Wash Co, Md. Hagarstown.

Robt Weakley has dcln'd a re-election to Cong from Tenn.

THU APR 4, 1811
Jas Byers, military store kpr, Springfield, Mass, Dec 31, 1810. Ltr to sec of war showing number of arms at armory of said place. Sam'l Annin, military store kpr, statement showing number of arms at armory at Harper's Ferry, Va, in yr 1810.

Ltr-in 1776: I was Capt in svc of the U S, attached to Genr'l Green's brigade then stationed on Long Isl. -Silas Tolbert.

Mrd: John Preston, Treas of Va, to Mrs Mayo, of Richmond, on Mar 30.

Mrshl's sale-all right, title & claim-etc of Jas Thompson to hse west of bldgs erected by Crookshank & Thomson on sq 461; writ from Crct Crt of Wash Co, D C, at suit of Dan'l Buzzard against said Thompson. -Wash Boyd, mrsh'l, D C.

Sale at Jas M'Cormack's dwlg, sideboard & looking glass, for tax due the Wash Corp by same. -Ez MacDaniel-col ward 2.

Mrsh'ls sale-all right, title & claim etc of Chrisopher S Thom, to lots 2 & 3 in sq 1666; writ issued from Crct Crt of Wash Co, D C, at suit of Jos Otis, use of Montgomery R Bartlett, against said Thom. -Wash Boyd, mrsh'l, D C.

SAT APR 6, 1811
Gen John Mason, of Gtwn, has rsgn'd his commission of Brig Genr'l of the Militia of the Dist of Columbia.

Mrd: Daniel Dulany, of Fairfax Co, Va, to Miss Sarah Ann Tingey, d/o Thos Tingey, Commandant of the Navy Yd in Wash, on Apr 4, by Rev Mr McCormick.

Died: on Apr 1, Dr John Willis, formerly of Wash, at his seat in Orange Co, Va.

North Star, Ver: Ravages of spotted fever took the lives of 5 persons in the hse of Capt Luther Bailey of Peacham last wk.

Prot Episc Chr will hold svc in the upper hall of the Treas Dept every succeeding Sabbath. -Andrew T McCormick.

For sale-negro man, prop of Chas Minifie, to satisfy taxes due the Wash Corp. -Henry M Queen, collector of 4th ward.

Sale-one brick hse in sq 253 for tax due the Wash Corp by Thos Webb. -Ez MacDaniel, coll 2nd ward.

Sale-one hse in sq 503 for tax due the Wash Corp by Israel & John P Pleasants. -Ez MacDaniel, coll 2nd ward.

Wm Shorter, negro-age 35, committed to Fredr'k Co, Md, jail; says he is free & came from Wash City. -Ezra Mantz, shrff.

TUE APR 9, 1811
London Gaz-Feb 16: the Prince Regent has appt'd Augustus John Foster, to be his Majesty's Envoy Extraordinary & Minister Plenipotentiary to U S of America; Mr Foster, is nphw to the Duchess of Devonshire & was sec to the America Legation.

Mrd: Mr Alexander Moore to Miss Ann M West, on Apr 4, by Rev Mr Gibson.

For sale or to let: hse presently occupied by Maj Wm Reily, next door to my residence. -John P Van Ness.

Zephaniah Farrell advertises for a partner in the manufacture of soap & candles, Wash City. Gilbert Docker, Gtwn, has lge supply of candles at his store.

For sale-or to let: grist mill in Fairfax Co, Va; 70 acs; good dwlg hse. -Wm Sheppard

For sale-one frame hse in sq 738, for tax due the Wash City Corp by Benj Bacon. -Zh Walker, coll 3d ward.

For sale-one frame hse in sq 758, for tax due Wash City Corp by Rich'd Delphy. -Zh Walker, coll 3d ward.

For sale-one hse in sq 283, for tax due the Wash Corp by John Davidson's heirs. -Ez MacDaniel, coll 2nd ward.

St Geo Tucker has rsgn'd his seat on the bench of the Crt of Appeals of Va.

Ladies with ltrs in the Wash Post ofc-Apr 1, 1811:
Mrs Kitty Adams	Miss Sally Bryson-(3)	Miss Eliz Brown
Mgt Christophe	Mrs Ann Colerick	Jane Coulson
Miss Fanny Clarke	Sarah Davis	
Jane Dillen c/o Ben Brian		Mrs Eliza Elliot
Miss Fairlie c/o Rich'd Derby		
Wm Far or Eliza Matticks		Miss Mgt Fowble
Miss Eliza Hazard	Ann Holmes	Fanny Hampton

Mrs P L Jones	Jane Isburn	Mgt Johnston
Mrs Kissuck	Rachel Keifer c/o Fred Brower	
Mary Lowry	Mrs Love	Fanny Martin
Eliz Maxwell	Mary Myers	Carey Ann Nicholas
Mary Pravote	Milly Perry	Rebecca Perkins
Rebecca Russ	Eliz Ross	Eliz Sandford
Sarah Sharlock	Sarah Stevens	Nancy Tanner
Darcus Anne Tolburt	Eliz Tabbs	Mary Tuckfield
Ann Viddler	Rachel Vermillion	Sarah Walker
Mrs Webb	Ann Warner	
Mgt Williams c/o Mrs Steele		Sarah Young.

THU APR 11, 1811
Orphans Crt of PG Co, Md. Ltrs of adm on est of John Mackall Gantt, late of PG Co, dec'd. -Mary S Gantt, admx, Fielder Gantt, adm.

Partnership bet Jas Bennett & Jas B Roddy, is dissolved by mutual consent; payments to Jas Bennett. -Wash City.

Va election-Thos Newton re-elected to Congress from Norfolk.

SAT APR 13, 1811
Orphans Crt of Montgomery Co, Md. Apr 12, 1811. Prsnl est of Rich'd Waters, late of said co, dec'd. -Mgt Waters, excx. Followed by sale of all prsnl est of Rich'd Waters-negro slaves, stock & furniture.

Partnership bet Isaac Tenny & Robt Ober is dissolved by mutual consent; payments to Robt Ober who will carry on the commission business.

Stone masons & pavers needed for bldg 2 stone bridges & paving ab't 40,000 yds in Richmond City, Va. -Benj Duvall, Jedediah Allen, com'rs-Richmond, Va.

Ranaway-Jack, mulatto man; from Upton Lawrence, Hagerstwn-Md.

John Hays, negro man, committed to the Fred'k Co, Md, goal; ab't 30 yrs of age; says he came from Winchester, Va; sold out of the goal & bght by David Casman. -Ezra Mantz, shrff.

TUE APR 16, 1811
Orphans Crt of Montg Co, Md. Apr 16, 1811. Prsnl est of John Lucas, late of said co, dec'd. -Jas B Higgins, exc.

For sale-one brick hse & lot in sq 16, for tax due the Wash City Corp by Jas Dunlop. Also, one brick hse & lot, west of sq 4, for tax due Wash Corp by Wm Lowrey. Also, one brick hse & lot in sq 118, for tax due Wash Corp, by Jas M Lingan. -Jos Bromley, coll 1st ward.

Orphans Crt of Calvert Co, Md. Ltrs of test on prsnl est of Rev Edw Gantt, late of said co, dec'd. -Thos C Gantt & Jos Wilkinson, excs.

Calvert Co, Md. Notice-trustees of Charlotte Hall School, in consequence of Mr John Kilgour's non compliance with his contract as steward-elected Oct 25, 1810; Jas Keech has been elected steward as of Mar 15, 1811 for remainder of the present yr.

THU APR 18, 1811
Mrd: Mr Jas D Barry to Miss Juliana Coombe, both of Wash, on Apr 16, by Rev Mr Matthews.

Mrd: Mr John G McDonald to Miss Ann Johnson, on Apr 16, by Rev Mr McCormick.

Orphans Crt of Chas Co, Md. Apr 18, 1811. Prsnl est of Henry Oswald Dyer, late of Chas Co, dec'd; formerly a resid of Gtwn. -Jeremiah Dyer, exc & adm.

Ezkiel Young, tailor, has commenced business in hse formerly occupied by Mr Edw Fendell, F St, Wash, D C.

Public sale-part of lot 3 in sq 289, prop of Lewis Clephan, for tax due Wash City Corp; also sale of lot 9 in sq 491, prop of Osborn Warner for same. -Ezl MacDaniel, coll 2nd ward.

Sale of one brick hse & lot in sq 1001, for taxes due Wash City Corp by Rich'd H Pignald. -Henry M Queen, coll 4th ward.

In Chancery-Wash Co, D C. Edmund I Lee, cmplnt, vs Robt Beverly, Byrd Beverly, Peter Randolph Beverly, dfndnts. Lee purchs'd of Byrd Beverly as agent & atty for Peter R Beverly, then residing in France, 1803, land in Culpepper Co, Va, 336 acs, @ $5 per ac; land resurveyed & there is only 240 1/2 acs. -Wm Brent, clk.

Sale at auction-all hsehld & kitchen furn & 2 frame hses & lots; at hse of Wm Spooner, nr the Navy Yd. -N L Queen-auct.

Sale-one frame hse & lot in sq 928, for taxes due Wash City Corp by Thos C Wright. -H M Queen, coll 4th ward.

Sale-one frame hse & lot in sq 406 for tax due Wash City Corp-prop of Andrew Thompson; one hse & lot in sq 406 for tax due Wash Corp, prop of Geo Thompson. -Ezl MacDaniel, coll 3d ward.

Sale-one brick hse in sq 651, for tax due Wash Corp, by Hugh Densley. -Zh Walker, coll 3d ward.

SAT APR 20, 1811
Died: Gen Stephen Maylan, of Phil, Apr 13, age 78 yrs; com'r of loans for dist of Pa.

Balt, Md County Crt: Judge Nicholson suspended Luther Martin for 12 months because of his manner in examining a witness.

Jas Corly, insolvent debtor, confined in Wash Co, D C, prison, for debt. -Wm Brent, clk.

TUE APR 23, 1811
City Cncl of Wash-Act of relief of Patrick Tuel, sum of $162.50, bal due P Tuel for work & labor on improving 6th St west.

Mrd: Mr Robt Polk, atty at law, of Wash, to Miss Penelope Maury, on Apr 16, by Rev Dr Belmain, at seat of Isaac Hite, nr Winchester.

Ranaway-Sam'l Richardson, age ab't 16 yrs, appr to boot & shoe mkng bus; bound by the Orphans Crt of Wash Co, D C; has relations in Worcester Co, nr *Snowhill*. -Jas Patterson.

H C Dargen informs her customers that she has mv'd from Bridge St to Jefferson St, Gtwn; millinery & fancy goods.

Orphans Crt of PG Co, Md. Ltrs of adm on prsnl est of her dec'd hsbnd, John H Beanes, late of PG Co. Exhibit claims to Horatio Clagett, Wm K Clagett or Hariet Beanes, admx, Piscataway.

Franklin Co, N C-interesting ltr by John Norwood, Justice of the Peace regarding Peggy Ingram, his neighbor, & d/o Mary Ingram; Peggy says she mrd Chas Morris ab't 11 yrs past, last Jan; Chas left & went to Norfolk, Va & cld himself Chas Devling; Peggy by her ltr of Jun last is a resid of the Federal City of Wash; Chas denies they were ever mrd.

THU APR 25, 1811
Turnpike Rds-Nathan Beach of Phil, Robt Harris & John Schoch of Harrisburg, Wm M'Candless & Adamson Tannehill of Pittsburg, appt'd comrs of rds from Harrisonburg to Pittsburg, Pa.

Mrd: Apr 9, in New Brunswick, N J, Capt Eli B Climson of U S A, to Miss Ann Maria Oliver, of that city, by Rev Dr Croes.

Died: on Apr 22, Mrs Keziah Dashiell, consort of Mr Thos E Dashiell, after a lingering illness.

Died: John Weatherburn, on Apr 21, Pres of the Mechanics' Bank of Balt.

Orphans Crt of Chas Co, Md. Ltrs of test on prsnl est of Sam'l Scott, late of Chas Co, dec'd. -Wilson Compton, exc.

Ranaway-Tom, negro boy; his mthr resides on Capitol Hill, Wash City. -Wm B Wright, living in Salem, Va, reward-$10.

SAT APR 27, 1811
Vessels that arrv'd at Port of Bourdeaux from Nov 1 to Feb 18, 1811:
brig-*New Oreans* Packet of & from N Y, R T Harris, mstr, Dec 2;
schn'r *Friendship* of & from Balt, Freeman Snow, mstr, Dec 6;
schn'r *Liberty* of & from Phil, John Scheer, mstr, Dec 30;
schn'r *Bird*, of & from Salem, John Evans, mstr, Jan 4;
schn'r *Lydia* of & from Boston, Wm Kelham, mstr, Jan 7;
brig *Female* of & from Balt, John Creagh, mstr, Feb 11;
ship *Traveller* of & from N Y, Rich'd Prendergast, mstr, Feb 12;
brig *Mile* of & from Balt, Rinaldo Johnson, mstr, Feb 12;
brig *Telemachus* of & from Salem, Chas Berry, mstr, Jan 24;
schn'r *Susan & Emeline* of & from Phil, I Hutchinson, mstr, Feb 11.

Mrd: Gilbert Devol, of Waterford, Ohio, to Mrs Ann Hatch, wid of Capt Elnathan Hatch, late of New London City, Con, on Apr 4, by Nath'l Hamilton. At his wedding his grchldrn were counted, number in this country was 53. -Spectator.

Jas Mosher chosen Pres of Mechanics' Bank of Balt, vice Mr Weatherburn, dec'd.

Crct Crt of the U S, Wash Co, D C, in debt. Postmstr Genr'l vs Jos Wheaton. Same vs Alex'r Cochrane, in debt; same vs Thos Gillis, in debt; same vs Jos Wheaton, in debt; same vs Rich'd Dinmore, in debt; same vs Jos Wheaton, in covenant. The award of Col John P Van Ness & Maj Caleb Swann, formerly given, shd be confirmed; deficiency in former award from Feb 16 to Apr 1, 1807. Award of $600 to Jos Wheaton for opening the horse path from Athens to Ft Stoddart, expenditures for carrying the mail-Nashville & New Orleans Route-$790, prsnl svcs on route from Apalache to Ft Stoddart-$3168.64, allowance-$355.55, horses, saddles-$1995, transportation of mail bet Wash City & Coweta from May 10, 1805 to Jul 10-$11,469.34, & bet Wash City & Apalachy Rvr from Jul 11, 1806 to Mar 31, 1807-$7912.40; advanced $24,690.00, bal due Jos Wheaton by P Mstr Genr'l, $1600.84. Judgment in all cases be entered for the dfndnts, without cost. -Geo Youngs, [Seal] E B Caldwell, [Seal]. Mar 22, 1811

Died: Henry Johnson, age 19 yrs, of Wash, on Mar 15, at N Orleans.

For sale-1 brick hse on sq 651 with ground, prop of Isaac Reed, for tax due Wash Corp. Also, one brick hse & part of lot 6 in sq 799, prop of Robt Cherry, for same. -Zh Walker, coll 3d ward.

Ranaway-Peter Colter, ab't 17 yrs of age, appr to hatting bus..--John Hemler, F St, Wash City.

To be sold-2 negro girls, prop of Wm Prout, for taxes due Wash Corp. -Henry M Queen, coll 4th ward.

For sale-1 brick hse in sq 847, for taxes due Wash Corp by Wm Small; & a frame hse in sq 917, for taxes due Wash Corp by Jos Bentley; & a frame hse & lot in sq 924 for taxes due the Wash Corp by Jos Slater. -Henry M Queen, coll 4th ward.

TUE APR 30, 1811
Died: Mrs Cath Loxley Smith, w/o John Smith, chief clk of War Dept, Apr 27, age 30 yrs, of consumption; languished for 16 mos.

Died: John Smith, on Apr 28, age 37 yrs, above mentioned; the parents of two infant sons consigned to one grave. Mr Smith, physician then lawyer in Somerset, Pa. In 1802 he accepted the station in the War Dept. [Earlier he had gone to Montreal but returned to his ntv country & New Eng.]

Thos Moore at the Tridelphia Cotton Factory, in Md, endorses Dan'l Pettibone's method of warming rms with heated air.

Va election-Gen John Hungerford elected to Congress by 6 votes over John Taliaferro, esq.

For sale-dwlg hse on Causeway St in Gtwn; built & formerly occupied by Andrew M'Donald, with lot; deed of trust from Andrew M'Donald. -Lewis Clephan.

Walter W Harwood, of PG Co, Md, applies for act of insolvent debtor; now in confinement for debt. -John R Magruder, jr.

Post ofcs discont'd in Mar 1811: Feely's store, Va; Highland Lick, Ky; East Chester, N Y; Norway Plains, N H.

Post ofc changes in Mar 1811.
Adams, N Y-David Perry, vice Mich'l Sterling, mv'd away;
Hestor, N Y-Rich'd Smith, vice Grover Smith, rsgn'd;
Hopkinton, RI-Jeremiah Thurston, vice R Wills, situation inconvenient;
Hanover C H, Va-Thos Priddy, vice B Oliver, mv'd away;
Greenville, M T-John G T Prince, vice Joshua Downs, dec'd;
White C H, Ten-Edmund Harrison, vice Jacob A Lane, rsgn'd;
Oxford, Va-Peter Nelson, vice Sam'l Terrell, rsgn'd;
Redfield, N Y-Aaron Butler, vice Amos Johnson, rsgn'd;
Hennicker, NH-Isaac Rice, vice Joshua Darling, rsgn'd;
Haddonfield, NJ-Sam'l Brown, vice M Runells, dec'd;
Upper Three Runs, S C-Jas Chron, vice Alex'r Smith, rsgn'd;
Mundellsville, Va-Wm R Almond, vice Wm S Marye, rsgn'd;
Gibson's store, Va-Bryant Toley, vice Wm Gibson, rsgn'd;
Milford, Del-Thos Glass, vice Sam'l Wright, dec'd;
Bowling Green, Ky-Thos H Robinson, vice A F Hubbard;

Gates C H, N C-Chas Townshend, vice Isaac Hunter, rsgn'd;
Jefferson, Ohio-D Coleman, vice Timothy Caldwell, rsgn'd;
Swansboro, N C-Andrew Wilson jr, vice M Backhouse, mv'd away;
Hamptonville, N C-Abner Carmichael, vice Thos Hampton, rsgn'd;
Tunkhannock, Pa-Elijah Barnum, vice Isaac Slocum, rsgn'd;
North East, Md-Benoni Williams, vice Wm Russel, rsgn'd;
Alfred, Maine-Jeremiah Goodwin, vice Thos Keeler, rsgn'd;
Sandisfield, Mas-Geo Hull, vice Elikim Hull, rsgn'd;
Hungrytown, Va-Jennings Robinson, vice G Y Stokes, rsgn'd;
Clover Dale Furnace, Va-Wm Gordon, vice Thos Evans, mv'd away.
New Post ofcs est in Mar 1811 & postmaster:
Long Meadow, Mas-Solomon Burt, Post mstr;
Hebron, Maine-Benj Chandler;
Bethel, N Y-Wm Brown;
Flinn's Fork, Ky-John Whitnall;
Hendrick's store, Va-Sam'l Hancock;
Lackawack, Pa-John Andesley;
Great Swamp, Pa-Theodore Woodbridge;
Okisons, Pa-Nichs Okison;
Honeoye, N Y-Nath'l Allen;
Levonia, N Y-Eli Hill;
Warsaw, N Y-Chas Sheldon;
Sheldon, N Y-Fitch Chipman;
Queen's town, Md-Nichs Hobbs;
West Farms, N Y-John B Gillespie;
Dover, N Y-Geo Casey;
Patterson, N Y-Henry B Lee;
Fallstown, N C-Wm Falls;
Barbary, N C-Elias Barber;
Sharon, Vt-Oliver Lathrop;
Salem, Pa- Theodore Woodbridge;
Newfane, Vt-Jason Duncan jr;
Wardsboro, Vt-Jas Tnfts, [as written];
Townshend, Vt-Chas Phelps;
Sullivan, N Y-Solomon Beebe.

THU MAY 2, 1811
Notice-Mr John Hemler, you advertised my son, Peter Colter, your appr to the hat bus, as a runaway; your wife ordered him to Frederick to her relations there to learn the blacksmith bus. -Peter Colter. [Calter chng'd to Colter in May 4, 1811 newspaper]

Natchez, Miss Ter, Feb 25. Ltr from Col Jas Callier to David Holmes, Gov of Miss, dt'd Tombigbee, Wash Co, Jan 15, 1811. I repaired to Ft Stoddert & gave Lt Col Rich'd Sparks a packet you entrusted to me; I raised 5 companies. Order arrived & the militia were to return to their homes-Jan 24. Miss Terr, Mar 19, 1811-falsehoods have appeared to things done in this part of the country; Col Kemper was arrested Dec 9 & was bailed on the 13th; Col Callier became security for his bro, Col John Callier; Dec 10 Maj Hargraves, with his party at Saw-Mill Creek were defeated. -Ltr not signed.

Blair M'Clenachan, appt'd by Pres of U S, com'r of Loans, for dist of Pa, vice, Stephen Moylan,dec'd.

SAT MAY 4, 1811

The ship-*Hebe*, commanded by Wm Ogle, was on Feb 21, 1811, taken possession of by French privateer, *Diligent*, commanded by Alexis Grassin; Ogle was compelled on Feb 22 to a bill for $10,000 in favor of Mr Hatfield Smith; persons are forewarned from receiving said bill as it was illegally extorted. -Wm Ogle.

TUE MAY 7, 1811

Wm McCoy, Rpblcn, elected to Cong from Va over Gen Blackburn, Federalist; John Montgomery, Rep in Cong from Md, appt'd Atty Genr'l of Md.

Merino sheep-prizes awarded on Apr 30: [Local] John Threlkeld, of Geotown, Columbia; Lawrence Lewis, of Woodlawn, Va; W H Dangerfield, of Notley Hall, Md; Thos Peter, of Tudor place, Columbia. Mr Parke Custis presided, Ludwell Lee, of Va, as senior, & Col Deneale & Dr Selden, as jr VPs; others there-Hon Jos Lewis, Judges Cranch & Fitzhugh, David Baillie Warden, M Ivanoff, Capt Cassin-U S N, Hon Ferdinando Fairfax, Dr Thornton, Gen Van Ness & Mr Simmons.

PG Co, Md-certify that Jos Willson, living nr Bladensburg, brought before me a stray sorrel gelding. -Geo Page, J P.

For sale-240 acs laid off in small farms, a mile from Wash on turn-pike to Alexandria. -W Cranch, Wash.

In Chancery-Apr 5, 1811. Petition of Wm M'Creery, actg adm of Stephen Wilson, for preference of his claim out of the proceeds of part of rl est of Wm Hammond & Wm King, sold by decree of this crt, on mortgage executed to Jos Clarke. -Nichs Brewer, Reg C C

Public sale-last will of Wm Bushby, dec'd; parcel of ground in Gtwn on Jefferson St with brick front & framed back bldg; & all leasehold int in lot 18 in sq 477 on M St, Wash City-the late dwlg place of said Wm Bushby, nr the Navy Yard.

David Ogden, insolvent debtor, confined in Wash Co, D C, prison for debt. -Wm Brent, clk.

Orphans Crt of Wash Co, D C. May 7, 1811. Prsnl est of Henry Craig, late of said co, dec'd. -Chas McNantz, adm.

Public auction-decree of High Crt of Chancery of Md. at Mc'Coy's Tavern, the rl est of John Spurrier, late of A A Co, dec'd; part of *Brown's Purchase*-ab't 5 to 600 acs; *The Anvil*-ab't 160 acs; *Spurrier's Interest*-13 acs; lands are ab't 13 miles from

Balt City; tavern occupied by Mr M'Coy at annual rent of $1450. -Beale Spurrier, trustee.

THU MAY 9, 1811
Newspaper, *The Time Piece,* is printed at St Francisville & edited by Jas M Bradford, in East La or West Fla Terr.

Died: Mr Henry Hope, of the noble family of Hope in Scotland; born in New Eng in 1736; at age 18 came to Eng to complete his education; became a partner with his uncles in Amsterdam; in 1780 on the death of his Uncle Adrian Hope, the whole hse devolved upon him to manage; in 1760 he took a tour with his 2 nieces, dghts of his sister Mrs Goddard; the eldest mrd Mr John Williams Hope, s/o Rev Mr Williams, of Cornwall; 2nd dght mrd John Landon, of Sandenhse, Oxfordshire; the youngest mrd Adm Sir Chas Pole, Bart; he settled on Harley St in Eng in 1794; Henry Hope died Feb 25 at age 75 yrs & is interred in Woodford, in Essex. -London, Mar 5.

Orphans Crt of Wash Co, D C. Will & prsnl est of Sam'l Young, late of said city, dec'd, ship carpenter. -Thos Young.

To rent or lease-land adj the city of Wash, next east of Joel Barlow. -Josias M Speake, living on the premises, Canton.

Laborers wanted to employ at his brick yard in Wash City. -Tench Ringgold.

SAT MAY 11, 1811
Died: Maj Laurence Butler, May 3, at his seat in this county; of Rev war; taken prisoner in Charleston, S C. -Winch Gaz

Arlington sheep shearing-premiums were awarded to the following for cloths: Mrs Ann Snowden, of Pr Wm Co, Va; Miss Delia Mc Afee, of Pr Wm Co, Va. Lambs shown by: Mrs Lee of Coton, Loudon Co, Va; D McCarty Chichester, of Fairfax Co, Va; John C Scott, of Strawberry Vale, Fairfax Co, Va; prop of Geo Mason, of Gunston, Fairfax Co, Va; John C Scott, of Strawberry Vale, Fairfax Co, Va. -Alex D Gaz.

Phil-May 9, 1811. Genr'l Moreau, on May 7, declared his intention to become a ctzn of the U S.

Wm Thumlert, successor to Rich'd Gaines, from Phil, has commenced the manufacture of ladies shoes in Bridge St, Gtwn.

To be sold-quantity of fence rails for tax due the Wash Corp by Abraham Young. -Henry M Queen, coll.

Washington Library: Jas Laurie, Pres & Moses Young, Treas.

Sale at auction-at store lately occupied by Mr Chas Vinson, in Bridge St; ab't 400 prs of leather shoes, groc, hack & horses. -John Travers, auct.

Jonathan Jennings re-elected to Cong from Indiana Terr.

TUE MAY 14, 1811
In N Y, Rensselear Co, Mr John Tallmadge, respected Federalist, has declared his dissent from nomination so far as relate to Abraham L Viele, whom he says is notoriously illiterate & ignorant in the extreme.

Appointments in the Militia of the dist of Col, May 8:
1st Legion-Walter Smith, Lt Col Com; Wm Brent, Geo Andrews, Jas Thompson, Geo Magruder, Majs;
2nd Legion-Chas McKnight, Capt; Jos H Mandeville, Horace Fields, Greensberry Griffith, John Cranston, Wm Ramsay, John Dulany-Lts;
Robt Conway-Cornet; Robt Gray-Ensign.

Mrd: Chisey Daniel, of S C, atty at law, to Miss Eliza Pugh Weightman, of Alexandria, D C, on May 9, in Raleigh, N C.

Died: on May 13, in N Y C, Rev Dr John Rodgers, senior pastor of the Pres Chr in N Y, age 84 yrs.

New mbrs to rep Va in the ensuing Congress: Thos *Israel, Jas Breckenridge, John Baker, Jos Lewis jr. [*Israel corrected to Thos Wilson, May 16th paper.]

N Y Gazette: regarding young man impressed from the brig *Spitfire;* I sailed from Portland, Maine, on Apr 27, 1811, bound to N Y with the owner, Josiah Ficket & his indented appr John Diguo, age 20 yrs, who was born in Cape Eliz, nr Portland & bound to the owner at age 9 yrs by his fr; he srv'd 11 yrs in the shipwrights bus. having never before been at sea; on May 1, we were brought to by a British ship of war and John Diguo was impressed. -John Neal, mstr of said brig. Any person that has doubts to the truth of the above, may call at Mrs Strangman's, 94 Pearl St, & converse with the owner, mstr, & a passenger, who put up at her hse.

Sale by auction-all hsehld furn & groc of Mr Dennis O'Conner, who is removing from the city; also the hse & lot, formerly the prop of Edw Scannell, nr the Navy Yd Mkt hse; also hse & lot on sq 406 on F St. -Chas Jones, auct.

Papers handed to Jas A Porter: Sir, take notice that I have countermanded all power I ever gave you as my atty; deliver to me all papers belonging to me or to Thos Jenkins, dec'd; deliver Lewis, negro man, now in your possession. -Francis Jenkins. [Jenkins appointed Porter-autumn of 1808].

Partnership bet John Hodges of Thos & Benj Hodges of Thos, is dissolved by mutual consent.

THU MAY 16, 1811
Wash Whig Soc: Dr Jas H Blake, chosen Pres; Maj Moses Young-VP, Dr Hanson Catlett-Treas & Caspar W Weaver-sec.

Wash Co, D C. Jas B Potts, of said co, brought before me a stray black mare. -Sam N Smallwood, J P.

For sale-ab't 200 acs on rd from Bladensburg to Annapolis, formerly cld *Baldwin's Tavern*. Terms by Basil Waring. -Sarah Waring.

Public sale-2 valuable negro men, a coachman & footman, prop of John P Van Ness for tax due Wash Corp. -Ezl MacDaniel, coll.

Jas A Porter writes a ltr regarding Francis Jenkins' ltr in May 14 newspaper. [Porter has an infirm wife & 5 infant chldrn; Jenkins has a wife]. Ltrs supporting Porter were sent by Thos Carpenter jr & G Boarman, M D-May 13 & 14.

Stephen W Gray, insolvent debtor, confined in Wash Co, D C, prison for debt. -Wm Brent, clk.

Public sale-1 brick hse & lot in sq 300, prop of Wm Duncanson, for tax due Wash Corp. -Ezl MacDaniel, coll 2nd ward.

Lost-horse & blk mare. -John Jones, nr Wash Bank-Capt Hill.

New Apothecary shop on Capitol Hill. -Thos Ewell

SAT MAY 18, 1811
For sale-so much of the sq 625, sufficient to pay taxes due Wash Corp; prop of Benj Oden. Also-lots 12 & 13, in sq 762, prop of Edw Plowden, for same. Also-lot 12 sq 700, prop of Wiseman G Keadle, for same. Also, a lot in sq 770, prop of Benj Bryan, for same. -Zh Walker, coll 3d ward.

Mgrs of the vaccine institute lottery, Balt, Md:
Wm Wilson	Robt Steuart	Luke Tiernan
Henry Shroeder	Aaron Levering	Sam'l Harden
Edw J Coale	Dr John Cromwell	Dr Wm H Clendinen
Jas W Collins	John W Glenn	Peter Hoffman, jr
Andrew Agnew	Alex'r McDonald	Edw G Woodyear
Dr Jas Smith		

For sale-merchant mill at Little Falls, 3 miles above Gtwn; hse is 50 X 48 & 3 stories high. Apply to Mr John Hersey in Gtwn or to Jos Dean, Alexandria.

For sale-brick hse on sq 742-all right, title & int of Rich'd Charles, for tax due Wash Corp; & a brick hse & lot in sq 651, prop of Thos Nevitt, for same. -Zh Walker, coll 3d ward.

Jesse C Palmer, insolvent debtor, confined in Wash Co, D C, prison for debt.
-Wm Brent, clk.

TUE MAY 21, 1811
Columbian Agric Soc exhibition held on prop of Thos Beall of Gtwn adj Mr Parrot's Rope Walk; premiums were awarded: 1-Gen John Mason, of Analoston Island, D C; 2 & 5-Jacob Gibson, of Talbot Co, Eastern Shore, Md; 3-Mr Roger Brook, of Montg Co, Md; 4-Wm Bowie, of PG Co, Md; 6-7 & 11-Mrs Eliz Bailey, of A A Co, Md; 8-Mrs Martha P Graham, of Dumfries, Pr Wm Co, Va; 9-Mrs Anna M Mason, of Analoston Island, D C; 10-Mrs Bruce, of Alleghany Co, Md; 12-Mrs Kimball of Fred'k Co, Md; 13-Mrs Mary Canby, of Montg Co, Md; 14-Mrs Sarah McCarty Mason, of Hollin Hall, Fairfax Co, Va; 15-Edw Eno, of Wash City; 16-Thos McGrath, of Wash City. Fine wool premiums-Gen Mason, Thos Peter, Bazil Darby, R Brook & Mr Chichester. Long wool-Messrs Marbury, Gibson, Wm Bowie, I Duckett. 5th premium-Thos Gibson, Dr Wm A Dangerfield, R Slaughter jr. Wm Marbury, J Kent. -Signed, W H Foote, J Threlkeld, Gerard Brookes, Thos Harwood of Benj, Rich'd K Meade, Basil Brooke, R M Boyer, John Davidson, John Hoye, Henry Childs. -David Wiley, sec, Gtwn, May 17, 1811. [Mrs Beall was thanked for her hospitality in the absence of Mr Beall.]

Vincennes, Ind Ter: last month a suit bet Wm Henry Harrison, plntf, vs Mr Wm McIntosh, dfndnt, for slander; verdict in favor of the plntff of $4,000 damages.

John Coalter, appt'd Judge of Crt of Appeals of Va, vice Judge Tucker, rsgn'd.

Balt & Phil, Pilot stages, through in one day; Balt to N Y in 2 days with 7 hrs sleep in Phil. Rich'd C Stockton, Balt; Wm B Stokes, Havre De Grace; Joshua Richardson, Alex'r Scott, Elkton; Wm Anderson, Chester; Wm T Stockton, Phil.

All persons indebted to est of John Smith, dec'd, late of this city & the Dept of War, to make payment immediately. -Sam Clarke, of Phil, adm; or Dr Phineas Bradley, of Wash City.

Sale at dwlg plantation of late Wm P Williams; order of Orphans Crt of Montg Co, Md: negroes, stock & furn. -Edw O Williams, adm of Wm P Williams, dec'd.

THU MAY 23, 1811
Tammany Soc of Wash. Grand Sachem-Dr Wm R Cozens; Sec-Wm Lambert; Treas-Henry Aborn. In N Y the Grand Sachem, Mr Clarkson Crolius, gave an oration on May 20.

Ranaway-Tom Brown, negro man ab't 24 yrs of age; secure him to Jashua Sedwich in Calvert Co, Md or to me in King Geo Co, Va. -Benj Sedwich.

Post ofc changes in Apr, 1811:
Lunenburg, Va-John Taylor, vice Jas Bagley, rsgn'd;
Queen Ann, Md-John Randall, vice Chas D Hodges, rsgn'd;
Milton, Vt-Jesse P Carpenter, vice Thos Dervey, mv'd away;

Norwich, N Y-Perez Randall, vice Haskall Ramsford, rsgn'd;
Darnes, Md-John Candler, vice Aaron Offutt, rsgn'd;
Nescopeck, Pa-John Briggs jr, vice Wm Baird, rsgn'd;
Glenns, Va-Benj Robinson, vice Christopher Garland, rsgn'd;
Vincennes, Ind Ter-Wm Prince, vice G W Johnson, rsgn'd;
Atsion, N Y-John Gregory, vice M Valentine, mv'd away;
Ft Edw, N Y-John F Gandall, vice Jas Rogers, dec'd;
Fairfield, Pa-Ezra Blythe, vice John McGinley, rsgn'd;
Beaufort, S C-Dan'l Parker, vice Jas Clark, rsgn'd;
Woodbury, N J-Chas Ogden, vice Benj Ruhlon, rsgn'd;
Woburn, Mass-John Wade, vice Ichabod Parker, mv'd away;
Elk Run Chr, Va-John Shute, vice Wm Shumate, rsgn'd;
Mt Airy, N C-Wm McCraw, vice M Lawrence, mv'd away;
Varennes, S C-Thos D Baird, vice Mark H Collins, mv'd away;
Conwayboro, S C-Joshua S Norman, vice Henry Durant, rsgn'd;
North Bend, Ohio-Jas Silver, vice John Hart;
Munroe N Y-Geo Wilkes, vice Edw B Tuthill, rsgn'd;
Price's Mills, Va-Thos A Hope, vice Otho W Callis, mv'd away;
Haverhill, N H-Moses Dow jr, vice Moses Dow, dec'd;
Smithfield, Va-Wilson Davis, vice J H Purdy;
West Union, Pa-Wm Russell, vice Jos Darlinton;
Eddyville, Ky-M Lyon, vice Chittenden Lyon, mv'd away.
New ofcs established in Apr 1811 & postmstr:
McIntosh's Bluff, Baldwin Co, Miss Tr-John B Chandler, postmaster;
Hamburg, Otego Co, N Y-Sam'l Root;
Buford's Bridge, Barnwell dist, S C-Mathew Moye;
Toland, Hampshire Co, Mass-Amos Phelps;
Dighton's Cross Rds, Mass-Sylvester Otwood jr;
Dryden, Cayuga Co, N Y-Jonathan Stout;
Virgil, Courtland Co, N Y-Zepher Moore;
Beaver Dams, Md-Jas Tucker;
Bethany, Wayne Co, Pa-Solomon Moore;
Winchester, Cheschire Co, N H-Henry Pratt;
West Port, Bristol Co, Ms-Isaac Howland;
Le Roysville, Jefferson Co, N Y-Le Roy De Chaumont;
Linden, Vt-Benj F Deming;
Burke, Vt-Geo W Denison;
BellyMeade, Vt-Sam D Blake.
Ofcs discont'd Apr 1811: Port Putnam, N Y & Grant's Lick, Ky.

For sale-part of lot 5 in sq 802 with 2 story brick hse; also one share in Wash Bldg Co; under decree of Crt of Chancery of Wash Co, D C, to pay debts of Jos Wheat, dec'd. -Geo Collard, trustee. N L Queen & Co, aucts.

SAT MAY 25, 1811
For sale-frame hse & lot on sq 84 for taxes due Wash Corp by Henry Suttle.
-Jos Brumley, coll 1st ward.

For sale-all prsnl prop of the late John W Warfield, at his late resid in Montg Co, Md; negroes, stock, furn, & farming utensils. -Alex'r Warfield, exc.

For sale-order of Orphans Crt of PG Co, Md; at dwlg hse of Seth Hyatt, negro boy, 7 yrs old, prop of the late Anderson Conaway, dec'd. -Elenor Conaway, Admx.

For sale-lots 2 & 3 on sq 38, Pa Ave, with improvements-cld *Pollock's Bldgs*. -Chas Jones, auct.

John Cotton Smith, appt'd Lt Gov of Conn; over Elijah Boardman, John C Smith, Chauncey Goodrich & John Treadwell.

For sale-brick hse & lot in sq 127, prop of Chas Cook's heirs for taxes due Wash Corp; also brick hse & lot in sq 74, prop of Henry Moscrop, for same. -Jos Bromley, coll 1st ward.

TUE MAY 28, 1811
John Tayloe, appt'd Maj of the Cvlry of this District, by Pres of the U S on May 22.

U S Gun Boat, 157, Lt John Kerr, Cmder, bound to St Mary's, May 17, dashed to pieces by the sea; drowned were: Lt John Kerr; Wm Tupper, boatswain; Jas Dogarthy; Oliver Corry, John Card; L Campbell; Bartholomew Fuller; Jos Daily; John Adams; Wm Trotter, *Jos Lucas; Wm Mackey, a boy; ____ Duboise. Saved were: Messrs Atwood of Md, Herriot of Gtwn, & Gyles, of Wash, all young men who had just entered the Navy as Midshipmen; & Mr Forneau, the pilot. -Charleston, May 18. *Charleston, May 20-Jos Lucas was saved by Mr Cahoone, the superintendent of the light hse.

Died: Capt Lewis Howard, of the Artillery, on Jan 13, 1811, at Island of Michilimackinac, Cmder of that fort.

Died: Col Miles Selden, near Richmond, on May 18.

Nath G Maxwell, residing in Wash City, obtained from Orphans Crt of Wash Co, D C, ltrs of adm on prsnl est of Robt W Goldsborough, late a purser in U S N, dec'd. -N G Maxwell, Wash.

Persons are cautioned against delivering any merchandize to me with out an order in writing. -Ch Minifie. N B-I left my dwlg hse, sundry lots to Mr Arthur Campbell, who is in possession. -C M, Wash City.

Info wanted of Henry Morgue Billington, otherwise Henry Morgue, born in London in 1788; in 1807 srv'd on his Majesty's sloop of war *Savage*, under name of Henry Mark, & then in the hunter sloop of war, Capt Fred'k Rogers. -Jos Price, 14 Stratton St, Piccadilly, London; John P Mumford, merchant, N Y; Sam'l Betton, Phil & John Price Betton, St Ann's Bay, Jamaica. To relieve the anxiety of his friends.

Orphans Crt of PG Co, Md: sale at *Brookfield,* late resid of Thos Contee, dec'd, part of his prsnl est-negroes, stock, furn. -Thos Contee Worthington, exc.

THU MAY 30, 1811
Mrshl's sale-all the est, right, title, int of Nicholas Voss to lot 8 sq 253, Wash City, with 3 story brick bldg & frame hse on F St & back bldgs; writs from Crct Crt of Wash Co, D C; suit of Benj Stoddert use of Abraham Vanbibbers, exc; & suit of Henry Shroder against the said Voss. -Wash Boyd-mrshl.

Mrshl's sale: on the premises, all right, title & int of Nathan Orme, to frame hse on sq 75 in Wash City, adj Dr Cousins, & hsedhld furn; writ from Crct Crt of Wash Co, D C; suit of Jas Moore against Nathan Orme, to satisfy the same. -Wash Boyd, mrsh'l, D C.

Mrshl's sale-on premises, all est, right, title & int of Benj Betterton to part of lot 23 in sq 101 with frame hse in Wash City; writ from Crct Crt of Wash Co, D C; suit of John Bridges against said Betterton, to satisfy same. -W Boyd

Henry Taylor applies to PG Co Crt, Md, for act of insolvent debtor; Taylor is in prison for debt only. -Dan'l Clarke, Test, John Read Magruder, clk PG Co.

New Book-*The Remains of Henry Kirk White,* late of St John's College, Cambridge, with an account of his life. -Robt Southey-2 vols.

SAT JUN 1, 1811
Mrd: Mr Rich'd Barry to Miss Eliza Cook, both of Wash, on May 30, by Rev Mr Matthews.

Mrd: Patrick Magruder, of Wash, clk of Hse o/Reps of U S, to Miss Martha Goodwyn, eldest d/o Col Peterson Goodwyn, Rep in Congress from Va, on May 28, nr Petersburg, Va, by Rev Mr Harrison.

Died: on May 3, Mrs Sarah G Smith, consort of Thos L Smith of Louisa Co, & eldest d/o Mathew Clay, of Va, age 22 yrs; dght, sister & wife.

Died: John Kilty, Adj Genr'l of Md, at Annapolis, May 27.

Jos Carter, applies for act of insolvent debtor of PG Co, Crt, Md, confined for debt. -John Read Magruder, jr clk.

For sale-deed in trust from Osborn Warner for paying debt due Dr John Douglass; all right, title, int & est in part of lot 9 in sq 491, Wash City, with framed dwlg & brick livery stable. -John Hewitt, trustee. Chas Jones, auct.

Orphans Crt of Chas Co, Md. Ltrs of adm on prsnl est of Col Gerard Briscoe, late of Chas Co, dec'd; also ltrs d b n on est of Benj Jamamien, late of Chas Co, dec'd. -Edw Briscoe & Eliz A Briscoe, adms of G Briscoe, & Benj Jameson.

Merino sheep for sale, at *Broom Lawn*, nr Alexandria; shipped some mos ago by Wm Jarvis. -J H Hooe. Gtwn

Lancaster Soc to build a school hse. -D Bussard, R Munroe, F S Key.

TUE JUN 4, 1811
Wonderful escape-Mr Jas Price, his wife & child; after a tree fell on their hse; living ab't 1 mile & a 1/4 S E of Waynesville, on May 2. -Lebanon, Ten.

Mrd: Miss Eliz Breckenbridge, 2nd d/o Jas Breckenridge, of Bottetourt Co, Va, & Edw Watts, of Campbell Co, May 7.

Died: Mrs Jane Thomas, w/o Col John Thomas, on Apr 16, age 91 yrs; spirited Whig. Tories attacked the hse of her hsbnd in 1779 & with her son & son-in-law, guarded it. Chaleston Ppr.

Henry W Magruder, of PG Co, insolvent debtor; confined for debt. -John Read Magruder, clk-PG Co, Md.

Norfolk, May 27. Altercation on Jun 1, between Mr Moses Myers & Mr Rich'd Bowden; Mr Sam'l Myers, s/o Mr Moses Myers, armed himself with a pistol when he heard of the injuries offered to his fr; went to Mr Bowden's store & shot him dead.

My wife Ellen Mulloney has eloped from my bed & board; do not give her any credit on my account. -Edw Mulloney.

Ranaway-Bob, negro man. -Isaac Stewart, lvng nr Port Tobacco, Chas Co, Md.

Lewis Morin has rec'd new goods for his store.

THU JUN 6, 1811
Schn'r *Ctzn,* to sail for New York for freight or passage. Apply to Jos Forrest, Wash. -Timothy Winn, N Y.

For sale-lots 21 & 22 in sq 688, prop of Adam Lindsay, for taxes due Wash Corp. -Zh Walker, coll 3d ward.

Walter Rodger, boy wounded on the frig, *President,* has been appt'd Midshipman in U S N.

Died: Lt Josiah Watson, on May 29, at his lodgings in Norfolk, attached to the U S brig, *Nautilus.*

Mbrs elected to City Council of Wash;
1st Chamber: Jas Hoban, Toppan Webster, John Davidson, Wm Worthington, Jas H Blake, Thos H Gilliss, Andrew Way jr, Walter Clarke, John Hewitt.

2nd Chamber: Alex'r McCormick, Geo Blagden, Elias B Caldwell, Jas D Barry, John Law, Matthew Wright, Jos Cassin, Gustavus Higdon, Wm Prout. Next 3 highest on the list: Jos Gales jr, Henry Herford, C W Goldsborough, John Dobbyn, Dan'l Rapine, Sam'l N Smallwood. Judges-Jas H Blake & Rich'd S Briscoe. Assoc Judges: Jos Stretch, T H Gilliss, Francis Clarke & Andrew Way jr. Judges of the Elec: Jos Forrest, Dan'l Rapine, Mathew Wright, Geo Blagdon, Gustavus Higden, Henry Ingle.

Germantown Acad conducted by Geo J Howell; at mansion of late Godfrey Dorfeuill; Mr Anthony Bouchard, teacher; Madam Bouchard will reside with her family in the institution. Apply in Phil to: Peter S Duponceau, Walter Franklin, or Anthony Morris; or to Geo J Howell, Germantown.

Thos Nicholson, of Gtwn, did on Apr 19, 1811, appoint Mr Isaac Hinkle, of Harrison Co, Va, his atty. Jun 5, 1811, I revoke, annull, & void same. -Thos Nicholson.

For sale-negro Jim, formerly the prop of Rd Cramphin, dec'd. -Cartwright Tippett, kpr of the goal.

Wm G Ridgely & Henry Childs have formed a co-partnership at store lately occupied by Ridgely & Riggs; assortment of seasonal goods.

SAT JUN 8, 1811
Population in the U S per census of 1810-7,238,421. Virginia-965,079; Md-380,546; Columbia-24,023.

For sale-a bay horse, prop of Benj Dulany, for taxes due the Wash Corp. -Zh Walker, coll 3d ward.

Henry Ingle, wishing to decline the hrdware business, offers his stock for sale; also 3 story brick hse on N J Ave. Steady employment to a journeyman cabinet mkr, apply to Mr H Ingle.

Marmaduke Dove, insolvent debtor, confined in Wash Co, D C prison, for debt-same for Robt Williams; same for Geo N Thomas. -Wm Brent, clk.

Mrd: Dr John Bronaugh to Miss Fanny Graham, d/o Mr Robt Graham, on May 30, by Rev Lee Massey, at Mr Robt Graham's seat in Pr Wm Co, Va.

Mrd: Mr Timothy Brundige to Mrs Mary Linton, at Dumfries, on Jun 2, both of Durnfries, by Rev Mr Chas O'Neal.

For sale-3 story brick hse & part of lot 5 in sq 461, prop of Crookshank & Thompson, for taxes due Wash Corp. Also a 2 story frame hse & part of lot 5 in sq 347, prop of Mark Stockwell's heirs, for same. Also a 2 story brick hse & part of lot 21 in sq 378, prop of Jas Gannon, for same. -Ezl MacDaniel, coll 3d ward.

Mrd: Mr Peter Gardner, of Wash City, to Mrs Mgt Green, of Balt Co, on Jun 3, by Rev Mr Richards.

TUE JUN 11, 1811
John Brewer appt'd Reg of Land Ofc for Western Shore of Md, vice John Kilty, dec'd.

Notice: Renewal of certificates in favor of Archibald Moncrieffe, of Balt, by Reg of the Treas. -Jos Forrest.

Mrd: Lt Anderson, of U S M & Miss Jane Willoughby, of Norfolk, on Jun 5, at Gosport.

Died: Col Geo Muter, fomerly Chief Justice of Ky, on May 9.

Ranaway-apprentices: Jas Samington & Lewis Pool; latter a ntv of St Mary's Co, s/o Mrs Pool, living in Gtwn. -W H P Tuckfield.

John Gassaway appt'd adjut Genr'l of Md.

THU JUN 13, 1811
Col Jon Williams has discovered that the rocks which obstruct the navigation of the Ohio, at Louisville, are petrified roots of trees.

Mrs Custis, at her hse on Pa Ave, will be grateful for the return of her music bk. Eliza P Law is written over many tunes.

Paper hangings for sale-AL Johncherez, crnr of Bridge & High Sts, Gtwn.

SAT JUN 15, 1811
Mrd: Mr Chas P Polk to Mrs Lucy Brockenbrough, of Port Royal, Va, Jun 14, by Rev Mr O B Brown.

N Y paper-A J Dallas jr, U S N, Jun 8-writes that he observed the fracas bet the President & Little Belt; the former had fired the first gun. -New York.

For sale-at Jas Johnson's, sundry hsehld furn, for taxes due Wash Corp. -Henry M Queen, coll 4th ward.

Ranaway-Frank, negro; from F W Hawkins, nr Port Tobacco, Chas Co, Md.

Sale-at Mr Wm Price's wharf, Fells Point, Balt, Md; a new ship built by the same & advertised by Messrs Von Kapff & Brune. -Thos Chase, auct, Balt, Md.

Orphans Crt of Wash Co, D C. Nathan Ball vs John Litle's heirs. Ratify sale by Sam'l Brooke, trustee, of lot 10 sq 222, in Wash City for $350-& part of lot 16 in sq 141, Wash City, for $472. -Wm Brent, clk.

TUE JUN 18, 1811
Post ofcs changes, May 1811.
Pughtown, Va-Wm Rayons, vice Wm M Holliday, rsgn'd;
Smithville, N C-Benj Blancy, vice Jno Conyers;
Wash, Va-Ralls Calvert, vice Jeremiah Strother, mv'd away;
West Brookfield, Ms-Hollis Hitchcock, vice Dan Merrian, rsgn'd;
Allen's fresh, Md-Edw Turner, vice Jas Swan, rsgn'd;
Dixon's Springs, Ten-David Cothran, vice T Dixon, rsgn'd;
Goshen, Ga-Jas E Food, vice Sam'l Davis, rsgn'd;
Hadley, N Y-Jno W Taylor, vice Benj Cowles, rsgn'd;
Broadalbin, N Y-N R Van Vranken, vice Jno Richards, rsgn'd;
Huntington, S C-Thos Martin, vice Turner Richardson, mv'd away;
Northumberland C H, Va-Jas Smith, vice I Anderson, mv'd away;
Shepherdsville, Ky-Jno W Beckwith, vice Jas Porter, rsgn'd;
Jacksonboro, S C-Jno Fabian Sr, vice Dan'l Miscalley;
Johnston, Pa-John Linton, vice John Beatty, rsgn'd;
Presque Isle, Pa-Robt Knox, vice Jno Gray;
Elizabethtown, Ten-Wm B Carter, vice Alfred M Carter, rsgn'd;
Landsford, S C-Hyder A Davie, vice W R Davie, rsgn'd;
Lincolnton, Ga-Jeremiah Walker, vice Thos Lamar, mv'd away;
Nashville, Ten-Robt B Currey, vice Robt Stothart;
McQueen's store, N C-Archd McQueen, vice J McQueen, rsgn'd;
Harrisburg, S C-Jas Harris, vice C Harris, rsgn'd;
Halifax, C H Va-Littlebury Royster, vice Andrew Clark, rsgn'd;
Thornsburg, Va-Edmund Foster, vice Jos Pollard, mv'd away;
Hart's Store, Va-David Young, vice Andrew Hart, rsgn'd;
Clarence, N Y-Archd S Clark, vice Asa Ransom, rsgn'd;
Eddington, Me-Henry Call, vice Park Holland, rsgn'd;
Rutland, N Y-Henry H Sherwood, vice John Read;
Bethlehem Crossrds, Va-John Stith, vice Spratley Williams, rsgn'd;
Bloomingsburg, N Y-Jas Lockwood, vice M Railey, mv'd away;
Northampton, C H Va-Rich'd Rodgers, vice John B Taylor, rsgn'd;
Mansfield Ct-Dan'l Bicknell, vice Roger Gurley, rsgn'd.
New ofcs-May 1811 & postmaster:
Casey C H, Casey Co, Ky-Nathan Miller, Postmaster;
Sudbury, Rutland Co, Vt-Thos White;
Prospect, Pr Edw Co, Va-Robt Venable jr;
Bloomsbury, Hallifax Co, Va-Mark Wilson;
Lockharts, LincolnCo, Ga-Jas Lockhart;
Solon, Courtland Co, N Y-Simeon Phelps;
Goshen Hill, Spartanburg dist, S C-Park Dugan;
Price's Store, Spartanburg dist, S C-Thos Price;
Sumner, Oxford Co, Me-Simon Barret jr;
German, Chenango Co, N Y-Stephen Pomroy;
Hartford, Pulaski Co, Ga-Solomon A Hopkins;
Clinton Kennebeck Co, Md-Gersham Flagg;
Roans Creek, Ten-Henry Hammond;
Abbington, Luzerne Co, Pa-John Miller;

Hartford, Susquehannah Co, Pa-Robt Chandler;
New Milford, Susquehannah Co, Pa-Nichs McCarty;
Seneca Mills-Jas L Lingan.
Ofcs discont'd: Fort Defiance, N C & Cross Keys, Va.

Bed of marble discovered nr Milford Harbor, New Haven, Conn; first specimens taken by Mr Baldwin, student in Yale Coll.

Mrd: Capt Viscoe S Doxey to Miss Eliza Goods, both of Alexandria, Jun 13.

Died: Genr'l Wm Eaton, at Brimfield, Mass, Jun 1; interred on Jun 4 with Military & Masonic Honors.

Wm Coleman, editor of the *N Y Evening Post*, has recovered of S Southwick, editor of the *Albany Register*, a verdict of $1500 damages, in a libel suit.

John Templeman, of Wash Co, D C, employed to construct a chain bridge over the Merrimack. -Newburyport, Dec 15. Directors of Essex Merrimack Bridge: Wm Bartlet, John Pettingal & Joshua Carter.

Soc for Encouragement of Domestic Manufactures for Fred'k Co, meeting held at *Friendly Grove Factory*, occupied by Mr Jos C Baldwin. Committee of Judges: Messrs A Magill, W Taylor, W Throckmorton, W Morris & A Holliday. Premiums awarded to: Mr W Alexander of Fred'k Co; Mr R K Meade; Mrs A Smith of Hackwood; Miss E McGuire of Winchester; Mrs Peggy Littler of Fred'k Co; Mrs Thos Lewis of Fred'k Co; Mrs E McAlister of Greenwood Mills; Mrs Mary D Washington of Hawthorn. Sheep Judges: Jared Williams, Joel Ward & Jas Singleton. Premiums to: Mrs David Ridgway; Mr R K Meade; Mr John Clevinger. -Lau A Washington, sec. Winchester, Jun 1. Meeting held May 28, 1811.

For sale-brick hse in sq 38, prop of Abigail Pollock for tax due Wash Corp; also brick hse & lot in sq 38, prop of Wm Stuart, for same; also frame hse & lot in sq 28, prop of Henry Luddington, for same; also frame hse & lot in sq 38, prop of Walter Barron, for same. -Jos Brumley-coll ward 1.

Runaway-John Baily, negro boy ab't 19 yrs of age; committed to Allegany Co, Md, jail; says he belongs to Sam'l Stone who lately remv'd from Va to Ky. -Wm Hilleary-shrf, Cumberland.

For sale-*The Orange Mills* in Orange Co, Va; & 12 negroes. -Tho Richards.

For sale-275 acs in Calvert Co, Md; with frame dwlg hse. -Walter Hellen.

THU JUN 20, 1811
Cowes, May 7-today, Mr Pinkney, his lady & 8 chldrn, embarked on board the American frig *Essex*.

Sam'l Saunders; ntv of Conn, has been dischg'd from the British sloop of war *Atalante* & sent to this place. -Norfolk, Jun 14.

Mrd: Dr Frederick May, of Wash, to Miss Julia Matilda Slacum, of Alex, on Jun 17, by Rev Mr Barclay, in Alexandria.

Died: Wm Dandridge Claiborne, age 55 yrs, in King Wm Co, Va, on Jun 11.

Died: Capt Law, U S A, in Miss Terr, of a lingering complaint, not long since.

Stray bay horse came to *Green Hill*, Mrs Digges. -Henry Gibbons, Basford.

Anthony Holmead, of Wash Co, D C, brought before me a stray bay horse. -Rich'd S Briscoe, a Justice of the Peace, Wash Co, D C.

SAT JUN 22, 1811
Died: Mr Peter Gardner, ship carpenter, a few days ago in Wash City.

Died: Sam'l Chase, a Judge of the Crct Crt of U S, on Jun 20, of a lingering disease, at an advanced age.

Died: Hon Joshua G Wright, of Wilmington, N C, on Jun 10, in Charleston, age 43 yrs, of consumption.

Wm Farrand, insolvent debtor, confined in Wash Co, D C, prison for debt. -Wm Brent, clk.

Public sale in Rockville-all right & est of Beale Ayton, an insolvent debtor; 1/4 part of 2 tracts of land, one in Hampshire Co, Va, 312 acs; other tract in Pa, cld *Sugartree Bottom,* 312 acs. -John Fleming, trustee.

For sale-hsedhld furn, prop of Wm Gray, for taxes due Wash Corp. -Zh Walker, coll 3d ward.

Reward-$10, for runaway, Jas Morris, appr boy to stone & brick laying business; has an uncle, Tom Morris, a tailor nr Leesburg, Loudon Co, Va. -Thady Hogan, Wash City.

Wool carding machine now in operation at the *Adelphi Mills.* -Issachar Scholfield, Adelphi Mills.

Luke Kent, insolvent debtor, confined in Wash Co, D C, prison for debt. -Wm Brent, clk.

Persons with claims against est of Peter Gardner, of Wash, dec'd, are to exhibit same. -Mgt Gardner, Wash.

TUE JUN 25, 1811

Mr Phineas Bond, many yrs the British Consul Genr'l for the middle & southern states, left Phil on Tue for England on board the ship *Susquehanna*, Capt Meade. He is succeeded by Mr Thos W Moore, Pro Consul.

Baton Rouge, Apr 29, 1811. Lt Col Z Pike of 4th Regt, U S infty is charged: unmilitary & unofficer-like conduct: 1-to publishing a list of promotions without authorization; 2-to assign companies to Capt Clinch & Capt Overton & to change the titles of the companies, Houston & Nicholas for those of Clinch & Overton, without authority. -J Gibson, Capt & Brig Ins. Apr 30, 1811: Z M Pike, Lt Col, writes a ltr of explanation. May 2, 1811: J Gibson, Capt & B inspec, writes a ltr releasing Pike from his arrest & is directed to resume his sword.

Died: Lt Col John Smith, of the 3d Regt of U S infantry, at his resid in Darlington dist, on Jun 6.

Jos Semmes is declining the tavern business on Jul 1.

St Louis, May 30-a few days ago a barn at the north end of this town, prop of Mr P Chouteau, was burned by Indians.

For sale-parts of lot 13 in sq 431, 7th St West, which leads from the mkt & past the poor hse. -John Sessford.

For sale-schn'r Polly, now at the Navy Yd. -Benj King, nr the Navy Yd.

THU JUN 27, 1811

Columbian Dragoons are ordered to parade on Jul 4th. -G C Washington, adj of the Columbian horse.

For sale-one frame hse on lot 7, in sq 348, subject to ground rent, prop of Theodore Mudd, for taxes due Wash Corp; also lot 7 in sq 378, prop of Walter S Chandler, for same; also lot 15 in sq 491, prop of B H Latrobe, for same; also part of lot 18 in sq 458, prop of heirs of Jas Maitland Sr, for same. -Ezl MacDaniel, coll 2nd ward.

SAT JUN 29, 1811

Died: Two veterans in Eng Lit: Wm Boscawen, translator of Horace, & Rich'd Cumberland, essayist & dramatic poet.

Notice-my wife Kitty Burns has left my hse without just reason. I will not pay any debts contracted by her. -Thos Burns.

Ranaway-Geo Beard, mulatto boy ab't 23 yrs of age. -Eleanor Johnson, nr Greencastle, Franklin Co, Pa.

Died: Col Henry Gaither, age 61 yrs, on Jun 22; ofcr of Rev war, having been in every battle [except Monmouth] which was fought by the American Army. -Spirit of '76.

Died: Henry Ridgeley, Assoc Judge of the 3d Judicial dist of Md, at his seat in Elkridge, A A Co, Md, on Jan 22.

Died: Mr Gurdon Chapin, cashier of the Bank of Alexandria, on Jun 26, after a lingering illness.

Corner stone of the Lancaster School hse was laid in Gtwn on Monday last; address by Rev Mr Sneethen of the Meth Chr; oration given by Mr Henry Beatty. -Gtwn.

Sale-deed of trust from Jas Hawkins Baynes, dec'd; plantation which the dec'd formerly resided, ab't 6 miles from Piscataway; 15 negro slaves, furn, wagon & harness. -Philip Stuart, Thos Mundell, Piscataway.

Strayed or stolen from the commons of *Greenleaf's Point*, Wash City, a sorrel horse. -Philip O'Mara, *Greenleaf's Point*.

TUE JUL 2, 1811
Wm Pinkney, our late Minister to Gr Britain, arrived in this country on frig *Essex* Capt Smith, passage of 49 days.

Died: Ann Burchan, formerly of Phil, age 80 yrs, on Jun 27, in Wash City.

Stolen or strayed, sorrel horse. -Jas Martin, Wash City.

Wanted-journeyman bkbinder. -F A Mayo, bkbinder, Staunton, Va.

Reward-$5 for Jos Casey, absconded apprentice to tayloring business, age ab't 16 yrs. -Dan'l Kealey, Wash City.

Wash Whig Soc Meeting at Davis' Hotel. -C Willis Weaver-sec.

THU JUL 4, 1811
Aug J Foster,was presented to the Pres of the U S, as Envoy Extraordinary & Minister Plenipotentiary from Gr Britain.

Thos Digges of Warburton, nr Piscataway, has a stray mare. -Wm Marshall, a Justice of the Peace for Md. [Henry Frazer, manager for Mr Digges].

For sale-auction: tenement in Gtwn, whereon Mr Clement Smith now resides; 4 adj lots, on Fayette St, Prospect St & Fall St. -Walter Smith, Gtwn.

Just rec'd & for sale-lemons & shrubs. -Lewis Labille, Pa Ave

In Chancery, Jun 21, 1811. Rich'd Duvall & Nathan Soper, vs Hannah West excx of Stephen West, John S Belt, Tobias Belt, Mary Hodges, Rich'd Belt & Beall Duvall. Bill to obtain a decree for return of money pd by Alex Duvall the fr of the cmplnt Rich'd, & the cmplnt Nathan Soper, to Stephen West late of PG Co, dec'd, for land cld *Recovery*, PG Co, Md. Original bill states that Jeremiah Belt, late of PG Co, dec'd, was indebted to said Stephen West & other persons; Alex Duvall, f/o cmplnt, did purchase of said West on behalf of himself & cmplnt N Soper part of said land; cmplnts have been evicted & turned out of possession of said land by John Belt the real owner. West is dead leaving his wife Hannah exc, who has possessed herself of his prnsl est; Alex Duvall is dead leaving Rich'd Belt his exc & heir at law; Hannah has refused to refund the purchase money; land was sold by West as agent of Belt ab't 1796 & money pd unto Mary Belt & Thos Belt, excs of said Jeremiah Belt, by said Stephen West's reps or to Tobias Belt, adm d b n with will annexed of Jeremiah Belt. John S Belt of A A Co, Md, Tobias Belt adm of Jeremiah Belt, Mary Hodges, Rich'd Belt, s/o Edw Belt, & Beall Duval of PG Co, Md, are heirs of said Jeremiah Belt. Rich'd Belt resides in Wash, D C. -Nichs Brewer, Reg Cur Can.

For sale-deed of trust from Jas Hawkins Baynes, dec'd, the plantation on which the dec'd formerly resided, ab't 6 miles from Piscataway; 200 acs & 15 negro slaves. -Philip Stuart & Thos Mundell, Piscataway, Md.

Mrd: Hon Robt Le Roy Livingston, mbr of Congress from N Y to Miss Anne Maria Diggs, d/o late Geo Digges, of PG Co, Md, at *Green Hill*, Jun 22, by Rev Dr Carroll, Archbishop of Balt. [2 splgs of Digges, Diggs]

For sale-mare, colt & horse, prop of Geo Burns, for taxes due the Wash Corp. -Zh Walker, coll 3d ward.

SAT JUL 6, 1811
For sale-lot 4 sq 119; lots 10 & 11 sq 1020; lots 2 & 3 sq 1045; lots 6, 7, 8, 9-sq 1020, part of lot 3 sq 118, prop of late John McElwee, dec'd, for paying his debts. -John Ott, trust.

Lewis Denham has leased the brdg hse at *Capon Springs*, Hampshire Co, was occupied by Mr Geo Leps for several yrs.

Notice-sale at hse of Mr Jesse Barns, Jersey Ave, all prsnl est of late Peter Gardner, dec'd. -N L Queen, auct.

Stolen or strayed-a bay horse. -Rich'd Bainbridge, Wash City.

TUE JUL 9, 1811
Runaway, Wickey, black woman; says she is the prop of John Bell of Montg Co, Md. -C Tippett, kpr of the jail. Also-John Johnson, black man, says he is free & born in State of N Y, age 24 yrs. Also-Wm Johnson, black man, age ab't 23 yrs; says he is free.

Ran away-Harry Dorsey, negro. Deliver to John Wilson of Henry, living in PG Co, Md, 2 miles from Bladensburg.

For sale-400 acs in Chas Co, Md; farm adjoins lands of Edw Hamilton, Sam'l & Wm Chapman & others; within 5 miles of Port Tobacco. -Teressa Semmes, Letitia H Hamilton.

THU JUL 11, 1811
Ladies with ltrs in Wash P O, Jul 1, 1811:

Charity Austin	Miss Priscilla Bayly	Mrs Cath Adams
Mrs Eliza Denoon	Mary Dinis	Mrs Casanave
Eliza Halley	Sarah McCarty	Mrs Mary Gaither
Sarah Murphy	Miss M Nicholson	Polly Madille
Mrs Zipp Porning	Nancy Prentiss	Mrs Mary Neale
Eliza Regen	Miss Susanna Spalding	Harriot Pierce
Mrs Ann Thomas	Sarah Young	Daceus Ann Talbut

Gideon Caprian, impressed on board his Majesty's ship *Guerrier,* was sent home to N Y after his fr wrote a ltr requesting same; John Digio, impressed, was also discharged; Josh Leeds will be discharged. -H Sawyer, Rear adm. Ltr from Sawyer to Thos Barclay, Halifax, Jun 25, 1811, followed.

Wash Acad-election will be held for 6 trustees. -Moses Young, Andrew Way jr & Jos Mechlin, Judges.

Info wanted-of Chas Segar, s/o late Henry Segar, of Kingdom of Bavaria; he will be informed of something to his advantage. In ltr dt'd Oct 18, 1803, the said Chas Segar announced his embarkation at Tonningen, with intent of proceeding to his Uncle-David Segar, merchant in Phil. -Dept of State.

SAT JUL 13, 1811
Died: Henry M Queen, of Wash, on Jul 12, age 31 yrs; he has left a widow & 3 chldrn.

Died: Lt Thos N Vaughan, U S Army, on Jul 1, board the brig *Botanic,* on his way from Savannah to Balt.

Wanted-journeymen hse carpenters. -Henry Keller, Middletown, Fred'k Co, Md.

TUE JUL 16, 1811
For sale-105 acs in Montg Co, Md, ab't 3 miles from Rockville with dwlg hse & stream cld *Capt John*, where Jas Moore formerly resided. -Miss Keziah Moore, lives on place.

Orphans Crt of Wash Co, D C. Ltrs of adm on prsnl est of John Greer, late of U S sloop of war, *Wasp, d*ec'd. -Wm M'Kee, adm. [Jul 13, 1811]

Died: Mr Eren Fisher of Dover, at Wardbury, Vt; poisoned by a bee while hiving a swarm of bees.

Notice-creditors of the late Capt Garret Barry of Wash City, dec'd; prsnl dividend will be made by Jas D Barry, adm.

THU JUL 18, 1811
F A Wagler is determined to wind up the mercantile business & will sell all his dry goods; he will be ready next month to attend to his former business of teaching music, piano forte.

Alexandria-Jul 11. The Bake hse of Mr John Young was struck by lightning on Jul 9th & Mr John Bowie, a young man, was struck & killed; Capt Pitts, Mr Marsteller & Mr Taylor were in the counting rm at the time.

Patent dt'd May 22, 1811 was obtained by John Ballthrope, Paris, Va, for *elevating & fastening window sashes by means of a spring instead of weights & pullies*.

Proposals will be rec'd for bldg a new church by the vestry of All Saints Parish, Fredericktown, Md. Apply to Wm M Beall or John Hanson Thomas, Reg.

SAT JUL 20, 1811
Mr Wm Rush of Phil, is at the head of a branch of the arts which he has himself created; his figures, forming the head or prow of a vessel & seem to draw the ship after them. Culpeper Crt hse, Jul 4, 1811.

Robt Brooke Voss, was orator of the day for the anniv of American Independence celebration.

For sale-lot 15 in sq 762; prop of Wm Gray, to satisfy Wash Corp. -Zh Walker, coll 3d ward.

For sale-633 acs cld *Indian Town*, in Chas Co, on Nanjemoy Creek, Md. -Theos Hargraves, Port Tobacco, Md.

Orphans Crt of Wash Co, D C-case of John Christian Heise, insolvent debtor, confined in Wash Co prison for debt. -Wm Brent, clk.

John Hewitt, atty at law, has taken M St Clair Clarke, as partner in the practice of law; F St, Wash City.

Orphans Crt of Wash Co, D C. Jul 18, 1811. Prsnl est of Jas O'Neal, dec'd. -P Moss.

Stolen or strayed from the commons of Wash, a cow; reward $3. -Timothy Bean, living nr the Great Hotel.

TUE JUL 23, 1811
Elected trustees of he Wash Acad-Jul 15: Sam'l H Smith, Gabriel Duvall, Revd Jas Laurie, Wm James, Thos H Gilliss & Jos Mechlin.

Died: Lord Melville, at Edinburg; there to attend the funeral of Lord President Blair; he slept at Lord Chief Barron's hse in George's square & was found dead in his bed; Lord Melville was mrd first to Eliz, d/o David Rennie, of Melville Castle; & secondly to Lady June Hope. He was 79 yrs of age.

W Marbury is declining business this fall & has goods for sale at his store in Bridge St, Gtwn.

Orphans Crt of Wash Co, D C-sale of silver plate, bedding etc, prop of late Sam'l Young, dec'd, to satisfy the creditors of his est. Sale at hse of Mr Shrub. -Thos Young, adm.

Mr Wm Cooper has an English piano forte for sale & a supply of music.

In Chancery, Jul 3, 1811-ratify sale by Solomon Davis of rl est of Solomon Simpson, dec'd; am't-$9990.29. -N Brewer-R C C.

THU JUL 25, 1811
Mbrs of The Soc of The sons of Erin, to attend the funeral of Andrew McClary, from his late lodgings at Mrs Suters, this morning. -Henry Whetcroft, sec.

Died: Capt Andrew M'Clary, sldr of the Rev, on Jul 24, in Wash City; many yrs a clk in Dept of War.

Died: Mrs Sylvia Russell, consort of Jonathan Russell, Charge D'affaires of U S-Paris; age 38 yrs, at Providence, R I a few days ago.

Died: Rich'd Penn, on May 27, in Richmond, England; formerly Gov of Pa.

Cash sale-parcel of free stone, prop of Robt Speeding, to satisfy hse rent due Adam Lindsay. -David Bates, constable.

Paul's Patent Columbia Oil sold by John Ott, Gtwn, & David Ott & Co, Wash City. First of the class of all pectorals & expectorants. Certificates: Elisha Soward, Balt, 16 Water St, Sign of The Plough-Sep 1809; Thos Elliot, Hook's Town Rd-Feb 12, 1809; Eleanor Elliot; Susanna Purden-Jan 15, 1811, Saratoga St, Balt; Wm Philips, Columbian Inn, Mkt St, Balt-Sep 6, 1803; Wm Peacock, Harrison's Creek, Balt-Apr 19, 1810; John Peacock, Thos Adams, John Clark, Balt-Apr 19, 1810; E Cath Walker, Mkt Space, Balt; Apalonio Walter, Lexington St, Balt; Kitty McClain, Phil-Jul 8, 1807. Thos Paul, late of Phil, now of Balt City, Md, is inventor & proprietor & appoints Dr John Love, of Balt City, druggist, his sole agent for U S of America, for 7 yrs beginning on Apr 23, 1810. Wit: Geo P Presbury, J P. Balt agents: Edme Ducatel, druggist, Balt Md; Henry Keerl & Son, 233 Mkt St, druggists; Jesse Talbot, druggist, Hanover & Mkt St; A Miltenberger, bk seller, Mkt St; John Vance & Co, bksellers, 178 Mkt St; G & R Waite's lottery ofc, St Paul's Lane, Mkt St; Messrs Warner & Hanna, Gay & Mkt St; Henry Dorry, druggist, Mkt St, Fell's Point; Nath'l Knight, bkseller, Fell's St; Easton-Thos H Dawson, druggist; Alexandria-Rich'd Litle, do; York Town-John Fisher, do;

Hagers town-Fred'k Miller, do; Frederick Town-John S Miller, do; Lancaster-Sam'l Fahrastock, do; Harrisburg-Sam'l Wiestling, do; Annapolis-Messrs Childs & Shaw, merchants; Phil: Thos Love at Dr Edwin A Atlee's, north 4th St; John Y Bryant, 2nd & Pine Sts, druggist; Jeremiah Morris, 293 Mkt St, do; Stephen North, 85 High St, do; N Y-R & R Waite, 38 & 64 Maiden La; Messrs John & Thos Clark, 91 Maiden La, druggists. -John Love, Balt, Jul 24.

Sale by auction-all hsehld furn of the late Capt Rankin, dec'd, at his late dwlg, 3 Bldgs. -Chas Jones, auct.

Died: on Jul 21, Thos Peter, s/o John, aged 17, in Gtwn, D C.

SAT JUL 27, 1811
Jonathan Lambert, late of Salem, Mass, mariner & ctzn thereof, on Feb 4, 1811, took possession of the islands of Tristan De Cunha, viz: The Great island & 2 others cld *Inaccessible & Nightingale*; solely for myself & my heirs; G island to be cld *Reception, Inaccessible* is now *Pintard* island, & *Nightingale* to be cld *Lovel* island. -J Lambert [Wit to signature: Andrew Millet.]

Orphans Crt of Wash Co, D C. Jul 26, 1811. Prsnl est of Chas Dent, dec'd. -Patrick Donahoe

Two cents reward-for runaway apprentice, Thos Steven, ab't 8 yrs of age. -M Young.

TUE JUL 30, 1811
A public dinner was given at Petersburg to Thos B Robertson, sec of Orleans Terr, now on a visit to his former place of residence.

Post ofc establishment changes in Jun 1811:
Manhus, N Y-Hezekiah L Granger, v Robt Wilson, dec'd
Nixonton, N C-John Pool, v Wm Albertson, mv'd away
Townsend, Ms-John H Loring, v Moses Warren, rsgn'd
Haw Rvr, N C-Benj A Rainey, v Benj Rainey, dec'd
Traveller's Rest, S C-Philip Meroney, v Jesse Edwards, mv'd away
Charlotte, N C-Afrew, v Jas Robb, rsgn'd
Wayne C H, Ky-Temple Poston, v Anthony Dibrell, rsgn'd
Woodstock, Vt-Alex'r Hutchinson, v John Carleton, rsgn'd
Cabel C H, Va-Chas Jessop, v Thos Buffington, rsgn'd
____ Pa-John Beitel, v Jos Rice, rsgn'd
Conway, N H-Dan'l Burrows, v Jas Russell
Fredericktwn, Pa-Henry P Pearson, v Chas Conyngham, mv'd away
Grant's Lick, Ky-John McLaughlin, v John G Fournoy, mv'd away
Saundersville, Ga-John Matthews, v Jas Walker, mv'd away
Evesham, N J-Sam'l Blackwood, v Henry Bennett, dec'd
Landaff, N H-Caleb Rix, v Nath'l Rix, rsgn'd
La Fourche, O T-Thos C Nicholls, v J Blanchard, rsgn'd
Laurenceburg, M T-Sam'l C Vance, v Jas Dill, rsgn'd

New ofcs established in June 1811 & postmasters:
Barbourville, Orange Co, Va-John Bradley, Postmaster
Port Watson Cayuga Co, N Y-Luther Rice, do
Bacon Castle, Surry Co, Va-R H Cocke
Ellisville, Nicholas Co, Ky-Jos Ellerbeck
New Hope, Spartanburg dist, S C-David Dantzlers
Ofcs discont'd: Lower Blue Lick, Ky & Round Bottom Mills, O.

Stockholders of the Va Copper Mine are cld to pay $10-one a share, to Jeremiah W Bronaugh, Gtwn. -Dan'l C Brent, Pres.

Case of Thos Carpenter, insolvent debtor. Creditors to exhibit their claims to Thos Carpenter jr, trustee. -Wm Brent, clk, Wash, D C.

THU AUG 1, 1811
Wash Co, D C-Chas J Nourse, insolvent debtor. Order of Hon Buckner Thruston, Ass't Judge of Crct Crt of D C. -Wm Brent, clk.

Died: Louis Claude Henry De Montmain, ancient Knight of St Louis, age ab't 70 yrs, at Charleston on Jul 14; born in Tonnerre, Dept of Yonne; was a planter of St Domingo island, but had resided in that city for 15 yrs.

Died: Mrs Eliz Hodnett of Wash, on Jul 29, age 53 yrs.

SAT AUG 3, 1811
Democratic Rpblcns of Annapolis, on Jul 30th, gave a tribute to Wm Pinkney,late Minister at London. -Balt America.

St Louis, La, Jun 27-Indian War. Mr Laline, Indian interpreter at Chicago, informs that savages are preparing for war; Indians murdered Clinton Hill; Mr Price was shot through the heart on his farm above the mouth of the Miss.

Sale-lot 17 in sq 634, by decree of Crct Crt of Wash Co, D C, as Crt of Chancery: to foreclose mortgages made by Amariah Frost to John G Ladd. -Chas Glover

College of Medicine of Md. Courses will be delivered by: John B Davidge, Jas Cocke, Nath'l Potter, Elisha De Butts & Sam'l Baker. [all M D's] -Jas Cocke, sec.

Ltr from Capt Wm P Coffin, of schn'r *Pauline*, to his owners in N Y, dt'd-Elsineur, May 30, 1811; regarding his encounter with a Danish privateer cutter from which he escaped with little damage.

J B Colvin, atty at law, may be consulted at Mrs Doyne's, Pa Ave, & will attend to prof business at crts for Wash Co, D C.

Wm H Hamer has hats for sale at his store on Pa Ave, next door to Mr Davis's Indian Queen Tavern.

Sale-at hse of Mr Pontius D Stelle, all his hsehld furn to satisfy rent due Dan'l Carrol of Dudn. -David Bates, cnstbl.

TUE AUG 6, 1811
List of land or lots with taxes due in St Mary's Co, Md:
Upper Resurrection Hundred
1807-8-9-John T Hawkins: part *Trent Neck*-175 acs; *Trent Neck*-1085 acs,-345 acs,-306 acs; *Indian Crk with Additions*-64 acs.
1807-Thos A Reeder: *Hepworth*-100 acs; *Falkirk*-165 acs; *Falkirk*-87 acs; *Boges Increase*-257 acs; *St Johns*-150 acs; *Plains of Jerico*-12 acs; 1807-8-*Haphazard*-304 acs; *Garden Spot*-6 1/4 acs; *Goslins Add*-21 3/4 acs; *Parting Path*-61 1/4 acs; 1807-*Delebrook Manor*-718 acs; *DeleBrook Manor*-365 1/4 acs. [Thos A Reeder]
Chaptico Hundred:
1807-8-9 Jas Johnston-heirs: *Chison* 94 acs, *Desart Party* 40 acs.
1807-8-9 Rich'd Mason-heirs: *Compton Purchase* 100 acs.
Upper St Clement's Hundred:
1809 Jas Knott-heirs: part *Hazard* 33 1/3 acs.
1809 Rich'd Bond-heirs: *Boston* 50 *Weems* 405 acs.
1806-7-8-9 Townsend Eden-heirs: *Bashford* 300 acs.
1807-8-9 Betty Ann Eden-hrs: *Bashford* 150 acs, Pt Neals Lot *Barrendoe* 292 acs.
1809 Notley Goldsmith: *Titchley* 50 acs.
1809 John Carpenter-heirs: *Mills Marsh* 140 acs.
1809 Eliza Jarboe: *Bayley's Risque* 93 1/5 acs.
1809 Jesse Thompson: *Friendship* 65 acs.
1809 Jesse Jordan-heirs: Pt *Bashford* 400 acs.
1807-8 Sam'l Keech-heirs: *Trumania* 50 acs, *Devonshire* 50 acs, *Stephens Good Luck* 50 acs, *Stephens Venture* 54 acs, *Ashcom's Green Field* 100 acs.
Lower St Clement's Hundred:
1807-8-9 Wm Bond-heirs: *St Clements Manor* 231 acs.
1809 Geo Bullock: *St Clements Manor* 50 acs.
1809 John Mattingley-heirs: *Snowhill* 100 acs.
1807-8-9 Jas Knott: Pt *Hazzard* 33 1/3 acs.
1809 Ignatius Fenwick-heirs: *Canoe Neck* 720 acs.
1807-8 Rich Mason-heirs: *Deynard* 220 acs.
Upper New town Hundred:
1807-8-9 Geo Howard-heirs: *Terry Wills* 130 acs.
1807-8-9 Wm Carpenter-heirs: *Crackburns Purchase* 99 acs.
1809 Martin French-heirs: *Twitten Ham* 100 acs.
1807-8-9 Repard Hopewell-heirs: *Scotland* 39 1/2 acs.
1807-9 Jos Howard-heirs: *Scotland* 12 1/2 acs.
1807-8 Rich'd Mason-heirs: *Leath* 80 acs, part of *Yieldingbury* 58 1/2 acs, *Hopton Park* 90 acs.
1809 Thos Mugg: *Long in Dispence & Farthing's Gift* 75 acs.
1807-8-9 Senaca Nelson-heirs: *Buckpart & Pomfret* 255 acs.
1807-8-9 Thos A Reeder-heirs: *St John's* 295 acs, *Reeder's Purch* 98 acs, *Young man's Venture* 344 acs, *Hamstead* 70 acs, *St John's* 100 acs, *Baptist's Hope* 38 acs, *Grave's Chance* 24 acs, *Fourth Addition* 209 acs, *Strap* 44 acs, *Westfield* 140 acs, *Middle Ground* 175 acs. 1809 Thos Shercliff's heirs: *Linstead* 80 acs, *Green's lot*

18 acs. 1807-8-9 Ign Thompson's heirs: *Linstead* 41 acs, *Addition* 50 acs, *White Acre* 60 acs.
1809 Geo Booth of Geo: *Hard Fortune* 106 acs.
1807-8-9 Thos Carberry: *Hopton Park* 155 acs.
1808-9 Wm Lansdale-heirs: *Ramble Hounslow & Strand* 988 acs. 1809 Icre Lancaster: *Lancaster's Discovery* 26 acs.
1809 Ign Mattingley-heirs: Pt *Willingham* 87 1/4 acs, *St Wms* 100 acs.
1809 John Daft-heirs: *Rockey Point* 100 acs.
1807-8 Francis Hager-heirs: *Febney* 95 acs, *Pomfret Fields* 152 acs. 1807-8 Bent Rily's heirs: *Dounham* 60 acs.
1807 Thos A Reeder-heirs: *Jas Addition* 158 acs, *Mill & Mill seat* 20 acs, Pt *Linstead* 9 acs.
1809 Jas Fenwick, Ch Co: *Inclosure* 112 acs, *Beaverdam* 92 1/2 acs, *Delebrooke* 57 1/2 acs.
1809 Edw J Heard: *Farm* 500 acs, *Tavern* 100 acs, *Plowdens Recovery* 96 acs.
1807-8 Mary Fenwick: *Fenwick Manor* 92 acs.
Lower New town Hundred.
1808-9 Mary Fenwick: *Well Found & Wheatley's Content* 132 acs.
1809 Rich'd Brown-heirs: *Chas Rest* 50 acs.
Harvey Hundred.
1807-8 Henry J Carroll of Somersett Co: *Smith's Discovery* 50 acs.
Poplar Hill Hundred.
1807 John Downs sr: *Devise* 1/2 of *Forrest of Dean & Abells Chance* 83 acs.
Upper St Mary's Hundred.
1807-8 Les Holliday's P Geo C'y: *No Name* 150 acs.
St Innigoes Hundred.
1809 Barnaby Rhodes-heirs: *Eliza Manor* 50 acs.
Ordered by John McWilliams, collector. Test: E J Millard, C C tax St M Co.
-John McWilliams, late collector of St Mary's Co, Md.

Sale by auction-sundry articles belonging to est of Capt Garrett Barry, dec'd.
-Nicholas L Queen, auct.

Wanted-a good gardener & farmer for my farm in Petworth nr Wash. -Apply to John Tayloe.

THU AUG 8, 1811
Remains of an elephant have been found on the shores of the York Rvr nr the seat of Mr Gawin Corbin, ab't 6 miles below Williamsburg.

Mrd: Mr Wm H Hamer to Miss Eliz Huddleston, all of Wash, on Aug 6, by Rev Ob B Brown.

Rich'd Ridgely, appt'd Assoc Judge of 3d Judicial dist of Md, vice R Ridgely, dec'd.

Suit of Robt Saunders & wife vs John Simpson & wife. J B Colvin writes the following from Chancery Records: Wm Andrews was f/o Priscilla Scott, formerly Priscilla Colvin, whose son I am; other chldrn left by Andrews was a dght, Eliz, reputed by the world to be illegitimate; Eliz mrd Dr John Simpson of Shippensburg, Pa. Robt Saunders of Harford Co, Md, mrd a dght of Wm Andrews. Suit was instituted over land that Simpson conceived that Saunders had not a legal title in 1800 or 1801. After this suit was pending for many yrs, that Dr John Simpson, thru my mthr, put into my possession a bond for conveyance of 75 acs of land, informing me that he gave that to me out of friendship, having mrd a dght of my grfr; my mthr's 2nd marriage was an unhappy one; I mrd in May 1801 & was poor; I offered the bond to Simpson but he refused to buy; when I told him I wld sell to someone else he took alarm; I was barely of age & terrified; I wld have been guilty of fraud if I had remained silent. I placed the ltrs on records of the Chancery Crt. Mr Hammond is the step-fr of Simpson's wife. My mthr died broken hearted at my hse in Fredericktown. -Wash City, Jan 8, 1810. [The character of Abm G Hammond is very bad; he is the h/o Mary Hammond, formerly Mary Lynchfield, & m/o Eliz Simpson, w/o John Simpson]. J Simpson writes that he will have no connection with John B Colvin, printer, or his mthr again. Jun 1810.

SAT AUG 10, 1811

For sale: order of Orphan's Crt of Wash Co, D C: all int of est of the late John M'Elwee, dec'd, for a term of yrs, in lots 25 & 26 in sq 378, Wash City; bet Pa Ave & E St. Apply to John Ott, Gtwn or Jas Kearney, F St, Wash, agents. -Rebecca McElwee, admx.

Strayed or stolen from the commons of Wash City-2 cows. Reward-$10. Geo Moore, Jas Hewitt, living nr the Centre Mkt.

Sale-all rghts, title, claim & int of Geo Adams in frame dwlg hse on S E crnr of lot 1 sq 784; ground rent $20 per annum. Writ of Fieri Facias, issued from Crct Crt of Wash Co, D C at suit of Wm C Newton. -W Boyd, mrsh'll. And all right, title, claim & int of Jas Eden in lot 13 sq 656 & lot 5 sq 744, at suit of Christiana Hamilton. -W Boyd, mrsh'l. Montg Co, Md.

For sale-at hse of Adam Robb, tavern kpr in Rockville, Montg Co, Md; rl est of late Wm Prater Williams of said Co: 800 to 1000 acs of land adj the said town, including the jail & part of the crt-hse sq; also some lots in said town. Apply- Upton Beall & Thos Wilson in Rockville & Walter C Williams. -Edw O Williams, agent for the heirs of the said Wm P Williams.

Wm Blanchard brought before me a stray gelding. -Walter B Beall, J P.

Sale-at Shumway's Tavern, Navy yd: all right, title, etc of John Hall in part of lot 1 sq 881 with brick hse; 5 writs of Fieri Facias from Crct Crt of Wash Co, D C; suit of Jas A Porter, Jesse Barnes, Geo Lake, Mich'l Quigley, Wm Prout. -Wash Boyd, mrsh'l.

Wm Richardson, Chas Co, Md, brght before me a stray mare. -Geo H Spalding, J P, Aug 3, 1811.

Ranaway-Tom Brown, negro man, age 24 yrs. -Benj Sedwick, King Geo Co, Va.

TUE AUG 13, 1811
Died: Mrs Maria Ringgold, consort of Gen Sam'l Ringgold of Wash Co, Md, & d/o late Gen Cadwallader, of Phil City; on Aug 1st, at Fountain Rock, after a short but severe illness.

Jos Carberry wishes to close the hatter's shop business. Mr John Queen will settle accounts. -Jos Carberry.

Strayed or stolen from Wash City, a sorrel horse. -John Douglass, living nr the Canal, N J Ave, Wash City.

Lost-$90 in bank notes at the theatre in Wash. -Hanson Catlett, Wash.

In Chancery, Aug 5, 1811. Ratify sale made by Sam'l Clagett, trustee; rl est of Chas Magruder, dec'd; land in Montg Co, Md, for $3,200. -Nichs Brewer, R C C

Public sale at hse of Edw Pye, Port Tobacco, Chas Co, Md; land lying in Cobneck, Chas Co, 360 acs, with dwlg hse. -Edw Digges. [Mr Wm Penn, living nr the land will show same.]

Col Return J Meigs sr is a resident of Tenn.

THU AUG 15, 1811
N Y, Aug 10. We are happy to announce the safe arrival in this city of Messrs Patrick & Wm Phelan, two of the persons taken in June last from on board the ship *Bellisarius*, on her passage from Dublin to this Port, by his Britannic Majesty's sloop of war, *Atalanta*. On the arrival of the *Atalanta* at Halifax, the following were remv'd to a sloop which sailed to St John's Island & were to be put on the est of Lord Jas Townsend: Rich'd, Jane, Jas, Mary & Jane King; John Gilbert; John & Eliza Birk; Thos Walsh; Thos Newman; Lawrence Current; Thos & Mary Bird; Valient & Cath Eliza Needham; Jos & Anne Gilbert; Ally Burton & Mich'l Murphy. The following cont'd on board the *Atalanta*: Rich'd Langar; Peter Foley; Jas Graham; John Dunn; Jas Costegan; Wm Turner; Edw Dore, Wm Morgan; Peter Courtney; Mich'l McHolland; Mathew Murphy; Wm Sutton; Bartle Turner; Edw Lately; Thos Walsh; Martin & Mich'l Bambrick.

For sale-2 lots in Wash City & 2 dwlg hses; 2 lots on L St with hses; 7 lots on K St with hse; hse on 5th St; land in Pa. -Levi White-has opened stores on Balt Rd & on Anapolis Rd.]

For sale-*The Farm*, 380 acs, late dwlg plantation of Jas Perry, dec'd, 2 miles from Montg Crt hse, with brick dwlg hse. Terms apply to Thos P Wilson at Mong Crt hse or to John Wilson or Rich Wootton, Montg Co, Md.

SAT AUG 17, 1811

Vt Rpblcn: Ltr from Judge Witherell, late of Vt, now of Detroit, to Gen Stark-Detroit, May 26, 1811. On examining the fort at this place I saw a brass cannon with this inscription-*John Stark-taken at Bennington, 16th of August, 1777*. He recalls the battled plains of Walloomsack, the ambuscade of Jul 31, 1763 where Capts Dalvell & Campbell fell, now cld *Bloody Bridge*. -J Witherell.

For sale-well known business stand on N J Ave, now in possession of Mrs Peeling, with brick hse & hsehld furn. -Chas Jones, auct.

Marietta, Aug 10: passed this place on Aug 5, Col Boyd's Regt of U S Troops destined for the station at Newport, Ky.

Creditors of Jas Neale, late of St Mary's Co, Md, dec'd, to exhibit their claims to Jas Forrest of Leonardtown. -Jas Walker, adm.

TUE AUG 20, 1811

Post ofc establishment & changes in Jul 1811:
Smithfield, N C-W W Hopkins, vice Robt H Helm, rsgn'd;
Brookhoen, N Y-Benj Hutchinson, vice Jehiel Woodruff, rsgn'd;
Danby, Vt-Jesse Lapham, vice Elisha Smithwick, rsgn'd;
Athens, Ga-Jas D Cole, vice Addin Lewis, rsgn'd;
Limintgon, M-Jas Frost, vice Wingate Frost, rsgn'd;
Montgomery C H, Va-John B Goodrich, vice Sam'l Shields, rsgn'd;
Lower Somers Point, N J-Jesse Somers, vice Andrew Godfrey;
Madisonville, Ky-Ed Cook, vice Joshua Barnes, rsgn'd;
Kinsale, Va-Geo Whitelock, vice John S Tapscott, rsgn'd;
Langford, Ky-Jas McClure, vice Henry P Buford, rsgn'd;
Sidney, N Y-Warram Willis, vice A G Siverly, mv'd away;
Brownsville, N Y-John M Canfield, vice B Skinner, mv'd away;
Quarlesville, Va-Rich'd Stith, vice John Stith jr, rsgn'd;
Enfield, N C-Jos Branch, vice John Branch, rsgn'd;
Orverton C H, Ten-John Kennedy, vice Benj Totten, rsgn'd;
Lebanan, Ten-Jas S Rawlings, vice Jonathan Picket, rsgn'd;
Cheraw C H, S C-Elias Gregg, vice John F Wilson, rsgn'd;
Westmoreland C H, Va-John Redman, vice John W Jones, rsgn'd;
Austinville, Va-Jas Saunders, vice Jas Newell, mv'd away;
Marion C H, S C-John McLane, vice A F Johnson, rsgn'd.
New ofcs est'd in Jul 1811 & postmasters:
Arrington's Tavern, Nash Co, N C-Rich'd Arrington, Postmaster;
Philips' Store, Nash Co, N C-Edwin Drake;
Milford, Hamilton Co,__-Jonathan Megrue;
Bargaintown, Gloucester Co, N J-Reuben T Baker;
Blue Anchor, Gloucester Co, N J-Josiah Albinson;
Plymouth, Luzerne Co, Pa-Chas Lane;
Hickory, Wash Co, Pa-Peter Nelle;
Circleville, Pickaway Co,__-Andrew Ensworth;
Lawsville, Susquehannah Co, Pa-Rich'd Barnum;

Pittman's, Darlington dist, S C-Philip Pittman;
Holland, Worcester Co, Mass-Benj Church.

Ofcs discont'd:
Somers Point, N J; Edgefield, Ky; German Flats, N Y.

Montevideo, Jun 10, 1811. Capts in port were to leave & steer towards B Ayres; order of Xavier Elio. 5 American merchants were to remain for benefit of the whole: Isaac Smith of Balt; Benj B Clark of Phil; Walter Nexsen of N Y; Wm Tufts of Boston; L Smith of Newburyport.

Ltr from Donald C Burkloe, on board schnr *Permela,* Jun 19, 1811, regarding marine volcano that burst thru the sea at St Michaels, one of the Azores. -Wilmington Gaz.

P Mauro intending to remove with his fmly to Balt, offers for sale his hse on Pa Ave & all his hsehld furn, piano forte & bay mare; also 4 lots on Pa Ave in sq 349; 4 lots on Pa Ave in sq 292. -Chas Jones, auct.

In Chancery. Wm Blanchard, John Vint & Thos C Wright, vs Mary Grace Craig Hall & Wm Stewart. Bill states that land in Montg Co was sold by Sam'l Craig to W Stewart who sold same to J Vint, who sold to C Wright, who sold to W Blanchard. Craig is dead, Mary G C Hall is his heir at law & she & Stewart reside out of Md. -Nichs Brewer, Reg C C.

For sale-123 acs of land, 3 miles from Bladensburg, title is indisputable; also hse & lot rent on Md Ave; & 2 sets of smith's tools. -Jos L Scholfield, Wash.

THU AUG 22, 1811
Paris-The Grand Duke of Baden departed this life on the 10th after a reign of 65 yrs; succeeded by his grson.

Died: Mr Wm Hyatt, in Falmouth, Va, Fri, the 23d instant. [Note-this is Aug 22nd paper-date above as written]

For sale-deed of trust from Henry Rose, dec'd; 3 tracts of land in Fairfax Co, Va- 350 acs, 170 acs, & 150 acs; adj the lands of Judge Fitzhugh, Wm Moss, Reps of John Moss-dec'd, Giles Fitzhugh & others. -R M Scott, Wm Moss.

So Carolina College-John J Chappel, chrmn of the standing committee of the brd of trustees. -Columbia, S C.

Wanted-9 or 10 journeymen shoe mkrs; apply on Capitol Hill, next door to Mr David Waterston's. -Alex'r Harper.

For sale-sundry furn at my present dwlg hse. -J T Frost.

Benson McCormick, insolvent debtor, confined in Wash Co, D C, prison for debt. -Wm Brent, clk.

For sale-hse #5 of the Seven Bldgs. -Leonard Harbaugh jr, nr the lower Gtwn bridge.

Mrd: recently, Mr Geo Kneller to Miss Mary Stettinius, all of Wash, by Rev Mr McCormick.

For sale-land where Elimelech Swearingen formerly resided in Montg Co, Md. -Jas B Higgins.

Notice-sale of frame hse on sq 742, prop of Job Smith, to satisfy taxes due the Wash Corp. Also a hse on sq 688, presently occupied by Wm Keefe, the prop of said Keefe, do. Also a hse & lot in sq 799 in Wash City, prop of Jas Calder, do. also 1/2 part of lot 9 in sq 758, prop of Jesse Burch's heirs, do. -Zh Walker, collector 3d ward.

Ranaway-Dick, mulatto man; nr the Eastern Branch, Wash City. -Lewin Talburtt.

For sale or rent-Ripon Lodge, ab't 1000 acs; 4 miles from Dumfries. Apply to Mrs Christian Blackburn, on the premises, or to P Blackburn, exc of T Blackburn, dec'd, nr Centerville, Fairfax Co, Va.

Partnership of Matthews & Lawrence, Morrocco manufacturers, was dissolved by mutual consent because of the declining state of health of Mr Matthews. John Lawrence to collect for the firm & will continue the business.

For sale-pew 27 in Rev A T McCormick's Church.

SAT AUG 24, 1811
Ltr dt'd Jul 30, 1811, from Return J Meigs on the death of Cherokee Chief, Black Fox who was of unmixed blood; died on Jul 16, 1811. Ltr from Rich'd Brown, Creek-Path, Jul 18, 1811, regarding same.

Rpblcn tkt for electors: PG Co, Md-Jos Cross & Robt W Bowie. Frederick dist- Roger Nelson & Joshua Cocken.

Reward-$10 for runaway, Benj Smith, appr boy to the blacksmith business. -Jos Scholfield, Wash.

For sale-*Porto Bello*, St Mary's Co, Md; 900 acs. -Wm Hebb, St Osyth, nr Wash City.

Ten cents reward for runaway, John Plant, appr to cabinet mkg business, ab't 19 yrs of age. -Wm Worthington

For sale for taxes due the Wash Corp: brick hse & lot in sq 74, prop of Thompson & Vietch; hse & part of lot 15 in sq 168, prop of O P Finley; hse & lot 3 in sq west of 14, prop of Chas C Jones; hse & lot 6 in sq 161, prop of Jas Serg McKim; hse & lot 10 in sq 86, prop of Jos Hodgson's heirs. -Jos Brumley, collector 1st ward.

For sale-frame hse & lot nr the ft of the bridge; presently occupied by Capt Benj Jarber & has been for past 14 mos. Apply to David Dobbyn, Pa Ave, or Mr Jarber. -C Jones, auct.

For sale-in Montg Co, Md, part of *Conclusion on Seneca,* 43 1/2 acs; Alleghany Co, part of *Town Creek,* 26 acs; part of *Hard Bargain,* 24 acs; part of *Peru,* 43 1/2 acs; part of land in Hampshire Co, Va, 92 acs; land cld *Deakin's Hall,* nr Bladensburg, PG Co, Md, 213 1/2 acs. Apply to Jas S Morsell, of Gtwn, D C. -John Addison.

For sale-at seat of late Rev Thos Harrison, Pr Wm Co, Va: all hsehld furn, stock & bks. -Philip Harrison, exc, Pr Wm, Va.

Died: Col John Nicholson, old Rev ofcr, age 71 yrs; on Aug 2, at Montgomery, Orange Co, N Y; friend of the brave & unfortunate -Genr'l Rich'd Montgomery.

Reward-$5 for runaway, Chas, negro boy, from Orchardfield on Aquia Crk, Stafford Co, Va. He belongs to Mrs Hannah Hardy & was hired by the subscriber. -W H P Tuckfield, Pa Ave, or A Dowson, N J Ave, Capitol Hill.

Reward-$30 for negroes, Jacob, Jude & Sally. -Talliaferro Shumate, Fauquier, nr Elk Run, Va.

TUE AUG 27, 1811
The People vs Edw Ferris & others. Indictment for a riot. Charge of the Hon De Witt Clinton, mayor of N YC; riot created in Trinity Chr during commencement of Columbia College; 8 indicted & only Wm G Graham pleads guilty; another, Chas Dickinson jr, must be acquitted as there is no evidence; Mr John B Stevenson, dfndnt & graduate, refused to comply with some corrections; other dfndts were Maxwell & Verplank.

THU AUG 29, 1811
Died: Mr Wm. ___att, in Falmouth, Va, on Aug 23.

SAT AUG 31, 1811
Died: Jos Clay, formerly mbr of Cong from Phil, at Phil on Jul 27. At the time of his death he was cashier of Farmer's & Mechanic's Bank.

Died: Thos Beatty, formerly of Gtwn, D C; in Wilmington, N C, on Aug 14.

Died: Thos Fitzsimons, at Phil, a few days ago, a merchant of that city. -Cincinnati, Aug 14.

A detachment of 8 cos of the 4th Regt of U S infantry, & 1 co of rifleman under command of Col John P Boyd, arv'd at the garrison at Newport, Ky on Fri last; and will proceed to Louisville & Vincennes, if advice from Gov Harrison should require them in quelling the Indian disturbances.

Anacostia Library Co-meeting at Mr Shumway's, nr the Navy Yard. -Benj Moore, librarian.

One dollar reward-for my son, John Overton, being under age, has runaway from my fatherly protection. John is a dark mulatto, 17 yrs of age. -Caleb Overton.

For sale-brick hse on Pa Ave, now occupied by Mr Chas Peale Polk; possession on Oct 1 next. -Thos Herty.

Runaway-John Collins, negro, ab't 26 yrs of age; says he belongs to Mr Rich'd Hamsley, of St Mary's Co, Md, who sold him to Mr Turner of Va, who was taking him to Carolina. -Matthias Shaffner, shrf of Wash Co, Md.

TUE SEP 3, 1811
Trustees of Stevensburg Acad have voted a vacancy in the professorship of the acad. -Chas Stuart Waugh, Principal, Culpepper Co, Va.

Ft Stoddert-Aug 17. U S Crt lately held for Wash dist, Miss Terr, Col Reuben Kemper & others, held to bail for planning & setting on foot an expedition against Mobile in Nov & Dec last, were released by the grand jury-they finding no bill.

For sale-decree of Superior Crt of Chancery, at Staunton, Va: brick bldgs & lot on Fairfax St, bet Prince & Duke, City of Alexandria; occupied at present by Mr Evan P Taylor & Mr Jacob Gregg. Com'rs: F Peyton, R Young, Wm Groverman

For sale-one negro man, prop of Hiram Belt, for tax due the Wash Corp. -Ezl MacDaniel, coll 2nd ward.

Ranaway-John, negro man; from John Francis Gardiner, living in Chas Co, Md. Reward-$15. -John F Gardiner, Gtwn.

Ranaway-Jess, black boy; says he belongs to Henry King on Eastern Shore of Md nr Newtown. -C Tippet, kpr of the jail.

For sale-hse formerly occupied by Jas Madison, now in possession of Mr O Pollock; with store & hse adj, occupied by Mr Wm Brown; also hse adj Benj H Latrobe, occupied by Dr Hunter; 3 hses on 7th St; 2 hses nr John McLeod's Seminary. Also 1,686 acs in Culpepper Co, Va; 9,000 acs in Lincoln Co, Ky; 1,000 acs of military land on Cumberland Rvr, & 1,000 acs at junction of Tenn & Ohio Rvrs. Apply to Capt Sam'l N Smallwood for city prop & to Nichs Voss, residing in Stafford Co, nr Falmouth, Va, for remainder.

THU SEP 5, 1811

Meeting of ctzns of Knox Co at Seminary in Vincennes, Jul 31, 1811: Col Ephraim Jordon appt'd Pres; Capt Jas Smith-sec; Gen W Johnson addressed the meeting; Adj Dan'l Sullivan introduced resolutions. -Indiana Terr, Vincennes.

Sir John T Duckworth, the new Govn'r of Newfoundland, has arriv'd at St Johns in the *Antelope*.

Died: Jas Mathers, Sep 2, Sgt-at-Arms & Drkpr to the Senate of the U S, age ab't 67 yrs. He suffered a fractured ancle in a fall into his cellar a few wks since; ntv of Ireland; emigrated some yrs prior to the Rev in which he took a part; he mv'd his family out of N YC & joined the American Army under Washington, till the close of the war; buried with honors of war on Tue last.

Partnership of Geo Collard & Wm H Ward was dissolved Jul last-bills will be in the name of Geo Collard.

Strayed or stolen-a black horse from my stable. -Henry Huntt, at the Marine Barracks, Wash City.

Sorrel colt was taken from my enclosure in Fairfax Co, Va, nr Pohick Chr. -Mary Hamilton.

SAT SEP 7, 1811

Admiralilty ofc-Jul 16. Ltr from Rear-Admr'l Sawyer, Cmder in Chief of his Majesty's ships on coast of N America, to John Wilson Croker, dt'd on board the *Africa*, Bermuda, Jun 11, 1811. He has enclosed a ltr from Capt Arthur Batt Bingham, Cmder of his Majesty's sloop *Little Belt*, regarding attack bet Cape Henry & Cape Hatteras, by U S frig, *President*, commanded by Cmdor Rodgers on May 16th last. Ofcrs, Petty ofcrs, seamen & Marines killed & wounded on board *The Little Belt*: killed-Sam'l Woodward, midshipman; Christ Bennet, Capt of foretop; Jacob Greaves, carpenter's crew; Thos Shippard, gunner's mate; Geo Wilson & Robt Liversage, able seamen; Jas Grey, Robt Howard & Rich'd Coody, ordinary seamen; John Pardoe, priv marine; Dan'l Kilham, landman. Wounded: *John Randall; *Nichs Manager; *Jas McQueen; *Jas Dunn; *Jas Lawrance; *John Richards; *Thos Ives; *Mich'l Skinners; *Wm Fern-[a boy;] *David Dowd; *Wm Harrold; Jas Franklin; Benj Angel; Peter McCaskett; Wm Andrews; Wm Weston; Edw Graham; Geo Dalany; Geo Roberts-[a boy;] Geo Shroad; Dan'l Long. [*Dangerously or severely.]

Impressed American seamen on board the British frig, *Guerriere*, Capt Dacres, at Halifax, Aug 25, 1811:
Thos Reed, a lad of Scituate, Mass;
Jacob Freeman, lad, of Edenton, N C, pressed Apr 8, 1811 from a coaster bound from Boston to N C;
Henry Brice, lad of New London, Conn, pressed Apr 22, 1811 from coaster bound from N London to N C;
Benj Hodges, of Salem, Mass;

Henry Brooks, black man of Fishkill, N Y, pressed from the *Chas Miller*, of Wiscasset, from Jamaica to N Y;
Jos Wright, lad of N Y, on board 3 yrs;
Geo Reed, of Phil, on board 2 yrs;
David Weston, of Fell's Point, Balt, on board 4 yrs.
[Sep 10 paper: Boston, Sep 3, impressed seamen in town on Fri, having arv'd on *The Ann:*-Freeman, Reed & Brico.]
Impressed America seamen on board the *Centurion* receiving ship at Halifax, Aug 25, 1811: Benj Johnson of N Y-pressed by sloop of war *Atalanta;* Nicholas Caston, black man, been on board the *Africa,* age 64, for 6 yrs; Jabez Choate, of Bridgeport, Conn, a supercargo of a Conn Vessel. -Patriot.

Proposals in writing for keeping in repair, by the yr, all pumps & hydrants in Wash. Apply to: Alex'r Kerr, Thos H Gilliss, Henry Ingle or Adam Lindsay. -Robt Brent, mayor.

Died: Mr John Hodgkin, age 40 yrs, Aug 26, on his passage from N Y to Alexandria; for many yrs was a resid of that town. He had gone north for his health, but died in Hampton Rds & was buried on Craney Island. He leaves a widow & 6 chldrn. -Gazette.

To rent-brick hse, late the prop of Mr Jas McCormick, nr the Great Hotel. -John Tayloe.

Orphans Crt of Wash Co, D C. Sep 7, 1811. Prsnl est of Geo Lambright, of Gtwn, dec'd. -Bysa Lambright, admx. [Tailors shears, geese & vest patterns, etc, incl'd]

Nichs B Vanzant, insolvent debtor, confined in Wash Co prison for debt. -Wm Brent, clk.

Jas Patterson, having declined the boot & shoe manufactory, has remv'd to brick hse fronting the West Mkt hse; offers shoes & boots for sale; & a few trunks. Also, the fee simple of a frame hse & lot 119 sq 19th St.

TUE SEP 10, 1811
Mrd: Mr John Norvell to Miss Mary Else Thurston, all of Balt, on Sep 5, in Balt, by Rev Mr Glendy.

Bank robbery in Charleston on Aug 24: Mr Benj Gray, of this city was arrested & examined before John H Mitchell, Justice of the Quorum. A negro belonging to Mr Gray was arrested by Wm Blacklock, & confessed the fact that he aided in the robbery. -Cour.

Died: on Sep 7, in Wash City, Mrs Ann Jarboe, age 56 yrs, w/o Mr B Jarboe.

Strayed or stolen from the commmons in Wash City-nrly black horse. -John Maul jr.

Ranaway-appr boy, Jason Casey, age bet 17 & 18 yrs; s/o Dan'l Casey who formerly resided in Chas Co, Md, but now lives in Wash City. -Nath'l Bradey, boot & shoe-mkr, Wash City.

My wife Eleanor McDonald has for almost 6 yrs past left my bed & board, & ever since lived in a state of adultery & debauchery. I am resolved never to cohabit with her or to contribute to her support. -Archibald McDonald, Wash.

Runaway-John, negro man; says he is prop of Mr Geo Ashton of King Geo Co, Va. -John Cord, Shrf, A A Co, Md-Annap.

Lost-note for $40.40 drawn by Jas Watson & endorsed B Wm Beall. -Morgan & Burgess, Gtwn.

THU SEP 12, 1811
Drowned: Mstr Benj King, s/o Mr Benj King, of the Navy Yard at Wash, on Sep 9. Young Benj, age 13 yrs, was sculling a small boat when he fell over-board. His fr, who was nearby, jumped into the water & tried to save him.

Md election: Anne Arundel Co-Lloyd Dorsey & Thos Sellman.
City of Annapolis-Nichs Brewer.
Wash Co-Martin Kershner & Frisby Tilghman.
Worcester Co-E K Wilson & G Hayward [Fed] & J Williams & G Purnall [Rpblcns].

Appointments made by The Pres of the U S on Aug 26 for the 1st Legion of the Militia of D C:
Capts-Rich'd D Briscoe, Jos Wheaton, Andrew Ross, Geo Way, Sam'l Speake, Wm McKee, Jas Veitch, John Minchin, Stephen Perry;
Lts-Edw Duvall, Thos Hyde, Henry Childs, Adam Whann, Lewis H Machin, Jeremiah Perkins;
Ensigns-Jas Corcoran, Benj F Mackall, Elisha W Williams, John Ingle.

Fredericktown, Md-Court Martial of Gen Wilkinson: Messrs R B Taney & J H Thomas, esqs, appear as cnsl for the Gen; trial to last ab't 2 mos; first meeting was Sep 2.

Died: Jos E Rowles, in Gtwn, on Sep 8, mbr of brd of Aldermen.

Russellville, Ky, Aug 23. Aug 11th the body of a man found nr Bowling Green, Ky, dead some days, is supposed to be Wm Loggins; he was on a visit to purchase land with other men; he appeared to have been murdered & had reins of a new bridle round his neck.

Notice-for sale for tax due the Wash Corp: frame hse & lot in square S E of square 267, prop of Cath Connell. Also lot 2 in sq 257, prop of Wm Esenbeck, for same. Part of lot 7 in sq 490, prop of David Oglesby's heirs, for same. Part of lot 6 in sq

380, prop of Alex'r Robinson's heirs, for same. Also a frame hse & lot in sq 466, prop of Notley Young, for same. -Ezl MacDaniel, coll 2nd ward.

Orphans Crt of PG Co, Md. Sale of prsnl est of Edw Swann, late of PG Co, dec'd; to satisfy his debts. -Henry T Compton, adm of Edw Swann.

Reward-$60 for stolen mare & horse. -Israel Janney, Stephen Wilson. Loudon Co, Va, 9 miles above Leesburg.

Wash Benevolent Soc of Young men-election of ofcrs: Jos Gales jr-Pres; Roger C Weightman-VP; Richmond Johnson-Steward; Alex'r McWilliams, Geo A Carroll & Richmond Johnson-Physicians. Directors for 2 mos: Ward 1-John D Barclay, Wm B Randolph, Thos V Huck; Ward 2-Geo Sweeny, John M Wightt, Isaac K Hanson; Ward 3-John P Ingle, Thos B Dashiell, Lewis H Machin; Ward 4-Edw Clarke, Jas Foyles jr, John Queen; Ward 5-John Suiclair, Robt Y Brent.
-R Johnson, sec.

SAT SEP 14, 1811
Mrd: on Aug 20, Craven P Luckett, of Louisville, to Miss Susan P Greenup, d/o Col Christopher Greenup, of Lexington, Ky.

The Court for the trial of Gen Jas Wilkinson: Gen Gansevoort- Pres; Cols Williams, Russell, Kingsbury & Beall; Lt Cols Wharton, McComb & T A Smith; Majs Porter, Nicoll, Stoddert, Swift & Armstead.

Died: on Aug 20, Danl McCormick, surg in U S N, at Cumberland Island, Ga.

Died: Hon Wm Williams, at Lebanon, Conn, age 80 yrs. Patriot of '76 & only surviving mbr of Congress from Conn, who signed the Decl of Independence.

Mrd: Mr Geo Greatwood to Miss Mary Oakes, both of this place, on the 12th inst. Late Montreal paper seems strongly allied to the romance of the forest. -Balance.

Willie Blount, re-elected Gov of Tenn; John Rhea, John Sevier & Felix Grundy, esqs, elected mbrs of Cong from Tenn.

Runaway-Jacob Harrison, negro, age ab't 35 yrs, committed to Fred'k Co, Md, jail; says he belongs to Wm Clagett of Wash, D C. -Ezra Manz, shrf-Fred'k Co, Md.

TUE SEP 17, 1811
Indian war-Gov Harrison will move from Vincennes ab't Sep 20th with an Army of Militia, & Col Boyd's Regt & Maj Floyd's Battalion of Regulars, to chastise the prophet & his tribe who live up the Wabash; volunteers are to send a note to Col Daveiss in Lexington by mail; each man having a good horse & armed with sword, pistols & knife; uniform: hat or cap covering with bearskin, blue cloth coatee, pantaloons, boots & spurs, pr of mockasons of tanned leather & soaled;-in each man's baggage.

To let-the well known stand for business lately occupied by Chas Jones, now in possession of Lewis Labille, on Pa Ave. -Chas Jones.

Orphans Crt of Wash Co, D C. Sale at hse lately occupied by Henry M Queen, dec'd, all his furn, negroes, horses, etc. -Nicholas L Queen, John Queen, adms.

Reward-one dollar for appr boy, Wm Leatch; has a bro living in Anne Arundel Co, Md. -Thos Wannell, boot-mkr.

THU SEP 19, 1811
Public dinner was given on Aug 17 to Hon Julien Poydras at New Orleans-our Delegate in Congress.

Died: Andrew Reid, a mbr of the Privy Cncl of Va, on Sep 2, at the seat of Dr Hare in Nelson Co.

Post ofc changes in Aug 1811:
Wiscasset, M-Orchard Cook, vice Wm Bowman;
Bath, N H-Ebenezer Carleton, vice John Baddock, mv'd away;
West Union, O-Wm Armstrong, vice Wm Russell, rsgn'd;
Willigton, S C-Jas Gamble, vice M Faddell, rsgn'd;
Mt Airy, N C-Wm Unthank, vice Thos Perkins, rsgn'd;
Stanford, K-Benj Munroe, vice Wm A Luckie, rsgn'd;
Cairo, S C-Jas Harris, vice Thos M Clure, mv'd away;
Chas City C H, Va-Sylvanus Gregory, vice Wm Singleton, rsgn'd;
Forks of Muskingum, O-Wm Whitten, vice Wm Lockard, rsgn'd;
Mt Vernon G-Robt G Rakestraw, vice Robt Burdell, rsgn'd;
Goochland C H, Va-Wm Perkins jr, vice Benj Derson, rsgn'd;
New Mkt, N H-Jeremiah Colcord, vice John Shute, mv'd away;
Holland, Ms-David Marcy, vice Benj Church, rsgn'd;
Calland's store, Va-Addison Armistead, vice Jabez Smith, rsgn'd;
Ranson's bridge, N C-Edmund Jones, vice B W Lucas, rsgn'd;
Galway, N Y-Solomon Rathbon, vice Martin Cook, rsgn'd;
Snow Hill, N C-Jas C Sheppard, vice Benj Evans, mv'd away;
Skinnersville, N C-Silas Long, vice John Rogers, rsgn'd;
Boothbay, Me-Edw Wilson, vice Dan'l Rose, rsgn'd;
Waterboro, Me-Humphrey Chadborn, vice Andrew Burley, dec'd;
Salem, N C-Gottleib Shober, vice N Shober, rsgn'd;
Northampton C H, Va-Keley Stott, vice Peter Rogers, dec'd;
Van Syckle's Store, N J-Aaron Van Syckle, vice Elijah Van Syckle, rsgn'd;
Hillsboro, N C-Thos Chancey, vice Wm Cain jr, rsgn'd;
Warrenton, O-Arthur Patterson, vice Jas Galbraith, rsgn'd;
Kent, C-Lewis Mills, vice Lewis St John, situation inconvenient;
Nassau, N Y-Jos Benedict, vice Thos R Benedict, rsgn'd;
Huron, O-Jabez Wright, vice Almon Ruggles, mv'd away.
New post ofcs-Aug 1811 & postmasters:
Williamsfield, Ashtabula Co, O-Jos J Brown, Postmaster;
Sharpstown, Salem Co, N J-Adam Cook;

Vermillion Huron Co, O-Almon Ruggles;
Hughes, Cumberland Co, Va-Geo Hughes;
Walnut Hills, Miss Terr-John Trumbull;
Warren, Miss Terr-Henry D Downs;
Liverpool, Cumberland Co, Pa-John Huggins;
Liverpool, Onandaga Co, N Y-Henry Case;
Northboro, Worcester Co, Ms-Benj Munroe;
Louisville, St Lawrence Co, N Y-Benj Willard;
Massena, St Lawrence Co, N Y-Calvin Hubbard;
French Mills, Clinton Co, N Y-Jas H Handsdall;
Bradleysville, Litchfield Co, Ct-Henry Wadsworth;
Jamesville, Onandago Co, N Y-Thos Rose;
Spencertown, Columbia Co, N Y-Cornwall Brush;
Chatham, Columbia Co, N Y-Calvin Pardee;
Bangor, Franklin Co, N Y-Henry Blanchard.
Ofcs discont'd: Drummondsburg, Va; Harrisburg, S C; Edisto, S C; Tarrantsville, S C; Claytonsville, N C; Hill's Iron works, S C; Voss's, Va; Harrison's Tavern, Va; Wash, Vt; Dyer's store, Va; McDanielsville, Va; Montague's, Va.

Fredericktown, Sep 14-Gen Wilkinson's trial: The Genr'l spoke & surrendered his sword which had been by his side for 25 yrs; Col Burbeck, Lt Col Freeman & Backus were excepted to by the Genr'l-they having expressed their opinions of guilt; their seats were taken by Majs Stoddart, Swift & Armistead. Walter Jones jr is Judge Advocate. Gen W pleaded not guilty.

Ltr to Robt Brent, mayor of Wash City-I enclose my commission as Sealer of Wghts & Meas; I have again entered the svc of my country in my former station as Mstr at Arms. I was long with Cmdor Rodgers; I am determined to hand powder as long as there is a shot in the locker. -John C Shindle.

Senate of Md-Electoral College of Md-all Rpblcns chosen: Wm Pinkney & Levi Hollingsworth, Balt; Wm McCreery, Balt Co; John Williams, Worcester; Solomon Frazer, Dorchester; Frederick Holbrook, Caroline Co; Edw Lloyd, Talbot; Jas Brown, Q Anne Co; Wm Hollingsworth, Cecil Co; Elijah Davis, Harford Co; Upton Bruce, Alleghany Co; Wm Thomas, St Mary's Co; Lloyd Dorsey, Ann Arundel Co; Moses Tabbs, Wash Co; Thos Hawkins, Fred'k Co.

Died: Mrs Martha Carr, age 64 yrs, Sep 3, at *Dunlora*-the seat of Mr Sam'l Carr of Albemarle. She was widow of Mr Dabney Carr & the sister of Mr Jefferson, late Pres of the U S.

Died: Mr Thos Anderson, at New Orleans, Aug 18, editor of *The Orleans Gaz.*

Died: Lt Sam M Lee, U S Light Dragoons, at New Orleans on Sep 21; ntv of Harford Co, Md.

Sale for tax due Wash Corp: lot 3 in sq 725 with improvements, prop of Jas R Dermott's heirs. Also hse & lot on sq 690, presently occupied by Chas H Varden, prop of Robt Campbell's heirs, for same. -Zh Walker, coll 3d ward.

Ranaway-Giles, negro; s/o Betty, a free woman who lives in Gtwn. -Chas Tyler jr, nr Centreville, Fairfax Co, Va.

John Robertson, insolvent debtor, of St Mary's Co, Md. -John Harris, clk.

SAT SEP 21, 1811
12th Cong-Senate: N H-Rich'd Cutts & Nichs Gilmam;
Mass-Jas Lloyd jr & Jos B Varnum;
Conn-Chauncy Goodrich & Sam'l W Dana;
R I-C G Champlin & Jeremiah B Howell;
Vt-Stephen R Bradley & Jonathan Robinson;
N Y-Obadiah German & John Smith;
N J-John Lambert & John Condit;
Pa-Andrew Gregg & Mich'l Leib;
Del-Jas A Bayard & Outerbridge Horsey;
Md-Sam'l Smith & Philid Reed;
Va-Rich'd Brent & Wm B Giles;
N C-Jas Turner & Jesse Franklin;
S C-John Gaillard & John Taylor;
Ga-Chas Tait & Wm H Crawford;
Ky-John Pope & Geo M Bibb;
Tenn-Jenkin Whiteside & Jos Anderson;
Ohio-Thos Worthington & Alex'r Cambell.
Hse o/Reps:
N H-Wm Hale, Sam'l Dinsmore, John A Harper, Elijah Hall, Geo Sullivan, Bartlett;
Mass-Josiah Quincy, Wm Reed, Rich'd Cutts, Ebenez Seaver, Ez Bacon, Chas Turner jr, Laban Wheaton, Leonard White, Isaiah L Green, Sam'l Taggart, Wm Ely, ____ Brigham, Abijah Bigelow, Barzillai Gannett, Peleg Tallman, Wm Widgery, 1 vacancy;
Conn-Lewis B Sturges, Jonathan O Mosley, Benj Tallmadge, Epa Champion, Timothy Pitkin jr, Lyman Law, John Davenport jr;
R I-Elisha R Potter, Rich'd Jackson jr;
Vt-Sam'l Shaw, Jas Fiak, Wm Strong, Martin Chittenden; jr, Pierre Van Cortlandt jr, Jas Emott, Thos B Cook, Robt Le Roy Livingston, Asa Fitch, Thos R Gold, Uriah Tracy, Dan'l Avery, Harmanus Bleeker, Arunnah Metcalfe, P G Porter, Wm Pond, Silas Snow;
N J-Adam Boyd, Jacob Hufty, Lewis Condit, Geo C Maxwell, Jas Morgan, Thos Newbold;
Pa-Adam Seybert, Wm Anderson, Jas Milner, Robt Brown, Wm Rodman, Jonathan Roberts, Wm Findley, John Smilie, Aaron Lyle, Robt Whitehill, David Bard, Roger Davis, Jos Lefever, J M Hyneman, Wm Piper, Abner Lacock, Wm Crawford, Geo Smith;
Dela- ____ Ridgely;

Md-Philip B Key, Jos Kent, Philip Stewart, Chas Goldsborough, Peter Little, Alex McKim, Sam'l Ringgold, John Brown, 1 vacancy;
Va-John Randolph, Hugh Nelson, Thos Gholson, Petersot Goodwyn, Th Newton, Dan'l Sheffey, John Hungerford, Edwin Gray, Jos Lewis jr, John Baker, Jas Breckenridge, John Dawson, Matthew Clay, Burwell Bassett, Thos Wilson, Wm A Burwell, John Smith, Aylett Hawes, John Roane, Wm McKoy, Jas Pleasants jr, John Clopton;
N C-Willis Allston, Wm Blackledge, Thos Blount, Jos Pearson, Archibald McBride, Nath'l Macon, Meshack Franklin, Rich'd Stanford, Wm R King, Lemuel Sawyer, Jas Cochran, Israel Pickens;
S C-D R Williams, Langdon Cheeves, Wm Loundes, Wm Butler, John C Calhoun, Elis Earle, Rich'd Winn, Thos Moore;
Ga-Geo M Troup, Wm W Bibb, Bolling Hall, Howell Cobb;
Ky-Rich'd M Johnson, Jos Desha, Henry Clay, Anthony New, Sam'l McKee, Stephen B Ormsby;
Tenn-John Rhea, Felix Grundy, John Sevier;
Ohio-Jeremiah Morrow.

Jacob Martin, hatter from Fredericktown, has commenced business on F St, in shop formerly conducted by John Hemler.

Dreadful calamity, Charleston, Sep 11. Tornado passed thru on Sep 15, blew on Mon & Tue; prostrated the flag at Ft Mechanic, unroofed Nath Russel's hse [furn lost;] Dr Alex Baron & the late Dr Chandler's hses were roughly handled; & hse occupied by Mr Henry Inglesby, mansion of the late Gen MacPherson, mansion of Hon Judge Desaussure, same. Deaths: Miss Mgt Cozzens, age 21 yrs, killed in hse adj Ft Mechanick; Dr Canton, ntv of France, killed by the falling of his hse in Beaufain St; Mr Peterson, ntv o/Germany, grocer, crnr o/Magazine & Mazyck Sts.

St Mary's Co, Md, Crt hse-application of Jos Edwards of Robt, of said co, insolvent debtor. -Jo Harris, clk St Mary's Co, Md.

Jos Pollard has remv'd to Louisville, Ky, where he keeps a commission ofc for transaction of all kinds of business.

Reward-$15 for Gerard Semmes, negro, ab't 21 yrs of age. -Basil Edelin, living in Upper Cedar Pt, Chas Co, Md; or to my bro, Walter Edelin, living nr Piscataway, PG Co, Md.

Runaway-Jerry, negro; says he belongs to Mr Wm Hartshorne of Fairfax Co, Va. -C Tippett, kpr of the jail-Wash Co, D C.

TUE SEP 24, 1811
Mr Edwmond C Genet, ntv of France, Minister to this country during the admin of Wash, mrd a dght of our VP & settled in N Y.

Wash Co, D C-Jos Beck, insolvent debtor, confined in prison for debt. -Wm Brent, clk.

Lord Berkeley's last will, Aug 21, 1810: Proved by Mary Countess of Berkeley; eldest son-Lord Dursley; to Augustus, Francis, Thos, Geo, & Craven; to Mary, Caroline, Emily, dghts; all at attaining age 21 yrs; Lord Dursley was left Berkeley Castle in Gloucester for life; L B's bro is adm Berkeley; to son, Maurice, his estates in Sussex Co. The hse of Lords on marriage at Berkeley Chr on Mar 30, 1787- alleged publication of banns in Nov & Dec 1784, & conclude that the title of Earl of Berkeley & family estates do not devolve to Lord Dursley, but to the 1st legitimate son after the marriage in Oct 1794. Lady Berkeley is the d/o Mrs Glassop Oofsbournby, Lincolnshire, formerly Mrs Cole. Jan 1787, Wm Fitznurding, natural s/o Earl of Berkeley, by Mary Tudor, was christened. Mary was the sister of Ann Ferred & another sister, Susan.

Booksellers-Jos Milligan in Gtwn; Robt Gray in Alexandria.

David Boudon, painter from Switzerland, draws profiles. [Wash City]

THU SEP 26, 1811
Lynn, Sep 14, 1811. I, John Twombly, sailed from Boston, Jan 7, 1811, on the ship *Hannah*, as mate, commanded by Jos Mudge, bound to Marseilles; Feb 21st was captured & eventually arv'd in Marblehead on Sep 13.

Died: Jul 29 at Devonshire hse, Piccadily, his Grace Wm Cavendish, Duke of Devonshire.

Died: Jas Belcher, Pugilist, champion of Eng, at his hse, the Coach & Horses, Frith St, Soho, age 81 yrs.

Died: Maj Wm Henderson, age 56 yrs, on Sep 9, Magistrate of Huntington,, Pa; entered the Army at commencement of Rev; taken prisoner at Battle of Long Island on Aug 28, 1776 & confined for 5 mos in British prison ship at N Y.

Died: Marquis Townsend on Jul 27 at Richmond.

Died: Mr Thos Bird, ntv of Eng, on Sep 18, age 37 yrs, & lately in svc of the U S Naval agency at Syracuse.

Dirs of the Mass State Bank, elected on Sep 16: Wm Gray, Henry Dearborn, Sam'l Dana, David Tilden, Jesse Putnam, Geo Blake, David Townsend, Wm Ward, Matthew Bridge, Jas Prince, Amasa Stetson & Wm Monroe.

Orphans Crt of Wash Co, D C. Est of Capt Andrew McClary, late of said co, dec'd. -John McClary, adm.

Consequence of the death of Henry Mill-following prop for sale: furnace & forge in Augusta Co, Va, 8000 acs; forge in Rockingham, nr 4000 acs. -Sam'l Miller & John Mestill, adms-Alex.

SAT SEP 28, 1811

Balt American-Henry Jackson & his family arv'd in this city; his dght, Mrs Bond, relict of Oliver Bond together with her 2 dghts & her sister, Miss Jackson, accompanied him.

Died: Mr J G Vassar, of Poughkeepsie, in consequence of mephitic gas. -late Phil Paper.

Died: Capt John Minchen, age 43 yrs, on Sep 23; many yrs a resid of Wash; ntv of Ireland; immigrated at an early age. He has left a widow & 4 children.

Died: Dr Rich'd Dinmore, formerly of Norwich, Eng, but latterly for many yrs a resid of Wash, on Sep 26.

Canandaigua, N Y, Sep 10-Execution of John Andrews, for murdering Nicholas, was held at Ovid, Seneca Co, Sep 6.

Orphans Crt of PG Co, Md. Est of Lucy Smith, of PG Co, dec'd. -Alex'r Philpot, adm.

Wm Brewer, living in Montg Co, Md, advertises for a teacher.

TUE OCT 1, 1811

Toasts on Jul 4 at Chilicothe, Ohio, were made by: Sam'l McCulloch, painter; John Baker, butcher; Rich'd Cavet, sadler; Wm Rutledge, bricklayer; Wm Smith, sawyer; Peter Day, blacksmith; Adam Holler, baker; Jas Foster, bk-binder; Sam'l Rogers, hatter; John L Tabb, cabinetmkr; John Douglas, weaver; Peter Spurk, watch & clock mkr; Thos Lloyd, taylor; Jack Rodgers, barber; John Gisfiden, shoemkr; Nichs Fisher, cooper; T W, ropemkr; Peter Parcel, printer.

Died: Mrs Ann Moore, the fainting woman, of Telbury, Staffordshire; existed 4 yrs without food & 3 without water; age 50 yrs; a few days ago. -London Paper of July.

Died: Saml Maclay, age 70 yrs, Sep 5, at his farm in Northumberland Co, Pa.

Died: Mrs Ann Darrach *Brush, w/o John C *Bush, age 35 yrs, in Wash, on Sep 29 of a pulmonary consumption. [*2-splgs]

Died: Mrs Caroline Plummer, age 23 yrs, Sep 13 nr Queen Ann, Md; w/o John Plummer & only d/o Mr David Shoemaker of Wash. She was mthr, wife, dght & friend.

Mrd: Mr Jos Taylor to Miss Zippera Katchem, both of Wash, on Sep 29, by Rev Mr Snethen.

Mrd: Mr Chas Geo Shaffer, printer, to Miss Eliz Slowman, both of Charleston, on Sep 16, at Charleston, S C.

D English is the cashier of the Union Bank of Gtwn.

Orphans Crt of Wash Co, D C. Oct 1, 1811. Prsnl est of John Minchin, dec'd. -Patience Minchin, admx.

For sale-family of negroes. -Jos Semmes of Gtwn.

THU OCT 3, 1811
Sale at auction-at hse of Mrs Dempsey: all her hsehld furn; gig sold at expence & loss of Chas Varden who did not comply with terms of the sale. -Nicholas L Queen, auct.

Sale by auction-at Mr Sam'l Williams's warehse: East India goods. -C O Muller, auct. Balt, Md.

Sale at auction-at hse of John C Brush, nr Pa Ave: sundry articles of hsehld furn & milch cow. -Chas Jones, auct.

For rent or sale-brick bldg, on ave leading from the Capitol to Gtwn; apply to Wm Worthington, who last occupied the same, or to Rich'd S Briscoe, residing nr the premises.

Orphans Crt of Wash Co, D C. Oct 2, 1811. Prsnl est of John Cummins, late of said co, dec'd. -John Davis of Abel, Alexander Cummins.

N G Dufief is a bkseller & stationer, no 26, So 4th St, Phil.

SAT OCT 5, 1811
W Little, of Pittsfield, Mass, has given $2,500 to Williamstown College to aid indigent scholars. -Bost Pat.

Mrd: Mr Jas Parsons, of Wash, to Miss Eliz Longden, of Gtwn, on Oct 3, by Rev Mr Addison.

Mrd: Mr John Smith to Miss Sarah Parsons, all of Gtwn, on Oct 3, by Rev Mr Addison.

Died: Dr Wm Upshaw, at New Orleans, on Sep 2, late surg of the 5th Regt of U S infantry; ntv of Va.

Died: Robt Alexander, 1st Lt of the Columbian infantry, architect, & late of Wash, at New Orleans, on Sep 3.

Orphans Crt of St Mary's Co, Md, Aug term, 1811. Petition of Janet Thompson, admx of Jas Thompson, late of said co, dec'd. -Jas Forrest, Reg of wills for St Mary's Co.

Died: Maj Genr'l Jas Green, on Sep 14, at Long Branch, N J.

Notice-sale of brick hse & part of lot 13 in sq 119, prop of J Welsh, for tax due Wash Corp. -Jos Brumley, coll 1st ward.

Sale by auction-frame hse nr the commercial store now in possession of W Johnson. -Chas Jones, auct.

Notice-sale of mahogany sideboard at hse of Henry Timms, prop of same, for tax due Wash Corp. -Zh Walker, coll 3d ward.

Notice-decree of High Crt of Chancery of Md: sale of ab't 175 acs, part of tract cld *Brown's Purchase*, being part of the rl est of John Spurrier, late of Anne Arundel Co, dec'd. -Beale Spurrier, trustee, Baltimore, Md.

Jenkin Whitesides, mbr of Senate from Tenn, resigned his seat.

TUE OCT 8, 1811

Strayed or stolen, grey horse; on Capitol Hill, Wash. -Mary King, widow of Patrick King, lately dec'd.

Order of Orphans Crt of PG Co, Md. Sale on the premises, prsnl prop of Aquila Beall, dec'd, of said co. -Sophia Beall, admx.

Dr Rich Dinmore, whose death was announced in a late Intelligencer: born in Norwich City, Eng on Dec 8, 1765; s/o a tradesman of that City; mrd Miss Shreeve in 1788 & settled in Watton. In 1797 he arrv'd in Washington with his wife & only child, whom he afterwards lost. He was reared by a wealthy uncle; opened a small school after going bankrupt; opened a grocery store in Gtwn; bec the editor of a newspaper in Alexandria; his wife died in Alexandria leaving an infant dght, their 16th child. The dght of his step mthr became his wife. Dr Dinmore died Sep 26, age 46 yrs.

Ladies with ltrs in the Post Ofc at Wash City, Oct 1, 1811:

Miss Cath Adams	Mrs Ruth Barlow	Mrs E Breckenridge
Miss Ann Clerklee	Mrs Cath Caldwell	Elicia Clark
Mary Douglass	Miss Ellis	Mary Enault
Lidy Fisher	Mrs Ann Green	Mary Gooding
Mrs E Huddleston	Mrs H Herman	Fanny Hamilton
Eliz Hunter	Amie Jones	Mrs Letty Lucas
Miss Eliz Lowe	Mrs Ann Lowry	Miss Agnes McQueen
Miss Ann R Mills-2	Miss Charlotte A Mortimer	
Mrs Maloy	Miss Mgt Nicholson	Eliz Orme jr
Mrs Eliz Perkins	Mrs Mgt C Smith	Mrs Eliz Sandford
Eliz Smith	Mrs Stewert	Sarah Triplett
Miss Martha Worthington		

Orphans Crt of Wash Co, D C. Est of Jas Van Zandt, late of said co, dec'd. -Jno McGowan, admr.

Public sale-Order of Crct Crt of D C: at his late store on Pa Ave, all stock of Nichs B Vanzandt, insolvent debtor; assortment of hrdware. -Andrew Way jr, trustee. Chas Jones, auct.

For sale at auction-all right, title, int & claim of Jas Johnston in 4 hses. -Nichs L Queen, auct.

Madison Mills to be sold; 16 1/4 acs; 3 miles of Orange Crt hse & 35 miles from Fredericksburg, Va. -Wm H Smith, on premises.

TUE OCT 10, 1811
Stevenson Archer, elected to Cong for Districts of Cecil, Hartford & Kent, in Md, vice John Montgomery, rsgn'd.

Princeton College: Hon degree of mstr of Arts was conferred on: Rev Thos Picton of Westfield, N J; Wm S Hamilton, Lt of 3d Regt of U S inf & aid to Brig Gen Wade Hampton; Mr Ebenezer H Cummings, A M of Athens Univ, Ga, was admitted Ad Eundem in this College. Dr of Divinity was conferred on: Rev John Brown, Pres of Ga Univ; Rev Robt Hall of Cambridge in Eng, Rev Jas Inglis of Balt, Md & Rev S Worcester of Salem, Mass.

Died: Mr Lewis Morin, Oct 3, ctzn of Wash City.

SAT OCT 12, 1811
Md election-Dorchester Co: Rpblcns-John Smoot & Frederick Smoot; Feds-Jos Ennalls & Edw Griffith. Annapolis City: Rpblcans-Dr Dennis Claude & Lewis Duvall.

Robt Getty, crnr of Wash & Bridge Sts, Gtwn, advertises liquors & groc.

Strayed or stolen from the commons in Wash City, a bay horse. -Zeph Farrell.

Sale at auction-four negroes, prop of Mary E Grayson, dec'd. -Spence Grayson, adm. Nich L Queen, auct. Gtwn.

Wm G Ridgley & Co have mv'd their store into hse lately occupied by Mr Romulus Riggs, Gtwn.

Orphans Crt of Wash Co, D C. Oct 3, 1811. Prsnl est of Ann Burch, late of Wash Co, dec'd. -John Craven, adm.

Wash City-Grand Lodge of D C: bros Valentine Reintzell, Amos Alexander, Alexander McCormick, Jos Cassin & John Richards, were appt'd deputies. -Jas Hewitt, Dep'y G sec.

TUE OCT 15, 1811

Died: Dan'l J Adams, ntv of Wilmington, Dela, on Oct 11, in Wash City.

Died: Ezra L'hommedieu, age 77 yrs, at his seat in Suffolk Co, N Y, in Sept; imbarked in the cause of the Rev, devoted 33 yrs of active svc to his country, in Congress & Senate.

Gtwn, S C-Fire from King to Broad St consumed the work shop of Mr Thos Dowdney, cabinetmkr. Store hses destroyed: Mrs Geo Heriot, Moses Myers, est of John Matthews & Mrs Martin.

Died: Capt Chas Jones, Oct 14, nr Centre Mkt, ctzn of Wash.

Runaway-Sam, negro; says he belonged to Anne Grey & then to Wm Elickson, both of Balt City; confined in Wash Co jail. -Matthias Shaffner, shrf of Wash Co, Md.

Will be sold-all right, title & int of Allen Simimpson in 794 acs; sundry Writs of Fieri Facias, issued from Montg Co Crt. -R W Fleming, shrf of Montg Co.

Edw Goddard, insolvent debtor confined in Wash Co, Md, prison, for debt. -Wm Brent, clk.

THU OCT 17, 1811

Memoirs of Benj West, Pres of The Royal Acad: born at Springfield, Dela Co, Pa, in 1738; ancestors were of the Soc of Friends-most emigrated to that state with Wm Penn; s/o John West who did not emigrate from Eng, Buckinghamshire 'til ab't 1714-15 & settled in Pa where he mrd & raised 10 chldrn, the youngest-Benj West; in 1760 Benj embarked for Italy to improve himself in art; in 1791, on the death of Sir Joshua Reynolds, succeeded him as Pres of the Royal Acad.

Arrv'd at Provincetown, Sat last, on schnr, *Betsey & Polly*, from Labradore, Mr Wm Stevenson of Tiverton, R I, who made his escape with 4 other Americans from the British sloop of war, *Hazard*. Mr S was taken out of the brig, *Undaunted*, of N Y-3 yrs since. -N Y Gaz.

Boston Patriot: Wm Parker, ntv of Boston, sailed from Norfolk on Jan 4, 1807, in the ship *Chas Carter*, John Tompkins, mstr, for London; impressed on Apr 3d & sent on the tender *Enterprize*; clearance from Mr Lyman, America Cnsl, was of no avail; met Admr'l Coffin & told him of my situation; he obtained my birth & baptism certificates from my mthr in Boston, no avail; attempted to desert & rec'd 296 lashes; 3 mos later I rec'd 164 stripes; sent to Lisbon on the *Belflour*; made a 3d & successful attempt at desertion. -Wm Parker, Boston, Oct 8, 1811.

Post ofc changes in Sep 1811:
Chester, Pa-Thos D Anderson, vice Aaron Coburn;
Mt Zion, Ky-Jonathan Taylor, vice Jas Latham, rsgn'd;
Bridge Branch, De-Jeremiah Jeffries, vice John Wilson, rsgn'd;

Marcellus, N Y-Erastus Humphreys, vice Jos Olmstead.
New ofcs est-Sep 1811 & postmaster:
Canve Camp, Tioga Co, N Y-Micah Spencer, Postmstr;
Wanesville, N C-Robt Love;
Colleton, St Geo dist, S C-David Riddlesperger;
Mearns Chapel, Nash Co, N C-M Lamon;
St Johns Plains, Orleans Terr-Rich'd Duvall;
Baton Rouge, Orleans Terr-Jas Chauveau;
Manshak, Orleans Terr-Jas Nelson;
Middleton, Fairfield Co, Ohio-Roswell Mills;
Buffaloe, Mason Co, Va-Peter Royston;
Marrs Bluff, Marion Co, S C-Jaques Bishop.
Discont'd post ofc: Arrington's Tavern, N C.

Mrd: Mrs Lewis H Machen to Miss Cynthia Pease, all of Wash, Oct 15, by Rev Mr Laurie.

Died: on Sep 14, John Sinclair, ntv of Ire, but many yrs a resid of Wash. Kind & affectionate hsbnd & fr.

Died: Maj David Zeigler, vet of Rev, at Cincinnati on Sep 24; after illness of more than 12 mos.

Notice-sale of part of lot 13 in sq 119, prop of J Welsh, for tax due the Wash Corp. -Jos Brumley, coll 1st ward.

Trunk turtle was harpooned by Mr Sam'l Coon, a branch pilot, ab't 30 miles S E of Sandy Hook; it weighed ab't 800 lbs & is a ntv of the East Indies. -N Y Paper.

Geo W Campbell, elected Sen of U S for Tenn, vice Jenkin Whitesides, resigned.

Md State elections-Worcester Co: T Williams, E K Wilson, R J H Handy, L Quinton-Feds. A A Co: W H Marriot, J S Belt, Dr Dorsey, Z Duvall, Rpblcns. Montg Co: Chas Evans, John H Riggs, Edw Owen, Abraham Jones, Feds.

For sale-Occoquan Mills, Va; ab't 8 miles below Mt Vernon; nr 1000 acs. Apply to Jas Campbell at Petersburg; Sam'l G Griffith of Balt; Jas Taylor jr of Norfolk; or Nath'l Ellicott & Luke Wheeler on premises.

Order of Orphans Crt of PG Co, Md-sale at late dwlg hse of Haswill Magruder, dec'd, nr Bladensburgh, all his prsnl est-furn, negroes, stock, etc. -Wm & Fielder Magruder, adms.

SAT OCT 19, 1811
Thos Ewell & others are about to establish a gun powder manufactory nr Bladensburg at *Stoddert's Mill*.

For sale-at late dwlg of Rich'd Brooke Lucas, dec'd, all his prsnl prop in St Mary's Co, Md; negroes, stock & furn. -Jas Forrest, exc, Leonardtown, Md.

Public sale-deed of trust from Dan'l McCarty & Mgt Matilda Snowden, his wife: 800 acs in Loudon Co, Va, cld *McCarty's Island & Sugar Land Tract*. Prop will be shown by Mr John W Bronaugh, Gtwn. -Elisha Janny, Jas Keith jr, Alexandria.

To rent-brick hse belonging to Wash Bldg Co, on F St nr the Roman Cath Chr. -Walter Clarke, sec appt'd in place of Mr Chas Jones, dec'd.

Stolen from the commons of Wash: a carriage horse. -Wm Simmons.

For sale-land in Ky, 4000 acs, 20 miles above Louisville. -Elie Williams, Gtwn.

TUE OCT 22, 1811
Notice-I intend to remove from Gtwn to my farm ab't 3 miles from the Capitol in Wash City & will educate ab't 10 boys. Apply to Rev Walter D Addison, of Gtwn, or to Sam'l Redout, of Annapolis. -John Addison.

To let-brick hse on sq 490, nr Pa Ave; lately occupied by Mr Robt Hepburn. -Aquilla D Hyatt, oppo the Indian Queen Tavern.

Died: Mrs Joanna Barry, relict of Jas Barry, of N Y; on Oct 18; mthr of two dghts, both dec'd.

Died: Francis Clark, ntv of Garragh, Londonderry Co, Ire; many yrs a ctzn of U S; last 8 yrs a merchant of Wash; on Oct 19, age 42 yrs; affectionate hsbnd & f/o 4 girls & 1 boy. His remains were interred Oct 20th with Masonic honors & attended by the *Society of the sons of Erin*.

Died: Mr John Herford, of the firm of Herford & Son, brewers of this city; on Oct 17; formerly a ctzn of Dublin, but lately of Wash.

Died: Moheer Ouder, in India; 2nd s/o Tippoo Saib; held state prisoner for some yrs & was detected in an attempt to escape; discharged a musket in his breast & died instantly.

Died: Maj Genr'l Jas Green, Oct 14, very suddenly.

Annapolis Races was won by Mr Wm B Bean's horse, Victory; awarded $300.

For sale-at hse of Mr John Cannon, 30 or 40 barrels of corn, tops & husks, stack of fodder & hay. -N L Queen, auct.

Jos Forrest & Geo Beall are appt'd auctioners in Washington.

THU OCT 24, 1811
To let by the yr-stand on crnr of C St facing the Centre Mkt. -Sam'l Stettinius.

Died: Jas M_s Campbell, Lt Col of the 22nd Regt of Militia of So Carolina & Senator from St Mathew's Parish, on Oct 7, at his plantation nr Congaree; age 60 yrs; born in County of Down, Ire; resided in S C for 43 yrs; sldr of Rev

Died: Thankful Dodge, w/o Mr Josiah Dodge, age 74 yrs, in Westmoreland, N H; lived 45 yrs in town.

Wm Ward has remv'd his store to the hse lately occupied by Dr Catlet, east of the Branch Bank; fancy goods.

Notice-persons having claims against the est of Eleanor Speake, late of Wash Co, D C, dec'd; bring same by May 1. -Mary Brooke, extx.

SAT OCT 26, 1811
Notice: I have cedar ware for sale at my shop in King St, Alexandria. -Loudon Campbell.

New Swisserland-situated on the right bank of the Ohio Rvr, in Jefferson Co, Indiana Terr; begun in spring of 1803 by some Swiss of the Canton of Vaud, formerly a part of Bern; 2,500 acs was purch'd under a law in favor of J Jas Dufeur & his associates, allowing them 12 yrs to pay for it from 1802; Mr F J Dufour's sister brought the art of tyeing straws together in making of hats to this country from Swisserland.

Wash Jockey Club Races, Oct 23; owners of horses: Joshua B Bond, John Tayloe, Bela Badger, Dr Thornton, Jacob G Smith, Phil Stewart, Col W Lyle.

Died: Hon Jas Bowdoin, at Boston, a few days ago, late Mnstr of U S to the crt of Spain.

Runaways, committed to Wash Co, D C, jail-negro Sukey, says she belongs to Thos Benson of PG Co, Md. also negro Joe, says he belongs to Henry Hunter of Tarborough, N C. -C Tippett, kpr of the jail for W Boyd, mrsh'l.

Persons indebted to Geo B Lindsay, insolvent debtor, are to make payments to Lund Washington, trustee.

Sale of negroes-at hse of Geo Jenkins, Chas Co, Md. -Philip B Key.

Ran away from the editor of the Intelligencer, Lancaster, Pa, apprentice, Jas Donnelly, ab't 14 yrs of age. -Wm Dickson.

TUE OCT 29, 1811
Canada paper-on Aug 24th, in Bristol, west side of the Canandaigua Lake, I killed 25 rattle-snakes. -Dan'l Wilder.

Mrd: Mr Sam'l Underwood, age 15 yrs, to widow Fanny Matthews, age 36 yrs, in Danville, Vt.

Mrd: Geo Watterston, to Miss Maria Shanly, all of Wash, on Oct 26, by Rev Mr Breckenridge.

Mrd: Mr John B Patterson, of Va, to Miss Cath W Goldsborough, at Cambridge, Md, on Oct 3.

Notice to ctzns of Wash-will commence my round to examine weights & measures & fire buckets. -Peter P Prevote.

Boot & shoe mkg will be carried on by Patience Minchin, successor to her late hsbnd; New Jersey Ave, Wash.

THU OCT 31, 1811
Boarding-Mrs Chisholm, in hse lately occupied by Sam'l H Smith, Pa Ave, Wash.

Roger's Vegetable Pulmonic Detergent-prepared by myself at my dispensary in Northampton, Mass. -Geo Rogers.

Sale at auction-at hse of Jas Mc Cormick jr; furn & remainder of a dry goods store. -Nichl L Queen, auct.

Wash Co, D C-In Chancery. John G Ladd, cmplnt, vs Amariah Frost, dfndt. Ratify sale by Chas Glover, trustee, of lot 17 sq 634, Wash, to John G Ladd, for $320. -Wm Brent, clk.

Orphans Crt of Wash Co, D C. Prsnl est of Lewis Morin, late of said co, dec'd. -Barbary Morin, admx.

Orphans Crt of Wash Co, D C. Oct 28, 1811. Prsnl est of Rich'd Dinmore, late of Wash Co, dec'd. -Bridget Dinmore, admx.

SAT NOV 2, 1811
Drowned: Capt Alexander Wilson, age 32 yrs, on Oct 20th in the Potomac, on his way to Richmond; was bro of the editor of the Sun & had lately returned from Eng; has left a wife, one child, mthr, 4 bros, & 1 sister.

Charleston, Oct 14. Loss of the schnr *Eliz City*, Capt Meriam, this port. Mr Jos D Broadbrooks, mate of said schnr, arrv'd here on the sloop *Eliza* with particulars of loss of the schnr & her Capt in a gale on Nov 2. Those who perished: Capt John H Meriam, formerly of the hse of Meriam & Perry; Mrs Fleming, formerly of Phil but residing lately at Nassau where her hsbnd recently died; Mr Uriah Noah, ntv of Phil, who had resided for a few yrs past in this city. Mrs Flemming was buried on St Simon's island.

Jos Bloomfield, re-elected Govn'r of N J, without opposition.

WED NOV 6, 1811
J Loga, Dentist & Oculist; nrly oppo the ofc of The Spirit of '76, Gtwn.

Mountjoy Bailey was elected door-kpr, in the Senate, vice Mr Mathers, dec'd. -Tue Nov 5.

THU NOV 7, 1811
Orphans Crt of PG Co, Md. Nov 5, 1811. Prsnl est of John Hancock Beans, late of PG Co, dec'd. -Polly B Magruder, admx d b n of John H Beans.

Sale at auction-at hse of Alex'r McCormick; furn etc. -Nich L Queen, auct.

Sale at auction per order of Orphans Crt of Wash Co, D C; at late dwlg of Jas Mathers, dec'd; sundry items. -John Coyle, Elias B Caldwell, admx.

Sale at auction-at resid of Mr John St Clair, dec'd: all hsehld furn, hay & boat. -Nich L Queen, auct.

For sale: *Shipwrights Wood Yd*, addition to Shipwrights Wood Yd, *Shipwrights Maggot, Woodbridge, Barbers, St Assard & Slingsbey*, adj each other, in Cob Neck, Chas Co, Md; ab't 400 acs. Apply to John B Boarm living in Gtwn. -Chas Chunn.

SAT NOV 9, 1811
Orphans Crt of PG Co, Md. Sale of 12 to 15 negroes at the late dwlg of Alice Duvall, dec'd. -Fredk P L Duvall, exc, PG Co, Md.

Hse o/Reps: 1-Petition of John Taliaferro, complaining of the undue election of John P Hungerford. 2-Petition of Benj Merrill & Alex'r Richards, merchants, of Newburyport, Mass-relief of the brig *Alex'r*, seized & condemned in Naples, Italy, Dec last.

Runaway-Jim White, negro man; committed to Anne Arundel, Md, jail; says he was sold by Mr Wicker, Dorset Co, Eastern Shore, ab't 12 mos ago; to Mr Thompson, of Ga, where he was carried & escaped. -John Cord, shrff, Anne Arundel Co, Md.

For sale-seat cld *Mountain Prospect*, residence of the late Robt B Voss, Culpeper Co, Va; 700 acs. Mr Geo Fitzhugh, who lives nrby, will show the land. -Sam'l Gordon, Sole exc. -Falmouth, Va.

W Cooper has remv'd his music store & printing ofc to Pa Ave, nrly oppo Mr Herford's Brewery.

Runaway-Sally Dangerfield, black girl, committed to Wash Co, D C jail; she says her mthr, Milly Wane, lives in Alexandria; says she is 14 yrs of age. -C Tippett, kpr of the jail, Wash.

La Gaz. Mr Charless, info has passed by Ft Machilimakinac; much is said ab't British traders; active smuggling by Robt Dixon, who arrv'd at Prairie Du Chien with several boats, he left with Roulette; they were guided by 100 Folles Avoines & 150 Puants. -A ctzn. St Louis, Oct 12, 1811.

To let-brick hse, lately occupied by Mr Cooper as a music store & printing ofc; on 11th St nr Pa Ave. Apply to Nichs King-Wash, or T C Wright-Gtwn.

Wash Co, D C-In Chancery. John P Van Ness, adm of Wm & Chas Laight, against John Blagge & the heirs & reps of Geo Walker. Bill states-on Jan 23, 1802, Geo Walker, being indebted to Wm & Chas Laight for $18,820.26; to secure payment conveyed lots in Wash City to John Blagge, in trust to sell said lots & discharge the debt; Wm & Chas Laight both died intestate; their rights have been granted to John P Van Ness, since which time the said Geo Walker also departed without any relatives or heirs; above sum is not pd; John Blagge is a resid of N Y C. -Wm Brent, Reg.

In Chancery, Oct 21, 1811. Hugh McGuire, vs Sam'l J Coolidge & Mary his wife, John Hepburn, Sarah Hepburn & Patricus Hepburn. Bill is to obtain decree for sale of lot with improvements in Upper Marlboro, PG Co, Md, whereof Frank Leeke died seized; F Leek died intestate leaving a bro, Sam'l Leeke, his heir, to whom his rl est descended; Sam'l, who is since dead, made a will leaving all his est to his Uncle, Sam'l Hepburn, who is since dead, leaving Sam'l J Coolidge & Mary his wife, John Hepburn & Sarah Hepburn of lawful age & Patricus Hepburn, a minor, his chldrn & legal reps. Frank Leeke died with no prsnl est, but died seized of the lot & improvements. Sam'l J Coolidge & Mary his wife, reside out of Md. -Nichs Brewer, Reg Cur Can.

Leg of Md: Tobias E Stansbury, chosen spkr of the hse of Delegates; John Brewer, Chief clk.

Edmund B Duvall, atty at law, has opened his ofc on G St.

Wm Hunter, chosen Senator of U S, for R I, vice Christopher G Champlin, rsgn'd.

New shoe & boot store-Pa Ave. -Andrew Coyle, Wash.

TUE NOV 12, 1811
Gtwn-sell or lease on ground rent, 190 ft on Fall St; also 190 ft on Pitt St, which fronts the river. -Frs Lowndes.

Hse o/Reps: 1-Petition of W & John Pearce, at Ft Stoddert, relief for heavy duties on goods at Mobile, while under the Spanish Gov't. 2-Petition of Sam'l Hanson, compensation for his svcs while employed in the Navy Dept.

Mrd: Mr Jas Carroll jr to Miss Achsah Ridgley, d/o Gen Ridgley of Hampton, a few evenings ago, by Rev Dr Bend.

Died: on Nov 6, at Phil, Mr Sam'l McCloud, ntv of Scotland & formerly a resid of Alexandria.

Died: Dr John Shore, coll of the port of Petersburg; at his seat in Nottoway Co, on Oct 20.

Died: Dr John Smith, on Oct 21, at Beaufort; principal of Beaufort College.

THU NOV 14, 1811
Rent or lease, tavern cld *Broad Creek*. Apply to Thos Wheat in Wash City. -Mary Moreland, PG Co, Md.

Boston Paper. To the public: some French frigs have orders *Burn, Sink or Destroy* all American vessels they can catch. Sep 19th I was brought to a French frig under English colors; I was robbed of my provisions, money, papers & clothes. Their seeing another vessel prevented them from burning the brig. -Elijah Beal.

Loss of Gun-Boat, No. 2: Command of Mr Lippincott. Sailed from Charleston on Sep 29th bound to St Mary's; Oct 4th they made Cumberland Island; hurricane gale on Nov 5th; those below forced open the hatches & the boat filled & instantly went down; John Tier was saved; persons lost:
John Lippincott, acting mstr, ntv of Pa;
*Wm Jas Gunning, midshipman of Wilmington, N C;
John Todd, do, of Charleston;
Francis Taylor, do, do;
Sam'l Liber, do, do;
Sam'l Robertson, boatswain;   Wm Wright, gunner;
Thos King, purser's Steward;   Sam'l Cameron, carpenter;
Mrs R Smith, ntv of Liverpool, going onto her hsbnd, a carpenter in the U S svc; & ab't 25 seamen.
*Gunning, a young man, leaves a widowed mthr. -Ed Reg.

Alexander Campbell, from Ohio, took his seat.

Congress. Senate, Nov 12. 1-Petition of Larkin Smith, coll of the Dists of Norfolk & Portsmouth, praying for additional compensation. 2-Memorial of Mathew Lyon, of Ky, fined & imprisoned under the Sedition law, praying renumeration.

Public auction at Rhodes' Hotel in Wash City; decree of Crct Crt of Wash Co, D C-as Crt of Chancery: in case of Thos Lawrason against Jas Patten, Eliz Wadsworth & others; brick hse on lot 18 sq 168 & part of said lot. -Chas Glover-trust.

SAT NOV 16, 1811
Hse o/Reps: 1-Petition of Jos Simons, of Phil, merchant, to receive drawbacks due to error of the collector, which were withheld from him. 2-Pet of Isaac Clawson of N Y, on drawbacks. 3-Pet of Thos & John Clifford of Phil, & Chas Wingman of

Balt, refunding money pd for duty on articles. 4-Pet of Mich'l Reap of N C, wounded sldr in Rev war-to be placed on pension list. 5-Pet of John Burnhan, taken prisoner by the Algerines some yrs ago, had an allowance made him by Congress, praying for further relief. 6-Pet of Anthony Crease of Alexandria, ntv of Gr Britain, intends on becoming a ctzn of U S, wants to hold land in Wash Co, D C. 7-Pet of John McCulloch, coll of the port of Balt, insufficiency of his emoluments. 8-Pet of Abraham Whipple, to be placed on pension list.

Nov 11, Gen Robt Bowie was elected Gov of Md. Elected Council: Dr Geo E Mitchell, John Stephen, Jas Britcher, Thos W Hall, Revardy Gheislin.

Orphans Crt of Wash Co, D C. Nov 14, 1811. Prsnl est of Jos E Rowles, late of said town & co, dec'd. -Sally Rowles, admx,

Orphans Crt of Wash Co, D C. Nov 16, 1811. Prsnl est of Chas Jones, late of said co, dec'd. -Prudence Jones, admx. Nichs L Queen, adm.

John Hugh of Gtwn appt'd as atty at law.

Chas H Plummer, of PG Co, Md, insolvent debtor, imprisoned for debt. -John R Magruder, clk, St Mary's Co Crt. [PG Co, Md, Crt, Sep term-1811]

TUE NOV 19, 1811
Gabriel Duval, present comp of the Treas of the U S, & Jos Story, of Mass, appt'd Judges of the Supreme Crt of the U S, by the President.

Hse o/Reps: 1-Petition of Archibald McCall, merchant of Phil, allowance of drawbacks withheld from him. 2-Pet of Selah Benton, Capt in Rev svc, asking for a pension. 3-Pet of Jas Forrest, of N Y, merchant, he had debts owing to him in the British W India Islands, $25,000, praying to import from them to that amount. 4-Pet of John Steele, Phil, increase of compensation.

Mrd: Mr Sam'l Robertson, of U S N, to Miss Eliza Murdoch, 2nd d/o late Col Murdoch of Gtwn, D C; on Nov 12, by Rev Mr Addison.

Mrd: Henry Fitzhugh, of Fauquier Co, to Miss Henrietta S Fitzhugh, d/o Hon Nicholas Fitzhugh, of Alexandria, in Fairfax Co, Va, Nov 14, by Rev Mr Maffitt.

Died: Mr Jabez Upham, late Rep in Cong for Mass; at Brookfield, Oct 31st.

Died: Wm White, sec of State of N C, on Nov 8th, in Raleigh, N C.

Died: Lt Robert Roberts, of the Regt of Artillerists, at Ft Johnston, Smithville, N C.

Died: Rinaldo Johnson, late of Aquasco, PG Co, Md, age 56 yrs, at Balt, Nov 12. His remains were deposited on Nov 14th in the fmly vault at Springfield, Balt Co, Md. [Tender hsbnd & indulgent fr]

Orphans Crt of St Mary's Co, Md. Oct 25, 1811. Prsnl est of Everard Taylor, late of said co, dec'd. -Jas M Taylor, adm.

Dissolution of partnership, by mutual consent; Thos Richardson & Co; payments to Richardson. -Th Richardson, Rich'd Parrott, Gtwn.

Persons are cautioned against leasing or purchasing of Wm H Washington, my island, known as *Alexander's Island*. The said Washington has no legal right, title or claim to the same. -Philip Alexander.

Orphans Crt of Wash Co, D C. Francis Clarke, late of said city, dec'd. -Eliz Clarke, admx. John McGowan, adm.

Orphans Crt of Wash Co, D C. Nov 15, 1811. Prsnl est of Geo Fenwick, late of said co, dec'd. -Mgt Fenwick, excx.

Public sale, at the plantation, St Mary's Co, Md, nr Leonardtown, late the farm of Geo Fenwick, of Gtwn, dec'd; stock, crop of corn & fodder, some furn, etc. -E J Millard, adm with the will annexed of Geo Fenwick, dec'd.

Mrs H Walker, F St, has fashionable millinery for sale.

THU NOV 21, 1811
Died: Miss Mary L Machen, of Wash, age 24 yrs, Nov 19, of a lingering & painful illness.

Affair of the Little Belt. Crt of Enquiry-Sep 2, 1811. Present-Cmdor Stephen Decatur, Pres; Capt Chas Stewart & Isaac Chauncey, mbrs. Witnesses: John Ord Creighton, on board the U S frig, *President,* on May 16th during the engagement with his Britannic Majesty's ship the *Lille* or *Little Belt.* Other witnesses: Capt Henry Caldwell, Raymond H J Perry, Andrew L B Madison, Jacob Mull, Henry Denison & Mich'l Roberts.

Died: lately, Geo Matthews jr, one of the Judges of the Superior Crt of the Terr of Orleans, in the Parish of Rapide, Orleans Terr; his lady died about the same time.

Crt at Rockville, Montg Co, Md: first meeting since the death of Henry Ridgely, esq; crape to be worn.

Hse o/Reps: Petition of Rich'd Crump, Jas Steptoe & others, to register their claims to lands in Ga.

Ranaway-Dick, negro man, calls himself Rich'd Thompson; formerly belonged to Mr Rich Watts. -Jas Walker, head of St Clement's bay, St Mary's Co, Md.

SAT NOV 23, 1811

Congress-Petition of Thos O Bannon, alteration in survey of land purch'd by him of the U S.

Rich'd Rush, of Phil City, appt'd comptroller of the Treas of the U S, vice Gabriel Duval, who accepted a Judicial appointment.

Died: Chas A Beatty, age 22 yrs, ntv of Gtwn, D C, & s/o Dr Chas A Beatty, of that place, on Oct 29th, at Wilmington, N C.

Thos O'Connor, of New York, preposes publishing History of Ireland, from the Union with Gr Britain in Jan 1801 to Oct 1811, by Francis Plowden, esq.

Ready made clothes, at the sign of the golden sheaf, on High St, Gtwn. -Rich'd Davis, Gtwn.

Hotel to let, Oct 1st next; now occupied by Wm Rhodes as a tavern. -Toppan Webster.

St Mary's Co Crt, Md, Aug term: Redmond Grace, of said co, insolvent debtor; confined for debt. -Jo Harris, clk.

TUE NOV 26, 1811

Leg of Ga: Matthew Talbot chosen Pres of the Senate; Robt Iverson, spkr of the Hse o/Reps.

D B Mitchell re-elected Govn'r of Ga over his opponent Gen Irvin.

Washington Dancing Assemblies. Mgrs appt'd: Robt Brent, Franklin Wharton, Wm Simmons, Thos Tingey, Dan'l Carroll, John Tayloe, Edw Coles, Edmund B Duvall, Wm Sanford, M St Clair Clarke, Rich'd Smith & Jas Eakin. Nov 26.

Columbian Agricultural Soc met on Nov 20th & the appt'd Judges were: Elie Williams, Thompson Mason, J Schnebly, Bernard Gilpin & Joshua Delapline. Prizes awarded by: Wm Marbury, Jas M Garnett, John Threlkeld, Wm S Nichols & Sam'l Fitzhugh. Prizes awarded to: Geo Calvert of PG Co, Md; Wm Stinbergen of Shenandoah Co, Va; Mrs Letitia Gilpin of Montg Co, Md; Mrs Sarah McCarty Mason of Hollin Hall, Fairfax Co, Va; Mrs Martha P Graham of Dumfired, Pr Wm Co, Va; Mrs Martha Lindsay of Fairfax Co, Va; Mrs Allice Wood, of Fairfax Co, Va; Mrs Eliz Maynadier, of Belvoir, Ann Arundle Co, Md; Mrs Wren of Fairfax Co, Va; Mrs E Leawright, of Va. Appt'd ofcrs of the Soc for ensuing yr: Osborn Sprigg, of Northampton, PG Co, Md; Thompson Mason, of Hollin Hall, Fairfax Co, Va; David Wiley, of Gtwn, D C. Standing Committee: John Mason, John Threlkeld, Robt Brent, Wm Cranch, Wm Marbury, all of Wash; Nicholas Fitzhugh, Wm A Dangerfield, Geo W P Custis, all of Alexandria; Wm Mason, of Chas Co, Md; Bernard Gilpin & Roger Brooke, of Montg Co, Md; Jos Kent, Geo Calvert, of PG Co, Md; Henry Maynadier & Chas Carroll of Carrolton, both of Ann Arundel Co, Md; Athanasius Fenwick, of St Mary's Co, Md; Sam'l Ringgold, of Wash Co, Md; Wm H Foote, Geo Graham, Rich'd M Scott, all of Fairfax Co, Va; Wilson C Seldon & Chas F Mercer, both of Loudon Co, Va; John Williams, Robt Graham, both of Pr Wm Co, Va; Dan'l C Brent & John J Brooke, both of Stafford Co, Va; Ferdinando Fairfax & John Dawny, both of Jefferson Cty, Va; Wm Stinbergen, of Shenandoah Co, Va. -David Wiley, sec, Gtwn.

Pblc sale-Order of Orphans Crt of PG Co, Md: at late dwlg of Moses Cawood, late of PG Co, dec'd; all prsnl prop-negroes, cattle, horses, etc. -Wm Marshall, exc.

Sale of negroes, deed of trust from Wm Digges, in order to close the trust; at *Melwood Park*, PG Co, Md, adj *Melwood*; seat of Mrs Digges. -Jo W Clagett, Philip B Key, trustees.

Confectionary & Distillery of Cordials, Eighth St, oppo the Marine Barracks. -Fred'k Cana & Co.

Sale at auction-at store of Enos D Ferguson; the remains of his store goods. -N L Queen, auct.

Orphans Crt of Wash Co, D C. Nov 23, 1811. Prsnl est of Nichs Lingan, late of said co, dec'd. -Rich'd Parrott.

Michael McCormick, insolvent debtor, confined in Wash Co, D C prison for debt. -Wm Brent, clk.

SAT NOV 28, 1811
Elegy on the death of M L Machen, who lately died in this city of consumption, at an early age;---Maria rests, to sigh no more---.

Shipwreck of schnr, *Hiram*, of Falmouth, Mass; on Oct 22, 1811; Barzillai Lewis, mstr; sailed from N Y bound to Wilmington, N C. Persons concluded to have been on board: Jas Perin-saddler, Sophia Perin, Hannah Perkins, Sophia Metcalf, Sam'l Metcalf, Sylvester Gridley-Sadler, John Fairman, Sam'l Meloy. -J W D Walsh, Justice of the Peace, D C C.

Ltr from Louisville, dt'd Nov 16: Action took place on Nov 7th bet the troops under Gov Harrison & the Indians under the prophet; killed in action-Col Daviess, Col Owen of Shelby, Col White of the Saline, Capt Spencer & both his subalterns, Capt Berry from Corydon & Capt Bain of the Regulars; Col F Geiger was shot thru the arm; Gov Harrison was shot thru his hat; Thos Randolph was killed dead. Also killed were Jas Summerville & Stephen Mars.

PG Co, Md, Crt. Jos R Hodges, of PG Co, insolvent debtor, confined for debt. -J R Magruder, clk

Ltr from Mr Wm Cobbett to Ephraim Pentland, of Pittsburg, Pa, dt'd Newgate, Aug 30, 1811. Regarding his imprisonment for 2 yrs. [Phil Paper]

His excellency Wm Hull, Govn'r of Mich Terr, arrived in Newton last wk with his lady & youngest dght. -Boston, Nov 21.

Post ofc changes, Oct 1811:
Feestown, O-Arthur Fee, vice Wm Fee, rsgn'd;
Montagues, Va-Sam'l Foster, vice Wm Montague, rsgn'd;
Liberty Hall, Ga-Jas Ware, vice W C Stokes, rsgn'd;
Stoyeston, Pa-Abraham Schell, vice John Lehmer, rsgn'd;
Sumpterville, S C-Wm McGee, vice Gershon Benbow, rsgn'd;
Rockingham, Vt-Jas Felt, vice Edw R Campbell 2nd, rsgn'd;
Leedstown, Va-John W Hungerford, vice Rob R Hodge, rsgn'd;
Quincy, Mass-Benj Vinton, vice Rich'd Cranch, dec'd;
Curretuck, C H, N C-Thos Morse, vice J Williams;
Barre, Vt-John Baker, vice Chapin Keith, rsgn'd;
Coeymans, N Y-Levi Blaisdell, vice Wm McCarty, rsgn'd;
Hermitage, Va-Garnett Andrews, vice Mark Andrews, rsgn'd;
Long Reach, Ky-Crawford Anderson, vice Vincent Anderson, rsgn'd.

New Post ofcs & postmstrs, Oct 1811:
Baton Rouge, N Orleans Terr-Jas Chaveau, postmstr;
Little Yox, Alleghany Co, Md-Wm Armstrong;
Nicholson Thornbottom, Pa-Caleb Roberts;
Paddy town, Hampshire Co, Va-Isaac McCarty;
Washington Duchess Co, N Y-Jos Thom;
Webbs, Stokes Co, N C-John Webb;
Olympian Springs, Montgomery Co, Ky-Cuthbert Banks;
Royalton, Worcester Co, Mass-Jos Easterbrooks;
Cataragus, Chetaugua Co, N Y-Foster Young;
Wheatsboro, Huron Co, Ohio-Nathan Wood jr;
Warren, Litchfield Co, Ct-Benj B Osborn;
Ellsworth, Litchfield Co, Ct-Dan'l St John.

Ran away-John, negro, from Benedict Boarman, in Chas Co, nr Bryantown, Md. -John Francis Gardiner.

Land for sale-2,000 acs in Loudon Co, Va. -Wm Dudley Digges, *Green Hill*, nr Bladensburg, Md.

Farm for sale-700 to 800 acs; in PG Co, Md; with dwlg hse; also hses & lot nr Bladensburg, cld the *Cross Roads*, adj the lands of Maj Williams & Messrs Berry's. My bro, Jas A Beall, & myself, will sell ab't 1,800 acs in Montg Co, Md. Jas A Beall is living on North West Branch. -J F Beall, residing nr Piscataway.

Died: Mr Jas Latimore, of Chas Co, formerly of PG Co, Md, on Nov 17th, after a short illness.

Died: Robt Treat Paine jr, age 38, at Boston, on Nov 13th.

SAT NOV 30, 1811
Orphans Crt of PG Co, Md. Sale at former dwlg of subscriber in PG Co; prsnl est of Edw Swann, late of said co, dec'd, to satisfy his debts. -Henry T Compton, adm

Runaway-Nancy Green, negro girl, age ab't 20 yrs, committed to Wash Co, D C, jail; says she belongs to Rich'd Bird of Smithfield, Va. -C Tippett, kpr of jail.

Orphans Crt of Wash Co, D C. Est of Robt Alexander, late of New Orleans & formerly of this city, dec'd. -Jos Cassin, exc.

Robt Chosley, of St Mary's Co, Md, insolvent debtor, confined for debt. -Edmund Key. -Jos Harris, clk, St Mary's Co.

Jos Boulton, of St Mary's Co, Md, insolvent debtor, confined for debt. -Jos Harris, clk, St M Co.

Public supplies will be rec'd at this ofc; usual articles of military supply. -Tench Coxe, Purveyor, Purv ofc-Phil.

TUE DEC 3, 1811
Mrd: Jos Pearson, Rep in Congress from N C, to Miss Eleanor Brent, d/o Robt Brent, of Wash, on Dec 2, by Rev Mr Plunket.

Mrd: Phineas Jannet, merchant, to Sally Hartshorne, d/o Wm Hartshorne, on Nov 21, at Friends Meeting in Alexandria.

Died: Col Henry Hopkins, Adj Genr'l of the Militia, at New Orleans, latter end of Oct; ntv of Md, born & educated in Balt; srv'd for some time in U S Army as a Subaltern & svr'l yrs as Adj Genr'l.

Died: Wm Orr, collector of the Port of Wash, on Nov 13, in Wash, N C.

H C Dargen & Co will open their store-French millinery, on Jefferson St, Gtwn.

THU DEC 5, 1811
Died: Stephen Benj Roe, a seaman of color, ntv of N Y; of the America Vessel, *Perseverance,* J C Aylwin, mstr, from New Orleans; died in the fever ward in this place; his bal remaining to those who are authorised to receive same. -Jas Maury, America Consulate, Liverpool, Sep 3, 1811.

Lexington, Va, Nov 17. The Militia of Rockbridge Co, the 8th Regt, met on Nov 14; in absence of Col Jas McDowell, it was commanded by Maj Jos Allen; strength of the Regulars exceeds 1,100; Maj John Alexander-Brigade Inspector. -Enq.

Sale at auction at my dwlg hse on Capitol Hill-hsehld furn, etc; also brick hse & lot. Also to rent, the hse I now live in. -Henry Tims.

SAT DEC 7, 1811
Hse o/Reps: Petition of Jane Deakins, of Alexandria, praying to be divorced from her hsbnd, John Deakins.

Died: Mr Geo Dobbin, printer, Dec 3, in Balt, age 38 yrs; one of the proprietors of *The American*; ntv of Ire, born in County of Monaghan, remv'd to this his adopted country, in 1798.

Died: on Dec 6, Mrs Mary E Norvell, age 18 yrs, consort of Mr John Norvell.

List of the killed & wounded of Clark Co, L T: killed-Jos Warnock, Thos Clendenen, Wm Fislar, Wm Hutchinson, Henry Jones & Wm Kelly; wounded-John Drummond, J Robertson, Thos Gibson, Col Bartholomew & Capt Norris. [Iindian attack, See Sat, Nov 28, 1811 paper] *Also killed: Col Owen of Ky, Col Davies & Lt McMahan; Thos Randolph & Col Isaac White, of the Cavalry. *Written by Wm Taylor, who had his horse shot from under him.

Endorsement of Mr Jonathan Findlay's School, Wash City. -Signed by Jas Laurie, Wm James, Phineas Bradley.

TUE DEC 10, 1811
Notice-my wife, Harriot, having eloped from my bed & board without provocation; forwarn all from harboring her or her child. -John Woolcott.

G W Smith, late Lt Govn'r, is chosen Govn'r of Va, over Jas Barbour, esq; votes-100 for Smith & 97 for Barbour.

Names & places of residence of American prisoners in Cape Henry, Hayti. Crew of the schn'r, *Hound,* taken Feb 6, 1811: Robt Harner-Phil; Thos Quail-Phil; Jas Wilson, N Y; Wm Smith, Norfolk; Sterling Waters, Easton, N Y; Jos Saunders, Kennebunk, Mass; Thos Robinson, Edenton, N C; Sam'l Brand, Bridgetown, N J; Memory Campbell, a black man, Norfolk. Crew of the schn'r, *Bee,* taken Aug 7, 1811: John Gilmore, Weatherfield, Con; John Mitchell, a black man, N Y; John Martin, do, do. Crew of the sloop, *Rebecca,* taken Aug 22, 1811: Anthony Beaumont, N Y; Henry Slaght, N Y; Sampson Curry, a black man, Boston.

Virtue of decree of Crct Crt of Wash Co, D C-Crt of Chancery. Geo King, Anna Marie Davidson & John B Evans, against, Ann Young, [widow] Sam'l W Young, Eliz Young, Susanna Young, Rich'd Young, John Young & Chas Young, heirs & reps of Abraham Young, dec'd; John Bell, Henry Pratt, John Ashley, Thos Willing Francis, John Miller jr, Jacob Baker, Adam King & Wm King. Sale of lots in Wash City, ab't 71 total; also land being part of *Chance, Hogpen Enlarged* & *Knock* in Wash Co, & out of the bounds of Wash City, sold by Abraham Young to Wm King. -Chas Glover, trustee, Nich L Queen, auct.

THU DEC 12, 1811
Edw Parker & Jos Delaplaine, bksellers, Phil, intend to publish an American Edition of the Edinburgh Encyclopedia.

Hse o/Reps: 1-Petition of Henry Waner, collector of Plymouth, Mass, praying for additional compensation. 2-Pet of Jared Shattuck was read & referred to committee. 3-Pet of Robt Kid, merchant of Phil, reimbursement of duties pd. 4-Pet of Ebenezer Rolins, merchant of Boston, to be pd drawback of coffee shipped from Boston to Gottenburg in 1810.

Caesar A Rodney has rsgn'd his appointment as Atty-Genr'l of the U S; Wm Pinkney, of Md, has been appt'd Atty-Genr'l.

There are now 13 steam boats. Livingston & Fulton built their first one in 1807.

Mrd: Dr Wm Hill to Miss Ann Smith, eldest d/o Dr Clement Smith, all of PG Co, Md, on Dec 3, at *Poplar Hill*, PG Co, Md, by Rev Mr Vergennes.

Boston Gaz: Mr Josiah Dunham published in the *Washingtonian*, printed in Windsor, Vt, that offers had been made by me to raise a sum for the education of my son, Zerah, this is incorrect. -Abias Colburn.

To be let, nr the Navy Yd-dwlg hse & store, lately occupied by Wilcox & Fitzgerald-Dry Good store. -Thos Holiday.

For sale: brick hse, lot 4 sq 951, K St by 9th; now in possession of Mr Jas Owner, Naval constructor. Apply to John Glasco at his hse at the end of Upper Bridge across Rock Crk.

Orphans Crt of Wash Co, D C. Dec 10, 1811. Prsnl est of Jas Craig, late of said city, dec'd. -Jas Cochran, adm. [Sale of all hsehld furn, 2 cows, 1 mare, cart & geers & 1 silver watch. -Nichs L Queen, auct.]

Lexington, Nov 30-Meeting of Lexington Lodge, No 1, Nov 18: Mbrs to wear mourning in respect to memory of Col Jos H Daviess, G Master of Masons for Ky, who fell in the defence of his country on the Wabash, Nov 7.

Died: Jas Fitzword Griswold, late a cadet in the Military School at West Point, & since a student of law; age 22 yrs, lately in Cincinnati, Ohio; eldest s/o Stanley Griswold, a Judge of the Illinois Territory.

State of Md-In Chancery, 1811. Anthony Reintzell, against, the adms & heirs of Peter Casenave & Amy Thrustom, Thos Robinson, Wm Robinson, Wm Pollard, Chas Pettet, Sam'l Crawford, John Barclay, Jacob Spier, Clement Biddle, Chas B Penrose & Wm Hutchison; dfndnts reside outside of Md. Bill to obtain a review & reversal of a decree before passed in a suit by the cmplnt against said dfndnts. -Nichs Brewer, RCC.

Died: on Dec 2, Jas Wm Lock Weems, of PG Co, Md, age 47 yrs.

I will give the highest price for a light waggon. -Thos Ewell

SAT DEC 14, 1811
Mrshl's sale: all right, title, int & claim of Clotworthy Stevenson, to lot 15 & all of lot 16 in sq 254, with dwlg hse; 2 writs of Fieri Facias issued by Crct of Wash Co, D C; suit of Wm DeNeale, adm of John Fowler; suit of Wm Woodcock & John Turner against said Stevenson. -Wash Boyd-mrshl.

TUE DEC 16, 1811
Geo B Williams of the township of Northampton, Berkshire Co, Mass, employs & moves by water 1 carding machine & 150 spindles; & by hand 410 spindles in woolen manufacture.

Philip J Hahn, 33 Wash St, Winchester, Fred'k Co, Va, makes & sells wool hats at 90 to 100 cents each.

Died: Mrs Martha Milledge, consort of Col John Milledge, late a Senator in Cong from Ga, on Dec 5th, of a lingering & severe illness.

Nath'l Williams, is elected by the Senate of Md, to fill the vacancy in their body occasioned by resignation of Mr Pinkney.

Post ofc changes, Nov 1811:
Campbell C H, Va-John Reid, vice Thos Reid, dec'd;
Sandusky, O-Jacob B Varnum, vice Wm Matthews, rsgn'd;
Kent, Con-Lewis St John, vice Lewis Mills, situation inconvenient;
Mifflinburg, Pa-Sam'l Geddis, vice Thos Youngman;
Watertown, N Y-Paul Hutchinson, vice Jos Clark, rsgn'd;
Barbourville, Ky-Gill Eve, vice John Logan, rsgn'd;
Westernport, Md-Lewis Dunn, vice Wm Price, rsgn'd;
Church Hill, Md-Wm Jacobs, vice R Rochester, dec'd;
Jefferson, Va-Wm K Spillman, vice Gabriel Tutt, rsgn'd;
Milledgeville, G-John Howard, vice John W Devereaux, rsgn'd;
Lewisburg, Ky-John Fisher, vice John Wier;
Danville, Ky-Benj Perkins, vice J Birney, rsgn'd;
Salem, Pa-Wm Woodbridge, vice Theodore Woodbridge, dec'd;
Beaufort, S C-Jas Clark, vice Dan'l Parker, rsgn'd;
Uxbridge, Mass-Sam'l Read, vice Sam'l Willard, dec'd;
Battletown, Va-Dan'l Annin, vice Bushrod Taylor, rsgn'd;
Milford Del-Matthew Rinch, vice Thos Glass, rsgn'd;
Middlehaddam, Ct-John Stuart, vice John H Peters, dec'd;
Augusta, Me-John Kimball, vice Nathan Weston jr, rsgn'd;
Greenville, Ky-Jos Winlock, vice P Redmon, rsgn'd;
Burgettstown, Pa-Andrew Stephenson, vice Thos Miller, rsgn'd;
Windham, N H-Sam'l Senter, vice Andrew Park, situation inconv;
Piscataway, Md-Gavin Hamilton, vice David Koones, rsgn'd;

Pittsville, Va-M G Hunter, vice Muscoe Garnett, rsgn'd;
Broadfield, Va-John Stoke, vice T S Dade, rsgn'd;
Burton, O-Gideon Finch, vice P Hitchcock, rsgn'd;
King & Queen C H, Va-Thacker Muier, vice A P Muse, rsgn'd;
Spring Hill, Va-Jas Moody jr, vice Jas Moody Sr, rsgn'd;
Harts Store, Va-John Smith, vice David Young, rsgn'd;
Milton, Va-Chas Vest, vice J Bennett, mv'd away;
North East, Md-Thos Maffit, vice B Williams, dec'd;
Lovington, Va-Chas Perrow, vice R L Talliaferro, rsgn'd;
Haley's Bridge, Va-Benj W Johnson, vice A DeBerry, rsgn'd;
Kingston, N H-Levi Bartlett, vice Simmons Secomb, rsgn'd;
Milton or Broadkill, Del-Eli Hall, vice S Wright, dec'd;
Grayson C H, Va-Robt Nicholls, vice Dan'l Coley, rsgn'd;
Westraysville, N C-John Bobbitt, vice Thos Philips, rsgn'd.

New ofcs & postmstr-Nov 1811:
Aldie, Loudon Co, Va-Peyton Cook, Postmaster;
Tewkesbury, Middlesex Co, Ms-Jacob Coggin;
Bear Garden, Fred'k Co, Va-Robt Rogers;
Cape Caphon, Fred'k Co, Va-John Copsey;
Little Cape Caphon, Hampshire Co, Va-John Higgins;
Anderson's, Fred'k Co, Va-Thos Anderson;
Parks, Fred'k Co, Va-Solomon Parks;
Leesville, Hampshire Co, Va-Stephen Lee;
Burlington, Middlesex Co, Ms-John Walker;
Bartlett, Stafford Co, N H-Obed Hall 2nd;
Davis's Tavern, Sussex Co, Va-Shepherd Davis;
Morgans, Muhlenburgh Co, Ky-Chas Morgan;
Canoe Camp, Tioga Co, Pa-Micha Spencer;
Double Branches, Pendleton Co, S C-Hugh Robertson;
Robertville, Barnwell dist, S C-Benj Brooks;
Reynolds, Lycoming Co, Pa-David Reynolds;
Putnam's, Tioga Co, Pa-Elijah Putnam;
Locke, Cayuga Co, N Y-Benj Williams;
Barnstead, Strafford Co, N H-Chas Hodgden jr;
Brookfield, Trumbull Co, O-Isaac Flower jr;
Vienna, Trumbull Co, O-Nathan B Derrow;
Shade Furnace, Somerset Co, Pa-Jos Vickroy;
Moryanns Forge, Somerset Co, Pa-Conrad Piper;
Williams' Store, Anson Co, N C-Edw C Williams;
Mcbees Ferry, Knox Co, Ten-Jos Evans;
Coal Mines, Chesterfield Co, Va-Isham Randolph;
Dripping Springs, Warren Co, Ky-Dan'l Maxwell;
Montgomery, Hamilton Co, O-Jos Toulmin.
Discont'd in Nov 1811: Reidsville, S C; Kanahwa, Va;
Nassau, N Y; Mitchell's Store, Va.

In Chancery-Dec 10, 1811. John Hoye & Leonard M Deakins, excs of Francis Deakins, against, Archibald Talbot & others. Bill to obtain a decree for the sale of equitable interest of Archibald Talbott, Elisha Hyland & the heirs of Paul Talbot, late of Wash Co, dec'd, in land in Wash Co cld: *Freestone* & part of *Take place, The Resurvey or Let Justice*. Francis Deakins & Wm Deakins were joint tenants of said land; Francis Deakins gave his bond of conveyance to Paul & Archibald Talbott; by the death of Wm Deakins the whole legal interest vested in said Francis's survivor & devisee, & the cmplnts as his excs, have authority under the will to convey the legal title; the interest of Archibald T was assigned to Paul Talbott; by agreement among the heirs of Paul T, all their interest was vested in Elisha Hyland-now in possession of same; Archibald Talbott resides in Ohio. -Nichs Brewer, Reg Cur Can.

David Holmes, Govn'r of Mississippi Terr, arrived in this city yesterday.

Wm Hawkins is elected Govn'r of North Carolina.

Public sale-decree of the Hon Chancellor of Md; at Montgomery Crt Hse: *Magruder's Farm, Addition to Turkey Thicket, The Mistake* & part of *Charles & Benjamin*; 5-6 miles from the Crt hse. Mr Levin Beall will show the premises. -Henry Williamson, trustee, Annapolis.

THU DEC 19, 1811
Mrd: Dr Francis Dade, of Orange Crt-hse, Va, to Miss Harriet Shepherd, in Alexandria, on Dec 12, by Rev Dr Muir.

Indiana Terr-Vincennes, Nov 23: Leg of the Terr met on Nov 11th; Jas Beggs was appt'd Pres of the Cncl & Genl W Johnston, spkr of the Hse o/Reps.

Maj Waller Taylor, who had his horse shot under him in the late engagement on the Wabash, is now in Wash City.

A charity sermon will be preached at the Methodist Chr by the Rev Mr Waugh on Sunday, next.

To be sold, lot of ground with hses, Pa Ave, crnr of 6th St West, presently occupied by R C Weightman; 2 story frame hse was built at an expense of ab't $1300; also a brick hse oppo the bldg cld the Hotel, but at present intended for the Genr'l Post ofc & Patent ofc; proprietor, Wm Duane, at Phil.

For sale: 22 lots in Wash City, devised by the late Sam'l Davidson, to Miss Pattison, of Cambridge, Md; being the whole of sq 186-except lots 1, 2, 3 & 18. -Chas Goldsborough, Wash.

Stolen from my waggon in Balt City, an iron grey mare; deliver same to Mr E Finly, merchant, Balt; to Mr Jno Keesly, merchant, Shepherdstown, Va. -Alex'r Peoples, nr Shippensburg, Pa.

Reward-$25 for lge dark hair trunk, stolen out of a bedrm at the boarding hse of Mr Speake, Pa Ave. -John Low

Notice-Mary Ellen Standford, my wife, having on Dec 10th, absented herself from my bed & board without any reason; left me to foster an infant child which requires the breast. I forwarn every person from crediting her on my acc't. -Mich'l Sandford.

Public sale-prop now rented by Mr Jos Ratcliffe on Water St, Gtwn; prop was advertised last May by Lewis Clephan, on deed of trust. Said sale stopped by filing a bill of injunction by Andrew McDonald. -John Travers, auct.

SAT DEC 21, 1811
Public sale-svr'l negroes, furn & some stock, etc. -Janet Thompson, admx of Jas Thompson, dec'd; St Mary's Co, Md, 4 miles below Leonard Town.

Abraham Whipple, late a Capt in the U S Navy, to be placed on the list of invalid pensioners; so disabled in the line of his duty, he is unable to support himself by labor; entitled to receive half the monthly pay of Capt, to commence from Jan 1, 1810. -H Clay, Geo Clinton. Apprv'd-Jas Madison.

Genr'l return of the killed & wounded under command of his excellency Wm Henry Harrison, Gov & Commander in Chief of the Indiana Terr, in action with the Indians nr prophet's town, Nov 7, 1811. Genr'l Staff killed-Col Abram Owens, Aid-de-Camp. Field & Staff wounded-Lt Col Jos Bartholemews; Lt Col Luke Decker; Maj Jos H Daviess; Dr Edw Scull; Adj Jas Hunter. U S infty, including the late Capt Whitney's Rifle Co, wounded-Capt W C Bean, since dead; Lt Geo P Peters; Lt Geo Gooding; Ensign Henry Burchstead. Col Decker's Detachment of Indiana Militia, wounded-Capt Jacob Warrick, since dead. Maj Redman's Detachment of Indiana Militia, wounded-Capt John Norris. Maj Wells's Detachment of Mounted Riflemen, wounded-Capt Frederick Guiger. Capt Spencer's Co, including Lt Berry's Detachment of Mounted Riflemen, killed-Capt Spier Spencer; 1st Lt Rich'd McMahan; Lt Thos Berry. -Nath'l F Adams, Adj of the Army.

Josiah H Webb, wounded in Creek Nation of Indians while carrying the mail of the U S from Athens, Ga, to New Orleans, to be pd $50 annually, to commence Jan 1, 1809, during his natural life. -H Clay, Geo Clinton. Apprv'd-Jas Madison.

Orphans Crt of PG Co, Md. Prsnl est of Jane Hawkins, late of said co, dec'd. -Jas G Wood, Josias Young, adms.

Orphans Crt of PG Co, Md. Prsnl est of Robt Young, late of said co, dec'd. -Jas G Wood, Josias Young, excs.

TUE DEC 24, 1811
Notice-proposal to publish *Washington Gazette* at the seat of the Nat'l Gov't. -Jas A Baynard jr.

Mrd: Wm Carroll, of Montg Co, Md, to Miss Henrietta M Williamson, d/o D Williamson, of Balt, on Dec 16, by Rev Dr Carroll.

Mrd: Christopher Hughes jr, to Miss Laura Smith, d/o Gen Sam'l Smith of Balt, on Dec 17.

Land for sale-400 acs within 3 miles of Gtwn; also #1 & 2, in Beall's Addition to Gtwn, ab't 6 acs; also a sq of 12 lots in *Beall's Addition.* Apply to Mr John Lee, atty at law in Gtwn. -Thos S Lee.

Hugh Maguire intends to open a school nr the Union Tavern; hopes his experience in teaching, his appointment with in St John's College & others, will be testimonials of his capacity. -Hugh Maguire, nr crnr of Cherry alley, Gtwn.

Orphans Crt of PG Co, Md. Sale at late dwlg of Jos Owens, of said co, dec'd: part of prsnl est. -Benj Owens of Ben, adm.

THU DEC 26, 1811
Mr Aaron Ogden, of Elizabethtown, N J, has constructed a boat to be propelled by steam.

Orphans Crt of PG Co, Md. Dec 17, 1711. Prsnl est of Thos Contee, late of PG Co, dec'd. -Thos Contee Worthington, exc.

In Chancery, Dec 16, 1811. Peter King, vs Jesse Carpenter & Ruth his wife, Thos Beall of Sam'l, John Boos & Sam'l M Linggan. Bill to obtain an injunction on a judgment obtained in Montg Co Crt; same was purchase money for land sold by Carpenter to Boos, which Carpenter had no title; Carpenter & his wife reside out of State. -Nichs Brewer, Reg C C.

Lost-a red Morocco pktbk on Capitol Hill. -S Stow.

SAT DEC 28, 1811
Died: Capt Robt Barron, an old & respectable inhabitant of Norfork, Va; on Dec 23rd at Mr Buller Cock's in Wash; a few days would have completed the 5th month of his 64th yr.

Wash. Brewery, at the old sugar hse, ft of N J Ave; malt liquors now ready for delivery. -J W Collet & Co.

Wanted-5 journeymen shoemkrs; apply to Alexander Harper, Capitol Hill, next door to Mr David Watterstone's.

Cabinet manufactory has remv'd from High St in Gtwn, to his shop adj the 6 Bldgs in Wash City. -Wm Worthington jr.

Ohio River lands for sale in Mason Co, Va; part of military survey, cld *Mercer's Bottom*, 1,304 acs; & 1,411 acs with grist mill, lately built by Mr Hereford, prop of the said tract. -Jas M Garnett, Pittsville, Essex Co, Va.

TUE DEC 31, 1811
Orphans Crt of Wash City, D C. Dec 31, 1811. Prsnl est of Capt Dan'l Adams, formerly of Delaware, dec'd. -Geo Sandford, adm.

Sale at late dwlg of Nichs Lingan, dec'd, in Gtwn; prsnl est including the sch'r, *Henry & Clement*. -Richd Parrott, adm.

Sale at auction-deed of trust from Geo Maxwell to me; part of lot 13 sq 119, Wash City. -Thos Brooke Beall, trust. -Forrest & Beale, aucts.

Lost-Morocco pkt bk with $230 in notes, chiefly on the Bank of Balt, and Pa. -Wm Machesney

Ranaway-Ned, mulatto man; formerly belonged to Mr Brook living nr Wash City & purch'd from him by Mr Jas Davis jr. -Hugh McCalley. Reward-$20.

Richmond, Dec 27. Fire in theatre in Richmond on Dec 26, left the city in tears. Some who perished: Geo W Smith, Govn'r; A B Venable, Pres of the Bank; Benj Botts 'wife & niece; Mrs Tayloe Braxton; Mrs Petterson; Mrs Gallego; Miss Conyers; Lt J Gibbon-in attempting to save Miss Conyers; Mrs E Page; Miss Louisa Mayo; Mrs Wm Cook; Miss Elvina Coutts; Mrs John Lesley; Miss M Nelson; Miss Page; Wm Brown; Miss Juliana Hervey; Miss Whitlock; Geo Dixon; A Marshall of Wythe-broke his neck in jump from a window; Miss Ann Craig; Miss Stevenson of Spottsylvania; Mrs Gibson, Miss Mariana Hunter; Mrs Mary Davis; Miss Gerard; Thos Lecroix; Jade Wade; Mrs Pickit; Mrs Heron; Mrs LaForest & niece; Jo Jacob; Miss Jacobs; Miss A Bousman; Miss M Marks; Edw Wanton jr; 2 Miss Trouins; Mrs Gerer; Miss Ellicott; Miss Patsey Griffin; Mrs Moss & dght; Miss Littlepage; Miss Rebecca Cook; Mrs Girardin & 2 chldrn; Miss Mgt Copeland, Miss Gwathmey, Miss Clay-d/o M Clay, mbr of Cong; Miss Gatewood; Mrs Thos Wilson; Wm Southgate; Mrs Robt Greenhow; Mrs Convert & child; Miss Green; Miss C Raphael; John Welch, a stranger, nphw to Sir A Pigott, late from Eng; Margaretta Anderson; Thos Frazier; Mrs Jerrod; Jas Waldon; Barack Judah-child; Nuttle-crpntr; Nancy Pattersen-colored; Fanny Goff & Betsy Johnson, do; Pleasant-mulatto woman. Philadelphia is a missing person.

Appt'd to secure info of ctzns & others who have fallen: Jefferson ward-Wm Rowlett, Jos A Myers & Sam'l Pleasants; Madison ward-Jedediah Allen, Robt McKin & Robt Pollard; Monroe ward-Thos Taylor, Anderson Barret & Thos Rutherford; Manchester-Wm Fenwick, Mr Clark & Mr A Freeland. Rev Mr John Buchannan & Mr John Blair are to prepare a funeral sermon for Wed next in the Chr on Richmond Hill.

National Intelligencer
Washington, D C
1812

THU JAN 2, 1812
Wilmington, Dec 28. Friends of Dr John Storey, age 54, late of Petersburg, Va, are requested to attend his interment at Friends Burial Ground in this borough, Dec 29. Dr S was disabled by a paralytick stroke. He remv'd to this borough in 1808 at the request of his bro, Abraham.

Sale at auction at hse of Mrs Hepburn, at the Wash Bridge; all her hsehld furn. -N L Queen, auct.

For sale or rent-hse nr the Navy Yd gate, on M St; lately occupied by Simon Green. -A Cheshire, at the Wash Bridge.

Notice: my wife, Eliz Davis Thompson, hath without provocation, turned me out of my own hse & other injuries to me did, too delicate to mention. I am determined not to pay any of her debts. -Andrew Thompson

For sale-rl est of Jos Wheat, dec'd: wharf on Eastern Banch, dwlg hse & lot. -Geo Collard, trustee; Forrest & Bell, aucts.

SAT JAN 4, 1812
Meeting held at Beckes's Inn, Vincennes, Dec 7, 1811. Col Luke Decker was appt'd chrmn & Maj Benj Parke, clk.

Hse of Reps: Petition of the widow of Genr'l Alexander Fowler, who came to this country in 1763, srvd in French War, he rec'd from Va warrants for 10,000 acs of land, never derived any advantage from them; relief is prayed.

Midshipmen at the Navy Yd are to wear crape in respect & sorrow, for Lt J Gibbon of the U S Navy, who perished in the fire in Richmond, Va, Dec 26

Mrs Finagan can accomodate boarders in her hse nr Capitol Hill.

Election for Gtwn Potomac Bridge Co, will be held at Simmes's Tavern in Gtwn. -Leonard Mackall, Treas.

Eloped from Newport, Chas Co, Md, John Thomas, mulatto slave; sometimes cld John Redman or Redmond. He went off with Betsey Harley or Harlow, a free mulatto woman & has left a lawful wife & 4 young chldrn. -Henry Pile, *St Thos' Manor* nr Port Tobacco, Chas Co, Md.

Wm A G Dade, esq, of Dumfries, is a candidate to rep the Senatorial Dist of Fairfax & Pr Wm, in the next Genr'l Assembly of Va.

Cash sale-sq 729; brick hse & lease of the lot for 10 yrs from last Apr; prop of P C F Boyert & Robt Long, under a distress for ground rent due Trescy Coyle, admx of Thos Coyle, dec'd, to satisfy writs against said Boyert. -David Bates, cnstble.

TUE JAN 7, 1812
Abraham S Venable, Pres of the Bank of Va, is gone; he left no wife or chldrn; he was lost in the theatre fire in Richmond City, Va, Dec 26. Other notes on victims: Mrs Botts was lost but her sr-in-law, Mrs Page was saved; Mrs Harvie has lost her dght, Juliana, her son, E J Harvie & her grdght, Mary Whitlock; Nancy Green, d/o the mgr, Mr Green, was lost; Mrs Robt Greenhow was lost; Mrs Patterson & Mr Wm Brown were overwhelmed by the crowd & perished; Mr John G Jackson was saved as well as Mr M W Hancock; Mr & Mrs Headlych & their son were saved; Mr Robt Greenhow was saved with his son; Mr Stetson jumped out a window & was saved; Mr & Mrs Gordon, who had 3 chldrn with them-were all saved. Mr Mathew Clay, esq, wrote a ltr requesting if the person of his dght cld be preserved until his arrival-he wished her to be interred in the family vault with her mthr & sister, the latter died May 3d last, age 21-5-11, the present Miss Clay was 16 yrs & 14 days of age.

Ofcrs of the Navy & Marine Corps are to wear crape as tribute of respect to Cmdor Nicholson, late Sr ofcr of U S Navy. -Paul Hamilton, Navy Dpt, Jan 6.

Mrd: on Jan 2, Mr John Barry, of Balt City, to Mrs Sarah Jackson, of PG Co, Md, by Rev Mr Breckenridge.

Died: Cmdor Sam'l Nicholson, sr, ofcr in U S N, aet 69 yrs, at Charleston, Mass on Sunday week.

Hse of Reps: 1-Pet of Stephen Burrowes, sldr in Rev, praying for compensation. 2-Pet of Ninian Pinkney, Capt in 1st Regt of infty, praying to be released from certain claims.

Runaway negroes, committed to Wash Co, D C, jail: John Wallis, age ab't 25 yrs, says he belongs to Joshua Smith at Ridgeley's Mill nr Balt, Md; also Harry, ab't 19 yrs of age, says he belongs to Rich'd Dement of Chas Co, Md. -C Tippett, kpr of jail for W Boyd, mrsh'l.

The funeral procession in Richmond for the theatre fire disaster victims began at Mr Edw Trent's on Main St where the remains of Mrs Patterson lay; at the cross st leading to the bank they were joined by the corpse of Juliana Harvie, who expired at her bro-in-laws, the cashier of the bank. The following are to be added to those who died: Miss Elvira Coutts, Mrs Picket, not wife of Mr G P; Miss Littlepage, Jean Baptiste Rezin, Thos Lecroix, Robt Ferrill, a mulatto boy. Expired since: Mrs John Boshard, Edw Jas Harvie, esq, from injuries rec'd in his efforts to save his unfortunate sister from the flames.

Died: lately, at Chalons, Fr M La Rochefocault Liancourt, intendant Genr'l of the schl of arts & manufactures.

I forewarn all persons from taking my assignment on any notes given by me to Stephen West, of PG Co, Md. I consider them nrly pd. Ambro E Updegraff.

Orphans Crt of Wash Co, D C. Will & prsn'l est of Edw Eno, late of said co, dec'd. -Thos C Wright & Sam'l Rogers, excs.

Ranaway, John Tanner, ab't 19 yrs of age, appr boy, by trade a blacksmith; supposed he has gone to New Crt Hse, Berkeley Co, Va, to an uncle by name of Jas Walker. -Thos Williams, blacksmith, nr the bank, F St, Wash City.

THU JAN 9, 1812
Public sale-Orphans Crt of PG Co, Md. Part of prsn'l est of Thos Magruder, dec'd: negroes, stock & furn. Upper Marlborough on the rd to the Poor Hse. -John Read Magruder, Polly B Magruder, adms.

Stolen-bear skin great coat, out of the entry of Aquila D Hyatt, oppo Mr Davis' Hotel.

Rich'd Rush, esq, Compt of the Treas of the U S, has reached Wash City.

Thos Corcoran, esq, was elected Mayor of Gtwn on Jan 6, for one yr.

Died: Mr Edw Eno, ntv of Eng, on Dec 27, 1811; many yrs an inhabitant of Wash; leaving a widow & 4 chldrn.

Died: Mr Jas McCormick sr, on Jan 4th in Wash City; ntv of Ire; age 45 yrs.

Jas Barbour, esq, of Orange [spkr of the Hse of Delegates] is elected Govn'r of Va for 1 yr, in place of the lamented Geo W Smith, esq.

Just published-*History of Maryland* by John Leeds Bolman. Price $2.50 bound.

School mstr wanted-apply at Pierce's Mill, Rock Crk, nr Gtwn. -Isaac Pierce.

SAT JAN 11, 1812
Col Boyd. Correction of a writer in the Va Argus. Col Boyd, of the 4th Regt U S infty, is ab't 42 yrs of age & was born in the neighborhood of Boston; rec'd his commission at ab't age 18 yrs; he rsgn'd & fixed his intentions upon the theatre of Asia; his namesake was Hugh Boyd; found svc among the Mahrattah. In India rank is designated by the # of men; Col Boyd had a Munsub of 10,000 cavalry; his Lt was Wm Tone, bro of the late Theo Wolfe Tone; he returned to his ntv country ab't 12 yrs ago; he mv'd thru this city with his regt.

Mrd: John *Durke, esq, of Balt, to Miss Mary W P Wheaton, of Wash, on Jan 4, by Rev Mr Breckenridge. [*Cld be Burke-type blurred]

Died: recently, His Highness Prince Geo of Brunswick, nphw of the King of England, in England.

Thos Eno is to collect moneys due to the est of Edw Eno, dec'd. Jan 3, 1812. -Thos G Wright, Sam'l Rogers. Witness to Sam Rogers-Jno Hewett.

Public sale-Orphans Crt of Wash Co, D C. Sale at the store of John McConnell & Co on Pa av; cloths, shoes & shoemkr tools; part of the prsnl prop of Francis Clark, dec'd. -N L Queen, auct.

Trespassing, a red cow & black bull calf. -J Knapp, Wash

Sale of negroes postponed. Professed negro buyers will not be allowed to become purchasers of the slaves. -Janet Thompson, admx of Jas Thompson, dec'd, nr Leonard town, St Mary's Co, Md.

TUE JAN 14, 1812
Virginia, to wit: Dan'l Adlington, Capt of the Schn'r, *Wm Henry*, belonging to Wm O'Neal of Wash, laden with goods from Phil to Alexandria; due to gale winds, lost the main boom on Dec 21; schn'r was cast on the bar of Smith Island Beach; the Capt & one of his men, Isaac Marrow, hath solemnly protested as above. Dec 27, 1811, John Gaffigon, Justice of the Peace for Northampton Co

Richmond, Jan 10-elected to fill the vacancies in the Privy Cncl: Genr'l Jas Wood; N H Claiborne; Robt Quarles; Peter V Daniel; John Campbell.

Auction: hse & lot in F St, formerly occupied by the Sec of State & now by Oliver Pollock, esq. -Forrest & Beale, aucts.

Runaway-Rich'd, negro man; formerly owned by Mr Templeman of Gtwn & lately by Mr Barlow. -Jos Wheaton.

Paul C Boyert, insolvent debtor, confined in Wash Co, D C, prison-for debt; trustee may be appt'd. -Wm Brent, clk.

Notice-Wm Grayson, of Gtwn, wants it known he has no interest or concern in establishing a gunpowder manufactury as previously advertised.

New York, Jan 11. In Col Constant's Regt, the 6th in the standing army, the following have rec'd their commissions: Jas Bailey-Lt, Jared D Smith-Lt, Benj Brower-Lt; Nath'l Sherman-Ensign; Henery Cook-Ensign, all of this city. -Geo Hodgson, Major.

THU JAN 16, 1812
Reward-$25 for Isaac Parker, ab't 25 yrs of age, black man; believed to be in or ab't Wm Carroll's, Montg Co, Md: or on his way to Cumberland to his fr. -Greenbury Barnes, Bladensburg.

C T Chapman offers $5 reward for return of his Italian grey-hound, which was enticed away from Alexandria by a man of color.

Orphans Crt of Wash Co, D C. Jan 16, 1812. Prsn'l est of John Hebron, late of said city, dec'd. -Abigail Hebron, admx.

Reward-$100 for 3 slaves: Jack, his wife, Betty, & their dght, Fanny; Betty has a mthr & bro living in Richmond; her bro calls himself John Hambleton. Jack formerly belonged to J Byad, Betty was purch'd of John Corbin. -John Wilson, committee of Jas A Glenn.

Phil Patent Floor Cloth Manufactory, Centre sq; Isaac Macauley, successor to Mr John Dorsey. Mr Macauley is in town for a few days.

SAT JAN 18, 1812
Orphans Crt of PG Co, Md. Prsn'l est of Isaac Barrett, of said co, dec'd. -Rich'd Barrett, adm.

Chas Co, Md, Crt, Aug Term, 1811. Petition of Martha Crismond, John *Amzeen & Hennry his wife, Leonard Martin & Ann his wife, Cath Dixon & Priscilla Dixon for a commission of partition under an act to direct descents, that John Ormes & Mary his wife, Sam'l Bacon & Sarah his wife, Jacob Dixon, Thos S Johnson & Teresa his wife, do not reside within the state of Md. -John Barnes, clk. [*The paper shows a space or ltr missing, _amzeen.]

Stray cows came to my farm-midway bet Wash & Bladensburg. -Thos Fenwick.

TUE JAN 21, 1812
Post ofc changes in Dec 1811:
King & Queen C H, Va-Thacker Muier, vice A P Muse, rsgn'd;
Kingston, Ten-John McEwen, vice Wm D Neilson, rsgn'd;
North East, Md-John Maffet, vice B Williams, dec'd;
Dix Hills, N Y-Lewis Wicks, vice Moses Blackley, rsgn'd;
Annville, Pa-Dan'l Henning, vice Henry Bowman, rsgn'd;
Petersburg, Va-Thos Shore, vice Jos Jones, rsgn'd;
Wysox, Pa-J W Piolett, vice D Ridgway, rsgn'd;
Mill Hall, Pa-Nathan Harvey, vice Benj Harvey, dec'd;
May's Landing, N J-Martin Synnott, vice Andrew Smiley, dec'd;
Keeler's Ferry, Pa-Asa Keeler, vice Wm Keyler, rsgn'd;
Greenville, Miss Ter-John H Carr, vice John G T Prince, rsgn'd;
Winchester, Ten-Thos D Wiggins, vice John Davidson, rsgn'd;
Corydon, Ind Terr-Wm Branham, vice Spier Spencer, dec'd;
Carnesville, Ga-John R Brown, vice M H Payne, rsgn'd;
Aquasco, Md-Thos R Johnson, vice Rhinaldo Johnson, dec'd;
Nottingham, Md-Robt Young jr, vice Robt Young, dec'd;
Salisbury, Mass-Seth Clark, vice Elijah Wadleigh, dec'd;
Lewisburg, Pa-Wm Hayes, vice C Baldy, rsgn'd;

Cabin Point, Va-Walter Spratley, vice Thos Peter, dec'd;
Wood C H, Va-Thos Neale, vice John Stephens, dec'd;
Lenox or Sullivan, N Y-Jos Bruce, vice E Caulking, rsgn'd;
Lovington, Va-Solomon Matthews, vice Chas Perrow, rsgn'd;
Chas City C H, Va-Wm Singleton, vice John Gregory, dec'd;
Annsville, Va-Wm B Pryor, vice John Atkinson, rsgn'd;
Dryden, N Y-Parley Whitmore, vice J Stout, situation inconvenient;
Goshen, Va-Rector Lowe, vice Wm Cook, mv'd away.
New ofcs established in Dec 1811 & Postmasters:
Boone's Sta, Fayette Co, K-Henry Moore;
Tompkins, Dela Co, N Y-John Ellsworth;
Colerain, Franklin Co, Mas-Isaac B Barber;
Charleston, Wash Co, R I-Jos Staunton jr;
Cross Rds, Colleton Dist, S C-N Nathans;
Lanierville, Brunswick Co, Va-Wm Gholson;
Sandy Fork, Mecklenburg Co, Va-Jos F Speed;
St Francisville, Mis Ter-Amos Webb;
Yellow Springs Tavern, Huntington Co-[no state]-David Moore;
Schooly Mount, Morris Co, N J-Wm Dillicker;
Reading, Middlesex Co, Mass-Nathan Parker;
Exeter, Otsego Co, N Y-Jared Munson;
Golden Grove, Greenville Co, S C-Chas Garrison;
Wilderness, Orange Co, Va-Armistead Gordon

Ofcs discnt'd in Dec 1811:
St John's Plains, O T; Merrick & Milton, N Y; Elam, S C; Cabot, Vt; Wmsburg, Pa; Mouth of Snickshinny Creek, Pa; Germainia, Va.

Leg of Delegates-re-elected: Jas Sykes, esq, spkr of the Senate & Cornelius P Comegy's, spkr of the Hse of Reps.

Dragoon orders-the Columbian Light Dragoons are to meet at Cooledge's Htl on Wed by order. -Geo W Lindsay, 1st Sgt.

Sale at auction-frame dwlg hse on lot 12 sq 1001 in Wash City; prop of John Bidt, dec'd. -Nichl Queen, adm.

THU JAN 23, 1812
Thos Ewell will have in operation in a few days, a salt petre refinery.

Meeting of Democratic Rpblcns was held of the 4th election dist of Cecil Co, Jan 7th; David Patten was chosen chrmn & W C Miller, sec.

Senate-1-Petition of Moses Austin & John R Jones, props of a lead mine in La; to incorporate Moses Austin & others; read & passed to 2d reading. 2-The case of the ship *Eliza Ann*, belonging to Esekiel Hubbel was passed to a 3d reading.

Runaway-Betty, negro woman; says she lately lived with Mr John Lefferson, of Jefferson Co, Va. -Matthias Shaffner, shrf of Wash Co, Md.

Died: on Jan 4, Mary Pinckney, w/o Maj Genr'l Chas Cotesworth Pinckney, age 60 yrs.

Hse of Reps: 1-Petition of Jonathan Earl & others of Mass, praying to import goods from England. 2-Mr Wm Edgar & Alex'r McComb pray relief for $29,600 pd in part payment for land in Western Terr of U S, unable to make payments, ask the amount pd be forfeited.

SAT JAN 25, 1812
Hse of Reps: 1-Petition of Peter Lacour & Co of N J, manufacturers of sand crucibles, praying for additional duty on imported articles of this kind. 2-Pet of John Hagerty & others of Balt, praying for remuneration in the case of a vessel improperly seized by the Coll of St Domingo.

Mrd: Mr John Erskine, printer, to Miss Caroline Belt, both of Wash, on Jan 23.

Mrd: Mr Thos Lewis to Miss Cath Jones, both of Wash, on Jan 23.

Runaway, Sam'l Davis, negro man ab't 27 yrs of age; says he srv'd time with Mr Wm Tremble of Balt City. -John Darnell, shrf of PG Co, Md.

Runaways-committed to Wash Co, D C, jail; Fortune & Sam, negroes; say they belong to Park & Chas Goodal, of Hanover Co, Va. -C Tippett, kpr of the jail.

TUE JAN 28, 1812
Gen Henry Dearborn, late Sec of War, now Coll of Port of Boston, has been appt'd a Maj-Genr'l in the U S Army, by the Pres of U S.

Verdict of jury in Dist Crt of Phil, in suit of Geo Fitler, vs Henry Probasco, for false imprisonment. Probasco committed Fitler to prison, refusing to take bail for 12 hrs for contempt of ofc, releasing him after 4 hrs; Judge stated that the power of a Justice of Peace to commit for contempts was not given by law.

Land for sale-where I now reside; ab't 1000 acs, 2 miles n w of Upr Marlborough, with commodious dwlg hse; will exchange for land in Ky; apply to my agent, Israel T Canby, nr Up Marl. -Ann Sprigg.

So Caroline commencement-Jan 2: Dr Maxey, Pres; Hon Sam'l Warren led the procession; spkr of the Hse of Reps, John S Richardson followed; John Drayton, Govn'r & Cmder in Chief, followed.

Land for sale-tract on which I now live; ab't 800 acs with dwlg hse; lying in Hampshire Co, Va; also a tract in Green Spring Valley nr the former, 250 acs; also a tract below Old Town, 250 acs; tract of 204 acs in Va; 5000 acs in parts of Ky. -Osborn Sprigg

Mrd: Mr John H Abert to Miss Ellen M Stretch, d/o Jos Stretch, esq, all of Wash, on Jan 25, by Rev Steven B Balch.

Public sale-Decree of Chancellor of Md-at Montg Crt Hse: *Magruder's farm* nr said Crt Hse. Mr Levin Beall will show same. -Henry Williamson, trust-Annapolis.

Fire Engines. I have been bred in Europe in the mkg of fire engines & carry my profession to Gtwn, D C. I constructed one for the fire Co in Fredericktown, Md. Apply to Mr Roch, coppersmith in Richmond, Va, who witnessed its construction. -John Achman, High St, Gtwn.

THU JAN 30, 1812
Mr Dan'l French has discovered a mode of mkg bricks out of the earth; a model may be seen at Mrs Wilson's, on Capitol Hill, Wash City.

Miss Quantril will open a Fancy Goods & Millinery Store at Mrs Vanzandt's, nrly oppo the Indian Queen Tavern.

PG Co, Md-I certify that Sam'l Magruder, of PG Co, brought before me a bay mare. -Geo Page, a Justice of the Peace.

SAT FEB 1, 1812
Mrd: on Jan 30th, Dan'l Sheffey, esq, Rep in Cong from Va, to Miss Maria Hanson, d/o Sam'l Hanson of Sam'l, esq, of Wash.

Senate-memorial of Thos Corcoran & others, in Gtwn, asking relief of Congress from legal injunction placed on improvements commenced in the channel of the Potomac Rvr, suggesting they might do injury to the bridge over said rvr.

Lands, mill & slaves for sale-will of Ralph Wormley, esq, of *Rosegill*, & decree in Chancery: 2 farms on Pomunkey Rvr, King Wm Co, cld *Queenfield*-400 acs & *Woody's*-409 acs; both part of Manskin Lodge est; Mr Jas Fox, Manskin Lodge, will show the prop. -Eleanor Wormeley, Carter Beverley, John Chew, adms. -King Wm.

Genuine family medicines, prepared by the sole proprietor, T W Dyott, M D, grson of the late celebrated Dr Robertson of Edinburg; sold in Phil at his family medicine warehse, 137 North E St, crnr of Race & North 2d Sts.

To rent-hse 5 of the Seven bldgs & small tenement on F St, nr the Lower Bridge over Rock Crk, Gtwn. -Leonard Harbaugh jr, nr the last mentioned premises.

Reward-$10 for sorrel horse that strayed from my stable. -John McGowan.

TUE FEB 4, 1812
To let-hse nr the Centre-Mkt, at present occupied by Jos Scholfield. [Followed in same advertisement of Thos Levering & Co-grocer]

Hse of Reps-Petition of Wm Ladd & John G Ladd, of Alexandria, praying to be released from a forfeiture incurred as securities in a certain case.

For sale-hses & lots, 1, 2, 3 & 4, the prop of the Wash Bldg Co. -Apply to Walter Clark or John A Wilson.

Orphans Crt of Wash Co, D C. Prsn'l est of Joshua Beall, late of said co, dec'd. -Archibald Van Horn, adm of Joshua Beall.

THU FEB 6, 1812

Stray horse came to the farm of Zachariah Berry; Jacob Gilman brought the horse before me. -Sam'l H Smith -Wm Brent, clk.

Congress in Senate: 1-Unfavorable report on the petition of Jacob Greer, bro & security of Jos Greer, a collector of the direct tax in N C, who prayed to be relieved from his securityship. 2-Pet of Arthur St Clair, praying for payment of a balance due him.

Charlotte Hall School. Rev Mr Wm Duke-appt'd Princ; Alex'r Keech & Neale H Shaw continue in their depts; Jas Keech is the Steward. -Neal H Shaw, Reg.

Mr Joel Barlow, America Minister at Paris, had his first audience of Bonaparte on Nov 17, when he presented his credentials.

Coshockton, Ohio, Jan 23, 1812. Earthquake was felt in this place for nrly a minute; Col Williams' chimney was cracked. -A Johnston.

Mantua mkg, millinery & plain sewing. Mary Davis, Capitol Hill, nr Mr Carroll's Row east of the Capitol.

Orphans Crt of PG Co, Md: sale of land or wood of which Wm Warman Berry died possessed; on Lower Bridge over the Eastern Branch to Upper Marlborough, 3 miles from Wash City. -Archibald Van Horn, PG Co, Md.

Orphans Crt of PG Co, Md. Public sale at the late dwlg of Elisha Fields, of PG Co, dec'd. -Mgt Fields, admx.

Reward-$40 for runaway, Isaac Lowe, negro man ab't 25 yrs of age. -Zachariah McCleney, living nr Mt Pleasant Ferry, A A Co, Md.

SAT FEB 8, 1812

Hse of Reps: Bill for relief of Selah Benton. Capt Benton srv'd the U S thru a great part of the Rev War; rec'd no wound in svc; contracted a disease in svc which had disabled him ever since; he is now 72 yrs old & very poor; to be allowed a pension of $20 a month.

Memory of a hero. Elegy on the death of Col of Cavalry, Jos Hamilton Daviess who died Nov 7, 1811 at Battle of Tippecanoe, fought nr the Wabash Rvr. Dedicated to Hon John Rowan, by Stephen Theodore Badin, Catholic Missionary, a friend to Mr Rowan & of the dec'd.

Gov Harrison, having relinquished the command of the army lately, & probably as an ofcr, left us forever. Affidavits-Signed:

Joel Cook-Capt 4th inft
R Burchstead-Ensign
Josiah Snelling-Capt 4th U S Regt infty
R C Barton-Capt 4th infty
O G Burton-Lt 4th infty
N F Adams-Lt 4th Rgt infty
Cha Fuller-Lt 4th Rgt infty
A Hawkins-Lt 4th infty
Geo Gooding-2d Lt 4th infty
Josiah D Foster-Surg 4th Rgt infty
Hosea Blood-actg ast Surg 4th Rgt infty
-Nat F Adams, adj of the army under command of Gov Harrison.

Jesse Kersey, a mnstr of the Soc of Friends, expects to attend the meeting at their meeting hse in Wash, Feb 9.

Benevolent Soc of Wash City elected ofcrs: Hon Wm Cranch-Pres; Jos Gales jr-V P; Geo Sweeny-Steward; Geo A Carroll, Alex McWilliams, Thos Patterson & Leonard Osborne-all physicians.

Mrd: Chas Carroll, esq, of Wash City, to Miss Mary Ann Carroll, d/o Henry H Carroll, esq, late of Balt Co, at *Sweet Air*, on Feb 4, by Rev Mr Edene.

Died: Mrs Eleanor Peter, relict of Mr John Peter, dec'd, at Gtwn, Feb 7th.

Whereas John Roads deserted my mail on Feb 1; if apprehended & brought to me a handsome reward will be given. -Sam'l Speake.

For Freight or Charter. New schn'r, *Mary*, Capt John Mathews-Mstr. Apply to Geo Beale, living on N J av nr Barry's wharf.

Jos Middleton, insolvent debtor, confined to Wash Co, D C prison for debt. -Wm Brent, clk.

TUE FEB 11, 1812

Died: on Feb 8, Mr Henry Childs, merchant, of Gtwn, after a short & severe illness. He had not reached his 25th yr & leaves a wife & one small child.

Died: on Feb 6, Mrs Mary Sprigg, w/o Benj Sprigg, of Wash City; age 25 yrs; her illness was long & painful. She was a fond dght, sister, wife, mthr & friend.

Hse of Reps: 1-Petition of Nath'l Coleman, ctzn of N J, who had been impressed on the English ship of War, *Mars*, praying for relief. 2-Petition of Caleb Hiorns of Boston, praying for permission to import certain goods purch'd in G Britain prior to Nov 7th.

Ltrs have reached Wash City announcing that Peter Sailly, esq, coll of the Dist of Champlain, N Y, has been killed by smugglers; the report current at Albany. We trust is not true; but if it be, punishment will be the reward of the offenders. [Feb 18th paper-his hse was broken into & Sailly is not dead]

Wash Co, D C-in Chancery. Thos Lawrason, vs Jas Patton & others. Ratify sale by Chas Glover, trustee; 2 hses on lot 18 sq 168 in Wash City; sold at public auction to Silas Butler for $600. -Wm Brent, clk.

Died: on Nov 7: Maj-Genr'l Thos Blount, Rep in Congress from N C, age 53 yrs, in Wash; vol in Rev army at age 16; leaves a widow & had no other family.

Farms for sale: the Va *Mingo Bottom farm* 1/2 mile below Stebenville, 650 acs, with dwlg hse, on the Ohio Rvr; the *Round Bottom Farm*, 710 acs, 8 miles from the Ohio Rvr. Apply to Zachs Biggs, living on the *Mingo Bottom Farm*, Brooke Co, Va.

For sale: slaves belonging to the est of the late Col John H Beanes; at *Hard Bargain,* late resid of the dec'd, 5 miles below Piscataway. -John Read Magruder, Polly B Magruder, admx. D B N of John H Beans.

Lands for sale-two deeds of trust from Henry Rose, dec'd; at Fairfax Crt Hse, 290 acs & 530 acs; lands adj Those of Wm Moss. -Rich'd M Scott, Wm Moss.

THU FEB 13, 1812
An Act passed to empower the Sec of the Treas to decide on the case of the ship *Eliza Ann*, belonging to Ezekiel Hubbel, & in the case of the ship *Mary & Frances* of Boston, belonging to Nath'l Goddard. E Hubbel purch'd the ship from Wm Lyman, acting agent of Joshua Jones & Edw R Jones of N Y, under firm of Joshua Jones & son.

Vacine institute lottery-State of Md. Mgrs:

Wm Wilson	Robt Steuart	Luke Tiernan
Henry Shroeder	Aaron Levering	Sam'l Harden
Dr John Cromwel	Dr W H Clendinen	Jas W Collins
John W Clan	Andrew Agnew	Alex McDonald
Ed G Woodyear	Ed J Coale	Peter Hoffman jr
Dr Jas Smith		

Hse of Reps: 1-Petition of Jos P Minnick & Thos Shipley, assigners of Wm & A M Buckley of Phil, praying to be exonerated from bal due U S for duties. 2-Petition of Augustus Watson, employed as a waggoner in the expedition against the insurgents in Pa, to be compensated for the loss of a horse.

Norfolk, Feb 3. Sat last the British ship, *Adventure*, under Capt Thos Lefavour, arrv'd from Liverpool bound for St Christophers.

Absconded from the hse of Mr Ball, 10 miles from Wash City on the Annapolis Rd-2 negro boys, Pertus & Perry. -Sam'l S Starns

Runaway negroes; committed to the goal of Dorchester Co, Md: Joshua, ab't 50 yrs of age; says he belongs to a widow Dent, of St Mary's Co, Md. Chas, age ab't 25 yrs; says he belongs to Jos Cullison of the same co. Uriah, ab't 37 yrs of age; says he belongs to Job Smith of same co. -John Newton, shrf of Dorch Co

Orphans Crt of Wash Co, D C. Feb 13, 1812. Prsn'l est & will of Eleanor Speake, late of said co, dec'd. -Mary Brooke, excx.

PG Co, Md, Sep 1811. Com'rs appt'd on the petition of Mary Ridgway, Francis Walker & Rachel his wife, & Sarah Hardy, if rl est of Ignatius Hardy wld admit of division; est cld not be divided; some of the said reps reside out of Md. -John R Magruder, clk, PG Co Crt.

Attention-commissioned ofcrs of the First Legion of Militia of the Dist of Col are to assemble at Rhodes's Tavern in Wash on Feb 15. -W Smith, Lt Col Com 1st B M D C.

SAT FEB 15, 1812
Hse of Reps: 1-Petitions & claims of Peter Endais; 2-Thos Wilson; 3-another for Simeon Knight; read & committed. 4-Petition of Thos Orr, assignee of Martin Andrews, read & committed

John Langdon has declined a re-election to Govn'r of N H; Wm Plumer, esq, is nominated by Rpblcns as a candidate to succeed him. [Erratum, Feb 22 paper: Wm King correct-not Wm Plumer]

Mrd: Mr F C De Krafft, of Wash, to Miss Harriot Scott, of Alexandria, on Feb 13, in Alexandria, by Rev Dr Muir.

Newburyport Herald-Mrs Chilley, of Seabrook, the past wk, safely delivered of four chldrn at one accouchement; weighing 22 lbs; 2 are living.

Public sale-all right, title, claim & int of P C F Boyert & Robt Long in small brick hse on Capitol Hill, sq 729; to satisfy ground rent due Teresey Coyle, admx of Thos Coyle, dec'd. -David Bates, cnstble.

Public sale-order of Orphans Crt of PG Co, Md; residue of prnsl est of Dr John Stuart, late of PG Co, dec'd; svr'l negroes. -Benj Hodges of Thos, adm.

My wife, Mary Wheeler, hath eloped from my bed. I am determined to pay no debts of her contracting. -Leonard Truman Wheeler.

Ranaway-Geo Wheatly, ab't 36 yrs of age, dark mulatto man; I bght him of Francis Wheatly of Chas Co, Md. Reward-$10. -Thady Hogan, Wash City.

TUE FEB 18, 1812
Hse of Reps. 1-Bill to authorise John Rutherford, of N C, to bring certain slaves into the U S, read & committed. 2-Mr D R Williams has obtained a leave of absence after today for remainder of the session. 3-Pres of the U S approved the acquital of Brig Gen Jas Wilkinson of charges alleged against him, & caused his sword to be restored to him.

Ranaway-Chas Gray, mulatto man, ab't 25 yrs of age, in St Mary's Co, Md. -Jos Dickson, residing in Lovingston, Nelson Co, Va.

Orphans Crt of Wash Co, D C. Application of John Murdoch for ltrs of adm, cum testaments annexo, on prsn'l est of Wm M Duncanson, late of Wash City, dec'd. -John Hewitt, Reg.

THU FEB 20, 1812
Crct Crt for Dist of Ga held at Milledgeville Dec 14, 1810 before the Hon Wm Johnson. Two men-Fluker & Morgan, were indicted for the murder of Strickland. The prisoners were discharged because the offence was committed in that part of Ga, the Indian title to which remained unextinguished; there existed no legal provision for a white man who murders a white man within Indian Terr; the crt ordered the prisoner to be discharged.

Henry Serratt was drowned when he upset his canoe with a fit, to which he had been subject to, nr the Navy Yd, Wash, Feb 19. He was a workman at the Navy Yd & was out gunning in the canoe.

Mrd: Casper Willis Wever, esq, of Jefferson Co, Va, late of this city, to Miss J Cath Dunlop, eldest d/o Andrew Dunlop, esq, by Rev Mr Denny, at Chambersburg, Pa on Feb 13.

Those indebted to the est of the late Benj Botts, are to make payment immediately; present claims for payment. -John Minor, Philip Harrison, acting excs.

Mrd: on Feb 15, Mr Jas Kelly of Wilmington, Dela, to Miss Mgt Watson of this place, by Rev Mr McCormick

Mechanics' Bank of Alexandria; com'rs:
Wm Veitch	Jas C Deneale	Dan'l Mcleod
Jas McGuire	Adam Lynn	Mark Butts
Jos Dean	Jas Sanderson	John Young
Isaac Entwisle	Robt Young	Peter Saunders
John Gird	John Longden	

Wash Co, D C. In Chancery. John P Van Ness, adm of Wm & Chas Laight, vs John Blagge & heirs & reps of Geo Walker. Ratify sales made by Chas Glover & Rich'd Forrest, the trustees. [no details] -Wm Brent, clk.

Mrd: on Feb 10, Dr Geo Boarman of this city to Miss L Dyer of PG Co, Md, by Rev Mr Young.

Died: Lt Lee Massey of the U S N, at Norfolk on Feb 7. He drowned when taking a false step on the bridge he was crossing.

Died: Gen Mich'l Bright, age 51 yrs, on Feb 9 at Phil; soldier of the Rev & for some time the past inspec of flour for the Port of Phil.

Died: Hon Wm Balfour, age 53, in Frederickton, New Brunswick, Maj-Genr'l on the Staff of the army in British America & lately Pres of Council & Commander in Chief of the Province of N Brunswick. -Montreal Gaz.

Committed to Wayne Co jail-David Butler, negro, ab't 35 yrs of age; says he was born in PG Co, Md & set free in Montg Co by Sam'l Owens; run off from Balt to New Orleans & sold to Wm Deuse living above Baton Rouge. -Wm Patton, shrf Wayne Cy.

Reward-$5.00 for lost or stolen silver watch case, mkr's name, Wm Chancellor, London #7315. -Thos Talbert, Navy Yd.

The subscribers propose to pblsh for their benefit & their sister Stanard, *Fifty Agricultural Essays.* -John M Carter, Jas B Carter, Gtwn. Price $1.50.

Ranaway-John, negro man, from Benedict Boarman in Chas Co, Md, nr Bryan Town, on Aug 1, 1811. -John Francis Gardner

Plattsburg, N Y, Jan 31. On Jan 29th, the dwlg hse of Peter Sailly, esq, collector of this place, was broken open by villains; Mr S shot & wounded Mr Jos Colberth, one of the intruders; the wound may be mortal.

Birth-Night Ball will be celebrated at Union Tavern, Gtwn, Feb 21. Mgrs: John Mason; John Cox; Wash Bowie; Geo Peter; Wm Whann; Geo C Washington; N W Worthington; R F Howe; J S Williams; John Lee; Rich'd Johns; John Marbury.

Proclamation by Robt Bowie, Gov of Md: $200 reward for the murderer of Vincent Le hermite, [barber] late of Balt City, Md.

SAT FEB 22, 1812
Post ofc changes in Jan 1812.
Buckstown, Me-Caleb B Hall, vice John Benson, rsgn'd;
Northampton C H, N C-Dempsey Taylor, vice Wm Brewer, mv'd away;
Bath, N H-Ira Goodall, vice Ebenezer Carleton, rsgn'd;
Plainfield, Vt-Amherst Simons, vice Silas Williams, rsgn'd;
Shoreham, Vt-Barzillai Carey, vice Reuben Baldwin, dec'd;
Denmark, N Y-Chas Squire, vice Willis Secomb, mv'd away;
Franconia, N H-Moses Atwood, vice John Punchard, rsgn'd;
Canaan, N H-Simeon Arvin, vice Esekiel Wells;

Charlotte Hall, Md-Jas Gardiner, vice Dennis Donlevy, rsgn'd;
West Chester, Pa-Jos Pearce, vice J B Remington, rsgn'd;
Greensburg, Pa-Mattison Hart, vice Geo Murray, rsgn'd;
Montague's, Va-Sam'l Foster, vice W Montague, mv'd away;
Maysville, K-John Roe, vice Moses Dalton, rsgn'd;
Pulaski, Ten-David Martin, vice Gabriel Bumpass, situation inconv;
Lee C H, Va-Isaac Dickenson, vice Allen Martin, rsgn'd;
Waterbury, Vt-Dan'l Lathrop, vice Calvin Deming;
Jaffrey, N H-Abel Parker, vice Sam'l Dakin, rsgn'd;
Rockingham, Vt-Horace Baxter, vice Jas Felt;
Greenwich, Ms-Jabez Colburn, vice Jos White, rsgn'd;
Burkesville, K-Jas Emerson, vice Chas Brooks, rsgn'd;
Port Wm, K-John B Bernard, vice Henry Winslow, rsgn'd;
Hackensack, N J-Abraham Westerfield, vice Jotham Baldwin, rsgn'd;
Richmond C H, N C-Archibald A McNeil, vice John W Cole, rsgn'd;
Rochester, N H-Wm Barker, vice Jos Clarke;
Vergennes, Vt-Jos Tomlinson, vice A Tomlinson, rsgn'd;
Cyprus Bridge, N C-Wm Hays, vice Oliver Prince, rsgn'd;
Averasborough, N C-Robt Droughon, vice Gerard Banks, dec'd;
Black Lick, Pa-John Lintner, vice Conrad Lintner, dec'd;
China Grove, S C-Jos S Edwards, vice Matthew Allen, rsgn;
Louisburg, N C-Rich'd Fox, vice Joel King, rsgn'd;
Nassau, N Y-John Griswold, vice Jos Benedict, mv'd away;
Sharon, N Y-Zachariah Keys, vice Zenas Pynnco, situation inconv;
Somers, N Y-Hackaliah Bailey, vice Milton Cushing, dec'd;
Centre Harbor, N H-Jonathan S Moulton, vice B Moulton.
Wilmington, N C-John Lord, vice John Bradley, dec'd;
Falmouth, Va-Edw Seddon, vice Thos Seddon, rsgn'd;
Groton, Mass-Abraham Moore, vice W M Richardson, rsgn'd;
Hadley, Mass-Sylvester Goodman, vice H Wilcox, rsgn'd;
West Cambridge, Mass-Thos Russell, vice Wm S Brooke;
Winchester, Tenn-Jas S McWhorter, vice John Davidson, rsgn'd;
Franklin, Tenn-Chas McCallister, vice T Masterman, mv'd away;
Litchfield, Me-Newcomb W Stephens, vice Wm Cleves, rsgn'd;
Hungrytown, Va-Jos Smith, vice G Y Stokes, rsgn'd;
Herkimer, N Y-David Holt, vice Elihu Griswold, dec'd;
Portsmouth, N H-Jonathan Payson, vice Mark Symms;
Nanjemoy, Md-Massey Sims, vice Wm Jackson, dec'd.

New Post Ofcs est'd in Jan 1812 & postmstr:
Webbsville, Orleans Terr-Amos Webb;
Brainard's Bridge, Ranselaer Co, N Y-M Brainard;
Ashby, Middlesex Co, Mass-Alex'r T Willard;
Schooly Mount, Morris Co, N J-Wm Dillicker;
Wolcott, Ashtabula Co, O-Isaac H Phelps;
Butler's Plantation, Orleans Terr-Sam'l McCatchon;
Godberry's Tavern, Orleans Ter-Jas Godberry;
Pleasant Valley, Fairfax Co, Va-Elijah Hutchinson;

Mullen's Ford, Franklin Co, Ga-Robt Hacket;
Dickeysville, Pendleton Co, S C-John Dickey;
Rich'dson's, Brunswick Co, Va-Jordon Richardson;
Puntytown, Harrison Co, Va-Jedediah W Goff;
North Amenia, Dutchess Co, N Y-Alex'r Neely;
North East, Dutchess Co, N Y-Stephen Eno;
Cowanesky, Tioga Co, Pa-Ira Kilburn;
Dover, Cayhoga Co, O-Phili Taylor;
Doylesville, Orleans Terr-Joshua F Doyle;
Lebanon, Washington Co, Ga-Rich'd A Blount;
Rose Mills, Amherst Co, Va-Henry Rose;
Perry Hill, Mecklenburg Co, Va-Wm Brickett;
Oak Grove, Lunenburg Co, Va-Thos Orgain.
[Mancher's Lick, Tenn P O discont'd in Jan 1812.]

Mrd: Mr Jacob Morgan, merchant, to Miss Ann Thompson, d/o Jonah Thompson, esq, all of Alexandria, Feb 19, by Rev Mr Meade.

Promotions, etc in old army. Inspector's ofc, Wash, Feb 12, 1812. Peace establishment.
Rgt of artl: Fabins Whiting of Mass; Sam'l Spotts of Dela; Thos Parker of Pa & Levi Whiting of Mass-appt'd 2d Lts, Feb 10, 1812.
Additional Military force: 3d Rgt of infty: 2d Lt Jos M Wilcox promoted to 1st Lt-rank from Jan 3, 1812. Ensign Wm Christian to 2d Lt vice Jos M Wilcox promoted Jan 3, 1812.
4th Rgt of infty: Ensign Phineas Wheelock to 2d Lt-Jan 3, 1812. Ensign Winthrop D Ager to 2d Lt-Jan 3, 1812. Ensign Shubael Butterfield to 2d Lt-Jan 3, 1812.
5th Rgt of infty: Ensign John Gassaway to 2d Lt- Jan 3, 1812. Ensign Henry O Hill to 2d Lt-Jan 3, 1812. Ensign John W Smoot, to 2d Lt-Jan 3, 1812. Adam Hays of Pa appt'd Surg-Feb 10, 1812.
6th Rgt of infty: 2d Lt to 1st Lt from Jan 3, 1812: Augustus Conant, Londus L Buck, Alex'r R Thompson, Geo W Runk.
7th Rgt of infty: 1st Lt to Capt, Mar 1, 1811: Cary Nicholas & Wm McClelland. 2d Lt to 1st Lt, Mar 1, 1811: Sam'l Vail & Geo C Allen. 2d Lt to 1st Lt, Elijah Montgomery, vice Jennings, dec'd, Jun 24, 1811. 2d Lt to 1st Lt, Feb 10, 1812-David McClelland.
Appt'd 2d Lts-Feb 10, 1812: Thos H Richardson of Ohio; Jacob Miller of Ky; Mich'l McClelland of Ohio; Sam'l Kercheval, do; Robt Todd, R S of Ky; Isaac Bickley, do; Etheldred Taylor of Tenn; Wm Snodgross of Tenn, Henry Helm of Ky.
Appt'd Ensigns Feb 10, 1812: Wm Prosser of Ohio; Jas Forsyth of Ky; John Hays of Tenn; Robt Guinea of Ky; John Meek of Ohio; John N Carrick of Tenn; Conrad Wolf of Ky; Elisha T Hall of Miss Terr; Thos Blackstone of Tenn; John Weaver of Ky.
Adam G Goodlet of Ky, appt'd Surg, Feb 10, 1812,
Rgt of rifleman: John Armstrong of Tenn & Lewis G A Armistead of Va, appt'd 1st Lts, Feb 10, 1812. Note: 2d Lt Wm Gamble-6th Rgt, declines. Ensign Benj Field, 1st Rgt infty, discontinued from Jun 1, 1811.

Ensign Hezekiah Wadsworth, 4th Rgt infty, struck from the rolls. -__ay Nicholl, adj & inspector. Richmond, Feb 18.

Nomination of Electors for Pres & V P of U S: Andrew Stevenson, spkr of the Hse, chrmn; Thos Ritchie appt'd Sec. Recommended as Electors-Richmond, Virginia:
Dist 1-Jos Godwin of Nansemond;
Dist 2-Benj Harrison, PG, Mt Airy;
Dist 3-Edw Pegram, Dinwiddie;
Dist 4-Rich'd Field, Brunswick;
Dist 5-Thos Reid Sr, Charlotte;
Dist 6-Mathew Cheatham, Chesterfield;
Dist 7-Landon Cabell, Nelson;
Dist 8-Chas Yancey, Buckingham;
Dist 9-Geo Penn, Patrick;
Dist 10-Wm G Poindexter, Louisa;
Dist 11-Spencer Roane, Hanover;
Dist 12-Streshly Rennolds, Essex;
Dist 13-Robt Taylor, Orange;
Dist 14-Gustavus B Horner, Fauquier;
Dist 15-Robt Nelson, York;
Dist 16-Mann Page, Gloucester;
Dist 17-Walter Jones, Northumberland;
Dist 18-John T Brooke, Stafford;
Dist 19-Hugh Holmes, Frederick;
Dist 20-Dan'l Morgan, Jefferson;
Dist 21-Archibald Rutherford, Rockingham;
Dist 22-Archibald Stuart, Augusta;
Dist 23-Andrew Russell, Wash
Dist 24-Jas P Preston, Montg;
Dist 25-Wm McKinley, Ohio;
Appt'd Central Corresponding committee:
Wm Wirt   Peyton Randolph   Andrew Stevenson
Thos Ritchie Sam'l Pleasants   Wm Mumford
Wm Brokenbrough

Wm Gray has peremptorily declined a re-election to ofc of Lt Govn'r of Mass. Wm Plumer, esq, is nominated by the Rpblcns as a candidate to succeed him.

A full pardon is granted to all individuals of the army, who within 4 mos, surrender themselves to the Commanding Ofcr of any Military Post within the U S or Terrs; & to those Marines who surrender to the Commandant of the Corps or to any ofcr Commanding a detachment. Feb 7, 1812, Jas Madison, Pres.

Lost-Pktbk, in Wash City. Apply to Mr Adolphus Plate, in 12th St.

For sale-bolting cloths. -Isaac McPherson, Balt, Md.

Wash Co, D C. I certify that Ignatius Hall, for Geo Peter, brought before me a stray sorrel horse. -Rd S Briscoe, Justice of Peace.

Ohio lands for sale-apply to Wm Wells of Springfield; Wm Montgomery or Mr John Gardner nr Vanesville. Levi Whipple of Springfield has a map. -Robt Underwood.

TUE FEB 25, 1812
For sale-Fancy ornaments at Miss Sinnott's Acad in 14th nr F St.

Died: Genr'l Francis Nichols, sldr of the Rev; on Feb 14, at Pottstown, Pa; made a prisoner after the assault of Quebec.

Imposter-Carter G Bradley, giving himslf out as connected with respectable families in Va; has written ltrs from Port Tobacco to Va Del in Congress.

New Drug & Medicine store, Wedderburn & Thornton-oppo Libby & Carne's, Fairfax St, Alexandria.

Died: Mr John Mills, some days ago in the vicinity of St Francisville, M T; one of the earliest settlers of the country; sldr of '76 & mbr of the convention of Fla.

Jas Moore has withdrawn his injunction & claim against bks, notes etc, lately assigned to U S by Mr Jos Wheation-the bks will soon be in the hands of Francis S Key for Collection. -Sexton & Williamson, Pa av

Hse of Reps: Petition of Joel Burt, coll of Oswego Dist, regarding the embargo laws-referred.

Died: Col Jos Ward, aged 75, at Boston on Fri wk.

Orphans Crt of Wash Co, D C. Prsnl est of Philip Mara, late of said co, dec'd. -Cath Mara

Names found in the charges against brig-Genr'l Jas Wilkinson at Genr'l Crt Martial at Fredericktown, Md, Sep 2, 1811:
Jos Ballinger at New Orleans & Frankfort, Ky, Dec 1789;
Philip Nolan, N Orleans, Autumn 1789;
La Cassagne at N Orleans, 1793-94;
Henry Owens, N Orleans, 1794;
Jos Collins, N Orleans, 1795;
Thos Power from New Madrid to Louisville, 1796;
Dan'l Clark, Loftus' Hgts, Oct 1798;
Aaron Burr, 1805-6.

THU FEB 27, 1812
An Act: Selah Benton, Capt in Rev army, to be placed on the pension list at $20 per mo to begin Jul 1, 1811; apprv'd-Jas Madison, Feb 21, 1811.

Hse of Reps. Petition of Stephen Fellow, wounded sldr of Rev, praying for an increase of pension which is now $5 per mo.

Land for sale-plantation in Montg Co, Md on which Wm Marley lately resided, ab't 250 acs. Thos Gittings will show the land. -Otho B Beall.

Ranaway-Isaac Dorsey, negro fellow, ab't 33 to 40 yrs of age, from John Winemiller, Montg Co, Md.

Wash Co, D C. In Chancery. Alex'r Cochran & others against Rebecca McElwee & others. Ratify sales by John Ott, trustee: to Zachariah Walker, lots 6 thru 11 in sq 1020 for $249; to Chas Glover, lots 2 & 3 in sq 1045 for $86; to Wm P Gardiner, lot 3 in sq 118 with improvements for $700; to Thos C Wright, lot 4 in sq 119 for $329.28. -Wm Brent, clk.

Land for sale: now in possession of Dr John Wootten, nr Rockville, Montg Co, Md; 203 acs. -Benj Berry.

SAT FEB 29. 1812
Died: Mr John Chapman, age 44 yrs, at his seat in Chas Co, Md, on Feb 21.

Died: Wm Newman Dorsett, aged 80 yrs, on Feb 10 at his farm nr Upper Marlborough, PG Co, Md.

Died: Mrs Jane Hanson, relict of John Hanson, esq, Del from Md in the old Rev Congress & Pres of that body in Phil, 1781-2. Mrs H died at Fredericktown, Feb 21, in 85th yr of her age.

Died: Genr'l Thos Matthews, at Norfolk, on Feb 20th; ctzn of same.

The *Wash Lancaster School* is now opened oppo the Great Hotel under Mr Henry Ould. -Wm Cranch, Bucknor Thruston, Thos H Gilliss, superintending committee.

Boot & Shoe Mkg-Sam'l C Dorman, lately from Balt, Md, has commenced the business in Mr Henry Tims' hse, next dr to Dr Jas Ewell's medical shop on Cptl Hill.

For sale-cranberries & lemons; also a cart or gig horse. -Wm Reily

Wm Norris, jr-tea-dealer & groc, #66, Mkt St, Balt, Md.

For sale-tract of land in PG Co, Md, ab't 100 acs with dwlg hse. Apply to Mr Geo Watterston on N J Ave, Mr John S Magruder in PG Co, or to the subscriber-Eliz Magruder.

My wife Anna has left my bed & board in an unbecoming manner. I forbid any person harboring, trusting, or dealing with her. I am determined not to pay any debts of her contracting, -John Barnes, Wash..

TUE MAR 3, 1812
Mrd: at *Sotterley* on Feb 25, Mr Wm G Ridgeley, merchant of Gtwn, to Miss Sophia Plater, d/o Col I R Plater of St Mary's Co, Md, by Rev Dr Duke.

An Act for relief of Thos O'Bannon; be permitted to withdraw his entry in the land ofc of Madison Co, Miss Terr, from the S E qrtr of section 2, Twnship 2, range one west; the money pd by him shall be credit on any purchase of public land in the same district, provided if range 2 has by error of the surveyor, marked range one. -H Clay, spkr of the Hse of Reps. Approved, Jas Madison.

Died: Mr Rich'd Weightman, aged 52, at Alexandria on Mar 1; inhabitant of Alexandria.

Congress-Hse of Reps: 1-Petition of Neil M'Ginniss of Phil City, praying remission of penalty of $75,000 incurred under the embargo laws-referred. 2-Petitions of Jane Deakins & of David Beek, of D C, praying for divorces-referred. 3-Pets of Jos Snelling & Henry Vanwey-unfavorable reports,

Orphans Crt of Wash Co, D C. Ltrs of adm d b n on prsnl est of Thos Jones, late of said Co dec'd. -Chas H Varden, adm

Supreme Crt of the U S; in the case of the schn'r *Exchange* vs John McFadon & Wm Greetham; reversed the decision of the Crct Crt, which reversed that of the Dist Crt of the U S for Pa.

Last Notice-having engaged in a different line of business, all persons indebted to me in store & shop acc'ts; settle with Mr Thos W Pairo in my absence. -F A Wagler.

Hse of Reps-Petition of Jane Deakins & David Beck, of this District, praying for divorces; report concludes that the prayer ought not be granted. Hse refused to print the report, vote 46 to 43.

Royal Free School. Borough Rd, Aug 31, 1811. Ltr to John Laird, esq. The ltr I rec'd of J Clagget & Alex'r Anderson, esqs, came when I just recovered from rheumatic illness; I was prevented from sending you a schoolmstr; I found but one young man but he was unwilling to leave England without his bro, a bro bound to him from his infancy, to whom he has been a foster parent since the decease of his mthr; the elder bro is Robt Ould; he & his bro, Henry Ould, have been my pupils; I hope it be my lot to visit America. -Jos Lancaster.

Notice-Decree of the Crct Crt of D C, as Crt of Chancery. Sale of all right, title, claim & int of Jas Thompson, & the heirs & reps of John Crookshank, dec'd, of & in the three 3 story brick bldgs on sq 461 in Wash City. -Dan'l Bussard, trust.

For sale-2 story brick hse in Wash City adj the dwlg of Mr Peter Hagner. -Jas Melvin, lvg in Gtwn.

THU MAR 5, 1812
Benevolent Soc of Wash City to meet at Davis' Htl this evening. -Geo Sweeney, Steward.

PG Co Crt-Rich'd L Humphreys of said PG Co, Md, insolvent debtor, in confinement for debt; to be discharged in April next. -John Read Magruder, clk.

For sale-22 lots in Wash City, which were devised by the late Sam Davidson to Miss Pattison of Cambridge, Md; being the whole of sq 186 except for lots 1, 2, 3, & 18. -Chas Goldsborough

SAT MAR 7, 1812
Hse of Reps. Petition of John Mason, of Gtwn, & the Corp & Turnpike Rd Co, of Gtwn, remonstrating against the cutting of a channel thru the causeway from Mason's island to the Va shore-referred to the Dist committee.

Resolved, that Allen B Magruder & Elegius Fromentin, agents from N Orleans Terr, be admitted within the hall of the Hse of Reps.

Heel shoes-just rec'd from Phil & Balt. -Andrew Coyle.

Reward-$20 for Ned Dines, mulatto lad; can be purch'd for $400 cash. -Ed H Pye.

Notice-creditors of Leonard Waring, late of PG Co, Md, dec'd; to rec their dividends of said est in Upper Marlboro on Sat. -Clement Holliday, adm.

Hse of Reps: 1-Petition of Elisha Winters, praying to be reinstated in the possession of land he is legally entitled & forcibly dispossessed by the Corp of N. Orleans-referred. 2-Unfavorable report on the petition of John Dixon.

Died: Thos S Bee, esq, at Charleston on Feb 18; one of the oldest inhabitants of that city & Judge of that Fed Dist.

Died: on Feb 15, Mrs Juliana B Wainwright, consort of Lt Wainwright, commanding U S M detachment in Charleston; aged 17 yrs & 5 mos, after a lingering illness. She was the y/d/o the late Gustavus Scott, of Md.

Public sale-order of the Orphans Crt of PG Co, Md. Prsnl est of Dr John Stuart, late of PG Co, dec'd. -Benj Hodges of Thos, adm.

TUE MAR 10, 1812
Hse of Reps: Petition of Geo Blagden & others for considerable amount for work done on both wings of the Capitol-referred.

Died: Mr John Read, on Mar 9, long a respectable inhabitant of this city. Burial from his late dwlg on Capitol Hill this morning.

Reward-$20 for appr boy, Rich'd Laymaster, to learn the hse carpenter trade; raised in Port Tobacco where he has a sister lvg, mrd to a Mr Cox or Coxen. -John Goszler, Gtwn.

Public sale-deed of trust from Geo Thompson, late of this town, to discharge a debt due by him; brick family hses nr the Bank. -Wm Morton, trust, Gtwn.

Notice-Property taxes are due Apr 1. Collectors: Jos Brumley, 1st Ward; Ezekiel MacDaniel, 2d Ward; Zachariah Walker, 3d Ward; John Queen, 4th Ward.

Caution-only my agents are authorised to grant printed licences to my patented improvements in the manufacture of flour. -Oliver Evans, Philadelphia.

Reward-$20 for negro woman, Priss, 46 yrs of age; she has a son living with Mr David Williamson in Balt. -Mary Crackels, Port Tobacco, Chas Co, MD.

THU MAR 12, 1812

An Act-Sec of Treas authorised to purchase of Winslow Lewis, his patent right to the new & improved method of lighting light-hses.

Public sale-order of Orphans Crt of Wash Co, D C; prsnl est of Walter Adams, late of D C, dec'd. Frame hse in sq 929 nr the Navy Yrd, carpenter's tools & hsehld furn. -Mgt Adams. Nichs L Queen, auct.

Ctzns of Wash City meeting; Dr Fred May, chrmn & Henry Herford, sec. Cmte for drafting a constitution for a Mutual Ins Co: Henry Herford, Nichs King, Moses Young, E B Caldwell & Geo Blagden.

Chas Simms was elected Mayor of Alexandria, vice Wm Herbert, who was rendered ineligible to a re-election.

Stolen-bay mare from the farm lately owned by Mr Mackubin in Patapsco Neck. -Amos Davis, lvg on said farm.

Public sale-hse & lot 15 in sq 163 on Pa ave. Enquire of John S Higden, nr the Seven bldgs. -Walter S Clarke

Public sale-all right, title & interest of R C F Boyert & Rob't Long in brick small hse in sq 792 in Wash City; sold because the purchasers did not comply with terms of sale to satisfy ground rent due Teresey Coyle, adms of Thos Coyle, dec'd. -David Bates, cnstble.

Orphans Crt of PG Co, Md. Ltrs of adm on prsnl est of Rinaldo Johnson, late of PG Co, dec'd. -Ann Eilbeck Johnson, admx.

Hse of Reps: Petition of Jas McIlhenny, of S C, praying exoneration from a judgment against him at the suit of the U S for violation of the law on importing slaves.

SAT MAR 14, 1812
There is a journal of Dan'l Bedinger on his voyage down the Mississippi. It begins with Dec 13, 1811 & thru Dec 22, 1811.

Mr John Braidwood has arrived in this country, a relative of the gentlemen of that name who have acquired celebrity by their Acad of the Deaf & Dumb established at Edinburgh, now at London.

Patent shot making & implements may be obtained from a person in the business for some yrs & quitted it for want of funds to carry on. -Mr R Libby, Alexandria.

Died: Mrs Martha Bowie, age 25 yrs, after a short illness on Mar 6, in PG Co; wife, mthr & dght.

Orphans Crt of Wash Co, D C. Prsnl est of Jas Mathers, late of said D C, dec'd. -John Coyle, Elias B Caldwell, excs.

Stock in Bank of Muskingum, Zanesville, Ohio will be opened under the super. of Jos Nourse & Robt Underwood. Comrs: Isaac Van Horn, Ebenezer Buckingham, Alexr McLaughlin & Geo Jackson; Davis' Htl on Pa ave, Wash, D C.

Orphans Crt of PG Co, Md. Prsnl est of Robt Young, late of said co dec'd. -Jas G Wood, Jos Young, excs.

TUE MAR 17, 1812
Stray yearling came to John Orr, nr the Great Hotel, Wash City.

Order of Orphans Crt of St Mary's Co, Md. Sale of prsnl prop of Jos Ford, dec'd, nr Leonardtown his late resid; 14 negroes, furn & stock. Also schn'r *Matilda-* *b*urthen ab't 70 tons. -Lewis Ford, adm.

Orphans Crt of PG Co, Md. Prsnl est of Wm Anderson, late of said co dec'd. -Sarah Anderson, excs.

Died: Rev Jas Madison, on Mar 6, in Williamsburg, Va; Bishop of the Prot Episc Ch in Va.

Hse & lot for sale: late the resid of Mr Benj Henry Latrobe, under a deed of trust from Robt Alexander, dec'd, to B H Latrobe & Jos Cassin. -B Henry Latrobe, trust. Forrest & Beale, aucts.

Peter Rogers-Sadler. From the green fields of Erin & tyranny to the green streets of Wash & liberty. He intends quitting the city ab't Jun 1st & wishes to be pd or pay his dealings before his departure; in the city nrly 3 yrs; advanced age. -U I M

Died: Lt Benjamin Franklin Read, U S N, ntv of Va; on Jan 27th last at Balize, on his return to New Orleans from a visit to Island of Cuba, for benefit of his health; died young; had much svc both before & since his captivity in Tripoli.

For sale-brick hse on sq 386; title unquestionable. -Ambrose Moriarty, Wash..

Public sale of 8 or 10 negroes; will not be sold to foreigners or their agents. -Fred P L Duvall, lvg nr Snowden's Iron Works, PG Co, Md.

Medical College lottery mgrs: John B Davidge, Jas Mosher, John Comegys, Robt Carey Long, B H Mullikin, D A Smith, Hall Harrison, W H Clendinen, Fielding Lewis, jr., Wm Gwynn, David Hoffman, Sam'l Baker, Jas Cocke, Jona Meredith, Jeremiah Sullivan, Midd'n B Magruder, Isaac Purnell, Benj Berry, Geo Winchester, John Crawford, G E Mitchill, P H Nicklin, Wm M'Mechen, J T H Worthington, Wm Jessop, Henry Thompson, Chas Alex'r Warfield, Chas Wirgman, Wm Lorman -Balt, Md.

THU MAR 19, 1812

Mrd: Wm T Barry esq, late a Rep in Congress from Ky, & Miss Cath Mason, d/o Stevens Thomson Mason, dec'd; at the seat of Mr Mason in Va by Rev Mr Dunn.

Died: Mrs Martha Ross, w/o Mr John Ross, of this city, on Mar 15 at age 32 yrs; after a very lingering illness. She leaves her hsbnd & 4 small chldrn.

For sale-ab't 80 lots in Wash City for exchange for land in Ky or Tenn. Apply to Rich'd Young, lvg with Mr Pairo, F St or to the subscriber nr Montg Crt Hse, Md. -Chas Young.

Union Circulating Library was opened 2 yrs ago by Jos Milligan.

Runaways committed to Wash Co, D C jail: negro Ned, says he belongs to Edw Pye of Chas Co, Md; negro Sam, says he belongs to Eliz Walker of PG Co, nr Vansville, Md. -C Tippet, kpr of the jail.

To let-brick hse on Pa ave, nr Rhodes' Tavern. Enquire of Cornelius M'Lean

Hse of Reps report on the petitions of Jane Deakins praying for a divorce from Wm Deakins her hsbnd, & of David Beck for a divorce from Ellen his wife. Report: the only object in view is to enable, respectively, to enter into new contracts of marriage; prayer of the petitioners ought not to be granted.

Pblc sale-order of Orphans Crt for Montg Co, Md; at late resid of Wm O'Neale, dec'd, 1 mile from the Montg Co Crt Hse; all prsnl prop-16 negroes, stock, furn etc. -Wm O'Neale, jr, adm

Hse of Reps: 1-Petition of Wm Garrard, $1,500 was recommended for this svcs as land Commissioner for the Terr of Orleans-referred to a committee. 2-Pet of Stephen Girard, merchant of Phil City, praying permission to enter his vessel, *Good Friends,* at some Custom Hse of the U S, vessel now at Amelia Island-referred.

The new mode of teaching our chldrn was introduced by Robt & Henry Ould, brothers, in Nov last, in Gtwn.

Boston, Mar 10-Capt Ockington has arrv'd at his home in this town from Europe. His vessel, *The Catharine,* was taken by the Danes; after a long detention was acquitted; soon after she was taken by a French Privateer & carried into Dantzie. 21 American seamen were impressed; Mr Frederic Soper, after a detention of 7 mos, escaped & has returned to his family in Cambridgeport. -Fed Paper.

SAT MAR 21, 1812
Hse of Reps: Petition of Levi Hollingsworth, copper manufacturer in Balt, Md, praying that a duty be laid on copper imported from foreign countries-referred.

Jas Greer has remv'd from Jefferson & Bridge to the Masonic Hall in Jefferson St; fresh supply of ale & beer.

For sale: frame dwlg hse oppo Wash Boyd. -Mgt Fennell, lvg in F St nr the Treas ofc, Wash City.

For sale-8,000 acs of land lying on the Mississippi, in the Dist of Baton Rouge, srvyd & patented in 1770 & 1772; 7,000 acs in Randolph Co & 3,000 acs in Harrison Co, Va, 2,400 acs in Ky. Property in this city will be taken in part payment. -Oliver Polock, Wash City.

Notice: Ignatius Waters, negro man ab't 50 yrs of age, committed to Frederick Co jail. He has a family lvg in Balt. -Ezra Mantz, shrf.

Ltr written by Presley Jas White & John Armistead White, of Culpeper Co, Va, Mar 9, 1812. Rg-feeding stock with different grasses to great advantage.

Rufutation of charges of Grand Jury of Baldwin Co, Miss Terr, against Harry Toulmin-ltr from Cowles Mead, spkr of the Hse of Reps of Miss Terr, has been referred.

Reward-$100-for conviction of the perpetrator; having had my 3 story brick hse on Pa Ave set on fire by design. -Peter Lenox.

TUE MAR 24, 1812
Orphans Crt of Wash Co, D C. Prsnl est of Garrett P Barry, late of said city, dec'd. -David Dobbin, exc.

Ball for the Poor-at Mr Crawford's New Assembly Rm, Mar 31. Mgrs:
John Mason	J S Williams	Geo Peter
John Lee	John Cox	Robt F How

Jas Melvin & Son, merchant taylors in Gtwn below the coffee hse.

Pa Electoral Tkt. Recommended by the Democ mbrs of the Gen'l assembly:
Chas Thomson-Montg Co	
David Mitchell-Cumberland	Mich'l Baker-Northern Liberties, Phil
Paul Cox-Phil City	Isaac Worrell-Phil Co
Jos Engle-Dela	Jas Fulton-Chester
Isaiah Davis-Montg	John Whitehill-Lancaster
Edw Crouch-Dauphin	Hugh Glasgow-York
David Fullerton-Franklin	Sam'l Smith-Adams
Robt Smith-Bucks	Nath'l Michler-Northampton
Chas Shoemaker-Berks	Jas Mitchell-Somerset
John Murray-Northumberland	Clement Paine-Ontario
Arthur Moore-Huntingdon	Abijah Miner-Greene
Henry Alshouse-Westmoreland	Jas Stevenson-Washington
Adamson Tannehill-Allegany	David Mead-Crawford

Hardware & Ironmongery-Geo Beale having purch'd the entire stock in trade of Mr Tunis Craven & will continue the sale at the store on Pa Ave -Geo Beale.

Oliver Whipple, Gtwn, advertises patent ornamental washes, to make stone, brick & wood of a white & greyish freestone color.

THU MAR 26, 1812
Robt Elliott, Capitol Hill, invites parents & guardians to attend an examination at his school rm on E Capt St.

Hse of Reps: 1-Petition of Elisha Thorndike, dec'd, Wm Haman & Benj Giles of Mass, praying indemnification for the loss of their vessel & cargo, illegally captured by the Spanish Ship of War in 1809-referred. 2-Pet of Jos Hilton of N H, comp for svcs as Rev ofcr-referred. 3-Pet of Sam'l, Jeremiah & John Peabody, of Mass, owners & Mstrs of schn'r *Equality*, praying for half of nett proceeds of cotton they found floating on the High Seas-referred. 4-Pet of Sam'l Tucker, comp for Rev svcs-referred. 5-Statement of Capt Sam'l Chew of N Haven, Conn; regarding supercargo on the brig *Thames* on Jan 19, 1812.

An Act to incorporate the trustees of the Gtwn Lancaster School Soc was approved by Jas Madison, Mar 19, 1812. Trustees: John Baird, Henry Foxall, Stephen B Balch, Robt Beverly, Robt Munroe, John McDaniel jr, David Wiley, Walter D Addison, Dan'l Bussard, Francis S Key, Walter Smith, John Abbott.

Reps of the Terr of Orleans in convention-providing for the admission of this country into the Union of the States was held Jan 28, 1812:
J Poydras-Pres
J D Degoutin Bellechasse
F Jh Le Breton Henderson
S Henderson
Bernard Marigny
Thos Urquhart
Sam'l Winter of Orleans Co
Jean Noel Destrehar
Andre La Branche of German Coast Co
Genezi Roussin of Acadia Co
Wm Wikoff jr of Iberville Co
Bela Hubbard jr
H S Thibodaux of Lafouche Co
S Hiriart of Pointe Coupee Co
Levi Wells of Rapides Co
P Bossier, Prud'homme of Nachitoches Co
David B Morgan of Concordia Co
Henry Bry of Ouachitta Co
Allan B Magruder
John Thompson of Oppelousas Co
Alex Porter jr of Attakapas Co
J Blanque
P Denis de la Ronde
F Livandais
Jacques Villere Watkins
John Watkins
Jas Brown
Michel Cantrel
L M Reynaud
Amant Hebert
Wm Goforth
St Martin
Thos F Oliver
Robt Hall
Chas Olivier
Jas Dunlap
Henry Johnson
W C Maquille
D J Sutton
Louis De Blanc

Attest, Eligius Fromentin, Sec to the Convention.

Med School lottery-Md. Tkts for sale from Kearny Wharton, Philip H Nicklin & J I Cohen jr. Lottery ofcs in Balt, Md.

Notice-sale of the prop of Robt Alexander, dec'd; hse & lot nr the Navy Yd, advertised by Mr B Henry Latrobe, will not take place.

Deserted: Robt Lewis, Pvt in the U S Regt of Light artl, 27 yrs of age, 5ft 11 1/2, by trade a seaman; born in Caroline Co, Va. Also, John McKenney, Pvt in U S Regt of Light artl, age 21 yrs, ab't 5ft 8, by trade a shoemkr, born in Ire. Also, Nicholas Foster, Pvt in U S Regt of Lght Artl, 23 yrs of age, 5ft 8, by trade a laborer, born in Cork Ireland. -G W Hight, Lt of Lt Artl.

Education-Robt Elliot will open a female acad on Apr 6th, E Capt St-Wash.

SAT MAR 28, 1812
Post ofc Changes in Feb 1812:
Newtane, Vt-Jonathan Ney vice Dan'l Kellogg, rsgn'd.
Enoesburg, Vt-Solomon Williams vice Solomon Dimmick, rsgn'd
Murraysville, N C-Wm Smith vice Samuel Murray, rsgn'd
Concord, Vt-John Frye vice Azarius Williams, rsgn'd
Guildhall, Vt-Jas Berry vice Jos Berry jr.
Berlin, Md-Adam Boughman vice Theodore Beall, rsgn'd

Dobson's X Rds, N C-Nath'l Shober vice Thos Adams, rsgn'd
Chas City C H, Va-Thos Gilliam vice Wm Singleton
Northeast N Y-Israel Reynolds vice Stephen Eno, rsgn'd
Wakefield, N H-John Wingate vice J G Hall, situation inconvenient
Lorraine, N Y-John Alger vice B Gates, mv'd away
Portsmouth, Ohio-Thos Waller vice John Brown, rsgn'd.
Eddington, Me-John Whiting vice Park Holland
Meadville, Pa-Henry Hurst vice Jas Gibson, rsgn'd.
Reedsville, S C-Colin Campbell vice N Reed
Snowhill, N C-Jas Porter vice Jas G Sheppard, rsgn'd
Green, N Y-Chas Josslyn vice David Fin
Rising Sun, Va-Walker Timberlake vice Sam'l F Morris, rsgn'd.

New Post ofcs established in Feb 1812 & Postmaster:
McCaulley's store, Montg Co, N C-John McCaulley
Reed's store, Moore Co, N C-D Reed
Paint Lick, Gerard Co, Ky-Wm Miller
Lombardy Grove, Meckienburg Co, Va-Wm Lydner
Phelps, Ontario Co, N Y-David McNeale
Riceville, Roane Co, Ten-Isaac Rice
Juliestown, Burlington Co, N J-John Fennimore
Pennfield, Ontario Co, N Y-Oliver Kingsbury
Oak Hall, Greenville Co, S C-Sam'l Richardson
Canterbury, Rockingham Co, N H-Jos M Harper
Northfield, Rockingham, N H-Alexander F Clark
Farnworth, Strafford Co, N H-John Page
Bolton, Chittenden Co, Vt-Jas Whitcomb
Highgate, Franklin Co, Vt-Peter Sax
Richford, Frankford Co, Vt-Henry James
Montgomery, Franklin Co, Vt-Sam'l Bernard
Ofcs discontinued in Feb 1812: Davisburgh, Ky & Pattonsburgh, Va.

Appointments in the new army:
Wm North of N Y-Adj Genr'l
Jas Winchester of Tenn-Brig-Genrl
Thos Pinckney of S C-Maj-Genr'l
Jos Bloomfield of N J-Brig-Genrl
Wm Polk of N C-Brig-Genrl

Com'rs appointed for establishing a new bank in Wash City;
John Tayloe
Jas D Bary
Jas Davidson
C W Goldsborough
John P Van Ness
Phineas Bradley
Jas H Blake
Buller Cocke
Andrew Way
Thos Tingey
Thos Munro
Elias B Caldwell
Washington Boyd
Roger C Weightman
Silas Butler
Walter Hellen
-Chas Carroll of Belle Vue-Pres. -Edmund Law, Sec.

Died: Mr Andrew Hanna, of the hse of Warner & Hanna of Balt, on Mar 26, at Balt, Md.

For sale-land nrly oppo Lower Marlborough, late the prop of John M Gantt, dec'd; ab't 1200 acs; also another tract of land, ab't 240 acs, adj Mr Clem Brooke's est. Apply to subscriber lvg in P G Co, Md. -Fielder Gantt, exc. M S Gantt, excx of J M Gantt, dec'd. P G Co Md.

Ranaway-Ralph Wotton, age 22 yrs, mulatto man; has a bro Rezin lvg in Phil. -Wm Bowie of Walter, nr Queen Ann.

For sale-a few hundred plants; Thos Main, shop on High St, Gtwn.

Orphans Crt of Wash Co, D C. Prsnl est of Chas McNantz, late of said city, dec'd. -Mary Ann McNantz, admx.

Cases determined by the Supreme Crt: 1-Thos Fitzimons vice Thos L Ogden. 2-Jas Welch vice Mandeville & Jamieson. 3-Md Ins Co vice Harman Le Roy. 4-State of N J on prosecution of Geo Painter vice Levi Wilson. 5-Nath'l Russel vice John Innis Clarke's excs. 6-Archibald Freeland vice Heron, Lenox & Co 7-Philip G Marsteller vice Archibald McLean. 8-Jas Welch vice Abraham Lindo. 9-John McIvin, assignee vice Lenox, Maillard & others. 10-Seth Barton vice Petit & Bayard. 11-Jas & John Dunlop vice Thos Munroe. 12-Josiah Fox vice Ebenezer Larkin. 13-Thos Beatty jr vice Thos Corcoran. 14-U S vice Aquilla Giles. 15-U S vice John Tyler. 16-Hezekiah Wood vice Davis. 17-Chesapeake Ins Co vice Jos Marcadin. 18-Jas Hughes vice Cleon Moore. 19-John McKim jr vice Peter G Voorhees. 20-U S vice Jonah Crosby. 21-David Davy's excs vice Abraham Faw. 22-Wm King vice Joshua Riddle. 23-Wm Wilson vice John Koontz. 24-Jos Ridge vice Robt Moss. 25-Jas Sheely vice Jos Mandeville. 26-Rich'd Conway's excs vice Walter S Alexander. 27-U S vice John Goodwyn. 28-Wm Morgan vice Anthony Reintzel. 29-U S vice Mich'l Hillegas' excs.

Festival of St Patrick was held Mar 17th at the Navy Yd; John Dobbin, Pres; Wm McKee-VP.

Ranaway, negro Ben, from John Montgomery lvg nr Bush Creek & adj Johnson's Old forge, Frederick Co, Md. Reward-$40. [Ben was brought as a child from PG Co, Md by Mr Zadock Brashears]

Indian hostilities, St Louis, Feb 15. An express arrv'd in town from Ft Madison & were fired on by the Indians; the family of Mr O'Neil was killed in St Chas Dist; 9 in number, mostly females, Mr O'Neil was in town at the time.

Wm H Hamer has an assortment of elegant hats for sale. [Local]

TUE MAR 31, 1812
Died: Capt Henry Caldwell, of Marine Corps, at Charlestown, Mass, on Thu fortnight.

Mrd: Thos Tonn, esq, one of the Judges of the Sup Crt of the U S, to Mrs Lucy Washington, sister of Mrs Madison, on Mar 29 at the resid of the Pres of the U S, by Rev Mr McCormick.

In Chancery-Wash Co, D C. Minifie, Frye & Spalding, against Geo Walker. Ratify sale to sundry persons of lots & premises for sum of $3,097.97. -Wm Brent, clk.

Died: Sam'l Tyler, on Monday a wk, at Williamsburg, Va. Judge of the Chancery for said dist.

Teacher wanted immediately. -Wm Marbury jr, nr Piscataway, P G Co, Md.

For sale-land, 350 acs in Fairfax Co, Va; also 1,000 acs in Monongalia Co, Va nr Morgantown. -Jas H Blake, Wash City.

Burnett grass seed for sale. -Thos Thorpe, Bridge St, Gtwn.

Public sale-for the benefit of Jesse C Palmer, insolvent debtor; 586 1/2 acs of land on Goully Rvr & Laurel Creek in Green Briar, Va. -Wm Wood, trust. Nichs L Queen, auct.

THU APR 2, 1812
In Chancery, State of Md: Dan'l Carroll of Huntingridge, Wash Van Bibber, Jos Heston, John Merryman, Caleb Merryman, John Mitchell, John Boyer Champayne, Job Smith, Edw Pumphrey, Zebulon Hollingsworth, Wm Hammond, & Jona Manro, vs Chas Carroll of Carrollton, Nichs Carroll, Dan'l Carroll of Duddington, Wm Smith, Isaac Van Bibber, Gordon Fortes, Wm Fortes, Louisa Lee Forbes & Robt M Forbes, Geo Carter, Robt Mitchell & Priscilla his wife, Spencer Ball & Betty Landon his wife, John Yates Chinn & Sarah Fairfax his wife, *Robt Beckley & *Julia his wife, *John W Belfield & *Frances Tasker his wife, Thos Ap Jones, Eliz Jones, Sophia Carter, *J Davis & *Sarah Tekell his wife, *Jos Belfield & *Jane his wife, Harriet Lucy Maund, Harriet Peck, John Carter Peck, Emanuel Peck & Tasker Carter Quinlan. Bill states that the Balt Co-the dfndnts, contracted to convey sundry tracts of land to the cmplnts, who have pd in part or in whole; Robt Carter, mbr of said company, by his will devised his int to the dfndnts, Geo Carter, Priscilla Mitchel w/o Robt Mitchel, Francis Tascar Jones, Thos Ap Jones, Eliz Jones, Jane Jones, Sarah Tekel Jones, Betty Landon Ball w/o Spencer Ball, Sarah Fairfax Chinn w/o John Yates Chinn, Harriet Lucy Maund, Julia Carter, Sophia Carter, Harriet Peck, John Carter Peck, Emanuel Peck, & Tasker Carter Quinlan, & to John Tasker Carter, & has since died, the said John Tasker Carter under his will conveyed his part of said lands to Wm Forbes, who is since dead, leaving dfndnts Gideon Forbes, Wm Forbes, Louisa Lee Forbes & Robt M Forbes all minors under age 21 yrs, his heirs at law. [*all reside in Va]. Others reside out of Md-serverally reside in Va. Minors: Eliz Jones, Sarah T Davis, Jane Belfield, Harriet Peck, John C Peck, Emanuel Peck, Tasker C Quinlan, Gideon, Wm, Louisa

L & Robt M Forbes. Bill is to obtain conveyances to the cmplnts for land so contracted to be sold to them. -Nichs Brewer, Reg Cur Can.

Died: Dr Wm Baker, on Mar 21, at Gtwn.

Notice-application for renewal of certificate 499 for 6 shares of Columbia Bank stock, issued in the name of Jos Queen, same lost or mislaid. -Ann E Queen.

David Holmes is re-appt'd the Govn'r of the Terr of Mississippi.

Orphans Crt of Wash Co, D C. Mar 25, 1812. Prsn'l est of John Read, late of said city, dec'd. -Marcella Read, admx. Jas Hoban, adm.

SAT APR 4, 1812
Rosanna Finnigan, insolvent debtor, Wash Co, D C. -Wm Brent, clk.

Wanted-journey saddlers. -John Peltz, Pa av, Wash City.

Stray cow taken up. -Jesse Howard.

For sale-potatoes at my store nr the Navy Yd. -John Dobbyn

Wm Jones, esq, of Phil, is appt'd Commissary-Genr'l of the U S Army.

Hse of Reps: 1-Petition of Bartholomew White, of Pa-he underwent difficulties in consequence of a prosecution against him in 1807, groundless suspicion of his being concerned in the conspiracy of Aaron Burr, expenses have nrly ruined him, motion was negatived-petitioner has leave to withdraw his papers. 2-Petiton of Thos F Reddick was read twice & committed.

Reward-$20 for Geo Wright, black fellow. Ranaway from Henry A Neale, lvg on Goose Crk, nr Port Tobacco, Chas Co, Md.

Capt Arthur Batt Bingham, who commanded the *Little Belt* at the time of her engagement with the American frig, *President,* has been promoted to Post Capt.

Crct Crt of Wash Co, D C-Crt of Chancery. Case of Jas McKenzie & others against Chas Minifie; public auction of 42 lots in Wash City. -Jas Davidson, Rich'd Forrest, trustees.

Cotton goods for sale. -Alex'r McCormick.

Rockville Acad lottery. Com'rs: Rich'd Anderson, Upton Beall, Honore Martin, Soloman Holland.

THU APR 7, 1812
Morgan Lewis, esq, is appt'd Qrtr-Mstr Genr'l of the U S Army.

Died: Hon Gunning Bedford, Judge of the Dist Crt of U S for Dist of Dela, at his country seat nr the town of Wilmington, on Mon week.

For sale-2 brick hses nr Barry's wharf. -Griffith Coombe or Geo Blagden, com'rs.

Hse of Reps: Petition of Jos Wellington Page, praying to be released from a judgment against him under the embargo laws as surety to a bond-referred.

New York-Apr 1. Wm Sampson, esq, was admitted in the Crct Crt of the U S, [present-Judge Livingston] to the rights of ctznship & degree of Cnsl of the Crt.

THU APR 9, 1812
Caution-Having obtained a patent for making bricks out of the earth, a Jas MacDonald, who lived in my family during my absence last summer at Richmond, having access to my papers etc, made a machine on the same plan; necessary steps have been taken to set aside the said MacDonald's patent. -Daniel French.

Wm Hull, esq, now Gov of Mich Terr, is appt'd Brig-Genr'l in the U S Army.

Wanted-proposals for ship timber. -Thos Tingey, Cmndnt, Navy Yd, Wash, D C.

Wash Co, D C. Sam'l Barnes, insolvent debtor, confined in prison for debt. -Wm Brent, clk.

Ladies with ltrs in the Wash. P O-Apr 1, 1812:

Eliz Barne	Miss Eliza Brown	Miss Louisa C Boiman
Miss Cecilia Coolidge	Miss Betsey Dines	Mrs Elizh Dempsie
Widow P Filschew	Miss Ann Greenwell	Mrs Anne C Morris
Mrs Patience Minchin	Mrs Eleanor Nargin	Mrs Eliz Orr
Anne Pane	Mrs Kesiah Rowles	Mrs C Smithers
Mrs Susan Van Zandt	Eliz Wright	Mrs Chlo Young.

Orphans Crt of PG Co, Md. Prsnl est of John Igleheart, late of said co, dec'd. -Rich'd Igleheart, adm.

Wm Hull, esq, now Govn'r of Mich Terr, is appt'd Brig-Genr'l in the U S Army.

Mrshl's sale-all right, title & claim of Levi White to lot 8 in sq 1046 & also sq 797 with improvement thereon; suit of John Vint against said White. -Wash Boyd, mrsh'l of D C

Wash Co, D C-In Chancery. Jas D Barry against Patrick Barry & the heirs of Garret Barry, dec'd. Bill is to foreclose a mortgage made by said Garret Barry on Mar 26, 1807 to said Jas D Barry, adj a lot sold by Thos Law to Mich'l Scott; also a lot G Barry purch'd of Mich'l Scott, Sep 9, 1805; it appears that Patrick Barry & other dfndnts are not residents of D C. -Wm Brent.

For sale-French burrs. -Isaac M'Pherson, Balt., Md.

Pressed Shot Factory-subscribers to Thos Bruff's solid shot business are to attend at his hse on Monday, Apr 13. -T Bruff

Rpblcn meeting at Albany City on Mar 27th; John Taylor, chrmn; W Ross, sec.

Members:
Peter Hurlbut	A J Hardenburgh	John Taylor
Nath'l Cole	O C Comstock	Thos Ludlow
Geo H Nellis	Jacob Teeple	Ebenezer White
Delevan Delance	Silas Holmes	H A Townsend
W Ross	Casper M Rouse	Henry Wells
Wm W Gilbert	John W Taylor	Isaac Ogden
Jas Boyd	Dan'l Hawkes	E Root
Jas W Eilkin	R Hubbard	F A Bloodgood
Peter S Van Orden	Benj Coe	Ezra Waite
John Fay	Chancy Hyde	Sam'l Campbell
Isaac Hayes	Avery Starkweather	Joel Keeler
Jas Guyon	Nath'l Allen	Philetus Swift
Bennet Bicknell	Israel Carl	Dan'l Crosby
Archibald McIntyre	Alex'r Livingston	Dan'l I Andrus
David Southerland	Abraham Rose	Alex'r Sheldon
Jacob Coddington	Seth Marvin	Henry Jansen
Zebulon Mott	Elnathan Sears	Dan'l H Burr
Henry Hager	Joshua Vanvleet	Araham Miller
J Bruyn	John Young	Asher H Moore
	Henry Yates jr	Nath'l Potter

Rpblcn meeting at Jacacks's Tavern, in Green St, Albany City, Mar 2, 1812; Reuben Humphrey, chrmn; John Ely, sec. Mbrs:

Sylvanus Smalley	Sam'l Haight	Walter Martin
Elijah H Metcalf	Sam'l Woodworth	Luther Rich
Jonathan Stanley jr	Billy Trowbridge	Wm Darrow
John Reddington	Rudolph I Shoemaker	John Ely
Edw P Livingston	Elisha Arnold	Lyman Hall
Halsey Rogers	Morgan Lewis	Robt Burch
Kitchel Bishop	Wm Taber	Humphrey Howland
Zacheus Colby	Stephen Close	John Kirtland
Jas Hill	Simeon Sayre	Barnet Mooney.
R Humphrey		

Morgan Lewis, esq, is appt'd Quarter-Mstr Genr'l of the U S Army.

SAT APR 11, 1812
Sale by auction of woolen goods. -C O Muller, auct, Baltimore, Md.

Beware of misrepresentations. Jas MacDonald writes that he is the patentee of improved form of brick making; not Dan'l French & that Jas Ray, atty for Dan'l French, circulated the insinuation.

Hse of Reps: 1-Petition of Mary Barrell, of Vt, stating that she was entirely dependent for support upon her son Capt Wm C Baen, who was killed in the late action with the Indians on the Wabash, praying relief. 2-Ltr was read from Jonathan Coleman, ntv born American ctzn, impressed on board the British ship of war, *Mars*, praying for interference of Congress in effecting his release.

Strayed or stolen-brown horse. -Wm Fletcher, Wash City.

Wash Co, D C. Hillary H Halsey, insolvent debtor. -Wm Brent, clk.

TUE APR 14, 1812
Ltr to Hon Mr Dinsmoor, mbr of Cong from N H: a son has been pressed on board a British war ship; he has been torn from the arms of his parents, bros & sisters; he is a ntv of this country---- Signed, your distressed friend & sister, Ruth Fling.

Ltr to Mr Dinsmoor laid before the Hse, addressed to him; State of N H, Cornish, Mar 12, 1812. Calvin Fling, my son, 20 yrs old last Jan, has resided in Prov of Canada these 3 yrs past as a journeyman saddler, in Montreal most of the time; ab't 2 wks ago, Henry Hall, of this town, says he worked in the same shop with Calvin Fling & that he was carried on board the British sloop of War, the *Rattler*; I did much for my country in the Rev War & was in svc ab't 8 yrs; I was in the Battle of Germantown, Nigh Phil; Battle of Mud Fort or Fort Miffin; in the Battle of Monmouth; I pray that my son can be released. -Lemuel Fling.

A new play for amusing & instructing little chldrn may be seen at Mr Milligan's bkstore in Gtwn & at Mr Rapine's on Capitol Hill. -Thaddeus Osgood.

THU APR 16, 1812
Died: on Apr 15, Miss Isabella Claxton, age 22 yrs, in Wash, d/o Mr Thos Claxton, many yrs past principal Drkpr to the Hse of Reps of the U S. Miss C died of consumption of the lungs.

Died: on Apr 13, Abel Janney, age 57 yrs, at Alexandria, long a respectable inhabitant of that place.

SAT APR 18, 1812
Orphans Crt of Chas Co, Md. Ltrs of adm on est of Rev Mr Sylvester Boarman, late of Chas Co, dec'd. -Chas Boarman, adm, Wash City, D C.

Mrd: Outerbridge Horsey, esq, Senator in Congress from Dela, to Miss Eliza Lee, d/o Thos S Lee, esq, of Gtwn; at Gtwn on Apr 16.

TUE APR 21, 1812
Mr Sylvanus Baldwin, of Montpelier, Vt, has arrv'd in Wash with the newly invented machinery for spinning flax & hemp.

Horse Farriery-R C Bainbridge, vet surg from England, has engaged in the tanning business at his yard, So Capt St, Wash.

Teacher wanted in the Rockville Acad. Apply to Rev J Breckenridge. -Jos Elgar, Sec, Montg C H, Md.

Died: Geo Clinton, V P of the U S, Apr 20, at his lodgings, Mr O'Neal's, in Wash City after an illness of ab't 4 wks. Funeral procession at 4 P M.

Levy Crt of PG Co, Md: Contract for bldg a stone bridge over Collington Branch, nr John H Hall's mill. Apply to Henry Waring, Wm B Beanes or John Hodges of Thos. -Upper Marlboro, Md.

Small Pox in Calvert Co, Md in Jan last. John Howes, a boatman, died of this disease on board his boat; he was attended by a young man, Wm Marcus, who had been vaccinated. Marcus, fearing for his own safety abandoned both Howes & his boat. The boat wrecked & Howes' body has not been found. When Marcus left the boat he took Howes' great coat & went to the hse of Mr Francis Wolf. He did not tell them of his situation & Mr Wolf, age 80 yrs, took sick on Feb 10th & died on Feb 19th. His disease was not ascertained before his death & thus cost the lives of many connexions. Elias Wolf, age 50 yrs, died Mar 18. John Yoe, age 64 yrs, died Mar 3. John Kent, age 50 yrs, died Mar 14. Lewis Harrison, age 40 yrs, died Mar 14. Jos Strickland, age 45 yrs, died Mar 11. Rich'd Hanse, age 63 yrs, died Mar 18. Benj Hanse, age 50 yrs, died Mar 29. Wm Yoe, age 18 yrs, died Mar 20. A child of Mr L Harrison died Mar 26 & another is dangerously ill. Those who were vaccinated, afflicted but recovered: negro Priscilla, age 56 yrs, belonging to Genr'l Jos Wilkinson; negro Frank, age 30 yrs, slave of Mr Levis Mackail; negro Isaac, age 30 yrs, slave of Mr Basil Brook; negro boy age 12 yrs, belonging to Mr Howe Sommerville. -Jas Smith, Dir of the Vaccine Inst for State of Md. Balt, Apr 4, 1812.

The mortal remains of the late Vice Pres, Geo Clinton, were interred at the burial ground nr the Navy-Yd in this city. Wash.

Orphans Crt of PG Co, Md. Sale at late dwlg of Zadock Jenkins, all prsn'l est of said Jenkins, 9 negroes, stock etc. -Archibald Jenkins, adm. Ann Jenkins, admx.

Hse of Reps: Petition of Ezra Weston & son of Duxbury, Mass, praying indemnification for a vessel captured by French frigs. -referred.

Ltr from Mr Thos G Watkins of Tenn, to Capt Jacob Elliston, of this county, dt'd Jefferson, Tenn, Mar 26. We have rec'd orders to march against the Creek Indians; they have killed 20 families on Elk Rvr. -Frankfort Paper. False alarm per a ltr dt'd Mar 27, 1812, Cairo; Nat'l Intell Paper of Apr 25, 1812.

Sweet Potatoes now landing at my wharf & shall retail. -Andrew Scholfield, Alexandria.

I found-a small bundle of gentlemen's clothing. -Apply to Remigius Burch, living nr the Center Mkt, Wash City.

THU APR 23, 1812
Valuable prop for sale-on the premises, 2 brick hses in Wash City, late the prop of Gen Washington, on N Capt St, lot 16 & parts of 6 & 7 in sq 634. -Philip B Key.

Thos Merryman/Maryman of Chas Co, Md, insolvent debtor, confined in prison for debt. -John Barnes, clk

Post ofc Changes in Mar, 1812:
Hillsboro, Md-Jas Seth, vice Francis Sellers, rsgn'd;
Oyster Bay, N Y-Jas Colwell, vice Jotham Weeks, mv'd away;
Newburgh, N Y-Aaron Belknap, vice Chester Clark, mv'd away;
Warren, Ct-John Tallmadge, vice Benj B Osborn, rsgn'd;
Watkinsville, Ga-Wm Waight, vice John Hopkins, mv'd away;
Holmes' Hole, Ms-Theodosius Parsons, vice Rufus Spalding, rsgn'd;
Hebron, N H-Stephen Goodhue, vice Wm Gale, rsgn'd;
Jamesville, S C-Maurice Power, vice Robt Dow, do;
Greenville, Miss Ter-Ab Bradford, vice John H Carr, do;
Hubbardstown, Ms-Clark Witt, vice Reuben Wheeler, do;
Rutherdordtown, N C-Geo Walton, vice Tench Cox jr, do;
Tazewell C H, Va-Henry P George, vice J George, do;
Monticello, N Y-John P Jones, vice Sam'l F Jones;
Newbury, Vt-Jos Smith jr, vice David Johnston;
Goshen, Ga-Sam'l Davis, vice Jas E Todd, rsgn'd;
Martinsville or Henry C H, Va-Thos Graves, vice Geo Hairston, do;
Big Lick, Va-Jas Brawley, vice Jas Echolls, do;
Gates C H, N C-Miles Riddick, vice Chas Townsend, rsgn'd.;
Williamston, N C-Jos Biggs, vice Sam'l Hyman, rsgn'd;
Manchester, Md-John Keefer, vice Sam'l Peters, rsgn'd;
Franklinton, O-Adam Hosack, vice Henry Brown, rsgn'd;
Mitchells store, Va-Thos Mitchell jr, vice Robt Merewether, do;
Stannardsville, Va-Robt Stringfield, vice Henry F Hume, rsgn'd;
Milwood, Va-John E Dangerfield, vice Bacon Burwell, mv'd away;
Chatham C H, N C-Wm Brantley, vice Jos Harman, do;
Urbana, Va-Parmenas Bird, vice John Darby;
Natchez, Miss Ter-John Hankinson, vice Noah Fletcher, rsgn'd.
New ofcs est'd in Mar 1812 & Postmaster;
Paris Furnace, Oneida Co, N Y-Jos Howard. Postmaster;
Canterbury, Kent Co, Del-Geo Guildersleive;
Milton, Miami Co, O-Jos Evans;
Millstone, Somerset Co, N J-Jacob Van Neste;
Dalton, Berkshire Co, Ms-John Chamberlaine jr;
Ellisville, Warren Co, N C-Jas Ellis;
Batchelor's Retreat, Pendleton Co, S C-John Lee;
Plough & Harrow, Augusta Co, Va-Mich'l Mouzy;
Littletown, Sussex Co, Va-Peter Booth;
Scituate, Providence Co, Va-Chas Angell;
Newbern, Wythe Co, Va-Henry Hanse;

Masonville, Dela Co, N Y-J Thatcher;
Hyde Park, Dutchess Co, N Y-Tobias L Stoutenburgh;
Paradise, Lancaster Co, Pa-Isaac F Lightser;
Henderson's Store, Northumberland Co, Va-name was ommited;
Greensburg, Green Co, Pa-John Crawford
Ofcs discontinued in Mar 1812: Tolland, Ms & Stockbridge, Vt

Thos Merryman/Maryman of Chas Co, Md, insolvent debtor, confined in prison for debt. -John Barnes, clk

Orphans Crt of Calvert Co, Md. Apr 15, 1812. Prsn'l est of Basil Brooke, late of said co, dec'd. -John H Brooke, exc of last will & test of the dec'd.

SAT APR 25, 1812
Died: Mr Jas Pease, age ab't 24 yrs, s/o Seth Pease, on Apr 21, in Wash, after a lingering illness.

Ltr from Mr Jacob B Varnum, dt'd Sandusky, Apr 9, 1812, to his fr Gen Varnum, Senator from Mass: regarding the murder by Indians of 2 batchelors-no names.

French shoes for sale. -John Laub, Gtwn.

Reward-$50 for runaway, Dennis, brown color. -Alfred Ewell, nr Dumfries, Va.

TUE APR 28, 1812
Congress in Senate: Petition of Thos Kelly of Phil, merchant, was owner of a brig, *Meteor*, captured by a British cruiser in Jun 1811 & condemned, praying relief.

Roger Griswold, esq, is re-elected Govn'r of Conn; at the election many Rpblcns have given their suffrage to Elijah Boardman, esq.

Va election: John Chapman Hunter & Alex'r Waugh, esqrs, Rpblcns, elected in Fairfax Co over Thos Blackburn & Haywood Foot, esqs, Fed Candidates.

John Gaither, having remv'd from Alexandria to Wash, has opened a shop nr the Center Mkt with a variety of silver ware, plated ware & jewellery.

Died: Wm Winchester, esq, age 62 yrs, in Balt, Apr 24th.

THU APR 30, 1812
Mrd: recently, Mr Wm E Williams to Miss Susan Cooke, d/o Wm Cooke, esq, in Balt, by Rev Dr Bend.

Hse of Reps: 1-Treas Dept is to allow to Wm Hubbell, collector of the excise tax, the sum of $1082.51 1/2, as credit against judgements obtained by the U S, against him. Approved-Jas Madison 2-Enacted that the heirs of Jos Harrison, late of Detroit, dec'd, be permitted to enter their claim to land in the District of Detroit. Approved-Jas Madison 3-Enacted that the following persons, claiming lands under Relief of Refugees from Canada & Nova Scotia, be entitled to quantities of land: 960 acs: Charlotte Hazen, wid/o Moses Hazen; Chloe Shannon, w/o Jas Noble Shannon & relict of Obediah Ayer, dec'd; heirs of Elijah Ayer & heirs of Israel Ruland. 320 acs: to:Elijah Ayer jr & heirs of Anthony Buck. 2240 acs: to heirs of Jas Boyd, 960 acs: to heirs of Nath'l Reynolds, heirs of Edw Antill & Joshua Sprague, 640 acs; to: Robt Sharp, John Fulton & John Morrison. 320 acs: to:Jas Sprague, David Dickey, John Taylor & heirs of Gilberts Seamans, dec'd, -Approved-Jas Madison.

Mrd: Rich'd Debutts, esq, eldest s/o Sam'l Debutts, M D of Mt Welby, PG Co, Md, to Miss Louisa F Dulany, d/o Benj Dulany, esq; on Apr 25, at *Shuter's Hill*, Fairfax Co, Va by Rev Dr Muir.

Died: Mr Elisha Winters, from Orleans Terr, on Apr 26, in Wash City, after a short illness; ab't 24 yrs since he left N Y City & settled in the western country; leaves a numerous family of chldrn & grchldrn.

Sale by auction-at hse lately occupied by Toppan Webster, oppo the Six bldgs; furn & Bks. -Toppan Webster. Forrest & Beale, aucts. Wash.

I am directed by the Cmder-in-Chief of the Militia of the State of Md, to require the ofcrs commanding rgts & extra battalions, to enroll all able bodied free white male ctzns from 18 to 45. -John Gassaway, Adj Gen.

An Act for the relief of Aaron Greeley; allow him $3 per mile for ea boundary line made in Dist of Detroit. -Approved, Jas Madison.

SAT MAY 2, 1812
John Fisher, esq, appt'd Judge of the Dist Crt of Dist of Dela, vice Gunning Bedford, esq, dec'd.

Ltr by Sam Brown, Lt in Col Arnold's Detachment to Quebec in 1775-dt'd-St Clairsville, Ohio, Apr 10, 1812. A short account of how Col Arnold got thro the wilderness to Quebec from Cambridge in 1775: we had 14 companies & upwards of 60 men in ea company, Rank & File-Col Arnold, Col Green, Col Enos, Maj Bigelow, Maj Meigs, Capts Morgan, Smith, Hendrick, Hanchet, Hubbard & Williams, Goodridge, Dearborn, Scott & McCobb, Thyer, Topham, Ward & Cobourne. [S Brown was a prisoner from Dec 31, 1775 until Aug 11 when we were sent to N Y on parole & were exchanged on the last of Jan 1777].

TUE MAY 5, 1812
Belmont Repository: Mich'l Baird or Baer, who lately lived nr Little York, Pa, was of German extraction; his fr left him a farm of 500 acs nr York. He kept a tavern for a number of yrs; mrd a wife & raised 4 chldrn. He amassed an estate worth $400,000; & died by hanging himself.

Revvard-$10 for runaway Stepney, mulatto man, age ab't 22 yrs. -Edw Ford, Fairfax Co, Va.

Mrd: Bernard Smith, esq, of New Brunswick, N J, to Miss Priscilla H Allein, d/o the late Wm Allein, esq, of Md; in Wash on Apr 26, at Dr Blake's, by the Rev Mr McCormick.

Died: Col Chas Mynn Thruston, age 74 yrs, Apr 21 at his seat nr New Orleans; ntv of Va having finished his education at Wm & Mary College; sailed for Eng in 1765 where he was ordained a Minister of the Episc Chr; returned to his ntv country; in 1777 he rec'd a severe wound in an engagement with the British troops nr the Brunswick Bridge in N J. Leaves a numerous & respectable family to regret his loss-among whom is Judge Thruston of Wash City.

Batavia, N Y. Apr 18. We stop the press to announce the intelligence of an armed British & Indian force on the Canada side of the Niagara Rvr; messrs Porter & Barton advised to remove their families.

Notice-all persons who have any business to transact with him, to call at Maj Hopkins' at *Greenleaf's Point*, before the 10th inst, on which day he will leave the city. -Jas Greenleaf, Wash City, May 4.

THU MAY 7, 1812
Hse of Reps: 1-Petition of Henry B & Chas Curtis, merchants of Boston; on Mar 23d last their brig *Adventure* was illegally captured & destroyed by Commander of a French ship of war-praying for relief -referred. 2-Petition of Jonathan Land, of Mass, his Vessel *Rover* was seized & condemned in Charleston, S C, for violation of importing slaves into the U S, praying restoration of said vessel.

Sheep Shearing-Arlington; Apr 30th; Mr Custis presided supported by Judge Cranch, Gov Lee, J C Herbert & Wm Herbert. Judges: Thos Sim Lee of Needwood, Md; John Tayloe of Mt Airy; Geo Graham of Lexington, Va; Jacob Morgan of Alex, D C. Rams displayed were property of: L Lewis of Woodlawn, Va; Geo Mason of Gunston, Va; Thos Peter of Tudor Place, D C; Wm A Dangerfield of Notley Hall, Md. Mrs Ann Lowden, Pr Wm Co, Va rec'd the prize.

London Paper; John Horne Tooke is no more; Tories have hated Mr Tooke since 1775; he was imprisoned as a libeler of his Majesty's Government.

Dragoon Head Quarters-Wash City. Cavalry inspection orders. Wm B Randolph, Q M S, acting as Adj of the Columbian horse.

Balt, May 5. A French cruiser captured the ship, *Congress*, of this port, bound to London & owned by Maj Biays.

Land for sale in PG Co, Md; nr Mr Philips' Mill, 300 acs with dwlg hse. Mr Mordecai Henerick lives on the premises. -G B Bitouzey.

For rent-a few convenient rms. -David Hopkins, *Greenleaf's Point*.

Louisville, Apr 17. Mr Hinton, who lived below Valloni, cld the *French Store* on Driftwood, fork of White Rvr, I. T; went on Apr 7th after his horses; not returning as expected, his bro & bro-in-law went in quest of him; his body was found lying in the rvr, he had been shot, scalped & stript. 2 young men by the name of Rogers were missing but returned. Col Bartholomew & company of 40 men have gone from Charleston; Maj or Capt Beck & his Co from Harrison Co, out to Driftwood. Col Robertson, [successor of Col Bartholomew rsgn'd,] rec'd orders to hold the militia in readiness. Maj Brown will leave Charleston on Mon next for Fort Knox; he has accepted a Lieutenancy in Capt Broker's Co of Rangers, who are to range from Ft Knox to Ft Harrison.

Public sale-deed from Levi White to me; lot of ground in Wash City in sq 797, with brick hse & a frame hse. -Sam Fitzhugh.

SAT MAY 9, 1812
Notice-committed to Frederick Co, Md, jail; Harry Dudley, negro, age ab't 28 yrs; says he belongs to the widow Ann Carter, nr Winchester, Va. -Ezra Mantz, shrf of Fred Co, Md.

Canandaigua, N Y-Apr 28. Maj J R Mullany, U S Army, arrv'd here on Wed last to superintend the recruiting svc in this District.

Hse of Reps: Bill for relief of Eli Whitney was twice read & committed.

Died: Blaize Cenas, esq, late shrf of the city & parish of New Orleans, on Mar 25th last, at New Orleans.

Hse for rent on Capitol Hill from Jun 22d next. -Edm Law.

Lancaster, May 1. Capt J Gibson has raised in this borough & neighborhood, one of the finest companies of recruits that we have seen for many yrs.

Carlisle, Pa, Apr 29. Capt Dan'l Hughes of the 1st Rgt U S infty marched from this place with 50 men.

Reward-$20 for Harry, negro man; ranaway from Mr J Mattingly to whom he was hired; could be nr Benedict, Chas Co, Md, where he was raised. -Jane G Cooke, Chaptico, St Mary's Co, Md.

TUE MAY 12, 1812
Orphans Crt of Wash Co, D C. Prsn'l est of Edmund Scannell, late of said city, dec'd. -Benj Bryan, adm d b n of E Scannell.

Died: Miss Eliz Smith, d/o Gen Sam'l Smith of Balt, on May 10th.

Jas M Varnum, esq, appt'd a Magistrate in Wash City.

Philip Barton Key, esq, declining re-election to Congress; A C Hanson, editor at Balt-the Fed Rpblcn Newspaper, is candidate to succeed him; also Wm Carroll, esq, Federalist, for some yrs a rep from his ntv Montg Co, Md.

Millinery. Mrs M Sweeny is at her old stand in F St, Wash City.

Chas Co, Md; Henry Anderson of said co, insolvent debtor. -John Barnes, clk.

St Mary's Co Crt, Md-Mar Term, 1812. Sam'l Strong & John Bransel, of said co; insolvent debtors. -Jo Harris, clk, St M Co Crt.

THU MAY 14, 1812

Mrd: recently, Dr Geo A Carroll, of Wash, to Miss Clarissa Mitchell, d/o Rich'd Mitchell, at the seat of said Rich'd Mitchell, esq, in Chas Co, Md. [no date]

Died: Jos Carlton, esq, on May 11th in Gtwn; by birth an English-man, but many yrs a resid of the U S; ofcr in the army during the Revolution.

Chillicothe, Ohio, May 2. Capt Wm Keys' Co of volunteers left this place for Dayton on Apr 27th to receive their arms & ammunition. Volunteers from Maj Dawson's Battalion, passed thro this town on the same day.

Dayton, Ohio, Apr 23. Capt Perry's Co of Rangers have rec'd orders to march immediately to Ft Lorimie.

Wash election for Aldermen & Common Cncl.
Superintending: Jas Briscoe, Jas Hoban, Jos Stretch
Ward 1: Jas H Blake, Phineas Bradley, Geo Way
Ward 2: Dan'l Rapine, Geo Blagden, Henry Ingle
Ward 3: Sam'l N Smallwood, Buller Cocker, Electius Middlton,
Ward 4: Robt Brent, Mayor.

Notice-Maj David Hopkins & Mr Nath'l P Bixby & none others, have authority to act in my name in what regards the small factory & factory store. -Jas Greenleaf, Wash.

Ltr from Geo W Erving, Spec Mnstr of the U S at Copenhagen, to Jonathan Russell, charge D'affaires of U S at Paris, dt'd Copenhagen, Aug 9, 1811. Brig *Hero*, H Blackler, Mstr of Marblehead, owned by Wm Blacker & sons, bound from Marblehead to St Petersburg. Brig *Radius*, B Lander, Mstr of Boston, owned by W Gray, from Newport, bound to St Petersburg. The two vessels arrv'd at Elsineur on Aug 6th. Aug 7th they were captured by a French privateer.

Hse of Reps: memorial of Thos Sheppard & others of Balt City; they were owners of a vessel which left Balt for Spain in 1809; in distress she put into Bordeaux in France where the vessel & cargo of tobacco was sequestered; later she was given up to the owners & again sailed for Balt; few days out she was captured by an Eng ship of war & carried into Eng & there condemned; praying relief.

Wanted-journeymen taylors. -Benj Burns, Capitol Hill, Wash City.

Chas Co Crt, Md. John Woods, of said co, insolvent debtor. -John Barnes, clk.

SAT MAY 16, 1812
Public sale-High Crt of Chancery. Land in St Mary's Co, Md, cld *Webet*, 62 acs, whereon Miss Sarah A Neale now resides. -Willy G Neale, trustee.

Reward-$20 for 2 negro women, Suck & Betsey; they left my plantation in Chas Co, Md. Heard they were employed by Mr Carberry of the Navy Yd. -Ed H Pye.

Hse of Reps-Petition of Jos Smith, of Alexandria, D C, merchant, praying relief for loss of tobacco shipped by him to Denmark that has been totally lost -referred.

Phil City-meeting of Democratic Ctzns on May 9, 1812, at hse of Jacob Zeilin, to consider public affairs; Thos Leiper, chrmn & John Geyer, sec.

John Langdon of N H & Elbridge Gerry of Mass are 2 gentlemen of whom we have heard the most said as successor to Clinton for V Pres.

Partnership bet Sam'l C Dorman & Edmd Rice, boot & shoe mkrs, was dissolved this day.

Wash Co, D C. Theophilus Hughes, insolvent debtor, confined in Wash Co prison for debt. -Wm Brent, clk.

Chas Co Crt, Md-Mar Term, 1812. Eliz Woods of Chas Co, insolvent debtor. -John Barnes, clk.

TUE MAY 19, 1812
Wash City, May 18. 82 mbrs of Cong convened to vote for V Pres-John Langdon rec'd 64 votes; Elbridge Gerry rec'd 16 votes; scattering-2 votes.

Mr Ekana Cobb, an ingenious sldr of the U S Army, is the inventor & patantee of a new mode of making blankets by the aid of machinery.

Mrd: John Thompson, esq, late a Rep in Cong from N Y, to Mrs Eleanor Curran, of Gtwn, D C, on May 16th.

Died: Mrs Gwynn Esenbeck, formerly of N J, in Wash City on May 9th.

Wash Bridge Stock for sale-enquire of Sam'l Eliott jr at the Bank of Wash.

Cincinnati, May 6-Express from Dayton. Gen McArthur has arrived there with svr'l cos of volunteers. Govn'r Meigs left here for Dayton yesterday-detachments under Genr'ls Gano & Cass will march for the same place tomorrow.

Circleville, Ohio, May 2. On Mon last, Capt B Fryatt, with a company of ab't 60 vols, left this county for the place of rendezvous, thence to Detroit.

Steubenville, Ohio, Apr 22. Indians killed 2 white men on Apr 3, Mr Giles & Mr Bissel who lived bet Pipe Creek & Sandusky Bay. The Indians were 3 in number of which one was captured & lodged in Cleaveland jail; trial is to day.

Public sale-the reversionary est in fee simple of 2/3rds of a tract of land in Fairfax Co, Va, now in the occupation of Mrs Mary Ferguson; adj the lands of Jas Sangster; ab't 140 acs; subject to the life est of Mrs Ferguson. -Thos R Ford.

THU MAY 21, 1812

Chas Co Crt, Mar Term, 1812. Joshua Mudd jr, of Chas Co, Md; insolvent debtor. -John Barnes, clk

Deserted-on May 19th, Geo Custis, Pvt in U S Rgt of Light artl, age 21 yrs, ab't 5ft 7, black eyes, black hair, dark complexion, by trade a laborer. Reward-$10. G W Hight, Lt of Light artil. He may have taken the stage to Balt.

Sat, May 16, 1812. Meeting of the mbrs of the Union Fire Co, viz: Jas Hoban-*Pres*; Andrew Way jr-*VP*; E McDaniel-*Treas*; Jas Kearney-*Sec;* Peter Lenox, S Stettinius, Henry Herford, C W Stephenson & C McLane-*engineers*; Jno Pelz, Z Farrell, Thos Wannel, Alex'r Smith, Walter Clarke, N Callan-*horsemen*; Wash Boyd, J M Varnum, T Carpenter, Geo Sweeny, Chas Glover, Andrew Coyle-*fire or lane men*; Thos H Gillis, David Ott, J Parsons, J Clarke, G C Grammar, Harvey Bestor-*Centinels*; Jas Ford, D Tweedy, John Frank, Geo Moore, Geo Cliver, Henry Smith, Jas Bennet, Ad Plate, Chas B Davis, Jonathan Appler-*laddermen*; Phineas Bradley, John McClelland, Benj Belt, Francis Coyle, S Bacon, E Travers, J Harbaugh, P Vallett, Chas Varden, Jas Moore, P Jas Moore, B & Wm McGee-*furniture-men*. [Wash, D C]

Congress in Senate-Bill for relief of Anna Young, heiress & rep of Col John Durkee, was read a second time & referred to Messrs Goodrich, Horsey & Tait.

Apr 29th. Fifty men, a part of Capt Colin Buckner's Co from Lynchburg, Va, arrv'd at Fredericktown under the Command of Lt John Jameson.

Died: Mrs Mary Bowie, relict of the late Walter Bowie, esq; age 65 yrs, at her seat in PG Co, Md, on May 16.

Potomac Co-meeting at Alexandria May 13th; Mr Jos Brewer was appt'd Treas to said co in place of Mr Jos Carlton, dec'd. -Gtwn, May 19.

SAT MAY 23, 1812

Balt, Md-Democratic meeting; Jos Nicholson, chrmn & Edw Johnson, Sec; regarding the great crisis.

Pa-Genrl orders: This day I have appt'd Nath'l B Boileau, John B Gibson, Wilson Smith & John Binns as my Aids-De-Camp, with the rank of Lt-Cols. -Simon Snyder, Harrisburgh, May 11, 1812.

Easton, Pa, May 16. Northampton patriotism-the Easton Light Infantry Co commanded by Capt Nungesser, 40 in complete uniform, have offered their svcs. A troop of Cavalry commanded by Capt Jarrett consisting of 50 also tendered their svc. A new company of riflemen commanded by Capt Gross, upwards of sixty, likewise; they are attached to the 71st Regt.

Johnston, N Y-May 12. Lt Page has recruited 20 men for the U S svc.

Died: on May 20, Capt Henry Washington of Alexandria, age 49 yrs.

Mrd: on May 21, Mr Wm P Bryan, s/o Guy Bryan, of Phil, to Mrs Maria H Swan, of Wash, by Rev Mr Laurie.

Mrd: Mr John P Dulany to Miss Mary Ann Debutts, on May 18th, at *Mt Welby*, the seat of Dr Debutts, in PG Co, Md, by Rev Mr Ralph.

Died: on May 21, Nicholas King, esq, city surveyor, age 41 yrs, suddenly in Wash; ntv of Eng but resided in this country since 1793; leaves a widow & 4 chldrn.

Hse of Reps: Bill authorising purchase of Winslow Lewis, his patent-right for a new mode of lighting light-hses; amended & $60,000 appropriated-agreed to & a third reading was ordered.

New York-May 14. The company commanded by Capt John M Bradhurst, of the 3d Regt of N Y artillery, was ordered to parade for the purpose of drafting 11 men; the men were told the object of the parade; informing them that vols wld be accepted in lieu of drafted men. The company of nrly 50 men unanimously volunteered their svcs to the Pres of the U S unconditionally.

Post Ofc changes in Apr 1812.
Chester, N J-Rich'd Hunt, vice John D Gardiner, rsgn'd;
Hebron, N H-Stephen Goodhue, vice Wm Gale, do;
Rutherfordton, N C-Geo Walton, vice Tench Coxe jr, do;
Newbern, N C-Thos Watson, vice Green Bryan, dec'd;
Huntington So, N Y-Selah S Carll, vice B K Hobart, rsgn'd;
Mendham, N J-Stephen Dod, vice Dan'l Dod, do;
Paint Lick, Ky-John Snoddy jr, vice Wm Miller, do;
Landisburgh, Pa-John Lightner, vice Wm Wilson, do;
Whiting, Vt-Cyrus Carpenter, vice Amos E Walker, situation inconv;
Westmoreland, N H-Edmund Brewster, vice John Brown, rsgn'd;
Pitch Landing N C-Starkey H Harrell, vice John Cooper, rsgn'd;
Richmond C H, N C-Peter H Cole, vice A McNeill, do;
Pine Grove Mills, Pa-Stephen Davis, vice David Nicholson, do;
U S Saline, Ind Terr-Jas Ratcliff, vice L White, do;

Manchester, Md-John Keefer, vice Sam'l Peters, do;
Warehse Point, Ct-Noah Smith, vice C Reynolds, do;
Ashbury, N J-Johnson Dunham, vice H Hankinson, do;
Sullivan, N Y-David Beecher, vice Solomon Beebe, do;
Painsville, O-Sam'l W Phelps, vice F Paine, do;
Bowling Green, Ky-Alex'r S Sharp, vice David H Robinson, do;
Abbeville C H, S C-Jas Taggart, vice Moses Taggart, do;
Pulaski C H, Ky-E B Porter, vice Wm J Sallee, do;
Charlotte Village, N Y-Frederick Bushnell, vice J Child, do;
Bath, N C-Tobias Butler, vice T Alderson, dec'd;
Cherry Valley, N J-Jabez Hammond, vice John Walton, rsgn'd;
Tappahanneck, Va-T Brockenbrough, vice Lawrence Muse, do.
New Ofcs est'd in Apr 1812 & postmaster:
Lehighton, Northampton Co, Pa-John Pryor, Postmstr;
Pattons, Augusta Co, Va-Mich'l Monzey;
Middlefield, Hampshire Co, Mas-Edmund Kelso;
Tuscarara Valley, Miflin Co, Pa-Jas Montgomery;
Otter Bridge, Bedford Co, Va-Edmund Read;
Mill Creek, Cavahoga Co, O-Eramus Mills;
Chickesawhay, Miss Terr-Josiah Skinner;
Indian Fields, Colleton Dist, S C-John Carr;
Smithfield, Providence Co, R I-Marcus Arnold;
Mechanickeburg, Cumberland Co, Pa-Jos Jones;
Augusta, Sussex Co, N J-Tho P Gustin;
Somerset Forge, Somerset Co, Pa-Peter Kimmell;
Wheat Plains, Wayne Co, Pa-G W Nyce;
Brick Chr, King & Queen Co, [no state]-D P Courtney.
Post ofcs discontinued: Ramsey's Mills, N C & Broaddus' Mills, Va.

Mrd: Casper Willis Wever, esq, of Jefferson Co, Va, late of this city, to Miss Cath Dunlop, eldest d/o Andrew Dunlop, esq, at Chambersburg, Pa, on Feb 13, by Rev Mr Denny.

Mrd: Mr Jas Kelly of Wilmington, Delaware, to Miss Mgt Watson of Wash, on Feb 15, by Rev Mr McCormick.

Hse of Reps: Petition of Jacob Snell, of Montg Co, N Y; his fr & only bro, under command of the late Genr'l Herkimer, at Oriskana, were both slain by British Tories & Indians, leaving their only son & bro a minor; on Oct 19, 1780 under the command of Col Brown, Jacob Snell rec'd a wound by a musket ball which lodged nr the shoulder blade; all his bldgs were consumed by fire by the British & their savage allies; his application soon after the close of the war to the Leg of N Y State was lost; prays Congress for a pension.

Mrd: Dr Geo Boarman, of Wash, to Miss L Dyer, of PG Co, Md, on Feb 10, by Rev Mr Young.

Died: Lt Lee Massey, of U S N, on Feb 7, at Norfolk; drowned when he fell into the river-having taken a false step from the bridge he was crossing.

Died: Brig Gen Mich'l Bright, sldr of the Rev & for some time past inspec of flour for the port of Phil; on Feb 9th, age 51 yrs, at Phil.

Died: Hon Wm Balfour, age 53 yrs, in Frederickton, New Brunswick; Maj-Genr'l on the staff of the army in British American, lately Pres of cncl & Cmder in Chief of the province of New Brunswick. -Montreal Gaz.

TUE MAY 26, 1812
Negroes wanted; also a blacksmith. -C Philips, at Weeping Willow Tavern, F St.

Horse, lost or stolen; brought by Mr Chester Bailey about 6 wks ago from Phil. Give the printer information on same.

Columbian Agric Soc: Fifth Semi-annual exhibit held in Woodland belonging to Thos Beall, esq, of Geo of this place. Judges of sheep: Hon Jos Kent, Hon John Taliaferro, Hon Thos Worthington, Clement Brooke & John Threlkeld, esqrs. Judges of manufactures: John Davidson, John Cox, Thos C Wright, Wm G Ridgeley & Wm Stewart, esqrs. Judges of ploughs: Isaac Pierce, Emmor Bailey, John Neeld, David Frame & Jos Canby, esqrs. Premiums awarded to: Genr'l John Mason of Annalostan Island, D C; Edw Lloyd of Wye, Talbot Co, late Gov of Md; Geo Calvert of PG Co, Md; Wm Marbury of Gtwn, D C; Mrs Martha P Graham, of Dumfries, Va; Mrs Sarah McCarty Mason of Hollin Hall, Fairfax Co, Va; Mrs Mary Anderson of Montgomery C Hse, Md; Mrs C Kimbol of Fredericktown, Md; Mrs Mgt Knode of Wash Co, Md; Mrs Maria Louisa Nourse, of Gtwn, D C; Mrs Neeld of Montg, Md; Wm Thornton of Montg Co, Md; Jas Brown of Montg Co, Md; Solomon Cassidy of Alexandria, D C. Other competitors: Roger Brooke, Basil Brooke, Lawrence Lewis, P G Key, Thos Peter & Bernard Gilpin. -David Wiley, sec.

The late Capt Lewis-particulars extracted from a ltr from American orniornithologist, Alex'r Wilson: I rode to Mr Grinder's where Lewis perished; Mrs Grinder told me of the event; this hse is 72 miles from Nashville; Govn'r Lewis arrv'd & asked to spend the night; he called for some spirits & drank a little; his 2 svts arrv'd; he ate supper; smoked his pipe; Mrs Grinder went to bed & after svr'l hrs heard 2 pistol shots; Lewis said, o madam! give me some water, & heal my wounds. Mrs G cld for the 2 svts & Lewis showed them where the bullet had entered; a piece of his forehead was blown off; he begged the svt to take his rifle & blow out his brains-he wld give them all the money in his trunk; he expired in ab't 2 hrs & was buried close by the common path. Mr G was not home.

Balt, Md, May 21-Genrl meeting of the committee of Democratic Delegates: Jos H Nicholson, chrmn & John Montgomery, sec.

Mbrs: A R Levering	David Fulton	Chas Bohn
Wm B Barney	John Montgomery	Wm Camp
Christopher Hughes jr	Benj Berry	Nathan Levering

J Wm McCulloh	John S Hollins	Jos Jamison
Jas Hutton	J A Buchanan	Lemuel Taylor
Luke Tiernan	Wm Wilson	J L Donaldson
L Hollingsworth	Jas Martin	Jas Wilson
T J Brown	Rich'd Mackall	Edw Johnson
Geo Stities	Jas Williams	Wm McDonald
Peter Diffenderffer	A Brisco	E G Woodyear
Hezekiah Niles	Jas Armstrong	Jos Smith
Dan'l Conn	John Kelso	Hezekiah Price
Geo Milleman	Jas C Dew	W Pechio
Jas Biays	David Burk	Geo Warner
Thornkike Chase	Timothy Gardner	Thos Shepperd
N F Williams	J H McCulloch	Christian Baum
Theodorick Bland		

Col Cuthbert has been dispatched to the fortress of St Augustine, to negotiate with the Commandant. -Savannah, May 14.

Died: Miss Mary Duckett, eldest d/o Isaac Duckett, esq, of PG Co, Md, on May 22, age 17 yrs; of pulmonary consumption.

Phil, Pa-May 20th. Meeting of the 1st Cong Dist of Pa; Wm Jones, chrmn & Jas West, sec. Committee: Robt Patterson, John Binns, Chas J Ingersoll, Jas Carson, John L Leib, Wm Duncan, Wm West, Frederick Hoeckly, A Hargesheimer, Robt McMullen, Jacob Holgate, T D Anderson, Jacob Richards & G G Leiper.

Election-Sam'l N Smallwood & Electius Middleton nominated Commissioners of elections are not residents of the 4th Ward, I do therefore appoint Jos Cassin & John Laws of Abel, to act as Judges, together with Mr Cocke. -Brent.

Millwrights wanted-apply to John Wark jr, nr Barry's wharf.

THU MAY 28, 1812
<u>New Army</u>-<u>Maj-Genr'ls:</u> Henry Dearborn & Thos Pinckney.
<u>Brig-Genr'ls</u>: Jos Bloomfield, Jas Winchester, Wm Polk & Wm Hull.
<u>Qrtr-Mstr-Genr'l</u>: Morgan Lewis.
<u>Deputy Qrtr-Mstr</u>: Bartholomew Shaumburg
<u>Hosp Surgs:</u> Garret E Pendergrast, David C Kerr & Jas Mann.
<u>Artl, 2d Rgt</u>: Col-Geo Izard; <u>Majs</u>: Geo C Mitchell & Wm Lindsay; <u>Surg</u>: Jacob De Lamotte; <u>Surg's Mate:</u> Wm Southall

<u>Capts</u>: Jesse Robinson	John Goodall	Jacob B I'On
Geo W Russell	Robt M Gill	Spottswood Henry
Isaac T Avery	Jos Sandford	Philemon Hawkins jr
Nathan Towson	Sam'l B Archer	Chs M Anderson
John Ritchie	Jos Phillips	
<u>1st Lts:</u>		
Henry Slaughter	Harold Smyth	Lowndes Brown
Thos M Randolph, jr	Adrian Niel	Jas G McDowell

Wm J Cowan / John Nevill / Peter Parsons
Robt R Ruffin / Henry K Craig / Jas H Deering
Jos H Larwell / John S Peyton / John Fontaine
Jonathan Kearsley

2d Lts:
Montg Newman / Jos Hook / Wm Tyler
Thos Winn / Robt Stewart / John W Kincaid
Jacob Warley / Lewis Morgan / Alex'r A Meek
Edwin Sharpe / Isaac Davis, jr / John Ruffin
Jas H Gamble

Third Artl. Surg's mates: Jos Eaton & German Senter

Capts:
Jas McKeon / Benj S Ogden / John W Gookin
John M Connelly / Alex'r S Brooks / Ichabod B Crane
Horace H Watson John Davis / Jas Elliot
Wm Van Deursen, jr

First Lts:
John M O'Conner / John W Green / Benj K Pierce
Moses J Chase / Jas Green, jr / Peter Pifer
Geo H Richards / Jeremiah L Tracy / Wm Card
Sam'l Weston / Luther Scott / John Farley
Barent Van Der Poel / Alex'r C W Fanning / Sam'l M Dewy
Silvester Churchill / Rich'd M Bailey / Benj Brearley
Wm De Peyster

2d Lieutenants:
Wm Shannon / Wm Henry / Chester Root
Greenleaf Dearborn / Wm R Duncan / Wm King
John P Bartlett / Thos C Legate / Henry A Torney
John Mountfort / Dan'l Smalley / Adam A Gray
Matthew Jenkins / Philip D Spencer / Jos H Rees

Cavalry, 2d Regt:
Col: Jas Burn / Maj: John T Woodford
Surg's Mate: Lewis M Bailey

Captains:
John Butler / Sam'l D Harris / Henry Hall
Sam'l G Hopkins / John R Stokes / Jas V Ball
Jos Selden / Stephen R Proctor / Chas Smith
Jonas Holland / John A Burd

First-Lieutenants:
Abel Wheelock / Archibald H Snead / Jas Hedges
John Nicholas, jr / Walter German / Gabriel Barbour
Benj Pratt / John D Hart / Beverly Turpin
Chas J Nourse

2d-Lieutenants:
Ira Williams / Benj Smith / David Evans
Thos S Johnston / Edw Conway / Fayette Roane
Walter Coles

Cornets:
Andrew McFarland   Harman Hays   Jas Martin
Jas Trippe   Armstrong McKinney   Benj Wilds

Infantry, 8th Regt:
Lt Cols: Wm P Anderson & Patrick Jack
Majors: Edmund P Gaines & Mossman Houston
Surg's mates: Wm Meriweather & Carlisle Humphries

Captains:
Jas M Anderson   Jas H Campbell   John A Rodgers
Robert Desha   Robt Butler   Alex'r Gray
Francis Armstrong   John Ballinger   Felix B Warley
Andrew H Holmes   Chas Crawford   Philip Cook
Wm Jones   David E Twiggs   Wm Chisholm
Wm O Allen   John T Chunn

1st-Lieutenants:
Otis Dyer   Tilden Taylor   Hamlin Cook
Obadiah Crawford   Isaac Walton   Hughes Walton
Don Carolus Dixon   Mich'l M Toomy   John M Smith
Wm Scott   Wm O Winston   Robt M Evans
Minor Sturges   Roswell P Johnston   Silas Stephens

2d-Lieutenants:
Beverly Martin   Jas Wilde   John Malony
Sam'l Scott   Uriah Allison   Jos D Smith
Jos Anthony   Robt Bentin   Wm Willis
Moses A Roberts   Thos C Porter   Julian Tortin
Avery Clark   Henry Rauchner   Taliaferro Richards

Ensigns:
Robt Caller, jr   Sam'l Coleman   C B Farott
Peter Lequex   Adam Peck, jr   Thos W Legge
Littleton Johnson   Jos Harrison   Jas Colson
Anthony W Putney

Ninth infantry.
Colonel Simeon Larned   Lt Cols: John L Tuttle & Eleazer W Ripley
Majors: Thos Aspinwall & Sam'l S Conner
Surg: Jos Lovell   Surg's mates: Jas H Bradford & Dan'l Cook

Captains
Seth Banister, jr   Benj Ropes   Eliha Jones
Jos Bucklin   Chester Lyman   Jos Treat
John Nye   Dan'l Libbey, jr   Chas Proctor
Jeremiah Chapman   Lemuel Bradford   Josiah H Vose
Chas E Tobey   Jos Grafton   Philip White
Ebenezer Thompson   Turner Crooker   Moses Hoit

First-Lieutenants:
Ebenezer Stuart   Dan'l Sheaver   Morrill Marston
Jonas Monroe   Ebenezer B Morse   Wm S Moore
Edmund Foster   Ebenezer White   Geo Bender
Lawson Kingsbury   Jas F Norris   Jared Ingersol
Jon h Perley   Wm Warren   Sullivan Burband

John Read, jr.　　　　　Jos Fuller
Second-Lieutenants:
Ebenezer Childs　　　　Ira Drew　　　　　　Shelton Felton
Thos Sturtivant　　　　　Stephen Turner　　　Azor Orme
Wm L Foster　　　　　　Lotan Smith　　　　　John Dawner
Peter Pelham　　　　　　Loring Palmer　　　　Edw White
David Perry　　　　　　Wm Bowman　　　　　John Fowle
Perez Loring　　　　　　Aaron Lewis　　　　　Sam'l L Allen
Henry Bender　　　　　　Thos Harrison
Ensigns:
Ebenezer Knox　　　　　Aaron Bigelow　　　　Francis Carr, jr
Geo Bender, jr　　　　　Elliot Claslin　　　　　Nath'l H Hall
Billings Otis　　　　　　Wm Brawning　　　　Dan'l Chandler
Edw Norton　　　　　　Otis Fisher　　　　　　Chas Foster
Jas Pratt　　　　　　　　Henry Wellington　　　Henry Draper
Lewis Norris　　　　　　Thos Bangs　　　　　　Wm Lyman
Henry Bates

Tenth infantry:
Colonel: Jas Wellborne
Lt Cols: Wm Drayton & Andrew Pickens, jr.
Majors: Laurence Manning & Wm Strother
Surg: Jas Norcum　　　Surg's Mate: Egbert H Bell
Captains:
Arthur Simpkins, jr.　　　Henry P Taylor　　　　Robt Cunningham
Matthew T Keith　　　　Thos W Farrar　　　　Geo Cloud
Jesse Copeland　　　　　Robt Mitchell　　　　　Jos Bryant
Philip Brittain　　　　　Oren Clinton　　　　　Thos J Robeson
Edw King　　　　　　　Mich'l I Kenan　　　　John Vail
Wm Taylor
First-Lieutenants:
Wm Winn　　　　　　　John W Farrow　　　　Thos C Hunter
Billups Gayle　　　　　Stephen Ford　　　　　Benj T Elmore
Geo Strother　　　　　　Wm Tisdale　　　　　　Chas Lutterloh
Alex'r King　　　　　　Hugh H Carson　　　　John Graham
Elias D Dick　　　　　　Jas Hamilton　　　　　Wm Ward
Montague G Wage　　　John McQueen　　　　Wm Rhodes
Wm Morris
Second-Lieutenants:
Robt Lamar　　　　　　Thos Reynolds　　　　John Watkins
Rich'd Thruston　　　　Jas A Black　　　　　　Sam'l B Carty
Wm N Miller　　　　　Edw Holliway　　　　　Hamilton Brown
Thos Barker　　　　　　Peter Summey　　　　　John Street
Emanuel S Hawkings　　Robt Mebane, jr.　　　Thos Molton
John Clinch　　　　　　Wm Bee　　　　　　　Arthur Fox
Ensigns:
John O Hara　　　　　　Alex'r Pagan　　　　　John Peebles
Thos Lane　　　　　　　John Miekle, jr　　　　Jas Roane
Anteony G Glynne　　　Robt Logan　　　　　　Wm Tyler

John Pritchard
John Devane
Rober Wynne

Anthony M Dickson
John S Todd
Yellis Mandeville

John Bird
John W Lawson

Eleventh infantry

Colonels: Isaac Clark   **Lt Cols:** Jonas Cutting & Moody Bedel
Majors: Timothy Dix, jr & Timothy Upham
Surg: Ephraim Brewster   **Surg's mates:** Jas Stark & Jacob B Moore

Captains:
Andrew McClary
Jonathan Stark
Geo Howard
Wm Walker
Jos Beeman
Chas Follet

Jos Griswold
John W Week
Peter Bradley
Sam'l Gordon
Sam'l H Holley

John McNeal, jr.
Seth Phelps
Festus Cone
Phineas Williams
Benj S Eggerton

First-Lieutenants:
John Bliss
Jonathan Eastman
John B Murdock
Valentine R Goodrich
Rufus Hatch

Rich'd Bean
Wm S Foster
Henry Dyer
Horace Hale
Ebenezer Grey

Sam'l Harper
Dan'l Henderson
Malachi Corning
Benj Smead
Elisha Ashley

Second-Lieutenants:
Jas Greene
Josiah Bartlet
Rufus Bucklin, jr.
Francis Cogswell of G

Ira Aldrich
Edw Gerald, jr
Wm S Heaton
Daniel Crawford

Jas Wells
Able Farewell
Walter Sheldon

Ensigns:
Jos Cilley
Newman S Clarke
Ephraim Shaylor
Jos Hutchinson
Thos Levake

Selah Bennet
John G Mann
Timothy Aldrich
Ezekiel Jewet
John V Barron

Fred A Sawyer
John Duncan
Jas C Tracy
Sam'l B Ladd

Twelfth infantry:

Colonel: Thos Parker   **Lt Cols:** Archibald F M'Niel & Jas P Preston
Majors: Thos Taylor & Isaac A Coles
Surg: Jas C Bronaugh   **Surg's mates:** Horace Wellford & Jos Berry

Captains:
Jas Gibson
Jas Charlton
Henry Branch
Robt C Nicholas
Emanuel I Leigh
Hodijah Meade

Thos M Nelson
Thos P Moore
Jas Paxton
Andrew L Madison
Willoughby Morgan
Archibald C Randolph

Lewis L Taylor
Chas Page
Rich'd Pollard
Josiah Woods
Mark Harden

First-Lieutenants:
Lewis B Willis
Spencer Hinton
John G Camp
Mathew M Payne
Angus McDonald

Wm Bailey
Thos Harris
Zackwell Morgan
Wm A Shelton
Rich'd P Fletcher

Chas Gee
Geo Vashon
Robt G Hite
Clement White
John P Duval

Abner S Lewis   Wm A Blount
Second-Lieutenants:
Dan'l Linn   Thos Howson   John Key, jr.
Jos G Wall   Geo Hatchet   John Kenney
Sam'l Hairstone, jr.   Wm Ligon   John A Howard
Thos Monroe   Robt Houston   Matthew Hughes
John Archer   John Towles   Geo Wyche
Rich'd Plummer   Thos C Wilwright   Geo Evans
Otho W Callis
Ensigns:
Jos Pettypool   Thos Grady   John Garret
Burwell Goodwyn   Jonathan Cox   Isaac Keyes
Jos Mcgavock, jr.   Sam'l Harris   Jos Shommo
Andrew Whitman   Baily Bruce   Wm H Godwin
Wm C Parker   Jas Glassell   Francis Jones
Edw B Randolph   Abner P Neale   Geo McLaughlin

Thirteenth infantry.
Colonel: Peter P Schuyler
Lt Cols: John Chrystie & Robt Le Roy Livingston
Majors: Jas R Mulany & Dan'l M Forney
Surg: Stephen D Beekman   Surg's Mate: John McCall
Captains:
Hugh R Martin   John Thompson   Willard Trull
Benj Tuckerman   Heman Finney   Joshua Weday
Thos Lyon   Peter Mills   Sam'l Campbell
John E Wool   Mindert M Dox
Abraham F Hull   Rich'd M Malcolm   Sam'l Youngs
Robt Helorig   Thos Delano   David Scott
John King   Henry Leaverworth   Rich Caldwell
First-Lieutenants:
John K Paige   Miles Greenwood   Jarvis K Pike
Wm Clarke   Jos Scoffield   Josiah Pamar
Benj D Pardee   John McCarty   Sam'l Colwell
Simon D Wattles   Azariah W Odell   Thos Donnelly
Ephraim F Gilbert   Geo G Phinney   Rich'd Goodale
Mich'l M Myers   Wessel Gansevocdt   Sam'l Chipman
John Campbell   Benj H Mooers
Second-Lieutenants:
Dan'l Huginin   Chandler W Drake   David Crofoot
Rololphus Simmons   Peter L Hogeboom   Dan'l B Wilcox
Rich'd H Root   Henry Whiting   Chas Stewart
Frederick Brown   Henry B Turner   Isaac Finch
Robt Crouse   Henry Stagg   Alfred Phelps
Hugh Robinson   John D Boon   Ira Wilcox
Rich'd M Harrison   Abijah Bennet   Jacob Sammons
John Brown, jr.   Waite Martin

Ensigns:

John Kirkby	Robt Morris	Geo Reab, jr.
Justus Ingersol	Sam'l R Hid	John Williams
Alphonso Whitmore	Zadock Morse	Jos H Dwight
Sam'l L Merchant	John Jones	Henry Male
Henry Dyoe	Wm C Enos	Ezra Post
Sam'l Tappan	Russel Eddy	John Gates, jr.
Ezra King	Rich'd Phillips	Levi S Burr

Fourteenth infantry:

Lt Col s: Wm H Winder & Chas G Boerstler
Majors: Jos Lee Smith & Robt M'Alla
Surg: Wm H Brown   **Surg's Mate**: Sam'l B Hugo

Captains:

Jas Brittain	Thos Montgomery	Robt W Kent
Kenneth McKenzie	Rich'd I Crabb	Sam'l Lane
Wm S Jett	Clement Sullivan	Byrd C Willis
Henry Grindage	Thos B Pottinger	Thos Sengster
John Macrae, jr	John Stannard	Wm McIlvain
Isaac D Barnard		

First Lieutenants:

Rich'd Arel	Thos Kearney	David Cummings
Peter Rich	Jos Marshall	Reuben Gilder
Jos S Nelson	Thos Gist	Jas McDonald
Benj Nicholson	Thos Post	Walter G Hays
Bernard Peyton	Thos Davis	John W Smith
John Caldwell, jr.	Jas McDowell	

Second Lieutenants

Jas Christie	Edw Wilson	John Becket
John B Sparks	John Waring	Thos Randal
Peter Magruder	Geo Murdoch	John Greene
John Martin	Russell Harison	Thos Blackwell
Benj Smith	Wm Stone	Wm Irvine
John M Thompson	Augustus M Shee	

Ensigns:

Jas H Gale	Rich'd Bennet	Wm G Saunders
Wm G Mills	Abraham Clark	Philip Wager
Kimmel Godwin	John B Hogan	Robt W Long
Thos H Saunders	Stephen T Donaldson	John Culbertson
Valentine P Lucket		

Fifteenth infantry:

Col: Dan'l Brown   **Lt Cols**: David Brearly & Benajah White
Majors: John V H Huych & Ephraim Whitlock
Surg: Fenn Denning   **Surg's mates**: Geo Mac Aray & Reuben T Baker

Captains:

Zachariah Rossell	Chas Carson	John Scott
Henry H Van Dalsem	Abraham Reynolds	Wm Battey
John L Hoppock	David Bartlet	John Sproul
Chas W Hunter	Peter Ogilvie, jr	White Youngs

Mordecai Myers
Henry B Armstrong

First Lieutenants
Jeremiah D Hayden
Jos L Barton
Aaron Sutphen
Stephen W Kearney
Robt Brett
John L Find
Patrick McDonough

Second Lieutenants:
Geo Henry
Rich'd Edsail, jr.
Philip C Whitehead
Archibald C Crary
Rich'd A Zantzinger

Ensigns:
Jacob Dickerson
Christopher Noyes
Jos Merry
Jas W Lent, jr
Jos Moore

Wm D Laurence
Geo G Steele

Wm Barnett
Jacob D Howell
Jeremiah Diman 3d
John Vallean
Abraham Per Lee
Israel Turner
Robt S Gardiner

Abraham Godwin, jr.
Sam'l McDougal
Benj Watson
David Curtis
Moses A Bloomfield

John Scott
Wm G Scott
Donald Frazer
Geo Keese

Moses Blackley
Wm Hodgers

John Hunt
Jas Piatt
Thos M Reed
Wm B Adams
Sam'l Haring
Geo McGlassin

David Riddle
Rich'd L Howell
John S Stake
Jos C Eldridge

Wm Coffie
Chas West
Jas W Sproat
Geo McChain

Sixteenth infantry:
Col: Cromwell Pierce   Lt Cols: Geo McFeely & Rich Dennis
Majors: Robt Carr & John McCluny
Surg: Sam'l Gilliland   Surg's Mate: Jones Davis

Captains:
Jacob Schener
Wash Lee
Wm Nicholas
Thos Biddle, jr.
Samson S Smith
Chas Kachlein
John Pentland

First Lieutenants:
Davis Espy
Jas Morrow
Jos Henderson
John Hazleton
Wm Morrow
Jas M Bailey
Thos M Church

Second Lieutenants:
Eli Thomas
Nathan McLaughlin
Jas McGee
Dominick Cornyn
Benj Byerly

Silas Amberson
Alexander McEwen
Henry Fleming
Robt Gray
Samson S King
Jacob Carmac

Terah Jones
Jonathan W Aitkin
Jas M Stewart
Willis Foulk
John Machesney
Sam'l Rutter
Frederick A Wise

Wm Sturges
Sam'l S Smith
John Cottrel
Geo W Ferguson
Thos N Powers

Dan'l McFarlin
David Millikin
Jas F McElroy
John H Bryson
Wm Mooney
Benj Foster

John Johnston
John Baldy
John Larkin
Thos Y Sprogel
Jas Huston
Archibald Kerr
Thos Lawrence

Thos Horwel
Adam King
Sam'l Weigly
Wm W Carr
Jacob Fetter

Francis D Cummins	Sam'l A Rippey	John Wise
David Blithe		

Ensigns:

John D Kehr	John Rham	Thos Wright
Frederick Messing	Robt R Maxwell	Jacob Whistler
John Canghran	John T David	Geo Metinger
Hugh May	John Armstrong	John R Guy
John Merrick		

Seventeenth infantry:
Col: Sam'l Wells   Lt Cols: Wm McMillan & John Miller
Majors: Geo Todd & Rich'd Davenport
Surg: Alexander Montgomery
Surgs' mates: Chas Marvin & Lyddal Wilkinson

Captains:

Geo Croghan	Wm Bradford	David Holt
Robt Edwards	Rich'd Hightower	Jas Duncan
Wm J Adair	Jas Meade	Jas Hunter
David C Irvine	Augustus L Langham	Robt Lucas
Wilson Elliot	Abraham Edwards	Jas Heron
Hugh Moore	Harris M Hickman	Chas Query

First Lieutenants:

John D Fleming	Benj Johnston	Robt Logan
Benj W Saunders	Alex'r Robertson	Stephen Lee
Thos C Graves	Thos J Overton	Sam'l Booker
Meredith W Fisher	Martin L Hawkins	Caleb H Holder
Lewis Howell	John Anderson	David Gwinne
Jas Campbell	Geo W Jackson	Henry Crittenden

Second Lieutenants:

Philip King	Thos Mountjoy	John T Redding
Parry Hawkins	Joshua Norvell	Ashton Garret
Jas Hackley, jr	Beverley Roy	Willis R Smith
Jonathan Rees	Henry Frederick	Philip P Price
Timothy E Danielson	Jos Watson	John Reeves
David Morris	Nimrod H Moore	Cyrus A Baylor

Ensigns:

John Whistler	John Milligan	Battle Harrison
Dan'l D Armstrong	Asher Phillips	John E Morgan
Philip S Sharer	Jas Legget	Jas Gray
Jos Duncan	Jas Mundy	Reuben Taylor
Thos S Morgan	Sam'l H Craig	Edmund Ship
Chas Mitchell	Thos Hawkins	

Ofcrs not arranged:
Col Lemnel Trescott & Lt Col John B Campbell [N B-the arrangement is only provisional & incomplete. Transfers will reduce the supernumeraries.]

Wm P Van Ness, appt'd by the Pres & Senate a District Judge of N Y State.

Lt Geo W Hight opened his recruiting rendezvous in Wash City a few wks ago.

Notice. Mr Stretch having declined acting as a Judge of election for the 1st Ward, Jos Bromley is appt'd; & Rich'd S Briscoe instead of Jas Briscoe. -R Brent.

French goods-sales by auction at Maj Tenant's wharf, Fell's Point, Balt, Md. -C O Muller, auct, Balt.

Fairfax Races will be run Jun 2nd next. -John Maddox, Fairfax Crt Hse, Va.

SAT MAY 30, 1812
An Act-to settle the account of John N Stout, of Ky, & allow him $87.15; his fees & compensation as a jailor, for committing, sub-sisting & releasing Archibald Hamilton, a prisoner of the U S. -Approved-Jas Madison.

An Act-for the relief of Thos & Wm Streshly; settle their accounts; late Collectors of the internal revenue in the Dist of Ohio; allowed further credits. -Approved-Jas Madison.

Ltr from a Gentleman of Clark Co,Iindiana Terr, dt'd May 15, 1812. Mr McGowan was murdered last Sunday at his own hse on White River; the 4th Regt of the U S infty are now marching from Vincennes to Cincinnati.

Hse of Reps: 1-Petition of Benj Connor, of N H; he has invented a portable bridge adapted to use of armies; he has a patent right; praying same may be purch'd for the use of the U S Army; read & referred. 2-Pet of Wm Peck, of R I, praying to be released from prison where he is confined for debt which he is unable to pay-referred.

St Louis, L T, Mar 2. Gov Howard rec'd info that two of his rangers, Jesse Vanbibber & Lewis Jones, being detached from Capt Boons' Co as spies; met 2 Winnebagoes a few days ago above Ft Mason; the rangers attacked & both Indians were killed; it is believed that these Indians were crossing the Mississippi as spies.

For sale-frame hse & lot fronting the Navy Yd mkt-hse; formerly occupied by Mr Jas Scannell. Terms-Dennis O'Conner. -Nichs L Queen, auct.

Strayed in Wash, 2 geldings. -S Goddard, living on Capt Hill

For sale-2 farms in St Mary's Co, Md; nr Leonard town, nrly joining ea other; ab't 200 acs, the place where Mr Jos Sewall, dec'd, formerly lived; also lot 1 in sq 1078 in Wash City; also land lying in the Third Dist of *Donation Lands*, Mercer Co, Pa. Persons wishing to see or purchase the St M Co land, apply to Capt Ignatius Manning, nr Leonardtown; the Mercer Co land-to John Finley, esq, nr Mercer Town; or Clement Sewall at the Gtwn Ferry, -Clement Sewall

Notice-Jas Maryman intends to apply to St Mary's Co Crt, Md, at Augt Term next, for the benefit of the insolvent laws of this state. -Jas Maryman, St M Co, Md.

Notice: Dan'l Peterson, negro boy, ab't 17 yrs of age, committed to Frederick Co, Md, jail; says he belongs to Mr John Simmons, nr Montgomery Crt-Hse in Md. -Ezra Mantz, shrff.

Wash Co, D C. Insolvent debtors confined in Wash Co prison for debt: Rufus Elliot & Jas Ewell. -Wm Brent, clk.

Latest from Portugal-Operations of the British in their attack on Badajoz, Mar, 1812. English lost ab't 4,000; ofcrs killed: Lt Col Rudge-5th Regt; Col Harcourt, 40th; Col Helder & Maj O'Hara. Wounded: Lt Gen Picton; Lt Gen Colville; Maj-Gen Kemp; Brig-Gen Hervey; Maj-Gen Bowers; Maj-Gen Walker; Lt-Col McLeed, 43d Regt; Lt-Col Gibbs, 52d; Lt-Col Aikin, 48th; Col Blackney, 74th; Lt-Col French; Majors Carle, Murphy, Maill; Cook & Alyed.

TUE JUN 2, 1812
New York, May 22. Recruiting has succeeded beyond the most sanguine expectations; in Orange, N J, Capt Reynolds has recruited 45 men; in Morristown, Capt Scott-54 men; at Trenton, Col Brearly-86 men; at Cedar Creek & Burlington-60 men; at Mt Holly & Aimville, ab't 45 men. In N YC, Col Chrystie-195 men.

Frederick Rpblcn meeting, May 16th, of Medley's Dist in Montg Co, Md. Laurence O'Neal, esq, chrmn & Mr Elijah Viers, sec; committee: John Cloyd, Benj White, Dr Wm Brewer, Alex'r Whitaker & Nathan White.

A ltr from Mr Nath'l Woodbury to his parents in Danvers, dt'd at Kegharni, in the So Sea, Sep 5, 1811, contained the melancholy report:-in Jun last the ship *Tonquin*, Thorn, Mstr, of N Y, lying at anchor at a village N Nootka Sound for the purpose of trade; a great number of Indians were on board & attacked the crew, killed all except the Capt & one more who flew into the magazine; seeing no possibility of escape, put fire to the powder & blew the ship to pieces & killed many Indians; at this time the boat was onshore & they tried to escape; their first landing was at Classet, where they were instantly shot. -Salem Gaz.

Jacob Leonard has just rec'd from N Y a few gold & silver epaulets-will sell low

From the Schenectady Cabinet-report for some time of the death of Lt Jonathan Thorn, of U S N; his parents reside in this city; [article from the Salem Gaz.] Another of the heroes of Tripoli is no more.

Richmond, Va-May 19. Requisition of the militia speeds with spirit in Va. All offices in line in regt volunteered-Capts A Turner & Sam'l G Adams will command; Capt John E Browne of Jas City Co, Lt Lindsay & Ensign Thos E Cowlet volunteered their svcs to their country in Williamsburg on May 7th.

Newark, May 26. Capt Arrowsmith has enlisted ab't 30 men.

Cincinnati, May 16. On Thu last the Cinc Light infty Co, commanded by Capt John F Mansfield, mv'd from this place for the genr'l rendezvous at Dayton. Brig-Genr'l Jas Findlay leaves town this morning for Dayton.

Public sale-on the premises, the frame stable, lately occupied by Wm Whodes, & must be taken off the ground this wk. -Forrest & Bealle, auct.

Steam Boats-the patentees offer licences to any individual or company, who may be inclined to build steam boats. -Robt R Livingston & Robt Fulton, N Y

Died: Mr Nicholas Carroll, an old & respectable inhabitant of Annapolis, on May 22nd at Annapolis.

Died: Mr Robt Oliphant, cashier of the branch bank of the U S at Norfolk; on May 20th, at Norfolk.

THU JUN 4, 1812
Phil, Pa-Stephen Girard, esq, has established a bank in this city, has executed & recorded a deed of trust to David Lenox, Robt Smith, Robt Waln, Jos Ball & Geo Simpson, esqs, to their survivors or heirs of such survivors. Copy of said deed may be seen by applying to Geo Simpson.

Public sale-order of the Orphans Crt of Montg Co, Md. Prsnl prop of Dr Rich'd Waters, late of said co, dec'd. -Mgt Waters, excx.

Anglo-savage war-from the Essex Register. Ltr from Lt Col Miller, commanding the U S Troops at Vincennes, rec'd a few days since by Capt Stephen Ranney, at Ft Sewall, Marblehead; acc't of recent massacres by the Indians nr Vincennes. Apr 11th Indians murdered Mrs Hutson & 4 small chldrn at their hse; a bro of Mrs Hutson was found dead; Mr Hutson was at a neighboring mill. Apr 21st, the family of Mr Mix was fired on, Mr Mix was shot dead, their youngest son shot in the knee & his arm broke by tomahawks; another son living close by ran off with his own wife & chldrn; the old lady, her dght & the wounded man beat off the Indians. Mr & Mrs Harryman & 5 small chldrn were murdered; a dght ab't 7 yrs of age, a dght ab't 9, twin sons ab't 3 yrs of age & a dght ab't 18 mos. Their closes relative was in Vt; Mr H was from Montpelier, Vt-mrd his wife there, her name was Olive Parker. Signed, Jas Miller, Lt Col 5th Regt infty. Capt Stephen Ranney, 4th Regt infty.

Williamson Co, Tenn. Justices of the Peace for said Co, Geo Hulme, John Crawford & Thos Garrett. John Bennet, an inhabitant of said co, says that on the 14th inst he was at the Crt Hse of Hickman Co & left there with 25 militia men commanded by Col Philips for Humphreys' Co Crt Hse; at Parker's, on Sugar Creek, Thos & Wm Gullidge told of 6 persons killed by Indians in McSimcs Bottom on Duck Rvr; Mrs Manly was shot in the knee & thru the jaw & scalped but was not dead; Capt Crawley's wife is missing; Mrs Manly's 9 day old child was thrown against the wall & is dead; her little son is also dead. The whole of the killed & missing belonged to Manley's family & Crawley's family. Certified by

John Coffee, May 13, 1812, that he knew John Bennett in North Carolina for svr'l yrs, before he remv'd to Tenn. Affidavits for John Bennett: G Hume, John House, Wm Hom, Geo Mansker & Wm Martin.

For sale or rent-the farm on which the late Judge Ridgely resided, on Elk Ridge, on the post rd from Balt to Wash City; 660 acs with brick dwlg hse. Apply to Sam'l Chase in Balt or Wm G Ridgely in Gtwn.

Indian hostilities. Ltr from Sam'l Goode Hopkins, esq, to his Excell Cha Scott, dt'd town of Henderson K. May 9, 1812. Recalls this day 2 weeks, of the murder of old Mr Meeks in the attack made on his family by the Indians. Mrs Harrison & the defenceless mbrs of the Govn'rs family arrv'd here by water last evening; they were accompained by the sick & wounded of the 4th Regt. Simpson.

For sale-the farm I live on ab't 3 miles from Montg Crt Hse, 600 acs with dwlg hse; also farm adj the above, 105 acs with dwlg hse. Wish to decline the farming line as I have not been brought up to it, reason the above is for sale. -Wm Blanchard, Montg Co, Md.

Bakers attention! Finding his health very much impaired, is desirous of retiring to the country for a time; for rent, my present dwlg hse on Capitol Hill with the bake hse & utensils. -Geo Burns.

For sale-hse hld furn at my residence on Capitol Hill, Lewis H Machen. -N L Queen-auct.

Wash City election: Aldermen & Cnclmen:

Ward 1 John Davidson	Wm Worthington, jr	Jas Hoban
Toppan Webster	Jas Hoban	
Ward 2	Wm James	Peter Lenox
Jas Hewitt	R C Weightman	Andrew Way, jr
Ward 3	Alex'r McCormick	Edmund Law
Dan'l Rapine	Geo Blagden	Benj G Orr
Ward 4 Jos Cassin	John W Brashears	Jas S Stevenson
Mathew Wright	John Dobbyn	

Ranaway-appr boy, John Hartlove, age 18 yrs; by trade a carpenter. -Cornelius McLean. Reward-$5.

SAT JUN 6, 1812
Union fire Co will meet this afternoon. -Jas Kearney, sec.

Ltr from an ofcr in the U S Army, dt'd Ft Harrison May 3, 1812. There are no families within 60 miles of this place, except Barnabas Lambert his son & 2 sons-in-law who remv'd from your county & are compelled to live in the Fort because of the Indians. Lt Albright rec'd orders to Ft Knox with Capt Posey's detachment; this will leave ab't 50 men. Gen Duncan McArthur has been elected Lt Col; Col

Jas Denny, First Maj; Wm Trimble, Second Maj, by the volunteer troops lately assembled at Dayton. They march in a few days for Detroit.

For sale-land in Shenandoah Co, Va, 990 acs; adj a tract of land purch'd by Jos Stover & Spengler of Robt McKay & others, formerly cld *McKay's Bottom*; also another tract on the other side of the rvr adj Jas Stinson's land. -Chas Sexton.

Foreign ofc, Feb 20, 1812. Earl of Liverpool to Mr Russel. Copy of an affidavit, sworn at Portsmouth by Eliz Eleanor Bowman, stating herself to be the w/o Wm Bowman, one of his Majesty's subjects, now detained against his will on the U S sloop, *Hornet*, at present at Cowes' Rd. [They mrd 6 yrs ago; Wm Bowman passed on board the *Hornet* by the name of Wm Elby].

Soc of the Sons of Erin will meet at 7 o'clock. -Jas Kearney, Sec.

Property for sale or to let on ground rent, on Mkt Space; also the hse & lot I presently occupy. -Sam'l Turner, jr. -Gtwn.

TUE JUN 9, 1812
Crt of Chas Co, Md-sale of rl est of Francis Dixon, late of Chas Co, dec'd; land is on the main post rd ab't 3 miles below town of Port Tobacco-87 acs; title is indisputable. -Luke F Matthews, John Digges, Francis Sewall. Chas Co, Md.

New York, Jun 5-Oliver Wolcott chosen Pres & Jonathan Burrall-cashier of the Bank of American.

PG Co Crt-Md. Petition of Colmore Pope, Fielder Pope & Francis Osborn & wife & Philip Soper & wife for division of the rl est of Jos Pope; Com'rs state that on account of the great number of parties concerned the lands cannot be divided; some of the reps live out of state. -John Read Magruder, clk, PG Co, Md.

Hse of Reps: Bill for relief of Col Jonathan Williams; of Clement B Penrose; of Lt Col Wm D Beall; all read a third time & passed. [individual bills]

THU JUN 11, 1812
Elkridge, Md-meeting at McCoy's Tavern, Anne Arundel Co; Rich'd Ridgely, chrmn & Dr Archibald Dorsey, sec: Meeting explained by Col R Dorsey, Dr Rich'd G Hockett, Thos Worthington of Nicholas, Dr Arthur Poe, Chas Hammond, Nichols Walker & John Dorsey. -Rg-the violation of our neutral rights by G Britain.

For sale-part of lot 9 in sq 290 on 13th St, with an unfinished frame hse; price $590. Apply to Mr Thos Hughes, Wash City, nr the premises. -Jos Jackson.

Wanted to hire by the yr-3 active lads. Enquire of J W Collet & Co, Brewers, N J Ave, crnr of L St, Wash City.

Sweel oil & claret for sale in his store in Gtwn. -Robt Getty.

Naturalization-meeting of the Soc of the Sons of Erin, to assist ntvs of Ireland obtain naturalization; committee: Moses Young, Jas Hoban, Robt Getty, Jas D Barry, Alex'r McCormick, Jas Kearney & Jonathan S Findlay.

Notice-intending to leave the city of Wash, & having svr'l hses & lots in said city, wishes to purchase a small farm for cash or exchange. -Nath Brady.

Public sale-order of Orphans Crt of Wash Co, D C. All prsn'l est of Jos Carlton, late of Gtwn, dec'd; furn, pistols & bks. -John Travers, auct. Gtwn.

Federal Mills-to lease; on Rock Creek, belonging to the est of Jos F Rowles, dec'd; 2 dwlg hses. Apply to John Heugh, Gtwn, atty in fact for admx of J Rowles.

SAT JUN 13, 1812
Annapolis Rpblcn meeting-May 30th. Wm Kilty, chrmn, & John S Skinner, sec. Committee: J Stephen, R Ghiselin, Lewis Duvall, Dennis Claude, N Brewer, W H Marriott & Jos Sand. Rgrdng our present crisis in Nat'l affairs.

Post ofc establishment changes in May 1812:
Asylum, Pa-Elias Vaughn, vice J M Piolett, mv'd away:
Bowling Green, K-Leander J Sharp, vice David H Robinson, rsgn'd:
Waynesville, N C-John Love, vice Robt Love, rsgn'd:
New Hampton, N J-Sam'l W Fell, vice H Dusenberry, rsgn'd:
New London, Va-Jas Penn jr, vice Jas Penn, rsgn'd:
Spread Eagle, Pa-Jas Watson, vice Edw Siter, rsgn'd:
Wayne C H, Ky-Jos Havens, vice Temple Poston, rsgn'd;
Bargaintown, N J-Ezra Baker, vice R S Baker, mv'd away:
Hope, N J-Barnabas Swayze, vice Jas Kinney, rsgn'd:
Deerfield St, N J-Sam'l Thompson, vice Jonathan Moore, rsgn'd:
Kingwood, Va-Rich'd Postle, vice J H Roberts, rsgn'd:
Kortwright, N Y-Martin Keeler, vice A Lawrence, rsgn'd:
Fruelstown, Pa-Jas McBride, vice Andrew Schooly, rsgn'd:
Danville, Vt-Timothy Follett, vice Ebenezer Eaton, rsgn'd:
Pattonsburg, Va-Thos Martin, vice Wm L Adams, rsgn'd;
Warham, Ms-Uzziel Dodge, vice Thos Barns:
Cabell C H, Va-Mark Russell, vice Chas Jessop, rsgn'd:
Russell C H, Va-Sam'l McDowell, vice Wm Flinn, rsgn'd:
Galway, N Y-Nathan Thompson, vice Solomon Rathbone, rsgn'd:
Nottingham, Md-Geo Armstrong, vice Robt Young, mv'd away:
Rough Crk Chr, Va-Sam'l Hannah, vice C Barshdale, rsgn'd:
Hillsboro, N H-John Burnham, vice M Starrett:
Lancaster, N Y-Fletcher Matthews, vice Jeremiah Foster, dec'd:
Centreville, S C-Jas Harrison, vice J McMullen, rsgn'd;
McQueen's store, N C-A McQueen, vice Jas McQueen, mv'd away:
Greensboro, Ga-Wiley Gershom, vice Robt Dale:
Northwood, N H-John Furber, vice John Harvey, rsgn'd:
Amherst, N H-Aaron Whitney, vice Eli Brown, rsgn'd;

Lincolnton, Ca-Lewis Stovall, vice J Walker, rsgn'd:
Conwayboro, S C-Robt Conway, vice Joshua S Norman, mv'd away;
Morristown, O-John Morrison, vice Robt Morrison, rsgn'd;
Hinesburg, Vt-Mich'l Hindsdall, vice Erastus Bostwick;
Hebron, N Y-Wm Root, vice Wm K Adams, rsgn'd;
White Plains, N Y-Francis Fowler, vice Wm Baldwin, mv'd away;
Sudlers X Rds, Md-Geo Maginnis, vice John Kennedy, dec'd;
Newport, Md-Matthew W Courtney, vice John McCulloch, rsgn'd;
New Rochelle, N Y-John Bennet jr, vice Dan'l Pelton, rsgn'd;
Brookfield, N Y-Henry Clark, vice Jos H Dwight, rsgn'd;
Amboy, N J-Robt Arnold, vice Simeon Drake, rsgn'd;
Mrsh'llville, Va-Alexander Boyd jr, vice Wm Boyd, rsgn'd;
Fitchburg, Ms-Calvin Willard, vice Jacob Willard, rsgn'd;
Fishkill landing, N Y-Thos Lawrence, vice Peter Folson, rsgn'd.

New Post ofcs est'd in May 1812 & postmaster:
Pharsalia, Chenango Co, N Y-Henry Weaver;
Berlinsville, Northampton Co, Pa-Jacob Stem;
Manchester, Claredon Co, S C-Geo J McCaulley;
Surrey, Hancock Co, Md-Edw J Jervis;
Madison Geauga Co, O-Phineas Mixer;
Booth Hill, Morris Co, N J Abraham Britton;
Cassadey Creek, Nicholas Co, Ky-Jas Gallespie;]
Bellville, Essex Co, N J-John Dow;
Aquackansack, Essex Co, N J-Peter Jackson:
Pompton, Morris Co, N J-Robt Colfax;
Patterson, Essex Co, N J-Henry Goodwin;
Stockholm, Morris Co, jr-Isaac Beach jr;
Mill Grove, Cabarrus Co, N C-Jas Pickens;
Baird's Forge, Burke Co, N C-Matthew Baird;
Orrington, Hancock Co, Me-Benj Nourse;
Turner's Mills, Caroline Co, Va-Dan'l Turner;
Yellow Springs, Green Co, O-Christopher Sroufe;
Naaman's Creek, Newcastle Co, Del-John Bellach;
Weston, Middlesex Co, Ms-Abraham Hews;
Manchester, Ontario Co, N Y-Nathan Barlow;
Baird's Tavern, Buckingham Co, Va-David Evans;
Elkton, Giles Co, Ten-John Hawkins;
Mayville, Chetaugue Co, N Y-Casper Rouse;
Alexander's, York Dist, S C-Obadiah Alexander;
Smith's Ferry, Ohio Co, Ky-Wm B Smith;
Richmond, Cheshire Co, N H-Job Bisby.
Ofcs discont'd-May 1812:
Highwassee, Ten & Little Cape Caphon, Va.

Fredericksburg, Va-meeting in Falmouth, Jun 12. Dr Chas L Carter, Mayor of the town, chrmn, & Garrit Minor, sec. Committee: Francis Taliaferro, Sen John T Brooke, Geo Buckner, John W Green, Geo French, Wm S Stone, Robt Stanard,

Thos Goodwin, Thos Minor, Wm Bernard, Wm Fitzhugh, Carter L Stevenson & Garret Minor. Regarding the attitude of Europe to our Government.

Return of recruits raised in Dist 4, Hdqrtrs, Canandaigua, under command of Maj J R Mullany, 13th Rgt of infty: Capt J McKeon-93; Lt John M O'Connor-23. Infty of the Line: Capt Minder M Dox-51; Capt Scot-20; Capt Morris-13; Lt Chipman-25; Lt Martin-22; Lt Clarke-37. Newburgh, Jun 2. Capt Oglivie has enlisted 50 sldrs in this village.

Orphans Crt of PG Co, Md. Sale of prsn'l est of Wm Smith, dec'd, at his hse in Bladensburg, PG Co, Md. -Zeph Farrell, adm.

Memorial to the Senate & Hse of Reps by inhabitants of N Y C; regarding the French burning our ships & continuance of the embargo.

John Jacob Astor	Isaac Heyer	Jos Otis
Sam'l Adams	Ralph Bulkley	Lewis Hartman
Howland & Grinnell	Sam'l Bell	Garret Storm
E Slosson	John F Delaplaine	Geo Bement
Israel Clason	Peter Stagg	S A Rich
John Slidell	David Taylor	Abraham Smith
Jas Lovett	John Kane	Wm Adee
Jos Strong	John Depeyster	Sam'l Marshall
Andrew Ogden & Co	John T Lawrence	Andrew Foster
Thos Storm	Thos Rich	Jos W Totten
Jacob Barker	Amos Butler	Wm Lovett
Isaac Schermerhorn	Ebenezer Burrill	Wm Edgar, jr.
Sam'l Stillwell	Jacob P Giraud	John Hone
Jos Strong	Amaso Jackson	Wm J Robinson
Abraham S Hallet	Joshua Jones	Elbert Herring
Frederick Giraud, jr.	Robt Roberts	John Crookes
Hugh McCormick	Gilbert Haight	John W Gale
John K Townsend	Leffert Lefferts	Alex'r Raden
Augustus Wynkoop	Thos H Smith, jr.	

Mrd: Peter Pedersen, esq, charge Des affairs & Cnsl Genr'l for his Majesty the King of Denmark to the U S, to Miss Maria Litchfield Scott, d/o the late Lewis A Scott, esq, of N Y, on Jun 3, at Phil by the Rgt Rev Bishop White.

Elected Directors of the Mechanics Bank of Alexandria:

Robt Young	Dan'l MacLeod	Mark Butts
Jas Sanderson	Isaac Entwisle	John Cohagen
Jas McGuire	John Gird	Adam Lynn
John Young	Jas C Deneale	Peter Saunders
Wm Veitch	Jos Dean	John Longden

Robt Young was elected Pres & Wm Paton jr, cashier. -Herald.

TUE JUN 16, 1812
Public sale-order of the Orphans Crt of Montg Co, Md. Prsnl prop of Jeremiah Berry, Sr, dec'd, at his late residence: negroes, horses, crop & a good still. -Jeremiah Berry jr, adm of Jeremiah Berry, Sr.

For sale-in virtue of a deed of trust to me by the late Geo Thompson, dec'd, to secure debts due to the Bank of Columbia; part of lot No. 30, on Falls St, with 3 story brick dwlg hse & ofcs now in occupation of Geo Johnson, esq-also part of lot 31 & part of lot 36. -C Smith, Gtwn.

For sale-at the late dwlg of John Read on Capitol Hill: carpenters tool & furniture. -N L Queen, auct.

Wash Co, D C. Case of Henry McCoy, insolvent debtor, confined in Wash Co prison for debt. -Wm Brent, clk.

THU JUN 18, 1812
Sweepstake race over Nashville turf. -Roger B Sappington, prop of said turf.

Mrd: John Milledge, long a Rep; Senator in Cong from Ga, to Miss An_Lamar of S C, a few days ago by the Rev Mr Garvi___. [incomplete page]

Pupils of Mr McLeod's School, nr the Navy Yd, address the guardians of our country. Male Dept: Benj F French, John A Chalmers, Clifton Wharton, Ebinezer Eveleth. Female Dept: Evelina McClain, Juliana Anders, Jane Sandford, Verlinda Burch.

Pendulum Mill machine patented; model at the Patent Ofc, Wash City. -Jos Lefever, Strasburgh, Lancaster Co, Pa.

SAT JUN 20, 1812
An Act-that war be and the same is hereby declared to exist between the United Kingdon of Great Britain and Ireland and the dependencies thereof, and the U S of America & their Territories. -Apprv'd Jas Madison, Jun 18, 1812.

Mrd: Mr Jos Milligan, of Gtwn, to Miss Ann McDonald, d/o Mr Alex'r McDonald, of Wash, on Jun 18, by Rev Mr Laurie

Died: Mrs Sarah McCormick, consort of the Rev Mr McCormick, on Jun 16, age 36 yrs; after a long & painful illness.

Orphans Crt of PG Co, Md. Prsn'l est of Chas Wood, late of said co, dec'd. -Sam'l Franklin, admr of C Wood. Public sale at the late dwlg ofc: wood; blacksmith's tools, 50 bushels of good charcoal & 3 or 4 negroes. -S Franklin.

Public sale-tract of land, ab't 300 acs; on the rd leading from Montg Crt Hse to the mouth of the Monocasy, 2 miles from Mr Wm Darnes's; Mr Henry Jones living nr the rd will show the above land. -Benj W Jones.

Proposals for completing the rd leading from Cumberland, Md, to Brownsville, Pa; info will be given by the Superintendent, David Shriver jr. Treas Dept.

Wash Co, D C. Fielder Parker jr, insolvent debtor, confined in Wash Co prison for debt; trustee to be appt'd. -Wm Brent, clk.

TUE JUN 23, 1812

Published Jun. 1812: *Corps of Engineers:* Wm Cutbush, Cadet of Mil Acad, promoted to 2d Lt, Mar 1, 1812.
Regt of artl: Capt Jas Read to Major, vice Moses Porter, appt'd Col of Light artl, Mar 12, 1812.
1st Lt Jas Reed to Capt, vice Jas Reed, promoted Mar 12, 1812.
2d Lt Milo Mason to 1st Lt, vice Alex'r La Neuville, rsgn'd Feb 29, 1812.
2d Lt Christopher Vandeventer to 1st Lt, vice Jas Reed, promoted Mar 12, 1812.
2d Lt John Fitzgerald to 1st Lt, vice John D Wyndham, dismissed Mar 14, 1812.
Jas W Rouse, appt'd 2d Lt, Mar 27, 1812
Rurgis B White, appt'd 2d Lt, Apr 14, 1812.
Peter St Medard, do, do, Apr 30, 1812.
Abel B Chase, do, do, Apr 30, 1812.
Jas Baker, do, do, Mar 1, 1812.
Jas L Edwards, do, do, May 7, 1812
First Regt of infantry:
1st Lt Dan'l Baker to Capt, vice Peter P Schuyler, appt'd Col in the additional Military force, Mar 12, 1812.
2d Lt Jas R Peyton to 1st Lt, vice Dan'l Baker, promoted Mar 12, 1812.
Ensign Lewis Bissell to 2d Lt, vice Jas R Peyton, promoted Mar 12, 1812.
Second Regt of infantry.
Ensign Lorreat Dufossat to 2d Lt, to rank from Jan 3, 1812.
Ensign Chas Vasse to 2d Lt, to rank from Jan 3, 1812.
Jonathan Bell, appt'd Ensign, Apr 14, 1812.
Landon C Bruce, appt'd Ensign, May 1, 1812.
Surg's mates:
Wm Ballard, Mar 24, 1812
Sam'l Dusenbury, Mar 25, 1812
Anthony Benezett, Mar 25, 1812
John H Sackett, Mar 25, 1812
Alex'r Wolcott, Mar 25, 1812
John T Priestly, Apr 25, 1812
Additional Military force of 1808.
Regt of Light artl:
Moses Porter, appt'd Col Mar 12, 1812.
1s Lt Andrew McDowell to Capt, vice John H T Estes, rsgn'd, Apr 1, 1812.
2d Lt Jas D Cobb to 1st Lt, vice Andrew McDowell, promoted, Apr 1, 1812.
Wm W Smith, Cadet of the Mil Acad, promoted to 2d Lt, to rank from Jun 1, 1812.
Regts of Light Dragoons.
1st Lt Alex'r Cummings to Capt, vice Jas Thomas, rsgn'd Nov 1, 1811.
2d Lt Geo Birch to 1st Lt, vice Alex'r Cummings, promoted Nov 1, 1811.
Dillon Thomas, appt'd 2d Lt, Mar 27, 1812.
Francis Belton, do, Mar 27, 1812.

Wm Neilson, do, May 1, 1812.
Louis Laval, do, May 1, 1812.
Jas Barton, do, May 27, 1812.
Third Regt of infantry.
Jas Smith, appt'd Ensign, Mar 27, 1812.
Tilman Turner, do, Mar 27, 1812.
Robt Goodwin, do, Apr 14, 1812.
Thos W McCall, do, Apr 30, 1812-declines.
John Martin, appt'd Ensign, May 27, 1812.
Fourth Regt of infantry.
John A Chandler, appt'd Ensign, Mar 27, 1812-declines.
Artemas Sibley, do, Mar 27, 1812.
Sam'l Armstrong, do, Apr 14, 1812.
Paul Peckham, do, May 15, 1812
John Ranney, do, May 19, 1812.
Amos Farnsworth, appt'd Surg's Mate, Apr 14, 1812.
Fifth Regt of infantry.
Wilson Prestman, appt'd Ensign, Apr 14, 1812.
Jas H Hood, do, Apr 30, 1812.
Geo D Snyder, do, Apr 30, 1812.
Tobias Stansbury, do, May 27, 1812-declines.
John Fendal, do, May 27, 1812.
Sixth Regt of infantry.
1st Lt Jas E A Masters to Capt, vice Jonathan Brooks, discont'd on rolls, Jun 4, 1812.
2d Lt Thos T Blauvelt to 1st Lt, vice Jas E A Masters, promoted Jun 4, 1812.
Ensign Thos D Jenkins to 2d Lt, to rank from Jan 3, 1812.
Isaac L Dubois, appt'd Ensign, May 1, 1812.
Seventh Regt of infantry.
2d Lt Thos R Richardson to 1st Lt, to rank from Feb 10, 1812.
Ensign Wm Prosser to 2d Lt, to rank from Feb 10, 1812.
Ensign Jas Forsythe to 2d Lt, to rank from Feb 10, 1812.
Isaac M Reilly appt'd Ensign, May 8, 1812.
Regt of Riflemen.
Jas Hamilton appt'd 1st Lt, Jun 4, 1812.
John Findley appt'd 2d Lt, May 15, 1812.
Henry Swearengen, do, May 15, 1812.
Edw Wadsworth, do, May 15, 1812.
Wm Townley, do, May 15, 1812.
Wm C Beard, do, May 19, 1812.
Geo Gray jr, do, Jun 4, 1812.
Surgeons:
Josiah D Foster, appt'd Hospital Surg, Apr 25, 1812.
David C Kerr, do, Apr 30, 1812.
Surgeon's mates:
Jas Stevenson, Hospital Surg's Mate, May 27, 1812.
Stephen Sutton, do, do.

Notes: Ensign John Hallam jr, of the 3d Regt of infty, declines.
Ensign Robt Guinea, of the 7th Reft of infty, declines.
Ensign Conrad Wold, 7th Regt of infty, resigned, May 4, 1812.
Ensign Wm Barnett, 6th infty, appt'd a Lt in the additional Military force of 1812.

London Courier-John Bellingham assassinated Mr Perceval on May 11th as he was entering the lobby of the Hse of Commons. The Coroner's Jury brought in a verdict of wilfull murder; A Gill-Coroner. Witnesses examined were: Lt Genr'l Gascoigne-mbr for Liverpool; Jos Hume-mbr for Weymouth; Henry Burgess-atty of Curzon St; & W Lynn-Surg; all esqrs. Thos Constantine Brookbank was Priv Sec to Mr P. Mrs Perceval & her 12 chldrn & Lord Arden, his bro, survive.

Runaway-committed to Wash Co, D C, jail; Peter Johnson, black man; says he was sold by Mr Tuckfield of Chas Co, Md, to a Mr Wood Fork, of Ga. -C Tippett, kpr of the jail.

New York, Jun 16. Capture of the ship *Egeria*, by the British ship of War, *Morgiana*. May 30th the ship *Egeria*, Capt Cock, of & for N Y from Copenhagen, having on board the passengers, Mr Lewis, Sec to & Bearer of Dispatches from G W Erving, Spec Mnstr at the Crt of Denmark, & Mr H Wilson. Whole crew, except for Capt Cock & the cabin boy, were put on board the *Morgiana*. Mr Lewis remained until Jun 4th; he was then put on board the *Sally & Mary*, Capt Luce of Boston, bound to Norfolk. Jun 9th, fell in with the brig *Dolphin*, of Boston, Capt R Williams, bound to N Y, who took him & Mr Higinbotham on board. John Paul, Chief Mate, was also put on board the *Sally & Mary*; Sam'l Maull, 2d do, Amos Brown, Wm Watson, Wm Myers, American ctzns, Elisha Whitten, Solomon Hartly-Capt Scott of the *Morgiana* promised to put the said John Zamas' crew on the next vessel he met.

Reward-$100 for Runaway, Harry, negro man, from Mr Mich'l Matot, to whom he was hired, nr Hagarstown, Wash Co, Md. Apply to Mr Jas Muir, Wm's Port, Md or to Edw Aprice, Chaptico, St Mary's Co, Md.

An Act-for relief of Wm Garrard, to be pd the additional sum-$1500 for his svcs as a land com'r in Orleans Terr. Approved-Jas Madison, Jun 10, 1812.

Reward-$30 for Aaron, negro, who absconded from my farm nr Queen Anne, PG Co, Md. -Isaac Duckett.

Reward-$20 for Nace, negro man, runaway. -John Spalding, nr Navy Yd, Wash.

Notice to the creditors of Jas Ewell, insolvent debtor; same to exhibit their claims. -Sam'l Burch, trustee. Wm Brent, clk, Wash

For sale-negroes belonging to the est of Mary E Grayson, dec'd, a man & a woman. -Spence Grayson, adm. Nichs L Queen, auct. Wash City.

Notice-I am informed that there is now offered for sale by Gerrard Snowden, who appt'd the trustee for that purpose, land cld *Snowden's Third Addition to his Manor & Snowden's Manor Engaged*, 1400 acs, that was devised by Rich'd Snowden jr to his wife during her life, & after her death to his bro, John Snowden & his nphw Sam'l Thomas; & the said J Snowden by his deed dt'd Mar 11, 1794, did with others, convey to me, Wm Holmes, of Montg Co, Md, a small part of the said land, [where the land is located.] I have pd for same & will not surrender same. -Wm Holmes.

THU JUN 25, 1812
Jeremiah O'Brian was the first Naval ofcr commissioned in the Revolution & now resides in Machias. -Ntv ctzn of New Hampshire.

Died: Jonathan Bayard Smith, esq, on Jun 16; interred on Jun 18 in the Presby Chr Yd in Arch St attended by mbrs of all the Masonic Lodges in the City. Mr S was born in 1741; his fr was a ntv of Boston, his mthr descended from one of the oldest families in Phil. -Aurora.

Mrd: Mr Sam'l Brook, First clk to the Treas of the U S, to Mrs Eliz Cheyney, formerly of Chester Co, Pa, on Jun 24th, at the Friend's Meeting Hse in Wash.

Orphans Crt of St Mary's Co, Md. Jun 15, 1812. Prsn'l est of Jeremiah Aderton, late of said co, dec'd. -Judith Attaway Aderton, admx.

Wash Co, D C-Case of Mary Shaw, insolvent debtor, confined in Wash Co prison for debt. -Wm Brent, clk.

SAT JUN 27, 1812
Rev Regular army-published for the gratification of public curiosity. List of General & Field ofcrs in the late army of the U S, who srv'd to the end of the war & were deranged in pursuance of acts of congs.

New Hampshire
Brig-Genr'l: Jas Reed & John Stark
Cols:

Ethan Allen	Geo Reid	Jos Cilley
Henry Dearborn	Seth Warner	

Lt-Cols:

Sam'l Stafford	Benj Titcomb	

Majors:

Gideon Brownson	Caleb Robinson	Jas Carr
Wm Scott	Amos Morrill	Benj Whitcomb

Massachusetts
Maj Genr'ls:

Wm Heath	Benj Lincoln	Henry Knox

Brig Genr'ls:

John Glover	John Greaton	John Patterson
Rufus Putnam	Mich'l Jackson	

Cols:
John Bailey
Gamaliel Bradford
Jeduthan Baldwin
Calvin Smith
David Cobb
Timothy Bigelow

Thos Marshall
Jas Mellon
Wm Sheppard
John Crane
Benj Tupper
Jos Vose

Thos Nixon
Jas Wesson
John Brooks
Benezer Sprout
David Hanley
Henry Jackson

Lt-Cols:
Barachiah Bassett
Sam'l Carlton
John Popkin
Henry Haskell
Elijah Vose

Ezra Newell
Andrew Peters
Wm Hull
Jos Thompson
Noah Littlefield

Dan'l Whiting
Tobias Fernald
Wm Stacy
Benj Holden

Majors:
Noah Allen
Wm H Baillard
Hedijah Baylis
Nathan Price
Matthew Clarkson
Lemuel Trescott
Caleb Gabos
Nathan Winslow

Robt Oliver
Moses Ashely
Wm Perkins
Sam'l Carr
Job Sumner
Sam'l Darby
John Wiley

Jos Pettingell
Isaac Pope
Thos Cogswell
John Spurr
Seth Drew
Sam'l Tubbs
Moses Knapp

Rhode Island
Maj-Genr'l: Nathaniel Green
Colonels:
Israel Angell
Henry Sherburne

Jeremiah Olney

Wm Barton

Lt-Cols:
Silas Talbot

Sam'l Ward

Majs:
Wm Blodget
Wm Peck

Coggleshall Olney
John S Dexter

Wm Bradford
Simeon Thayer

Connecticut
Maj-Genr'ls:
Israel Putnam
Brig-Genr'l:

Sam'l H Parsons
Jedediah Huntington

Cols:
Philip B Bradley
Heman Swift
Return J Meigs
Sam'l B Webb

Elisha Sheldon
Thos Grovenor
Sam'l Willis

Zebulon Butler
Isaac Sherman
Josiah Starr

Lt Cols:
Ebenezer Gray
Jonathan Johnson
David Humphreys
Jonathan Trumbull

Thos Hobby
Hezekiah Holdridge
David F Sill

Jos Hait
John Sumner
Ebenezer Huntington

Majs:
Albert Chapman
Benj Tallmage
Eli Levenworth
Robt Warner
Elisha Painter

Benj Throop
Sam'l Johnson
Theodore Woodbridge
Abner Pryor
Jos A Wright

Wids Clift
Amos Waldridge
Dan'l Lyman
John P Wyllis
David Smith

New York
Maj-Genr'l: Alexander McDougall
Brig-Genr'l: Jas Clinton

Colonels:
Donald Campbell
Philip Cortlandt
Goose Van Schaick
Frederick Weisenfelts

Jas Livingston
Wm Malcolm
Peter Gansevoort

John Lamb
Lewis Dubois
Marinus Willett

Lt-Cols:
Jacobus Bruen
Robt Cochran
Cornelius Vandyke

Ebenezer Stevens
Wm S Smith
Rich'd Livingston

Benj Walker
Udney Hay

Majors:
Sebastian Bauman
Stephen McDougall
Geo C Nicholson
Sam'l Logan

Lewis Morris
John Davis
John Graham

Jas Rosecranse
Nicholas Fish
Rich'd Platt

New Jersey
Brig-Gen'l: Elias Dayton

Colonels:
John N Cummings
Oliver Spencer

Israel Shreeve
Matthias Ogden

Ephraim Martin

Lt-Cols:
John Conway
Henry B Livingston

Eleazer Lindsley
David Rhea

Jonathan Forman

Majors:
Jeremiah Bruia
Rich'd Cox
Nath'l Bowman

Wm Barber
Ichabod Burnett
Sam'l Reading

Jos Bloomfield
John Ross
John Burrowes

Pennsylvania
Maj-Genr'l: Arthur St Clair
Brig-Genr'ls:
Edw Hand

Anthony Wayne

Wm Irvine

Colonels:
Dan'l Broadhead
Rich'd Butler
Stephen Moylan
Jas Chambers
Andrew Porter
Adam Hubley

Francis Johnston
Robt Magaw
Henry Bicker
Geo Nagle
Rich'd Hampton

Fred'k Vernon
Wm Butler
Lewis Nicola
Thos Craig
Walter Stewart

Lt-Cols:
Stephen Bayard

Francis Mentges

Lewis Harmer

Caleb North
Josiah Harmar
Tench Tilghman
Majors:
John Armstrong
Thos D Moore
Isaac Craig
Francis Procter
David S Franks
Geo Tudor
John Hulings

Sam'l Hay
Christopher Stewart

Wm McPherson
Thos Church
Jas Moore
Moore Fontleroy
Jas Reid
Jas Hamilton

Thos Robinson
John Murray

Wm Alexander
Francis Murray
Evan Edwards
Jas Parr
Jas Grier
Jeremiah Talbot

Delaware
Colonel: David Hall
Lt Col: Jos Vaughan
Majs:
Nath'l Mitchell   John Patten

Maryland
Maj Genr'l: Wm Smallwood
Brig-Genr'ls:
Mordecai Gist   Otho H Williams
Cols:
Peter Adams   Nath'l Ramsey   John Gunby
Thos Woolford   John E Howard   Ludwick Weltner
Josias Cawel Hall
Lt Cols:
Uriah Forrest   Levin Winder   Edw Tillard
Majors:
Benj Brooks   Thos Lansdale   Wm Dent Beall
Thos H Luckett   Wm Brown   John Lynch
John Davidson   Jas McHenry   John Eccleston
Alex'r Roxbury   Aquilla Giles   Henry Hardman
Jonathan Silliman

Virginia
Maj Genr'l: Horatio Gates
Brig Genr'ls:
Peter Muhlenberg   Chas Scott   Dan'l Morgan
Geo Weedon
Cols:
Geo Baylor   Chas Harrison   Abraham Buford
Wm Heth   Burges Ball   Levin Joynes
Wm Davies   Henry Lee   Wm Darke
Geo Matthews   Christian Febiger   John Nevill
Nath'l Gist   Wm Russell   John Gibson
Jas Wood   Anthony W White   John Green
Lt Cols:
Rich'd C Anderson   Thos Posey   Sam'l I Cabell
Rich'd Taylor   Jonathan Clark   Oliver Towles
Edw Carrington   Benj Temple   Thos Gaskins

Wm Washington	Sam'l Hopkins	John Webb
Gustavus B Wallace	Sam'l Hawes	John Jameson

Majors:

Peter B Bruin	David Hopkins	John Belfield
Wm Lewis	Wm Cunningham	Wm Moseley
Wm Croghan	John Poulson	Rich'd Call
Chas Pelham	Andrew Waggener	Thos Ridley
Jos Eggleston	Smith Snead	Sam'l Finley
David Stephenson	Geo Gilchrist	John Swan
Thos Hill	Wm Taylor	John Hays
John Wyllis	Jos Crockett	Christian Holmer

North Carolina
Maj Genr'l: Robt Howe
Brig Genr'l: Jethro Sumner
Cols:

Jas Armstrong	Archibald Lytle	Thos Clarke
John Patten	Selby Harney	Jas Thackston
Gideon Lamb		

Lt Cols:

John Armstrong	Hardy Murfee	Wm Davidson

Majors:

Reading Blount	Thos Hogg	Thos Donohoe
Griffith I M'Ree	Geo Doherty	John Nelson

South Carolina
Maj Genr'l: Wm Moultrie
Brig-Genr'l: Isaac Huger
Cols:

Bernard Beckman	Francis Marion	Chas C Pinckney

Lt Cols:

John F Grimke	Wm Henderson	Wm Scott

Majs:

Edmund M Hyrne	Isaac Harleston	Ephraim Mitchell
Thos Pinckney		

Georgia
Brig Genr'l: Lachlin McIntosh
Cols: Sam'l Elbert   John McIntosh
Majs:

John Habersham	Jos Lane	Philip Lowe

Foreign ofcrs:
Maj Genr'ls:

M Duportail	Marquis La Fayette	Baron Steuben

Colonels:
Thadeus Kosciusko & ____Laumoy

Lt Cols:

____Cambray	Lewis De Fienry	____Gouvion
____Gimot	John Ternant	____Wiebert

Majs:

Ferdinand De Brahm	J Murnan	Geo Shaffner

___ Villfranche
States unknown: Col Moses Hazen & Lt Col Edw Antill

Baltimore paper: all ctzns are to preserve the order & peace of the community; [Chief Justice, Mayor, subscribers & Justices of the Peace]. Signed: John Scott, John Aisquith, John F Harris, Jas Wilson, Edw Johnson, Geo G Presbury, Owen Dorsey, Edw Woodyear, D Fulton. R R Richardson, Adam Fonerden, Baltzer Schaeffer, Sam'l Young, John Dougherty, Sam'l Vincent, Edw Aisquith, Jno S Abell, Thos C Jenkins, Enos W Griffith, Ferd Gourdon, Jno Bankson.

Mrd: Mr Sam'l P Todd to Miss Rebecca A Dawson, d/o Mr Joshua Dawson, of Wash, on Jun 25, by Rev Stephen B Balch.

Passengers pressed by the British frig. *Morgiana*, Jun, 1812.

Hugh O'Brien	Teague McFeaden	Sam'l Corbet
Jas Cresholm	Peter Kelly	Jas Williams
John Drummend	Patrick Curry	Sam'l McIntire
Robt Fletcher	Dan'l Ronno	John Begley
Martin Beill	Con Finn	John Wilson
Edw Doherty	Brian Hapan	Peter Hoan
Mich'l McCormick	Wm Stevenson	Robt Stevenson
Patrick McCallum	Manus McFadden	John Ward
Manus Connor	Hugh Doherty	Brian Quigley
Patrick McGuire	John Bresland	Wm Ward

[Passengers were Irishmen headed for the shores of America]

Sale at auction-all stock in trade of Thos Hughes & Co in F St; whiskey, herrings, sugar, furn, carriages. -N L Queen, aucts.

Public sale-order of Orphans Crt of PG Co, Md. Prsn'l est of Hedwick Holliday, late of PG Co, dec'd. -Sarah Ann Holliday, admx. [Sale at her residence]

TUE JUN 30, 1812
An Act-for releif of Clement B Penrose, a commissioner for right of persons claiming land in La Terr, the sum of $500. -Approved, Jas Madison, Jun 17, 1812.

Fourth of July celebration in Balt, Md-Wm H Winder to read the Dec of Indep; Jos H Nicholson, the Dec'l of War message from the Pres; Wm Pinkney, an oration.

In Chancery, Jun 9, 1812. Peter Kemp, vs Jesse Carpenter & Ruth his wife, Thos Beall of Sam'l, John Boos & Jas M Lingan. Bill to obtain an injunction on judgment in Montg Co Crt by said Carpenter use of Beall against the cmplnts for relief; same was a bond given by Boos with the cmplnt as security to said Carpenter & assigned to Beall of Sam'l; bond was part payment of money for land sold by Carpenter to Boos, to which he had no title. Carpenter & wife reside out of state. -Nichs Brewer, Reg Cur Can.

Patent corset maker, Mrs Edwards, from Phil, has same for sale at the store lately occupied by Mr Pairo.

THU JUL 2, 1812
Merchants of Phil consider bldg a ship of war; Mr Jacob Gerard Koch subscribed $5000 as a gift. -Press.

Louis Pise, portrait painter & drawing mstr, will teach same in Gtwn, on Jefferson St, 3 drs below the lodge. Info to Mr Ez King, nr the Post Ofc.

Strayed or stolen, a black horse, from the Commons of Wash City. Reward-$10. -Geo Frank, Capitol Hill, Wash City.

Orphans Crt of Dorchester Co, Md. Jun 8, 1812. Prsn'l est of Thos Ecclestion, late of said co, dec'd. -Jas Kemp, adm.

Settlement of the prsnl assetts of the late Capt Dan'l J Adams, dec'd, on Jun 25th. -Geo Sandford, adm cum test ann. Wash City.

For sale-last will of Robt Means, dec'd, all the lands of the testator in Ohio & Ky. -Dan'l Call, exc. Richmond.

SAT JUL 4, 1812
Hse of Reps: Bill for relief of Anna Young, heiress & rep of Col John Durkee, dec'd, was read a third time & passed.

Edw A Barnum, a sailor, was wounded in a affray at a brdg hse in N Y in James St, died Jun 29th.

WED JUL 8, 1812
Thos Flournoy, esq, of Ga, appt'd a Brig-Genr'l in the U S Army by the Pres & Senate. Col Thos Cushing of the U S Army, is appt'd Adjut Genr'l. Col Alex'r Smyth of the U S Army, is appt'd Inspec Genr'l of the U S Army.

Henry A S Dearborn, esq, appt'd coll of the Port of Boston, vice Gen H Dearborn, rsgn'd.

Acts passed at the first session of the Twelfth Congress, relief of :
Josiah H Webb	John Burnham;	Thos F Riddick
Wm Gerrard	John N Stout	Ninian Pinkney
Thos O'Bannon	Thos Wilson	Thos Orr
Clement B Penrose	Aaron Greeley	John Thompson
Wm Hubbell		

Mr Sam'l Carswell, esq, of Phil, appt'd Commissary-Genr'l of the army.

Died: Brig Gen'rl Peter Ganssevoort jr, age 62 yrs, 11 mos, 16 days; on Jul 2 at Albany.

Sale at auction-at hse occupied by Hon Augustus J Foster, late Mnstr Pleni & Ambassador from his Britannic Majesty, all the said Minister's furn. -Nichs L Queen, auct. Wash City.

Wash Co, D C. Tunis Craven, insolvent debtor, confined in Wash Co prison for debt. -Wm Brent, clk.

Reward-$5 for strayed or stolen bay mare from the Wash City Commons nr the Navy Yd. Info to Mr Thos Foyles. -Philip Otterback.

Balt Hospital in order for reception of patients; infirmary almost complete, asylum for lunatics is finished. Mr & Mrs Gatchel are the steward & matron & have long experience in Pa Hosp. Physicians: Drs Celin MacKenzie, Jas Smyth, Wm Gibson, Geo Brown, Miles Littlejohn, John Coulter, John Campbell White, John Crawford, Solomon Birkhead, P Chatard, John Cromwell, Ashton Alexander. Visitors: John Hillen, Jas Mosher, Wm McDonald, Wm Ross, Jacob Miller.

PG Co, Md. Creditors of John M Burgess & Geo W Willett, insolvent debtors, are to hand in their accounts. -Chas E Burgess, trustee.

SAT JUL 11, 1812
John Armstrong, esq, late Minister to France, appt'd a Brig-Genr'l in the U S Army.

TUE JUL 14, 1812
Fauquier & Pr Wm Cos, Va-4th of July meeting at the field of Maj Tho Hunton; Jno Love, esq, chrmn; Capt Jno Hampton, [of the vol Troop of Cavalry], sec; volunteer toasts by Dr Gustavus B Horner & Augustine Jennings.

Havre-De-Grace, Md, Jul 4, 1812-Capt Thos Courtney's Co assembled on Union Green; Mr Wilmer delivered an oration. Volunteers: Capt Thos Courtney, Lt John O'Neill; also Capt Bennet Barnes, a Vet of '76.

PG Co, Md. Jos Willett residing at the town of Vansville, brought before me a stray bay horse. -Gabriel P Van Horn.

Ltr of Col Martin of SmithCo, to Lt Col W P Anderson, dt'd Jun 22, 1812.
-to inform you that my son, Jos A Martin, enlisted as a sldr in the U S Army; w/o my knowledge. My friends sent his name to the War Dept requesting an appointment; I had not intended such an application be made.
[See reply]
W P Anderson, Lt-Col of Eighth Regt, U S Army, replies that he had already directed Capt Gray to order him to this place, to perform the duties of adjut.
-W P Anderson, Nashville, Jun 20, 1812.

Aaron Burr has given notice in the New York Prints, of his having opened a law ofc in that city.

Ltr from gentleman at Carthage, Ten. Capt Gray has enlisted 50 good men. The true spirit reigns; the old worthies who inhabit it do wonders. -Maj Tilman Dixon, Col Wm Martin, Col Walton, etc.

Died: Mr Thos Carberry, age ab't 68 yrs, on Jul 12th.

Reward-$20 for negro woman slave, Susan; calls herself Suckey Boardley, age ab't 40 yrs; she has a mthr-in-law in Balt, Md; she formerly belonged to Mr Jas Miller, merchant of Bladensburg, now a resident of Glasgow, Scotland. -Ann Tilley

Nashville examiner. Ltr from Lt Jos Anthony to Lt Col W P Anderson. Smith Co, Jun 21, 1812. I enlisted 18 men last wk:.....

Jas Ellis	Chas Wilson	John Green
Thos Henderson	Wm Jones	Stephen Dallas
John Brawner	Wm Lorance	Wm Linvill
Wm Talbot	__asant Talbot	Enoch Wemberly
___ Stafford	__os Romark	___ Murfrey
___Potter	__ram Britton	___phen Johnson

[Page incomplete]

Ladies with ltrs in the Wash City Post ofc, Jul 1, 1812.

Mrs Anne Adams	Mrs Chloe Butler	Matilda Berry
Mrs Eleanor Connor	Mrs Sarah B Crawford	Miss Davis
Mrs A Dent	Mrs Douglass c/o Mrs Doin	
Mrs Fenwick	Miss Helena Fenwick	Jane Finget
Miss Anna Greenwell	Mrs Ann Green	Martha Gordon
Mrs Emmery Genious	Miss Frances M Halsey	Fanny Hampton
Mrs Harrison	Miss Mary Isaacs	
Miss Lucy Kenney	Miss Jerushan Lyman	Miss Ann Lee
Miss Ellen Lucas	Mrs Eliza May	Mrs Cath Mara
Mrs Mary A McNantz	Mrs Manigault	
Mrs Maloy, c/o John Glasco		
Mrs Eleanor Perks	Mrs Mgt Patterson	
Miss Mary Peters	Mrs Eliz Rhodes	
Mrs Sharlot Rowels	Priscilla Shorter	
Mrs Mary E Sandford	Mrs West	

THU JUL 16, 1812
An Act for the relief of Anna Young, sole heiress & rep of Col John Durkee, dec'd; his 7 yrs half pay & interest thereon. Approved, Jas Madison, Jul 1, 1812.

Trustees of the Wash Acad, Wash Co, D C: Jas Laurie, Wm Cranch, Wm James, Silas Butler, Sam'l N Smallwood, Dan'l Rapine & Alex'r McCormick.

An Act for relief of Jas Wilkinson-that from Mar 16, 1802 be allowed for transportation of his baggage, for fuel, same compensation as is now allowed to other Brig Genr'ls in the svc of the U S. -Approved, Jas Madison, Jul 1, 1812.

Willton, Conn, Jul 7, 1812. Capt Peter Bradley has enlisted ab't 50 men in the past wks.

SAT JUL 18, 1812

Died: Mr David Sommerville, sculptor, Jul 17, of consumption. Ntv of Scotland & has resided for 8 yrs in Wash City; leaves a widow & infant offspring. Funeral from his late dwlg hse nr the Centre Mkt today.

Reward-$10 for Joe, mulatto man, prop of Mr Marcus Lattimore of Chas Co, Md. -J Thompson, Wash City.

Runaways committed to the Wash Co, D C, jail: negress, Nancy-says she belongs to Rich'd Wooten, Montgomery, Md; & negress, Mary. -C Tippet, kpr of the jail.

Jas Williamson, of Staunton, Va, has a printing press & type. He wishes to go into operation; he needs a man to come & take interest in the press & publication of a wkly paper as he has no knowlege of printing. -J Williamson.

Taken up-a stray bay horse. Josias Jones, at Mr Brent's Mills. Wash.

For sale-600 acs in Chas Co, Md, called *Cliffden*; with small brick dwlg hse. -Thos Hawkins.

Reward-$50 for Ben, mulatto boy. -Tilghman Hilliary, living in PG Co, Md.

TUE JUL 21, 1812

Pres of the U S appt'd the following Justices of the Peace for Wash Co, D C:
Sam'l Smith   Nicholas Young   John Ott
Nathan Luffborough   John Threlkeld   Thos Corcoran
Thos Peter.

Notice-a gold watch was left with Matthew Wright.

Sale at auction: 2 frame dwlg hses belonging to Mrs Coyle, admx of Thos Coyle, dec'd, on Capt'l Hill; & a set of blacksmith's tools. -N L Queen, auct.

THU JUL 23, 1812

Notice-the partnership of Wight & Moore is hereby dissolved. The lumber yd will be carried on by G Moore.

Sec of War is to place the following invalid pensioners of U S, on the pension list:

Sam'l Allen	$2 per mo	beginning Nov 15, 1811
Nehemiah Levitt	$2.50 per mo	Dec 28, 1811
Wm Powers	$2.50 per mo	Jan 7, 1812
Wm Cushing	$10 per mo	Nov 25, 1811
Wm Leaver, alias Lavar	$2.50 per mo	Dec 6, 1811
Oliver Russel	$2.50 per mo	Apr 6, 1808

Joel Fox	$2.50 per mo	Feb 27, 1811
Isaac Durand	$2.50 per mo	Aug 31, 1811
Aaron Peck	$3.33 1/3 per mo	May 20, 1811
Hezekiah Baily	$5 per mo	Jan 19, 1812
Jonas Hobart	$2.50 per mo	Nov 16, 1810
John Philips	$4 per mo	Jul 10, 1811
Elisha Fanning	$2.50 per mo	Dec 26, 1811
Sam'l Leonard	$2.50 per mo	Mar 9, 1811
Sylvester Tilton	$2.50 per mo	Feb 3, 1812
Mahlon Ford	$20 per mo	Mar 7, 1812
Randolph Clarkson	$2.50 per mo	Mar 16, 1812
Stephen Carter	$3.75 per mo	Feb 16, 1811
Geo Pierson	$2 per mo	Jan 27, 1812
Andrew Bartle	$2.50 per mo	Oct 12, 1811
Philip Krugh	$2.50 per mo	Dec 9, 1811
Andrew Johnson	$5 per mo	Feb 15, 1812
John Harbeson	$3.33 1/3 per mo	Feb 25, 1812
Edw Leary	$5 per mo	Aug 1, 1811
Dan'l McCarty	$4 per mo	Feb 16, 1811
Thos Rogers	$2.50 per mo	Apr 4, 1811
Reuben Plunket	$2.50 per mo	Jun 7, 1811
Jas Bridget-	do	Oct 7, 1811
Mich'l Reap	do	Apr 20, 1811
Henry Weems	$5 per mo	Nov 15, 1811
Malcom Keys	$4 per mo	Nov 15, 1811
Jas Armstrong	$5 per mo	Nov 15, 1811
John Martin	$2.50 per mo	Nov 15, 1811
Robt Elder	$3.33 1/3 per mo	Jul 19, 1811
Jasper Tomiton	$2.50 per mo	Dec 10, 1811
Robt Patterson	$20 per mo	Jul 12, 1811
Virgil Poe	$2.50 per mo	Sep 23, 1811
John Jacobs	$5 per mo	Jul 5, 1811
Thos Hickman	$2.50 per mo	Jan 12, 1811
Jos Shaw	$2 per mo	Jan 13, 1812
Jos Todd	do	Jan 14, 1812
Dennis Laugelan	$2.50 per mo	Aug 24, 1811
Geo Adams	$5 per mo	Jan 29, 1812
Sam'l Newell	$8 per mo	Mar 2, 1811
Thos Wyatt	$2.50 per mo	Jul 24, 1811
Perry Floyd	do	Feb 15, 1812
John Kirk	do	Sep 21, 1811
Jas Crawford	$6 per mo	Sep 12, 1811
Wm Haile	$1.66 2/3 per mo	Nov 19, 1811
Jos Gilmore	$1.75 per mo	Oct 9, 1810
Ethelrod Cobb	$2.50 per mo	Nov 19, 1811
John Taylor	$3.75 per mo	Mar 12, 1812
John Reynolds	$3 per mo	Jul 13, 1810
Henry McFarlane	$2 per mo	Feb 11, 1809

Name	Amount	Date
John Elliott	$2.50 per mo	Dec 26, 1811
John Williams	$5 per mo	Mar 2, 1812
Thos Scotland	do	Dec 10, 1810
Luke Guyant	do	Sep 21, 1809
Dan'l Evans	$2.50 per mo	Mar 13, 1812
Dan'l Rady	do	Apr 16, 1806
John Jordan	$7.50 per mo	Dec 14, 1811
Jacob Seay	$5 per mo	Oct 16, 1811
Amos Lewis	$2.50 per mo	Oct 29, 1811
Benj Fry	$5 per mo	Sep 17, 1810
Benj Collington	$2.50 per mo	Apr 25, 1812
John Johnson	$3.50 per mo	Jan 6, 1812
Patrick Coleman	$5 per mo	Apr 12, 1810
John Garner	$2.50 per mo	Jan 29, 1812
John Bair	$8 per mo	Apr 8, 1811

Increase of pensions to those already on the pension list of the U S:

Name	Amount	Date
Joshua Haynes	$4 per mo	Mar 16, 1811
Nath'l Leavitt	$5 per mo	Mar 16, 1811
Ebenezer Carlton	$5 per mo	Jan 13, 1812
Robt B Wilkins	$5 per mo	Jan 20, 1808
Jas Crummer	$5 per mo	Feb 19, 1812
Jonathan Jotham	$5 per mo	Sep 8, 1808
Wm Warren	$7.50 per mo	Nov 4, 1811
Jonathan Stephens	$2.50 per mo	Feb 27, 1811
Luke Aldrich	$2.50 per mo	Oct 26, 1811
Gustavus Aldrich	$5 per mo	Dec 16, 1811
Levi Chadburn	$5 per mo	Mar 19, 1812
Stephen Barnum	$5 per mo	Jul 3, 1810
Gorsham Dorman	$5 per mo	Jul 3, 1810
Dan'l Bouton	$15 per mo	Mar 14, 1810
Israel Dibble	$3 per mo	Jun 27, 1811
Heber Smith	$5 per mo	Oct 7, 1811
Nathan Hawley	$4 per mo	Aug 22, 1811
David Hurd	$5 per mo	Oct 7, 1811
Amos Skeet	$5 per mo	Jun 21, 1811
Moses Raymond	$5 per mo	Nov 8, 1811
Isaac Buell	$3.75 per mo	Nov 15, 1811
Ransford Avery Ferris	$5 per mo	Mar 2, 1812
Azel Woodworth	$5 per mo	Feb 13, 1812
Jonathan Woolley	$5 per mo	May 16, 1809
Jos Tyler	$5 per mo	May 11, 1809
Nehemiah Pierce	$5 per mo	May 11, 1809
Sam'l Eyers	$5 per mo	May 11, 1809
Oliver Darling	$5 per mo	May 11, 1809
Ebenezer McIllvein	$5 per mo	May 11, 1809
Dan'l Russell	$5 per mo	May 11, 1809
Asa Gould	$5 per mo	May 16, 1809

Wm Hazletine	$5 per mo	May 12, 1809
Dan'l Brown	$5 per mo	May 11, 1809
Amasa Grover	$2 per mo	May 16, 1809
Jos Huntoon	$13.33 1/3	Sep 22, 1808
Philo Stoddart	$3.33 1/3	Oct 7, 1811
Dan'l Staunton	$3.75 per mo	Sep 12, 1810
Elijah Knight	$5 per mo	Aug 1, 1809
Aaron Stiles	$5 per mo	Nov 16, 1811
Morris De Camp	$5 per mo	Apr 17, 1812
Ambrose Lewis	$3.75 per mo	Mar 9, 1811

Nocholas Barth, alias Barrette,-$11.25 per mo-Jan 24, 1812 -Approved, Jas Madison, Jul 5, 1812.

Wash Co, D C. Crct Crt, Jun Term, 1812. Sam'l N Smallwood, cmplnt, vs heirs & adms of Jos Wheat, dfndnts. Ratify sale made by Geo Collard, trustee; part of sq So of sq 802 in Wash City with wharf & appurtenances belonging to the dec'd-sold to Franklin Wharton for $2200. -Wm Brent, clk.

Late bank of the U S-Dividend of 7% to holders of shares in same. -G Simpson, cashier, Phil, Jul 18.

Robt Munro, crnr of Mkt & Water Sts, Gtwn, advertises groc, etc, for sale.

SAT JUL 25, 1812
Biographical memoir of the late Nicholas King, esq; ctzn of Wash City, lately surveyor of the city; Mr K was of a respectable family, not only in Yorkshire, Eng, where his family & relations more immediately existed but in other parts of Eng; the writer met the fr in 1786; Mr K migrated to this country in 1793 & for a short time was a resid of N Y & Phil; he came to Wash in spring of 1796. -not signed.

Died: Geo Wash Varnum, esq, s/o Genr'l J B Varnum, age 33 yrs, at Lovingston, Va, on Jul 8th.

Sale at auction-at the hse occupied by Sam'l Smith in Carroll's Bldgs east of the Capitol; hsehld furn. -Sam'l Smith; N L Queen, auct.

Form to be used by alien enemies; instructions from the Dept of State. Same to be rec'd by the Mrsh'l in person, by John A Wilson or Henry M Wilson, Deputy mrshl; in Alexandria Co, by Dan'l Minor or Wm Fox, Deputy mrshls. Excerpts: - I, a. b., a ntv of Eng, do hereby report myself.age 30 yrs.resid of the U S ab't 15 yrs; I have a wife & 4 chldrn; on Jun 10, 1812 I made declaration to the Crct Crt of my intention to bec a ctzn of the U S. -Wash Boyd, mrshl of D C.

Passengers for England with permission of the Gov't apply to C N Buck or L Krumbhaar, in Phil.

Orphans Crt of Wash Co, D C. Jul 23, 1812. Prsn'l est of David Sommerville, late of said co, dec'd. -John McGowan -Ezl MacDaniel

Notice. Ltrs of adm on est of the late Nicholas King. Persons having claims are to present them. -Margaretta King, admx of N King.

For sale-the whole of the furn in the 3 brick hses at present occupied by Mrs Lane on N J av. -Forrest & Beale, aucts.

Ran away-Jerry Myers, mulatto negro, age bet 30 & 40 yrs; formerly the property of Jas McCormick jr. -Myers & Appler, Wash City.

Sale at auction-at the hse of Joshua Dawson, 13th St, west, next to Dr Blake's; hsehld furn, etc. -Nichs L Queen, auct.

Sale at auction-at the hse of Mr Ball at the Ten Bldgs; hsehld furn. -Nichs L Queen, auct, Wash City.

TUE JUL 28, 1812
Died: Capt Henry Whitby, in England, age 30 yrs; he commanded the *Leander* when she fired on one of our coasters & murdered John Pierce, an American sailor.

Wash City, D C-Cnc'l. Mich'l Lowe is to receive $100, the inspec of tobacco in Wash City shall receive the annual sum of $150, payable quarterly to begin Jun 10, 1812. Geo Blagden, Pres Pro Temp of the Brd of Common Cnc'l. Alex'r McCormick, Pres of the Brd of Aldermen. Approved, Dan'l Rapine, Mayor. Jul 22, 1812.

THU JUL 30, 1812
Elected trustees to the Wash. Acad: G Duval, P Bradly, Th H Gilliss, Robt Underwood, J Mehlin, J Patterson & Jas Davidson.

American vessels captured by H B M ships of war & carried into ports of G Britain bet Feb 20 & May 29, 1812.
Brig Don Roderick, of N Y, D C Gillies, Mstr
Schn'r John, S O Beckford, Mstr, from Boston
Schn'r Hotspur, of Balt, Jas Knowles, Mstr
Sch Sarah Gladston, B Chase, Mstr, from Balt.
Ship Snipe, John Sheer, Mstr from N Y.
Brig Clio of N Y, J Goodday, Mstr
Brig Eclipse, C A De Sheils from Balt.
Schn'r Betsey of Boston, John High, Mstr.
Schn'r Martha of Phil, Jas Lister, Mstr.
Schn'r Vesta of Balt, Cock, Mstr.
Ship Lark of Phil, Hutchinson, Mstr.
Brig Tigress of Balt, Thos Lane, Mstr.
Schn'r Grace Ann Green of N Y, Northrup, Mstr.
Schn'r Fairy of N Y, Philip I Quereau, Mstr
Brig Lucy, of Salem, John Evans, Mstr.
Schn'r Arrow, Durkey, Mstr, bound to Balt.

Brig Zenobia, Skiddy, Mstr, bound to N Y.
Schn'r Falcon, Wilson, Mstr, from Balt.
Friendship, Peter Mood, Mstr, bound to Phil.
Schn'r Betsey, of Marblehead, Mullet, Mstr, from Marblehead.
Ship Genr'l Gates, Warner, Mstr, bound to N Y.
Schn'r Young Connecticut, of N Y, Waterman, Mstr.

Wash Co, D C. Case of Chas P Polk, insolvent debtor. -Wm Brent, clk.

Gov Meigs, Genr'l Thos Worthington & Jeremiah Morrow, have been appt'd by the Pres of the U S, Spec Com'rs to hold a cncl with the Indian Chiefs of Ohio & east of the Mississippi, at Piqua town, in this State, on Aug 1. -Scioto Gaz.

Wm H Hamer, Hatter, Pa av nr the Centre Mkt.

SAT AUG 1, 1812
Post ofc changes in Jun 1812:
Falmouth, Ms-Chas Sandford, vice Jas Hickley, dec'd.
Butler's Plantation, O T-M Le Bone, vice Sam'l McCutchen, rsgn'd.
Morgan, O-Jesse D Hawley, vice T R Hawley, do.
Lloyd's, Va-Thos Matthews, vice B H Munday, do.
Crewsville, Va-Walter Crew, vice Micajah Crew, do.
Randolph C H, Va-Ezekiel Paxson, vice John M Hart, do.
Middleton Point, N J-Cornelius Vanderhorf, vice John Mott, dec'd.
Edenton, Ga-John Smith, vice Henry Barnham, rsgn'd.
Bent Creek, Va-Andrew White, vice Wm G Freeland, rsgn'd.
Dorchester, S C-Henry Clayton, vice Rich'd Maynard.
Jamesville, S C-John Brock, vice Robt Dow, rsgn'd.
Narragagus, Me-Jos Adams, vice Thos Archibald, rsgn'd.
Beckhamsville, S C-John Kidd, vice Wm C Beckham, rsgn'd.
Harvard, Ms-Stevens Hayward, vice Wm L Foster, mv'd away.

New Post ofcs-Jun 1812 & postmaster.
Middleton, Monmouth Co, N J-Wm Murray.
Greenville, Greene Co, N Y-SToddart Smith.
Durham, Greene Co, N Y-Sam'l Hotchkiss.
Ranselearville, Greene Co, N Y-Eli Hutchinson.
Bethlehem, Greene Co, N Y-Dan'l Mead jr.
Denmark, Ashtabula Co, O-John Dibbell.
Russell, St Laurence Co, N Y-Pliney Goddard.
New Baltimore, Greene Co, N Y-Noah Wheeler.
Rouseville, Delaware Co, N Y-John C Dewitt.
Black Heath, St Clair Co, Il Ter-Wm Alexander.
Bear Gap, Northumberland Co, Pa-Henry Fisher.
Lehigh Gap, Northumberland Co, Pa-Henry Bowman.
Kirk's Mill, Lancaster Co, Pa-Timothy Kirk.
Murray, Gennessee Co, N Y-Wm H Ward.
Riga, Gennessee Co, N Y-Rich'd Dibble.

Parma, Gennessee Co, N Y-John D Higgins.
Smalley's, Livingston Co, K-Jas M Runyon.
Orange, Essex Co, N J-Dan'l P Stricker.
Loveton, Balt Co, Md-John Ridgley.
Mill Rose, Amherst Co, Va-Henry Rose.
Bradford, Millsboro Co, N H-Dan'l Moore.
Brown's Turnpike, Albemarle Co, Va-Brightberry Brown
Ofc discontinued in Jun 1812-Pittman's, S C.

Mrd: G W Campbell, esq, Senator in Cong from Tenn, to Miss Hannah Stoddert, d/o Benj Stoddert, esq, of Bladensburg, a few days ago, in this vicinity, by Rev Mr Balch.

Wm Isabel, Prince St, Alexandria, has hair mattrasses for sale.

Reward-Six cents for appr, [to brick laying & stone mason work,] Hugh Mooney, ab't 13 yrs of age, s/o Mr Neale Mooney, of Alexandria, Va. -Robt Brown.

TUE AUG 4, 1812
A bay horse was taken away from a runaway. -A Cheshire, at the Wash Bridge.

Rpblcn Convention-Trenton, Jul 10. Maj Gen Benj Ludlow, Pres; Geo Cassedy, Sec. Committee: Lewis Moore of Bergen; John Lindley of Essex; Solomon Doughty of Morris; Jas J Wilson of Hunterdon; Nathan Stout of Somerset; Bernard Smith of Middlesex; Wm Garrison of Monmouth; Jos McIllvaine of Burlington; Ezra Baker of Gloucester; Ezel Pierson, of Cumberland & Merriman Smith of Salem.

Died: Mr Sam'l Judson Coolidge, on Jul 30th, age 43 yrs, after a long & painful illness; a fond hsbnd, fr & bro.

Laborers wanted at the Powder Yard. -Fielder Parker.

Died: Geo Jefferson, esq, late American Cnsl at Lisbon, on Jul 20th, at sea; he was on his way home in the *Diana* when attacked by a fever in the brain. He was a relation of the late Pres & formerly a merchant in Richmond.

Sale at auction-at the hse of Pontius D Stelle, all his hsehld furn, for rent due Jas Moore. -Nichs L Queen, auct.

Meeting at the Navy Yd on Jul 31, 1812; Mr Wm Sanford, chrmn; John Davis of Abel, sec; Mr Townsend, foreman shipwright; Benj King, mstr blacksmith; Shadrach Davis, mstr Joiner; Wm McKee, armorer; Mr Cocke, Navy store-kpr.

THU AUG 6, 1812
Patriotism-Mr John H Deubell, merchant, of this city, has fitted out a schn'r of 113 tons & tendered the same to the Revenue Dept for U S svc. -Savannah Paper.

Ltr from Robt Wallace jr, Aid-De-Camp to Gen Hull, dt'd-Sandwich, Upper Canada, Jul 12, 1812. Shall move down to Malden where all the British ships & forces are concentrated; Jul 14, 1812-we are prepared to attack Ft Malden; Jul 17, 1812-writing from his Majesty's Dominion. We arrv'd without a battle.

The undersigned were mbrs of the Bladensburgh Militia Co in the early yrs of the Rev; their uniform was green turned up with buff & in 1775 or 1776 the Co procured a stand of colors to correspond with their uniform. -Benj Stoddert; Benj Berry, Ensign to said Co ab't 1780; Zachariah Berry.

For sale-land, deed of trust dt'd Feb 12, 1810 & recorded in PG Co, Md, executed by Marsham Waring, late of said co, for debts due Waring to the Bank of Columbia; at the late dwlg hse of said Waring, lands which he died possessed in said co, ab't 750 to 850 acs. -Walter Smith, Gtwn.

To rent or lease for a term of yrs: the farm on which Hezekiah Wood now lives, ab't 2 miles from the Capitol. -John Breckenridge, oppo Seven Bldgs.

Orphans Crt of Montg Co, Md-sale at late resid of Thos Swearingen, dec'd, 3 miles from Montg Crt Hse; all prsnl prop-3 negroes, cattle, horses, furn. -Eliz Swearingen, admx of Thos Swearingen, dec'd.

Zachariah Maccubin of Montg Co, Md, applying for benefit of the act for relief of sundry insolvent debtors, confined in prison for debt. Rich H Harwood, assoc Judge, Anne Arundel Co, Md [Montg Co Crt in recess.] -Upton Beall, Ck M C C

SAT AUG 8, 1812
Capt John Cassin of the Navy, honored with the command of the Navy Yd at Gosport, Va, ab't to leave this city & proceed to his station. Oliver Pollock, upwards of 60 yrs of age, a Rev Patriot, offered himself a volunteer, to serve in the ranks. Wash City.

Concord, N H, Jul 28-ab't 300 recruits under Lt Col Bedell marched from this place for Burlington, Vt last Thu.

For sale-250 acs in PG Co, Md. -Jas Beck, PG Co, Md.

For sale-healthy negro woman. Apply to Jno Peltz, nr this ofc, Wash City.

TUE AUG 11, 1812
Crct Crt of Wash Co, D C-Crt of Chancery. John Skyren & Chas L Nevit, cmplnts, vs Abram Lindo, Geo Gillingham, Elisha Gaden & Thos Fitzgerald, dfndnts. I will set up & expose for public sale, lots in Wash City: lot 11 in sq 168; lots 3, 4, 6, 10 & 11 in sq 219; lots 1, 2, 3 in sq 458. -Robt King, trust. Nichs L Queen, auct.

Runaway-committed to Wash Co, D C, jail: negress Mary; says she belongs to Mgt Crafford of PG Co, Md. -C Tippet, kpr of the jail for W Boyd, mrshl.

Orphans Crt of PG Co, Md-sale at John H Hall's Tavern in Upper Marlborough; hse srvnts & hsehld furn. -Dennis M Burgess, adm.

John W Eppes, esq, of Va, is a candidate for Congress; his address is in the Richmond Papers.

THU AUG 13, 1812

Report to Edw Johnson, esq, Mayor of Balt City, Md. S H Moore & Thos Rogers, clks. Commotion in Balt on Jun 22nd; Dr Gale was shot & killed; Alex'r C Hanson, an editor of the paper that caused great irritation came into town; he stayed on Chas St at the late dwlg of Mr J Wagner, his partner. Boys began throwing stones & guns were fired from the hse; the occupants surrendered themselves to the Civil Authority: viz-Alex'r C Hanson, Gen Henry Lee, Jas M Lingan, Wm Schnroeder, John Thompson, Wm B Bend, Otho Sprigg, Henry Kennedy, Robt Kilgour, Henry Nelson, John E Hall, Geo Winchester, Peregrine Warfield, Geo Richards, Edw Gwinn, David Hoffman, Horatio Bigelow, Ephraim Gaither, Wm Gaither, Jacob Schley, Mark U Pringle, Dan'l Murray & Rich S Crabb. After their removal the hse was injured & the furn destroyed & dispersed.

Committee of the City cncl-Balt, Md.:

Adam Fonerden	Jas Carey	Wm Steuart
Thos Kell	Jas Calhoun	John C White
Wm McDonald	Henry Payson	
Joined by:		
Jas A Buchanan	Wm Wilson	Peter Little
W Cooke	Wm Gwynn	Thorndike Chase
Lemuel Taylor	Robt Gilmor	S Sterret
John Montgomery.		

Wm C C Claiborne, esq, chosen Govn'r of the new State of Orleans.

For sale or rent-brick hse nr crnr of 12th St & Pa Ave, Wash City; next dr to the resid of Dr Geo A Carroll & oppo Mrs Morin. Apply to Mr A Coyle, nr the Centre Mkt, to Dr John Ott, Gtwn, or to P Mauro, Balt. -P Mauro

SAT AUG 15, 1812

Pittsylvania Co meeting, Jul 31, 1812; Dan'l Coleman, chrmn; Wm Tunstall, Sec. Committee: Geo Tucker, Thos H Wooding, Francis Dabney, Rich'd Johnson, Thos H Clark, Jesse Leftwich, Jas Soyars, Wm Clark, Champney Terry, Nath'l Wilson, Moses Hutchings, Jos Carter, Stephen Coleman & Wm Wimbish, who withdrew.

Reward-$20 for runaway, Jos Isaac, negro man ab't 20 yrs of age. -Kidd Morrell, Vansville, Md.

TUE AUG 18, 1812
Capt Christopher R Petty, of Newport, R I has been appt'd super of the Navy Yd at Charlestown, vice Capt Bainbridge, appt'd to the *Constellation*. -Patriot.

Sam'l Carswell, esq, of Phil, merchant, has rsgn'd the ofc of Commissary Genr'l to the U S Army.

Town meeting-Wash City, D C. Thos Corcoran, Mayor, chrmn; John Lockerman, sec. Committee: Jas S Morsell, Chas A Beatty, Abner Ritchie, Dan'l Reintzel, Thos L McKenney, Ninian Magruder, Wm S Nichols, Geo Magruder, Thos T Gantt, Nichs Hedges, Vincent King, Dan'l Bussard, Joel Brown & Chas A Burnett.

Hdqtrs-Boston, Mass-Aug 5, 1812. Maj Genr'l Henry Sewall is appt'd to command the Eastern Division of the Militia, which was detached by order of Apr 25th last, consisting of all the detached Militia in District of Maine. -Wm Donnison, Adj Gen.

Ltrs rec'd from Upper Canada on capture of Ft Michillimackinac; the Ft capitulated to U S on Jul 15th; Capt Roberts at our head with part of the 10th R V Battalion; Mr Crawford had command of ab't 200 Canadians, Mr Dickenson-143 Sioux, Forlaveins & Winebagoes; myself ab't 280 men, Attawas & Chippewas. My son, Chas Longlade, Augustin Nolin & Machello Caddotte, jr, rendered me great svc. -Signed, John Askin, jr-Strkpr, Dep.

For sale at Tomlinson's Htl, all rght, title, etc of Jas Johnston in dwlg hse nr the Wash Bridge, for ground rent due Anne Cassanave. -David Bates, cnstbl.

Surplus of the call on Gtwn Potomac Bridge Stock, held by each-

Geo Aitkin-$2.25	Bronsal & Niles-$3
Thos Clarke's est-$2.50	Francis Deblock-$20
Uriah Forrest's est-$20	John Garnett-$8.50
Farris & Stocker-$38	Jacob Hoffman-$20
Harrison & Sterret-$31	Henry Holdship-$25
Monagn Hagan-$23	Jos Hardy-$7
Hudson & Yorke-$25.50	Eusha Janney-$18
Thos Law-$19	Dominick Lynch-$19
Eliz McDonough-$14.50	Alex'r I Miller-$11
Jas C Neilson-$30	Thos Natt-$9.50
Pierce & Turner-$15	Isaac Pollock-$17.50
Thos Patton-$8	John Reid-$32
Jas Reid-$8	Ritchie & Beatties-$15.50
Wm Vaughan-$21.50	Wallace & Muir-$28.50
Henry & Clement Lawrence-$15	

Blanket manufactory erected in Gtwn. -Elkanah Cobb & Dan'l Bussard & Co

THU AUG 20, 1812
For sale at the hse of Henry Tims, a sideboard & lkg glass, taken as prop of

said Tims, to satisfy taxes due the Wash Corp. -Z Walker, coll 3d Ward.

Mrshl's sale. All rght, title, etc, of Levi White in part of sq 797, also sq 766. Also all rght, title etc of Stephen Parry to hses on lot 2 sq 879. Also the title & int of Henry Timms to a brick hse on sq 690 on so B St. Prop is sold to satisfy a judgement in favor of John Vint, against the said White, Parry & Timms. -Wash Boyd, Mrsh'l D C.

Stray mare taken by the subscriber at Bladensburg, Md. -Watkins Scott.

Runaways committed to Wash Co, D C, jail: Wm, negro; says he belongs to Gen Jas Breckenridge of Bottetorte Co, Va. Also negro Tom; says he belongs to John Bailey, esq, of Fredericktown, Md. -C Tippet, kpr of the jail

Proclamation-Exec of the State of Pa hath demanded of the Exec of Md, Jos Roche, Thos Kennedy, John Oram & Jas Oram, as fugitives from justice, alleged to be at large in Md; charging same with felony in kidnapping 3 negroes from Phil City viz. Solomon Luff, Rich Bailey & Gabriel Jackson. -Robt Bowie, Aug 3, 1812.

Mrd: Mr Alban Clark, of Wash, to Miss Sarah-Ann Mudd, of PG Co, Md, on Aug 17 by Rev Mr Henry.

New York-the Hse of Benj Austin, esq, of Boston, was on Thu last attacked by persons unknown-more mobocracy. -N Y-Aug 13.

Med College lottery now drawing in Balt; tkts may be purch'd from: Kearney Wharton, 8 South St; Philip H Nicklin, 202 Markes St; J I Cohen jr, Med Coll lottery ofc, 110 Mkt St, Baltimore, Md.

Cncl of Appointment met at Albany, N Y, & appt'd Dewitt Clinton A Maj-Genr'l in the Militia of N Y; & Thos Addis Emmet, Atty-Genr'l, vice Matthias B Hildreth, dec'd.

Final dividend. T H Gilliss, adm of Stanley Byus, dec'd, prepared to make final settlement.

Orphans Crt of PG Co, Md: sale at Henry Hall's Tavern in Upper Marlborough, to the highest bidder, a woman & 5 chldrn. -Edw N Calvert, grdn to Maria Tibbins.

SAT AUG 22, 1812
Valuable stock of dry goods for sale. -Wm G Ridgely, Gtwn.

Act for relief of the heirs of Chas Jones, dec'd, late of Wash City, did on May 9, 1811 obtain a license as auctioneer for 1 yr, & by his decease, 5 mos later, was deprived of the benefit thereof; Treas to pay $58.33 for unexpired time.

Newburgh, Aug 11. Co of Artl under Capt Henry Butterworth, infantry under

Capt Alexander Denniston & Chas Birdsall of this town, have by ordered by the Govn'r to be in readiness on Aug 15 to march to N Y.

Wash Co, D C, to wit: John L Naylor, cmplnt, vs Sam'l Hanson of Sam'l Ameriah Frost & Sam'l Treat, dfndnts-in Chancery. Bill is to obtain title to lot 3 sq 947, Wash City, which was sold in 1800 to Uriah Forrest & Sam'l Hanson of Sam'l; trustees, under decree of High Crt of Chancery of Md, at public sale, to said Ameriah Frost, for $143.50, who gave bond Jul 11, 1800 W Jas Piercey & Sam'l Treat, his securities; obligors failed to pay the said bond & suit was brought; Sam'l Treat was the only one taken, for whom the cmplnt & Robt Cherry became spec bail; judgment obtained against Treat at Dec term, 1805. Ameriah Frost & Sam'l Treat are not residents of D C. -Wm Brent, clk.

Kentucy election: for Govn'r-Col Shelby, 15,297 votes & Col Slaughter, 5,996 votes. Lt Gov: Mr Hickman-10,607; Mr Bradford-1,839 votes; Mr Ewing-1,205 votes; Mr Crutcher-463 votes. Congress: 1st Dist-Jas Clarke; 2d do-H Clay; 3d do-R M Johnson; 4th do-Jos Desha; 5th do-Genr'l Sam'l Hopkins; 7th do-Sam'l McKee; 8th do-John Simpson [over Stephen Ormsby;] 9th do-Thos Montgomery; 10th do-Wm P Duval. 6th Dist remains to be heard from. Not certain ab't Sam'l Hopkins in 5th.

Post ofc changes, Jul 1812:
Greenville, Ky-Jas Weir, vice Parmenas Redman, rsgn'd. .
Peacham, Vt-John Mattocks, vice Abner Crossman, do;
Greenwich, Mass-Roger West, vice Josiah White, do.
Bridgewater, N Y-Isaiah Bunce, vice Dan'l Rindge, situation inconvenient.
Huntingtown, Md-Thos H Wilkinson, vice Lewis Sutton, rsgn'd.
Concord, Del-Thos Adams, vice Mich'l Stewart, dec'd.
Ft Miller, N Y-Peleg Bragg, vice Solomon Smith, rsgn'd;
Wrightsboro, Ga-Thos Dooly, vice Jno Hardin, mv'd away.
Murraysville, Md-Wm Murray, vice Wm Smith, rsgn'd.
Galway, N Y-Martin Cook, vice Nathan Thomson, do.
Greensburg, Ky-Thos M Emerson, vice W H King, dec'd.
Madisonville, Ky-M Caldwell, vice Edw Cook, mv'd away.
Richmond, R I-Geo B Pitman, vice Sam'l Clark, rsgn'd.
Ripton, Ct-Philo Judson, vice Chas De Forrest, mv'd away.
Rocky Springs, N C-Wm Dearing, vice Jas H Dearing, rsgn'd.
Attleboro, Pa-Isaac Gillam, vice Robt Croasdale, do.
Beckamsville, S C-John Kidd, vice Wm Beckam, do.
Canajoharry, N Y-Abraham Wimple, vice Martin Rueff, do.
Winchester, Ky-Robt Clark, vice Mordecai Gist, do,
Scottsburgh, Va-Stephen Cook, vice John B Scott, do.
Piscataway, Md-Rich'd L Humphreys, vice Gavin Hamilton, do.
Stanford, Ky-Jas Helm, vice Benj Monroe, do.
Lincolnton, Ga-J Walker, vice Lewis Stovall, mv'd away.
Loveton, Md-John Ridgeley, vice Thos Love, rsgn'd.
Big Lick Va-Wm Wilson, vice Jas Echolls.

Darlington C H, S C-Moses Saunders, vice David Mason, dec'd.
Haw River, N C-Thos Scott, vice B A Rainey, rsgn'd.
Bethlehem X Rds, Va-John W Stith, vice John Stith rsgn'd.

Post ofcs established in Jul 1812 & postmaster:
Bruce's, Rockingham Co, N C-Chas Bruce.
Patrick, Rockingham Co, N C-Ebenezer Patrick.
Fishing Ford, Bedford Co, Ten-Rich'd Hooper.
Old Salt Hse, Lincoln Co, Ten-John Kelly.
Exeter, Luzerne Co, Pa-Naphtali Hurtbut.
Keg Spring, Murray Co, Ten-Jonathan S Stanfield.
Mill Farm, Caroline Co, Va-Dan'l Turner.
Jackson, Louisa Co, Va-Elisha Jackson.
Point Harmer, Wash Co, O-Geo Dunlevy.
Minerva, Livingston Co, Ky-Jas M Runyon.
West-North-East, Duchess Co, N Y-Stephen Thorn.
Ofc discontinued in Jul 1812: Yellow Springs, Pa.

Wash Co, D C-In Chancery. John Woodward vs Thos Gamble. Bill is to procure foreclosure & sale of ground in Holmead's Addition to Gtwn in Wash Co, D C, late Montg Co, Md; prop on New & Beall Sts; mortgaged by the dfndnt to the cmplnt-136 pds 3 shillings & 3 pence with int from Feb 14, 1799. Thos Gamble not a resid of D C. -Wm Brent, clk.

Savannah, Aug 6. We learn that 2 patriots, Jas Hollingsworth & Dan'l Pritchard, were shot dead by Indians belonging to the Lotchway Tribe, Creek Nation; both were tomahawked & scalped.

Buffaloe, Jul 28. Spy in custody: Elijah Clark, a subject of his Majesty in Upper Canada was lurking on this side apparently as a spy. Judge Barker & Capt J Wells & others arrested him in Mr Lay's hse. Also arrested were Aaron Brink & David Lee who were examined by Col Swift & Maj Miller. All await for a crt martial to be ordered by Maj Gen Hull.

Phil, Pa-Aug 15. We understand that Peter L Berry, Bryant Drum, John Warr & Edw Kirby were brought before the Mayor, virtue of a warrant from Montg Co, on charge of assault & battery on Mr Sowers, printer, in Norristown.

St Mary's Co, Md-meeting. Col Henry Neale, chrmn; Jas Forrest, sec. Cmte: John Rousby Plater, Raphael Neale, Athanasius Fenwick, J Hopewell & Wm C Somervill. Regarding lawless & violent proceedings recently in Balt City, Md.

TUE AUG 25, 1812
Frederick Co, Md. Rpblcn ctzns convened at the hse of Mr Justinian Mayburry, in this town on Aug 14; Genr'l Roger Nelson, chrmn; Dr Wm Tyler, sec; Jos Miller, David Kemp, Peter Zollinger & John Cook to rep the voters of Fredr'k. Genr'l Sam'l Ringgold be recommended to the voters of the 4th Dist; Mr Francis

Hollingsworth to rep 3d Dist; Joshua Cockey recommended as candidate for electors of Pres & VP.

Teacher wanted-for private family in the country; $300 per annum & his accommodations. Apply to Dr Jas H Blake, Wash City.

St Mary's Co, Md-Orphans Crt, Aug Term 1812. Francis Simms, adm of Anthony Simms jr, late of St Mary's Co, dec'd, is ordered to give notice required by law for creditors. -Jas Forrest, Reg wills for St M Co, Md. [Notice followed]

Phil, Pa-Aug 22. The remains of Capt John Heard of the British brig, *Ranger*, were interred with that respect which honor & valor even in an enemy can never fail to inspire; Capt Heard was captured with his brig by the priv armed schn'r, *Matilda,* of this port. He died of the wound he rec'd. The Phil Blues under Col L Rush performed the funeral honors. -Aurora.

Dissolution of the partnership of Stettinius & Kneller, by mutual consent. -Sam'l Stettinius. Geo Kneller-Wash.

Ranaway-Jack Brown, negro man, age ab't 24 yrs. -Elias Gray, living in PG Co, Md.

Notice: sale of all right, title, claim & int of Ignatius Howe in a frame hse, adj the hse of John A Burford, at which sale John A Burford became the highest bidder at $330 & not complying with the terms; the said hse will be sold at the loss & expense of Mr John A Burford. -N L Queen, auct.

THU AUG 27, 1812
To the public-the colors displayed by the Bladensburg Co in Battalion, Col Thos Bowie, are British colors. -Jos Cross & Christopher L Gantt, PG Co, Md.

New London, Aug 9. Mon last, Mr A Henderson of Va & Mr Stewart of N Y, landed here from on board the ship *Fanny,* Jennings, of N Y, 35 days from Greenock, Scot.

Wm Henry Harrison, Govn'r of the Indiana Terr, we learn, has been appt'd a Brig Genr'l in the U S Army.

For sale-400 acs in Huntingdon Co, Pa. -Lancaster & Knott, Gtwn.

Sale at auction-at the late resid of Mr Chas McNantz, dec'd, a parcel of hsehold furn & tools. -N L Queen, auct.

Drs Pendergrast & Ross, of the U S Army, will go with the Hon S L Mitchill to Schooley's Mntn, on the Musconecunk in N J, & examine the silicious stone; determine if same is suitable for the manufacture of flints. -Jos Bloomfield, Brig Gen Command. [Topographical info rec'd from David Heath jr & Henry Plum.]

Wash Htl opened on this day on Pa Ave nr the Treas ofc. -John Macleod.

Land for sale-51,202 acs in Va; 46,702 acs of the said quantity lies in Randolph Co nr Beverly, remaining 4,500 acs lay in Monongahela Co, Va; titles are indisputable & entered regularly as early as Jul 1785. -Apply to Robt Ober, Gtwn.

Ft Wayne, Jul 20. On Jul 4th, Little Turtle breathed his last at his Camp nr Ft Wayne; gout was his disorder. I had him buried on the 15th with the honors of war. -B F Stickney, Indian agent [to John Johnson, esq, agent for Indian affairs].

For rent-hse in F St, lately occupied by John Hewitt, esq. -Eliza Clark.

Runaway committed to Frederick Co, Md jail; John Herbert, mulatto man ab't 21 yrs of age; says he belongs to Mr Jonas Thompson of Gtwn, D C. -Ezra Mantz, shrff.

In Chancery, Aug 19, 1812. Ratify the sale of Zachariah Waters, trustee, for the sale of rl est of Godfrey Waters; sum of $2709.10. -Nichs Brewer, Rg.

SAT AUG 29, 1812
Chillicothe, Aug 19. One Regt of riflemen, under Lt Col John Allen; the 1st Regt of infty under Lt Col John M Scott; & the 5th Regt of infty under Lt Col Wm Lewis, have marched from Ky to join the N W Army in Canada; this body of 1800 strong are under Brig Genr'l Payne. 400 regulars, recruited in Ky, marched at the same time for the same point under Col Wells. At Urbana, they will form a junction with 900 Ohio vols under brig Genr'l Tupper & 100 Regulars, recruited in Ohio, under Capt Langham.

Boston town meeting. Wm H Sumner, esq, read the resolves; Geo Blake made a motion; Sam'l Dexter spoke. Voted: Hon Harrison G Otis, Hon John C Jones, Hon Christopher Gore, Dr John Warren, Jos Head, Wm Sullivan, Sam'l Parkman, Chas Jackson, Hon E St Loe Livermore, Hon Dan'l Sargent, Hon Artemas Ward, Wm Parsons, Hon Thos Dawes, Theodore Lyman, Arnold Welles, Jas Perkins, Warren Dutton, David Sears & Benj Gorham. -Benj Weld, Moderator; Thos Clark, clk.

Carriage for sale-enquire of Mr John Davis, Indian Queen. Wash City.

For rent, hse lately occupied by the subscriber, adj Mr Thos H Gilliss, on 14th St West. Apply to Wm James, 13th St, next door to Dr Blake.

To tanners: by last will of David Somerville, dec'd, sale of a tan yard, sq 642 in Wash City, together with 21 lots in said sq; with brick dwlg hse. -John McGowan, Ezl MacDaniel, excs.

Eloped from my bed & board, my wife Mary Jeffers, on Aug 25th without any cause. I am determined not to pay any debts of her contracting. -Matthias Jeffers.

Rockville Acad will open for students in Latin & Greek languages, mathematics etc, on Oct 12th; under Rev Sam'l Martin, late of Slate Ridge, Pa; 10 pds per annum. -Jos Elgar, sec, Montgomery Crt Hse, Md.

TUE SEP 1, 1812
Montg Co, Md, meeting, Aug 29, 1812. Robt Smith, cld to the chrmn; Robt Wallace, sec. Committee: Jos Elgar, Dr Jas Anderson, Wm Wilson, Maj K Gettings. Dr John Wootton, Col Jas B Brookes, John Adamson, Chs Young, Jesse Leach, Lloyd Magruder, Rich'd West, Grandison Catlett & Nicholas W Dorsey.

Natchez, Jul 29. Meeting held Thu last; Beverly R Grayson, chrmn; Capt Hunter Holmer, sec.

Phil, Aug 28. Callender Irvine, esq, is appt'd Commissary-Genr'l of the U S in place of Sam'l Carswell, esq, rsgn'd.

New York, Aug 27. Crt-Martial held lately on Governor's Island, Peter Beam, ntv of Long island, a sldr belonging to the garrison was convicted of desertion & sentenced to be shot; he deserted 5 times & enlisted 3 times & rec'd bounty; at the awful moment-the prisoner rec'd a pardon.

THU SEP 3, 1812
I certify that Wm Blanchard brought before me a stray bay mare; Aug 29, 1812. -Walter B Beall, Justice of the Peace.

Reward-$50 for runaway, John White alias Robt Green, mulatto man ab't 24 yrs of age; he belonged to Mr Benj Drew, of Smithfield, Va, who sold him to Mr Wm Young nr Richmond, Va. -Wm Crawford, Union Tavern, Gtwn.

Died: Louis Bonaparte, late King of Holland, aged 40; in Gratz, Silesia, about the middle of Jun last.

Orphans Crt of Wash Co, D C. Sale of all prsnl prop of the late Edw Eno, dec'd, at his late dwlg; hsehld furn & butchering business articles. -Thos C Wright, Sam'l Rogers, excs.

Hdqtrs at Detroit, Aug 16, 1812. Genrl orders: Brig Genr'l Hull announces to the N W Army, he has been compelled to agree to the following Articles of Capitulation. Camp Detroit, Aug 16, 1812. Surrender of Ft Detroit, entered into bet Maj Gen Brock, his Britannic Majesty's forces & Brig Gen Hull of the U S Army. [Not a shot was fired & the ofcrs & men were so indignant at this dastardly conduct of their Genr'l that they actually shed tears-Sep 8 nwspr]
1-Troops will be prisoners of war
2-All public stores, arms & documents will be given up.
3-Pvt persons & prop will be respected. [All was plundered-Sep 8 newspaper]
4-Agreed that the Detachment from Ohio, on its way to join this Army; & one sent from Ft Detroit under Col McArthur, to be included in the above

stipulation. 5-the Garrison will march out at 12 o'clock this day & the British forces will take immediate possession of the fort. -J M Dowl, Lt Col Militia B A D C. L B Gegg, Maj A D C. Approved: Wm Hull, Brig Gen, commanding the N W Army. Jas Miller, Lt Col 5th U S infty. E Brush, Col 1st Regt Michigan Militia. Approved, Isaac Brock, Maj Gen. Montg Co, Md.

Died: M Sonnini, the celebrated traveller, lately, in France.

Sale at auction-at hse formerly occupied by Cmdor Tingey; assortment of hsehld furn. -Forrest & Beall.

Mechanic's Bank of Alexandria; notification to stockholders of one dollar per share is cld for. -Wm Paton jr, cashier.

Reward-$20 for runaway, Nancy, negro woman; formerly the prop of Stanley Hoxton, residing in Alexandria; she was raised by Miss Brook of PG Co, Md. -Jos Costigan, Wash.

SAT SEP 5, 1812
Grand Number lottery-Susquehanna Canal, 2d Class; Drawing in Balt, Md. Mgrs: Robt Gilmor, Wm Smith, Mark Pringle, Sam'l Smith, Wm Cocke, Hugh Thompson, John Swan, David Williamson, Wm Patterson, Robt Oliver, Stewart Brown, John Sherlock, John E Hollin, Arch McCalister, Sam'l Sterrett.

Chilicothe, Aug 22. Genr'l Hull sent ab't 150 vols to protect the U S mail from Detroit to the rapids, & to reinforce Capt Brush; when they arrv'd at Magawga they were fired on & among those killed was Capt McCulloch; Capt Ulry was wounded & taken prisoner.

Note to Col Jos Sterrett: whereas, Edw Johnson, John Scott, Job Smith & John F Harris, Justices of the Peace of Md, have recommended me to order Militia to preserve the peace of the State. [Signed] J Stricker, Br Gl 3d Brig M M. Balt, Jul 28, 1812. The orders to Maj Barney & Col Harris were in similar terms.

For sale-brick hse on sq 78; oppo the West Mkt Hse. -Wm O'Neale

Norfolk, Aug 29. On Thu last 70 men, raised by & under the command of Capt Sam'l B Archer, embarked on the Ferguson's Packet of Princetown.

Sale at auction-at hse lately occupied by Sam'l J Coolidge, dec'd, on Capitol Hill; 5 female slaves, 7 doz silver spoons, ladles & candlesticks. -Moses Young, trustee; Nichs L Queen, auct.

Public sale-order of Orphans Crt of Calvert Co, Md. Prsnl prop of Basil Brooke, dec'd, at his late residence: negroes, stock, furn, etc. -John J Brooke, exc of B Brooke. [Also 1,000 acs of Patuxent land in Calvert Co, Md]

Sale at auction-at hse of Andrew Coyle, hsehold furn & nrly new piano. -Eliz Chisholm. -N L Queen, auct.

To be sold-variety of hsehld furn & hse for term of seven yrs. -Mary McNamara, admx of Cornelius McDermott Roe. -Nich L Queen, auct.

Reward-$5 for strayed or stolen bay gelding. Deliver to Jos Thomas nr Gen Van Ness's wharf. -J Thomas

Died: Mrs Belinda Crawford, age 115 yrs; in Richmond. Mrs C was 18 yrs old on Apr 22, 1715; she remembered because of the total Eclipse of the Sun.

Died: Rev Favell Hopkins, of Huntingdon, age 87, in England.

Died: Sir Francis Molyneaux, age 75 yrs, in London; forty yrs a gentleman usher of the Back Rod to the King of Eng.

TUE SEP 8, 1812
Killed & wounded on board the U S frig *Constitution,* Isaac Hull, esq, Capt, in action with H M S *Guerriere*, Jas R Dacres, esq, Capt, on Aug 20, 1812.
Killed: Wm S Bush, 1st Lt of Marines
Seamen:

| Jacob Sago | Robt Bruce | John Brown |
| Jas Read | Caleb Smith | Jas Ashford0 |

Wounded:

Chas Morris, 1st Lt, dangerously	John C Aylwin, mstr, slightly
Rich'd Dunn, seaman, dangerously	Geo Reynolds, o s, dangerously
Dan'l Lewis, o s, dangerously	Francis Mullen, Marine, slightly.
-Isaac Hull, Capt. T J Chew, Purser.	

Killed & wounded on board the *Guerriere*:
Wounded:

Capt Jas T Dacres	Bartholomew Kent,
Lt Robt Scott, Mstr.	Sam'l Grant, Mas Mate
Jas Enslie, Mid	John Little, seaman
Jas Miller, o s	Henry Verderie, o s
Hugh McKinley, o s	Jas Morris, seaman
T Harringtor, arm'rs mt	Wm Mee, arm'rs mt
Peter Stempstead, o s	Peter Peterson, o s
Ralph Williams, o s	Henry Holt, o s
Wm Somers, o s	Wm Millington, o s
Pat Murphy, Qr Gun	J Cromwell, Qr Mas
Mat Reardon, o s	John Campbell, o s
John Southgate, o s	Henry Dent, o s
Stephen Kelly, boy	John O'Hare, o s
Philip Dwyer, o s	J Smith, 3d seaman
K McDonald, seaman	Alex Ferguson, o s
Geo Meather, seaman	Jas Crooker, seaman

David Lewis, o s
Jos Lushwood, o s
Geo Reed, seaman
D McMechen, Carpt's crew
G Emmerson, sail mak
J Jameson, seaman
John Bruntlot, seaman
R Baily, 1st mate
Sam'l Miller, seaman
John Fake, Marine
John Goss, Marine
Wm Cooper, Marine
Thos Chambers, Marine
Wm Ryan, Marine
John Robson, Marine

John Hibbs, o s
Robt Taylor, o s
Wm Jones, o s
Wm Cooper, seaman
Lawrence Norman, seaman
Wm Hall, seaman
J Sholer, bo mate
J Copeland, seaman
Roger Spry, Marine
Melchis Archer, Marine
Edw Daking, Marine
Sam'l Long, Marine
Jos Fountain, Marine
Thos Couther, Marine
Wm Jones, Marine

Killed:
H Ready,
2d Gun'r Mt Henry Brown, o s
Robt Rogers, seaman
Wm Baker, o s
Wm White, seaman
J A Fox, Sgt Marine
Rich'd Chusman, handsman
Wm Brown, 2d Seam

2d Lt J Smith,
G Griffiths, Qu Gunner
J Tuck, o s
Alex Cowie, Seaman
J Woodcock, Marine
John Peterson, Seam.
T Pratt, Marine

Missing:
Jas Johnston
Ben Haworth
Jas Johnson 3d
Marine John Griswell
Wm Raysdon
John Jacobs
Lt Roberts
John Newman

Moses Vingen
Jas Greenwood
Cpl Webb,
Jas McGill
Wm Hammock
Lt Jas Pullman
John Fravit
Mr Garton

Robt Scott
Wm Cole
Robt Winn
Jas Batterwitch
A Joaquin
John Hosey
Jas Guy
Robt Mittwoft

The account of the proceedings of H M S *Belvidere*, Rich'd Byron, Capt, Jun 23, 1812 and the President, Cmdor Rodgers. [Ltr from Capt Hull to the Sec of the Navy]: Killed, Wm Gould, seaman; wounded, John Hill, [Armourer] mortally, Jos Lee [Sea.] severely Geo Marlon [ships Cpl] badly, Lt Bruce & Jas Kelly, Jas Larmont [Sea] slightly.

Died: Robt Underwood, Sep 6, in Wash City; many yrs a clk in Treas ofc of U S.

Legionary order. The First Legion of Militia of D C is divided into 3 Btlns:
1st-Maj Geo Magruder; companies: Capt Brown, infty Capt A King, infty Capt Ross, infty
Capt Nourse, infty to which are attached: Capt Stull's Rflmen & Capt Ruth, Rflmen, Lt infty.
2d-Maj Wm Brent; companies:

Capt McKee, infty Capt B King, infty Capt Moore, infty
Capt Parry, infty to which are attached: Capt Cassin's, Lt infty & Capt Young, Lt infty
3d-Maj Jas Thompson; companies:
Capt Briscoe, infty Capt Speake, infty Capt Wheaton, infty Lt Com Bester, infty to which are attached:
Capt Davidson, Lt infty & Capt Lenox, Lt infty.

New York-Sep 1. Military Parade-Aug 31st the 1st brigade of N Y State Artl, Gen Morton, paraded in broadway in respect to the 2d brigade on svc at Ft Richmond for the defence of this city. Troops on svc-the following companies: Capt Walkers, Artl, from Albany City:

Wigton-from City of Hudson	Stocking from Village of Catskill
Nelson-from Poughkeepsie	Butterworth from Newburgh
Dubois from Village of Catskill	Pierson from Athens.
Wilson from Poughkeepsie	Lawson from Poughkeepsie
Denniston from Newburgh	Birdsail from Newburgh
Bulkley Com of Lt infty from Albany	

Rich'd Duvall, Coll of the County Taxes for PG Co. Md; list of taxes due.
Upper Marlborough, Charlotte & Mt Calvert Hundreds:
Dennis M Burgess, 1 1/2 lots imprv'd in Upper Marlborough; $15.26
Sam'l Hepburn-heirs, prt of *Maiden's Dowry & Grey Eagle Enlarged*, 392 acs; $13.59
Mrs Shirley, part of *Adventure*, 51 acs; $34.08
Arnold Livers, lot in Upper Marlborough; 45 cents.
Frank Seek jr-heirs, 1/2 imprv'd lot in Upper Marlborough; $10.15
Hugh Maguire, prt of *Darnall's Chance & Addition*, 12 acs; $2.43
Francis Piles, prt of *Brooke Hill & Cuckhold*, 100 acs; $11.
Sam'l W Magruder-heirs, 1/3 lot in Upper Marlborough; 15 cents.
John Roger-heirs, 1/2 lot in Upper Marlborough; 45 cents
John Selby, prt of *Leith*, 96 acs; $2.76.
Rich'd Sprigg-heirs, West River, 1 lot in Upper Marl; 59 cents.
Dennis Scott-heirs, 1 1/2 lots imprv'd in Upper Marl; $16.49
Thos Tillard-heirs, prt of *Mt Calvert Manor*, 30 acs; $1.41
Jane Ruquhart, prt of a lot in Upper Marl; $1.17.
Lingan Wilson, 1 lot imprv'd in Upper Marl; $2.06
Mattapang, Wash & Prince Frederick Hundreds:
John Adams jr & wife, *Quicksall*, 128 acs; $2.19.
Rich Brightwell, *Ridgeway* or *No Name*, prt of *Padgett's Rest*, 279 1/2 acs; $4.62.
John Bunce, *Runaways*, 3 acs; 12 cents.
Jas Bates heirs, Pt of *Coolspring Addition*, prt of *Forrest*, 173 1/2 acs; $3.32
Thos Buchanan-heirs, 1 lot imprv'd in Nottingham; $1.19.
Fielder Bowie-heirs, *Tanyard & Reed's Meadows*, 29 acs; $1.19
Ignatins Boone, 1 lot imprv'd in Nottingham; $12.55
Alexander Contee, 3 lots imprv'd in Nottingham; $62.39.
Henry Compton, prt of *Dunbar*-20 acs; *Taylorton*-150 acs; prt of *Taylorton*-50

acs; Pt of *Crooked Lane*-12 acs; part of *Crooked Lane*-5 acs; prt of *Dunbar*-2 acs; part of *Taylorton*-5 acs; $20.46.
Henry T Compton, prt of *Coschangs*, 75 acs; prt of *Pascum*, 168 1/2 acs; $7.44.
Arthur Campbell, *Hogpen Addition Enlarged* & prt of *Forrest*-186 1/4 acs; *Forrest Enlarged*-4 1/2 acs; 73 cents.
Benj Contee, prt of *Coolspring* & *Forrest Sherwood*-21 acs; 25 cents.
John Campbell, prt of *Hogpen* & *Sasser's Green*-100 acs; $4.21.
Wm Cooke, prt of *Wright's Park*-43 acs; prt of *Reed's Swamp*-21 acs; 59cents.
Jane Davis, prt of *Coolspring Addition* & prt of *Forrest*-186 3/4 acs; $26.40.
Wm M Eversfield-heirs, prt of *Brookfield*-360 acs; $9.38
Sarah A Gibbon, *Terra Excultabalus*-100 acs; $4.05.
Mary A Gates, prt of *Anchong Hills*-234 acs; $8.76.
Thos Gardiner, prt of *Thatham*-6 acs; $1.56.
Wm Grindall, prt of *Taylor's Course*-210 acs; $3.63.
Dr Thos Gantt, prt of *Terrell & Bowling Green*-174 acs; prt of *Terra Excultabalus*-4 1/2 acs; $4.47.
Geo H Gantt, prt of *Londo Derry*-100 acs; $5.73.
John Hughes, prt of *Good Luck*-79 1/2 acs; $4.36.
Thos Hodgkin, 1 lot in Nottingham; 30 cents.
Rebecca Letchworth, prt of *Brooke Crt*-200 acs; $3.19.
Rich'd Lee, *Reed's Swamp*-125 acs; $1.52.
John Linthicum, prt of *Beans's Landing* adj Nottingham-1/8 ac; 37 cents.
Jas Mewbern, prt of 1 imprv'd lot in Nottingham; $1.88.
Wm Mayhen, prt of *Colebrooke*-196 1/2 acs; $14.53.
Alex'r Magruder-heirs, prt of *Coschargs*-125 acs; prt of *Coschargs*-449 acs; $25.88.
Chas L Nevitt-1/2 lot improv'd in Nottingham; $2.30.
John F A Prigg-heirs, prt of *Trueman's Hills*-280 1/2 acs; prt of *Pleasant Hill, Addition to Ditto, & Addition to Prevention*-70 acs; *Addition to Sterling Park & Strife*-379 3/4 acs; *Walls Refuse*-30 1/2 acs; *Walls Refuse Enlarged*-3 acs; $9.22.
David D Paggett, prt of *Londonderry*-100 acs; 93 cents.
Nichs B Sansbourg-heirs, *Tan-Yard & Wiglel's Park*-200 acs; $3.87.
Jas Swann-heirs, *Ludford's Gift* & prt of the *Hatchets*-198 acs; $23.72.
Edw Swann, *Anchong Hills*-15 acs; 26 cents.
Nathan Smith, 1 lot imprv'd in Nottingham; 40 cents.
Eliz Trueman, prt of *Buttingham*-312 acs; $29.22.
Levin Watson, prt of *Poplar Hills*-30 acs; $4.61.
King George & Grub Hundreds:
Henry Achison, prt of *Jessamine*-36 acs; $6.27.
John Adams, 1 lot imprv'd in Piscataway; 85 cents.
Chas Boarman, prt of the Upper prt of *Wynn's Chance*, prt of *Indian Fields* & prt of *Gardiner's Meadows*-98 3/4 acs; prt of *Wynn's Chance & Indian Fields*-80 3/4 acs; $3.58.
John Bowling-heirs, prt of *Piscataway Manor & Downes Neglect*-267 1/2 acs; $6.72.
Rich'd Brandt, prt of *Market Overton*-175 acs; $5.26.
Rich'd Boarman, prt of The *Ridge*-270 acs; $6.26.

Nicholas Blacklock-heirs, *Blacklock's Venture*-125 acs; prt of the *Widow's Trouble*- 100 acs; prt of *Gantt's Enlargement Enlarged*-268 1/2 acs; prt of *Strife & Boston*-135 acs; prt of *Strife*-142 acs; $85.81.
Sam'l Berry, prt of *Aix*-116 acs; prt of *Wynn's Chance*-46 1/4 acs; $6.82.
Mary Clagett, prt of *Market Overton*-100 acs; *Tyler's Discovery*-210 acs; $11.56.
Jas Clerklee & wife, prt of *Beal's Reserve*-310 acs; $3.60.
Sam'l Chapman, 1 lot imprv'd in Piscataway; $8.86.
Thos Clagett, 1 lot imprv'd in Piscataway; $1.76.
Geo Dyer, *Edelen's Hogpen Enlarged*-200 acs; $1.99.
John Dyer-heirs, *No Name*-100 acs; prt of *Leith*-4 acs; $23.61.
Geo W Dent, prt of *Nickhim in Deerrange & Meadows*-100 acs; $8.52.
Henry Davidson, 3 lots in Piscataway; $16.13.
Erasmus Gantt, *Brentwood Farm*-100 acs; $1.39.
Henry Glassgow, prt of *Wynn's Middle Lot*-53 acs; 98 cents.
Theodore Glassgow, prt of *Wynn's Middle Lot*-78 acs; $5.40.
Sam'l Jay, *West Qrtr Enlarged*-337 acs; prt of *Limpster*-67 1/2 acs; $3.38.
Eliz Hollery, prt of *Exeter*-243 1/2 acs; $4.50.
Wm Jenkins, 1 lot imprv'd in Piscataway; $2.27;
Elvira Handy, prt of *Leith*-1ac; $5.03.
Eliz A Hilton, prt of *Jessamine*-77 acs; $2.23.
Thos James-heirs, prt of *Vineyard*-200 acs; $4.02.
Nath'l Newton, prt of *Prevention & Inclosure*-30 acs; prt of *Apple Hills*-170 acs; *Jos & Ann*-339 acs; prt of *Plymouth*-170 acs acs; prt of *Wheeler's Hope*-265 acs; *Hazzard*-106 acs; prt of *St Luke & Eliz & Longcoat Enlarged*-98 acs; $28.45.
Benj Mitchell of Notley, prt of *Thos & Sarah*-132 acs; $9.42.
Rev Geo Ralph, prt of *Limpster*-63 /12 acs; *West Qrtr Enlarged*-337 acs; $31.87.
Walter Rankin, prt of *Jessamine*-27 1/2 acs; $53.
Rich'd B A Webster, prt of the *Ridge*-73 acs; $1.24.
<u>Piscataway & Hynson Hundreds:</u>
Geo Beall of Geo, *Tenley's Chance*-106 acs; *Baynes 1st & 2d lots*-60 acs; $21.93.
Rich'd H Courts, prt of *Radford's Chance*-402 acs; $6.86.
Judson M Clagett-heirs, prt of *Dublin*-197 acs; prt of *Stoney Harbor*-100 acs; $60.61.
Benj Dulany, prt of *Battersea*-40 acs; $2.20.
Jesse Greenwell-heirs, prt of *Silver Hills*-213 acs; $2.45.
Dan'l Hurley, prt of *Weaver's Delight*-93 acs; $2.66.
John Hepburn, prt of The *Outlet*-70 acs; $1.78.
Geo Hardey, prt of *Refuse*-45 acs; 78cents.
Chas Jones [Millwright], *Leonard's Lot*-65 1/4 acs; $4.12.
Mary Jones, *Leonard's Lot*-65 1/4 acs; $7.21.
Thos Jenkins of Dan;l, prt of *Oxmantown & Maiden Bradley*-278 acs; prt of *Magruder's Choice*-90 acs; prt of *Refuse*-45 acs; prt of *What You Please*-34 acs; $4.18.
Chas King, a small prt of svr'l tracts-2 acs; $7.39.
Mich'l Lowe, prt of *Forrest*-24 acs; prt of *Soper's Rest Enlarged*-95 acs; $9.79.

Henry H Lowe, prt of *Lanham,s Delight*-84 acs; prt of *Soper's Rest Enlarged*-25 acs; $14.76.
Philip Lee, prt of *Magruder's Plains*-8 acs; 15cents.
Solomon Lanham, prt of *Hunter's Fields*-94 acs; $3.27.
Mich'l Love & Leonard Soper, *Fishing Island*-3 3/4 acs; $6.14.
Dan'l Morriss, *Coxen's Rest*-100 acs; 95 cents.
Wm Mansfield, prt *Insley's Discovery*-75 acs; $2.66.
Eliz McDonough, prt of *Major's Choice*-57 1/2 acs; $3.76.
Jas Moore heirs, prt of *Silver Hills*-215 acs; $6.48.
Wm Masters, prt of *Silver Hills*-27 acs; $1.01.
Dan'l Moxley, prt of *Oxen Hill Manor*-10 acs; $1.58.
Jas Rudd, prt of *Magruder's Choice*-111 acs; prt of *Goodwill*-34 acs; $1.95.
Dan'l Purl, prt of *Magruder's Plains*-71 acs; $5.26.
Sarah Smith, *Loudon's Pleasure*-33 1/2 acs; 47 cents.
David Stone, prt of *Chance*-166 acs; $2.12.
Wm O Sprigg, the *Levels Enlarged*-604 acs; $22.60.
Lewin Tallenet, prt of *Gleaning*-124 acs; $2.46.
John Wheat, *Coolspring Addition*-100 acs; $2.97.
Mary Wade, prt of *Hunter's Folly*-44 acs; $5.29.

New Scotland, Oxen & Bladensburg Hundreds:
Hiram Belt, *Nicholas' Hunting Qrtr*-10 1/2 acs; prt of *Gamefield*-7 1/2 acs; $6.48.
Sam'l D Beck-heirs, 2 lots imprv'd in Bladensburg & adj land; $21.24.
Patrick Dougherty, 1 lot imprv'd in Bladensburg; $2.99
David Ferguson, prt of 1 lot imprv'd in Bladensburg; $3.14.
Jos Gordon, prt of *Second Thought*-76 acs; $2.54.
Thos Gantt, prt of 3 lots imprv'd in Bladensburg; $12.80.
Jas Johnson-heirs, prt of one lot imprv'd in Bladensburg; $4.51.
John Murray, *Land Above*-26 acs; $1.17.
Randolph Morris, prt of *Pleasant Spring Enlarged*-110 acs; $3.09.
Wm Syclebothom-heirs, prt of *Hogpen*-65 acs; $5.69.
Wm Stewart, 7 lots imprv'd in Bladensburg & adj land; $39.56.
Jesse Taylor, 1/2 ac adj Bladensburg; 80 cents.
Rev Notley Young, prt of *Brother's Joint Iinterest Enlarged* & a Mill-50 acs; $7.06.
Dr John Stonestreet, *Cadmune*-113 acs; *Name unknown* nr Bladensburg-3 acs; $1.75.

Rock Creek & Eastern Branch Hundreds:
Jeremiah Berry, hse & lot in Bell town; $1.07.
Francis Deakin-heirs, prt of *Resurvey on Miller's Beginning*-105 acs; $16.07.
Geo Frank, *Frank's Adventure*-20 acs; $1.85.
Janot Hopkins, *New Bermingham Manor*-976 acs; *Resurvey on Martin's Fancy*-73 acs; prt of *Isaacs Park*-50 acs; prt of *Piney Grove*-14 acs; *Maple Swamp*-9 acs; $12.29.
Eliz Jones, prt of *Elizabeth's Portion*-41 1/4 acs; $5.48.
Andrew Leitch-heirs, prt of *Deakins Hall Little Meadows, Force Put & Paint Branch*-235 1/2 acs; $2.94.
Nicholas Lingan, prt of *Gilead*-76 acs; $1.92.
Chas Tilley, prt of *Black Ash*-4 acs; 11 cents.

Sycebothom William-heirs, hse & lot in Bell town-2 acs; $1.26.
Horsepen & Patuxent Hundreds:
Benj Beall, *Timberland*-189 acs; $5.22.
Zachariah Baldwin-heirs, prt of *Strife*-254 1/2 acs; *Moore's Cultivation*-12 acs; prt of *Strife*, prt of *Peaches Meadows & Evan's Range*-66 1/2 acs; $5.35.
Wm Brogden, 2 lots adj Queen Anne-1 1/4 acs; $19.02.
Francis Carrick, prt of *Carrick's Industry*-33 acs; $2.96.
John Rustin-heirs, prt of *Essington*, adj Queen Anne-1ac; $2.23.
[total: $1105.43] -Rich'd Duvall, collector of Prince George Co, Md.

Detroit is taken! Our volunteers & heroes of Tippecanoe, are prisoners of war. Capt Wm Keys of the first company of Chillicothe vols has just arrv'd in town from Detroit & confirms that Hull has shamefully, ingloriously & disgracefully surrendered to the British & Indians.

Elkana Cobb & Dan'l Bussard are erecting a fulling mill & enlarging their Blanket Factory at Paint Mills, 12 miles from Gtwn; fulling & dying will be executed.

THU SEP 10, 1812
Store & dwlg hse to let: on F St, now occupied by Mr Lynde Elliott. -Jas Hoban.

Notice-persons endebted to est of Geo W Varnum, dec'd, late of Lovingston, Nelson Co, Va, are to make settlement. -Jas M Varnum & Solomon Matthews, adms.

Urbana, Ohio, Aug 26. Orders by the Commander in Chief. Headqrtrs, Urbana, Aug 19. Brig Genr'l Edw W Tupper has been called to take command of the forces now collecting from the svr'l divisions of the State of Ohio. -R J Meigs, Govn'r-Ohio.

Richmond, Va. Sep 5. Patriotic meeting; Jas Barbour, chrmn; Wm Munford, sec. Committee to receive contributions:

Jas Wood	Thos Ritchie	Alex M'rae
Wm Foushee Sr	Christopher Tompkins	Hugh Davis
Robt Greenhow	Wm Dandridge	Jas Brown
Benj J Harris	Sam'l Pleasants	Rich Anderson
Chas Hay	John Hayes	Wm Fenwick
Jas W Winfree.		

Committee on Rules & Regulations:

Chas K Mallory	John Robertson	John Campbell,
Wm Brockenbrough,	Wm W Hening	Gervas Storrs
Nath'l H Clairborne,	Gurden H Bacchus	Peter V Daniel, ,
John Seabrook	Wm Hay jr	

Arrived Aug 24th in an open boat from Havanna, via Amelia, Americans: Warren Waterman of New London; Robt Robinson of N Y; Joshua Wing of Boston; Christian Miller of N Y & Redman Chase of Charleston-all seamen.

Public sale on the premises, lot 1 & 2 in sq 771 with improvements; prop of Jas D Barry, for taxes due the Wash Corp, which accrued in the name of John Craig, Jas Crawford, Wm Rush & others. -J Walker, coll-3rd ward.

Reward-$20 for Jos Carter, age ab't 22yrs, & Christian Dick, alias Alex'r Smith, age ab't 22 yrs. Carter states himself to be ntv of Jefferson Co, Va, & marched to this place from Frederick Town as a substitute to a draughted militia. Dick, also a substitute, says he is a ntv of New Eng. -Thos C Worthington, Com. 2d comp, infty at Ft Severn, Annapolis.

Black varnish for boots & shoes may be had at the drug stores of David Ott, Wash City, Dr Ott & Geo Bohrer, Gtwn, & Rich'd Latile, Alexandria.

SAT SEP 12, 1812
Mrs Hopkins, late of Phil, has opened a boarding school for young ladies; the *Frederick-Town Seminary*, Md.

Trustees of the public schools will meet on Mon next. -Jas Kearney, sec. Wash.

TUE SEP 15, 1812
Died: Capt Ulry, Capt Gilcrease, Capt Boersiler & Capt McCulloch of the Ohio vols, on Aug 4th, at the Battle of Brownstown. -Chilicothe, Sep 2.

The Deer Creek Vols under Capt McNemar & the vol mounted riflemen under Col Jas Dunlap, both from this county, marched from Urbana for Ft Wayne. The ctzns of Ross County have furnished 7 vol companies. -Chilicothe, Sep 2.

Thos Richardson has declined his mercantile pursuits in Gtwn & requests all persons indebted to him to make payment.

Henry Herford & Ed Stephens, late of N Y, have commenced the groc business on Pa Ave

Lancelot Griffin insolvent debtor, confined to Wash Co, D C, prison-for debt. -Wm Brent, clk.

G C Grammar & Co inform their customers that they have mv'd from Pa Ave to F St in the hse lately occupied by Thos Hughes & Co: groc, wine, cotton, etc.

Extract of a ltr from the Journal of Com Rodgers; [H M S *Belvidere*, Rich'd Byron, Capt, Jun 23, 1812 & Cmdor Rodgers] Endeavoring to get alongside of the enemy the following persons were wounded or killed; some by the bursting of our own gun, viz: <u>Killed:</u>

John H Bird, Midshipman	John Taylor jr, Midshipman
	Francis H Dwight, Marine

<u>Wounded:</u>

Cmdor Rodgers	Thos Gamble, Lt, severely
John Heath, Lt of Marines, slightly	Matthew C Perry, Mdshpmn, slightly

Frank Ellery, Mdshpmn, slightly   Jas Beasley, Qrtr-gunner, slightly
Lawrence Montgomery, Mdshpmn, lost his left arm
John Barrett, Qrtr-gunner, severely
Andrew Matthews, Qrtr-gunner, slightly
Jordan Beebe, Armorer, slightly
John Clapp, seaman, slightly
Geo Ross, seaman, slightly
Wm Thomas, ordinary seaman, slightly
Neil Harding, ordinary seaman, slightly
John Berry, ordinary seaman, slightly
Henry Gilbert, ordinary seaman, slightly
John Smith, 5th, boy, slightly.
Note: Greater part of the wounded have since nrly recovered.

Jas W Johnston has commenced business in the store formerly occupied by Mr Grammar, Pa Ave: grocery & spirit line.

Public sale at hse of Walter Hellen in F St, formerly occupied by Hannah Walker, hsehld furn, millinery, etc; prop of Hannah Walker, under a distress for hse rent due to Walter Hellen. -Geo Miller, cnstble.

Wash City lots for sale for taxes due thereon up to the yr 1811.

John Benson	lots 2-3-4 in sq 374	$5.10
John B Beall	lot 2 in sq 490	$5.98
Wm Brogden	lot 1 in sq 608	$6.24
Mathias Corlass	lots 5-6 in sq 532	$7.42
John Craig	lots 5-6 in sq 538; lot 12 in sq 780	$14.41
Benedict Calvert	lot 13 in sq 610	$6.99
Martha Hall	lot 8 in sq 606	$7.01
Wm Kain	lots 17-18-19-20-21 in sq 534	$23.80
Sarah Porter	lots 8-9-13-14 in sq 258	$23.12
Basil Waring	lot 13 in sq 603	$4.88
Maximilian Haysler	whole of sq 582	$112.78

Peter Godfrey & others, whole of sq 483 & numerous other lots [listed]; $85.52.
Henry Thompson, lot 4 in sq 290; lot 17 in sq 348; lot 17 in sq 457; $35.31.
Wash Tontine, many lots in numerous squares [listed]; $1,174.47.
-Ezekiel MacDaniel, Coll 2d ward.

THU SEP 17, 1812
Wash City lots for sale for taxes due thereon up to the yr 1811.
John Appleton, s/o sq 505-whole; lot 10 sq 608; lot 10 sq 610; lot 5 sq 654; lot 6 sq 564; lot 20 sq 702; $61.10.
Sam'l Blodgett; numerous lots in various sqs [listed]; $337.03.
Stuart Brown, prt 3 of sq 256; lots 2-6 sq 378; $39.18.
Ball & Ford, whole of sqs 328-383-412-467-471; lots 2 thru 8 sq 325; $224.84.
John Baltzer-heirs, lot 3 sq 577; lot 3 sq 579; lot 3 sq 581; $12.42.
John Basset, lot 23 sq 253; lot 11 sq 321; lots 2-8-11 sq 792; lots 5-6-9 sq 874; $22.64.

Jacob Cist, lot 2 sq 320; lot 24 sq 533; $8.87.
Wm Campbell, lot 18 sq 101; lot 9 sq 172; whole of sqs 465-468-469-470-485-498; $303.75.
Wm Deakin-heirs, lot 4 sq 83; lot 4 sq 124; whole of sq 506; $80.27.
Solomon Etting, numerous lots in various sqs [listed]; $88.63.
Jas Fenwick, whole of sq 439; $25.68.
Thos Fenwick, whole of sqs: 497-505-548-E548-E of E548-E549-931; lot 13 sq 621; lot 3 sq 667; lots 7 thru 23 in sq 672; lots 5 thru 19 in sq 1051; $90.25.
Robt Hay, lot 6 sq 288; $6.30.
John Johnson, lot 18 sq 254; $20.61.
Chas Johnson, lots 16 & 17 in sq 378; $18.32.
Chas Lowndes, lots 14-19-20 in sq 293; lots 3-4-14- in sq 323; $113.46.
Dominick Lynch, numerous lots in various sqs [listed]; $80.60.
Wm Lorman, lots 5-21-23 in sq 514; lots 4-8-19-24-25-26 in sq 515; $13.75.
Owen McDermot Rowe, lot 6 sq 253; $19.24.
John Mason, lots 3-4 sq 254; lot 4 sq 294; lots 1-2 sq 407; lots 9-10-11 in sq 408; lots 3-4 in sq 489; lot 3 sq 701; $71.89.
Jacobus Merson, whole of sqs 326 & 410; $41.76.
Moris & Nicholson assignees, numerous lots in various sqs [listed]; $729.28.
John Mercer, lot 2 sq 86; lots 1-6-7-8 in sq 433; lots 12-13 in sq 456; lot 6 sq 493; $39.65.
Henry Massey, lots 1-2-3-4-10-11 in sq 452; $11.60.
Wm Matthews, lots 2-3 in sq 488; $10.42.
Martin & Ward, numerous lots in various sqs [listed]; $49.08.
Oden & Burn-heirs, lots 1-3-5-7 in sq 518; lots 1-3-5 in sq 570; lot 1 sq 572; lots 2-4-6 in sq 573; $873.40.
John A Oswold, prt of lot 7 in sq 456; $5.46.
Isaac Pollock, lots 19-20 in sq 38; prt of lot 3 sq 256; lots 17-28 in sq 258; lots 2-3 in sq 288; lots 2 sq 457; lots 3-19 sq 533; $160.66.
Pratt, Francis & others, lots 18 thru 24 in sq 33; lot 1 sq 84; lots 1-2-7-8 in sq 145; lots 1-2-3 in sq 146; lot 4 sq 147; lots 9-10-11 in sq 168; lots 6-7-10-11-12-15-16 in sq 258; whole of sqs 266, 268, 269; & other numerous lots in various sqs: $3457.12.
Paleskie & Gardiner, lots 2-24-27 in sq 231; lots 5-9-10-22 in sq 296; lots 11-18-27-35-39 in sq 417; lots 20-23-25 in sq 499; lots 13-14-21-22 in sq 529; $33.60.
Geo Pickett, lots 2-3-4-5-16 in sq 319; lots 2-3-4-16 in sq 345; $15.60.
Robt Pollard, lots 3-4 in sq 378; $20.28.
Jes & Isaac Perkins, lot 1 sq 408; lots 5-6 sq 533; $47.94.
Walter Smith, lots 2-5-6-15 in sq 348; $60.51.
Sam'l Sterret, 5 sqs with various lots; $203.66.
Wm O Sprigg, prt of lot 7 in sq 489; prt of sq 503; $12.60.
Comfort Sand, numerous lots in various sqs: $55.74.
Mr Gues, lots 1-2 in sq 38; lot 4 sq 258; lot 23 sq 378; lot 3 sq 457; lots 15-16-19-20-23 in sq 490; lot 18 in sq 533; $74.35.
Anthony Van Mannick, lot 5 sq 458; lots 12-13-16 in sq 532; $21.12.
Wm Whetcrofft-heirs, lot 4 sq 403; prt of lots 3-4 in sq 432; lots 6-7 in sq 458; lot 6 & prt of lot 7 in sq 461; $51.24.

Nicholas Young, whole of sqs: 353, 437, 391, 415, S415, 508, 439, 709, N931, 932, 933, 908, 909, 808, 1049; lots 1-2-9-10-11-12 in sq 776; lots 3-4-6 in sq 777; lot 12 sq 653; lots 5 thru 14 in sq 856; lots 7 thru 10 in sq 959; lots 1-2-3-4-11-12-13-14 in sq 1002; lots 1-2-6 in sq 1050; $135.68.
Sale to commence on Dec 17th next. -E MacDaniel, col 2d ward.

Commanding ofcrs of compaines not included in the genr'l order of Aug 15th:
Henry Shippen, Capt Comp'y Yagers, brig 1, div 4.
Wm Adams, Capt Troop of Horse, brig 2 div 6.
Jacob U Snyder, Capt, Troop of Horse, brig 2 div 6.
Robt McGuigan, Capt, Light infty, brig 2 div 9.
Isaac Vandevender, Capt, Rifle Co, brig 2 div 11.
-Simon Snyder, Govn'r of the Commonwealth of Pa.

Rpblcn Tkt for mbrs of assembly for PG Co, Md: Jos Cross, Sam'l Sprigg, Henry Culver & Geo W Biscoe.

Extract of a Ltr from Lt Hanks, dec'd, late Commandant of Michillimackinac to Genr'l Hull, dt'd-Detroit, Aug 4, 1812: rgrdng the surrender of the same on Jul 17 to Capt Chas Roberts of the Britannic Majesty's forces; Capt Daurman was sent to watch the motions of the Indians & met the British forces & made a prisoner & put on his parole of honor. -Porter Hanks, Lt of Artl.

Ltr to the Indian Dept to the Sec of War, dt'd Detroit, Aug 6: rg-Michillimackinac: Robt Dickson, Indian trader & John Askin jr, Indian agent, & son commanded the Indians; those who commanded the Canadians are: John Johnson, Crawford, Pothier, Armitingen, La Croix, Rollette, Franks, Livingston & others, all Indian traders. Ltr not signed.

Americans on board the British Gov't schn'r, *Holly*, lately arrv'd at N Y as a cartel or flag of truce: John Myers of Ga; John Barker & Chas Keith of Pa; Peter Swarthy of Mass; Cornelius Martin of N Y. Some have not seen their friends for 10 yrs.

Died: Mrs Sarah Wheeler, age 53 yrs, on Sep 9 in Wash City.

Died: Genr'l Geo Matthews, Rev Patriot & late agent of the U S to the Floridas; he died a few days since in Augusta, Ga, on his way to Wash City.

Died: Christopher Gadsden, of the U S brig *Vixen*, on Aug 28th, age 32 yrs.

Elected to Rep Ky in the 13th Cong: *Jas Clarke, Henry Clay, Rich'd M Johnson, Jos Desha, *Sam'l Hopkins, *Solomon P Sharpe, Sam'l McKee, *John Simpson, *Thos Montgomery & *Wm P Duval. [*New mbrs]

SAT SEP 19, 1812
Paris, Ky, Sep 5. Gov Harrison to take command of the Army of Ky; the Army was at Lebanon, Ohio, Mon last. Col Jas Smith, of Indian memory, one of the

black-boys of Sideling-Hill expedition, in Pa, who is nrly 80 yrs of age, has gone to join our Army.

British Treat the prisoners with barbarity: Cpt Fuller of the 4th Regt was told to take the middle of the road by British Maj Simmons; Capt Snelling applied for permission to speak to his lady [with whom he had been connected only a few days] & was tauntingly refused; Lt Goodwin of the 4th Regt had to witness the exhibition of American scalps; the hses of Messrs Atwater & Naggs, & McDonald's store at Detroit were plundered. -From the Albany Register.

Sam'l Finley calls for volunteers of Ross & adjacent counties.

For sale-the establishment of the Lynchburg Star; two good presses; and an Almanac. -Jas Graham, Lynchburg, Va.

Frankfort, Ky, Sep 5. Col Simrall left this place with 4 companies of vol cavalry- ab't 300 men, on their way to Ohio; prior to leaving they elected Capts McDowell & Jos Simrall, Majors; & Dr Smith of Shelbyville, Surg. Capt Arnold's Co of vol mounted riflemen, nrly 70 in number, raised in this county, left here on Mon. Capt Quarles' Co from Pulaski, ab't 60 men, arrv'd in this place Tue, destined as above; it has joined Col Jenning's Regt. Cols Barbee & Jennings regts passed thru Gtwn to join the Army in Ohio. Col Barbour's Regt has marched for Kaskaskia to the relief of Edwards.

Professor wanted-at the *Acad of Stevensburg*. -P Hansbrough jr, Pres, Stevensburg-Va.

For sale-prop on 11th St occupied by Jas B Herd. Apply to Patrick Toole, *Greenleaf's Point*, or C Stephenson. -Roger Toole, Wash. Cty.

TUE SEP 22, 1812
Wash City lots for sale for taxes due thereon up to the yr 1811 inclusive:
Addison, Thos G, lots 4-5-6 sq 705; $30.62
Addison, Henry, lot 11 sq 611; $6.00
Appleton, Henry, lot 9 sq 611; lots 6-7-8 in sq 654; $27.28.
Barnetts, John-heirs, part of sq 651; $17.05.
Baily, Wm, lot 5 sq 652; $7.71.
Barnes & Rudgate, lot 10 sq 601; lot 1 sq 611; lot 6 sq 661; lot 20 sq 165; lot 4 sq 666; lot 1 sq 702; $36.27.
Bean, Wm, lot 12 sq 652; $3.77.
Biddle, Clement, lot 7 sq 598; lot 6 sq 601; lot 3 sq 702; $15.82.
Boon, Francis, lot 1 sq W553; lot 3 sq 555; $24.
Beall, John, part of sq 799; lot 7 sq 104; $16.50.
Bean, Quintain, lot 15 sq 799; $1.82.
Bradford, Henry, lot 3 sq 650; $2.40.
Brown, Jas, lots 1 & 14 in sq 661; $18.71.
Brice, John, lot 2 sq 667; $2.00
Bushel, Wm, lot 6 sq 692; $15.40.

Barksdale, Wm, lot 8 & 9 in sq 702; $4.52.
Bartlet, Rich'd, part of sq 695; $7.12.
Coates & others, various sqs & lots [listed]; $96.74.
Carroll & Oden, various sqs & lots [listed]; $98.22.
Carroll, Oden & N Young-heirs, lots 6-7-8-9-10-11-18 thru 23 in sq 673; $2.70.
Caldwell, Chas B, lots 8 & 9 in sq 569; 90cents.
Carroll, Chas jr, lot 3 sq 599; lot 5 sq 611; lot 2 sq 652; $21.19.
Carroll, Daniel-heirs, lot 3 sq 611; lot 2 sq 653; lot 7 sq 661; lot 7 sq 667; $27.92.
Carrol, Eliz, lot 7 sq 609; lot 2 sq 613; $10.86.
Coolidge, Judson, lot 1 sq 652; $7.69.
Campbell, John, lot 2 sq 654; lot 21 sq 665; lot 3 sq 666; $13.42.
Conway, Rich'd, lot 6 sq 658; $2.00.
Craig, Jas, lot 3 sq 661; lot 13 sq 665; lot 11 sq 666; $6.00.
Cooper, Cyrus, lot 8 sq 667; $2.50.
Chase, Sam'l, lot 2 sq 661; $9.35.
Clagett & Mason, lot 9 sq 703; $9.25.
Crammond, Jas, lot 22 sq 729; $9.38.
Chandler, Jacob, lot 3 sq 734; $2.
Deakin, Francis-heirs, lot 8 sq 663; $2.50.
Dick & Stuart, lot 10 sq 598; lot 6 sq 662; lot 2 sq 702; $30.92.
Dulany, Walter, lot 8 sq 603; lot 2 sq 611; lot 4 sq 614; $11.30.
Digges, Jos, lot 1 sq 599; lot 18 sq 652; $13.71.
Dick, Thos-heirs, lot 7 sq 704; $3.84.
Eden, John, lot 13 sq 656; lot 5 sq So of 744; $14.97.
Earle, Jas, lot 7 sq 664; $7.38.
Frost, Amariah, lot 17 sq 634; $14.87.
Fenwick, Ignatius-heirs, lots 1-9 or 19 in sq 655; lots 1-11-12 in sq 657; $55.14.
Fowler, Job, lot 15 sq s/o 667; $4.06.
Fowler, Joh, lots 1-2-3 East of So of sq 667; $2.24.
Griffin, Sam'l, lot 9 sq 728; lot 6 sq 200; lot 6 sq 456; $36.19.
Graham, Rich'd, lot 6 sq 655; lot 16 sq 608; $18.27.
Holliday, Jas, lot 4 sq 605; $20.15.
Holliday, Thos, lot 19 sq 702; $3.84.
Hill, Henry, lot 4 sq 650; lot 14 So of sq 667; lot 2 sq 704; $28.07.
Hall, Jonathan, lot 4 sq 656; $7.89.
Hemmersly, Wm, lot 10 sq 657; lot 10 sq 667; lot 2 East of sq 667; $20.61.
Harrison, Wm, lot 1 So of sq 667; part of s/o S-sq 667; lot 1 E of s/o S sq 667;$7.6-
Hepburn, John, lot 19 sq 703; $10.01.
Henderson, Rich'd, lot 10 sq 704; lot 14 sq 610; $18.19.
Jennifer, Daniel, lot 1 sq 607; lot 8 s/o sq 744; $5.92.
Jennings, Thos, lot 11 sq 665; lot 13 sq 666; lot 14 sq 703; $20.12.
Johnson, Jas jr, lot 8 sq 705; $6.
Leidler, Eliza, lot 1 sq 605; lot 15 sq 653; $10.22.
Leeke, Francis, lot 6 sq 611; Ot 5 sq 665; $11.78.
Lux, Darby, lot 8 sq 661; lot 11 So of sq 667; $13.72.
Lux, Wm, lot 1 sq 667; lot 1 East of sq 667; $9.80.
Lawson, A, lot 6 sq 708; lot 15 sq 608; $19.05.

Laird & Mason, lots 1-15-16 in sq 745; lots 17-18 in sq 846; lots 1 thru 5, 23 thru 34 in sq 876; lots 1-2-3-4-34-35-36 in sq 1043; lots 3 thru 8 & 11 & 12 in sq 1046; lots 1 thru 5 & 26-27-28 in sq 1047; $40.26.
Lynch & Sands, lots 4-5-6-7-21-22 in sq 555; $1.88.
Merryweather, Reuben, lot 10 sq 609; $2.94.
McQuakin, Wm, lot 16 sq 611; $2.88.
Mewbern, Jas, lot 20 sq 652; $7.79.
Mackey, Ebenezer, lot 7 sq 656; &8.23.
Moylan, Stephen, lot 10 sq 702; lot 18 sq 703; lot 1 sq 606; lot 12 sq 608; $54.54.
Neale Jas of Bennet, lot 2 sq 599; lot 10 So of sq 667; $8.79.
North, Rich'd, lot 12 sq 691; $3.84.
Nicholl, Henry, lot 14 sq 728; $29.96.
Oden & Notley Young-heirs, lots 1 thru 5 & 12 thru 17 & 24 in sq 620; $26.63.
Parkinson, Edw, lot 2 sq 609; $5.93
Patton, Jas, lot 3 sq 665; $3.
Parks, Andrew, lot 5 sq 667; $4.74.
Phillips, Nath'l, lot 6 sq 728; $4.30.
Ross, David, lot 8 sq 609; $1.92.
Riddle, Matthew, lot 4 sq 603; lot 2 sq 660; lot 4 sq 602; $18.24.
Ringgold, Mary C, lot 15 sq 611; lot 7 sq 660; $9.06.
Russell, Wm, lot 16 sq 703; $15.92. [Cont'd]
Ringgold, Hillary, lot 9 sq 705; $4.19.
Rutter, Thos, lot 34 sq 569; $4.08.
Stephens, John, lots 10-11 in sq 569; 96 cents.
Speare, Jos, lots 33 & 36 in sq 569; 48 cents.
Sidebotham, Wm, lot 8 sq 607; lot 13 sq 705; lot 21 sq 88; $6.42.
Stewart, John-heirs, lot 3 sq 653; lot 7 sq 606; $2.06.
Smith, Wm, half of lot 7 sq 654; 96 cents.
Saver, Dan'l, lot 8 sq 655; $5.98.
Stewart, Chas, lot 11 sq 667; lot 7 E of sq 667; $13.46.
Turner, Thos, lot 12 sq 611; $1.92.
Thomas, Evan, lot 5 sq 662; $3.50.
Tompkins & Minor, lot 13 sq 691; $6.84.
Thompson, Dan'l, part of sq 766; $3.25.
Washington, Wm A, lot 7 sq 607; lot 9 sq 609; lot 10 sq 653; lot 7 sq 663; lot 3 sq 664; lot 4 East of sq 664; lot 8 sq 704; lot 2 sq 606; $32.33.
Wharton, Thos, lot 9 E of sq 667; $3.50.
William, Jas, lot 12 sq 705; lot 2 S of S of sq 667; $5.04.
Walker Young & Prout; lots 2-3-7-8-9 sq 809; $3.11.
Washington, Lund, lot 2 sq 705; $13.75.
Ward, Jas, part of lot in sq 580; $2.22.
Wharton, Jas, lot 6 sq 609; lot 9 sq 667; lot 10 sq 705; $19.88.
Oct 20th next will be sold - part of lot 9 in sq 758, with improvements thereon, taken as prop of Jane Burch. -Z Walker, Col 3d Ward.

New York, Sep 17. U S ship of war, *Alert*, commanded by Lt Jas P Wilmer, arrv'd in this port Sep 16th, 14 days from St John's Newfoundland, with 232 American prisoners. She was captured Aug 13 by Capt Porter of the U S frig, *Essex*, who on the 19th stripped her of all her armament except one gun, & sent her as a cartel to St John's with her ofcrs, crew & other English p o ws amounting to 120 men.

Mrd: Mr Elisha Riggs of Gtwn, to Miss Alice Lawrason, d/o Mr Jas Lawrason, of Alexandria, on Sep 17th by Rev Wm H Wilmer.

Died: recently, Mrs Jane Presly Herford, relict of Mr John Herford, dec'd, age 55 yrs, in this city after a long & severe illness. [no date]

Died: Lt Hetchcote J Reed of the U S Navy, at Savannah, lately; ntv of N J; distinguished himself in the mediterranean under Cmdor Preble.

Md Electoral Tkt: Rpblcn Candidates-
Anne Arundel Co & Balt & Annapolis Cities-John Stephen & Edw Johnson. Calvert & part of PG & Montg Cos-John Johnson. 4th Elec Dist [Wash & Frederick]-Frisby Tilghman & Joshua Cockey. Balt Co-Tobias E Stansbury.

Sandwich, Aug 7, 1812. On Aug 4th Maj Van Horn, of Col Findlay's Regt of Ohio Vols was detached from this Army with the command of 200 men to proceed to the River Raisin; at Brownstown the Indians had formed an ambuscade & the Maj's detachment rec'd heavy fire; the whole detachment retreated in disorder. Killed: Capt Gilchrist; Capt Ullery; Capt McCallough of the Spies; Lt Pentz; Ensigns Roby & Allison & 10 pvts. Capt Boerstler, wounded since died.

Return of killed & wounded in the action fought nr Maguago, Aug 9, 1812: 4th U S Regt: Capt Baker of the 1st Regt of infty; Lt Peters of the 4th; Ensign Whistler of the 17th-doing duty in the 4th; Lt Silly. -Wm Hull.

Post ofc changes in Aug 1812.
Danville, Vt-Asa Peabody vice Timothy Foilette, rsgn'd..
Danville, Va-John Ross, vice Jos Barnett, rsgn'd.
New Geneva, Pa-John Davenport, vice J W Nicholson, rsgn'd.
Middlebrook Mills, Md-Tho Saunders vice J M Lingan, dec'd.
Bethlehem, X Rds, Va-Spratley Williams, vice John W Smith, mv'd away.
Cumberland C H, Va-Rich'd Cunningham, vice Rd Cunningham jr, rsgn'd..
Skinnersville, N C-Sam'l Skinner, vice Silas Long, rsgn'd..
Hay-Mkt, Va-Elishab Evans, vice Wm Robinson, dec'd.
Greensburg, N Y-John Dean, vice Jos Cutler, rsgn'd..
Stagville, N C-John Wilkins, vice Dan'l Cameron, rsgn'd.
Ellisville, Ky-Wm McClenachan, vice Jos Ellerbeck.
Fairton, N J-Jas Clarke, vice Thos Burch, dec'd.
Monmouth, Me-John A Chandler, vice John Chandler, rsgn'd..
Manchester, Va-Thos Tredway, vice Wm B Clarke, rsgn'd.
Henderson, Ky-Sibella Husband, vice John Husband, dec'd.

New Post ofcs established in Aug 1812 & postmaster.
Sedgwick, Hancock Co, Maine-Dan'l Bigford.
Greensborough, Mechlenburg Co, Va-Alex'r B Prinyear.

Bristol, Hartford Co, Cont-Lott Newell.
Bolton, Tolland Co, Cont-Saul Alford.
Leverings, Phil Co, Pa-Aaron Levering.
Williamsville, Niagara Co, N Y-Jonas Williams.
Longacoming, Gloucester Co, N J-Thos Wright.
Wells's, Beauford Dist, S C-John Wells.
Deposit, Delaware Co, N Y-Wm Butler.
Clay Crt Hse, Clay Co, K-John H Slaughter.
Champs Race Ground, Pr Wm Co, Va. [no name]
Richmonds, Chester Dist, S C-Jas Richmond.
Lewisville, Chester Dist, S C-Thos S Mills.
Rochester, Gennessee Co, N Y-Abelard Reynolds.
Tunbridge, Windsor Co, Vt-Elijah Tracy.
Allenton, Montgomery Co, N C-Frederick Randle.
Ratesville, Breckenridge Co, K-Wm Pate.
Ofc discontinued in Aug 1812: Holland, Mass.

Wanted-a clk in the Surveyor Genr'l's ofc south of Tenn. Apply to Thos Freeman, Purveyor's ofc, Wash City.

The Bank of Columbia has declared a dividend. -Wh Whann, cashier.

Reward-$100: Ranaway Harry, negro, on Oct 19, 1810 from Mr Michl Malot, to whom he was hired nr Hagars-town, Wash Co, Md; deliver to Mr Jas Muir, Williamsport, Md or to the subscriber, Chaptico, St Mary's Co, Md. -Edw Aprice.

THU SEP 24, 1812
Appointments in the Navy of the United States:
John H Dent Sr-Mstr Commandant to Capt, vice Sam'l Nicholson, dec'd.
David Porter, John Cassin & Sam'l Evans-Mstr Commandant to Capts.
G W Reed-Lt to Mstr Commandant.
Acting Lts to Lts:

Jas Wilson	John B Nicholson	B V Hoffman
Wm Peters	Geo Budd	Thos A C Jones
John M Funk	Jos S MacPherson	John Porter
John Shubrick		

To be Pursers:

Edwin T Satterwhite	Robt Ormsby	Edw Fitzgerald
John B Timberlake	Rich'd C Arther	J R Wilson
Jas H Halsey	Isaac Garretson	Gwynn Harris
Sam'l Robertson	Sam'l Hambleton	Clem S Hunt
Thos I Chew	John R Greene	Robt C Ludlow
Nathl Lyde	Thos Shields	Robt Pottinger
John H Carr	Sam'l Maffit	Lewis Deblois
Alex'r P Darragh	Edwin W Turner	Henry Dennison
Ludlow Dashwood	Geo S Wise	F A Thornton
Humphrey Magrath		

To be Navy agents: at Newcastle-Jas Riddle; in Tenn-Wm Helms.

Corps of Marine. Rich Smith, sr-1st Lt to Capt vice Capt H Caldwell, dec'd.
2d Lts to 1st Lts:
Robt Moseley   Jas Brown   Chas S Hanna
Alex'r Sevier   Alfred Grayson   Wm Strong
John Urquhart   John Heath   Sam'l Bacon
To be 2d Lts:
Benj Hyde of Dist of Col.   Lyman Kellogg of N Y
Sam'l E Watson of Ky   Lloyd Luckett of Md
Wm L Brownlow of Tenn   Joshua Prime of N Y
Rd L Smith of Va   Moses A Roberts of Ga
Sam'l Bacon of Pa   Wm Hall of N C
Thos Arrowsmith of Pa   Newman S Clarke of Vt
Neil A McKinnon of N Y   F B Bellevieu, of Orleans
T Raimond Montegut, of Orleans   Wm Cowan of Va
John Contee of Md   Francis Sterne, of Ky
Rich'd Steward of Va   H B Breckenridge of Ky
P Bouche De Grand Pre of Orleans
Surgeons:
Thos Harris of Pa;   Robt Miller of Va.
Surgeons' mates:
Usher Parsons of N H   Sam'l Jackson, of N Y
Wm C Whittlsey of N Y   Peter Christie of N Y
John Young jr of Md.   Herman M Clark of Conn
John D Armstrong of Ky   Donald Yeates of Md

Ltr from Dan'l Landon to Chas Peltier, contractor's agent, dt'd Ft Wayne, Aug 24, 1812. We are all confusion since you left us; Indians show hostility; I shall not venture from the garrison; ab't 300 Indians here & they plunder everything; your garden as well as mine is destroyed; your store hse broken open this day; Piatt tells me they took your sugar; perhaps I may never see you again.

Frankfort, Ky, Sep 12. Families killed by the Indians: Morris' family-5 persons; Collins' family-7 persons; Payne & family-8 persons; young Collins was wounded; all were buried by Col Robinson & his party.

Md Rpblcn Council Chamber, Annapolis, Sep 7, 1812. Publish the documents. They show the correctness & propriety of Genr'l Stricker's official conduct, during the late occurrences at Balt. -Robt Bowie.
Affidavits:
Wm B Barney, Maj 5th C D Md Militia;
John Shrim, Capt, 1st Co 5th Regt Md Militia, Aug 24, 1812;
Dan'l Conn, Capt, Rpblcn company, Balt, Aug 24, 1812;
Robt Lawson, Lt of Capt Conn's Co, Aug 25, 1812;
John Stricker, Brig Gen 3d brig Md Militia, Balt, Aug 29, 1812;
Davice Harris, Lt Col, 1st Regt Artl, attached to 3d brigade Md Militia;
W Vance, Capt, Rifle Co 5th Regt, Balt, Aug 22, 1812;
Ar Levering, Lt Comdt, Balt I B, Aug 28, 1812;
John Keller, B M V, Balt Aug 22, 1812. -Your humble svt-R K Heath.

Jacob Hilbus, organ builder, G St, nr the Treasury, Wash City.

Notice. All indebted to subscriber are to make immediate payment. -Thos Baker.

Flannels for sale-just rec'd from New Eng. -Jos O'Brien & son, Alexandria.

SAT SEP 26, 1812
Civil ofcrs appt'd or re-appt'd with consent of the Senate in it's last session: Edw Hearsey-to srvyr of the Miss Dist & inspec of Rev for Port of N Orleans. John Coburn, re-appt'd Judge of latter. Oliver Wayne Ogden, re-appt'd mrsh'l of the Dist of N J. Jas Prince, re-appt'd mrsh'l of Mass Dist. Nathl Holland of Va-to Coll of the Dist of Cherry Stone & Inspec of Rev for Port of Cherry Stone, vice Isaac Smith, rsgn'd. Thos L Shannonhouse of N C-to srvyr & Inspec of the Port of Nebiggen Creek, N C, vice Jas L Shannonhouse, dec'd. John Andrews to be srvyr of the Port of Cincinnati, Ohio. Reuben Attwater-re-appt'd Sec of the Mich Terr. John Clay of Orleans Terr-to srvyr of the Customs for Miss Dist & Inspec of the Rev for the Port of New Orleans, vice Jas Lovell, rsgn'd. John Mitchell of Pa-to cnsl of the U S at St Jego De Cuba. Robt K Laury of Md-to cnsl of the U S at Port of Laguira, Caraccas. Thos Bourke of Ga-to srvyr of the Dist of Savannah & Inspec of the Rev for Port of Savannah, vice Edw White, dec'd. Wash Boyd, reappt'd mrsh'l of the Dist of Columbia. Josiah Simpson of N J, to Judge of the Miss Terr. Oliver Forward-to Coll of the Dist of Buffaloe Creek & Inspec of Rev for the Port of Buffaloe town, vice Erastus Granger, rsgn'd. Dempsey Jones of N C-to srvyr of the Port of Swansborough & Inspec of the Rev for said Port, vice Thos Dudley, dec'd. Massey Simms of Md-to srvyr of the Port of Nanjemoy & Inspec of the Rev for the same, vice W Jackson, dec'd. John Fisher of Dela-to Judge of the Dist Crt of Dela, vice Gunning Bedford, dec'd. Elias Glenn of Md, to atty of the U S for that Dist, vice Thos B Dorsey, rsgn'd. Wm Sprigg of Ohio-to Judge of latter, vice Otho Shroeder, dec'd. Wm White of Pa, to Com'r of loans for the U S in State of Pa. Aaron Nassert of N J, to Coll of the Dist of Perth Amboy & Inspec of the Rev for same. David Hopkins of D C-to Justice of the Peace for Wash Co, D C. Thos Speyer of N Y-to cnsl of the U S at Stockholm, Sweden. Dominick A Hall from Judge of the Dist Crt of Orleans Dist, to Judge of the Dist Crt of La, Jno R Grymes, from atty for the U S in Orleans Terr to atty for the U S in La. Peter L B Duplessis, from mrsh'l in Orleans Terr to mrsh'l in La. Jno Caldwell of Indiana Terr-to Receiver of public Monies for land ofc of Kaskaskia. David Holmes-re-appt'd Govn'r of the Miss Terr. Wm Augustine Linton-to Coll of the Dist & Inspec of the Rev for the Port of Dumfries. Beverly Daniel-re-appt'd mrsh'l of the Dist of N C. Thos H Blount of N C-to Coll of the Customs for the Dist of Wash & Inspec of the Rev for the Port of Wash. Jos Wilcox of Ohio-to srvyr & Inspec of the Rev for the Port of Marietta. Benj Homans of Mass-to be cnsl of the U S at Tunis. Wm G Miller of Pa to be cnsl of the U S at Monte Video. Rich'd B Jones of Pa to be cnsl of the U S at Tripoli. Henry A S Dearborn of Mass to Coll for the Dist of Boston. Walter Bradley of Conn to Coll for Dist of Fairfield & Inspec of Rev for the port. Thos S Singleton of N C to Coll for Dist of Oc__cock & Inspec of Rev for the Port. Thos Chapman of S C to Coll of the Dist of Gtwn, So C

& Inspec of Port for same. Henry Coffin of N Y, to srvyr & Inspec of the Rev for the Port of Cape Vincent. Jas Fish of Vt-to Judge of Indiana Terr, v Henry Vanderburg, dec'd. Sam'l Smith of D C-to Receiver of pblc Monies for Dist of Pearl River, Miss Terr. Thos L Ha---y jr of R I, to be cnsl of the U S at Buenos Ayres.

Newport, R I-Sep 2. Privateer *Rossie*, Com J Barney, arrv'd here last night; the schn'r *Rossie* sailed from the Chesapeake on Jul 15th in company with an American ship, his prize, from Liverpool to N Y; the *Rossie* has taken 15 prizes, one being the British frig *Guerriere*.

Meeting in Phil, Pa on Sep 12: Thos Leiper, esq, chrmn; Geo Bartram, sec. Committee for the Assembly: John Connelly, Wm J Duane, Thos Sergeant, Lewis R-sh & Jacob Mitchell.

Select Council:
John W Thompson	Wm Warner	Jas Vanusen
Jos Morris		

Common Council:
Thos Leiper	Alex'r Cook	Jeremia Hornketh
John Steel	Levi Gerret	Adam Eckfeldt
Seth Craige	Wm Smiley	Liberty Brown
Jas Cutbush	Walter Daltzell	Edw Smith
M.Alphonson	C Ireland	Sam'l Wetherill jr
Chas Johnson	Francis Mitchell	Randal Hutchenson
Capt John Mollowny	Timothy Matlack	Chas J Ingersol
Jos Barnes	Jas Carson	

Rpblcn Tkt for mbrs of the Leg in Calvert Co, Md: Wm Holland; Dan'l Kent; John Gray & Thos C Gantt.

Geo W Briscoe informs his Rpblcn friends of PG Co, Md, that his peculiar situation precludes his being a candidate for the State Leg. Wm G D Worthington, esq, has been nominated as a substitute.

Meeting in Middlesex, Ontario Co, N Y: Geo Green, esq, chrmn; Rich'd M Williams, sec; Sam'l T Church & Dan'l Gainsey, committee.

New Orleans, Aug 21. Gale commenced on Wed night: Mr Paulding's unfinished brick hse in Chartres St blown in; brick store of Messrs Talcott & Bowers, in Chartres St demolished-Mr Talcott escaped in time; Mr Donaldson's hse, Faubourg St Mary-unroofed; Mr Fry's brick store, Faubourg St Mary, blown down; Mr Musson's brick store, Canal St, blown down; Mr Erkin's brick store, Chartres St, blown down; hse in Chartres St nr Messrs Kenner & Co, partly blown down; Mr Lester's brick bldg, Bourbon St, same. Vessels damaged or destroyed: brig *Mary* of Pittsburgh-lost both masts. Ship *Missouri*, Balt-little damage. Brig *Archimedes*, much damaged. *Polacre Divina Pastora*-much damaged. U S brig *Enterprize*, ashore. Brig *Wm,* Newport-damaged. U S brig *Viper*, much damaged. Schn'r *Liberty* of N Orleans, sunk. Brig *Wm & Mary*-damaged. Ship *Dryad* of

N Y, damaged. Brig *Mechanic*, Kennebunk. Ship *Alfred* of Newburyport, damaged. Ship *Jane* of N Y. Brig *Sally Ann* of N Y, damaged. Brig *Hope*, N Y, injured. Sloop *Wm & Mary* of Charleston, sunk. Schn'r *Betsey* of Boston, much injured. Brig *Reliance* of Charleston, irreparable. Privateer *Buckskin*, lost. Privateer *Felix*, ashore-damaged. Ship *Paragon* of N Y, damaged. Ship *Iris* of N Y, ashore & damaged. Ship *Juno* of N Y, ashore. Schn'r *Wm*, Newport, damaged. Schn'r *Flora*, Duxbury, damaged. Brig *Maid*, Boston, destroyed. Ship *Eliz*, of N Y, little damage. Ship *Agricola*, New Bedford, dismasted. Ship *Eldrich*, N Y, damaged. Schn'r *Astrea*, Salem, damaged. Ship *Genr'l Knox*, Portland, dmg'd. Schn'r *Mary*, Ky, lost masts & bowsprit. Ship *Suffolk*, N Y, ashore & dmg'd. Ship *Ceres*, N Y, ashore-dmg'd. Ship *Oliver-Ellsworth*, N Y, dmg'd. Ship *Henry Seawell* of Eliz City, dmg'd. Sloop *JoAnna* of Warren, dmg'd. Ship *Washington*, irreparable. Schn'r *Atlas* of N Orleans, dmg'd. Schn'r *Clara* of N Y, dmg'd. Brig *Juno* of Salem, damaged. Ship *Nancy* of Boston, damaged. Schn'r *Cumberland*, destroyed. U S Ketch *Etna*, sunk. Schn'r *Mary Ann* of Whiting, dmg'd. Brig *Rolla*, damaged. Ship *Remittance*, Otho, brig *Sumatra*-all of N Y, damaged. The ship *Harlequin*, Capt Coffin, from N Y, just below the English turn-on Wed night; 2 of her sailors were on shore making it fast, when the ship took a sheer, upset & sunk; every soul on board perished.

<u>Sale of Wash City lots for taxes on Dec 28th:</u>
Bernard, John, lot 12 sq 105; $10.51.
Bartleman, Wm, lot 9 sq 122; $2.84.
Beall, Thos & Leo M Deakins, lot 2 sq 124; $3.72.
Barry, Zachariah, lot 14 sq 142; $4.04.
Bawn, Benj, lot 5 sq 218; $1.42.
Brodeau, Ann, lots 1 thru 8, 19 & 20 in sq 20; lots 7-8-9 in sq 33; lots 1-2-6-7-8-16-17-18 in sq 247; lot 15 sq 634; lots 1 thru 6 & 30 in sq 950; lots 1 & 4 in sq 976; $39.60.
Conyngham, John, lot 1 North of sq 4; lot 8 sq 5; lots 22-23 in sq 16; $24.10.
Custis, Geo W P, lots 1-2-3-4 in sq 21; $18.32.
Curry, Jas, lot 2 sq 54; $5.96.
Callaham, John-heirs, lot 2 sq 172; $1.10.
Cazanave, Ann, sqs 232 & 233 all 265 whole sq 267 part 1 lots 3 thru 16; $89.33.
Dennison, Robt, lot 11 sq 79; $13.46.
Emery, John-heirs, lots 1 & 22 in sq 218; part of sq 731; $2.86.
French, Ariana, lot 4 sq 27; $2.36.
French, Geo-heirs, lots 4 thru 9 in sq 27; lot 8 sq 104; $42.72.
Fisher, Azariah-heirs, lot 1 sq 57; sq 122 of 6; $9.93.
Fitzgerald, Thos, lot 7 sq 80; $9.30.
Fisher, Jas, lots 19 & 20 in sq 169; lot 2 sq 634; $26.90.
Gaither, Henry, lot 1 sq 14; lots 1-2-3 in sq 104; lots 22-33 in sq 127; $29.34.
Hughs, Christopher, lot 6 sq 169; $10.11.
Hoe, John, lots 1-2-16 in sq 225; $10.56.
Jones, Thos-heirs, lot 9 sq 63; lots 1 & 14 in sq 120; lot 1 sq 121; $36.56.
Jones, Leonard-heir, lot 23 sq 166; $6.51.
Jameson, Walter, lot 12 sq 78; $3.67.
Kemp, Mary, lot 3 sq 56; $2.76.

Kesler, Andrew, lot 12 sq 79; $13.19.
King Nicholas, Va, lot 14 sq 81; $3.94.
Kimshaw, Nichs, lot 19 sq 88; $9.01.
Kerr, Ann, lots 1-2-7 sq 196; lots 5 thru 12, 21 thru 28 in sq 197; lots 3-4-7-8-9-13-14-17-18-19 in sq 198; lots 3-4-7-8-9-13-14-17-18-19-20 in sq 199; lots 2 thru 7, 14 thru 20 in sq 214; sq 216 all; lots 2 & 5 in sq 254; lot 1 sq 487; lot 13 sq 489; lot 2 sq 604; $109.84.
Ludlow, Dan'l, lots 4 & 9 in sq 231; lots 23 & 24 in sq 296; lots 4-24-26 in sq 499: $6.24.
Mantz, John, lot 17 sq 88; lot 10 sq 102; lot 7 sq 143; $13.16.
Mcgrath, Wm, lot 1 sq 61; $8.78.
Miller, Peter, lot 6 sq 62; $3.25.
Murdoch, Geo, lot 3 sq 63; lots 2 & 3 in Sq 71; lot 6 Sq 143; lot 6 Sq 569; lot 4 Sq 570; $10.46]
Morris, Benj, lots 23 & 24 in Sq 77; $11.41.
Marshall, John; Hopkins, J; & Marshall, Jas; lots 1-2-7-8-9-12-13 in Sq 219; $20.66.
Moyer, Jacob, lot 8 Sq 80; lots 12 & 22 in Sq 88; lots 4 & 5 in Sq 141; $58.59.
Murdoch, Eleanor, lot 11 Sq 80; $2.76.
Marr, Va, lot 7 Sq 122; $16.13.
Mason, Geo-heirs, lots 8 thru 12 in Sq 106; $16.21.
Merky, David, lot 6 Sq 142; $12.52.
Martin, Luther, lots 13 thru 18 in Sq 143; $17.64.
Pierce, Thos, lot 7 Sq 101; $19.02.
Powell, Curshbert, lot 4 Sq 168; $10.07.
Rose, Robt, lot 25 Sq 38; $3.
Rednover, Matthias, lot 8 Sq 79; $13.19.
Stone, John-heirs, lots 17 & 18 in Sq 24; $11.92.
Shaaff, Arthur, lot 3 Sq 81; lot 12 Sq 214; $4.56.
Schnebley, Henry, lot 1 Sq 83; $18.92.
Snowden, Sam'l, lot 2 East of sq 87; lot 2 Sq 608; lot 1 Sq 610; $4.23.
Sayle, John, lot 5 Sq 103; $7.09.
Sluby, Nicholas, lots 7 & 8 in Sq 105; $5.16.
Scott, Gustavus-heirs, lots 9 & 10 in Sq 77; lot 8 Sq 120; lots 22-23 in Sq 172; $53.17.
Shell, Christian-heirs, lot 6 Sq 124; $10.50.
Southgate, John, lot 13 Sq 170; $3.92.
Stewart, Walter-heirs, lot 3 Sq 219; lots 8 thru 11 in Sq 200; $21.11.
Shaw, Ann, lots 1 & 2 in Sq 119; $3.30.
Stoddart, Benj, numerous lots & sqs: $448.20.
Stoddert & Templeman, lots 2-3-4-22-27 in Sq 101; $10.02.
Thompson Ezra & Smith, Isaac, lots 17-18-19 in Sq 69; $2.46.
Thomas, John Chew, lot 9 Sq 142; $23.57.
Threlkeld, John, lots 11-29 & 30 in Sq 105; lots 8-9-10 in Sq 119; $40.70.
Templeman, John, lot 1 Sq 12; lot 8 Sq 153; $1.18.
Weems, John Dr, lots 5 thru 9 in Sq 27; $41.53.
Waring, Marsham, lots 3 & 4 in Sq 57; lot 10 East of Sq 88; $21.77.
Wash Assoc, Sq North of 137 all; $1.14.

Wilson & Dennis, lots 4 & 5 in Sq 142; $21.89.
Winder, Levin, lots 6-7-8 in Sq 218; $7.15. [-Jos Brumley, Col 1st Ward]

The laws of the Dist of Col authorise aliens to purchase & hold landed property & every species of rl est in the city & county of Wash in said District.

Public sale: part of lot 3 in sq 141, with improvements, prop of Smith, Calhoun & Co. Brick dwlg hse on lot 6 in sq 141, prop of Jas McKim. Part of lot 13 in sq 119, with improvements, prop of Jas Welch. Above property sold for taxes due the Corp of Wash City. -Jos Brumley, Coll 1st Ward. Sale on Oct 26th at McLeod's Hotel.

Auction sale at hse of Dr Patterson on F St; hsehld furn. -N L Queen auct.

Deserted: from my recruiting rendezvous in Stanardsville, Orange Co, Va, on Sep 11, Benedict Athon, a sldr ab't 23 yrs of age; occupation-school mstr. Reward-$10. -Micajah Lynch, Lt 20th Regt inf U S A.

For sale-at the hse of Rich'd Charles-hsehold furn; for taxes due the Wash Corp. -John Queen, Coll 4th Ward.

TUE SEP 29, 1812
Manufacture in England: Birmingham & neighborhood-Mr Thos Attwood, High Bailiff of Birmingham; Mr Wm Whitehouse, nail-ironmonger of West Bramwich; Mr Thos Potts, merchant of Birmingham; Mr Jos Shore, same; Mr Jas Ryland, manufacturer of coach harness & saddle furniture, of Birmingham; Mr Rich'd Spooner, Banker of Birmingham.

D R Williams, esq, has declined being a candidate for a seat in the 13th Congress from So C.

In Alexandria a company of more than 60 men are ready to obey the call of their country; Jas McGuire chosen Capt; Robt Smith-Lt & Chas L Nevitt-Ensign.

Died: on Sep 25, Mrs Rachael Hyatt, age 35 yrs, in Wash City, of a short but severe illness.

Orphans Crt of Wash Co, D C. Sep 24, 1812. Prsnl est of Wm Bond, late of the city, dec'd. -Ann Bond, admx.

Reward-$1,500 for those attemprting to destroy the Gunpowder Mills. -Thos Ewell, Wash.

Reward-$50 for Tarleton, negro man, alias Wallace; raised by Mr Fowler in Chesterfield Co, nr Manchester, Va; was again the prop of Mr Rubeau, a Frenchman; again the prop of Mr Wm Fulcher, of Richmond, of whom he was purch'd & brought to So C. -John Lowry, Fairfield Dist, S C, nr Winnsborough.

THU OCT 1, 1812
Manufacturers in England: Mr Wm Blakeway, lamp manufacturer, Birmingham; Mr Thos Messenger, brass founder, of same;
Mr Henry Dunbar, button make, of same;
Mr Geo Room, japanner, of same;
Mr Robt Fiddian, brass candlesticks, of same;
Wm Bannister, plater, of same; Thos Osler, glass-toy & button-mkr, of Birmingham; Jos Stanley, screw-mkr, of Woolverhampton;
Thos Blidge, jappanner, of same; Benj Cook, jeweller & gilt toy mkr, of Birmingham;
Thos Clarke, webbing, braces & toys, of same; Benj Smith, heavy steel toys, of same;
Joshua Scolfield, American merchant, Birmingham;
Mr Tho Milward, spoon-mkr, same; Mr John Bailey, merchant, of Sheffield.
Mr Geo Naylor, merchant, of Sheffield.
Mr Ebenezer Rhodes, manufacturer of cutlery, Sheffield.
Wm Bannister, plater, Birmingham.

List of Genr'l ofcrs of the U S Army:
Maj-Genr'l:
| Henry Dearborn | Thos Pinckney | |
Brig-Genr'l:
Jas Wilkinson	Thos Flournoy	Wade Hampton
John Armstrong	Jas Winchester	John Chandler
Jos Bloomfield	Wm H Harrison	Wm Hull
John P Boyd		

Qrtr-Mstr-Genr'l: Morgan Lewis
Adjut-Genr'l: Thos Cushing
Inspec-Genr'l: Alex'r Smyth

Proclamation: during the action bet his Majesty's frig *Guerriere* & the yankee cock boat, cld the *Constitution*, on Aug 19th last, the following persons deserted their post & not heard of since:

Jas Johnston	Moses Virgen	Benj Henworth
Jas Greenwood	Wm Cole	Jas McGill
3d Cpl Webb, marine	John Griswell	Jas Butterwitch
Wm Rayseon	Wm Hammock	Robt Mittwoft
A Joaquin	John Jacobs	Lt Jas Pullman
Mr Garton	John Newman	Robt Winn
Jas Guy	Robt Scott	Lt Roberts
John Flavitt	John Hosey	
-Halifax, Sep 10, 1812	-signed, Dacres.	

Mrd: Mr Jonathan Appler to Miss Ann Maddox, both of Wash, on Sep 29th, by Rev Mr Breckenridge.

Mrd: Mr John A Barcley, merchant, to Miss Rebecca O C M'Crea, step-dght of Adjut Genr'l Thos H Cushing, U S Army, both of Phil, in Phil, on Sep 17, by Rev Mr Doake.

Died: Capt John Fenno Mansfield, age 25 yrs, on Sep 14 in Ohio, of a malignant fever; remains interred on the 15th in the new burying ground with the honors of Masonry & war; he belonged to the sacrificed army of Gen Hull; he returned from Detroit with his company on the 7th. -Ohio paper.

Albany Register of Sep 22. State trial at crct crt, at Norwich, Chenango Co; trial of Gen David Thomas, treas of this state, alledged to bribe Casper M Rouse, to vote for the incorporation of the Bank of American, in the senate of this state. Verdict-not guilty. Judge Van Ness presided.

For sale-elegant assortment of artificial flowers. -John Rose jr, Navy Yd.

Snuff & Tobacco ware hse. -P L Duport, Gtwn.

Rich'd Davis, sign of the golden sheaf, High st, Gtwn; assortment of cloths for sale.

Sale of Wash City lots on Apr 2. for taxes due thereon up to the yr 1811:
Alleson, Robt, lot 7 sq 63; $3.58.
Avidths, J B, lot 5 sq 107; $3.38.
Carmack, Dan'l, lots 9-11-12-13 in sq 40; $11.24.
Clark, Sam'l, lot 14 sq 74; $2.20.
Campbell, Hugh, lot 2 sq 39; $8.82.
Crawford Jas jr, lots 26 & 28 in sq 231; $2.34.
Camp, John, lot 1 sq 88; $5.95.
Duer, Jas, lot 10 sq 54; $16.47.
Davidson, Elias, lot 16 sq 80; $7.99.
Flick, Andrew, lot 5 sq 80; $1.38.
Feltwell, Wm, lots 25 & 26 in sq 126; lots 10 & 11 in sq 568; $9.08.
Gangaware, Michl, lot 2 sq 62; $2.65.
Goulding, Frederick-heirs, lot 6 sq 76; $11.85.
Goil, Henry, lot 12 sq 89; $1.00
Gott, Christopher, lot 1 sq 105; $1.90.
Gilpin, Bernard, lot 11 sq 142; $1.86.
Geouges, Arnold, lots 12 & 13 in sq 224; $5.82.
Haga, Jonathan, lot 8 sq 56; $2.76.
Hindmand, Wm, lot 2 sq 43; lot 1 sq 60; lot 3 sq 83; lot 6 sq 120; lot 9 sq 665; $21.90.
Hackett, John, lot 24 sq 88; $9.04.
Holstien, Geo, lots 16 & 17 in sq 81; $20.40.
Kirk, Jas, lot 6 sq 61; $8.58.
Klinger, Henry, lot 6 sq 80; $19.75.
Kesler,Dan'l, lot 11 sq 81; $2.40
Kruger, Lodowick, lot 1 sq 89; $1.56.
Link, Andrew, lot 11 sq 84; $5.04.
Matthias, John, lot 4 sq 60; $6.32.

McDade, John, lot 9 sq 81; $10.82.
Middart, John, lot 14 sq 84; $1.38.
Parry, Edwards lot 5 sq 161; 62 cents.
Reclimair, Aaron, lot 2 sq 61; $2.04.
Ragan, Dan'l, lot 16 sq 88; $4.97.
Robinson, Wm, lot 20 sq 88; $8.97.
Robinson, Henry, lot 17 sq 184; $1.12.
Reeder, Geo, lot 3 sq 102; $2.76.
Reed, Wm, lots 1-3-8-10 in sq 231; $4.90.
Ratcliff, Sarah, lots 8-9-10 in sq 166; $19.24.
Shaw, Capt John, lot 10 sq 40; lot 23 sq 122; lots 19 & 20 in sq 143; $19.08.
Stoker, Mich'l, lot 14 sq 84; $2.96. [cont'd]
Smith, Amos, lot 3 sq 88; lot 3 sq 89; $5.76.
Swingle, Geo, lot 7 sq 88; lot 7 sq 89; $9.97.
Seybert, Philip, lot 23 sq 88; $8.11.
Skinner, Edw, lot 12 sq 122; $12.55.
Shippin, Thos l, lot 29 sq 155; 76 cents.
Stall, Henry, lot 7 sq 144; $8.07.
Sutton, Robt, lot 13 sq 222; $4.80.
Tompton, Jacob, lot 3 sq 62; $2.72.
Tabbs, Barton, lot 27 sq 126; 76 cents.
Umbults, Henry, lot 5 sq 120, $12.55.
Ward, Jas, lots 1-2-3 in sq 49; whole ofsq 580; n of 580 part; lot 14 sq 878; $3.32.
Waugh, W & E, lot 6 sq 122; $6.69.
Walker, Henry, lot 9 sq 143; $12.78.
Wayman, Chas-heirs, lots 8 & 9 in sq 196; lot 9 sq 117; $21.03.
Youman, Elias, lot 3 sq 104; $9.47.
Wason, Geo-heirs, lots 8 thru 12 in sq 106; $7.53.
Vanbibber, Abraham, lot 2 sq 2; lots 17 & 18 in sq 172; $11.52.
Taylor, Jos-heirs, lot 9 sq 222; $8.48. -Jos Brumley, coll 1st ward.

SAT OCT 3, 1812
Elisha Padgett, insolvent debtor, confined in Wash Co, D C, prison-for debt. -Wm Brent, clk.

<u>Sale of Wash City lots on Dec 29th for taxes due Wash Corp up to 1811:</u>
Brown, Thos, lots 9 & 16 in sq 825; $4.84.
Berry, Zachariah, lots 18-19-20 in sq 847; $7.80.
Bauhay, Wm, half lot 1 in sq 978; $1.80.
Ball, Jos, sq 988; $3.34.
Beterman, Alex'r, 25 ft front sq 878; $2.20.
Carrol & Prout, lots 6 to 18 in sq 882; $73.26
Crawford, Davis-heirs, lots 1 to 7 in sq 849; $40.93.
Carlton, Jas, lot 19 sq 949; 62 cents.
Cope, Jasper, sq 974 3000 sq ft; $1.20.
Cooper, Wm, lot 5 sq 1043; $4.95.
Clark, Wm, sq 996; $1.32.
Barnard, Elliott-heirs, lots 2-3-4-8-9 in sq 864; lot 3 sq 1067; $1.66.

Evans, Evan, lots 12-13 sq 1020; lot 13 sq 1046; lot 6 sq 1047; lot 7 sq 1123; $7.78.
Fuller, Oliver, sq 825 30 ft front; $8.30.
Farrington, Lewis, lot 1 sq 879; $5.70.
Frye, John, lots 1 to 14 in sq 919; lots 1 to 12 in sq 938; lots 13 to 16 in sq 938; lots 3-4-5 13 to 18 in sq 986; lots 11 to 19 in sq 1042; lots 5 to 12 in sq 1066; $72,85.
Gantt, Thos T, lots 13 & 14 in sq 1023; $26.81.
Genners, Chas, sq 1114; $3.
Hart, Barnard, lots 3 thru 7 & 11 thru 13 in sq 963;$2.26.
Howard, Henry, lots 8 & 14 in sq 983; $6.39.
Ingraham, Nath'l, lots 21 to 25 in sq 1047; $9.30.
Lynn, Adam, lot 6 sq 1023; $6.18.
Michell, John, lots 14 & 15 in sq 978; $10.02.
Moscrop, Henry, numerous lots in various sqs; $4.04.
McElwee, John, lots 6 to 11 in sq 1020; $6.10.
Maltby, Sarah, lots 19 & 20 in sq 1020; $1.50.
Morris Nicholson & Prout, lots 1 & 2 in sq 1149; 34 cents.
Parrott, Rich'd, lot 10 sq 874; $1.52.
Perry, Edw, lot 3 sq 1148; lot 4 sq 1149; lots 1 & 2 in sq 569; $2.28.
Prout, King & Carroll, lots 3-4-5 & 7 to 16 in sq 977; $108.51.
Slater, David, lots 11 & 12 in sq 610; lot 4 sq 904; lot 5 sq 928; lot 4 sq 975; lot 3 sq 976; lot 13 sq 768; $51.80.
Slater, Thos, lot 5 sq 840; 60 cents.
Stockwell, Mark-heirs, lots 8 & 9 & half of 10 in sq 845; $4.86.
Sanford, Wm, lot 8 sq 1123; $4.09.
Slater, Hy, lot 6 sq 876; $9.54.
Slater, Ann, lot 5 sq 904; $6.51.
Slater, Sarah, lot 6 sq 904; $9.50.
Stans, Francis, lot 33 sq 1043; 34 cents.
Smith, And, lot 1 sq 1045; lots 6-7-20-21 in sq 1077; $34.35.
Thomas, Rich'd, lots 1-2-15-16 in sq 846; lots 18-19-20 in sq 569; lots 1-2-17 in sq 17; lot 11 sq 142; $33.57.
Thompson, Eliz, lot 9 sq 1067; $1.89.
White, Bensan, sq 825, 18 ft front; $2.66.
Walker, Geo, numerous lots in various sqs; $313.35.
Walker & Wheeler, lots 1-5-6 in sq 1025 east; $43.91.
Wheeler, Eliz, sq 1067 south, 225 ft front; $22.12.
Walker, Jas jr, numerous lots in various sqs; $94.90.
Wilson, Wm, lot 10 sq 864; lots 10 to 14 in sq 1048; $23.46.
Wormley, Jas, lots 4-5-9 in sq 1048; lots 16 to 22 in sq 1112; lots 3 & 4 in sq 1121; lot 9 sq 1122; $1.28.
Weighman, Chas-heirs, lot 9 sq 1117; $1.20.
Willink, Wm & Jas, sq 916; lots 3-4-5-9 in sq 964; lots 1 & 5 in sq 942; lots 1-2-3-9-10-11-12-13-20-21-22 in sq 987; $1.90.
Ward, John, lots 11 & 12 in sq 996; lots 14 to 18 in sq 1020; lots 1-2-3-11-12 in sq 1023; $32.24.
Young, Benj-heirs, sqs 848, 329, 413, 355, 354, 389, 390; lot 6 sq 602; $159.84.

Yeaton, Wm, sq 902 22 ft front; $3.74.
Young, Abraham-heirs, numerous lots in various sqs; $33.59.
Young, Wm, numerous lots in various sqs; $22.41.
Young, Mordeica, numerous lots in various sqs; $24.77.
Young, Mary of Wm, numerous lots in various sqs; $22.58.
Young, Ann, numerous lots in various sqs; $24.33.
-John Queen, col 4th ward.

Manufacturers in England:
Mr John Buckley, manufacturer, of Saddleworth;
Mr Thos Greenwood, cotton & woollen manufacturer, of Halifax;
Mr Jas Holforth, cotton spinner at Leeds;
Mr Wm Midgley, woollen manufacturer of Rochdale, Lancashire;
Mr Wm Walker, woollen manufacturer of Rochdale;
Mr Wm Hastings, woolen manufacturer of Rochdale;
Mr Henry Hoyle, woollen manufacturer at Rosendale;
Mr Rich'd Turner, flannel manufacturer, Haslingden, nr Rochdale;
Mr Francis Platt, merchant & woollen manufacturer, of Saddleworth;
Mr David Sheard, blanket & flushing manufacturer, of the parish of Dewsbury;
Mr John Oxley, woollen merchant of Wakefield;
Mr Joshua Beckett, trustee of the cloth hall at Leeds;
Mr Ralph Stevenson, of the potteries;
Mr Wm Thompson, woollen manufacturer, of Rawden, nr Leads;
Mr Josiah Wedgwood, of the potteries;
Mr Jos Walker, merchant, at Leeds;
Mr Christopher Lawson, woollen merchant of Leeds;
Mr Josiah Wedgwood, of the potteries;
Mr Jos Walker, merchant, at Leeds;
Mr Christopher Lawson, woollen merchant of Leeds;
Mr Thos Dennison, woollen manufacturer, a trustee of Cloth Hall, at Leeds.

Madison electoral tkt: [Richmond, Va. Sep 26, 1812]

Jos Goodwyn of Nansemond	Benj Harrison of Mt Airy, PG Co
Edw Pegram of Dinwiddie	Rich'd Field of Brunswick
Thos Reed sr of Charlotte	Matthew Cheatham of Chesterfield
Thos M Randolph of Albemarle	Chas Yancey of Buckingham
Geo Penn of Patrick	Wm G Poindexter of Louisa
Spencer Roane of Hanover	Robt Taylor of Orange
Sthreshley Rennolds of Essex	Gustavus B Horner of Fauquier
Robt Nelson of York	Mann Page of Gloucester
Walter Jones of Northumberland	John T Brook of Stafford
Hugh Holmes of Frederick	Dan'l Morgan of Jefferson
Andrew Russel of Wash.	Chas Taylor of Montgomery
Wm McKinley of Ohio	Archibald Rutherford of Rockingham
Archibald Stuart of Augusta	

Note: Jas P Preston of Montgomery has accepted a commission in the U S army in rm of Landon Cabell who declined accepting the appointment, Thos M Randolph of Albemarle is on the tkt.

Genr'l Sam'l Findley has been elected Col of a regt of mounted riflemen. Gen Jos Kerr has been elected Major.

Died: Geo Fred'k Cooke, esq, age 57 yrs, at N Y on Sat, a celebrated tragedian.

Richmond, Va. Mbrs of the central corresponding committee for election of Jas Madison:
Thos Ritchie
Sam'l Pleasants
Wm Wirt
Wm Mumford
Wm Brockenbrough
Peyton Randolph
Andrew Stevenson

TUE OCT 6, 1812
Manufacturers in England:
Mr Jas Kay, cotton & woollen manufacturer, nr Bury, in Lancashire.
Mr Geo Palfreyman, manufacturer & caliCo printer of Manchester.
Mr Thos Cardwell, manufacturer of small wares, at Manchester.
Mr John Grundy, jr, woollen manufacturer of Bury, Lancashire.
Mr Jos Weight, manufacturer & buyer of cotton goods at Manchester.
Mr Timothy Wiggin, genr'l exporter of manufactures to American.
Mr Shakespeare Phillips, merchant of Manchester.
Mr Jeremiah Bury, cotton manufacturer of Stockport.
Mr Thos Withington, merchant of Manchester.
Mr Thos Leach, hosiery manufacturer at Leicester.
Mr John Bentley, muslin manufacturer of Stockport.
Mr Wm Drayton, stocking manufacturer, of Leicester.
Mr John Bentley, muslin manufacturer, of Stockport.
Mr John Wood, cotton manufacturer, of Bolton in the Moors.
Mr Thos Short, hosiery manufacturer, at Hinckley, in Leicestershire.
Mr John Parkes, worsted manufacturer, at Hinckley, Leicestershire.
Mr Thos Holt, of Liverpool, prop of glass-works at Warrington.
Mr Herbert Broom, carpet manufacturer at Kidderminster.
Mr Rich'd Watson, carpet manufacturer at Kidderminster.
Mr Wm Okill,-salt works of Cheshire.
Mr Walter Fergus, linen trade of Scotland for 30 yrs.
Mr John Honyman, church warden of the Parish of Spital Fields.
Mr Wm Hale, in the silk trade & treas of the Parish of Spital Fields.
Mr Geo Stevenson, in the silk trade, of Spital Fields.
Mr Sam'l Woods, of London; sale of the cloths of Gloucestershire, etc.

For sale-4200 bushels of coal; laying at Rich'd Parrott's wharf, Gtwn. -Wm O'Neale, Wash City.

Died: Mrs Sophia Mercer, w/o John Francis Mercer, on Sep 25th at *West River farm*; the seat of her ancestors for svr'l generations.

Died: Robt Moss, age 34 yrs, on Oct 1 at his seat in Fairfax Co, Va.

Teacher wanted-apply to Wm Brewer, a few miles below the mouth of the Monocacy, in Montg Co, Md.

To rent, brick hse now occupied by Overton Carr, on Va Ave. May be had Nov 1 next. -Sam'l N Smallwood.

Robt Long, insolvent debtor. Oath to be administered-Wash Co, D C. -Wm Brent, clk, Oct 6.

THU OCT 8, 1812
Merchants in England: Mr Jos Brooks Yates, merchant, Liverpool.
Mr John Richardson, American Commission merchant of Liverpool.
Mr Wm Rathbone, Mr Wm Alex'r Brown & Mr Thos Thornely, merchants of Liverpool.
Mr Thos Holt, Soc for bettering the condition of the poor at Liverpool.
Mr John Richmond Jaffray, merchant of London.
Mr Henry Hinckley, insur broker of London.
Mr John Fry, managing clk of the Hse of MacKenzie, Glennie & Co in London.

The editor of this paper has taken Mr Wm W Seaton, late joint conductor, [with Mr Jos Gales Sr] of the Raleigh Register, into business with him. From Nov 1st next, the Nat'l Intell will be conducted under the firm of Gales & Seaton.

For sale-schn'r, *Virginia*, rigged for the coast or Europe. -E & J Handy, crnr of Congress & Water St wharf. Gtwn.

Public sale of ab't 31 lots in various sqs; per will of Mr Jos Carleton, late of Gtwn, dec'd. -John Laird, exc-Gtwn.

Reward-$10 for John Bulman, seaman, ab't 40 yrs of age; deserted from John Williams, mstr of gunboat 74.

Land for sale per will of Sam'l Turner, esq, dec'd; farm in Montg Co, Md, late the resid of said dec'd, ab't 700 acs. -Tho & Sam'l Turner, excs.

Runaway committed to the Wash Co, D C jail; Sarah, a black girl; says she was sold by Mr Geo Hillary of PG Co, Md, to a trader of negroes. -C Tippet, kpr of the jail.

SAT OCT 10, 1812
Federal Convention at Staunton, Va, has nominated Rufus King of N Y, as candidate for the ofc of Pres; Eldridge Gerry as V P; Jared Ingersol of Pa & Wm Davie of S C also named.

St John's College wishes to engage a Principal; salary $1000 per annum. -Sam'l Ridout, sec'y.

Richmond, K. Sep 19. On Sep 15th the ctzns of Madison Co were addressed by Capt R A Sturgus, G Walker & Gen Green Clay; 3 companies of mounted vols rallied for their country; they marched for Louisville yesterday.

Pa Electoral Tkt:	Chas Thompson	Isaac Worrell
Paul Cox	Mich'l Baker	Jos Engle
J Davis	Jas Fulton	Edw Crouch
John Whitehill	David Fullerton	Hugh Glasgow
Robt Smith	Sam'l Smith	Chas Shoemaker
Nath'l Michler	John Murray	Jas Mitchel
Arthur Moore	Clement Paine	Jas Stevenson
Henry Alshouse	David Meade	Abiah Minor
Adamson Tannehill	David Mitchel	

Committee Rm, Phil, Sep 16. Ctzns of same: Jacob Holgate, John Binns, John Geyer, John Porter. [Regarding the Presidential election]

For sale-all hsehld furn of Chas P Polk, in F St. -Wm Reily & Thos Hughes, trustees.

PG Co, Md. Henry Yost, of Bladensburg, brought before me a stray sorrel gelding. -Thos Bowie.

Mrd: Geo Wash Biscoe, esq, to Miss Hannah S Oden, 2nd d/o Benj Oden, esq, on Oct 1, by the R R Bishop Clagett, PG Co, Md.

To rent-a 2 story brick hse on 10th St nr the theatre. -E B De Kraft, or Mr Jas Moore, next door to the premises.

Orphans Crt of Wash Co, D C. Oct 10, 1812. Prsnl est of Robt Underwood, late of said city, dec'd. -John Underwood, adm.

TUE OCT 13, 1812
An act for the relief of Wm Hewitt; by Council of Wash City; $150 for svcs as clk of the First Chamber of the City Cncl bet Jun 1811 & 1812. -Jas Hewitt, Pres Pro Tempore; Alex'r McCormick, Pres of the Brd of Aldermen. -Approved, Sep 5, 1812, Dan'l Rapine, Mayor.

Ladies with ltrs in the Wash Post ofc, Oct 1, 1812:		
Miss Polly Adams	Mrs M Magruder	Eliz Shorter
Mgt Adams	Mrs Muse	Sophia Smith
Ms Sally Carter	Eliz R B Mayhen	Mrs Smith
Mary Danning	Mrs Eliz Mitchell	Mgt C Strother
Mrs Fisher	Mrs Eliz Maxwell	Mary Thompson
Anna Greenwell	Mrs Maloy	Nancy Turner
Ann Green	Abigail Osborn	Jane Posey
Mary Ann Tolbert	Mrs Nancy Holmes	Hopeful Toler
Mary Jeffery	Mrs Eleanor Purkins	Ann Thomas

Mrs Docia Long	Mrs Nelly Purts	Ann White
Mrs Linkins	Miss L Peterson	Miss Mary White
Mrs Sarah Winder	Mrs Eliz Long	Sarah Robertson
Mrs Elinor West	Sarah Lambert	Mrs Simpson
Mrs Amelia Short	Mrs Martha Young	Mrs J Lindsay
Mrs Mary White c/o Mr Hollaway		

Mrd: Mr Wm McKee to Mrs Grace McCormick, both of Wash City, on Oct 11, by Rev Mr Addison.

Public sale: 1-whole of sq south of 173, with improvements; prop of David Burns' heirs. 2-a brick hse & lot in Sq 118, prop of Jas M Lingan. Both sold for taxes due the Wash Corp. -Jos Brumley, Coll 1st Ward.

Staff of the 1st Legion: Geo Peter, Adjut; Wm Whann, Qrtr Mstr; Clement Smith, Paymstr; Dr Fred'k May, Surg; Dr John Ott, Surg's Mate; E Cummings, Qr Mstrs Sgt; John Simpson, Fife Maj. -Wm Smith, Lt Col Com First Legn, Mil Dist Col. Gtwn, Oct 10, 1812.

Died: Lt Sam'l G Blodget, age 28 yrs, commander of gunboat 46, on Sep 29th, together with 8 of her crew. Seamen who drowned: Dennis M'Stay, Thos Joice, Jonas Fisk, John Dutcher, Sam'l Holly, Morris Smith, John Howard & Josiah Simmons. [Severe gale on south part of the Island of Conannicut. -Newport]

THU OCT 15, 1812
Died: John Smith, esq, clk in the Treas Dept of the U S; formerly an ofcr in the Marine Corps; buried with the honors of war on Oct 12.

Died: Rev David Wiley, Postmstr of Gtwn, D C; Oct 7th at Fayetteville, N C.

Died Wm Wood, esq, late his Britannic Majesty's Cnsl for Md; Oct 10 at Balt, Md; after a short illness.

Died: Col Henry Conway, on Sep 10th, at his seat in Greene Co, East Tenn-his death occasioned by the sting of bees. He was interred on Sep 12th; a Rev hero; entered the svc in 1776 & continued therein until the close of the war.

Wash Brewery, bottom of N J Ave, ice order rec'd by Dan'l Rapine, Capitol Hill & at the brewery. -J W Collet & Co

Article on impressed seamen-2 gr nphws of Genr'l Washington were impressed. John & Chas Lewis-John was discharged in Feb 1812 after 3 applications; very badly used during detention, deserted twice & flogged twice. Chas also applied 3 times & was discharged in 1811; he alleged in the first case that he was a ntv of Quebec & in the other that he had voluntarily entered.

S W Gray to resign the ofc of Constable for Wash Co; he has committed his unfinished business to the care of Mr Brooke Edmonson.

SAT OCT 17, 1812
Ezekiel Bacon & Josiah Quincy, of Mass, declined a re-election to the 13th Cong.

Lost-a sorrel horse; reward $5. -John Glasco, Wash City.

Reward-6 cents for Nicholas Osborn who ran away on Oct 10th. -John Mulloy.

Wash Co, D C. Gustavus Howard; insolvent debtor oath to be administered on Oct 24. -Wm Brent, clk.

Public sale-Decree of High Crt of Chancery; at Mt Calvert, negroes, stock, furn, parcel of land cld *Beall's Gift* & one cld *Mt Calvert Manor;* both in PG Co, Md. -Trueman Tyler, trustee.

TUE OCT 20, 1812
Queen Ann Co, Md-election returns:
Congress: Robt Wright-811   Sam W Thomas-275
Delegates to the Genr'l Assembly:
Th Wright of S-689 votes   Sam Sturges-654
Thos Emory-681 votes   Robt Stevens- 619

Poughkeepsie, N Y, Oct 14. Yesterday two companies of U S Cavalry arrv'd in this village, viz: Capt Burd's Co from Bedford Co, Pa, 80 men; & Capt Hall's Co from Md, 40 men; under the command of Maj Woodford.

Died: on Oct 12, John Smith, esq, age ab't 38 yrs, in Wash, ntv of Letterkenny, in the Kingdom of Ireland; formerly a Lt in the 10th U S Regt of infty & many yrs a clk in the Treas Dept; after a violent illness of twelve days. He was buried with Military Honors, being accompanied to the grave by the Union Light infty, Capt Davidson, of which he was 3d ofcr, & the Nat'l Guards, Capt Lenox.

*Travellers take care-*my trunk from behind my carriage was stolen bet Alexandria & Oscoquan Mills; clothing, Marine ofcr full dress uniform, $100 in Va bank notes & a ck drawn in my favor from the Wash Bank on the Bank in Petersburgh, Va. Apply to Lt Col Wharton, of Wash City. -Alex'r Sevier.

THU OCT 22, 1812
Wash Library open from 3:30 to 5 P M. -Jonathan S Findlay, Librarian.

Mr Dedier, of Balt, passenger on the ship *Ferox,* from Bristol, England, which left Port on Sep 6, bears dispatches from Mr Russel, our charge Des Affairs in London.

Boarding Hses: Mrs Doyne, Wash City. Mrs Dinmore on Pa Ave.

Pa elections. *Lancaster Co.* Rpblcn Federal:
Jas Whitehill-2684   Jn Gloninger-3568
Jacob Bucher-2659   A Slaymaker-3563

Cumberland Co: Robt Whitehill-2553
Jas Duncan-1110 D Rose-1465
Wm Crawford-2532 Ed Crawford-1096
Berks Co: John M Hyneman-2312

Post ofc changes in Sep 1812:
Haymarket, Va-Thos Noble, vice Elishab Evans, rsgn'd..
Skinnersville, N C-Sam'l Skinner, vice Silas Long, mv'd away.
Boone C H, K-Joshua Whittington, vice Jno Love, rsgn'd..
Barbourbille, K-Overton Baker, vice Gill Ev, mv'd away.
Calland's store, Va-Jabez Smith, vice Addison Armistead, rsgn'd..
Granville, O-Dan'l Baker, vice Wm Gavit, do.
Triadelphia, Mr-Jos E Bentley, vice Isaac Briggs, do.
Hartland, Vt-Sam'l F Fielding, vice David H Sumner, do.
Jemappe, Va-John Woodford jr, vice Jno Woodford, do.

New Post ofcs established in Sep 1812 & Postmaster:
Marion, Twiggs Co, Ga-Martin Holt
Miller's Ferry, Randolph Co, Ill T-Newton E Westfall
Yancy's Mills, Albemarle Co, Va-Ralph H Yancy
Mamoronock, West Chester Co, N Y-David Rodgers
Oakham, Worcester Co, Mass-Jos Fobes
Becket, Berkshire Co, Mass-Asabaird
Ewingville, Christian Co, K-Finis Ewing
Mouth of Black River, Wash Co, O-Jno S Reid
Oblong Society, Litchfield Co, Conn-M Hitchcock
New River Ferry, Green Briar Co, Va-Aaron Halloway
Aquiarun Mills, Falmouth Co, Va-Aaron Halloway

Died: Jos Bryan, esq. Sep 5, at his seat on Wilmington island, nr Savannah, Ga; a few yrs ago. He was a Rep in Congress from the State of Ga.

Sale at auction-furn, etc, at Mrs Mary Lane's. -Forrest & Beale, aucts.

Stephen Sanger petitions Chas Co Crt [Md] for Act of insolvent debtor. -John Barnes-clk.

Canandaigua, Sat Eve, Oct 10. Brave sailors & ab't 200 vols went from Buffaloe on Oct 8-9 in boats & took the British vessels, the brig *Adams* [surrendered at Detroit] & the *Caledonia*, which were lying under the protection of the British Fort Erie; captured ab't 50 prisoners. Oct 9th the battery commenced & Maj Wm H Cuyler, aid to Gen Hall, & Maj Mullany, of the 23d Regulars, were riding down the beach, a shot struck Maj Cuyler & instantly killed him.

Stray or stolen-a black horse from the City Commons. -Toppan Webster

Miss Nutting has opened a Millinery at Mr Peltz's.

John S Bridges, Confectioner & Distiller of cordials; opposite Wm Morgan's groc store, Bridge St, Gtwn.

SAT OCT 24, 1812
John Barker, esq, is elected Mayor of Phil City.

Augusta, Ga, Oct 9. Tue last a detachment of vols & drafted Militia, under Capt Wm Cumming of the Rpblcn Vol Blues, marched from this place for Sandersville.

Mrd: Mr John MacDaniel Sr, to Mrs Eliz Beall, all of Wash City, on Oct 20th by the Rev Mr Breckenridge.

To let-2 story brick hse on 19th St West; presently occupied by Mr John Haw. -Jane Lenthall, nr the premises.

Funeral Masonic Procession in Wash at Christ Chr; sermon by Rev Bro McCormick; death of esteemed brother John Williams, late a Capt in the Marine Corps, who fell by the hands of savages & negroes on Sep 11, 1812.

Jos Semmes has remv'd to that elegant & commodious 4 story dwlg on Water St; the Columbian Inn, Gtwn; accomodations will be satisfactory.

TUE OCT 27, 1812
St Louis, Lou. Oct 3-the Governor has dispatched 200 mounted volunteers up the Illinois in search of Indians. Abraham Keickley, of St Chas, was found scalped nr one of the family forts.

North-Western Army. Ft Defiance, Oct 3, 1812-under command of Gen Winchester: in Sept a skirmish ensued with the Indians & our advanced party-killed: Ensign Liggett of the 7th Regt Regulars; Alex'r McCoy, of Gtwn, Scott's Regt. Wyatt Stepp, Guy Hinton, Wm Bevis & Wm Mitchell, all of Woodford-volunteers in Capt Virgil McCracken's company.

Albany Gaz-Oct 20. Attack on the heights of Queenstown by the American Troops; Oct 13, Col Solomon Van Rensselaer, at the head of 300 Militia & Lt Col Christie at the head of 300 Regulars of the 13th Regt embarked in boats to dislodge the British from Queenstown; Col Van Rensselaer rec'd a wound thro his right thigh soon after landing; Lt Col Christie rec'd a wound in the hand; on the attack the number killed is considerable on both sides; the Americans lost many prisoners, most are wounded. Among the prisoners are Lt Cols Scott, Christie & Fenwick of the U S Troops, Gen Wadsworth & Col Stranahan of the Militia. Maj Genr'l Brock of the British was slain; on Oct 14th arrangement was made bet Van Rensselaer & Genr'l Sheafe for the liberation of all Militia prisoners on parole, not to serve during the war.

Hd-qrtrs, Lewiston, Oct 15. Ltr to Stephen Lush, esq. Your son, Maj Lush, was in the battle of yesterday; acted as aid to Col Van Rensselaer; he is well but exhausted; Brock has fallen, his Aid-De-Camp mortally wounded. -John Lovett.

Army of the U S. Ofcrs of the old Army have rec'd Brevet Commissions; shall have srv'd for 10 yrs in any one grade in the Army:

*Brig Genr'l Jas Wilkinson   Col Henry Burbeck
Lt Col Constant Freeman   Maj Wm Macrae
Capt Nehemiah Freeman   Capt Lloyd Beall
Maj Zebulon Pike   Capt John Whistler
Capt Hugh McCall

*now ranks as Maj Gen by virtue of this promotion.

Volunteers from Petersburg, Va, 102 ctzns, under Capt Rich'd Mcrae, marched for Canada on Wed last.

Zachariah Macubbin of Montg Co, Md; praying for act of insolvent debtor. -Rich'd H Harwood.

Upton Beall, Ck M C C. Aug 7th. Camp at Greenbush, Oct 20, 1812. Prisoners taken by the enemy are Lt Col Fenwick of the Flying Artl, thrice wounded, Lt Col Scott of the 2d Regt U S Artl, Lt Bayly of the 3d Regt of U S Artl, Lt Col Chrystie of the 13th infty & Maj Mullany of the 23d infty. Capt Gibson of the Fying Artl is either dead or a prisoner.

Ctzns of the U S now in Copenhagen: Nathl Jackson
B Hathaway   Rich'd Law   Wm R Russel
Sam'l Somis   Amos Dennis   R J Cleveland
Wm Williams   John Eveleth   Jos Brown
Thos Laing   John Connell   Anthony Moffat
Peleg Congdon   Adam Champion   Wm Law
Henry Peters   [Copenhagen, May 12, 1812.]

Lemuel Dickerman of the State of N Y, has patent dt'd Jul 18, of a machine for the shearing & laying the knap of cloth. Jul 25th he sold the right of using & vending machine to Henry Knowles, of Gtwn, D C.

One dollar reward-for runaway, apprentice boy named John Johnson, ab't 16 yrs of age. -Jilson Noel.

Mrs M Sweeny has rec'd her fall & winter goods; at her old stand on F St.

Thos Main is about to remove his nursery to another station from High St, Gtwn.

THU OCT 29, 1812
U S frig *Constellation,* Oct 24, 1812. Ltr regarding boys at the age of 10 or 12 on board ships of War. Signed by: Midshipmen-Jno H Bell, Chas F Stallings & Phila J Jones. Also signed by: Robert E Searcy, Thos W McCall, Jno T Ritchie, Wm L

Rogers, Jos Tattnall, Pollard Davis, Chas A C Thompson, Edw Innes, Jos Thompson, John Cook, Geo W Gray, Chas S McCauley, & Benedict Higdon.

For sale at the hse of A D Hyatt, Pa Ave; hsehld furn. -N L Queen, auct.

THU OCT 29, 1812
Jas Webster of Phil is publishing a superb print of the engagement bet the American frig *Constitution*, Capt Hull, & the British frig *Guerriere*, Capt Dacres, from a painting by Mr Thos Birch. Phil, Oct 24.

SAT OCT 31, 1812
T Wm Freeman advertises Great National Prints for sale; 51 Chesnut St.

Died: Wm James, esq, age 41 yrs, on Oct 27th; for many yrs a principal clk in the Treas Dept; hsbnd & fr.

The Pres has conferred the Brevet Rank of Maj on Capt Z Taylor, of the 7th Regt of infty, for his defence of Ft Harrison.

A stray horse came to my livery stable on Oct 28th. -John Carnes, N J Ave.

TUE NOV 3, 1812
Ltr to Hon Paul Hamilton, Sec'y U S Navy from Capt Jesse D Elliot-Black Rock, Oct 9. To my ofcrs & men I fell under great obligation; to Capt Towson & Lt Roach of the 2d Regt of artl, Ensign Prestman of the infty, Capt Chapin, Mr John McComb, Messrs John Town, Thos Dam, Peter Overstocks & Jas Sloan, resident gentlemen of Buffalo, for their soldier & sailor like conduct. I lost one man, one ofcr wounded, Mr John C Cummings, Acting Mdshpmn, a boyonet thru the leg. Sailing mstr Geo Watts, performed his duty in a mstrly style. -Jesse D Elliot

Wash. Jockey Club, Oct 27th. Sweepstake won by Mr Luffborough's filley, Columbia, by Col Tayloe's Oscar-trained by Mr Chas Duvall. 2d-Maj Bean's B C by 1st Cnsl; 3d-Gov Wright's B C Red Bird, by Oscar; 4th-Mr Ridgely's R C by 1st Cnsl; club purse won by Maj J Robert's b h Defiance, bred by his owner in Culpeper Co, Va & trained by Mr C Duvall of PG Co, Md; 2d-Maj Hoomes C C Tuckahoe by do; 3d-Mr J B Bond's c h Financier; Capt Ridgley's c m Indiana & Mr Daffin's Vingtun.

Mrd: Mr Alexander Estep to Mrs Barbary Morin, both of Wash City, on Nov 1, by Rev Mr Breckenridge.

Died: Capt Robt Denny, at Annapolis on Oct 23d; Auditor-Genr'l of the State & Auditor of the Crt of Chancery, age 65 yrs. Soldier of our Rev.

Died: Genr'l John Mitchell, at his farm in Chas Co, Md, on Oct 11th; sldr of the Rev service.

Died: Skelton Jones, on Oct 28th, at Richmond, a young Virginian. He was some yrs since editor of the *Examiner* & engaged in completing *The History of Va-* commenced by Mr Burk. -Enq.

Died: Roger Griswold, esq, Gov of Conn, on Oct 25th, at Norwich, Conn.

Steam Boat establishment bet Gtwn & Alexandria; B Henry Latrobe, agent for Messrs Livingston & Fulton.

Wash Co, D C-In Chancery. Hyde & Thomson vs Chas Crookshank & others. Dan'l Bussard, trustee, sold the property ordered by this crt on Jan 23, 1812; sum-$1550. -Wm Brent, clk.

Troop orders. The Wash Troop is ordered to muster at the Centre Mkt on the 7th. -Capt R Collet, orderly Serg.

Aaron Ogden is elected Gov of the State of N J.

Result of the late election for mbrs of congress in the State of Conn:
Hon John Davenport, jr-10,162	Benj Tallmadge-10,631
Timothy Pi-Ki-10,341	Jonathan O Mosely-9,872
Lewis B Sturges-10,076	Lyman Law-9,476
Nathan Smith-751	Sam'l B Sherwood-402
Sylvanus Backus-422	Nathl Perry-402
Epaphroditus Champion-9,572	Ebenezer Huntingdon-235

Reward-$10. Deserted from a rendezvous at Fairfax Crt Hse, under the Command of Lt Hairston, on Oct 15th, Thos Austin, a sldr in the U S Army, age 21 yrs. -John Macrae, Capt 20th Regt U S infty. Dumfries, Va.

THU NOV 5, 1812
Chauncey Goodrich, esq, chosen a Senator of the U S from Conn for 6 yrs from Mar 4th next.

Dudley Chace, esq, is chosen a Senator of the U S from Vt, for 6 yrs ensuing Mar 4th, vice Stephen R Bradley, whose term of svc expires.

Edw Johnson, esq, has been re-elected Mayor of Balt, by unanimous vote.

Auction sale-entire stock of hardware-at his store in Bridge St. -Evan Jones.

SAT NOV 7, 1812
Genteel pvt brdng at Mrs Nicholas King, next door to Judge Duvall's.

Geo Kneller has opened his new Dry Goods & Groc store on Pa Ave.

Reward-$100 for my hse svt who absconded on Oct 11th-Jos Michaels. He is a negro slave raised by me from a child. -Dan'l Lee, Winchester, Va.

Ofcrs taken prisoner in the Battle of Queenstown: Lt Cols-Fenwick, Scott & Christie; Capts-Ogilvie, *Machesney & *Gibson; Lts-Turner, Clarke, Bayley, Kearney, *Randolph, McCartey, Phelps, *Totten, Carr, Sammons, Finch & Huginnin; Ensign-Reab. Capt Wool, the hero of the heights of Queenstown, is 26 yrs of age. *Since exchanged. Lt Valleau was killed; Ensign Morris was killed, he is bro to Lt Morris of the frig, *Constitution*.

Reward-$25 for negro woman, Betsey, whose sister lives with Mr Villard, at *Greenleaf's Point*. -Christ L Gantt, living nr Bladensburgh, Md.

TUE NOV 10, 1812
Battle of Queenstown from a N Y paper: killed-Capt Nelson, 6th Regt of infty; Lt Valeau of N Y-scalped by an Indian; Ensign Morris, 13th infty. Mortally wounded-Lt Col J R Fenwick of First Light Artl; Lt A Phelps, 13th infty. Wounded: Col Christie, 13th infty; Capt Wall, 13th do; Lt Clark, 23d do; Capt Lawrence, 13th do; Ensign J Lent, 13th do. Prisoners: Brig Gen Wadsworth of militia; Maj Spencer, do; Col Scott, 2d Artl; Maj J R Mullany, 23d infty; Capt Ogilvie, 13th do; Capt Machesney, 6th do; Capt Gibson, First Light Artl; Capt Brown; Capt Bacon; Lt Turner, 13th infty; Lt R M Bayly, 3d Artl; Lt Kearney, 13th infty; Lt Randolph, 1st Light Artl; Lt McCarty, 23d infty; Lt Fink, 13th do; Lt Hugmin, 13th do; Lt Reab, 13th do; Lt Chamberlin, U S Army, Mass.

Cong election-Artemas Ward, Fed, elected from Boston, vice Josiah Quincy, who declines re-election. Wm Reed, Fed, is re-elected from Essex So Dist. Timothy Pickering, Fed, from Essex North Dist. Nath'l Ruggles is elected, vice Eben Seaver, in Norfolk Dist. Wm Baylies, Fed, elected vice Chas Turner jr, Rep from Plymouth Dist. Laban Wheaton, Fed, re-elected. Elijah Brigham & Abijah Bigelow are re-elected.

Ga Cong election-all Rpblcns: Geo M Troup, Wm W Bibb, Bolling Hall, *John Forsyth, *Wm Barnett, *Thos Tellfair. *New members.

Fall & winter goods. Wm O'Brien at his store nr the Navy Yd.

Franklinton, Oct 19. Gen Harrison arrv'd in town on Oct 12th from Urbana. Gen John G Jackson, Capt Clarke, Capt McCally, Capt Davidson, Dr Jackson, & others arrv'd here from Clarksburgh, Va, on Oct 18. Capt Markle's Troop of Horse from Pa & Capt Pierce's Troop from Zanesville, lately arrv'd. Brig Genr'l Joel Leftwich, with 1500 troops from Va, is expected in a few days. Col Simerall's Regt & Capt Garrard's Co of cavalry from Ky, to arrive soon.

Mrd: Mr Owen McGlue, bkbinder, to Miss Mary King, both of Wash, on Nov 8 by Rev Mr Matthews.

Notice-Geo, runaway, negro, committed to Frederick Co, Md goal; says he belongs to Mr Jas Brown, nr Staunton, Va. -Morris Jones, shrf Fred'k Co, Md.

In Chancery, Oct 14, 1812. Rich'd Owings & Abraham Freear, vs John Hoge & others. Bill to obtain an injunction to prevent the sale of lands as directed by a decree of this crt; bill filed by Francis Deakins & Benj Stoddart against Nathan Waters & others; decree was passed for sale of rl est of N Waters for money due by Waters to the dfndnts; Owings purch'd the rl est of Waters; Owings has since sold said rl est to Freear; Deakins hath departed; John Hoge resides out of Md. -N Brewer, R C C.

New school-Addison Belt will commence teaching on F St.

Seasonable goods for sale-Thos Baker, Gtwn # 10.

Ltr rec'd by Sec of the Navy from Com Rodgers: U S frig, *President*, at sea. Oct 17, 1812. On Oct 15th nr the Grand Bank, this ship, the *Congress*, captured the British King's Packet, *Swallow*, Jos Morphew, Cmder, bound from Kingston, Jamaica, to Falmouth. -John Rodgers-to Hon Paul Hamilton, Sec of the Navy.

Mrd: Mr Dillon Hodgson to Miss Priscilla Dixon, both of this city, on Tue, Nov 10th by Rev Mr Matthews.

Hse of Reps: memorial of Benj M Pratt, of Ill Terr, remonstating against what he states to have been the illegal return of Shadrach Bond as delegate to Cong from that Terr; referred to the committee of elections.

Mrshl's sale: part of lot 3 in sq 320 with frame dwlg hse; writs of fieri facias, issued from Crct Crt of Wash Co, D C; one at suit of Adam & Geo King against Jos Dove, & the other at the suit of Mary Ann Fenwick, against Dove & others. -Wash Boyd, mrsh'l.

For sale-lot 4 in sq 552 with improvements, prop of Jas Graham; & lot 1 in sq 696 with improvements, prop of Robt McMahon, for taxes due Wash Corp. -Zach Walker, coll 3rd ward.

The ship *Brutus*, John Fenno, mstr, with her cargo, litigated to Jens Tobias Samuelsen, & other privateer Captains, as a good prize. Apr 7th 1812. Signed W Legel; N Terbol; N Y Henrigues, Copenhagen, Apr 8, 1812, Translator Royal [Danish].

Arrv'd the Flag of truce, *Lark*, from Plymouth, Eng; sailed Sep 30th: passengers-Jonathan Russell, esq, late charge D'affairs at the Crt of London; John Spear Smith, esq, of Balt, former, do; John E Howard jr, esq, of Balt, Pvt Sec'y; M Diroff, attached to the Russian Legation in the U S.

Jas Melvin & Son-merchant tailors; Bridge St, Gtwn.

Orphans Crt of PG Co, Md. Nov 12, 1812. Prsnl est of John Jackson, late of said co, dec'd. -J M Jackson sr, adm.

Notice-the Levy Crt of Wash Co, D C, will be in session at Union Tavern, Gtwn; hearing of appeals under late assessment of prop in said co. -John Mountz, clk Levy Crt.

For sale per decree of Crt of Wash Co, D C; the Federal Mills & 27 1/2acs adj; prop of the late Jos E Rowles, dec'd. Also half lot of ground on High St, 40 ft front with frame store hse, occupied as a groc by Messrs Kirby & Wells. -John Heugh, trust.

SAT NOV 14, 1812
Hse of Reps: Petitions of Eliz Collins, Wm Daniel, John Darby, Sam'l Davis, Hezekiah Carter, Robt Cocks, Edwin Lewis & sundry inhabitants of Mississippi Terr; praying extension of time of payment for lands purch'd of the U S-referred to committee.

Federalists, N J, electors of the Pres & V P: Matthew Waldren, Wm B Ewing, Franklin Davenport, Jacob Losey, Wm McGill, Elias Conover, Andrew Howell & Jonas Wade.

Wm Barnett, elected a Rep to Cong from Ga, vice Howell Cobb, rsgn'd.

Federals appt'd Executive Cncl of Md: Benj Stoddert of Bladensburg; A C Magruder of Annapolis; Walter Dorsey of Balt; Bond Martin of Cambridge, Wm W Ward, of Elkton.

Notice-stray brindled steer came to my place nr Rock Creek Chr. -Benj Belt.

Public sale-Decree of High Crt of Chancery, at Mt Calvert, PG Co, Md: 12 negroes, sheep, hogs, furn, & all right, title & int of Agnes Brown & John H Brown, to part of 2 tracts cld *Beall's Gift & Mt Calvert Manor*, PG Co, Md; to raise sum with int from Mar 25th 1809. -Trueman Tyler, trustee.

Edw Goddard, insolvent debtor, confined in Wash Co, D C, prison for debt. -Wm Brent, clk.

TUE NOV 17, 1812
Proposal-for publishing in the Balt City, a daily Rpblcn Nswpr, to be entitled, the *Baltimore Patriot*, by Ebenezer French; late one of the editors of the *Boston Patriot*.

Electors from New York:	Jos C Yates	Simeon De Witt
Archibald McIntyre	John H Hogeboom	Gurdon S Mumford
Jacob Delamontagnie	Philip Van Cortlandt	John Chandler
Henry Huntington	John Woodworth	David Boyd
Cornelius Bergen	Jos Perine	Chauncey Belknap
John Dill	David Van Ness	Robt Jenkins
Michl S Vandercook	Geo Palmer jr.	Jas Hill
Wm Kirby	Henry Frey Yates	Tho H Hubbard

John Russell   Jas S Kip   Jotham Jayne
Jonathan Stanley jr   Wm Burnet   Geo Rosecrantz

Saddler's Shop-directly oppo Davis's Hotel. -Jno Peltz.

B H Romlinson has remv'd from Brighton Hse to the City Hotel, Capitol Hill, Wash.

Trinity Church lottery-Mgrs: Alex'r McKin, Wm McMechin, Wm Price, John Snyder, Jos Allender & Hezekiah Price. Balt, Md. -Nov 13.

THU NOV 19, 1812
Legislature of Delaware chose the following electors: Jas L Clayton, Ebenezer Blackiston, Jas Sykes & Thos Fisher; all Federal.

David Howell, esq, appt'd a Dist Judge of the U S for the Dist of R I, vice D L Barnes, dec'd.

Ltr from Maj Genr'l S V Van Rensselaer, of the Militia of N Y, to Brig Genr'l Smyth, of the Troops of the U S. Buffaloe, Oct 24, 1812. Having this day rsgn'd to you the command of the Army on the Niagara frontier, & being the eve of my departure for Albany. I recommend to your notice the svc of: Capts Wool & Ogilevie; Lts Kearney, Carr, Huginin & Sammons of the 13th infty; Lt Randolph of the Light Artl, who volunteered his svcs & commanded the Van-Guard; Lts Rathbone & Gansevoort of the Artl.

Ltr from Mr Henry Dennison, of the U S brig *Argus*, to the Sec of the Navy. Phil, Nov 11, 1812. Arrv'd here last evening in the ship *Ariadne* of Boston, cleared from Alexandria for Cadiz; detained by the U S brig *Argus*, Capt Sinclair, for being under British licence; fell in with the British cruizers, sloop of war *Tartarus* & brig *Colibri*; the latter put on board of us 9 American seamen. -Henry Denison.

Congress in Senate, Nov 18, 1812. Allan B Magruder, a Senator from La, produced his credentials & took his seat.

Ltr from Capt Moon, of the Privateer *Sarah Ann*. Nassau, New Providence, Oct 14, 1812. Six of my crew, claimed as British subjects were this day taken out of jail & put on H M brig, *Sappho*, & sailed for Jamaica; they were as follows: 1-David Dick, seaman, born in North of Ireland, resided in U S since 1793, srvd 10 yrs in the U S Navy on board the frigs; *Chesapeake*, *President*, *Constitution*, *John Adams* & schn'r *Enterprize*, & Gun Boat # 2. David Dick, shoemkr, in Alexandria, is his uncle; he entered on board the *Sarah Ann* in Baltimore. 2-John Gaul, seaman, says he was born in Marblehead, Mass, where his parents, bros & srs now reside, is mrd & his wife, Mary Gaul, lives in Roosevelt St, no 37, has a regular discharge from the U S Navy by Capt Hugh G Campbell, dt'd at St Mary's, Ga, Aug 14, 1812; has srvd on board the U S brig *Vixen*, Gunboats 10 & 158; Gaul is 2 7 yrs of age, he entered on board the *Sarah Ann* in Savannah. 3-Michael Pluck, o seaman, says he was born in Balt, his parents are dead, but he is known by Wm

Doulan; Thos Turner & McDonald, all of Balt, has a sister in Pawhose whose name is Ann Welsh; was never at sea before; he is 26 yrs old, boarded the *Sarah Ann* in Baltmore. 4-Thos Rogers, seaman, says he was born in Waterford in Ire, has resided in the U S & was duly naturalized, copy filed in the custom-hse in Balt- is known by Jos Carey & Tom Rogers, Cork Cutter, both of Balt; has a wife & 3 chldrn in Balt; boarded the *Sarah Ann* in Balt. 5-Geo Roberts, a coloured man & seaman. I know him to be a ntv born ctzn of the U S; he had documents & free papers; he boarded the *Sarah Ann* in Balt, where he is mrd. 6-Sonty Taylor, boy, says he was born in Hackensack, N J; says Jane Snowden, of Savannah, Ga, is his mthr; Taylor is 15 yrs old; boarded the *Sarah Ann* in Savannah. -Rich Moon, late Cmder of the Privateer, *Sarah Ann*. [N B-We understand the mrshl of S C has detained in custody 12 British subjs as hostages for the safety of the above ctzns of U S.]

Charleston, Nov 2. Arrv'd British brig *Francis Blake*, Coffin, prize-mstr; captured on Oct 17th in sight of St Thos by privateer schn'r *Nonsuch*, Capt Levely, of Balt; killed: D Christian, Lewis Reily & David McCarty, seamen. Wounded: Mr Wilkinson, sailing-mstr, since dead; Chas Cook-dangerously; Chas Arrel, R Manning, Peter Nelson, Nicholas May & Zacharia Fuller. Loss on enemy's vessels is not known.

Wash Co, D C, to wit: Wm Prout, cmplnt, vs Sam'l W Young, Eliz Roach, Susannah Young, Chas Young & Rich'd Young, Geo King, John B Evans, Ann Maria Davidson, Adam King & Wm King. In Chancery. Bill to obtain a cnvync to the cmplnt from the heirs of Abraham Young, dec'd, of land-108acs & 1/2ac in co & dist aforesaid & in Wash City land cld-*Chance* & part of tract cld-*Hog Pen Enlarged*, & part of tract cld-*Knock;* also to obtain a decree for sale of the other moiety of said land to satisfy a claim due to the cmplnt. Abraham Young, now dec'd, being seized of land on or ab't Jan 1792 agreed to sell one moiety of said land to Wm King & the other moiety to cmplnt; the latter two agreed to pay the said Wm Young. Wm King became an insolvent debtor in 1797 & Adam King is now his trustee. E Roach, Susannah Young, Sam'l Young, Chas Young, John B Evans & Ann M Davidson do not reside in Wash Co, D C. -Wm Brent.

Steam boats for sale-apply to H Bleecker, Capitol Hill, Wash.

Wash Co, D C. Act of insolvent debtor will be administered to Alban Howe; also to Jas Williams. -Wm Brent, clk.

Ranaway, mulatto man slave, Isaac; he left me nr Wilmington, N C. -Rezin Royal, Sampson Co, N C. Info may be given to W R King, mbr of congress at Wash.

SAT NOV 21, 1812
Congressional elections-Pa. The following are chosen to Rep this state in the 13th Cong:

Wm Crawford	Robt Brown	Jonathan Roberts
David Bard	Robt Whitehill	Wm Piper
*Sam'l D Ingham	Wm Findley	*Jas Whitehill
	Adam Seybert	Wm Anderson

*Chas J Ingersol	*John Conrad	Roger Davis
Jno M Hyneman	*Adamson Tannehill	Abner Lacock
*Isaac Smith	*Jared Irwin	*Hugh Glasgow
*Aaron Lyle	John Smilie	*John Gloninger

[*New members] All Rpblcns except Mr Gloninger, whose politics are doubtful, elected by Rpblcn votes.

So-Carolina-all Rpblcns to Rep this State in the next Congress:

Langdon Cheves	John C Calhoun	Elias Earle
Wm Lowndes	*David R Evans	*Sam'l Farrow
*John J Chapell	*Theodore Gourdine	*John Kershaw

[*New members}

Wm J Lewis, esq, of Mt Athos, nr Lynchburg, Va, has undertaken to raise a Regt of volunteers.

Wm Wood, silver-smith & jeweller, nrly oppo the Marine Garrison, nr the Navy Yd.

Wanted to purchase, a few shares of bank stock in Wash or Gtwn. -Thos H Gilliss, nr the Treas Dept.

Order of Orphans Crt of PG Co, Md. Sale of all the prsnl est of John Jackson, late of said co, dec'd; negroes, stock, etc. -J M Jackson jr, adm.

The Pres of the U S re-appt'd the following Justices of the Peace for the 2 counties in the Dist of Columbia, viz, for Wash County:

Robt Brent	Thos Peter	Wm Thornton
Jos Sprigg Belt	Thos Corcoran	Rich'd Parrott
Thos Fenwick	Nichs Young	John Ott
Sam'l L Smallwood	Sam'l H Smith	Dan'l Rapine
John Threlkeld -		
For Alex County	Geo Gilpin	Abraham Faw
Chas Alexander jr	Jonah Thompson	Cuthbert Powell
Alex'r Smith	Jacob Hoffman	John McKinney
Robt Young	Jos Dean	Amos Alexander
Clement Sewell	Rich'd Libby	John Richards
Henry O'Reilly -	Elisha Cullen Dick	

TUE NOV 24, 1812
Electors chosen by the Leg of Ga: Gen Stewart, Henry Graybill, Chas Harris, John Rutherford, Oliver Porter, Henry Mitchell, John Twigg & John Howard, esqs.

Chas Tait, esq, is re-elected a Senator of U S from Ga beginning Mar 4th next.

Ltr to Paul Hamilton, Sec of the Navy, from Isaac Chauncey, Sacket's Harbor, Nov 13, 1812. In our passage thru the Bay of Quanti, I discovered a schn'r at the Village of Armingstown-she would have delayed our chase of the Royal George-I had Lt MacPherson burn the schn'r. We also took the schn'r *Mary Hall* from Niagara. In our affair we lost one man, Mr Arundel, who was wounded & fell overboard & drowned. Isaac Chauncey [Ltr was enclosed with ltr from Mr S T Anderson, to the Sec of the Navy].

THU NOV 26, 1812
Post ofc changes in Oct 1812.
Lincolnton, N C-David Reinhardt vice Vardry McBee, rsgn'd..
Conwayboro, S C-Henry Durant vice Robt Conway, do.
Clough Mills, S C-R Mills vice Jas Mills, dec'd.
Jefferson, N C-M Ray vice Geo Bower, rsgn'd..
Middlebury, Vt-Wm Stade jr, vice Geo Cleveland, do.
May Ann Forge, Pa-Jos Vickroy, vice Conrad Piper, do.
Shade Furnace, Pa-Philip Bier, vice Jos Vickroy, do.
Hartford, K-Chas Mccreary, vice Warner Crow, do.
Cowanesky, Pa-Wm Lindsley, vice Ira Kilbourn, do.
Craftsbury, Vt-Harvey Scott, vice Thos Kingsbury, do.
Nassau, N Y-John Griswold, vice Chester Griswold, do.
Christianville, V-Henry D Hicks, vice Signal Abernathy, do.
Schoharie Bridge, N Y-John F Gasley, vice John C Blanchard, do.
Wash, O-Peter Umstot, vice Simon Beymer, do.
Waddell's Ferry, N C-Jas Gaches, vice Edmund Waddle, do.
Kingwood, Va-Rich'd Postle, vice John S Roberts, do.
Cleveland, O-Ashbell W Walworth, vice John Walworth, dec'd.
Chatham C H, N C-John Mebane, vice Wm Brantley, dec'd.
West Brookfield, Mass-Josiah Carey, vice R Hitchcock, rsgn'd..
Barnwell C H, S C-John Carr, vice Edmund Brown.
Spotsylvania C H, Va-Jos Carter, vice Joshua Long.

New Post ofcs established in Oct 1812 & postmstr:
Gorham, Ontario Co, N Y-Parley Gates
West River, Ontario Co, N Y-Michl Pearce
Middlesex, Ontario Co, N Y-Rich'd M Williams
metheun, Essex Co, Mass-Moses How
Poland, Cumberland Co, Me-Ebenezer Simonton
Big Springs, Gennessee Co, N Y-Alex'r McDonald
Chesterfield C H, Chesterfield Co, S C-John Craig
Bentley, KenhawaCo, Va-Geo Bentley
Madison, Jefferson Co, Ind Ter-John Seering
Smockville, Jefferson Co, Ind Ter-Sam'l Smock
Charleston, Clark Co, Ind Ter-John Douthett
Allen's Ferry, Franklin Co, Ind Ter-John Allen
Wayne C H, Wayne Co, Ind Ter-Wm F Sackett
Duncansville, S C-Hansford B Duncan
Willow Grove, Sumpter Dist, S C-Matthew Bradley jr
Dubose Ferr, Darlington Dist, S C-Dan'l Dubose
Carter's Crossing, Darlington Dist, S C-Elias Welden
Ford's on Pearl River, Miss Ter-John Ford

Nixon's, Miss Ter-Henry Nixon
Butler C H, Butler Co, Ky-Jas Love
Isbelville, Logan Co, K-Geo Isbell
Worcester, Wayne Co, O-Thos G Jones
Morris' Flatts, Madison Co, N Y-Bennett Bicknell
Head of Cow Neck, Queen Co, N Y-Wm Allen
Kites Mill, Shenandoah Co, Va-Martin Kite
Overalls, Shanandoah Co, Va-Wm Overall
Humbough, Frederick Co, Va-John Humbough
West's, Caswell Co, N C-Benj C West
Hull's Store, Harrison Co, Va-M Givens
Tagwaddles, Madison Co, N Y-Lemuel Covel
Humburger's, Rockingham Co, Va-Tobias R McGahey
Mrsh'lls, Allegany Co, Pa-John Marshall
salem X Rds, Westmoreland Co, Pa-Hugh Bigham
Youngstown, Somerset Co, Pa-Alex'r Johnston
Wilson's, Somerset Co, Pa-Thos Wilson
Murray's, Westmoreland Co, Pa-Jeremiah Murray
New Castle, Beaver Co, Pa-Jos J Boyd
Bricelands X Rds, Wash Co, Pa-Jas Briceland
Loughlin's town, Westmoreland Co, Pa-Jas Clark
Cadiz, Jefferson Co, O-Jos Harris
Dearing, Hillsboro Co, N H-Russel Tubbs
HaN Cock, N H-John Whitcomb
Antrim, Hillsboro Co, N H-Jas Campbell
Newport, N H-Arnold Ellis
Plymouth, Litchfield Co, Ct-Apollos Warner
Weare, N H-Rich'd Philbrick

Hse of Reps: Petition of David Lamb of Charleston, remission of penalties incurred by importation of British goods into the U S.

Died: Lt Robt Cherry, of the 2d Regt of the U S Army, formerly a merchant in Wash; his death was from a fall from his horse on Oct 27th at Ft Stoddert; he laid in a state of stupor until he expired on Nov 1st. His remains were interred with Military Honors on Nov 2d.

Land auction at Davis's Hotel, Wash City-Parcels of land in Ohio, the prop of the late Wm Eaton. -Gideon Granger.

SAT NOV 28, 1812
Orphans Crt of Wash Co, D C. Nov 26, 1812. Prsnl est of Mary Rose, late of said city, dec'd. -John P Ingle, adm.

For sale-brick tenement on Va Ave, Wash City. -Overton Carr, in the Wash Bank, or to Wm Hebb, PG Co, Md.

Commited to the goal of Harford Co, Md-Sam'l Ritchey, negro man, about 27 yrs of age; says he belongs to Jas Ritchey of N Y. -Benj Guyton, shrf of Harford Co, Md. Bell-Air, Harford Co, Md.

North Carolina electors:
Wm H Murfree	Jas Mebane	Kedar Ballard
Jas Ranney	Jas Bright	Thos D King
Jas W Clarke	Francis Locke	Monford Stokes
Thos Davis	Kemp Plummer	Hutchins Burton
Jonathan Hampton	Jos Winston	Henry Massen

Mrd: G R A Brown, esq, of Pr Wm, Va, to Miss Caroline Esminard, of Balt, on Nov 24th, by the Rev Mr Roberts.

Ltr from Lt Claxton to his father; on board the *Cartel*, New York, Nov 25, 1812. -Just returned from our captivity of 2 or 3 wks-you have heard of our action with the sloop of war *Frolic*; particulars in Capt James' ltr; I have been sick since we left Delaware & not able to assist my brave comrades; will stay 2 days here & 4 in Phil & shortly embrace you all at home.

Died: Theodorick Armistead, esq, Navy agent at Norfolk, age 36 yrs; at Norfolk on Nov 20th.

Sale by auction-at the warehse occupied by Mr Geo Hoffman, 2 So Chas St, Balt: sundry goods, cloths, quilting, etc. Baltimore, Md.

Horatio Lanham has harbored 2 negro men, Bob & Abram, the prop of Martha Jenkins of PG Co, Md. I am authorised to take said Martha Jenkins with her prop into my care. I forewarn all persons from harboring or medling with them. -Francis Jenkins.

TUE DEC 1, 1812
Deserted from Fredericktown Barracks, on Nov 23, 1812, Geo Shawaker, a recruit in the 1st Regt of U S Light Dragoons; born in Phil Co, age 26 yrs. -Geo Birch, Lt 1st Reg Lt Drag. Reward-$10.

Electors for the State of Md:
Tobias E Stansbury	Edw Johnson	John Stephen
Edw Lloyd	Thos W Veazy	Thos Worrell
Dan'l Rentch	Edw H Calvert	Henry Williams
	Henry H Chapman	Littleton Dennis

Ltr from Capt Jones, late of the U S sloop of war, *Wasp*, to the Sec of the Navy, dt'd-N Y, Nov 24th, 1812. Cruise terminated in the capture of the *Wasp* on Oct 18th; Lts Biddle, Rodgers, Booth, Mr Rapp & Mr Knight acted with courage & promprtness.

Thos G Addison, esq, chosen a mbr of the Exec Cncl of Md, vice Benj Stoddert, who declined the appointment.

Ltr from Col Edmund P Gaines, U S Army, dt'd Knoxville, Nov 16, 1812. War with Lower Creeks seems now to be inevitable. 5,000 men could subdue the whole nation. 2,500 infty should make an establishment at the Hickory Ground.

Water Wheel, new invention by Sam'l Brouwer, of N YC. Apply to Sam'l Brouwer or Dan'l Ryckman of N Y C or to Barnes H Smock, at present in Wash City .

Wash Co, D C-In Chancery. *Wm Raborg jr & John Hearn, cmplnts, vs Jas D Barry, surviving exc of Jas Barry dec'd, the heirs & reps of Joanna Barry, dec'd, who was widow & legatee of the said Jas Barry. Heirs & Reps of Ann Gould Barry, the d/o said Jas Barry, & Jas Barry & David D Barry, Robt Barry & John D Barry named in the will of said Jas Barry, & heirs & reps of Edmund Scannell, dec'd, & of Garrett P Barry, dec'd, which Edmund & Garrett are legatees named in the will of said Jas Barry, dec'd; dfndnts. After death of Jas Barry & payment of his debts, his rl & prsnl prop was devised to the dfndnts, or part of them; prsnl est not sufficient to pay his debts; Joanna Barry & Ann C Barry, 2 of the excs having died, the said Jas D Barry did not conceive himself authorised to sell & convey the rl est without the decree of the Crt of Chancery; the dfndnts except Jas D Barry, are residents without the Dist of Col, & out of the jurisdiction of this court. -Wm Brent, clk. [Raboy chng'd to Raborg in Dec 8, 1812 newspaper].

Lots for sale, authorised by the excs of Wm Hunsby, esq, dec'd; prop lying in Wash City; indisputable titles from the original proprietor of Carrollsburg, to the late owner, purch'd 40 yrs since. -Tench Ringgold.

THU DEC 3, 1812
Notice-Renewal of certificate 343 for $3000 Louisiana; to credit of Wm Holland; by the Treasury of the U S. -Jas Davidson.

Prop for sale on Pa Ave; formerly occupied by Genr'l Turreau & recently by Mr Foster, the British Minister. Apply to Mr Crawford in Gtwn or to Peter Ham, Sharpsburg, Md.

Died: Lt Wm Peters, of the U S Navy, age 27 yrs, at St Mary's, on the 3d inst.

Died: John Dunlap, esq, of Phil, on Nov 27th, age 66 yrs.

SAT DEC 5, 1812
Oath of insolvent debtor, to be administered to Ignatius Edelin, Wash Co, D C, crt rm. -Wm Brent, clk.

Military memoranda. Supplies employ a train of nrly 100 waggons & teams. They are conducted by Capt Jos Wheaton, of the Qrtr-Mstr Genr'l Deprt, an old Revolutionary ofcr. -Pittsburg, Nov 26.

Baltimore made chariot for sale-may be seen by calling Messrs Baum & Pritceard, coachmakers, Gtwn.

Detailed acc't of Col Dan'l Newnan's late expedition against the Fla Indians. New Hope, St John's, Oct 19, 1812. Engagements bet the Lotchaway & Alligator Indians & the Gavols; arrv'd upon St John's ab't Aug 15. Sep 24th we left St John's, Capt Humphrey's Co in front, Capt Ford's Co under command of Lt Fannin in the centre, & Capt Coleman's Co with Cone's detachment under the command of Lt Broadnax in the rear; skirmishes with the Indians-one man killed & 9 wounded; brave ofcrs & men under my command: Capt Hamilton, who volunteered as a Pvt, his Co having left him at the expiration of their time, Lt Fannin, Ensign Hamilton & Adj Harden, Sgts Holt & Attaway, Lt Broadnax, Ensign Mann, Capt Cone who was wounded in the head; Lt Williams; Sgt Hawkins & Cpl Neil of Coleman's Co; Sgt Maj Reese; Capt Humphries Co, Lt Reed, Sgt Fields, Sgt Cowan & Sgt Denmark. -Dan'l Newnan, Pittsburg, Nov 26.

Naval Ball at Tomlinson's Hotel. Mgrs: Chas Carroll of Belle Vue, Robt Brent, Cas W Goldsborough, Thos Tingey, Sam'l Miller, Edw Coles, Henry Huntt & Edmund B Duvall.

Ranaway-negro Rich'd, committed in the pblc jail of Dorchester Co, Md; says he is a slave of Rich'd Gillum of Hampton, Va; about 40 yrs of age; says he has a wife named Sally & 4 chldrn at Widow Moore's on Back River. -Thos J Pattison, shrf.

TUE DEC 8, 1812
Hon Wm Eustis tendered his resignation of the ofc of Sec of War.

Nomination of Wm H Harrison, esq, as Brig Genr'l confirmed by the Senate of the U S to take rank from Aug 22d last.

Congress-Thos Posey, Senator from La, appeared & was qualified & took his seat.

The partnership under firm of Walter Gody & Co is dissolved. -Walter Gody. Wm Thomson.

Partnership between Cashell & Baker is being dissolved, it will in the future be carried on by Cashell & Lagary.

THU DEC 10, 1812
New wholesale & retail grocery. Rich'd Parrott & Co, Water St, Gtwn.

Walter Gody, Tin & Iron Plate worker, will continue to carry on his business on Bridge nr the crnr of High St, Gtwn.

Lands for sale-at Capt Williams Tavern, Dumfries; land in Pr Wm Co, Va, devised by the late John Gibson for the payment of his debts; 1,624 acs on upper side of Cedar Run; 158 acs on the lower side of Cedar Run. Mr Jenkins residing thereon will show the lands. -John Spence, Jas Reid, excs of John Gibson. Dumfries, Va.

Lawrence Hayes, insolvent debtor, confined in Wash Co, D C, prison, for debt.
-Wm Brent, clk.

Congress in Senate-Petition of Jas D Wolf & others of R I, owners of private armed vessels, complaining of grievances & praying relief.

Died: Harry I Todd, M D, age 24 yrs, eldest s/o Judge Todd of Ky; at Bedford, Pa on Nov 29th.

Naval Victory-Oct 25th, the frig, *United States*, under cmnd of Cmdor Decatur, off New London, captured the British frig, *Macedonian*, Capt John Carden. Killed on our side: John Mercer Funk-Lt; John Archibald-carpenter; Thos Brown & Henry Shepherd, seamen; Wm Murray, boy; Mich'l O'Donnell & John Roberts-Marines.

Rappahannoc Acad, Caroline Co, Va. Trustees desirous of engaging a President for the next yr; at least $1000 salary. -John Taylor, J Bankhead, Reuben Turner, Hay Battaile, Chas Taliaferro. -Port Royal, Va.

Runaway-Henny Hicks, negro woman ab't 18 yrs of age. I bought her of Mr Gilbert Docker, Capitol Hill, Wash City. She originally belonged to the est of Notley Young, dec'd, when Mr Docker bought her & has relatives in Queen Anne. -Wm Kean

Jas Cooper, insolvent debtor, confined in Wash Co D C, prison, for debt.
-Wm Brent, clk.

SAT DEC 12, 1812
Hygelia Acad, Haymarket, Pr Wm, Va, to open in Jan. -Thos Turner, Pres. Edmond Brooke, sec'y.

John Stokes brought before me a stray sorrel horse. -Dan'l Rapine, J P-Wash.

Hse of Reps: 1-Petition of widow & heirs of Leonard Marbury, Col in the Rev War, praying for remuneration for advances made & svcs rendered; referred. 2-Petition of B W Crowninshield & others of Salem, owners of private armed vessels, praying a revision of the act concerning prizes, etc,-referred.

Killed & wounded in the capture of H B M ship, *Macedonian*, Capt John Carden, by the *United States*, Stephen Decatur; on Oct 25th, 1812.
Killed:
Thos Brown-N Y, seaman	Henry Shepherd-Phil, seaman
Wm Murray-Boston, a boy	Michael O'Donel-N Y, pvt marine
John Roberts-N Y, pvt marine	

Wounded:
*John Mercer Funk-Phil, Lt	*John Archibald-N Y, carpenter's crew
Christian Clark-N Y, seaman	Geo Christopher-N Y, ordinary seaman
Geo Mahar-N Y, ord seaman	Wm James-N Y, ord seaman

John Laton-N Y, pvt marine   [*since dead]
Permit me to take particular notice of my 1st Lt, Wm H Allen; he has srv'd with me upwards of 5 yrs. -Signed, Stephen Decatur.

John Grimes, insolvent debtor, confined in Wash Co, D C, prison-for debt. -Wm Brent, clk.

Re-elected Governors: Jas Barbour, esq, of Va; & Wm Hawkins, esq, of N C.

Journeymen cabinet-makers wanted. -Wm Worthington jr.

TUE DEC 14, 1812
Died: Mr John Evans, age 56 yrs, on Dec 12th, in Wash City.

Abner Lacock is chosen a Senator of the U S from Pa, vice Aaron Gregg, whose term will expire Mar 4th next.

David Stone is chosen a Senator of the U S from Congress, vice Jesse Franklin, whose term of svc will expire on Mar 4th next. [D Stone-100 votes; A D Murphey rec'd 73 votes & Thos Davis-12 votes].

Buffaloe, Nov 20, 1812.
Expedition under Col Winder of the 14th Regt, to storm the enemy's batteries opposite to Black Rock; 10 boats set out under command of Lt Angus; 5 boats landed commanded by Capt King, late of the 5th Regt, with Capt Morgan of the 12th infty, Capt Dox, of the 13th & Capt Sproull with Capt Angus & Sam'l Swartwout as volunteers. Batteries from Ft Erie to Chippewawere silenced the brave Capt Watts of the Navy, 2d in command to Capt Angus, fell; Lt Scisson is badly wounded; Mr Graham, s/o Col Graham, has his leg broke; Mr Carter, of N Y, is wounded in the arm; Capt Dox is slightly wounded; Capt King was made prisoner together with ab't 10 men; after this affair the force under Genr'l Smyth prepared to embark; Maj Noon is in command, attached to Col McClure. 300 Pa & 100 Balt volunteers, & the N Y & Albany Rifle Corps compose the Reg't.

Wm A Lilly, Pr Edw Co, Va, advertises he has always been successful in curing cancer.

Mrd: recently, Capt Thos Tingey, Commandant of the Navy Yard in Wash City, to Miss Ann Delany, d/o Daniel Delany, esq, of Alexandria. [No date]

Mrd: His Excellency Wm C C Claiborne to Miss Bosque, d/o late Bartholomew Bosque, merchant of New Orleans, on Nov 8th by the Rev Fr Antonie.

Died: Dr Wm Burke, Oct 3d, ab't 35 yrs of age; the great champion in the patriotic cause of So America; his manuscriprts may at a future period adorn the pages of the history of the present Revolution of our so hemisphere.

Died: Capt Geo Thomas, s/o Benj Thomas, of Balt City, age 23 yrs; on Nov 6th at Sunbury, state of Ga, where he commanded the U S Gun Boat 3. His young widow & an aged father lament his death.

Died: Hon David Campbell, one of the Judges of the Miss Ter; on Nov 21st at Wash, Rhea Co, Ten; age 65 yrs.

Died: Wm Polk, Chf Judge of 4th Judicial Dist of Md; on Dec 2d, in Somerset Co

Died: John C Holcomb, late a Midshipman & a victor of the *Wasp*, on Nov 18th, after a few days illness on his passage from Bermuda to the U S.

Wm Norris jr, Tea dealer & grocer, 66 Mkt St, Balt, Md.

Young men of bravery & patriotism, desirous of serving their country as a soldier, are invited to join the 14th Regt, commanded by Col W H Winder. -Timothy Dix, Maj 14th U S infty, superintending the recruiting svc for said Regt at Balt, Md. [$16 on entering the svc; $8 per month; $24 on discharge & 160 acs of land.]

Land for sale in Montg Co, Md, nr Peter Kemp's Mill; ab't 140acs. -Solomon Myers.

For sale-cord wood. Apply to J Levy nr the sq; or to Archibald Lee, Gtwn.

THU DEC 17, 1812
Lost-silver watch, Liverpool made; on Turnpike Rd on Alexander's Island. Reward-$5. -Geo Cheshire.

New Port, R I, Dec 10th. The ctzns of this town witnessed the arrival in this port of the late British frig *Macedonian*, John S Carden, esq, Cmder, a prize to the *United States* frig, Cmdor Decatur.

Baltimore American of Dec 15: Capt Wm Davidson, late mstr of ship *Melantho*, of the port of Balt, returned from Halifax & told of his capture on his homeward passage from Valparayso on the Coast of Chili. He was captured on Sep 17, 1812 by the British frig *Spartan*, carried into Halifax, was a prisoner of war until Nov 19th; treatment was disgraceful.

Raffle on Dec 24th, set of china; may be seen at Mrs Mary Anne's, Bridge St, Gtwn.

SAT DEC 19, 1812
Official report from Geo McFeeley, Lt Col commanding Ft Niagara to Brig Genr'l Smyth, commanding the Army of the Centre. On Nov 21st heavy cannonading opened on this garrison at & in the neighborhood of Ft George; at times the town of Newark was in flames; Capt McKeon commanded a 12-pounder; Capt Jacks of the 7th Regt Militia Artl commanded a 6-pounder; Lt Rees of the 3d Regt Artl had command of an 18-pounder; Capt Leonard of the 1st Regt U S Artl took command

after Lt Rees was bruised in the left shoulder by a part of the parapet falling on him; Lt Wendel of the 3d Regt Artl had command of an 18 & 4 pounder; Dr Hooper of Capt Jacks' company Militia Artl had command of a 6-pounder; the wife of one Doyle, a private of the U S Artl, [Made a prisoner at Queenstown,] I cannot pass over. During the cannonading she attended the 5-pounder; Lts Gansevoort & Harris of the 1st Regt U S Artl, had command of the salt battery at Youngstown mounting an 18 & a 4 pounder; Lt Harris from his 4 pounder, sunk a schn'r which lay at their wharf; Lt Col Gray commanded the artl; to Dr West of the garrison, Dr Augan of the 14th Regt U S infty, & Dr Craige of the 22d U S infty, I offer my thanks. Our killed & wounded amount to 11.

Killed:
Sgt Jones-1st Regt U S Artl   Pvt Stewart-22d Regt U S infty
Sgt Salisbury-3d Regt U S Artl   Pvt Lewis-1st Regt U S Artl

Wounded:
Lt Thomas-22d Regt U S infty
Pvt McEvoy-1st Regt U S infty   Pvt Bowman-14th Regt U S infty
Pvt Welsh-1st Regt U S infty   Pvt Campbell-1st Regt U S infty
                                    Pvt Ray-3d Regt U S infty
Pvt Woodworth 7th Militia Artl [Only 2 of the above men were killed by the enemy's shot, the rest by the bursting of a 12 pd in the s e block sse, & by the spunges of the guns on the north block hse, & at the salt battery.

Dr E Fendall, surg dentist from Balt, Md, has just arrived in this place, where he will continue until the 22d. Make application at Mr Crawford's Bar, Gtwn.

Mrd: Mr Robt Smith to Miss Hannah Walker, both of Wash City, at Fredericksburg, on Dec 13th, by Rev Mr Wilson.

Lost-a round top trunk; presumed to be at some of the stage ofcs north of Alexandria; contained papers for Philip Harrison, W A Linton & the journals of the Senate of Va for Wm A G Dana. Reward-$10. -Burr Harrison, Dumfries, Va.

TUE DEC 22, 1812
Jos Alston, esq, is elected Govn'r & Eldred Simpkins, esq, Lt Gov of S C.

Jedediah K Smith, esq, chosen Senator in Congress from N H, vice Chas Cutts, esq, whose term expires on Mar 3, 1813.

Massachusetts Reps in the 13th Congress:
Levi Hubbard	Artemas Ward	Wm Richardson
Wm Reed	Sam'l Taggart	Timothy Pickering
Dan'l Davey	Abijah Bigelow	Wm Ely
Elijah Brigham	Laban Wheaton	Wm Bayles
John Reed	Cyrus King	Nath'l Ruggles
Sam'l Davis	Abiel Wood	Geo Bradbury
[one vacancy]		John Wilson

Land for sale, nr New Lisbon, Columbia Co, Ohio; 320 acs. Shown by the subscriber on the premises. -Gideon Hughes.

Mrshl's sale-all right, title, int & claim of Nicholas Voss in lots 3-4-5 & part of lot 6 in sq 846, Wash City; prop seized by virtue of two writs of fieri facias, issued from Crct Crt of Wash Co, D C; one at suit of Rich'd Nally, other at suit of Benj Bryan use of Nicholas Travers, against said Nicholas Voss. -Wash Boyd, mrshl.

Promotions in the Corps of Engineers:
Lt Col Jos G Swift to Col, vice Williams, rsgn'd., to rank Jul 31, 1812.
Maj Walker R Armistead to Lt Col, vice Swift, promoted, rank Jul 31, 1812.
Capt Wm M'ree to Maj, vice Armistead, promoted, rank Jul 31, 1812.
1st Lt Jos G Totten to Capt, vice M'ree, promoted, rank Jul 31, 1812.
1st Lt Sam'l Babcock, to Capt, vice Partridge, dec'd, rank Sep 20, 1812.
2d Lt Thos P Finley to 1st Lt, vice Totten, promoted, rank Jul 31, 1812.
2d Lt Frederick Lewis to 1st Lt, vice Babcock, promoted, rank Sep 20, 1812.
Jas Gadsden, appt'd 2d Lt of Engineers, Dec 2, 1812.

Mrshl's sale-all right, title, int & claim of Geo St Clare to sundry improvements on lot 4 in sq 928 in Wash City, the lot on ground rent; prop seized by virtue of two writs of fieri facias, issued from Crct Crt of Wash Co, D C; one at suit of Zachariah Walker, other at suit of John Hollingshead & Co against the said St Clare. -Wash Boyd, mrshl, D C.

Wet nurse wanted-apply at the dwlg of John Wilson, nr the Presbyterian Church on F St, Wash City.

THU DEC 24, 1812
Notice-I intend to apply to St Mary's Co Crt, at next term, for benefit of the insolvent laws of this State. -Jas Maryman, St Mary's Co, Md.

Leg of Ky convened on Dec 7th; Jos H Hawkins was chosen spkr of the Hse.

PG Co, Md-I certify that Sam'l Hanson, of PG Co, brought before me a stray bay gelding. -Notley Maddox, one of the Justices of the Peace, PG Co, Md.

Dayton, Ohio, Dec 2. Genr'l Harrison is engaged in collecting supplies for his army; Jas Logan, the half-blood Shawanoe Indian, who had been acting as a spy in Genr'l H's Army for some time past, was severely wounded last wk by some of his countrymen, while nr Ft Defiance, in company with Capt Jonny & another Indian. His wound is said to be mortal.

Short-hand system-while in Europe in 1792, a system of short hand was published in Phil; said to be the system used by Mr Lloyd in taking down the debates of congress; I am now about to print the same for use of schools. -Thos Lloyd. Certificates may be seen by Mr Jared Ingersoll, Jas Carson & H C Byrne of Phil.

Montg Co, Md-came to the plantation of Mr Wm Holmes, of said co, a sorrel mare. -John Yewell, overseer.

TUE DEC 29, 1812

Post ofc changes in Nov. 1812.
Meredith, N H-Stephen Parley, vice Jonathan Ladd, rsgn'd..
Trent Bridge, N C-Simon Fosure jr, vice J Howard, do.
Tunkhannock, Pa-Chas Otis, vice Elijah Barnham, dec'd.
Alford's Store, Ga-Collin Alford, vice Allen Alford, dec'd.
Pickensville, S C-Elisha Hamlin, vice Rich'd Tarrant, rsgn'd.,
Wellsboro, Pa-Benj W Morris, vice Sam'l W Morris, rsgn'd.
Belle Air, Md-John Reardon jr, vice John Reardon, do.
Crewsville, Va-Walter Crew, vice Micajah Crew, do.
Aurora, N Y-Eleazer Barnham, vice Walter Wood, do.
Liberty Hall, Ga-Hudson J Ware, vice Jas Ware, do.
Hendersonville, S C-Lewis Hogg, vice John Henderson, do.
Frankford, K-Dan'l Wesiger, vice M Springer.
London Grove, Pa-Jonas Pusey, vice Lea Pusey, rsgn'd..
Front Royal, Va-Gabriel Tutt, vice P Senseney, do.
Hackett's town, N J-Silas C Ayres, vice Benajah Gustin, do.
Wash, Miss Ter-Robt H Morrow, vice Sam'l L Winston.
Salisbury, Md-Robt Lemon, vice Rich'd Lemon, rsgn'd..
Miller's Tavern, Va-Jas Evans, vice Mich'l Samuel.
Middlesfield, Ms-David Mack jr, vice Edmund Kelso, mv'd away.
New Lancaster, O-Chas R Sherman, vice Sam'l Coates.
Jefferson, O-Timothy R Hawley, vice Elijah Coleman, mv'd away.
Bakersfield, Vt-Asadean, vice John Maynard, rsgn'd..
Rain's Tavern, Va-John Rain jr, vice Tarleton Williams, mv'd away.
St Inigoes, Md-Peter U Thompson, vice Wm Tarleton.
Gates C H, N C-Dan'l Southall, vice Mills Riddeck, rsgn'd..
North Norwich, N Y-Edw Salter, vice Pardon Morris, mv'd away.
Dover, Del-Cornelius Schee, vice Jas Schee, rsgn'd..
Champion, N Y-John M Henderson, vice Stephen Hubert, dec'd.
Vassalboro, Me-L Lathrop, vice Thos Odivine.

New Post ofcs established in Nov 1812 & Postmaster:
Cook's Law Ofc, Elbert Co, Ga-Jos Cook
Chesterfield C H, Chesterfield Co, S C-John Craig
Broad Creek, Kent Co, Md-Wm L Bewley
Selsertown, Miss Terr-Edmund Andrews
West Boylestown, Worcester Co, Mass-Peter Holmes
Princeton, Worcester Co, Mass-Sam'l Stevenson
Cash-Clapp settlement, La Ter-John B Murray
Canton, Starke Co, O-Thos Taylor
Union, Loudon Co, Va-Seth Smith
Mosser's, Starke Co, O-Abraham Mosser
Mt Hope, Shanandoah Co, Va-P Senseney
Groton, New London Co, Conn-Thos Avery
Lyme, Grafton Co, N H-Arthur Latham
Ft Defiance, Wilkes Co, N C-Wm Davenport
Lewellyn Mills, Culpepper Co, Va-John Strother jr
Humphreyville, New haven Co, Conn-John T Wheeler

Martinsburg, Hopkins Co, K-Jas Baker
Sandy Point, Wayne Co, N C-Gabriel Sherod
Mt Pleasant, Jefferson Co, O-Jas Judkins
Franklin C H, Indiana Ter-Wm H Eads
Marlboro, Windham Co, Vt-Jonas Whitney
Port Slade Creek, Currituck Co, N C-Wm Parmale
Torrington, Litchfield Co, Conn-Nath'l Smith

Reps to the 13th Cong from the State of Ohio:
John McLean   John Alexander   Duncan McArthur
Jas Kilbourn   Jas Caldwell   John S Edwards
[all Rpblcns]

Died: on Oct 24, 1812, Edw Church Nicholls, age 66 yrs, at Donaldsonville, La; ntv of Eng; entered as a student to the Jesuits College at St Omers; returned to Eng & then embarked for America; from close of the war until 1801. He practiced law in the State of Md; to his chldrn he was a kind & indulgent parent. -La Gaz.

The gallant Col Fenwick of the U S Light Artl, has so far recovered of his wounds as to be able to travel.

Died: on Dec 22, in Orange Co, N Y, Gen Jas Clinton, age 76 yrs; ofcr in the Rev Army.

Fire engines-the subscriber informs that he has been bred in Europe, to the making of engines; carries on the profession in the city of Wash; apply to Mr Roch, a copper smith in Richmond, Va. Patent rights for sale. -John Achmann.

Orphans Crt of Wash Co, D C. Application of Owen McCue for ltrs of adm on prsnl est of Albert Johnson, John Holmes & Henry Frazize, seamen, late of the U S brig, *Enterprize*, dec'd. -John Hewitt, Reg wills.

Peter Shorter, my hsbnd, a free man of color, remv'd from Wash City ab't 3 yrs next May in the svc of Gen Sumprter, Sen from S C; reported my hsbnd may have been sold as a slave; $100 for person or persons who may procure my said hsbnd in Wash; the papers of his freedon being deposited with Wm Lance, esq, Charleston, S C, atty at law, by Capt Jos Middleton. -Amelia Shorter.

Notice-claims against the est of the late Capt John Williams, of the U S Marine Corps, dec'd, are requested to bring same to the subscriber. -Nath'l P Williams, adm of John Williams, dec'd. Stafford Co, Va.

Willford Knott, insolvent debtor, confined in Wash Co, D C, prison, for debt. -Wm Brent, clk.

THU DEC 31, 1812
Pianos for sale at W Cooper's Music & Book store, Pa Ave.

Robt Smether invented an improvement in bridles; Rev O B Brown to vend his patent right within D C; applications to Mr Brown living on North E St, nr the Genr'l Post ofc. -Robt Smether is about to go to Richmond.

Boarding & Lodging-Mrs Odin's, #6, in the Seven Bldgs, Wash City.

Miss Squire will open a school for young ladies, in the hse now occupied by Mr John Haw, 19th St West, bet F & G Sts. Apply at Mrs Lenthall's, F St North.

Died: on Dec 30, in Wash City, John Smilie, Rep in Congress from Pa, age ab't 71 yrs; ntv of Ire, arriving in this country at an early age; was engaged in the Rev war both in civil & military capacities. Funeral will take place this day at half past 2 o'clock from the Capitol.

Died: on Dec 19, Wm Loughton Smith, of S C, suddenly, at his country resid.

Drum beating, useful & complete system, by Chas Sashworth, approved by the War Dept; for sale at W Cooper's Music & bk store, Pa Ave.

Wash Co, D C. Dec 28th, 1812, John Henning, of Wash City, nr the magazine, brought before me astray bay mare. -Sam'l N Smallwood, a Justice of the Peace for said co.

Hon Paul Hamilton has resigned the ofc of sec of the Navy.

Lt Col J Chrystie, of the 13th U S infty, one of the brave few who earned a name at Queenstown, arrived in Wash on Tue.

Genr'l P B Porter's transactions at Black Rock appeared in the Buffaloe paper & will be copied into our next paper.

Stockholders of the Wash. Bldg Co will meet on Jan 5th at Davis' Htl. -Walter Clarke, sec.

The partnership of Ringgold & Heath is dissolved by mutual consent; manufacture of cordage will in the future be conducted by the said Ringgold. -Tench Ringgold, Nath K Heath.

Lost-gold watch key of gold with ltrs M C engraved. -Mat Clay, on Capt Hill.

For sale-2 likely negroes: man ab't 21 yrs of age & a boy ab't 13. -Oliver Barron, PG Co, Md, 5 miles from Bladensburg on the Annapolis Rd.

Daily National Intelligencer
Washington, D C
1813

FRI JAN 1, 1813
Orphans Crt of Wash Co, D C. Prsnl est of Albert Johnson, John Holmes, & Henry Frazize, seamen, late of the U S brig *Enterprize*, dec'd. -John Hewitt, rg o/wills.

New dry good store on Pa av, Wash City. -Geo Kneller

Stephen Sanger, of Chas Co, Md; insolvent debtor. -John Barnes, clk.

Lands for sale, at Capt Wms Tavern, Dumfries, Pr Wm Co, Va; devised by the late John Gibson for payment of his debts: 1,624 acs on Siatz-run branch; 158 acs on French's branch. -John Spence, Jas Reid, excs of John Gibson, Dumfries, Va.

Sam'l Ritchey, age about 27 yrs, negro, committed to Harford Co, Md goal. Says he belongs to Jas Ritchey of N Y. -Benj Guyton, shrf of Harford Co, Md. [Bell-Air]

Died: John Smilie, ntv of county of Down, in N Ire; came to the then colony of Pa in 1762, settled in Lancaster Co with his wife & 3 chldrn. His wife & a son & a dght with their families survive him. Mr S was 71 yrs of age & died of typhus fever. Zealous patriot of 1776. [No date]

Committed to goal of Fred'k Co, Md; Geo, age 26 yrs, says he belongs to Mr Jas Brown nr Stauntion, Va. -Morris Jones, shrf, Fred'k Co, Md.

Mrsh'l sale, part of lot 6 in sq 320, with dwlg hse; suit of Adam & Geo King against Jos Dove, & the other at the suit of Mary Ann Fenwick against said Dove & others. -Wash Boyd, mrsh'l.

Notice-claims against the est of the late Capt John Williams, U S M C, dec'd. -Nathl P Williams, adm of John Williams, dec'd. Stafford Co, Va.

John Ball of PG Co, Md; insolvent debtor. -Daniel Clarke, Jan 1.

Orphans Crt of Wash Co, D C. Prsnl est of John Evans, of said city, dec'd. -Robt Evans, John Evans, adms.

SAT JAN 2, 1813
Died: on Nov 9, in New Orleans, Wm S Thom, formerly a resid of Wash City.

Orphans Crt of PG Co, Md. Ltrs of adm on est of Sam'l Fowler, dec'd. -Mgt Fowler, admx.

Thos Jones Waters, of PG Co, Md; insolvent debtor. -John Read Magruder, clk.

MON JAN 4, 1813
Hygeia Acad-school of learning to be opened on Jan 1st. -Thos Turner, Pres. Edmond Brooke, Sec. Haymarket, Pr Wm Co, Va.

Peter Shorter, a free man of color, was remv'd from Wash City about 3 yrs next May in the svc of Gen Sumpter. I will pay $100 on procuring my said hsbnd in Wash City; papers of his freedom being deposited with Wm Lance, Charleston, S C, atty, by Capt Jos Middleton. -Amelia Shorter

TUE JAN 5, 1813
Mrd: on Dec 31, by Rev Mr M'Cormick, Mr Andrew Forrest to Miss Ann H More, both of Wash City.

Gen Alex'r Smith, of the Army of the Centre, passed thru this place on Wed last, on his way from Niagara to his resid in Wythe Co, Va. -Martinsburg, Va, Jan 1.

Paul Hamilton intends shortly to leave Wash City; Tench Riggold or N G Maxwell, empowered to rec & settle demands against him.

WED JAN 6, 1813
For sale-lands in Ohio & Ky; virtue of last will of Robt Means, dec'd. -Dan'l Call, exc, Richmond, Jul 19.

For sale-350 acs in PG Co, Md. Immediate possession cannot be given, as the plantation is under lease of 5 yrs to Thos Magruder, at 4000 pds of Tobacco per yr, 2 of which expired on Dec 31, 1812. -Jos Peach, nr Vansville.

THU JAN 7, 1813
Stockholders of the Commercial Co of Wash; Directors elected Mon last:

Moses Young	Chas W Goldsborough	Geo Blagden
Alex'r Kerr	Thos Tingey	Adam Lindsay
Henry Ingle	Thos Young	Peter Miller
Toppan Webster	Wm Prout	John McGowan-Pres

Stray calf at the plantation of Thos Patterson, nr Wash.

Superb laces & veils, shawls etc. -Wm G Ridgely, Gtwn. Ad.

The Levy Crt of Wash Co will sit at the Union Tavern in Gtwn on Jan 11. -John Mountz, clk.

FRI JAN 8, 1813
Returns of the Vt Election at Montpelier, the seat of gov't. Rpblcn Tkt has majority of 233 votes. Mbrs elected:

Jas Fisk	Wm Strong	Wm C Bradley
Ezra Butler	Chas Rich	Rich'd Skinner

Wash Co, D C, in Chancery. Pres, Dirs & Co of the Bank of Col, against Sarah Rowles & others. Ratify sale of rl est by John Heugh, trustee, of Jos E Rowles, dec'd. -Wm Brent, clk.

SAT JAN 9, 1813
Hse o/Reps. Petitions of Sam'l Barrett, John Frothingham, Arthur Tappan, & H D Searle, stating they are ntv born ctzns of the U S, & prior to the war against Gr Brit, were engaged in mercantile business in Montreal, Canada. Their property was seized by the revenue ofcrs; pray restoration of same.

Miss S Evans has opened a school for young ladies, in the hse belonging to Mr Dan'l Carr, 4th door north of Dr Thos Ewell. Wash City.

To rent-hse lately occupied by Mr John Evans, adj Gen Van Ness's, on Pa av. For terms apply to J P Van Ness or S Evans, Capt Hill. Wash City.

Potomac Steam Boat Co, Jan 2. Meeting at Tripplett's Tavern in Alexandria; John Cook, chrmn; B H Latrobe, clk; John Dawson, Pres. Dirs: John Davis, of Wash City; John Withers, of Alex; Carey Selden, of Potomac Crk; Robt Lewis, of Fredericksburg, Va.

Orphans Crt of Montg Co, Md. Prsnl est of Wm Viers, sr, late of said co, dec'd. -Lier Veirs. [2 splgs of Viers-Veirs]

Young men of bravery & patriotism are invited to join the 14th regt U S infty, commanded by Col W H Winder. You will rec $8 per mo, $16 bounty; 3 mos pay on discharge, & 160 acs of val land. Those who have debts will, on enlisting, be free from all civil arrests, & the law for inflicting the degrading punishment by stripes is abolished. -Timothy Dix, super, Balt, Md.

MON JAN 11, 1813
Trustees of Rappahannoc Acad: John Taylor, J Bankhead, Reuben Turner, Hay Battaile, Chas Taliaferro. Port Royal, Va, Dec 10.

Edw Dyer & Co have this day opened a wholesale & retail dry good store; a few drs above Messrs Silas Butler & Co, Wash City, Navy yd, Jan 8.

TUE JAN 12, 1813
Benevolent Soc of Wash City, meeting this evening. -Geo Sweeny, Jan 12.

Caution-notes of hand, ea for $13, made payable to T Williams, ea is fully satisfied; said to be in the possession of Wm O'Neale, or of some other individual in this city. Same to be speedily surrendered. -Sam Hoot, Wash, Jan 12.

Info wanted of Mr Boon Van Ostade, in the U S army from Aug 1806 to Aug 1812, under the name of Chas Williams. His family is anxious to ascertain whether he is now living or dead. Communicate to the editors of this paper.

Orphans Crt of PG Co, Md. Prsnl est of the late John Fairall, dec'd; pblc sale on Feb 2. -Robt Fairall, adm.

Jos Powell, Sen, of PG Co, Md, insolvent debtor, now in confinement for debt. -John Read Magruder, clk.

WED JAN 13, 1813
Wm Jones, of Pa, appt'd Sec of the Navy of the U S, by the Pres & Senate.

Died: on Oct 16, Rich'd Moss, qrtr-mstr on the frig *Pres*. He informed Cmdor Rodgers that he had a wife & 3 chldrn in Boston, dependent on him for support.

Strayed or stolen-2 carriage horses. Deliver to Dan'l C Brent, nr Aquia, Va, reward $20. -Thos L L Brent.

Pblc sale of lots & sqs in Wash City, to satisfy taxes due Wash Corp thru 1811:

John Benson	John B Beall	Wm Brogden
John Craig	Benedict Calvert	Martha Hall
Wm Kain	Sarah Porter	Henry Thompson
Wash Tontine	Maximilian Haysler	Basil Waring

[Lots & sqs included in the paper.] -Ezekiel MacDaniel, coll of 2d Ward.

Pblc sale of lots & sqs in Wash City, to satisfy taxes due Wash Corp thru 1811:

Robt Alleson	J B Avidths	Dan'l Carmack
Sam'l Clark	Hugh Campbell	Jas Crawford, jr.
John Camp	Jas Duer	Elias Davidson
Andrew Flick	Wm Feltwell	Mich'l Gangaware
Fred'k Goulding-hrs	Rev Mr Goulding	Henry Goil
Christopher Goir	Bernard Gilpin	Arnold Geouges
Jonathan Haga	Wm Hindman	John Hackett
Geo Holstein	Jas Kirk	Henry Klinger
Dan'l Kesler	Lodowick Kruger	Andrew Link
John Matthias	John M'Dade	John Middart
Edwards Parry	Aaron Reclimair	Dan'l Ragan
Wm Robinson	Henry Robinson	Geo Reeder
Wm Reed	Sarah Ratcliff	Capt John Shaw
Mich'l Stoker	Amos Smith	Geo Swingle
Philip Seybert	Edw Skinner	Thos L Shippin
Henry Stall	Robt Sutton	Jacob Tompton
Barton Tabbs	Henry Umhults	Jas Ward
Wayman Chas-heirs	Elias Youman	Fred'k Wilzall
Abraham Vanbibber	Jos Taylor-heirs	Walker Henry
W & E Waugh	Eliza & Josias W Watson	

-Jos Brumley, coll of 1st Ward

THU JAN 14, 1813
For sale-lge brick hse & lot on S Capt st, Wash. -Chas H Varden

Ladies w ltrs in the P O, Wash City, Jan 1, 1813:

Mrs A M Alston	Miss Eliza Brown	Mrs Jane Beall
Mrs E Brown	Henrietta Bilbo	Obedience Bryan
Miss Matilda Berry	Eliz Clarke-2	Cath Cassell
Cath Cale	Miss Adelle Colmes	Susan Derick
Mrs Ann Davi	Betsey Fowler	Mrs Lidy Gary
Eliz Goodrick-2	Mrs Ann Green	Ann Hall
Ceceila Hall	Mrs Hart	Gwynn Harris
Mrs Ann Jones	Miss Ann Lee	Miss Lyon
Miss Barbary Low	Mgt Mitchell	Mary Neal
Mary Ann Parsons	Margt Parsons	Mary Eliza Quinto
Melinda Stewart	Mrs Shorter	Mgt St C'air
Rosa Shanks	Sally Toole	Eleanor West-3
Sarah Winder	Mary D White	Miss Jane Young

Killed or wounded in the battle of Massassinwa on the 18th inst & in the skirmish on the 17th. 17th-Serjeant Jas Wright, in Capt Hopkins's troop, killed. Sgt Thos Smith, wounded, since dead; in Capt Elmore's troop of Ky Vols. 18th-Capt Hopkins's troop of regulars, wounded: Lt Jas Hedges; Pvts Thos Robinson-badly; John Holecroft-badly; John May-slightly; John Fain-badly; Thos Salsbury-badly. Killed in Capt Marcle's troop of Pa Vols: Lt Dan'l Watts; Pvt Jas Griffin. Wounded, Cpls Henry Breneman, badly; Robt Skilly; sadler Jas Smith; Pvt Thompson Carnahan, since dead; Robt Campbell, dangerously; Finlay Carnahan, badly; Wm Logue; Jos Chambers, badly; Jas Selby; Thos Porter, badly; John M'Carman, badly; Robt Cooper; David Braden; John Bennet. Capt Garrard's troop of Ky Vols, killed: Pvts Thos Bedford & Beverly Brown; wounded: lt Edmund Basey; Lt David Hichman; Q M Sergt Strother G Hawkins; Sergeant G Edwards; farrier T M Cormel; Pvts Henry Wilson, Moses Richardson, Thos Easton, badly; Wm Scott, mortally; & Thos Webster. Capt Peirce's troop of Ohio Vols, killed Capt Bennoni Peirce; & Pvt Daniel Cummingham; wounded-Pvt Wm Morrow. Lt Warren's troop of Pa Vols, cornet Greer-wounded. Cornet Lee's troop of Mich Vols, wounded: Pvts David Hull, Mich'l M'Dormot, Cyrus Hunter. Capt Elliott's Co of U S Infty, wounded: Pvts Walter M'Allister, Henry Walter, Thos Wattington. Capt Butler's Pittsburgh Blues, killed: Pvt John Francis Lousong; wounded, Cpls Elliott & Reed; Pvts Jos Dodds, Isaac Chess. -John Payne, 1st Lt. Ky Vol L Drag & Adj to Detch'mt.

In Chancery-ratify sale of prop mortgaged to Wm B Beans by John H Brown, made by Trueman Tyler, trustee. -Nichl Brewer, rg c c.

To be sold, Jan 18, at the dwlg of J Gideon, 12th st west, Wash, hsehld furn, etc. -Jas Young. N L Queen, auct.

Just rec'd from N Y & Phil, chewing Tobacco & snuff. Duport's Snuff Store, Bridge st, nr the Union Tavern, Gtwn.

FRI JAN 15, 1813
John Peter is chosen Mayor of Gtwn.

Mrd: at N Y, on Jan 9, Isaac Hull, of the Navy, late cmder of the *Constitution* frig, to Miss Ann M Hart, d/o Elisha Hart, of Saybrook, Conn.

SAT JAN 16, 1813
Clover seed, hrdware, calicoes, for sale. Thos W Pairo, F st, Wash.

Ranaway-mulatto man, Bob, 23 yrs old. -Jas Beck, Fredericksburg, Va.

MON JAN 18, 1813
Died: in Loudoun Co, Va, on Jan 12, Abraham Barnes Thompson Mason, esq. in his 52d yr.

Salem Register of Jan 9-impressment. Deposition of Mr Isaac Clark, of this town, who has been torn from his family & country & for 3 yrs compelled to serve on board his Britannic Majesty's ships of war, is entitled to an attentive perusal. Clark was born in the town of Randolph, Norfolk Co, & sailed out of Salem about 7 yrs ago; impressed from the ship *Jane* of Norfolk, on Jun 14, 1809.

TUE JAN 19, 1813
For sale-60 doz prs of elegant cotton hose. Rich'd Davis, High st, Gtwn.

To rent-frame hse & lge garden, nr the Capitol on Md av; none but orderly persons need apply. Enquire of Jos Scholfield, Wash.

Sale at auction of the prsnl est of John Richter, dec'd. Groceries, hsehld furn, 3 work horses, his brick storehse, dwlg hse & frame ware hse, crnr of King & Alfred sts. -A C Cazenove, exc, Alexandria, Jan 19.

Pblc sale of frame hse nr the Wash Bridge, with leasehld est of the lot. -Geo Burns. N L Queen, auct.

WED JAN 20, 1813
Wanted to purchase-a few U S Military Land Warrants. -H Northup, at the sign of the Wheat Sheuf, Gtwn.

Following ofcs of the army & militia of the U S, made prisoners of war at Detroit, Queenstown & elsewhere, duly exchanged for ofcrs, non-com ofcrs, drummers & pvts, taken on board his Britannic Maj's transport *Samuel & Sarah*, on Jul 11, 1812, viz: Brig Gen Wm Hull, Cols Duncan M'Arthur, Jas Findley, & Lewis Cass; Lt Cols Jas Miller, John R Fenwick, Winfield Scott, & John Christie; Maj Jas Taylor; Capts Nathan Heald, John Whistler, Henry B Brevoort, Josiah Snelling, Robt Lucas, Abraham F Hull, Peter Ogilvie, Wm King, Joel Cook, & Return B Brown; 1st Lt Chas Larrabee; 2d Lts Jas Dalliba & Dan'l Hugunin. -T H Cushing, Adj Gen, Wash City, Jan 18, 1813.

Drum Beating by Chas S Ashworth, apprv'd by the War Dept, for sale at W Cooper's Music & Bk Store, Pa av, Wash. $2 sgl, & $18 per doz.

Phil, Jan 15, 1813. Info respecting Mr Boon Van Ostade, known as Chas Williams; was a sergeant in the 6th regt of infty, & arrv'd from N Orleans in Mar last; was a clk in my ofc. He died in Apr with pneumonia [or pleurisy] about 9 days from the first attack. -Francis Le Baron, Surg U S Army.

THU JAN 21, 1813
St Geo Tucker, the erudite commentor on Blackstone, is appt'd Judge of the U S for the Va dist, vice John Tyler, dec'd.

Died: on Jan 9, John Tyler, judge of the U S for the dist of Va.

Died: on Jan 9, in her 48th yr, after the warning of but a few short hrs, Mrs Mary Semmes, consort of Mr J Semmes, of Gtwn; leaving a sorrowful hsbnd & numerous relatives & friends.

Hse o/Reps. Petition of Thos Simpson of N H, an ofcr of the Rev army, praying for arrearages of pension.

FRI JAN 22, 1813
Horse strayed from the hse of Mr S Lewis, nr the Dept of War; horse recovered, but the saddle is missing; reward. -Mr David Dobbin, Pa av, Wash.

Wanted-a lady to manage a female acad about to be established in Port Royal. Apply to Newton Berryman, Postmstr, Port Royal, Va.

SAT JAN 23, 1813
Gun Powder Mills now in operation. Experiments were made by John T Frost, & in some instances the ounce has thrown the 24 pd ball 300 yrs, never failing to send the ball the required proof of 200 yds. Fielder Parker, J P of PG Co, Md, made oath on same; sworn before Thos Bowie. Navy Yd, Oct 28, 1812, Thos Tingey examined same. Bladensburg, Jan 16, 1813; Geo Calvert & Rich'd T Lowndes examined same. B Neal examined same for the frig *Constellation.* -Thos Ewell.

Clarksburg, Virg, Jan 11. Mr David Cram, lately a resid of this place, contrived a machine for cutting limber. -Byestander.

For sale-22 lots in sq 186, directly in front of the Pres' hse. C Goldsborough, agent for the proprietor.

Info wanted of Mr F Jones, who came to this city on Dec 10 last; age about 45 yrs. He put 2 horses in my hands for a sale, while he went to Balt on some business for his bro. C R Green, auct, Horse Mkt, Balt.

Wm McGee, insolvent debtor, in Wash Co prison for debt. -Wm Brent, clk.

Orphans Crt of PG Co, Md. Prsnl est of John Fairall, dec'd; sale Feb 2. -Robt Fairall, adm.

MON JAN 25, 1813
Hse o/Reps. Bill for relief of John Dixon & John Murray, was read a 3d time & passed. Petitions of Joshua Berry & Stephen Kingston were referred to committee.

TUE JAN 26, 1813
Jesse Bledsoe is chosen a Senator of the U S from Ky for 6 yrs, from Mar 4th next.

Hse o/Reps. Memorial of Chas Rockwell, agent of Jas Dickson, of Savannah, stating that he is the owner of property, recently imported from G Britain, which comes within the provisions of the non-importation act.

Orphans Crt of PG Co, Md. Prsnl est of Zadoch Jenkins, late of said co, dec'd. -Archibald Jenkins, adm; Ann Jenkins, admx.

Money was found nr the Navy Yd on Jan 9. Apply to Robt Armistead, nr the Navy Yd.

WED JAN 27, 1813
P O changes in Dec 1812:
Burkesville, Ky-John M Emerson v Jas Everson, rsgnd.
Groton, Con-Elijah Bailey v Thos Avery, rsgnd.
Cayuga, N Y-Reuben S Morris v Hugh Buckley, dec'd.
Jefferson, N H-Wm Plaisted v Sam'l Plaisted, rsgnd.
Yorktown, Pa-Peter Spangler v Jacob Spangler, rsgnd.
Beaufort, N C-Thos Cook v Bryan Hellen, rsgnd.
Chickasaw Agency-Thos M'Coy v Jas Neilly, mv'd away.
Roan's Crk, Tenn-Reuben Thompson v Henry Hammond, dec'd.
Milledgville, Ga-John W Devereaux v John Howard, rsgnd.
Barbourville, Va-Wm Douglass v Jacob Bradley, rsgnd.
Ward's Bridge, N Y-Isaac Smith v Thos M'Neill.
Urbanna, Va-Paremenas Bird v John Darby residence too distant from ofc.
Strasburg, Pa, Dan'l Kendrick v J Caldwell, rsgnd.
Great Crossings, Ky-Thos Henderson v Mareen Duvall, mv'd away.
Hermitage, Va-Philip G Todd v Mark Andrews, rsgnd.
Brown's store, Va-Dan'l Brown v Ammon Hancock, rsgnd.
Jefferson, N C-John O Johnson v C Ray, mv'd away.
Shaftsbury, Vt-Henry Huntington v P Jones.
Falmouth, Va-Philip Alexander v Ed Seddon, dec'd.
Lewistown, Del-Peter Hall v Jno Thompson, rsgnd.
Edgefield C H, S C, John Simkins v Jesse Simkins, mv'd away.
Ridge, S C-Jesse Simkins v Jno Simkins, declines.
Hartford, Ga-John Howard v S A Hopkins, rsgnd.
Union, Me-Ebenezer Alden v Wm White, rsgnd.
Winton, S C-Gareson M Smith v Wm Duer, rsgnd.

Littleton, Mass-Thos Read v Jno Adams, rsgnd.
Watkins Stone, Ga-Sam'l Watkins v Robt H Watkins, mv'd away.
Barnwell C H, S C-Barnett H Brown v Edmd Brown, rsgnd.
Hull's store, Va-Thos Kincaid v Robt Given, rsgnd.
Averasboro, N C-Jonathan Smith v R Droughon, rsgnd.
St Tamany's, Va-Jas M'Gowan v E Magowen, rsgnd.
Plymouth, Pa-Geo Lane v Chas Lane, mv'd away.
Warrenton, Ga-Philip Dewel v Geo Hargrove, rsgnd.
Mercersburg, Pa-Wm B Gutherie v Jas M'Coy, rsgnd.
May's Landing, N J-John Morrow v Martin Synott, dec'd.
Hartford, Md-John Johnson v E Nowland, rsgnd.
New Offices est'd in Dec, 1812 & postmstr:
Verona, Oneida Co, N Y, Jos Grant
Martinsburg, Hopkins Co, Ky, Jas Baker.
Albright, Orange Co, N Y, Dan'l Albright.
Blacks & Whites, Nottaway Co, Va, John Morgan.
Pidgeon Run, New Castle Co, Del, Wm Polk.
Kingston, Somerset Co, Md, Jesse Adams.
Huttonsville, Randolph Co, Va, Jonathan Hutton.
Lassellsville, Mont Co, N Y, Wm Lassell.
Walnut Grove, St Clair Co, Ill Ter, Thos Todd.
East Falls of Machias, Wash Co, Me, John C Talbot.
Piney Grove, Southampton Co, Va, Jacob Barnes.
Chagrin Rvr, Geauga Co, Ohio, Christopher Colson.
Eaton, Preble Co, Ohio, Alex'r C Lanier.
Rutland, Gallia Co, Ohio, Eli Stedman.
Danielsville, Madison Co, Ga, Jas Long.
Orrsville, Pendleton Co, S C, Wm Orr.
Sheetz Mill, Hampshire Co, Va, Chas Marshall.
Philipsburg, Clearfield Co, Pa, John Lorain.
Narrows of Lackawaxen Crk, Wayne Co, Pa, Wm Kimble.
Salisbury, Montg Co, N Y, Amos Griswold.
West Mexico, Oneida Co, N Y, Jos Bailey.
Union Mills, Fluvanna Co, Va, Walker Timberlake.
South Hero, Grand Isle Co, Vt, Malvin Barnes.
Jenner, Somerset Co, Pa, John Dennison.
Chatham, Columbia Co, N Y, Elijah Hurlbut.
Hall x Rds, Harford Co, Md, Crispin Cunningham.
Discontinued offices:

Harrison, Ill terr	Bear Garden, Va	Cape Caphon, Va
Little Cape, Caphon, Va	Leesville, Va	Parker's, Va
Anderson's, Va	Rising Sun, Va	

Orphans Crt of PG Co, Md. Prsnl est of Wm Smith, late of said co, dec'd.
-Zephaniah Farrell, Jan 27.

W M Hamer, hatter; Wash City.

Tracts of land in Baton Rouge, on the Miss, srvyd & patented in 1770 & 1772; also tracts in Randolph Co, Harrison Co, Va, & in Ky, for sale. Each recorded in the name of Oliver Pollock, Wash City.

THU JAN 28, 1813
Crct Crt of D C, in Chancery. Sale of prop of the late Col Henry Gaither, hse & lot formerly occupied by Ross & Getty as a groc store, at this time by Robt Getty, on Bridge st. Also lots 22 & 23 in sq 127, & lots 2 & 3 in sq 104, in Wash City-call on Jas S Morsell, Gtwn, who will give satisfaction as to the title. Lots no 2 & 3 in sq 104 are occupied by John Knapp, as grdn. -Benj Gaither, Dan'l Gaither, trustees.

Died: on Jan 23, at the residence of his son, in Morrisville, Bucks Co, Geo Clymer, Pres of the Bank of Phil.

Ja A Porter has declined the practice of law in the Dist of Columbia.

FRI JAN 29, 1813
Died: at Laguira, Spanish Maine, Sam'l Helms, a ntv of Conn, on Dec 5, of dysentery. He aided in securing the liberties of his country under Washington. He recently arrived in Laguira, with a view of recruiting his shattered fortune. Also in Nov last, on passage from Laguira to St Thos, Timothy Phelps, lately a merchant of Newhaven, Conn.

SAT JAN 30, 1813
Lorenzo Dow, God willing, will preach at the Capitol tomorrow morning.

Wm Kennedy, Rpblcn, is chosen to rep Congress from N C, vice the decease of Gen Thos Blount.

Meeting of the Common Cncl of Wash, on Mon. -Pontius D Stelle, Sec.

MON FEB 1, 1813
Boarding & lodging at Mrs Odlin's, #6 in the Seven Bldgs, Wash City.

Wm Steuart, insolvent debtor, confined in Wash Co prison. -Wm Brent-clk.

Impressed seamen now on board the *Dragon*, viz:

Thos Edmons, R I	P Williams, Middletown, Conn
Ezekiel Morton, Mass	Jos Cann, Va
Jas Goodman, N Y	Geo Gray, R I
Wm Hannah, N Y	Jas Balfour, Virg
John Wood, N Y	S Ward, N J
S White, N Y	

Proposals for publishing a newspaper in the city of Albany, to be entitled *The Albany Argus*; decidedly Rpblcn. -Jesse Buel

TUE FEB 2, 1813
Orphans Crt of Wash Co, D C. Prsnl est of Abner Cloud, late of said co, dec'd. -Susanna B Cloud, admx; Everard Gary, adm.

Confined in Wash Co prison for debt; insolvent debtors: Jos McMurray, Levi White, & Allen Scott. -Wm Brent, clk.

Columbia Turnpike Rd; from nr Ellicott's Lower Mills, towards Gtwn in D C. Com'rs: John Ellicott, o/John; P E Thomas; Nicholas G Ridgely; Geo F Warkfield.

THU FEB 4, 1813
Mrd: on Feb 2, by Rev Mr M'Cormick, Col Fielder Dorset, of PG Co, Md, to Miss Amelia T Beall, of Wash Co, D C.

Subscriber, being encouraged to reside in this place, informs those who contemplate to build, that he will execute according to their own plans, or he will present them plans. His work can be viewed in the much admired staircase in Capt John Peter's new hse in Gtwn. Apply at the resid of Mr Jeremiah Merrill, High st, Gtwn. -Daniel Sutherland.

FRI FEB 5, 1813
Acting lts commissioned as lts in the Navy:
Wm Finch   Alex'r Claxton
Wm B Shubrick   Glen Drayton
Enos Davis   Benj W Booth

Stockholders of the Mechanics Bank of Alexandria, to meet on Mar 8. -Wm Paton, jr, cashier.

Eloped: apprentice boy, Robt Maitland, aged 16 yrs. Reward .06 & a handful of Brick-bats. -Jas Maitland, bricklayer, Wash City.

SAT FEB 6, 1813
Died: at Dumfries, on Jan 31, Mrs Fanncy C Heath, w/o Jas C Heath, & eldest d/o the Rev M L Weems. She was in her 17th yr; her illness was but short.

Reward-$4, for a sorrel mare who strayed away on Jan 17. -John F Heffnoman, Marine Barracks.

Crct Crt of D C. Jas A Porter, insolvent debtor. -Wm Brent, clk.

MON FEB 8, 1813
Died: on Jan 22, Sam'l Ashe, aged 88 yrs; venerable ctzn & vet patriot; at his seat on *Rocky-Point*, New Hanover Co, N C, after a few days illness.

TUE FEB 9, 1813
Miss Charlotte Ann Taylor will commence a female brdg school & acad on Feb 15, at the hse of Gen Van Ness, nr Pa av, Wash.

Died: at Champlain, on Nov 22, of pleurisy, occasioned by fatigue & exposure on the march from Plattsburgh, Capt Rich'd Caldwell, 25th reg U S infty, late of Orange co. He fell in the prime of life; & genuine sorrow mingled with the last sad honors over his grave.

WED FEB 10, 1813
Chilicothe, Feb 2. Horrid disaster. Gen Winchester was killed & his body mangled in the most horrid manner by the Indians.

THU FEB 11, 1813
Votes of the Electors: Jas Madison, of Va, 128 votes; Dewitt Clinton, of N Y, 89 votes-for Pres. For V P-Elbridge Gerry, of Mass, 131; Jared Ingersoll, of Pa, 68.

Died: at Newbern, N C, on Jan 24, Mrs Lydia Allen, consort of Vine Allen, atty at law of that place. She has left a family of chldrn, and an affectionate hsbnd.

FRI FEB 12, 1813
Died: at Detroit, on Dec 29, 1812, Jas Henry, an American gentleman, long a resid of that place. On Dec 31st his remains were interred in the English burying ground, attended by a numerous concourse of his fellow-ctzns.

One cent reward for John Craton, appr to the baking business. Esias Travers.

Prop for sale in Wash: Brick hse on F st,occupied by Jas A Porter, atty. Brick hse on 12th st, occupied by R Brown. Small brick hse in the middle of 2 acs of land, on Va av, occupied by Mich'l Lowe. Brick store-hse on L st, occupied as a grocery & china store by M Shanks. -Wm Hebb, PG Co, nr the Eastern Branch Bridge.

SAT FEB 13, 1813
Runaways committed to Wash Co jail, D C: Betsey Baker, alias Betsey Gillis, age bet 30 & 40 yrs, yellow complexion; believe her name is Sarah & that she belongs to Mr Brown, of Pr Wm Co, Va. Also, Sam Harver, negro, 30 yrs of age, raised in Phil. -C Tippett, for W Boyd, mrshl, Wash.

MON FEB 15, 1813
Died: on Jan 29, at his seat in A A Co, Md, Dr Chas Alexander Wakefield, in the 62d yr of his age.

Pblc sale of the cargo of the Swedish brig *Stockholm*, on Ramsay's Wharf, Thu. -P G Marsteller, V M, Alexandria.

Mr John Scotti, ladies & gentlemen's hair dresser, will arrive in Wash on Feb 15.

For sale-valuable rl & prsnl prop, at his present resid, 6 miles from Hagerstown; 26 negroes, 200 head of cattle, 200 head of hogs. Probable sale of the stills & apparatus with about 225 acs of grain. Land in Wash Co, Md-840 1/2 acs, with stone dwlg hse; merchant mill & saw mill. -Jos Sprigg, Wash Co, Md.

TUE FEB 16, 1813
Fresh fruits just rec'd. David Ott & Co, Pa av, Wash, & John Ott, Gtwn.

Orphans Crt of PG Co, Md; sale at the late resid of Marsham Waring, dec'd; all prsnl est of same. -Marsham Waring, exr, PG Co, Md.

Lands for sale of which Wm W Berry died possessed; 150 acs in PG Co, Md, at the shop of Henson Marshall, nr the premises. -Archibald Van Horn, Com'r.

John Staples, insolvent debtor, confined in Wash Co prison. -Wm Brent, clk.

WED FEB 17, 1813
Mrd: on Feb 16, by Rev Mr M'Cormick, Gen Sam'l Ringgold, a Rep in Cong from Md, to Miss Maria Antoinette Hay, d/o Geo Hay, esq, of Richmond.

For sale-3 story brick hse on Pa av, now occupied by the Hon Jas Monroe, Sec of State. Apply to Mr Andrew Ross, nr the Union tavern, Gtwn, or Timothy Caldwell, 214 Race st, Phil.

For sale-seats for mills, in & nr Petersburg, Va. -John Grammer, Edw Mumford, Rich'd N Venable, Edw Dillon, Thos A Morton.

THU FEB 18, 1813
Wm H Ward, insolvent debtor, confined in Wash Co prison. -Wm Brent, clk.

Calvary orders-Feb 16: so prepared as to be ready for duty, if it should prove requisite, at the sound of the trumpet. -Geo C Washington, adj of clvry, Wash.

Henry W Magruder intends to apply to the judges of the First Judicial Dist of Md, of PG Co crt, in Apr, for benefit of the insolvent laws of this state.

FRI FEB 19, 1813
Mrd: lately, by the Rev Mr M'Cormick, Mr Geo Mason, of Fairfax Co, Va, to Miss Eliza Mason, of same county.

Died: in Apr, 1812, at New Orleans, John B Treat, & on Jan 5, 1813, at the same place, Sam'l Treat, formerly of Mass, brothers.

Berry's store & tavern in Montg Co, Md will be sold; 3 acs, but adjoining is 1,000 acs which may be used for a farm. -Edw Berry.

David Boudon, painter, has remv'd into F st, where he paints miniatures on Ivory, & profiles on parchment. Wash City.

Wash Co, D C, in Chancery. Jas McKenzie & others v Chas Minifie. Ratify sale by trustees, Jas Davidson & Rich'd Forrest, am't $1644.12 1/2. -Wm Brent, clk.

SAT FEB 20, 1813
Gtwn Birth Night Ball is Feb 25. Mgrs: John Mason, Robert F Howe, Ch Worthington, Elie Williams, John Cox, Thos Gantt, John Hoye, Joh Marbury, R M Boyer, & John Lee.

For sale-negro woman named Hesther [or Esther] taken as the prop of Jas Nevitt, to satisfy taxes due the Wash Corp. -Z Walker, coll of the third Ward.

Ranaway-appr boy Robt Stephenson, reward-five cents. -John Bing.

MON FEB 22, 1813
Law bks, just rec'd, for sale. Jos Milligan, bkseller, Gtwn.

TUE FEB 23, 1813
Killed on board the U S frig *Constitution*, under command of Wm Bainbridge, in an action with his Brit Maj's frig *Java*, Henry Lambert, Cmder, Dec 29, 1812.

Smn: Jonas Ongrain	Jos Adams	Mark Snow
Patrick Conner	Barney Hart	John Cheves
John D Allen	Wm Cooper	
Pvt marine-Thos Hanson	Signed: Robt C Ludlow, purser.	

P O changes in Jan, 1813:
Jefferson, Indiana Ter, Willis W Godwin v Jas Lemmon, rsgnd.
Newport, R I, Benj B Mumford v Jacob Richardson.
Hillsboro, Va, Sam'l W Young v Mahlon Roach, rsgnd.
Vincennes, Ind Ter, John H Hay v Wm Prince, do.
Herculaneum, L T, Elias Bates v Chas C Austin, do.
Shoals of Ogechee, Ga, Wilson Bird v Wm Bird, dec'd.
Shelbyville, Ky, Isaac Watkins v Wm Bullock, rsgnd.
Lower Somers Point N J, John Somers, jr v Jesse Somers, do.
Middleton Upper Hses, Ct, Josiah Sage v Sam'l Rose, dec'd.
Cross Keys, Va, Sam'l Johnson, v B W Johnson.
Point Harmar, Ohio, Jos Wilcox v Geo Dunlevy.
Waynesboro, N C, Benj W Caswell v Nicholas Washington, rsgnd.
Willow Grove, S C, Jas Bradley v Matthew Bradley.
Baton Rouge, O T, Isaiah Nelson v Jas Chaveaux.
La Forche, O T, Jas R Wilson v Thos Nicholls, mv'd away.
Robbstown, Pa, John Nicholls v Jos Vankirk, rsgnd.
Murray's Mills, Pa, Sam'l Dunbar v Jeremiah Murray, declines accepting.
Hicksford, Va, Wm A Wardlow v Nathaniel Land, rsgnd.
Keene, N H, Jos Buffum v B M Atherton, do.
Enfield, Ct, John C Pease v Wm Dixon, do.
Gtwn, Me, Mark L Hill v Andrew Reid, do.
Overton C H, Ten, Joel Mabry v John Kennedy, do.
Hardwich, Mass, Sam'l F Cutler v Wm Cutler, do.
Lyrne, Ct, Chas Smith v Marshfield Parsons, dec'd.
Dover, Ohio, Asahel Porter v Philo Taylor, rsgnd.
Mayville, N Y, Anselem Potter v Casper Rouse, dec'd.

Smyrna, N Y, Chester Hammond v Sam'l Gutherie, rsgnd.
York C H, S C, jas A Whyte v John Feemster.
Sandy Point, N C, Alex'r Carter v Gabriel Sherrod, declines.
Danville, N Y, Wm B Rochester v Jared Irwin, dec'd.
Sampson C H, N C, Owen Holmes v Michael Sampson, dec'd.
Buffaloe, Va, Lawrence A Washington v Peter K Royston, mv'd away.
Montpelier, Vt, Joshua Y Vail v L Baldwin, mv'd away.
Dinwiddie C H, Va, Wm Dunn v Thos Field, rsgnd.
New ofce est'd in Jan 1813 & postmstr:
Temple, Hillsboro Co, N H, Benj Whiting.
Watkinsville, A A Co, Md, Isaac Watkins.
Birdsville, Burke Co, Ga, Sam'l Bird.
Bengal, Oneida Co, N Y, Wm Smith.
Mexico, Oneida Co, N Y, Calvin Tiffany.
Scriba, Oneida Co, N Y, Hiel Stone.
Wmstown, Oneida Co, N Y, Sam'l Freeman.
Furnace, Oneida Co, N Y, Marshall Fairsville.
Wilmington, Clinton Co, Ohio, Isaiah Morris.
New Hope, Wayne Co, N C, Nicholas Washington.
Alford, Richmond Co, N C, Warren Alford.
Wmsville, Niagara Co, N Y, Isaac Bowman.
Speedwell Mills, Barnwell dist, S C, Thos G Lamar
Moore's Town, Burlington Co, N _, Thos Porter.
New Boston, Champaign Co, Ohio, Jas Tomplin, jr.
Blackwater, Princess Ann Co, Va, Wm Holt.
Mohontongo, Northumberland Co, Pa, Jacob Achord.
M'Allisterstown, Miffin Co, Pa, Thos Gallagher.
Milton, Stafford Co, N H, Levi Jones.
Big Springs, Wash Co, Md, Jas Kirkpatrick.
Fotheringale, Montg Co, Va, Geo Hancock.
M'Gaheystown, Rockingham Co, Va, Tobias R M'Gahey.
Oppenheim, Montg Co, N Y, Ezekiel Belding.
Norway, Herkimer Co, N Y, Josiah Smith.
Salisbury, Orange Co, N Y, John Caldwell.
Ofcs discontinued: Reynolds, Pa; Leapers Fork, Ten.

WED FEB 24, 1813

Crct Crt of D C, to wit: petiton of Sarah Crookshank & Chas Glover, adms of the est of John Crookshank, dec'd, who died intestate in 1803, leaving the petitioner, Sarah Crookshank, his widow, & Ann, Chas, John & Rich'd Crookshank, his surviving chldrn, who are under the age of 21 yrs. In Feb 1795 the dec'd purchased of Thos Afflick, part of lot 40 in Gtwn, for $1,600. Afflick died in 1797, leaving no heir or legal rep. Crookshank pd to said Afflick, in his life time, $968, with bal pd to the adms of Afflick. In Feb, 1795, Crookshank sold part of said lot to Jas Melvin, of Gtwn, for $640, part of which only has been pd, & no legal title can be made there-for. Pray for appointment of a trustee. -Wm Brent, clk.

Orphans Crt of Wash Co, D C. Prsnl est of John Smith, late a clk in the Treas & of Wash Co, dec'd. -Chas Glover, adm.

THU FEB 25, 1813
Irishmen of Wash City wish to celebrate the Birthday of their tutelar Saint; meet at the hse of Mr David Dobbin, on Sat. Wash.

FRI FEB 26, 1813
Crct Crt of D C-sale of 2 story frame hse on High st, 3 drs above the store of Renner & Buzzard, at present occupied as a groc store by John B Goddard, also 30 ft of ground, the eastern half of lot 49, on *Beall's Addition*, with a small frame hse, the prop of Jeremiah Hazel, dec'd, on Mar 23. -Thos B Ball, Dan Kenner, Th Beatty, jr, com'rs. N B-Apply to Philip Buzzard, High st, Gtwn, for viewing prior to sale.

Young Paymstr, brown stud horse, prop of Isaac Pettit, will be sold on Mar 3, to satisfy a debt due to Geo Burns, obtained against Thos Nevitt. -Geo Burns.

Last notice-claims against the est of Edw Eno, dec'd. -Thos C Wright, Sam'l Rogers, adms, Gtwn.

SAT FEB 27, 1813
Died: in the West Indies, a few wks ago, Lt Reld, U S Navy, late cmder of the brig *Vixen,* which was captured & carried in by the frig *Southampton.*

Orphans Crt of Wash Co, D C. Prsnl est of Benj Patterson, late of said co, dec'd. -Nathan Lufborough, adm.

For sale-the land on which I reside nr Orange Crt Hse, Va, 700 acs; with dwlg hse. -Robt H Rose, Orange Co, Virg, Feb 10, 1813.

MON MAR 1, 1813
Balt [Md] hosp lottery mgrs:

Jas Hindman	Jas Calhoun	Jas Smith
John Walraven	Nicholas Brice	Stewart Brown
Edme Ducatel	P Chatard	Jas Bosley
		Colin Mackenzie

Fifty dollars reward-for runaway, Dick, bright mulatto negro man. -Joshua Chilton, living in Montg Co, Md, nr Conrad's Ferry.

TUE MAR 2, 1813
Army appointments by the Pres & Senate, to be Maj Genr'ls of the U S Army:

Jas Wilkinson	Wm H Harrison	Wm R Davie
Wade Hampton	Aaron Ogden	Morgan Lewis

Affidavit of Medard Labbadie, late resid nr the rvr Raisin, Mich terr. Re: the action on Jan 22, 1813, bet the American forces, Gen Winchester, & the British, Canadians & Indians, said to be commanded by Col St Geo.

WED MAR 3, 1813
Mrd: at Alexandria, on Mar 2, Rich'd Wallack, of Wash City, to Miss Ann Simms, d/o Chas Simms, of Alexandria.

THU MAR 4, 1813
Jas Madison, Pres of the U S; tk the oath of ofc on Mar 4; copy of speech followed.

Died: on Feb 22, in his 66th yr, Rich'd Ponsenby, for many yrs a resident of Bladensburg,

Settlement of est of Rebecca Nally, dec'd, on Mar 20. -Sam N Smallwood, ex'r.

Loudon land for sale, [Va] belonging to Wm D Digges. 2,000 acs-*Short Hills*; & *Valley Tract*, nr Leesburg, 1100 acs. -E Mason, atty in fact, Stafford Co, Va.

FRI MAR 5, 1813
Ranaway-from Ellicott Mills, Md, on Feb 26, Perigrine Johnson, about 17 yrs of age, apprentice to the black-smith's business. -Aquilla Hitchcock.

Hse of Reps-1-Sec of Treas is authorized to pay John Dixon, $329.84, with 6% int, per annum, from Jan 1, 1785 being settlement on certificate #596, issued by Andrew Dunscomb, late com'r of acc'ts for Va, on Dec 23, 1786, to Lucy Dixon, who transferred the same to John Dixon. 2-John Murray, rep of Dr Henry Murray, be allowed the amount of 3 loan-ofc certificates, $2,000, etc, with int from Mar 29, 1782, issued in the name of Henry Murray, signed Francis Hopkinson, treas of loans, countersigned Thos Harwood, am't to be pd to said John Murray. - H Clay, spkr of the Hse o/Reps. 3-Relief of & release of John Redfield, jr, of N Y C, insolvent debtor, from jail. 4-Sum of $500 be pd to Reuben Attwater, as additional allowance for his svcs, as sec of Mich terr, & com'r of land claims. -Wm H Crawford, Pres of the Senate, pro temp, Feb 25, 1813. Apprv'd, Jas Madison

SAT MAR 6, 1813
Notice. Whereas my wife, Nancy Mitchell, having behaved herself in a clandestine manner, very much against my interest, I have thought proper to forwarn all persons from harboring or crediting her on my account, as I will not pay any debts of her contracting hereafter. -Martin Mitchell, Wash, Mar 6.

MON MAR 8, 1813
For sale-some valuable negroes, at the town of Port Tobacco, Md; per deed of trust to Henry S Yater.

TUE MAR 9, 1813
Obit notice-Hon Robt R Livingston, late Chancellor of this state, ambassador to France, expired at his seat in Clermont, on Thu last, at age 70 yrs, we believe. He had lingered some time under a paralytic stroke. Livingston introduced the Merino sheep to this country; also known in the invention & establishment of the steam boat. -Columbian.

Civil appointments proposed by the Pres & confirmed by the Senate, during the late session of Congress:
Ninian Edwards, re-appt'd Gov of Ill Terr.
Thos Posey, of La, to Gov'r of Ind Terr, v Wm H Harrison, rsgnd.
John Gibson, re-appt'd Sec of Ind Ter.
Jas Scott, of Ind, to Judge of Ind Terr.
Geo Poindexter, to Judge of Miss Terr.
Silas Brent, of Terr of Mo, to Judge of that Terr, v John Coburn, rsgnd.
David Howell, of R I, to Judge of the Dist of R I, v David L Barnes, dec'd.
Asher Robbins, U D Atty for dist of R I, v David Howell.
Titus Hutchinson, to U S Atty for dist of Vt.
Thos Rutter, re-appt'd Mrshl of dist of Md.
Isaac P Hutchinson, of Pa, to Cnsl at Lisbon, v Geo Jefferson, dec'd.
Benj C Wilcocks, of Pa, to Cnsl at Canton.
Josiah Meigs, of Ga, to Srvyr Genr'l of U S, v Jared Mansfield, rsgnd.
Cornelius P Van Ness, of Vt, to Coll of dist of Vt, & inspec of Rev for Allburgh.
Ashel W Walworth, of Ohio, to Coll of dist of Erie & inspec of port of Cayahoga.
Jesse M'Call, of La, to Coll of dist of Teche, inspec of port of Nova Iberia.
Ezra Baker, of N J, to Coll & Inspec of dist & port of Great Egg Harbor.
Roger Enos, of Vt, to Coll & Inspec for dist & port of Mumphreymagog.
Jeremiah Bradbury, of Mass, to Coll & Inspec for dist & port of York, in Maine.
Benj Wilmot, of Md, to Srvyr & Inspec for port of Easton.
Hampton M'Intosh, to Naval Ofcr for dist of Savannah.
John Fawn, of Va, to Navy Agent for port of Norfolk, v T Armistead, dec'd.
Henry Elkins, of Mass, to Naval Ofcr for dist of Salem & Beverly.
Columbus Lawson, of La, to Reg of Land Ofc for Eastern dist of La.
Lloyd Posey, of La, to Rec'r of pblc monies for Land Ofc of Estrn dist of La.
Wm Garrard, of La, Rec'r of pblc monies for Land Ofc of Western dist of La.
John Reed, of Miss, Reg of Land Ofc of Madison Co, in Miss Terr.

Reward-$200, for my hse servant, Jos Michaels, who absconded in Sept last; seen at Bath, Berkeley Co, on his way to Pa. He is a slave of light complexion & raised by me from a child. -Dan'l Lee, Winchester, Va.

WED MAR 10, 1813
Good riding horse for sale for the benefit of the creditors of Wm Stewart. -Ben S Forrest, trustee, Gtwn.

THU MAR 11, 1813
Among the losses in the action of the 18th & fell on the 22d: Col John Allen, Maj Elijah M'Clannahan, & Capt John H Woolfolk. -J Winchester, Brig Gen U S A, Fort Geo, Upper Canada, Feb 11, 1813. [Ltr to Sec of War]

Mrd: on Mar 9, by Rev Bishop Asbury, Mr Sam'l McKenny to Miss Maryann Foxall.

PG Co Crt, [Md]-petition of Josias Simpson & Ann Bryan, for division of rl est of John Simpson; same cannot be divided due to size of land & number of interested parties. -John Read Magruder, Clk P G C C.

FRI MAR 12, 1813
Hse o/Reps. An act for the relief of reps of Sam'l Lapsley, dec'd. Settle the acc't of John Lysle & Mgt his wife, late Mgt Lapsley, widow & admx of Sam'l Lapsley, dec'd; be pd $1,000 & $1,360, & int from Mar 22, 1783, issued in the name of Sam'l Lapsley by the com'rs of the army acc'ts for the U S on Jul 1, 1784. -H Clay, spkr of the Hse of Reps. Wm N Crawford, Pres of Senate, pro temp. Apprv'd-Jas Madison, Mar 3, 1813.

Wanted-2 blacksmiths. Apply at G Beall's Nail Factory, nr the Navy Yd, Wash.

Sale-per deed of trust to Thos Holliday & Shadrach Davis; 2 story brick hse & lot on 8th st, Wash, adj the tavern of Mr Drummond. -Nichols L Queen, auct.

SAT MAR 13, 1813
Philip Wirt, insolvent debtor, confined in Wash Co prison. -Wm Brent, clk.

Dwlg hses to be rented. Apply at Tomlinson's Htl, or to Nathaniel P Bixby at *Greenleaf's Point*. -Jas Greenleaf, Wash City.

MON MAR 15, 1813
Law Books, just rec'd by Edw J Coale, 176 Mkt St, Balt, Md.

TUE MAR 16, 1813
Died: at Gtwn, in this Dist, on Mar 10, Gen Thos Meason, of Union Town, Pa, who arrived there last wk, having by exposure on his journey taken a violent cold, which caused his death.

Hse o/Reps. 1-Act for the relief of Susannah Wiley, of Gtwn, D C; the sum of $500, as comp for the svcs of her late hsbnd David Wiley, employed by the Post Mstr Genr'l to survey rd leading from St Mary's, Ga, to Wash City. 2-Gold medal to be presented to Capt Wm Bainbridge, of the frig *Constitution*. 3-Release of Nath'l G Ingraham, Alex'r Phoenix & Wm Nexsen, jr, of N Y C, confined in debtors prison of said city & county.

Copy of ltr, dt'd Algiers, Sep 1, 1812, from Francis Garcia to his wife; an individual captured in the brig *Edwin* of Salem, is printed. He names Capt Smith & Mr Laraby, & conditions of imprisonment. -Balt Patriot

Ignatius Edelin an insolvent debtor, Wash Co, D C. Clotworthy Stephenson appt'd his trustee. -Wm Brent, clk.

Pblc sale of lots 13 & 15 in sq 253, with a good brick hse; deed of trust from Jos Wheaton. -Sam'l Eliot, jr.

Ltrs respecting Mr Daniel Pettibones' air stoves; Mr A Daschkoff, Russian Mnstr, Wash, Mar 7, 1813; Hon Rich'd Rush, Compt of the Treas, Wash City, Mar 8, 1813. Signed, F S Key, John Ott, Danl Bussard, John Abbot, Wm Morgan.

Union Bank of Gtwn; meeting at Mr Semmes' Tavern. -D English, Cashier.

WED MAR 17, 1813
The undersigned believes attempts have been made to rob him of his legal right to his *Steam Distillery*; feels compelled to take every legal step which the laws of the U S will justify to support his Patent. -Wm Gamble, Capitol Hill, Wash, D C.

Pblc sale at the hse of Mr Sylvester Shumway, at the Navy Yd, a variety of hsehld & kitchen furn. -N L Queen, auct.

Pblc sale at Union Tavern in Gtwn, ground in Holmead's addition to Gtwn, in the case of John Woodward against Thos Gamble. -Chas Glover, trustee.

THU MAR 18, 1813
Biographical sketch of Capt Isaac Hull; born at Derby, Conn, s/o the gentleman who distinguished himself in the capture of some whale boats in the Sound during the late war.

Runaway, negro Simon, lately bought of Mr Scott, of PG Co, Md; reward-$30. -Thos Ewell

Mrd: in Centerville, on Mar 9, by Rev Jeremiah Moore, Geo Wash Lane, of Fayette Co, Pa, to Miss Frances T Adams, of Fairfax Co, Va.

Fielder Parker, jr, insolvent debtor; Henry B Joy, trustee. -Wm Brent, clk, D C.

Tract of Land cld *Long Meadows*, on boundary line of the city & Turnpike rd to Balt, purchased for the purpose of selling half of it. -Thos Ewell

Passengers on the Swedish ship *Redligheten*, Capt Hanson, from London, & 29 days from Kingston, Jamaica, in Ballast, to Lenox & Maitland. John Wallace, late mstr of the schr *Three Friends;* Wm Shields, of brig *Cyrus*; Geo Hazleton, of N Y; A P Aner, of brig *Dorothea*; Edwin T Satterwhite, purser of the late brig *Vixen*; Sam'l Horsely, surg of do; Jas Conlon, midshipman of do; Jacob Small, surg of privateer *Jos & Mary*; Russel Stevens, of schr *Mary*; Wm Orr, of do; Chas Hurst, of *Three Friends*; Z Washington, of *Vixen*; Edw Patten, boy, of the *Jos & Mary;* Ben Melhado, of Charleston; Jas Hanna, surg of the *Saratoga,* & ____ Stran, of Phil. N Y, Mar 13.

FRI MAR 19, 1813
Jos Etter, insolvent debtor, confined in Wash Co prison. -Wm Brent, clk.

Reward-$100; the shop of Chas E Eckel, watchmkr, Gtwn, D C, was opened by a false key on Mar 9th, & watches [itemized list] were taken.

Reward-$40, for two mulatto fellows, Jesse & David. Deliver to Geo Sweeny, Pr Wm Co, Va.

SAT MAR 20, 1813
Six cents reward for appr boy, Jonas Granger, about 20 yrs of age, absconded on Mar 15. -Barton Harriss, Montg crt hse, Md.

Wanted-a journeyman cabinet-mkr. - B M Belt.

P O changes, Feb 1813:
Salina, N Y, John P Sherwood v Nehemiah H Earle, rmv'd.
Zelienople, Pa, John Shriver v Andrew M'Clure, rsgnd.
Hanover C H, Va, John Thornton, jr, v Benj Hooper, situation inconvenient.
Stroudsburg, Pa, Sam'l Gummere.
Little Falls, N Y, Sam'l Smith v Wm Alexander, dec'd.
Trumansburg, N Y, Herman Camp v C Comstock, rsgnd.
Millerstown, Pa, Henry Walters v Thos Cochran, do.
Enfield, N C, John H Bailey v Wm Bradford, rsgnd.
Greenup C H, Ky, Sam'l L Crawford v Joshua Bartley, rsgnd.
Concord, Mass, John Keys v John L Tuttle, do.
New Canton, Va, Thos Pittman v Wm Woodson, do.
Hendersonville, Va, Isaac Oliver v Sam'l B Iter, do.
Carnesville, Pa, Caleb Trevor v John B Trevor, do.
Lunenburg C H, Va, Miles Jordan v Jas Bagley, do.
Farnham, Va, Mickel Saunders v Geo Saunders, do.
Bethlehem, Pa, Francis C Kampmann v Geo Huber, dec'd.
Broadfield, Va, Jeremiah B Jett v John Storke, dec'd.
De Kalb, N Y, Potter Goff v J B Benedict, rsgnd.
Carver, Mass, Jas Ellis v J Shaw, situation inconvenient.
Estill C H, Ky, Elijah Broaddus. Re-establishment.
Bridgewater, N Y, Absalom L Groves v D Rindge.
Bath, N C, John R Hoyle v T Butler, mv'd away.
Thornsbury, Va, Robt Foster v Edw Thornton, rsgnd.
Louisburg, N C, Robt J Taylor v Rich'd Fox, do.
Darien, Ga, Scott Cray v Jas Hamilton, do.
Jacksonboro, Ga, Wm T Killbee, v A Newman.
Houstonville, S C, A S Duvall, v C Houston, rsgnd.
Colchester, Va, Thos Morgan v P Waggoner, dec'd.
Wentworth, N H, Wm Moore v Caleb Keith, rsgnd.
Butler C H, Ky, David Morrison v J Love.
Palmyra, Ten, Wm L Brown v S Vance.
Marrs Bluff, S C, John W Thompson v Jaques Bishop, mv'd away.
Harrodsburg, Ky, Jos M'Murtry v Wm M'Bride, rsgnd.
Chenango Point, N Y, Wm Woodruff v J M'Kinney, mv'd away.
Madison, Ga, John Conyngham v Abraham M'Afee, dec'd.
Canisteo, N Y, Geo Hornell, jr, v Geo Hornell, dec'd.
Paradise, Pa, David Wetmore, jr, v J T Lightner, rsngd.

New ofcs & postmstrs: So Canna, Litchfield Co, Conn, Wm M Burrall.
Bloody Run, Bedford Co, Pa, Philip Campher.
Wilmington, Fluvanna Co, Va, Geo W Richardson.
Morganfield, Union Co, Ky, Ebenezer Briggs.
Beach Grove, Luzerne Co, Pa, Nathaniel Beach.
Dixville, Henry Co, Va, Thos Dix.
Harmony, Sussex Co, N J, Thos Stewart.
Litchfield, Grayson Co, Ky, Wm Conningham.
Boxford, Essex Co, Mass, Parker Spafford.
St Martins, Worcester Co, Md, Sam'l Showell, jr.
Newberry, Burlington Co, N J, Wilson M'Gowan.
Provine, Clarke Co, Ind Ter, Wm Provine.
Trapp, Talbot Co, Md, Wm Dickinson.
North Western Camp, army of the U S, Jas Abbott.
Isle Hooket Falls, Rockingham Co, N H, Rich'd Ayre.
Scataquoy Village, Hillsborough Co, N H, Jas Parker.
Goffstown, Hillsborough Co, N H, Thos Jamison.
Owosgo, Cayuga Co, N Y, Stephen Chiles.
Pleasant Valley, Duchess Co, N Y, Amasa Angell.
Blooming Grove, Orange Co, N Y, Sam'l Moffatt.
King Wm Mills, King Wm Co, Va, John Segar.
Bridgefield, Shelby Co, Ken, Wm Bridgewater.
Augusta, Oneida Co, N Y, Sam'l Chandler.
Nesbitt's Iron Works, Spartansburg Dist, S C, Wilson Nesbitt.
Ewingsville, Rutherford Co, N C, Hugh Guise.
Caruthsville, Lincoln Co, N C, John Caruth.
Mooresboro, Rutherford Co, N C, Lemuel Moore.
Ofcs discontinued: Sidney, N Y; Little Britain, N Y.

Neal McNantz, insolvent debtor, confined in Wash Co prison. Wm Brent, clk.

MON MAR 22, 1813
Land for sale-deed of trust from Alex'r Lithgou to Chas Tyler & Alex'r Lithgou, jr: 800 acs nr Dumfries with dwlg hse. -Philip Harrison, atty in fact for Chas Tyler & A Lithgou, Dumfries, Va.

Reward-$5 for strayed Bay Mare. Basil Club, nr Booth's wharf in Wash City.

TUE MAR 23, 1813
Mrd: at the hse of John B Colvin, in Wash City, on Mar 22, by Rev Mr McCormick, Mr Kennedy Burns, Merchant of N Y, to Mrs Charlotte Creusa Rowe.

Died: in Wmsburg, Va, on Mar 8, Hon Wm Nelson, one of the judges of the genr'l crt of this commonwealth, prof of law & police in Wm & Mary Un, in his 54th yrs.

Died: at Ft Moultrie, on Feb 10, Capt Addison Bowles Armistead, of 1st Regt U S Artl; srv'd his country in the army for 18 yrs. His remains were interred at Ft Johnson, on Mar 13, with military honors. -Charleston Pa.

For sale-three lg brick hses, joining each other on Water st, nr the middle of this town. -Sabret Scott, Gtwn.

Committed to the goal of Fred'k Co, Md, runaway, Sam Anderson, a dark mulatto man, about 23 yrs of age. He says he belongs to Mr Geo Peter of Gtwn, D C. -Morris Jones, Shrf, Fred'k Co, Md.

WED MAR 24, 1813
Muster roll found on the *Macedonian*, after her capture by the *Decatur*, & impressed Americans on board that frig, 2 of whom were killed, another drowned at sea. Christopher Dodge, American, aged 22; Peter Johnson, American, aged 21; John Alexander, of Cape Ann, aged 29; C Dolphin, of Conn, aged 22; Maj Cook, of Balt, aged 27; Wm Thompson, of Boston, aged 20, drowned at sea; John Wallis, American, aged 23, killed in the action in the Macedonian; John Card, American, aged 27, killed in the action in the Macedonian. -Bos Chr.

Whereas my wife Nelly Barnes has left my bed & board without any provocation, I therefore forbid all persons trusting her on my acc't, as I will pay no debts of her contracting after this date-I do also forewarn all persons harboring her at the risk of the law. -Peter Barnes, Wash City, Mar 24.

Pblc sale at the new bldgs of Simon Meade, oppo Mr Andrew Way's, the prnsl est of the late Archibald Sager, dec'd, consisting of carpenter & joiner tools. -Dr Rapine, Simon Meade, excs.

Stray cow came to my prop. -Bridget Connelly, nr Walter Jones, Wash, Mar 24.

THU MAR 25, 1813
Died: suddenly, in Gtwn, Oliver Whipple, cnslr at law, formerly of Hampton, nr Portsmouth, N H. Mr W slept at his ofc, & was in the practice of only dining at his brdg hse; he had been absent from Fri the 12th to Mon the 15th. Search found him dead in his ofce; probable that he died on Sun. Remains were interred on Tue, Mar 16. -F R.

Pblc sale of lots in Wash City; Crct Crt of D C, sitting in suit bet Chas Minifie, John Fry, & Sam'l Spalding, cmplnts, & Geo Walker, dfndnt. Purchasers at sale of Jan 17, 1812, failed to pay the purchase money; resale on Apr 3. -P B Key, Wm Brent.

FRI MAR 26, 1813
Orphans Crt of Wash Co, D C. Prsnl est of Peter Prevote, late of said co, dec'd. -Mary Prevote, admx, Mar 25, 1813.

SAT MAR 27, 1813
Died: on Jan 4 last, in his 33d yr, Capt Geo Wash Reed, at Spanishtown, in the island of Jamaica; y/s/o the late Pres Reed, of Pa. The *Vixen* was the first he ever

had independent command of was captured by the *Southampton* frig. He was shipwrecked & died a prisoner among strangers.

To the editors, Mar 25, 1813. Ltr regarding impressed seamen. In 1803, & bound for Bombay, I beheld my countrymen in the svc of the E India Co, John Carr & John Brown, both of Newport, R I. Carr, whose fr is a mechanic in Newport, had been in navy svc for 8 yrs, & was transferred to the *Glatton* in 1803. J Brown was a sailor, a mrd man with 3 chldrn in Newport, & in cruel bondage for 7 yrs. I called on his fr, a shoemkr, when I returned in 1807 to American. -Nath'l G M Senter.

Notice-sale of lot 16 in sq 1046, prop of Chas Minifie, with 2 story brick hse. Lot 1, in sq 847, with a 1 story brick hse, the prop of Wm Small. Both to satisfy taxes due the Corp of Wash City. -John Queen, Coll of 4th Ward, Wash.

MON MAR 29, 1813
Mrs M Sweeney rec'd a few handsome straw bonnets as patterns for her spring assortments. Mar 25.

TUE MAR 30, 1813
Died: in Wash City, on Mar 15, Alvin Converse, a ntv of Staffford, Conn. His distant relatives may rest assured that Alvin met with every attention on the bed of sickness that his situation demanded; he was truly faithful to his employer, & peculiarly obliging in his manner.

Thos Hughes & E Lindsley have entered in the business, under the firm of Hughes & Lindsley, liquors & groceries. Store oppo the Indian Queen Hotel.

Henry V Hill & Chas R Belt have commenced the cabinet business on Capitol Hill, in the hse lately occupied as a cabinet-mkr's shop by Mr Henry Ingle, Wash.

Notice to creditors of Henry O Dyer, of Chas Co, Md, dec'd. -Jeremiah Dyer.

Wash Co, D C. I certify that Ann Casanave, of said co, brought before me a stray bay mare. -T Fenwick, J P.

WED MAR 31, 1813
Com'rs of the Wash Turnpike Co: *Gtwn, D C*-John Mason, Wash Bowie, Thos Peter, Clement Smith & Dan'l Bussard. *Wash City*: Chas Carroll, Daniel Carroll of Dudn, Wm Brent, Tench Ringgold, Robt Brent. *Rockville*: Upton Beall, Thos P Wilson, Brice Selby, Honore Martin, & Rich'd Anderson. *Fredericktown*: John M'Pherson, John Graham, Geo Baer, Francie Mantz, & Henry Kuhn. *Elizabethtown*: Wm Fitzhugh, Moses Tabbs, Upton Lawrence, Frisby Tilghman, & Otho H Stull.

THU APR 1, 1813
Wash Library meeting on Apr 5. -John C Steiner, Librarian.

David Ott & Co, garden seeds. Pa av, Wash City.

FRI APR 2, 1813
Biographical sketch of Arnold Henry Dohrman, died at Steubenville, Ohio, on Mar 21, in his 65th yr, leaving a wife & 11 chldrn. Committee of Foreign Affairs-Mr D, merchant of Lisbon, hath from the commencement of the present war, manifested a warm & steady attachmen to the cause & interest of the U S. He assisted a number of American prisoners carried into the ports of Portugal with money & other necessaries. He arrv'd in this country in 1783.

Fire on Mar 23, Easton, Md, discovered in the kitchen of the hse occupied by the widow Sewell, belonging to Mr Bennett, spread till it came to John G Emory's hse, & the hse lately occupied as the Monitor's ofc; devasting Mr Applegarth's carriage-mkr's shop; destroying 43 hse, but no lives were lost.

Died: on board the U S frig, *Constitution*, at sea, on Jan 28, of wounds rec'd in the action with the *Java*, John Cushing Alwyn.

Hartford Mercury announces the death of Joel Barlow, a ntv of this state. Mr Barlow died in Cracovia, Poland, on his return from Wilna to Paris on Dec 26 last.

SAT APR 3, 1813
Judges in the election in the Third Ward of Wash City, on Apr 5, to fill the vacancy of Benj G Orr, rsgnd. -Thos Dunn, Robt Collett, Jas Young.

Columbian steam boat for sale-at Tyber creek wharf. H Bestor, treas.

Headqrtrs Wash, Mar 3, 1813-John P Van Ness, Brig Gen Mil Dist Col.
Dates of commission: John Tayloe, Lt Col Com'dt, Jan 30, 1813; Major [vacant.]
Columbian Dragoons: Wm Thornton, Capt-Jun 6, 1811; John Law, First Lt, do; vacant-2d Lt; Samuel Burch, Cornet, Jun 6, 1811.
Gtwn Hussars: John Peter, Capt, Jun 6, 1811; J S Williams, First Lt, Jun 15, 1811; Wm G Ridgely, 2d Lt, May 30, 1812; Jas Cassin, Cornet, do.
Wash Light Horse: Elias B Caldwell, Capt, May 30, 1812; R C Weightman, 1st Lt, do; N L Queen, 2d Lt, do; W B Randolph, Cornet, do.
Alexandria Dragoons: J H Mandeville, Capt, Jun 6, 1811; Wm H Maynadier, 1st Lt, no date; John Dulany, 2d Lt, May 8, 1811; Robt Conway, Cornet, do.
Adjutant-G C Washington; Qrtrmstr-Wm Crawford; Paymstr-Daniel Brent; Surg-Dr G Clarke; Sgt Maj-Nicholas Worthington; Qrtrmstr-not yet appt'd.

MON APR 5, 1813
Sam'l Prioleau, an old & respected inhabitant & ntv of Charleston, died in that city on Mar 23d, in his 71st yr. After the fall of Charleston, with a band of patriots, at St Augustine, he was made to sustain all the sufferings heaped upon him by the enemy. His wife & family of young chldrn were banished from their home & transported to Phil.

Crt Martial of trial of Lt Sam'l B Ellis, of First Legion, acquitted him of the charge exhibited against him, & the Pres of the U S approved his sentence; his sword will be returned to him. -Gen John P Van Ness; John Cox, Brig Maj-Militia of D C.

Those indebted to Thos Baker are to come forward to S Baker & Edw Dyer. Settlement at Mrs Coolidge's brdg hse, next dr to Dr John Ott's, Gtwn.

TUE APR 6, 1813
Ladies with ltrs in the P O at Wash City, Apr 1, 1813:

Mary Berry	Nancy Butler	Mrs Mary E Benton
Mrs Anna Coats	Eliza Ervin	Eliz Frankling
Mary Healy	Ann Handy	Eliz Hooper
Ann Hodge	Jane Johnson	Eliza M Love
Eliz Lyon	Clarissa Mattingly	Rebecca C Mackall
Mrs Mason	Mrs Eliza Oiliver	Sarah Robinson
Mary B Rogerson	Mrs Suns	Nancy Thomas
Maria Vanzandt	Susanna Warwick	Mary Y White
Sarah Wood	Martha Williams	Mary D White

WED APR 7, 1813
Died: on Mar 21, at the hse of John T Mason, of Lexington, Ky, Mrs Mary Armistead Howard, consort of Gov Howard.

Robt Saunders, of Wmsburg, appt'd by the Exec of Va, a judge of the Gen Crt, to supply the vacancy occasioned by the death of Judge Wm Nelson.

Thos Fenwick of Wash Co, D C, brought before me a trespassing horse. -Robt Brent

THU APR 8, 1813
Sale at the hse of Jos L Scholfield, nr the city P O, groceries, crockery, Smith's tools, & a Hackney carriage. -Jos Forrest, auct.

PG Co, Md. Jos Wilson, jr, of said co, brought before me a stray sorrel horse. -Thos Bowie, Bladensburg Mills.

Notice: Capt Theophilus Bowie, late cmder of the schn'r Alexandria, has been dischg'd from our employ. -Wm Ball, Balt; Bede Clements, Alexandria.

For sale-lot 21 in sq 665; lot 3 in sq 666; lot 2 in sq 654, in Wash City, late the prop of Mr Francis Campbell, dec'd. Sale at the late resid of the dec'd in Annapolis city.

Thos Essom proposes to commence teaching vocal music at Christ Chr, nr the Navy Yd, on Apr 6, & at the usual place in Gtwn.

FRI APR 9, 1813
Bank of Columbia has declared a 8% dividend. -Wm Whann, cashier.

Mrd: on Mar 27, by Rev Mr McCormick, Mr John C Brush to Mrs Mary Doyne, both of Wash City.

Mrd: on Apr 8, by Rev Mr McCormick, Mr G C Grammer to Miss Eliza Doyne, both of Wash City.

SAT APR 10, 1813
D C-on Jun 1, 1812, Francis S Key, Pres of Gtwn Lancaster School, deposited in this ofce a bk, the right he claims as proprietor in the following words: American Edition of sets of Lancaster Lessons, [etc.] -G Deneale, clk, D C.

Nancy Brown, mulatto woman, committed to Fred'k Co, Md, jail, as a runaway; age about 25 yrs. Says she was manumitted by Mr Jas Armstrong, who resides at the head of McElderry's dock in Balt city. -Morris Jones, shrf, Fred'k Co, Md.

MON APR 12, 1813
Va election returns: *Princess Ann Co*-Swepson Whitehead, 189 votes; Thos Newton, 108 votes. *Richmond Co*-J P Hungerford, 111 votes; John Taliaferro, 99.

TUE APR 13, 1813
Mrd: at Norfolk, on Apr 3, by Rev Mr Symes, Mr Benj Bryan, Sailing Mstr of the U S frig *Constellation*, to Mrs Mgt Haynes.

Ranaway, negro, Nick, age 56 yrs old, from Josiah Prather, living in PG Co, Md, nr Vansville-reward $20.

Crct Crt of Wash Co, D C. Mrshl's sale of 2 story brick hse on sq 690, fronting on So B st, the lot on ground rent; suit of Thos Baker & Elisha Riggs, against Henry Timms & others. -Wash Boyd, Mrshl, D C.

WED APR 14, 1813
Wash Co, D C. Philip Webster brought before me a stray bay horse. -Nicholas Young, J P. Philip Webster, mgr for Dr John Shaeff.

Schn'r *Gen Armstrong*, Guy R Champlin, cmder, of N Y, mounts guns-Mar 11, 1813, against frig. Killed: John Lenox & Ansel Waters, of New London; Geo Deravere, Isaac Hedges, & Jos Johnson, of N Y; John Dial, black, of Alexandria. Wounded-Philip Wiseman, of Providence, R I, since dead. Wounded dangerously: Capt Guy R Champlin; Anthony Frances, Peter Pegau, Andrew Bells, Jas Williams, Peter La Reuse, John Martin. Slightly: Henry Betts, prize mstr; Amos Wright, Abraham Deravere, David Blinn, Geo B Bush, Jas Coffin, Henry Fombell, & Dan'l Charies [black man.]

Va election returns. Charlotte Co for Cong: John Randolph-345; John W Eppes-177. Ise of Wight Co: Jas Johnson-278; Edwin Gray-25. Fred'k co: John Smith, Rep-357; Robt Page, Fed-153. To Jas Pleasants, jr, John Dawson, Thos Gholson, Peterson Goodwyn, there is no opposition in their respective districts. Loudon co:

John Love, Rep-165; Jos Lewis, Fed-484.

THU APR 15, 1813
A monument was erected by Mrs Barlow to the memory of her hsbnd, Joel Barlow, Mnstr of the U S at Paris, dec'd, at Zarnowitch, Poland, Dec 26, 1812.

Died: on Apr 14, Mr Rich'd Barry, painter of Wash City, aged about 34 yrs. Funeral from the hse of Mr Orlando Cook at 3 o'clock this day.

FRI APR 16, 1813
Dirs of the Wash Library:
Jas Laurie [Pres]	Thos H Gilliss	Moses Young
Jonathan S Findlay	Geo Way	Wm Parker [Treas]
Jos Stretch	John C Steiner [Lib]	

SAT APR 17, 1813
Bozman's History of Md, 3 yrs after its settlement. Geo Calvert then Gov of the province in the yr 1638; Mar 14-bill for the attainder of Wm Clayborne; Thos Smith cld to the bar; depositions produced of John Tarbison & Arthur Brooks. Then departed out of the Hse, Capt Cornwaleys, Cuthbert Fenwick, Wm Lewis, John Nevill, Anthony Cotton, Edw Fleete, & Cyprian Thoroughgood. The Hse mv'd to inquire of the death of Wm Ashmore, Ratcliff Warren, John Bellson, & Wm Dawson. The name of the dissentient mbr appears to be John Halfehide. Jrn'l of the Hse-Mar 15: then was fined to the lord proprietor Thos Baldridge, 40 lb tobacco for striking John Edwards.

Rich'd Cutts appt'd Super Genr'l of Military Supplies.

Pews for sale in Christ Chr, Vestry of Wash Parish. -Henry Ingle, Reg.

Patent Lever watches for sale. Jacob Leonard, Gtwn.

Blacking shop to open on May 4 nr Wash Tavern. -John B Adams & Co.

Orphans Crt of PG Co, Md. Sale of prsnl prop of Wm Ponsonby, dec'd; valuable bks & furn. -Jas McCormick, adm.

MON APR 19, 1813
Died: on Wed wk, in his 76th yr, at his residence, nr the borough of Harrisburgh, Cumberland Co, Robt Whitehill, for many yrs, & at the time of his decease, a mbr of Cong from Pa.

Pontius D Stelle, insolvent debtor, confined in Wash Co prison. -Wm Brent, clk.

TUE APR 20, 1813
Mrd: in N Y, on Apr 13, by Rev Mr Bowen, Nathan Sanford, U S Atty for the dist of N Y, to Miss Mary E M Isaacs, d/o Col Ralph Isaacs, of Ga.

Died: on Apr 4, at his seat in Westmoreland, Va, the Hon Rich'd Parker, one of the Judges of the Genr'l Crt, of that state, in his 84th yr.

Died: in Weymer, Germany, in advanced age, the celebrated poet Wieland, cld the Virgil of Germany.

Crct Crt of Wash Co, D C. Pblc sale in Wash City, 2 lots in sq 742 on N J av; in the case of Jas D Barry, against Patrick Barry & the heirs & reps of Garret Barry, dec'd. -Jas Davidson, Chas Glover, Trustees.

For sale-3 valuable servants. -Ann Lee

WED APR 21, 1813
Tribute of respect to the memory of John Hart, Jos Williams, & Hannibal Boyd, 3 of the crew of the *Hornet* Sloop of War, who lost their lives in an attempt to save part of the crew of the *Peacock*, a British vessel they had just captured-she sunk & the whole perished together. -Americanus, Apr 12, 1813.

Wash Co, D C. Anthony Thornton, insolvent debtor, confined in Wash Co prison. -Wm Brent, clk.

THU APR 22, 1813
Extract of a ltr from Walter Jordan, a non-commissioned ofcr of the regulars at Ft Wayne, to his wife in Allegheny Co, dt'd Ft Wayne, Oct 19, 1812. Re: attack by Kickapoo & Wynbago Indians.

Phil Freeman's jrnl of Tue-announcement of the death of Dr Benj Rush, who died on Monday, of typhus fever; a patriot of the Revolution.

FRI APR 23, 1813
Died: at Newark, N J, on Apr 18, from wound rec'd from the accidental discharge of a pistol on Monday wk, Geo Chas Herford, Cashier of the Bank at Newark, in the 32d yr of his age.

For sale-valuable snug little farm, about 80 to 100 acs, within 4 miles of Gtwn; land in the District. I will also sell a hse & lot on Gay st. -Jos S Belt

SAT APR 24, 1813
Reward-$15 for strayed bay horse; raised in Wash Co, Pa; mgr-Mr Francis Clements, living nr Bladensburg. -Wm Dudley Digges.

MON APR 26, 1813
Money lost bet Wash City & Balt city, Md. -Exum Newby, Perquimines Co, N C.

Orphans Crt of PG Co, Md. Sale of prnsl prop of Nathan Prather, dec'd, 2 miles from Vansville. -Walter Prather..

York, Pa, Apr 17. Trial of Sam'l Harman, & Eliz Eaton, m/o Sam'l Harman, on an indictment for the murder of Mgt Harman, w/o said Sam'l Harman; who died on Feb 27 last. Verdict of the jury-Eliz Eaton guilty of murder in the first degree; Sam'l Harman in the second.

For sale-negro man cld David, prop of John A Burford, to satisfy taxes due the Corp of Wash. -Z Walker, col 3d Ward.

TUE APR 27, 1813
John S Bridges manufactures cordials, cakes & confectionary, nr the coffe hse, Gtwn.

P O changes in Mar, 1813:
Mechanicksburg, Pa, Jacob Krout v Jos Jones, mv'd away.
Sempronius, N Y, Rowland Day v Gershom Morse, rsgnd.
Ossippee, N H, Moses Colby v D Gilman, situation inconvenient.
Canfield, Ohio, Elijah Wadsworth v Harman Canfield, mv'd away.
Claytonsville, N C, David Johnson v Lambert Clayton, do.
Newburyport, Mass, Chas Turner, jr v Caleb Cross.
Hamilton, N Y, Thos H Hubbard v John A Smith, rsgnd.
Pulaski, Ten, Henry Hogan v David Martin, do.
Duanesburg, N Y, John Titus v Ichabod Fuller, do.
Peru, N Y, Asa Elmore v Henry De Lord, mv'd away.
Grand Isle, Vt, Abraham H W Hyde v E Beardsley, rsgnd.
Bennington, Vt, Henry Robinson v O C Merrill, do.
Parkinson's ferry, Pa, Geo Wyeth v Adam Hailman, dec'd.
Strasburg, Va, Sam'l Gardner v Alex'r Hite.
Middlebrook Mills, Md, Edw Trail v T Saunders, dec'd.
Pocotaligo, S C, Wm Martin v Matthew Mullen, mv'd away.
Cairo or Craigfont, Ten, John Brown v J Winchester, absent.
Great Bridge, Va, Bressie Lewis v Thos Bartee, rsgnd.
Lower Somers' Pt, N J, Gideon Leeds v John Somers, jr, situation inconvenient.
Canterbury, N H, Ezekiel Morrill v Jos M Harper, rsgnd.
Lewisville, S C, Geo Gill v Thos S Miles, rsgnd.
Willingboro, Pa, Jonathan Dimon v Chas Dimon, rsgnd.
Madisonville, O T, Allan D Thorn v Jas Gaines, mv'd away.
Coatesville, Pa, Isaac Coates v Moses Coates, rsgnd.
Hadley, N Y, Chas Carpenter v John W Taylor, rsgnd.
Carnesville, Ga, Wm Terrill v John R Brown.
Waterford, Pa, Enoch L Anderson v Enoch Anderson, rsgnd.
Moorestown, N J, Gilbert Page v Robt Anan, mv'd away.
Dubose's Ferry, S C, Elias Dubose v Dan'l Dubose, rsgnd.
Solon, N Y, Chester Allen v Simon Phelps, do.
Harwinton, Conn, Joel Bradley v Wm Woodruff, do.
Maysville, N Y, Chas B Rouse v A Potter.
Short Creek, Va, Rich'd Simms v Sam'l Chambers, rsgnd.
Yarmouth, Mass, Joshua Hamben v Henry Thatcher, situation inconvenient.
Wheatsboro, Ohio, Revee Wood v Nathan Wood, dec'd.

Gorham, N Y, Rodolphus Morse v Parley Gates, dec'd.
Jericho, N Y, Dan'l Underhill v Fred'k A De Zong, rsgnd.
Middlefield, Mass, Edmund Kelso v J Mack.
Allison's store, Ga, Jos Hundley v Wm B Allison, rsgnd.
Danville, Pa, Rudolph Sechler v Dan'l Montgomery, dec'd.
Newville, Pa, Andrew M'Cord v H Adams, rsgnd.
Averasboro, N C, Dusher Shaw v John Smith, do.
Montgomery C H, Md, Enoch Busson v Thos P Wilson, do.
Woolwich, Me, Robt Wright v Sam'l Trott, situation inconvenient.
Sutton, Mass, Jacob March, jr v Estes Howe, rsgnd.
Granville, N Y, Henry Bulkeley v Stephen Thorn, dec'd.
New Salem, Mass, Nahum Bryant v Obadiah Townshend, dec'd.
Salem, N Y, Geo Reab v Wm Gray, mv'd away.
Greensboro, Md, John Matthews v Robt Fountain, mv'd away.
Winchester, N H, Jonas Bruce v Henry Pratt, rsgnd.

New ofcs est'd & postmstrs-Mar 1813:

So Salem, West Chester Co, N Y, Gould Hawley.
Little River, Buncomb Co, N C, Epaphroditus Hightower.
Centre Camp of the Army of the U S, Jos B Varnum, jr.
Sidney, Kennebeck Co, Me, Stephen Springer.
Webster, Lancaster Co, Pa, Joshua Webster.
Bell Air, Lancaster dist, S C, Fowler Williams.
Brown's Mill, Miffin Co, Pa, Wm Brown, jr.
M'Cullochsville, Union Co, S C, Jas M'Cullock
Middletown, Fred'k Co, Va, Jacob Danner.
Schellsburg, Bedford Co, Pa, Jacob Schell.
Village Hill, Nottoway Co, Va, Abraham Buford.
Barkhamstead, Litchfield Co, Conn, Judah Roberts.
Bowler's, Essex Co, Va, Wm Smith.
Barnardstown, Franklin Co, Mass, Gideon Ryther.
Assumption, Lafourch Co, La, Bela Hubbard.
Hebron, Tolland Co, Conn, John T Peters.
Hollow, Dutchess Co, N Y, Wm Germond.
Randolph, Broome Co, N Y, Jas Moore.
Sparta, Ontario Co, N Y, Sam'l Stillwell.
Sackett's Harbor, N Y, Sam'l Shaw.
German Coast, German Co, La, Sam'l M'Cutchen.
Montrose, Cumberland Co, N C, John Graham
Readsboro, Clearfield Co, Pa, Alex'r Read.
Durham, Northampton Co, Pa, Morgan Long.
Hop Bottom, Luzerne Co, Pa, Putman Catlin.
Marietta, Lancaster Co, Pa, Sam'l Bailey.
Hyattstown, Montgomery Co, Md, Lemuel Nicholls.
Felizville, Cumberland Co, Va, Newton Ford.
Ofcs discontinued: Marlboro, N Y; Istapatchy, Miss terr; Bursontown, Pa.

Died: on Apr 19, at Buckland, the seat of John Love, in Pr Wm Co, Virg, Sam'l Love Watson, eldest s/o Mr Jas Watson; mortally wounded by the passage of a wheel of a loaded wagon over his breast.

WED APR 28, 1813
Zephaniah Farrell has obtained an auctioneer licence for Wash City; his residence is on Pa av, Wash City.

THU APR 29, 1813
For sale-valuable water lot, lot 1 in sq 705, on the Eastern Branch. -Geo A Carroll.

Bath Berkeley Springs, Va, nr Martinsburg. Subscriber-Robt Bailey. [Ad]

FRI APR 30, 1813
Mrd: at Balt, on Apr 27, by Rev Arch-Bishop Carroll, Dan'l Brent, of Wash City, to Miss Eliza Walsh, d/o Robt Walsh, of Balt, Md.

Scows, truck wheels & wheel barrows, prop of Jas Cochrane, to be sold in the basin of the Canal on Tue. David Bates, auct, Wash ad.

Wash Co, D C. Thos B Dyer, insolvent debtor, confined in the Wash Co prison. -Wm Brent, clk.

SAT MAY 1, 1813
Orphans Crt of Wash Co, D C. Prsnl est of Rich'd Barry, late of said city, dec'd. -Peter Lenox, exc.

MON MAY 3, 1813
Nat l Advocate-documents worthy of attention regarding impressment. Beekman Ver Plank Hoffman, of Poughkeepsie, lt in U S navy; lt on the frig *Constitution* in the action & capture of the Guerriere, etc. Dt'd Apr 16, 1813, B V Hoffman. Rich'd Tompkins, ntv of Ulster, oppo Pouchkeepsie, on board the frig *Warren*, Wm Kelly Capt, for Cork. Rich'd [X] Tompkins, Apr 17, 1813.

Runaway-Emanuel Groomes, negro about 36 yrs of age, committed to Fred'k Co, Md, jail; says he belongs to Mr Sam'l Chase o/Balt city. -Morris Jones, shrf, Fred'k Co, Md.

TUE MAY 4, 1813
Biog of Mr Joel Barlow, Mnstr Pleni of U S of American; born in 1735, in Reading, Conn; mrd in 1781, Miss Baldwin of New Haven, sister/o the senator of that name.

Died: on Apr 21, at Annapolis, Rev Ralph Higginbotham, long the V-Princ of St John's College of that state, & a mnstr of the Eng Episc Chr.

Wash Co, D C. Wm B Carrier appt'd trustee for the creditors of Albin Howe, insolvent debtor.

Sale of numerous lots in Wash City, by the excs of David Peter. -Sarah Peter, Geo Peter, L H Johns.

WED MAY 5, 1813
To be sold for their jail fees, at the Wash Co jail, Betsey Baker alias Betsey Gillis, negro, about 40 yrs of age; & Sam Hanson, negro, about 27 yrs of age. -C Tippett, for W Boyd, mrshl.

Jas Laurie is Pres of the Wash Library.

THU MAY 6, 1813
Impressment: Elijah Sterling is a ntv of Dorchester Co, in this state, where svr'l of his relations live; he seems to have little chance of seeing any of them shortly, except a bro in our svc, whom he may meet one day in battle. -Jas H M'Culloch. [Ltr followed dt'd Port Royal Dock Yd, 1813, *Dear Uncle*.]

Reward-$100 for Anthony, negro slave, prop of the late Wm B Page, dec'd; age about 28 yrs. -Thos Swann, Edmond I Lee, admrs of Wm B Page, dec'd, Alexandria.

FRI MAY 7, 1813
Meeting of the Ctzns of Wash City, Alexandria & Gtwn, on May 5, 1813; Gen Robt Young cld to the chair; Jos Gales, jr, Sec. Mgrs appointed:

of Wash:
John P Van Ness	Jas H Blake
Walter Jones, jr	Sam'l H Smith
Patrick Magruder	

of Gtwn:
Chas A Beatty	Chas Carroll of Belle Vue
Thos Corcoran	Jas S Morsell
John Ott	

of Alexandria:
Robt Young	Francis Peyton
Adam Lynn	Jos Dean
Amos Alexander	

of Md:
Robt Bowie	Jos Kent
Lloyd Magruder	

of Va:
Thompson Mason	Wm Moss
John Thos Ricketts.	

SAT MAY 8, 1813
Furnished Hse & Stable, to let. Apply to Thady Hogan, on the premises, North F st, nr St Patrick's Chr, Wash City.

Mrd: on May 6, by Rev Mr M'Cormick, Mr Jonathan Elliot to Miss Sarah Evans, both of Wash City.

Ralph Charlton informs his friends & the pblc that he continues to keep his old established stand on 7th st, nr the Navy Yd; good supply of Porter, Ale & Cider.

Land for sale, by excs of the late David Peter, at the Union Tavern, Gtwn, on Jun 7: *Carderock*-1704 1/2 acs; *The Hay Park*, 40 acs; *Dowl's Discovery*, 127 acs; part of *Jas' Park*, 149 acs; *The Ferry Landing*, 22 acs; part of a tract of about 220 acs cld *The Resurvey on Honesty*. These lands adjoin ea other, not exceeding 9 miles from Gtwn. Call on Mr Barton Duly who lives nr them. -Sarah Peter, excx; Geo Peter, L H Johns, ex'rs.

Crct Crt of Wash Co, D C. Case of John P Van Ness, adm of Wm & Chas Laight, of John Blagge, & the heirs & reps of Geo Walker, having on May 21, 1812, by virtue of said decree, sold at pblc auction property in Wash City to Jos Forrest; to Zachariah Walker; to Jos Gales, jr; to Geo Beale; to David Bates; to John J Mumford; purchasers failed to comply with terms of sale. Said prop will be resold on May 19 at Tomlinson's Htl, Wash City. -Rich'd Forrest, Ch Glover, trustees.

MON MAY 10, 1813
From the bay-the British have burnt the small town of Gtwn & Frederic, Cecil Co, Md. Gtwn x Rds, Kent Co, May 3, 1813. Last wk a party of the enemy landed at Mr Geo Medford's, at Plump Point, in Werton, & robbed his meat-hse, hen-hse & sheep-fold; they even went into the kitchen & stole the furniture.

Ranaway-Thos Mitchell, appr to the *Tayloring Business*; age 16 yrs. -Dan Kealey

Crct Crt for Wash Co, D C, in Chancery. Leonard M Deakins & John Hoye, excs of Francis Deakins, dec'd, against Jas White, John Breckenridge & Eleanor Breckenridge. Sale of 225-47-160 acs of land, parcels of tracts cld *Pleasant Hills* & *Mt Pleasant*, in the neighborhood of Wash & Gtwn, alloted to the dfndnt, Jas White, in the division bet him & the dfndnt, Eleanor Breckenridge, of their gr-fr, Jas White's est. -Geo Johnson, trustee, or to John Hoye, both residing in Gtwn.

TUE MAY 11, 1813
Jas M Varnum requests that all persons who belong to the infty company he commands, will assemble this evening. Wash Item

Land for sale-250 acs bet Alexandria & the Wash bridge. -W Cranch

Wash Co, D C. Zachariah Collins brght me a stray gelding. Wm Waters-J P.

Militia of the Dist:
Maj Genr'l John P Van Ness
Brig-Genr'ls: Robt Young & Walter Smith
Adj Gen-John Cox

Assist Inspec Gen-Geo Peter
Brig Majors-Philip Triplett, John S Williams
Colonels: Geo Magruder, Wm Brent, Wm Allen Dangerfield.
Lt Cols: Jas Thompson, Michael Nourse, Adam Lynn
Majors: Lawrence Hoot, Adam King, Joel Brown
Capts of Infty:
Chas L Nevitt   David Whann   Josias M Speake
Rich'd Johns   Joe Cassin   John Hollingshead
Elisha W Williams   Craven T Payton   Geo Fitzgerald
Alex'r Hunter
Capt of Riflemen: Horace Field
Capt of Artl-Benj Burch
Lts of Infty:
Edw Edmonston   Abraham Wingart   John Fowler
Henry Beatty   Chas Warren   Wm Morton
Thos L M'Kenny   Bernard H Tomlinson Ambrose White
Thos W Peyton   Levin Moreland   Leonard Adams
Gustavus Harrison   Robt Smith   Alex'r L Joncherez
Lt of Rifleman-David Mankins
First Lt of Artl-Alex'r M'Cormick
2d Lt of Artl-Shadrack Davis
Lt of Grenadiers- John Goddard
Ensign of Grenadiers-Geo Riffle
Ensign of Riflemen-Francis Hucorn
Ensigns of Infty:
Gustavus Alexander   Marsham Jameson
John Mitchell   Jas B Holmead
Wm Williams   Francis Lownds
Robt B Kirby   John Gildy

Extract of a ltr from New London to the Editor of the *Columbian*, dt'd May 3, 1813. Re: Alfred Carpenter, ctzn of Norwich, Con; & finding & rescuing his son, John Carpenter, from 5 yrs of slavery. Other Americans on board the *Ramilies*, in the same situation as himself, viz: Wm Banks of Hampton, Va, 5 yrs in svc; Edw Ried, of Nantucket, 13 yr in svc; John Clements of same, or N Y; John Nicols, of N Y. The frig *Orpheus* sent ashore at New London a few days ago 30 American prisoners, of whom two were impressed seamen.

Wilmington, N C, May 1. On Tue, Capt J S Oliver, of this town, of the privateer *Genr'l Armstrong*, was shot & killed by Mr Evans.

WED MAY 12, 1813
Ltr from Cmdor Isaac Chauncey to the Sec of the Navy, Hon Wm Jones; U S ship *Madison* at anchor off York, Apr 27, 1813. Re: Brig Gen Pike was killed.

Notice-regarding the return of Music Bks lent to sundry persons by Mr Jos Hughes, during his life; leave same at the store of Hughes & Lindsley, oppo Davis Htl.
-Local Notice.

Died: on May 10, Mrs Rebecca Moore, in her 69th yr, a ntv of Tyrone Co, Ire, & for the past 9 yrs a resident of Wash City.

Romulus Riggs, commission merchant, goods on consignment. Gtwn

THU MAY 13, 1813
Escape from a British Prison Ship. Ctzns of the U S of America, viz: Sam'l G Parker, ntv of Boston; Thos W Nelson, ntv of N Y; John H T Estes, ntv of Va; John Harman, ntv of Pa; Robt Bond, ntv of N Y; Sam'l Wright, ntv of Conn; Jacob Anderson, ntv of Mass; Pleasant Scott, colored, ntv of Va; Thos M'Kezy, colored, ntv of Phil; being prisoners on board the H B M ship *Goree*, lying at Bermuda isle.

Mrd: at Alexandria, on May 11, by Rev Mr Norris, Dr Thos H Kent, of Bladensburg, Md, to Miss Anne Maria Peyton, d/o Francis Peyton, of that place.

Notice-comfort to travelers, Neabsco Htl, Pr Wm Co, Va; halfway bet Alexandria & Fredericksburg. -Zebulon Kankey, resident.

FRI MAY 14, 1813
The ltr of John Crawford, a ntv American seamen, who was born in Wilmington, Dela, will show the cruel treatment board the ships of Great Britain.

Extract of a ltr from Mr John O'Neill, who was taken at Havre de Grace, bravely fighting alone in the cause of his adopted country, to a gentlemen in this city, dt'd May 10.

For sale-3 story brick hse on F st in which I reside. -Wm Thornton, Wash City.

Lands for sale-500 acs in Alleghany Co, adjoining the noted tavern of John Simpkins; tract was located in 1774 by the late Col Archibald Orme, for his own use; $4 per ac. -T Beall, of Geo, D C.

SAT MAY 15, 1813
Mrd: on May 11, by Rev Mr Breckenridge, Mr Archibald Chesheur to Miss Rosanna Shanes, both of Wash City.

MON MAY 17, 1813
Property for sale-the whole of lot 18 in sq 348, in Wash City, on 10th st, with 2 story framed hse. Prop formerly owned & occupied by A B Woodward. All persons indebted to me are to make payment to Mr Jas Hewitt. -Jos Woodworth

Mrd: nr New Glasgow, Amherst Co, Va, on Apr 15, by Rev Chas Crawford, E Fletcher, to Miss Maria Antoinette Crawford, d/o Wm S Crawford.

TUE MAY 18, 1813
Mrd: at *Selby Cliffs*, in Calvert Co, Md, on May 13, by Rev Mr Wilmore, Craven T Peyton, of Alexandria, to Miss Eliza Beckett, of the former place.

Notice: Jos Woodworth who advertised his hse & lot on 10th st for sale on Thu next, I hereby forwarn all persons from purchasing any of said prop at their peril, as I have ever reason to believe him insane. -Ann Woodworth

P O est'd in Apr 1813 & changes:
Columbia, N Y, Joshua Lamb v Geo Clark, dec'd.
Chester, N Y, Solomon B Fox, v Gavriel Fox, rsgnd.
Hamilton, Ms, Isaac D Brown, Dan'l Brown, do.
Weymouth Works, N J, Lewis M Walker, v Wm Erwin, do.
Armagh, Pa, Jas Elliot, v Wm Parker, situation inconvenient.
Dunsburg, Pa, Jas Grier, v Francis Fergus, dec'd.
Blackwater, N C, Thos Lawrence, v Wm Holt, rsgnd.
Danville, Ky, Dan'l Barbee, v B H Perkins.
Knowlton Mills, N J, Elisha Lambert v Jacob Kerr, rsgnd.
Dover, Del, Augustus M Schee, v Jas Schee, dec'd.
Centreville, Va, Benedict M Lane, v Jno Hanning, rsgnd.
Hartford, Ga, Jos Wood, v J Howard, do.
Easton, Pa, Philip H Mattes, v John Knauss, dec'd.
Belfast, Me, Benj Whittier, v Thos Whittier, rsgnd.
Deerfield, N H, Enoch Butler, v Benj Butler, dec'd.
Cumberland C H, Ky, Milton King, v Jno M Emerson, rsgnd.
White Haven, Md, Jacob Ayres, v Littleton Ayres, do.
Lanesville, Va, Wm Palmer, v John Keene, do.
Conway, N H, John Hill v Dan'l Burrows, dec'd
Nottingham, Md, Wm G D Worthington, v Geo Armstrong, rsgnd.
Milton, Ohio, Enos Terry, v Jos Evans, do.
Middlefield, Ms, David Mack, jr, v Edmund Kelso, do.
Port Tobacco, Md, Ignatius Semmes, v R D Semmes, do.
Village Hill, Va, Thos Clark v Abrm Burford, do.
Machias, Me, Saml A Morse, v R H Bowles.

New P O est'd in Apr, 1813, & postmstrs:
Stony Point, Albemarle Co, Va, Nath'l Bumley.
Oxford Furnace, Sussex Co, N J, Jno P Robeson.
Mt Pleasant, Halifax Co, Va, Wm H Chalmers.
Lower Sandusky Garrison, Ohio, Jedediah Burnham.
Colchester, Chittenden Co, Vt, Barachus Farnham.
Bulletsburg, Boone Co, Ky, Lot North.
Alstead, Cheshire Co, N H, Enoch Darling.
Kindale, Stark Co, Ohio, Thos Roach.
Walpole, Norfolk Co, Ms, Levi Maxcey.
Grangerville, Harden Co, Ky, Arthur McGaughay.
Cross Rvr, West Chester Co, N Y, Thos Smith.
M'Allister's x Rds, Ten, Thos Batson.
Petersville, Fred'k Co, Md, Gafton Duvall.
Watsboro, Lunenburg Co, Va, Gill Wain Watts.

Ofcs discontinued in Apr 1813:
Montpelier, N C; Berlin, Md; Newville, Bucks co.

WED MAY 19, 1813
Stephen Ormsby, mbr of the last Cong, is elected to the 13th Cong from Ky, v John Simpson, a mbr elect, who was killed in the battle at Rvr Raisin.

Notice-whereas my wife Victoria has eloped from my bed & board without any just cause, this is to forwarn all persons from trusting or crediting her on my acc't, as I am determined not to pay any debts of her contracting from this date, or be in any way answerable for her conduct. -Peter Varon.

THU MAY 20, 1813
Killed at the siege of Camp Meigs, of the 5th inst; Majs Stoddard & Hukill. Maj Stoddard died of lock-jaw, from a fragment of a shell which struck him in the thigh. -J O Fallon, Actg Asst Adj Genr'l.

Land for sale on Jun 5; part of tract cld *Waring's Grove*, 199 1/2 acs, contiguous to the lands of Dr Jos Kent & Mr Fielder Gantt, with improvements. -Eleanor Waring, Ann Waring, PG Co, Md.

FRI MAY 21, 1813
Hugh Caperton-elected to Cong from the new dist in Va by a majority of 129 votes.

SAT MAY 22, 1813
Reward-$10-deserted from my Co of the 36th Regt U S Infty, at Wash City, on May 17, 1813, a sldr-Fred'k Brown, enlisted on May 12, in this place, by Ensign Clark; age 22 yrs, 5ft 7in, born in Germany. -Thos Carbery, Capt 36 Rgt U S Infty.

MON MAY 24, 1813
Brdg-Mrs Suter can accommodate 8 or 10 gentlemen with boading, crnr of F st oppo the Treas Ofc. Wash City.

TUE MAY 25, 1813
Died: at Pomons, Balt Co, Md, on May 17, after a short illness, Rev Geo Ralph, in his 61st yr.

WED MAY 26, 1813
Died: on May 22, Capt David Whann, of Gtwn, a respectable merchant of that place. He was on Monday interred with military honors.

THU MAY 27, 1813
Commission issued from PG Co, Md, crt; for valuation & division of the rl est of the late John Jackson, of said co. -Thos Bowie, John Wilson, Rich'd Ross, Kidd Morsell, John Chew.

For sale-12 to 15 hundred bushels of ice; also a few hundred bushels of potatoes. -John Dobbyn.

Caution-whereas Wm Holland, of Calvert Co, Md, holds my bond dt'd May, 1810; caution to all persons from taking an assignment of said bond, as I have a claim, which I mean to plead in discount against said bond. -Fielder B Smith

Boot & Shoe Manufactory. Jas Patterson has taken his son, Wm Patterson, into partnership with him, at their store on Pa av, Wash.

FRI MAY 28, 1813
Ltr from Lt Col Mitchell, dt'd Sackett's Harbor, May 14, 1813. Re-the death of Capt B Nicholson, Aid-De-Camp to the late Gen Pike. He was mortally wounded with the Gen at the battle of York, in Upper Canada, on Apr 27. He was landed here from the ship *Madison*, & died on May 13, & was buried with Gen Pike yesterday with military honors. [Capt Benj Nicholson was born in Aug, 1788, & was the fifth & only surviving s/o the late Benj Nicholson, of Balt Co, Md.] [Gen Pike was killed by the explosion of a magazine.]

Sale in Gtwn of lot 31, in the old town, not taken away by the opening of Prospect & Fred'k sts; also part of lot 40 on Duck Lane with a 2 story frame hse; now in the occupancy of Mrs Thompson; all the right, title, & int of Geo Thompson, dec'd. -Clement Smith, trustee; John Travers, auctioneer.

SAT MAY 29, 1813
Lost on Jan 17, at the stage ofc at Fredericksburg, a trunk with ladies apparel. Deliver to Wm Crawford's tavern, Gtwn. -Eleanor Williams.

Norfolk, May 25. Died yesterday of a wound rec'd from a centinel in Ft Nelson, Mr Wm Ball, jr, adj of the 4th militia regt.

MON MAY 31, 1813
Thos Gittings of Montg Co, Md, brought before me a stray mare. -Robt Edmonston, J P.

TUE JUN 1, 1813
Election will be held at Mechlin's School Rm on Jun 7, for 2 aldermen & 3 cnclmen. -Jos Brumley, Jos Stretch, Wm Waters, Com'rs.

Ranaway-Thos Carter Burton, aged 19 yrs, appr to skin dressing & breeches mkg business. -Henry Tutwiler, Post-mstr, living in Harrisonburg, Rockingham Co, Va.

Geo Boyd, insolvent debtor, confined in Wash Co jail. -Wm Brent, clk.

For sale-a frame hse on Capitol Hill with a lease of the lot for 6 yrs. -Jno Peltz.

WED JUN 2, 1813
Nathaniel Russel, insolvent debtor, confined in Wash Co jail. -Wm Brent, clk.

THU JUN 3, 1813
Mrsh'ls sale of claim & int of Nicholas Voss to lots 3, 4, & 5 in sq 846 in Wash City; at the instance of Edw A Price, against said Voss. -Wash Boyd, Mrshl, D C.

FRI JUN 4, 1813
Re-appt'd to compose the Levy Crt of Wash Co, D C:
Sam'l H Smith	Nicholas Young	Nathan Luffborough
John Threlkeld	Thos Corcoran	John Ott
Thos Peter		

Wash Hotel, opened on Pa Av nr the Treas, Wash City. -John Macleod.

Died: at Richmond, on May 30, Mr Wm Monroe, merchant, of Boston, on his return from Petersburg, when by the turning over of the stage, his right arm was shattered, which although amputated, produced lock-jaw. He has left a widow & 3 young chldrn.

Mrsh'ls sale of the claim & int of Hanson Hedges & Fanny Hedges to part of lot 7 in sq 491, in Wash City, with small frame hse on Pa av. -Wash Boyd-mrshl.

Wash Co, D C. Today Theophilus Hughes brght before me a stray bay mare. -Sam'l H Smith, J P.

SAT JUN 5, 1813
Land & hses for sale, at Montg C H, Md, now occupied as a tavern by Mr Robb; also a lot of ground at Medley's, with dwlg hse; also 500 acs in said co. -Honore Martin, Rockville, Md.

MON JUN 7, 1813
Election at Drummond's tavern, for 1 Alderman & 3 Common Cncl men, to rep Ward 4, Wash City. -Jos Cassin, Gustavus Higden, Buller Cocke, com'rs.

TUE JUN 8, 1813
Application of John M'Cullock, of Chas Co, Md, for benefit as insolvent debtor. -John Barnes, clk.

Rockville Acad in Montg Co, Md. J Elgar, Sec.

WED JUN 9, 1813
Paper hangings, at his Boot & Shoe Store, oppo the Indian Queen tavern, Pa av, Wash City. -Andrew Coyle.

Forty dollars reward for a pr of carriage horses, strayed or stolen, from the commons of Wash City. -Andw Hunter, Navy Yd.

Mrd: on Feb 17, at the Chateua of his Excellency John Quincy Adams, Mnstr Pleni from the U S of American to the Crt of St Petersburg, Wm Steuben Smith, Sec of Leg, to Miss Cath Johnson, sister to Mrs Adams, the Mnstr's Lady.

THU JUN 10, 1813
Wash City election on Jun 7. Aldermen:

Stephen Pleasenton	Jas Hewitt	Wm Emack
Jos Cassin		

Common Cncl:

Rich'd S Briscoe	John Graham	Wm Worthington
R C Weightman	Thos H Gillis	Chas Glover
Electius Middleton	Thos Howard	Edmund Law
Shadrach Davis	Geo M'Caulay	Thos Holliday
-Dan'l Rapine, Mayor		

Wash Co, D C, in Chancery. Jas D Barry against Patrick Barry & heirs & reps of Garret Barry, dec'd. Ratify sale by Jas Davidson & Chas Glover, trustees, of prop decreed to be sold to Overton Carr, for $2,500. -Wm Brent, clk.

Return of the killed & wounded on board the squadron under command of Cmdor Isaac Chauncey, in the attack upon York, Apr 27, 1813. Ship *Madison*-wounded: John Campbell, seaman; Rich'd Welch, ord, both black. Schn'r *Ontario*: Benj Hacker, seaman, wounded; John Rattler, do. Schn'r *Growler*, John Stimas, seaman, wounded; John Peterson, o s, wounded. Schn'r *Conquest*-killed, John Hatfield, midshipman; killed-Benj Quereau, sail-mkr. Schn'r *Scourge*-Lemuel Bryant, o s, wounded. Schn'r *Raven*, Israel Clark, o s, blackman, killed.

FRI JUN 11, 1813
Died: at Boston, during the last wk, O Augustus Page, !st Lt of the frig *Chesapeake*, aged 28 yrs; entered the Navy in 1798; s/o John Page, of Caroline Co, Va, & has left 4 bros & numerous acquaintance to deplore his loss.

Died: at his residence in Northumberland Co, Va, on May 20 last, after a short illness, Col Jas Moore, an ofcr of the Rev; entered the army in 1775 at age 18 yrs as a capt in the Pa line. Exemplary as a hsbnd & fr. The tears of a widow & 10 chldrn bedew his grave.

John Turner, of PG Co, Md, insolvent debtor. -John Johnson, Judge

Sale of patent rights to flax & hemp spinning mach. -N Foster, Patentee.

Reward-$50, for runaway, Jas, negro man, about 25 yrs of age. -John Teisher, living nr Hagerstown, Wash Co, Md.

SAT JUN 12, 1813
Biog of Cmdor Stephen Decatur, of French descent, by the male line; gr-fr was a ntv of La Rochelle, France, & mrd a lady of R I. His fr, Stephen Decatur, was born in Newport, R I, & when a young man remv'd to Phil, where he mrd the d/o an Irish gentleman by the name of Pine; he died in Nov, 1808. Stephen Decatur, his son, was born on Jan 5, 1779, on the eastern shore of Md, where his parents had

retired; they returned to Phil when he was a few mos old. Lt Jas Decatur was a bro of Stephen Decatur.

John Donnell is chosen Pres, & Jas Sterrett-Cashier, of the new bank cld the City Bank of Balt.

Mrd: on Jun 10, by Rev Mr Brown, Mr Andrew Tate, of Phil, to Miss Sarah Borrows, of Wash City.

Dissolution of the partnership bet Thos L M'Kenney & Sam G Osborne, by mutual consent; the former will continue the business. -Gtwn

Wash Co, D C. Jas Brown, insolvent debtor, confined in Wash Co jail. -Wm Brent, clk.

MON JUN 14, 1813

Runaway committed to Wash Co, D C, jail, Bazil Lee, black man; says he belongs to Miss Jane Contee, at Mr Wm Keith's, in Alexandria; age about 21 yrs. -C Tippet, jailor for W Boyd, mrshl.

Orphans Crt of PG Co, Md. Pblc sale of a negro woman & her child, part of prsnl est of Jesse Handey, late of said co, dec'd. -Ann Handey, Matthew Moore, jr, adms.

Deserted from the Camp Ground in Wash City, on Jun 6, a drafted militiaman, Chas Stewart, of fair complexion. Wm Minor, Capt in 36th Regt Infty.

TUE JUN 15, 1813

Jas H Blake was yesterday elected Mayor of Wash City for the ensuing yr.

Dividend of the prsnl assets of Edw Eno, dec'd, will be made on Jul 10, at the hse of Thos C Wright, in Gtwn, D C. -Thos C Wright, Sam'l Rogers, excs.

Female Acad-Miss Charlotte Ann Taylor has remv'd to G st, westward of Dr Elzy's dwlg hse. Wash City.

To let-a genteel 2 story brick dwlg hse, half way bet the War Ofc & the mouth of the Tiber. -John P Van Ness.

WED JUN 16, 1813

Lands in Ohio & Ky, for sale; per last will & testament of Robt Means, dec'd. -Dan'l Call, exc, Richmond, Jul 19.

THU JUN 17, 1813

Ranaway-white girl, an appr about 13 yrs of age, on May 6 last; reward ten cents. -Jane Noel, living at *Greenleaf's Point*.

FRI JUN 18, 1813
For rent-svr'l dwlg hses at *Greenleaf's Point*. -Nath'l P Bixby, *Greenleaf's Pt*.

Sale at auction-the remainder of stock of grocs; sale at Mr T Kenna's on Thu, nr the Navy Yd. -N L Queen, auct.

Orphans Crt of Wash Co, D C. Prsnl est of Robt Anderson, late of said co, a gunner in the Navy of the U S, dec'd. -Henry Burford, exc.

SAT JUN 19, 1813
St Mary's Co, [Md] Crt; application to Hon Edmund Key, one of the judges of the first Judicial dist of Md, by petition in writing, of John Mattingly, Jos Mattingly, Chas Thompson, of said Co: praying the benefit of insolvent laws of Md. -Jo Harris, clk. St Mary's Co Crt.

Whereas my wife Jane has left my bed & board w/out my leave or consent, I hereby forwarn all persons from giving her credit on my acc't, as I am determined to pay no debts of her contracting, nor be accountable for her conduct. -Rich'd Jackson, Fairfax Co, Va.

MON JUN 21, 1813
Albany, Jun 15. Col Backus died of the wounds he rec'd on the 29th; he was buried on Thu last, with the honors due a distinguished patriot & sldr.

Died: on Wed last, at his seat nr Richmond, Gen Jas Wood, late Gov of Va, a Rev patriot.

My long & continued ill health, will compel me to relinquish my present pursuits-I therefore offer for sale, the Printing Ofc & establishment of the *Peersburgh Intell*; established for 27 yrs, one of the oldest. -John Dickson, Petersburgh, Va.

TUE JUN 22, 1813
Lt Col John Mills fell at the head of his regt, on May 29, 1813, in the gallant defence of Sackett's Harbor.

Sale of the best beaver hats; at his new hat manufactory, High st, Gtwn. -John Hagerty, jr.

WED JUN 23, 1813
P O establishment-changes in May 1813:
Conway, N H, John Hill v Daniel Burrows, dec'd.
Gallatin, Ten, Jas Robb v Jos H Conn, rsgnd.
Port Eliz, N J, John Dunham, v Stephen Willis, do.
Stockbridge, Ms, Augustus Sherrill v Horatio Jones, dec'd.
Hollis, Me, Ellis B Usher v Isaac Lane, rsgnd.
Fruitstown, Pa, John F Derr v Jas M'Bride, dec'd.
Winchester, Ky, Thos Pickett, v Robt Clarke, rsgnd.
Middleburg, Ky, Henry Russell, v Edmund Guthrie, do.

Sacketts Harbour, N Y, Elijah Fields, jr, v Hart Massey, mv'd away.
Jerseytown, Pa, Nicholas Funston, v Andrew Haslet, rsgnd.
Westraysville, N C, Sam'l Westray, v John Bobbit, do.
Otis, Ms, Bavil Seymour, v Roderick Norton, rsgnd.
Montg C H, Ga, Simon Hadley, v Daniel M'Intosh, rsgnd.
Baton Rouge, O T, Jas Converse, v Isaiah Nelson.
Pittsylvania C H, Va, Wm Rawlings, v Thos Rawlings, rsgnd.
Tioga, Pa, Thos Putnam, v Elijah Putnam, do.
Craftsbury, Vt, Munnis Kenny, v Harvey Scott, do.
Delhi, N Y, Wm H Etting, v H R Phelps, do.
Skaneatiles, N Y, John Ten Eyck, v Wm J Vandenburgh, dec'd.
Winchendon, Ms, Jos Jewett, v Amos Goodhue, rsgnd.
Quincy, Ms, Mottram Vesey, v Benj Vinton, dec'd.
Mattamuskeet, N C, Abner Pasteur, v Hugh Jones, rsgnd.
Winchester, Ten, Jas Estill, v Thos D Wiggen, do.
Alfred, Me, Jas Goodwin, v Jeremiah Goodwin, rsgnd.
Lower Sandusky Garrison, O, Wm M'Connell, v Jedediah Burnham, rsgnd.
Peterboro, N H, Jonathan Smith, v Sam Smith, do.
Essex, N Y, Wm Rolfe, v Peter Dorrin, dec'd.
Sillwater, N Y, Geo Palmer, v Henry Metoalf.
New Lancaster, O, Jacob D Dietrick, v Sam'l Coates.
Somerset, K, Henry L Mills, v W J Sallee, mv'd away.
Paris, Me, Russel Hubbard, v Levi Hubbard, rsgnd.
Mendham, N J, Abner Dod, v Stephen Dod, mv'd away.
Wheatsboro, O, Jas R Cowan, v Rael Wood, dec'd.
Madisonville, K, Baxter D Towns, v Thos Cardwell, rsgnd.

New ofcs est'd in May 1813 & postmstr:
Upper Sandusky, O, John M'Clelland.
Friendship, Lincoln Co, Me, Jos H Beckett.
Haywoodsboro, Chatham Co, N C, John A Ramsay.
Ballsville, Powhattan Co, Va, Isham Ball.
Cherry Plains, Wake Co, N C, Ludovic Alford.
Mobile, Miss Ter, Jas B Wilkinson.
Weare, Rockingham Co, N H, Sam'l F Peterson.
Danielsburg, Spottsylvania Co, Va, John Daniel.
Londonderry, Chester Co, Pa, Ziba Vickars.
Hampton Falls, Rockingham Co, N H, Edw Langmaid.
Springfield, York Co, S C, John Spring, jr.
Legonier Valley, Westmoreland Co, Pa, Wm King.
Ottsville, Bucks Co, Pa, Matthew Ott.
Ofc discont'd: Dighton x rds, Md.

Wash Co, D C: Geo Barcley, insolvent debtor, confined in Wash Co prison.
-Wm Brent, clk.

Strayed or stolen; brown horse, off the Commons of Wash City; prop of Sam'l Cloakey, of said place.

Land for sale in Montg Co, Md; 200 acs; 2 miles below Mr Wm Darnes. Apply to Mr Henry Jones, living thereon; or to Benj W Jones, in Gtwn, D C.

THU JUN 24, 1813
Died: at his seat, on the Susquehannah, 3 miles from Harrisbugh, on Tue last, Gen Mich'l Simpson, aged about 80 yrs. He is honorably spoken of in Henry's acc't of the band of heroes in the campaign against Quebec, in 1775.

FRI JUN 25, 1813
Wash Artl to meet on Jun 26. -Benj Burch, Captain.

SAT JUN 26, 1813
St Mary's Co, Md. Com'rs appt'd on the petition of John B Stone, whether the rl est of Wm Hatton Stone, late of St Mary's Co, dec'd, wld admit of division; same is not admitted for division. All reps of dec'd to appear in St Mary's Co crt, except Eliz Stone, who, it is represented, resides out of this state. -Jos Harris, clk.

Died: on board the U S frig *Chesapeake*, on Jun 5, Capt Jas Lawrence, fighting in defence of *Free trade & sailor's rights*, aet 30. No ofcr in our Navy of his age has seen more or harder fighting, & a more patriotic spirit never ascended the skies.

Orphans Crt of PG Co, Md. Prsnl est of Jas Forbes, late of said co, dec'd. -John Forbes, adm, subscriber of the Hghts of Savoy, nr Aquasco Mills.

Reward-$10, for horse that strayed from the commons nr the Navy Yd. John Davis, of Abel.

Wash Co, D C. Wm Dixon, insolvent debtor, confined in Wash Co prison for debt; trustee to be appt'd. -Wm Brent, clk.

MON JUN 28, 1813
Ranaway from John C Heise, living in Gtwn; negro man, Gusty Hall, about 19 yrs of age.

Reward-$5, for strayed red cow. -Peregrine Warfied, living in Gtwn.

Extract from a ltr from the Surgeon of the *Chesapeake*, dt'd Halifax, Jun 8. Capt Jas Lawrence mortally wounded-died Jun 4; Lts Augustus C *Ludlow & Cox wounded but doing well. Lt Ballard died in 15 or 20 mins after receiving his wound. The mstr, Mr W N White, & midshipmen Weaver, Nichols, Berry, & Abbott were wounded but are doing well. Capt Broke of the *Shannon* is likely to recover. [*Ludlow died per paper of Jun 29, aged 21, at Halifax.]

TUE JUN 29, 1813
Capture of the frig *Chesapeake*, Jun 1, 1813. Mr Edw J Ballard the 4th Lt & Lt Jas Broom of the Marines, fell early in the action. -Geo Budd, ltr to the Hon Wm Jones, Sec of the Navy, Wash.

Died: at New Alexandria, Westmoreland Co, Pa, on Jun 17, Gen Wm Reed, Adj-Genr'l of the Militia of Pa.

My creditors take notice that I have given up debts & prop five times more than I owe, & shld be glad to receive back my debts & property. -Levi White.

State of Md, in Chancery, Jun 25, 1813. Jas Brookes & others vs John Cottle & Sarah his wife, Jas Brookes, Giles Brookes, Johnsee Brookes, Wm Brookes & Eliza Brookes, heirs of Jas Brookes. Re: distrbution of rl est of Mary Brookes on Aug 10. -Jas P Heath, Reg C C/

WED JUN 30, 1813
Protest of the minority of the Leg of Mass; dt'd Boston, Jun 16. Signed: John Holmes, Wm Moody, Solomon Aiken, Joshua Prentiss, John Hart, Ambrose Hall.

Killed in the action of the U S frig *Chesapeake* with the British frig *Shannon*, Jun 1, 1813.

*Wm A White	Pollard Hopewell	John Evans
Courtland Livingston	Abraham Cox	Geo C__yton
Sterling Clark	Danl Burnam	Alex'r Marinor
Thos Evans	John Miller	Dan'l Martin
Robt Bates	Jas Woodbury	Wm Russell
Harris Ball	Andrew Williams	Jos Simonds
John W Duggin	Davis Bias	Henry Munroe
Josiah Shatfield	Chris Houston	John Phillips
Benj Esday	John Reed	Michael Kelly
Sam'l Mullin	Mich'l Sawyer	John Carter
Sam'l M Perkins	Jos Judith	John Jones
Marines:		
Jas Broom	Thos Wheaton	Benj Morrison
John Milligan	John German	John Muntress
Jas Treanor	Jacob Preston	Philip Bryant
Redmond Barry	Robt Standley	Delany Ward

*Sailing mstr, aged 26, ntv of Rutland, Mass; Wm Augustus White.

THU JUL 1, 1813
Reward $10 for strayed or stolen, bay horse. -John Graham

FRI JUL 2, 1813
P O Ws on parole in the parish of Beaufort, nr Quebec, Jun 5, 1813: Jas Winchester, Brig Gen, U S Army; Wm Lewis, Lt Col-5th Regt Ky Militia; Geo Madison, Maj Rifle-Regt Ky Militia; Joshua Conkey, Capt-N Y Militia; Lewis Godard, Lt-N Y Militia; Wm C Beard, Lt-U S Rifle Regt; John G Clark, 5th U S Infty; David P Polk-Ensign, 12th Regt U S Infty.

Wash Co, D C, case of Wm Fitzgerald, insolvent debtor, confined in Wash Co prison. -Wm Brent, clk.

Wash Public Baths-on C st, Wash City, est'd Apr 9, last. -F Shuck.

SAT Jul 3, 1813
Thos Hurdle, insolvent debtor, confined in Wash Co prison. -Wm Brent, clk.

MON Jul 5, 1813
For sale or rent-the hse next dr to W Cooper's bk-store. -Geo Moore.

WED Jul 7, 1813
The co-partnership of H H Edwards & G Bestor is this day dissolved. -Wash

Reward $20-for strayed or stolen horse, from the Wash City commons.
-G C Grammer & Co.

Epaulettes, etc, just rec'd & offered for sale. -Jacob Leonard

THU Jul 8, 1813
Portsmouth, N H, Jun 25. Treason-on the 22d inst, Sam'l York, jr, of North Yarmouth, Me, mariner, was arraigned at the Crt Hse, at the complaint of Capt Thos M Shaw, Wm Clagget, & the D A, in support of the cmplnt, in behalf of the U S & Edw Cutts jr, & Wm A Hayes, cnsl for the respondent. York was commited to prison, & detained until discharged by order of law.

The partnership of Jeremiah Boothe & Jos Johnson, is dissolved by mutual consent; render accounts to John N Brashears, at the Navy Yd. -Local Item.

FRI Jul 9, 1813
Brewery in Wash City to be sold or let. -J W Collet.

Alex'r Phoenix, of N Y C, & Wm Nexsen, jr, insolvent debtors, long confined in jail for debts due to the U S, which they are unable to pay, are to be discharged.
-H Clay, spkr of the Hse of Reps, E Gerry, V P. Approved, Jas Madison.

SAT JUL 10, 1813
Ladies with ltrs in the P O at Wash City, Jul 1, 1813:

Rebecca Angel	Mrs Maria A Baker	Mrs Eliza Berry
Mrs Jane Beall	Mrs Charlotte Cozens	Mrs Eliza Clarke
Mrs Mary Duffy	Miss Charl De Niroth	Mrs Mgt Ewell
Mrs Sally Evelith	Mrs Sarah Edwards	Ann Green
Miss Eliz Hooper	Charity Hutchins	Nancy Homes
Miss Mary I Hanson	Mrs Fanny Hodges	Mrs Fanny Hamilton
Widow Jenkins	Mrs Julia Jones	Jane Johnson
Mgt Kortright	Mrs Mudge	Miss Mary Macdaniel
Bridget M'Dermott	Mrs Eliza Nowland	Mrs Nowland
Mrs M A Polock	Miss Louisa Power	Rebekah Russ
Mary Robb	Mrs Mary Sinclair	Rosa Shanks

Mrs Wm Staines   Mrs Sarah G Smith   Mrs Sarah Sims
Mrs Ellender Smith

Notice-John Shreve & Chas Myers have commenced the *Tinning Business*, at the crnr of High & Gay sts, Gtwn; under the firm of Shreeves & Myers.

MON JUL 12, 1813
Examination of the pupils of Charlotte Hall School [Md] on Jul 26. -Wm Duke, princ.

TUE JUL 13, 1813
Adam Whann has commenced the hrdwre & cutlery bus, for the use of the family of David Whann, dec'd, in co-partnership with Benj F Mackall, under the firm of Whann & Mackall. -Adam Whann.

Fifty dollars reward for Bay Gelding stolen from a pasture of Mr Wm Prestman's nr the Spring Gardens. -Sam'l Dorsey. Horse may be delivered at Dubois's stable, Balt, Md.

Mrshl's sale-at M'Leod's Tavern, all the right, int, claim & prop of Henry Aborn, as garnishee of Abraham Lindo, to lots 9 & 10 in sq 168, in Wash City. Re: suit of Esther, admx of Archibald Gardiner, against Henry Aborn. -Wash Boyd, Mrshl -D C.

WED JUL 14, 1813
Furs for sale, at the warehse of Messrs Bowie & Kurtz. Enquire of R H Johns, Gtwn.

Henry O Middleton informs the pblc that his Mineral Water apparatus is now in operation for ctzns of Gtwn & Wash.

THU JUL 15, 1813
Reward-$10, for runaway, Levi Chancy, about 17 yrs of age, appr to the joiner & hse carpenters business. His parents live in A A Co, Md. -Aaron Nally.

FRI JUL 16, 1813
Valuable Wash City prop for sale; the whole crnr of a sq on which Mr R C Weightman now lives; the price is $6,000. Enquire at this ofc.

SAT JUL 17, 1813
Runaway, Henrietta Green, negro woman, says she is 37 yrs of age & manumitted by Mrs Eliza Nixon about 7 yrs ago. Since her manumission she has resided with Capt Sam'l W Sterrett, of Balt city. -Morris Jones, shrf, Fred'k Co, Md.

Died: on Jul 16, in Wash City, Robt H Nicholls, a clk in the War Dept, in his 28th yr, after a short illness. He was distant from his relatives, where no bros or sisters' tears flowed around his grave.

TUE JUL 20, 1813
A full company of the most respected gentlemen in Chas Co, Md, exempt by their advanced age from svc, yesterday mustered at Piscataway, under command of the Wm D Beall, late a Col in the U S army.

WED JUL 21, 1813
Josias Cox, insolvent debtor, confined in Wash Co prison. -Wm Brent, clk.

Annual meeting of the stockholders of the Potomac Co, will be held at Union Tavern, Gtwn, on Aug 2. -Jos Brewer, Treas.

THU JUL 22, 1813
Daniel Rapine & Jonathan Elliot have entered into the copartnership in the printing business; ofc in a hse on Capt Hill, nr D Rapine's bkstore.

FRI JUL 23, 1813
American manufactured goods; 172 Mkt st, Balt, Md. -Jno C Buckland.

SAT JUL 24, 1813
Elected on Jul 19 to the Permanent Institution for the education of youth in Wash City: Gabriel Duvall, Jas Laurie, Elias B Caldwell, Geo Blagden, Jas Davidson, & Jos Mechlin. Judges of Election-Jos Mechlin, Moses Young, & Henry Ingle.

Wanted to purchase, a good young wench, that has been brought up in a family; 16 or 20 yrs old. Call on Mr Edw Viduler in the Navy Yd.

TUE JUL 27, 1813
Hse o/Reps-an act for the relief of Thos Sloo, a com'r appt'd to examine the validity of claims to land in the dist of Kaskaskia, the sum of $500.

Died: in Augusta, Maine, on Jul 6, Mr John Gilly, at age 124 yrs; born in the west of Ire, a few miles from Cork, migrated to America about 70 yrs ago. He has left a large family; youngest child is in his 25th yr.

Dividend declared on est of Wm Smith, dec'd, late of Bladensburg, PG Co, Md. -Zeph Farrel, adm.

WED JUL 28, 1813
Wanted: a lad to learn the hatting business, from 15 to 16 yrs of age. -Wm H Hamer.

Reward-$50, for negro slave, Bill Guy, ranaway from Salubria, nr Hagerstown, Wash Co, Md, on Jul 14; bet 18 & 21 yrs of age, raised by Mr Benj Harrison of West Rvr, at which place he has a mthr & relatives. -O G W Stull, Wash Co, Md.

Strayed, from Federal Mill, nr Gtwn, a grey mare. -John White

THU JUL 29, 1813
Brd of aldermen & board of Common Cncl appt'd by the Mayor:
Sam'l N Smallwood   Alex'r M Williams
Franklin Wharton   Andrew Hunter
Wm Matthews   Moses Young
John Haw
 [Previously elected-Gabriel Duvall, Jos Mechlin, Jas Laurie, Jas Davidson, Elias B Caldwell, Geo Blagden.]

FRI JUL 30, 1813
Ranaway-negro man, about 6' high; $30 reward. -Wm Taylor, Jefferson Co, Va, nr Shepherdstown. [No name given.]

SAT JUL 31, 1813
The subscriber has remv'd his dry goods store to one of Mrs Clarke's hses in F st. -Alex'r Cochrane.

MON AUG 2, 1813
Orphans Crt of Wash Co, D C. Prsnl est of Wm Sanford, late of said city, dec'd. -Jos Cassin, adm.

TUE AUG 3, 1813
Some Acts passed at the 13th Cong: relief of Thos Denny; Alex'r Scott; Alex'r Phoenix; Thos Sloo; Edwin T Satterwhite; John Jas Dufour; David Henley; Joshua Dorsey; & Geo Lyon.

Died: on Aug 2, after a short illness, Miss Charlotte Abercrombie, of the Theatre in Wash City, aged 16 yrs & 3 mos. Funeral today from Mrs Deery's, Pa av.

WED AUG 4, 1813
Reward-$1, for runaway, Hugh Moony, aged about 14 yrs, fair complexion, appr to the bricklaying bus; absconded from Alexandria. -Robt Brown, F st, bricklayer.

THU AUG 5, 1813
To let-the groc store lately occupied by Mr Fred'k Cana, in 8th st. -Buller Cocke.

The subscriber has the right, title, interest, for the mkg, selling & using the spinning machine, invented by Messrs Luther Bissel, Justus Hinman, Luke C Hinman, & Benoni Gains, their patent for same obtained Jun 19, 1813. Geo Sweeny, at the P O, is authorised to dispose of such rights. -John Goulding

Died: at Ft Geo, in Upper Canada, on Jul 22, of a fever, Col John Christie, of the U S Army. Col C entered the army originally in 1808.

Died: at Sackett's Harbor, on Jul 16, Lt J H Sparks, an ofcr of the army; of typhus fever, a ntv of Md.

FRI AUG 6, 1813
Stray cow & calf came to my farm a few days ago. -Thos Fenwick.

SAT AUG 7, 1813
Piano forte from the manufactory of Mr Jas Stewart, of Balt, for sale. Just rec'd, W Cooper, Pa av, Wash City. Other musical instruments & new music advertised.

Orphans Crt of Wash Co, D C. Prsnl est of Wm Sanford, late of said city, dec'd. -Jos Cassin, adm.

Found-bet Wash City & Ft Warburton, a case of surgical instruments. Apply to John B Forrest, Navy Yd.

MON AUG 9, 1813
Mrd: on Aug 6, by Rev Noble Young, the Rev A T M'Cormick to Miss Hannah Pleasonton.

Died: On Fri last, Mr Joshua J Moore, chf clk in the Land Ofc of the U S, a worthy & amiable man, who has left a large family to lament their loss.

Died: at Balt, a few days ago, Mr Sam'l Stettinius, merchant of Wash City. He was a respectable & useful ctzn, & has left a numerous family.

TUE AUG 10, 1813
For sale-an elegant carriage. Apply to Robt Ellott, Capitol Hill, Wash.

Info of ctzns of Balt, Md, by Cmdor Gordon; U S schn'r *Patapsco*, of Hawkins Point, 6th Aug 1813. Re: Jas Martin, born in Harford Co, Md, late of the schn'r *Laurestenus;* Thos Mason, born in Harford Co, of the privateer *Rolla;* & Jas Riggen, of Somerset Co, Md; concealing themselves from the enemy on Kent Island.

Deserted on Aug 1, on march from Ft Warburton to Queen Ann's, PG Co, Md, Ephraim M'Laughlin, about 27 or 28 yrs of age; fond of playing the fiddle; enlisted in N C, nr the mountain. -G Cloud, Capt 10th U S Infty.

Deserted from camp nr Queen Anns on Aug 3, Matthew Childress, about 40 yrs of age, & Jas *Calson. Childress' family lives in Surry Co, N C or Patrick Co, Va. *Colson was enlisted in Buckingham, N C, or Pittsylvanis Co, Va. Reward-$10 for ea. -G Cloud, Capt 10th U S Infty. [*2 splgs]

WED AUG 11, 1813
Strayed on Jul 10, from the Centre Mkt, Wash City, a sorrel filley. Reward-Jas W Johnston.

FRI AUG 13, 1813
Died: on Aug 1, at his residence in St Mary's Co, Md, the Hon Wm Thomas, Pres of the Senate of Md.

Deserted on the march from Ft Wash to Annapolis on Aug 3, the following pvts in the 5th regt of the U S Infty:
Alex'r Eaton, aged 18 yrs, laborer, born in Loudon Co, Va.
Geo Green, aged 13 yrs, wheelwright, born in Pr Wm, Va.
Wm Dudley, aged 35 yrs, sailor, born in Curituck Co, N C.
Jas Whaling, aged 20 yrs, sailor, born in Ireland.
Manuel Tillman, aged 27 yrs, born in Burke Co, Pa.
Wiley Meggs, aged 27 yrs, farmer, born in Norfolk Co, Va.
-Signed: Geo M Brooke, Capt, 5th U S Infty.

Boarding-Mrs King, wid/o the late N King, having completed an additional bldg to her dwlg hse in G st, Wash.

SAT AUG 14, 1813
Rpblcn nominations for the mbrs of Assembly-Md.
Calvert Co: Rich'd Ireland, Stephen Johns, John G Mackall, W Hungerford.
Dorchester Co: H P Wagganian, Geo Lake, A S Stenford, Wm Groghegan.
Talbot Co: Sam'l Stevens, Dan'l Martin, John Bennett, Jonathan Spencer.
Caroline Co: Th Saulsberry, Th Culbreth, Peter Willis, John Boon.

MON AUG 16, 1813
Jervase Markham, about the yr 1600, published a work titled-the *English Hsewife*, containing the inward & outward virtues which ought to be in a complete woman.

Strayed or stolen, from the enclosure of the old tan yd, nr Capt Hill, a bay horse. Reward-$20. -Lawrence Hayes, Bank of Wash.

TUE AUG 17, 1813
Rpblcn nominations for mbrs of Assembly-Md.
Cecil Co: Dan'l Sheredine, Th W Veazey, Th Williams, John Groome.
Kent Co: Wm R Steuart, Jas Harris, Wm Moffett, Benj Massey.

Luther Martin is appt'd Chf Justice of the Crt of Oyer & Terminer & goal delivery of Balt Co, Md.

Died: on Aug 12, at Greencastle, Pa, during a journey hoping to re-establish her health, Mrs Eliz Laurie, d/o the late Rev Jas Scott, Musselburgh, Scotland, & w/o Rev J Laurie, of Wash City; whose loss will be felt by her hsbnd & 4 infant chldrn, her offspring.

Reward-$100, for runaway Solomon Jones, a negro fellow; may be on the way to Phil where he has a son. Reward if delivered in Raleigh, N C. -Lewis S Muse.

Orphans Crt of Wash Co, D C. Prsnl est of Joshua J Moore, late of said city, dec'd. -Eliz Moore, admx.

For sale-all the right, title, int, of Jos Woodworth, at his hse & in lot 18 sq 348; subject to a mortgage in favor of Geo Moore, for $500; to satisfy Wm O'Brien. -Geo Adams, Cnstbl.

WED AUG 18, 1813
Died: on Aug 12, Sam'l Osgood, naval ofcr of the port of New York.

I will sell a carriage & 4 horses. -Mary Stettinius, admx of Sam'l Stettinius, dec'd.

THU AUG 19, 1813
To be placed on the pension list of invalid pensioners of the U S:

Benj Randall	rate of $5 per mo	beginning on Feb 11, 1813
Geo Hill	$3.25 per mo	beg on Feb 25, 1813
Leonard Clarke	$5 per mo	beg Jan 18, 1813
Geo Shannon	$8 per mo	beg Jan 1, 1813
Hezekiah Thorndike	$3.33 1/3d	beg May 1, 1812
Benj Brockway	$2.50 per mo	beg Dec 11, 1812
Paul Bebee	$3.75 per mo	beg Jan 7, 1813
Zachariah Sherwood	$2.50 per mo	beg Dec 13, 1809
Braxton Carter	$3 per mo	beg Jan 1, 1813
Patrick Logan	$2.50 per mo	beg Jan 1, 1813
Jos Davidson	$2.50 per mo	beg Jan 23, 1812
John Jourdan	$5 per mo	beg Aug 26, 1812
Jas Russell	$5 per mo	beg Nov 21, 1812
Nathaniel Henry	$15 per mo	beg Jan 1, 1813
Abraham Merryfield	$5 per mo	beg Feb 15, 1813
Joshua Patrick	$2.50 per mo	beg Jun 1, 1813
Jonathan Morris	$10 per mo	beg Jun 14, 1813
Sam'l White	$2.50 per mo	beg Apr 12, 1813

Increase in pension-to the sum herein annexed to their names:

Ebenezer Bean	$2.50 per mo	beg Jun 9, 1812
Sam'l Morrell	$3.75 per mo	beg Sep 11, 1812
Moses Trussel	$5 per mo	beg Sep 25, 1812
Sam'l le Count	$5 per mo	beg Nov 20, 1812
Josiah Jones	$5 per mo	beg Jan 25, 1813
Stephen Everts	$5 per mo	beg May 18, 1812
Amazian Chappel	$3.75 per mo	beg Feb 7, 1811
Sam'l Stillman	$3.75 per mo	beg Nov 28, 1812
Israel Dibble	$4 per mo	beg Dec 12, 1812
Sam'l Sawyer	$4.50 per mo	beg Dec 12, 1812
Jacob Williams	$2.50 per mo	beg Jan 11, 1813
Benj Tower	$5 per mo	beg Jan 27, 1813
Younger Grady	$5 per mo	beg Jun 8, 1811
John Talman, alias Tallman	$5 per mo	beg Feb 1, 1813

Lost on Aug 18 bet Mr Long's Tavern on Capitol Hill & Davis' Tavern, Pa av, 3 deeds of land; one of Thos Drane, jr; one of Nathaniel Jones, & one of Jesse Willcoxer. Reasonable compensation-leave at Mr Long's Bar. -Wash Drane.

Balt Patriot. Habeas Corpus-Dan'l Wells, an infant, by Geo Mackenzie, vs John Kennedy. Petitioner was an infant under age 21, & above age 18 yrs, an appr to Geo Mackenzie. Aug 10th he was arrested by sldrs, under orders of John Kennedy. Decision-he is in legal custody, & must be remanded to his ofcr, & conducted to camp.

Reward-$20, for strayed or stolen bay horse. -Francis Wayne, Navy Yd, Wash City.

FRI AUG 20, 1813
Died: on Aug 19, in Wash City, of a lingering disease, Mr Wm Kean, in his 35th yr, a ntv of Moira, Ire. Funeral from his late dwlg hse nr the P O, this day.

SAT AUG 21, 1813
Reward-$20, for Jas Stewart, an appr to the shoemkg bus, 15 or 16 yrs of age; his mthr, Mary Ann Stewart, lives nr the Navy Yd, Wash. He may call himself Jas Howard. -Jacob Janney, Ocoquan.

MON AUG 23, 1813
<u>Civil appointments, confirmed by the Senate during the last session of Congress:</u>
Dominick A Hall, to dist Judge for La.
Morton I Waring, to mrsh'l of S C.
Thos Lehre, to Com'r of Loans for S C.
Robt Fairchild, re-appt'd Mrshl fo dist of Conn for 4 yrs.
Jas Brobson, re-appt'd Mrshl of dist of Dela for 4 yrs.
Peter F Dubourg St Colombe, to coll for Port of Orleans, La.
Chas Harris, to U S Atty for dist of Ga.
Wm I M'Intosh, to Coll of Customs & Inspec of Rev for Brunswick.
Wm Clarke, to Govn'r of Mo terr.
Henry Dodges, to Mrshl of same.
Nathan Pope, of Ky, to Sec of Ill Terr.
Jas Rush, of Pa, to Treas of the Mint of the U S.
Edw Wyer, of Mass, to Cnsl at Rigu, Russia.
Thos D Anderson, to Atty of U S in Miss Terr.
John Hanes, to Mrshl in same.
Wm Spriggs, of Mo, to Judge in Ill Terr, v Alex'r Steward, rsgnd.
Elijah Sparks, to Atty of U S in Indiana Terr.
John Vawter, to Mrshl of same.

Jas Morgan, re-appt'd Srvyr for port of Murfreesborough in N C.
Wm Mears, Atty of U S for same.
Philip Fouche, to Mrshl in same.
Nath'l W Strong, of N Y, to Cnsl of U S for port of Bartholomews.

TUE AUG 24, 1813
Mrd: on Aug 19, Chas Glover to Miss Jane Cocking, d/o Mr Wm Cocking, of Wash City.

Died: in Wash City, on Aug 20, Mrs Martha Nevitt, consort of Mr C L Nevitt, of Alexandria.

Died: in Gtwn, on Aug 20, Mrs Harriet Peter, consort of Maj John Peter, aged 22 yrs.

Died: at *Chesnut Hill*, Fairfax Co, Va, on Aug 19, Mrs Cath Brown, aged 61 yrs, relict of the late Dr Wm Brown, of Alexandria.

Six cents reward for runaway-Mich'l Garetty, aged about 17 yrs, indented appr. -Nicholas Cassady, Wash, nr the Navy Yd.

WED AUG 25, 1813
Laborers wanted; 80 to 100 able bodied axe-men. -Andrew Bartle, wharf & bridge bldr, Alexandria.

Mrd: on Aug 23, by Rev Mr Laurie, Mr Seth Hyatt, to Mrs Jane Somervell, both of Wash City.

Changed in the P O, Jul 1813:
Cuckooville, Va, Robt Barrett v Robt Barrett jr, rsgnd.
Bent Crk, Va, Wm Price, v Andrew White, do.
Royalton, Vt, Asa Edgerton v Zebulon Lyon.
Bradford, Vt, Thos Currier, v David Hartwell.
Newport, Pa, John Kelly, v Thos N Sloan, dec'd.
Clay C H, Ky, Stephen Gibson v J H Slaughter, mv'd away.
Attakapas, La, Wm Armstrong, v Jos Parrot.
Snicker's Gap, Va, Notley C Williams, v Levin Stephens, rsgnd.
Fla, N Y, Geo Smith, v D Lamater, mv'd away.
Chesterfield C H, Va, John P Crump v V Winfree, jr, dec'd.
New Lisbon, Ohio, Geo Endley, v Thos Rowland, rsgnd.
Charlotte, Ten, Chas Barnes, v John Read, do.
Burke, Vt, Matthew Cushing v Geo W Dennison, do.
Pembroke, N Y, Jos Lester, v Jas Richardson.
Fork Shoals, S C, John W Harrison.
Remson, N Y, Heman Ferry, v S Hutchinson, situation inconvenient.
Penn's Sq, Pa, C Humphreys, v John Thomas.
Bowling Green, Ky, David H Robinson, v J Sharp, rsgnd.
Youngstown, Pa, Sam'l White, v Alex'r Johnson, do.

New ofcs est'd in Jul 1813 & postmstrs:
Fishing Crk, Wilkes Co, N C, John Conyngham.
Parishville, St Lawrence Co, N Y, Dan'l Hoard.
Kingsbury, Wash Co, N Y, Jonathan Bellamy.
North Adams, Berkshire Co, Mass, Nathan Putman.
Ports Ferry, Marion Co, S C, Jas Bellune.
Murfreesboro, Knox Co, Ten, Joel Childers.

Fair View, Erie Co, Pa, Calvin Cole.
St Helena, Wilkinson Co, La, Wm Spiller.
St Tammany's, Wilkinson Co, La, Benj Collins.
West Brooks, Bladen Co, N C, A C Miller.
Somerville, Fauquier Co, Va, Thos Samuel
Cold Stream Mills, Hampshire Co, Va, Sam'l P White.
Concordia, Concordia Co, La, Jas Dunlop.
Catahoula, Rapid Co, La, John Hall.
German, Chenango Co, N Y, Ebenezer Hill.
Fairfield, Columbiana Co, Ohio, John Crosier.
Frayser's tavern, New Kent Co, Va, Beverly Frayser.
Byrdtown, Cape Girardeau Co, Mo Ter, Jos Sewall.
Duplin Old Crt Hse, Duplin Co, N C, Dan'l Kenan.
Walden, Caledonia Co, Vt, Leonard Farrington.

Orphans Crt of Chas Co, Md. Prsnl est of John Parnham, late of said co, dec'd. -Geo D Parnham

THU AUG 26, 1813
Pblc sale of rl est of Jas Barry, dec'd, lying in D C, on Oct 25. -Robt Brent, Elias B Caldwell, Trustees.

Strayed from the commons in Wash, a Buffaloe cow. -John Hayre, tavern kpr, nr the Navy Yd; reward-$5.

FRI AUG 27, 1813
Creditors of the late John Litle, dec'd, to appear on Sep 3 for their dividends. -Sam'l Brook, adm & trustee.

SAT AUG 28, 1813
Reward-$5, for strayed or stolen bay mare. Basil Clubb, living nr Booth's wharf.

MON AUG 30, 1813
Ice for sale at the Ice Hse. -Lewis Deblois.

Died: at Phil, on Aug 23, after a short illness, Alex'r Wilson, author of the American Ornithology & other literary works.

TUE AUG 31, 1813
Orphans Crt of Wash Co, D C. Prsnl est of Joshua J Moore, late of said co, dec'd. -Eliz Moore, admx.

R Cashell, jeweler, F st, Wash. To let-the hse 4 hses above the Union Bank, Gtwn.

WED SEP 1, 1813
PG Co, Md, tax list-Aug 10, 1813. Lands, lots & hses on which county taxes remain unpaid. Upper Marlbro, Charlotte & Mt Calvert Hundreds.
Sam'l Hepburn-heirs   Arnold Livers   Grace Lyon-heirs

Mrs Thirley	Frank Leek, jr-heirs	Hugh Maguire
Francis Piles	John Rogers-heirs	John Selby
Rich'd Spriggs	Dennis Scott-heirs	Thos Tillard-heirs
Sam'l W Magruder-heirs	Jane Urquhart	Lingan Wilson

Mattapany, Wash, Pr Fred'k Hundreds:

John Adams, jr	Rich'd Brightwell	John Burwell
Wm Sprigg Bowie-heirs	Jas Bates-heirs	Benj Contee
Thos Buchanan-heirs	Fielder Bowie-heirs	Fleming T Compton
Arthur Campbell	John Campbell	Wm Cook
Jane Davis	Mary Eversfield	Sarah A Gibbons
Wm M Eversfield-heirs	Geo Gibbons	Mary A Gates
Thos Gardiner	Wm Grindall	Dr Thos Gantt
Geo H Gantt	Thos Hodgkins	John Hughes-heirs
Rebecca Litchworth	Rich'd Lee-heirs	John Linthicum
Jas Mewbern	Susanna Magruder	Wm Mayhew
Alex'r Magruder-heirs	Chas L Nevitt	David D Padgett
John F A Prigges-heirs	Rich'd Richards	Elisha Richardson
Dan'l Smallwood	Edw Swann-heirs	Edw Swann, jr.
John Smith	Rich'd Skinner	Nathan Smith
Nicholas B Sunsberry-heirs	Jas Swann-heirs	Eliz Trueman
Dan'l Townshend	Levin Watson	Jas Wilson-heirs
Wm Wilson-heirs	Robt Young-heirs	

King Geo & Grub Hundreds:

Henry Atchison	John Adams, jr	John Bowling-heirs
Chas Boarman	Jas H Baynes	Zachariah Burch
Rich'd Brandt	Rich'd Boarman	Hepburn Berry
Nicholas Blacklock-heirs	Sam'l Berry	Mary Clagett
Sam'l Chapman	Thos Clagett	Jas Clerklu & wife
Geo Dyer	Geo W Dent	Wm Lewis Dent
Henry Davidson	Electius Edelen-heirs	Henry Glasgow
Edw Gantt	Theodore Glasgow	Eliz Holley
Thos & John Holley	Elvira Hardy	Eliz A Hilton
Wm Jenkins	Thos Lane-heirs	Benj Mitchell
Nathaniel Newton	Revd Geo Ralph	Walter Rankin
Rich'd A B Webster		

Piscataway & Hynson Hundreds:

Geo Beall of Geo	Rich'd H Courts	Benj Dulany
John M Clagett-heirs	John Dodson-heirs	John Galworth
Jesse Greenwell-heirs	Dan'l Henley	John Hepburn
Geo Hardy	Ann Jenkins	Mary Jones
Chas Jones [millwright]	Thos Jenkins of Dan'l	Francis Jenkins
Chas King	Mich'l Lowe	Henry H Lowe
Philip Lee	Solomon Lanham	Dan'l Morris
Mich'l Lowe & Leonard Soper	Wm Mansfield	Eliz M'Donough
Jas Moore's heirs	Wm Masters	Dan'l Moxeley
Jas Rudd	Dan'l Paul	Sarah Smith
Sarah Shanby	Dr John Shaaff	David Stone
Lewin Talburt	John Wheat	Mary Wade

New Scotland, Oxen, & Bladensburg Hundreds:

Hiram Belt	Sam'l D Beck-heirs	Zacharish Brown, jr
Isaac Banot-heirs	Wm Bruce-heirs	Wm Danford-heirs
Henry Bradford-heirs	Patrick Daugherty	David Ferguson
Jos Gorden	Thos Gantt	Cath Helmes
Dr Alex Mitchell-heirs	John Murray	Randolph Morris
Nath Popen, sr-heirs	Dr John Stewart-heirs	Jesse Taylor
Wm Sydebothem-heirs	Wm Stuart	John Tilley-heirs
Wm Thomas	Rev Notley Young	

Rock Creek & Eastern Branch Hundreds:

Wm Bailey	Jeremiah Berry's heirs	Henry Cheeney
Francis Deakins-heirs	John Free	Geo Frank
Eliz Jones	Andrew Leitch-heirs	Nicholas Lingan
Wm Sydebothom-heirs	Chas Tilley	John Turnbull

Horspen & Patuxent Hundreds:

Benj Beall-heirs	John Igleheart-heirs	
Philip Nicholl-heirs	Banuck & Isaac Duckett	John Rustin-heirs

Collington & Western Branch Hundred:

Mary Burgess   Elias Harding

-Rich'd Duvall, Collector of PG Co, Md.

Died: on Aug 7, in his 62d yr, nr Warm Springs, whither he was going for the benefit of his health, Gen John Martin, 1st brig U S militia; ofcr during the Rev.

Reward-$25, for negro man, Isaac Davis, about 40 or 50 yrs of age. -Thos Getsendanner, living in Montg Co, Md, about 4 miles from the Crt-hse.

THU SEP 2, 1813

Died: on Aug 31, Mrs Mary Wharton, consort of Col Franklin Wharton. Funeral from her late residence this afternoon.

Wash Co, D C. Wm M'Concklin, insolvent debtor, confined in the Wash Co prison for debt. -Wm Brent, clk.

FRI SEP 3, 1813

Runaways committed to Wash Co, D C, jail: Patsey Simpson, mulatto, aged 32 yrs. Negroes Jacob [ab't 12] & Betsey Thomas [ab't 15]; they say they belong to Nicholas Carr, of Balt, Md. -C Tippett, for W Boyd, Mrshl.

Notice-claims against the est of Elisha Berry, late of PG Co, Md, dec'd, to make known the amount to Beal Ayton. -Ann Berry, excx, Upper Marlboro, PG Co, Md.

SAT SEP 4, 1813

Funeral sermon for Mrs Wharton at the Prot Episc Chr, by Rev Andrew T M'Cormick, on Sunday.

MON SEP 6, 1813
Alexandria, Sep 4. Duel fought bet Com Barney & L Taylor, both of Balt, in Alexandria. Mr Taylor was wounded, but not considered dangerous.

TUE SEP 7, 1813
Runaway committed to the Fred'k Co, Md, jail-Stephen, mulatto man, age about 42 yrs; says he belongs to Mr Sam'l Robinson, of Montg Co, [*Goshen Mills*] Md. -Morris Jones, shrf, Fred'k Co, Md.

Wash Co, D C. Peter Mills, insolvent debtor, confined in Wash Co prison for debt. -Wm Brent, clk.

WED SEP 8, 1813
Died: at Savannah, on Aug 22, Mr Geo Tomlin, U S N, commanding Gun-boat 153, aged 30 yrs.

Wash Co, D C, to wit: Jun term, 1813. Benj Gaither & Dan'l Gaither, trustees of Col Henry Gaither of said Co: ratify sale of rl est to Andrew Ross, of said co, of brick hse & lot in Gtwn for $9,300. -Wm Brent, clk.

Reward $1 for Wm Leach, appr to the shoe making bus, who absconded on Aug 21. -Thos Wannall

THU SEP 9, 1813
Mrd: on Sep 7, by Rev Mr Breckenridge, Mr Jas Bowen to Miss Ann Cook, both of Wash City.

FRI SEP 10, 1813
Wash Co, D C. Jas Ridgway, insolvent debtor, confined in Wash Co, prison, for debt. Trustee appt'd. -W Brent, clk.

SAT SEP 11, 1813
To be rented-fishing landings at Gisborough. Proposals rec'd by Mr Philip Webster, residing therein. -J T Shaaff

MON SEP 13, 1813
Extract from a memorial to the Sec of State by Jas Orm, Jos B Cook, Thos Humphries, mstrs of American vessels, who were P O Ws in Eng, & returned to the U S in the cartel ship *Robinson-Potter*. Rg: treatment of our countrymen [P O Ws] by the British.

The Fairfax Jockey Club Races will commence on Sep 23. John Maddux, prop of the course, Fairf C H, Va.

TUE SEP 14, 1813
Killed: Nathl Garren, on board the U S brig *Enterprize*, in engagement with the British brig *Boxer*, Sep 5. -Edw R M'Call, Senior ofcr.

Two of the crew of the late U S sloop of war *Wasp*, detained by Capt John Beresford, British ship *Poictiers*. John M'Cloud, mrd in Norfolk in 1804 or 05, has wife & 4 chldrn there. John Stephens, in svc about 5 yrs. -Geo S Wise, purser.

WED SEP 15, 1813
Mr Dan'l Brown, grocer of Charleston, a ntv of R I, but for 20 yrs a resident of Charleston, was found dead in his bed chambers, his body burnt.

THU SEP 16, 1813
Portland, Sep 12. The remains of the gallant Wm Burrows, late Cmder of the U S brig *Enterprize*, & of his brave competitor Sam'l Blyth, late Cmder of the British brig *Boxer*, will be entombed in the town today.

Mrd: on Sep 14, by Rev Mr Brown, Mr John Bailey to Miss Cath Borrows, all of Wash City.

Jun term, 1813. Crct Crt of D C to allot dower to the widow of Jer Hazel who died intestate. -Wm Brent, clk.

Deserted from the garrison on Sep 8, Uriah Ray, a pvt in the 2d Artl; aged 28 yrs; born in Nantucket, Mass; has relations in Balt. -John Ritchie, Capt, 2d Artl Com Ft Wash.

FRI SEP 17, 1813
Six cents reward for runaway, Jas Wiss, age about 18 or 19 yrs, appr to the plastering bus. He was employed a few days by Mr Jos Chick, plasterer, in New Mkt, Fred'k Co, Md. -Alex Carmichael, Gtwn.

SAT SEP 18, 1813
Depos regarding the landing of the British at Fredericktown, Md, 1813. Depositions of Jonathan Greenwood, aged 30 yrs, resident of Fredericktown, Md; of Capt John Allen, of same, aged about 51 yrs; of Joshua Ward, aged 44, living nr same; of Toilus Robertson, aged about 34 yrs, living in Cecil Co: of Moses N Cannon, aged 32 yrs; of Jno T *Veazy, being in the fort at Fredericktown on May 6, under the command of Col Thos W *Veazey; of Frisby Henderson, J P of Cecil Co: of Cordelia *Pennington, lvg in Frenchtown; of Delia *Penington. Others who appeared before the J P:

	John W Etherington	Dela F Heath
John V Price	Henry E Coalman	Sam'l Dixon
Joshua Greenwood	Robt H Maxwell	Wm Etherington
John Loftis	John Etherington	John Duffoy
Mosses N Carson	Hezekiah [x] Dowlin	Elias See

Jos Davis. Depo of Rich'd Barnaby, of Fred'ktown, Cecil Co, Md, aged 48 yrs. Francis B Chandlear, of same, aged about 39 yrs. -H B Penington, J P for Cecil Co, Md. Signed on Jun 10, 1813, Cecil Co, Md. [*2 splgs]

MON SEP 20, 1813
Statement of Jacob Gibson, of articles taken by the British, on his property at *Sharps Island*, on Apr 12, Easternshore, Md. -Wm Harrison, J P-Talbot Co, Md.

TUE SEP 21, 1813
Depos-attack on Havre de Grace, May 3; Wm T Kirkpatrick regarding Capt Lawrence who plundered the town. Sworn before Elijah Davis, J P for Harford Co, Jun 25, 1813; Jas Wood & his account; Roxana Moore-fled for her safety, her hsbnd not being home, her chldrn with her including her baby under 2 mos. Rich'd Mansfield, a ctzn of Havre de Grace, & his son, his hse was plundered & set on fire. Others named-Jas Sears, age 17 yrs; John O'Neil, a naturalized Irishman.

WED SEP 22, 1813
Died: on Sep 13, in Frederic Co, Va, Edmund Randolph, after a few days illness.

I wish to sell my farm in Fairfax Co, Va, nr Mr Wrens tavern, 248 acs. Apply to Everard Gray, Gtwn, D C, or to Susanna P Cloud.

THU SEP 23, 1813
Killed on board the U S squad under command of O H Perry, in action of Sep 10, 1813, on board the *Lawrence*:

	John Brooks-Lt	Henry Laub-Mids
Christian Mayhew, -Qrtrmstr	Jas W Allen-seamn	Jos Kennedy-seamn
John C Kelly-pvt	John Smith-seamn	Wm Cranston-o s
Andrew Michael-seamn	John Hoffman-o s	Chas Pohig-seamn
Nelson Peters-seamn	Jas Jones-seamn	John Rose-seamn
Jas Carty-sle mkr's mate	Thos Butler-seamn	Jas Brown-seamn
Wilson Mays-carp mate	Ethelred Sykes-landsmn	Jesse Harland-pvt
Philip Starpley-cpl marines	Abner Williams-pvt	

Killed on board the *Niagara*:
Peter Morel-seamn   Isaac Hardy-o s

P O changes in Aug. 1813:
Hartland, Vt, Aaron Willard, jr v D H Sumner, dec'd.
Eastham, Ms, Jos Mayo v Hardin Knowles, rsgnd.
Barbourville, Ky, Wm Patton v Overton Baker, do.
Ft Massac, Ill Ter, Jas Weaver v A Skinner, do.
Chalk Level, Va, John Stone jr, v Sam'l Stone, do.
Cold Spring, N J, Daniel Hughes v Aaron Eldridge, do.
Clarksboro, Ga, John Loving v Sam'l Gardner, mv'd away.
Kenhawa C H, Va, Patrick Kenon v Wm Whittaker, rsgnd.
Westmoreland, N Y, Jos Jones v Noah Levins, do.
Greenville, Va, Sam'l Finley v Robt Mitchell, do.
Jones Store, N C, Benj Riggon v Rich'd Jones, do.
Ft Stephens, Ohio, Geo Pease v Wm M'Connell, do.
Salem, Ky, Douglas J Puckett v Sam'l C Haskins, do.
Kingstree, S C, Patrick Cormick v W Murray, dec'd.
Waynesville, Ohio, David Pugh v Sam'l Highway, rsgnd.
Overton C H, Ten, John Kennedy v Joel Mabry, do.
Topsfield, Ms, Cyrus Cummings v N Cleveland, do.
Riceboro, Ga, John Baker, v A Forrister.

Ca Ire, Va, Henry Rivers v S Lemoine, rsgnd.
Beverly, Ms, John Burley v Farnham Plummer, do.
Pomfret, N Y, Jacob Houghton v Sam'l Berry, do.
New ofcs est'd in Aug 1813 & postmstrs:
Stonesboro, Green Co, Ky, Nimrod Stone.
Spanish Grove, Mecklenburg Co, Va, Wm Garner.
Wmsboro, Barnwell dist, S C, Wm M'Williams.
Pownal, Burlington Co, Vt, Josiah Wright.
Graceham, Fred'k Co, Md, John Creeger.
Lewisville, Brunswick Co, Va, Wm S Lane.
Springfield, Loudon Co, Va, Amos Skinner.
Smith's Store, Spartanburg dist, S C, Wm Smith, jr.
Springfield, Hamilton Co, Ohio, John Baldwin.
M'Cutchensville, Pickaway Co, Ohio, John M'Cutchen.
Ofcs discont'd in Aug 1813:
Gee's Bridge, Va   Black Water, Va   Cuthensville, Ohio

FRI SEP 24, 1813
Died: on Aug 16, at New Orleans, Deniel Clark, Merchant of that city.

SAT SEP 25, 1813
Mrd: on Sep 23, by Rev Mr Breckenridge, N P Bixby to Miss Mgt Sinclair, both of Wash City.

To be sold at the farm of the late Tobias Belt, PG Co, Md, nr Thos Magruder's tavern, negroes, stock, furn, etc. -Rebecca Belt, Jonathan Belt, adms o/same

Reward-$50 for runaway mulatto man, Billy Jackson, age about 20 yrs of age. -Fleet Smith, Leesburg, Loudon Co, Va.

Wash Co, D C. Geo Barnes, insolvent debtor, confined in Wash Co prison, for debt. -Wm Brent, clk.

Listing of items taken by the British in St Mary's Co, Md, nr Point Lookout, Jul 26 last, is in the paper. Victims were:

Wm & Eliz Smoot	Ann Bennett	Capt Wm Smith
Jas Kirk	Robt Duncanson	Josiah Biscoe
M'Kay Biscoe	Tyler Thomas	Benj Williams
Robt Armstrong	Modecai Jones	Elwiley Smith

MON SEP 27, 1813
Boarding. Subscriber is desirous of taking a few genteel boarders; his accomodations are good & terms moderate. -Pendleton Heronimus, Beall st, Gtwn.

TUE SEP 28, 1813
Escaped from the depot of P O Ws, at Pittsfield, on Sep 21: 1-Walter Kerr, lt Glengary regt, born at Niagara, aged 22 yrs, 6' 2, taken on May 27, nr Ft Geo.

2-Alex'r Greig, ensign 8th King's regt, aged 20 yrs, 5' 9 1/2, born at Quebec, taken in May last at Sacket's Harbor. -Thos Melville, jr, Dep Mrshl Mass Dist, & Agent of Prisoners, Pittsfield, Mass.

WED SEP 29, 1813
Jos S Collins & Co has est'd a Printing Ofc in Gtwn on Bridge st, nrly oppo the store of Mr W Morgan.

THU SEP 30, 1813
Wash Co, D C, in Chancery. John Woodward vs Thos Gamble. Ratify sale of prop sold by Chas Glover, trustee, to Wm Crawford, who hath assigned same to Edgar Patterson, for $147. -Wm Brent, clk.

Wash Co, D C, in Chancery. Minifie, Frye & Spalding vs Geo Walker. Wm Brent & Philip B Key, trustees in this case, sold prop to Jos S Lewis & Chas Glover, for $1,140.86. -Wm Brent, clk.

FRI OCT 1, 1813
Ranaway-Ham Cook, mulatto man, age bet 26 & 30 yrs. -Jas Gordon, lvg in Fauquier Co, Va, nr Middleburg.

The John Bull story of the late Capt Jas Lawrence having been born in Bristol, Eng, is very like a whale. Capt Jas Lawrence, s/o John Lawrence, of Burlington, N J, was born in 1776; his hse directly oppo Powell's Acad. I was intimate in the family of Mr John Lawrence, who was the eldest s/o Elisha Lawrence, of Chestnut Grove, Monmouth Co, N J. His gr-fr might have been born in Eng; he was upwards of 70 yrs when I first met him, & I understood that Elisha Lawrence & his bro, John, were among the first settlers in Monmouth Co, N J. Statement founded on unquestionable authority. -W G.

Died: at his residence in Fairfax Co, Va, on Sep 23, Col Wm Payne, in his 62d yr.

Camden Co, N C-Rpblcn meeting on Sep 20, 1813; Nathan Snowden, chrmn; Malachi Sawyer, sec. Rg-official conduct of David Stone, Sen in Cong from N C.

SAT OCT 2, 1813
Public sale of numerous acticles at Wm Shepard's Ware-hse, Newbern, N C, on Oct 11 next. -Edw Pasteur, Wm Shepard, agents, Newbern, N C.

MON OCT 4, 1813
Previous to my departure from Wash, I have endeavored to settle all claims upon me. Should I have omitted to do so in any instance, address me at Pittsburg, Pa. -B H Latrobe.

Mrsh'ls sale; title etc of Chas Minifie in prop in Wash City; at the suit of Wm Prout against Chas Minifie. -Wash Boyd, Mrshl D C. Oct 4, 1813

TUE OCT 5, 1813
Grand Nat'l Lottery. Mangers in Wash City:
Fred'k May   Edmund Law   Gr'th Coombe
Dan'l Carroll of D'n Thos Law   Peter Miller
Jas D Barry
Sole agent of Balt, Md-Eli Simkins

Bigspring Estate for sale on the premises nr Leesburg, Loudoun Co, Va, on Dec 28; 1,260 acs. -Geo W Ball, Fayette Ball, Chas B Ball, heirs & devisees of B Ball, dec'd. Leesburg, Loudoun Co, Va.

WED OCT 6, 1813
Ranaway-John & Harry, both of black compeletion. John was hired from the reps of the est of the late Mr Thos Mason of Woodbridge. -Thos Harrison, lvg in Pr Wm Co, nr Dumfries, Va.

THU OCT 7, 1813
Ladies with ltrs in the P O at Wash, Oct 1, 1813:

Claressa Baldwin	Miss Sarah Barns	Mrs Ann Brodeau
Jane Baker	Eliz Bradley-2	Mrs Mary Bruff
Mary Choular	Miss F Campton	Charlotte Cannady
Mrs Ann Crain	Betsey Clark	Eliz Clark
Lidia Dorsey	Eliza Duvall	Mrs Derey
Eliz Farnow	Sofia Fouenan	Mrs Green
Cath A Glaves	Susannah Jenkins	Cath Johnston
Mgt Ingram	Mary H Lee-3	Miss Lythea
Susan Mosher	Eliz Kelly	Mrs Ann Morgan
Sarah Miles	Mary Purrel	Ann Phenix
Kitty Rounds	Madame Rotland-3	Betsey Ross
Mary Simes	Eliz Singos	Ann Stewart
Hannah Sprigg	Mrs Strike	Mary Ann Stettenius
Mary Shelhamer	Miss Stewart	Mrs Ann Tareman
Mrs Thompson	Mrs M Vand Zant	Mrs A D Wallack
Mary Washington	Susan Warwick	Martha Warren
Matilda Young	Martha Young	

Reward-$100 for Sam, negro, bound to a blacksmith. -John Threlkeld

FRI OCT 8, 1813
A return of the American prisoners who were tomahawked by the Indians subsequent to the battle at Frenchtown, Jan 22, 1813:
Pascal Hickman, Capt   Jas E Blythe, Pvt   Chas Gerles, do
Thos S Crow, Pvt   Dan'l Darnell, do   Thos Ward, do
Wm Butler, do   Henry Downy, do   John P Sidney, do
-Isaac L Baker, Ensign 2d U S infty

Valuable prop for sale at the Union Tavern, Gtwn; prop of the late Gen Jas M Lingan; tract cld *Haerlem*-185 acs; *Spring Hill*-21 acs, country seat of Henry Foxall; & numerous other lots. -W Smith, trustee

SAT OCT 9, 1813
Ten dollars reward for the apprehension of Thos Hasett, a sldr in the 38th regt of Infty; deserted from my rendezvous in this place, Sep 25; ntv of Va, painter by profession, aged 23 yr; has resided in Calvert Co, Md for svr'l yrs. -John Brookes, Capt 38th Regt U S Infty, Upper Marlborough, PG Co, Md.

Mrsh'l sale of *Clear Drinking*, 50 acs, in Montg Co, Md, seized as the prop of Chas C Jones, at suit of Oliver Evans. -Thos Rutter, Mrshl, Balt.

Died: at Fredericksburg, on Sep 28, Larkin Smith, Coll of the Port of Norfolk.

MON OCT 11, 1813
Mt Vernon mills for sale; rebuilt in 1801; with dwlg hse; 100 acs with 120 acs nrby, Kent Co, Dela. -Henry Molleston, Camden.

TUE OCT 12, 1813
Runaway, Joseph, mulatto boy; says he belongs to Mr Benj Perry, nr Gtwn, D C. -Morris Jones, shrf, Fred'k Co, Md.

WED OCT 13, 1813
Notice-came to the subscriber's inclosure on *Greenleaf's Point* Sep 2, a red cow & calf. -John Wheat.

THU OCT 14, 1813
I certify that Saml S Schaney brght before me a small white horse. -T Fenwick-J P

Obit of fallen naval hero, Thos Claxton, midshipman on board the *Lawrence,* Capt Perry, on Lake Erie, on Sep 10. Young Claxton was a ntv of Phil, but for the last 13 yrs a resident of Wash City; s/o Mr Thos Claxton, ofcr of the Hse of Reps, & bro to Lt Alexander Claxton. He was in his 19th yr; wounded with an 18 pd cannon shot on the right shoulder, lingering 27 days; he expired on Oct 7.

Wash Co, D C. Sale of est & effects of insolvent debtor, Hanson Hedges, by Wm H P Tuckfield, the trustee, on Nov 30th.

FRI OCT 15, 1813
Orphans Crt of Montg Co, Md. Prsnl est of Eliz Offutt, late of Montg Co, Md, dec'd. -Baruch Offutt, exc.

Died: at *Belle Field*, PG Co, Md, the seat of B Oden, on Oct 8, Mrs Hannah Sophia Biscoe, after a short & painful illness.

SAT OCT 16, 1813
Died: on Oct 7, in his 42d yr, at the residence of Mr Travers Daniel, sr, in Stafford Co, Dr John Moncure Daniel, Senior Hosp Surg, U S military svc.

MON OCT 18, 1813
Mrd: in Fauquier Co, Va, on Oct 15, Jas L M'Kenna, Cashier of the Bank of Alexandria, to Miss Ann F Randolph, d/o Col Robt Randolph, of said co.

Strayed from Centreville, on Aug 16, a chesnut sorrel horse; raised above Harper's Ferry. -John Hampton, Buckland.

Wash Co, D C, in Chancery. Bennet Jarboe vs Rich'd B Brashears. Bill is to obtain a decree for the sale of a part of lot 1 in sq 348, Wash City, formerly sold by the cmplnt to the dfndnt & cnvy'd to him, on which is due $55. Brashears resides out of D C. -Wm Brent, clk.

Deserted-from the hosp at *Greenleaf's Point*, Geo Ebert, born in Mass, enlisted in Balt, aged 18 yrs, seaman. Wm Powers, born in Alexandria, Va, age 18 yrs, laborer. -Jas Haslett, Capt in 38th Regt U S Infty.

TUE OCT 19, 1813
Died: on Oct 15, Capt Thos Tretcher, of Alexandria, in his 53d yr, after a long & painful illness. This gentleman had the honor of sailing the world around with the celebrated Capt Jas Cook.

WED OCT 20, 1813
Trustees of Newbern Acad, N C, advertise for a principal. -Francis Hawks, Pres; Jas G Stanly, Sec.

THU OCT 21, 1813
To be sold at Neabsco, nr Dumfries, Va, 70 to 80 head of cattle. -Anderson Boughton, agent for Col Tayloe.

Seasonable good for sale by Seth Hyatt, jr, at his store, Pa av, Wash City.

Lease for sale-*Mt Washington,* 40 acs, on Gtwn Turnpike rd, halfway bet that place & Alexandria. -Mariam Ball

FRI OCT 22, 1813
Stenographer wanted for about 10 or 12 wks at the ofc of the Md Rpblcn, Annapolis, Md; capable to take down the debates in legislature. -Jehu Chandler

Val land to be sold; on Chas' Branch, PG Co, Md; about 700 acs; formerly belonged to Henry Brookes. -Ann Berry, excx of Elisha Berry.

Mrd: on Tue wk, by Rev Dr Bowen, Francis Jeffrey, editor of the *Edinburgh Review*, to Miss Charlotte Wilkes, d/o Chs Wilkes, cashier of the Bank of N Y.

Mgt Fauble, insolvent debtor, confined in Wash Co prison. -Wm Brent, clk.

SAT OCT 23, 1813
Mrd: on Oct 20th, by Rev Dr Muir, Mr John H Crease, merchant, to Miss Jane P Newton, both of Alexandria.

MON OCT 25, 1813
Narrative of Thos King, an American seaman, who escaped from a British ship at Bermuda. King is a ntv of S C, & at this time 21 yrs of age, having followed the sea for the 9 yrs past on the gun-brig *Vixen*-commanded by Geo Wash Reed. -Thos King, Aug 27, 1813, Wash City, D C.

Wash Co, D C. Case of John Goldsmith, insolvent debtor, confined in Wash Co prison, for debt. -Wm Brent, clk.

TUE OCT 26, 1813
Wash Co, D C. Thos Belt brought before me a stray mare; taken up on the farm of Benj Belt. -Sam'l H Smith, J P.

Sale by auction-2 story brick hse, presently occupied by Mr Thos Keithly, on part of lot 1 in sq 952, nr the Navy Yd gate. -David Bates, auctioneer.

WED OCT 27, 1813
Strayed or stolen-two bay mare horses. I purchased them of Mr Crostree, of Waynesborough, Pa. -Geo Beall, lvg in Wash City nr the Marine Barracks.

To rent-my store hses at *Allen's Fresh*. -Jno Campbell, Chas Co, Md.

THU OCT 28, 1813
Orphans Crt of PG Co, Md. Prsnl est of Robt Wall, late of said co, dec'd. -Mary Wall, admx.

To rent-my store hses at *Allen's Fresh*. -Jno Campbell, Chas Co, Md.

FRI OCT 29, 1813
Illumination-celebration in Phil on Thu for the capture of Gen Proctor's army by the U S army under Gen Harrison; most conspicuous was the hse of Jacob G Koch, crnr of 9th & Mkt sts.

Mrd: on Oct 12, in Hagerstown, Daniel Sprigg, of Wash Co, to Miss Eliza Chesley, late of Gtwn.

Died: on Oct 23, at the hse of Mr Wm Whann, of Gtwn, Mr Sam'l Moffitt, a Purser of the U S Navy.

Reward for mislaid silver watch, maker's name Hugh Cunningham, Dublin, no. 490. Patrick Ferrall, nr the Navy Yd, Wash.

Will be sold on Oct 30, the fast sailing Schn'r formerly owned by Jos B Parsons, dec'd. -Eliz Parsons.

Orphans Crt of Wash Co, D C. Prsnl est of Jos B Parsons, late of said city, dec'd. -Eliz Parsons, admx.

Strayed or stolen-a pointer dog, Trim; five dollar reward- -John T Abert.

SAT OCT 30, 1813
Ltr dt'd Chillicothe, Oct 22, 1813. We are told that Brig Gen Tecumseh is certainly killed; & a Maj of the Ky Militia had a rifle with him which he said was Tecumseh's.

Died: in Wash City, on Oct 28, Mrs Mary Clarke, consort of Mr Walter Clarke, of this place. Her funeral will take place from her late residence today.

Died: at So Kingstown, R I, on Fri wk, the Hon Freeman Perry, aged 88, gr-fr of the gallant Com Perry.

Died: at Beaufort, S C, on Oct 13, Prentiss Willard, capt in the corps of engrs in the U S svc.

MON NOV 1, 1813
Died: on Oct 25, Jas Cocke, M D, Prof of Anatomy in Md Un.

TUE NOV 2, 1813
Lost, bet the race ground & Wash City, 2 sets of silver castors. Info or leave them at Mr Tomlison's htl on Capt Hill; shall rec a reward of $5, & will bestow charity on a poor unfortunate cartman. -Jos Russell.

WED NOV 3, 1813
Runaway-Isaac Howard, negro man, committed to Fred'k Co, Md, jail; says he belongs to Mr Jas Ogg, of Balt Co, Md. -Morris Jones, shrf of Fred'k Co, Md.

Notice to all persons having claims against the est of Nathan Prather, dec'd; exhibit same by Feb 1. -Walter Prather, exc.

Land for sale at the Crt Hse, in Dumfries, Pr Wm Co, Va; tract cld *Douglass Hill*, the residence of the late Alex'r Lithgow; 800 acs, with dwlg hse. Sale on deed of trust from Alex'r Lithgow to Chas Tyler & Alex'r Lithgow, jr. -P Harrison, atty.

PG Co, Md, Crt. Com'rs deny division of est of John Jackson; petitioned by Jasper M Jackson. -John Read Magruder, clk.

Reward-$5. For strayed horse; deliver same to Edw Owen, on F st, Wash City. -John Bontz.

THU NOV 4, 1813
Removal-Patrick Rodgers, sadler, has remv'd his shop from the ft of Capt Hill, to the hse adjoing Mr Coyle's shoe store. Wash

Orphans Crt of PG Co, Md; sale at the late residence of Benj Owens, dec'd, of PG Co, nr *Crow's Mill*; furn, stock, etc. -Archibald Edmonston, adm w a.

For sale-farm cld *Rockhall Mill*, in Fauquier Co, Va, 4 to 500 acs, prop & late residence af Minor Winn, dec'd, with 2 story stone dwlg. Shown by John W Winn, who resides nrby. -John W Winn & Isham O'Bannon, excs.

FRI NOV 5, 1813
Biog of Com Oliver H Perry, eldest s/o Christopher Raymond Perry, formerly of Newport, R I, but for some mos a resid of this town. Midshipman about 1798; has 3 bros also in the navy, 2 are lts on board the *Pres*; the other, the youngest, about 13 yrs of age, was on board the *Lawrence*. Perry is now 28 yrs of age, having been born in Aug, 1785; mrd a few yrs since to Miss Mason, d/o the late Dr Mason, of Newport, by whom he has one son. [Norwich Courier]

Pblc sale of lot 5 in sq 599, prop of Basil Waring, for taxes due the Wash City Corp, up the yr 1812 inclusive, $5.48 with costs. -Ezl Macdaniel, coll 2d ward.

SAT NOV 6, 1813
Mrd: on Nov 2, at the hse of Mr Edwin Dulin, Fairfax Co, Va, Mr Jas B Catter, of Gtwn, to Miss Maria Dulin.

Runaway-Frank mulatto man, committed to Fred'k Co, Md, jail; says he belongs to Gen Hugh Douglass from Leesburgh, Va. -Morris Jones, shrf, Fred'k Co, Md.

MON NOV 8, 1813
Died: in Ky, on Oct 22, Gen Chas Scott, in his 74th yr, after a lingering illness of some mos; svc in the rev war.

Died: in Boston, on Sat wk, Hon Theophilus Parsons, Chf Justice of the Sup Crt of Mass, aged 63 yrs.

Bargain offer-I will take $1000 cash for tract cld *Terrel Green & Bowling Green*, in PG Co, Md, 173 1/2 acs; with good dwlg hse lately rebuilt at cost of $600. Land is 7 miles from Nottingham. Address John Gantt, nr Lower Marlborough, Calvert Co, or to the subscriber in Balt city. -Geo F Janney.

TUE NOV 9, 1813
Mrd: in Phil, on Nov 4, Mr John Norvell, Editor of the *Balt Whig*, to Miss Cath Cone.

Mrd: on Nov 4, in Phil, Mr John Norvell, Ed of the *Balt Whig*, to Miss Cath Cone.

A Patriot of Seventy-Six. Pleasant Grove, Stokes Co, Oct 20, 1813. Col Jos Winston, of N C, is presented a sword by Hon Bartlett Yancey, as a testimonial for his conduct on Oct 7, 1780, at King's Mntn.

Died: on Sat last, at his residence in the Western Precincts, in his 53d yr, Daniel Delozier, many yrs srvyr of the Port of Balt.

Sam'l West intends to petition the Gen Assembly of Md for the right of Wm West's heirs to part land cld *Two Bros*, part of the addition, & part of *Rocky Point Fortified*.

Orphans Crt of PG Co, Md. Ltrs of adm on est of Archibald Elson, late of said co, dec'd. -Martha P Childs, admx.

WED NOV 10, 1813
Reward-$20, for runaway, Rich'd Brown, a sldr in the svc of the U S, dark hair & red whiskers, born & raised in Rockbridge Co, Va. -H Cross, Lt 42d U S Infty.

THU NOV 11, 1813
Biog of Lt Wm Burrows; born in 1785 at Kinderton, nr Phil, the seat of his fr, Wm Ward Burrows, of S C. In Jun, 1813, he was appt'd to the command of the brig *Enterprise*, at Portsmouth; killed in his 29th yr.

For sale-lot on Mkt Sq, Gtwn; all the right, title, etc of Jos Carleton, dec'd, to a part of same orig lot adjoining, & binding on the property in possession of Mr Peter Meem, with the frame stable on it. -John Travers, auct.

Orphans Crt of Wash Co, D C. Ltrs of adm on the prsnl est of Thos Maine, late of said co, gardener, dec'd. -Wm Bunyie.

Election to be held for one Alderman of the First Ward, vice Stephen Pleasanton, rsgn'd. -Wm Waters, Jos Bromley, Wm O Neal.

FRI NOV 12, 1813
Orphans Crt of PG Co, Md. Sale at the late dwlg plantation of Thos Hays, of said co, dec'd; the whole of his prsnl est. -Fielder Hays, Osborn Vermillion, adms.

SAT NOV 13, 1813
Died: at his farm, at the falls of Paint, [Ohio,] on Nov 2, Gen Nathaniel Massie; one of the oldest settlers in Ohio, & proprietor of the town of Chilicothe.

For sale-a frame hse for ground rent, due to Daniel Carroll of Dudn, on part of lot 5 in sq 771, formerly leased to Mr Henry How, dec'd. Sold by-David Bates.

Reward-$10 for runaway, Zachariah Walker, appr to the Blacksmith trade, age about 18 yrs. -Jos Walker

Nov 12th Anthony Holmead brought before me a stray mare. -Jas M Varnum, J P.

MON NOV 15, 1813
Squadron crt martial will sit at M'Leod's Tavern, Wash City, for trial of all defaulters on Nov 20. -John Peter, Maj C D C Gtwn.

Mrd: on Nov 11, by Rev Wm H Wilmer, Mr John Corse, one of the Editors of the *Herald*, to Miss Julia G Talbot, all of Alexandria.

Two hundred dollars, board & washing, for a teacher, sober & attentive man. -Wm Brewer, nr Poole's store, Montg Co, Md.

Allen Taylor, of PG Co, Md, brought before me a stray mare. -Wm Marshall, J P.

Orphans Crt of PG Co, Md. Sale on the farm where Elsworth Bayne now lives; all the prsnl est of John Bayne, dec'd. -Elsworth Bayne & Edw C Edelen, adms.

TUE NOV 16, 1813
Tribute of respect to the memory of Gen Z Montgomery Pike, Ft Geo, Aug 30, 1813; Lts Geo M'Glassin, Rich'd L Howell, & Ensign Wm Coffie, to be a committee to draft rules for that purpose.

WED NOV 17, 1813
Died: at Charleston, a few days ago, Peter Freneau, late Com'r of loans for S C.

To Rent-3 story brick hse on Jefferson st; warehse & wharf on Water st, lately occupied by Mr Robt Ober. Apply to Sam'l M'Kenney, Gtwn.

Pblc sale at the hse now occupied by Tristram Dalton, nr the Marine Barracks, who is about to remove from Wash City to the Eastward. -Geo Beall, auct.

Stolen-2 pktbks at the hse of Henry Lansdale, in Montg Co, Md, on Fri last. -Wm Locke, & Jas Davis, both nr Hagerstown, Md.

THU NOV 18, 1813
Mrd: on Nov 16, by Rev Mr M'Cormick, Mr Henry Chas *Lewis to Miss Caroline Charlotte De Carnap, both of Wash City. [*possible-part of page is blurred.]

Gen Chas Scott, lately dec'd, was, says the *Ky Reporter*, the last Rev Ofcr of his grade; he engaged at age 17 yrs as a common sldr in the war which terminated by the peace of 1763.

Orphans Crt of Wash Co, D C. Prsnl est of Nath'l Wilson Maddox, late of said co, dec'd. -Notley Maddox, adm.

FRI NOV 19, 1813
On Nov 15, at the rear of Ft Norfolk, Wm Proctor, 35th U S regt, was executed for desertion. Willoughby Meggs & Jos Poole, 5th U S Regt, & Lemuel Jackson, Morgan's Rifle Regt, sentenced for same; order suspended. -Ledger

On Oct 17, three dghts of Mr Benj Harrison, ages 9, 11, & 14, drowned when a canoe upset on Toogalo rvr, nr the mouthh of Chauga. His 16 yr old dght was rescued by a negro belonging to Mr Cheatham of Ga.

Impressed by the British on Lake Ontario: Wm Kelly, shoemkr, of the 14th U S Infty, residence in Cecil Co, Md; emigrated to the colonies before the Rev, srv'd as sldr in the Pa line during that war, age 52 yrs; pressed on board the *Melpomene*. Also John Todd, a ntv of PG Co, Md, of the 14th; pressed on board the *Regulus*.

Wm Waters elected an Alderman for the First Ward, vice Stephen Pleasanton, rsgnd. Wash News.

SAT NOV 20, 1813
Sale of land in Chas Co, Md, whereon the late Wm D Briscoe resided, & now in the occupation of Mrs Sally Briscoe; about 500 acs. -Edmund Key, trustee.

MON NOV 22, 1813
Co-partnership in the rope & twine business, factory on *Greenleaf's Point*. -Daniel Renner & Nath H Heath.

TUE NOV 23, 1813
Died: at Harrisburgh, Pa, on Nov 16, in his 71st yr, Maj Gen Andrew Porter, Srvyr Gen of that state.

Stray black mare came to the farm of Mr Dudley Digges, on Oct 30. -Wm Rabbitt.

WED NOV 24, 1813
For sale-3,000 pr of shoes. Isaac Tenny, Gtwn.

Orphans Crt of PG Co, Md. Prsnl est of Jas Forbes, late of said co, dec'd. -John Forbes, adm.

THU NOV 25, 1813
Died: at Bladensburg, on Nov 22, after an illness of 5 wks, Mrs Ann Maria Kent, consort of Dr Thos H Kent, of that place, & d/o Col Francis Peyton, of Alexandria. This excellent young woman was only in her 18th yr & mrd but 6 mos. Her remains will be buried in the family burial ground nr Alexandria.

FRI NOV 26, 1813
Biog of Jas Broom, first Lt of Marines, on board the *Chesapeake*, about 24 yrs of age, killed in the action with the Shannon, on Jun 1. Born in Wilmington, Dela, s/o Maj Abraham Broom. His bro, Chas, age about 18 yrs, is now a Lt of Marines; his youngest bro, Thos, is a cadet at West Point.

SAT NOV 27, 1813
Nicholas B Van Zandt brought before me a stray horse. -R S Briscoe, J P, Wash.

MON NOV 29, 1813
To his Excellency Martin Chittendem, *ordering the Militia of the 3d Brig in the 3d Div of the Militia of Vt, now doing duty in N Y state, to return to their residence. While we are in actual svc, your power over us is suspended. Signed:*

Luther Dixon-Lt Col	Elijah Dee, jr-Maj.
Josiah Grout-Maj	Chas Bonnet-Capt
Jesse Post-Capt	Elijah W Wood-Capt
Elijah Birge-Capt	Martin D Follet-Capt
Amasa Mansfield-Capt	T H Campbell-Lt
G O Dixon-Lt	Francis Northway-Lt
Joshua Brush-Lt	Daniel Dodge, Ensign
Sanford Gad Comb-Capt	Jas Fallington-Qr Mstr
Shepard Beals-Lt	John Fasset-Surg
Seth Clark, jr-Surg's Mate	Thos Waterman-Capt
Benj Follet-Lt	Mesa Hill-Surg's Mate

TUE NOV 30, 1813
For sale, by deed of trust from Jos Wheaton to me, lots 13 & 15 in sq 253 in Wash City, with good brick hse. -Sam Eliot, jr.

Appt'd mgrs of the lottery, by the Mayor, Wash City, for bldg 2 pblc schools & a penitentiary in Wash City:

John Davidson	Thos Munroe	John Hewitt
Wash Boyd	Andrew Way, jr	Jos Gales, jr
Wm Brent	John Law	Sam'l N Smallwood
Buller Cocke	Wm Prout	John Dobbyn

Died: in Wash City, on Nov 27, Mrs Mary C Ringgold, consort of Tench Riggold. Funeral sermon at the Cath Chr in Gtwn, tomorrow.

Runaway-Wm, negro man, says he belongs to Sam'l Wilson of Berkeley Co, Va; age about 17 yrs. -Henry Sweitzer, shrf of Wash Co, Md. Hagerstown, Md.

Land for sale on Fredericktown rd, 93 acs; farm of 141 acs; & farm adj both with 480 acs. Apply to Wm Blanchard on the premises, or Wm Cocking, Wash City.

WED DEC 1, 1813
Ofcrs killed in the action at Wmsburg in Upper Canada on Nov 11, 1813, viz: Lt Wm W Smith of the Light Artl; David Hunter, 12 Regt Infty; Edw Olmstead, 16 Regt Infty. Brig Gen Leonard Covington, mortally wounded, since dead.

THU DEC 2, 1813
For Rent-the place I now live on, bet the toll-gate & the Capitol; about 10 acs well enclosed. -Jos Forrest

FRI DEC 3, 1813
Sam'l W Beck, of PG Co, Md, insolvent debtor, in confinement for debt; trustee to be appt'd. -John Read Magruder, clk

For sale-part of *Haddon*, north of the turnpike rd leading from Wash to Bladensburg; divided into 2 parts, ea part $2,000. -Jas Clerklee, Bromont, nr Allen's Fresh, Chas Co, Md.

Mrd: at Boston, on Nov 27, by Rev J S J Gardiner, Chas Stewart, Cmder of the U S frig *Constitution*, to Miss Delia Tudor, d/o the Hon Wm Tudor.

Boarding hse opened on Pa av, Wash, D C. -Alex Estep

SAT DEC 4, 1813
Mrd: in Fredericktown, on Nov 30, by Rev Patrick Davidson, Mr David Ott, of Wash City, to Miss Mary Ritchie, d/o Col John Ritchie, of Fredericktown.

Plated ware for sale-manufactory, 29 N Gay st, Balt, Md. -Geo Tharp, slvr pltr.

MON DEC 6, 1813
Stolen out of my stable, a lge Sorrel horse; reward-$10. -Jos Ratcliffe

TUE DEC 7, 1813
Boots & Shoes Manufactory, oppo the Union Bank of Gtwn. -Benj Mayfield

Wm Elliott proposes publishing, in Wash City, an evening newspaper, to be entitled *The Wash Gazette*.

Died: lately in the state of Ohio, after a severe illness, Capt Sam'l Price, of the 1st Regt U S Light Artl.

Died: a few days ago, at Cincinnati, on his return from Detroit, having srv'd in the late campaign as Adj to the 28th U S Regt, Lt Rich'd Price.

Patrick Frazier has been appt' Chimney Sweep for the !st & 2d Wards, Wash City; Rich'd Sheckles for the 3d & 4th Wards.

Runaways-John Pride, negro, age about 30 yrs; Jack Gardiner, negro, age about 26 yrs. They say they belong to Mr Thos Turner of Pr Wm Co, Va. -Moris Jones, Shrf, Fred'k Co, Md.

WED DEC 8, 1813
Proposals for publishing in Wash City, a monthly work, to be entitled *The American Historical & Political Register*, by Wm F Warnick.

THU DEC 9, 1813
N J Fredonian. Lt Wm W Smith who fell in the action of Nov 14, was a ntv of our state, & a bro of B Smith, P Mstr of this city; was appt'd at age 14 a Cadet at the Military Acad at West Point. At the time of his death he was but 18 yrs of age.

Died: on Dec 2, in his 50th yr, after a lingering consumption, at Slash Creek, Lt Col Elisha Jones, of PG Co Militia [Md]-leaving a lg family.

Orphans Crt of Wash Co, D C. Prsnl est of Peter Dent Moore, late of said city, dec'd. -Louisa Moore, admx.

FRI DEC 10, 1813
Boarding hse opened on Pa av, Wash City. -Alex Estep

SAT DEC 11, 1813
The body of Capt Fairbanks Comstock, of this place, who was drowned in New Longon Harbor on Oct 20, was found on Marth'a Vineyd on Nov 13. -Courier [Wash City column]

Orphans Crt of PG Co, Md. Ltrs test on est of Peter Meem, dec'd. -Lawson Pearson, adm.

Mary Bowie, Wm Bowie, Adms of Walter Bowie vs Geo Tyler, Tobias Tyler & Wm Tyler, in Chancery, Nov 22, 1813. Rg: sale of rl est of Robt Bradley Tyler, now dec'd. On Apr 14, 1792, Walter Bowie became the surety of Robt B Tyler for the payment of the sum of 690 pds 5 shillings current money; the said Bowie dischg'd the said bond; Robt B Tyler has since died intestate leaving rl est, which has descended to the dfndnts his sons & heirs at law. Wm Bowie & Mary Bowie, adms, have filed their peition, stating that Wm Tyler, dfndnt, now resides in Va. -Jas P Heath, Reg Crt Chancery.

Ad-Mr Geo Murren has been engaged for one half my line of stages from Dumfries to Alexandria; the business will be conducted by him, who resides at Wood Lawn for that purpose. -John Tayloe.

Wanted-a sober steady man to drive a hack carriage. -John Bridges, Gtwn.

Montg Co Crt, [Md]. Sale at the dwlg plantation of Zachariah Gatton, late of said co, dec'd; 353 3/4 acs. Wm Willson, Sam'l West, Sam'l Willson, Robt P Magruder, Com'rs.

MON DEC 13, 1813
Robt T Leech appt'd Srvyr Gen of Pa, vice Gen Andrew Porter, dec'd.

Louisville, Ky, Nov 23. The Bagging Factory of Mr Jas S Bate, 6 miles from this town, has been destroyed by fire.

For sale-Jewelry, watches, gold & silver cases, etc. -Jacob Leonard, Gtwn.

Reward-$10 for Jas H Hankins, fair complexion, aged 37, deserted from the subscriber's rendevous at Clarksburg, Montg Co, Md, on Dec 4, enlisted sldr; cabinest mkr. -Robt Beall, Lt 14 Reg U S Infty.

TUE DEC 14, 1813
Wanted to purchase-U S Military Land Warrants. Apply to Henry Northorp, of Zanesville, Ohio, or to Mich'l Nourse, Wash City.

Runaway, Will Lee, mulatto man, committed to the A A jail; age about 25 yrs. -Solomon Groves, Shrf of Anne Arundel Co, Md.

Liberal wages for negro men to be employed on the Works of the Potomac Co, for the yr 1814. -Josias Thompson, Superintendent for said co.

For sale or rent-the hse I lately erected on sq 533, fronting on C st; also the whole of sq 563. -Nath'l H Heath.

For sale-the farm on which I reside, on Wash Turnpike Rd, upwards of 300 acs, with small 2 story frame dwlg. -Thos Fenwick

Petition in writing of Sam'l W Beck, for act of benefit of insolvent debtor. -John R Magruder, clk PG Co, Md.

WED DEC 15, 1813
Wm O'Neale has built an additional hse containing 20 rms completely furnished; bet the Pres' Hse & Gtwn, Wash City; rms by day, wk or month.

Orphans Crt of PG Co, Md. Prsnl est of Philip Waters, late of said co, dec'd. -Jos Cross, adm. [Pblc sale at the farm of Philip Waters, dec'd, nr Thos Magruder's Tavern, on Jan 12, 1814.]

THU DEC 16, 1813
Orphans Crt of Wash Co, D C. Prsnl est of Jos B Parsons, late of said city, dec'd. -Eliz Parsons, admx.

Ltr from Capt David Porter to Hon Wm Jones, Sec of the Navy, Wash.
List of deaths, since my departure from the U S, on board the *Essex:* [Pac Ocean]
Dec 3, 1812, Levi Holmes, seaman, palsy
Jan 24, 1813, Edw Sweeny, o s, old age.
Jan 24, 1813, Sam'l Groce, seaman, contusion of brain by a fall from the main yd.
Mar 1, 1813, Lewis Price, Marine, consumption.
Apr 4, 1813, Jas Shafford, gunner's mate, accidental gun shot-wound of the lungs.
May 25, 1813, Dr Robt Miller, surg, disease of the liver.
May 26, 1813, Benj Geers, qr gr, inflamation of the stomach.
Jun 29, 1813, John Rodgers, qr gr, fall from the main yd.

Thos Hooper, insolvent debtor, confined in Wash Co prison for debt. -Wm Brent, clk.

FRI DEC 17, 1813
Jas Barbour has been re-elected Govn'r of Va.

SAT DEC 18, 1813
Mrd: at Woodville, nr Winchester, Va, on Dec 14, by Rev A Bamain, Mr Jos Gales, jr, of Wash City, to Miss S Juliana M Lee, d/o Theodorick Lee.

Mrd: on Dec 15, by Rev Mr Breckenridge, Mr Noah Fletcher to Miss Betsey Pease, d/o Seth Pease, all of Wash City.

MON DEC 20, 1813
Copy of a ltr from Maj Gen Thos Pinckney to the Sec of War, dt'd Hdqrtrs, 6 & 7th dists, Milledgeville, Dec 7, 1813. Rg-dispatches from Gen Floyd, commanding the troops of Ga, on the expedition against the Creek Indians.

TUE DEC 21, 1813
Complete assortment of clothes at my store, High st, Gtwn. -Rd Davis.

WED DEC 22, 1813
Hse o/Reps. Petitions: 1-Thos Hartwell, of N H, for pension for injuries rec'd whilst an ofcr in the rev army; referred. 2-Mary Cheever, of Mass, her 2 sons, John & Jos P Cheever, were killed whilst sailors on the frig *Constitution*, in her engagement with the British frig *Java*, praying for support. 3-Pet of Jonathan Davis & others of Mass, owners of the cargo of the Spanish ship *Patriota*, for restoration of said cargo seized by the rev ofcrs in port of N Y. 4-Pet of Daniel Carne, presented at the last session was referred to the Cmte of Claims.

Mrd: on Dec 9, by Rev Mr Breckenridge, Mr Morduit Young, of Alexandria, to Miss Eliz T Beall, of Wash City.

H M S *Plantagenet*, Rd Lloyd, captain, cruizing off N Y, Nov 21. Petitions of American ctzns held on board: Jas Killigan, of Phil, srv'd 7 yrs in the hatting business, appr in 1787 to Adam Champfer, in Elfrith's alley, Phil. Turned over to Fred'k Krider in 2d st; mrd the d/o Robt Jordan. My mthr was, Rebecca Riding, wid/o Thos Riding, my step fr, who sat me up in business in Callowhill st, Phil, where I carried on business for some time, then I followed the sea. I hear my mthr died in 1805, & the property she left me is in the hands of Mr Thos Rimmer, shoemkr. My wife's bros are Sam'l Jordan & Alexander Jordan. 2-Pet of Jos Parker, ntv of Va, seaman, has srv'd at Norfolk, Va; sailed with Capt Barron who commanded the frig *Chesapeake*; personally knew Stephen Decatur.

$50 reward for runaway, Jerry, negro man, prop of John Wager, of Harper's Ferry; age about 21 yrs, can speak Dutch, excellent boatman. -Henry Garnhart, nr Charles-Town, Jefferson Co, Va.

THU DEC 23, 1813
Hse o/Reps. 1-Petition of Rebecca Hodgson, wid/o Jos Hodgson, was referred to the Cmte of Claims. 2-W H Peake, of Fairfax Co, Va, praying comp for svcs & monies advanced during the Rev War, referred. 3-Pet of Thompson Maxwell, guide to Gen Hull's army, referred.

Died: very suddenly, on Dec 17, at this seat in Bladensburg, Benj Stoddert, who was Sec of the Navy during Mr Adams' administration.

Orphans Crt of PG Co, Md. Sale at Bladensburg of the prsnl est of Wm Bruce, late of said co, dec'd; negroes, hsehld furn, etc, on Dec 24. -John Sutherland, adm.

Orphans Crt of PG Co, Md. Sale at the plantation of Nath'l Weems, dec'd, nr Upper Marlboro, Md; negroes, stock, hselhld furn, farming utensils, etc, on Jan 17. -Violetta Weems, admx.

SAT DEC 25, 1813
Chancery Crt, Md. Pblc sale of all the right, title, int, & est, of the late Gen Jas M Lingan, or his heirs, in *Middlebrook Mills & Estate*; 548 acs in Montg Co, Md. Mr Griffith Henderson lvng on the premises, & Mr H Waring, adjacent thereto, will show same. -W Smith, Trustee.

Mrd: at the seat of Mrs Lowndes in Bladensburg, on Dec 21, by Rev Mr Norris, Mr Wm B Jackson to Miss Eliza B Lowndes, d/o Mrs Dorothea Lowndes, all of that place.

Died: at Lexington, Ky, on Dec 5, Maj Levi Hukill, of the U S Army, after a short illness; srvd in the staff of Gen Harrison, during nrly all his operations to the N West-was with the Genr'l at Ft Meigs.

Died: on Nov 29, Capt Jesse Copeland, of the 10th U S Infty.

Died: at Plattsburg, on Nov 28, Capt Jos Bryant, of the 10th U S Infty.

New Orleans, Nov 18. Suicide on Sat last, Cadet Jeano, shop kpr, Frenchman by birth, age about 55 yrs.

Orphans Crt of Chas Co, Md. Sale at the village of Newport, Chas Co, Md, on Jan 18, 40 val slaves, late the prop of Eliz Price Winter, dec'd. -J Campbell, adm.

TUE DEC 28, 1813
Obit notice-among the many brave spirits who have fallen, during the last campaign, Maj Levi Hukill, ntv of Md; entered the army in 1808 as a Cornet, in the 1st regt of light dragoons; died on Dec 5, at Lexington, Ky.

Died : at Phil, on Dec 21, Mrs Eleanor Taylor, w/o Jas N Taylor, of Wash City.

Reward-$100, for negro, Jas, age about 22 yrs; absconded from my farm, PG Co, Md, nr Queen Anne. -Isaac Duckett

WED DEC 29, 1813
On Wed evening, the large manufacturing mill, on Swift Crk, nr Petersburg, Va, belonging to Mr Wm Rowlett, was consumed by fire; loss about $15,000.

For sale-part of lot 10 in sq 378, on 10th st, Wash City. -Henry Ryan, on F st.

THU DEC 30, 1813
Listing of all the patients cured of cancer by Wm A Lilly, Edward, Va, Dec 14, 1813.

Albany, Friday. We stop the press to say that an Express just arrived, who left Buffalo on Tue, with the horrid intelligence, that on Sunday, about 3,000 British regulars, militia & Indians, crossed the Niagara rvr, carried the Ft by storm, & murdered the whole garrison, except for 3.

FRI DEC 31, 1813
Boston, Dec 24. Ltr from Mr Chas Pierce, Editor of the *Centinel*, dated Portsmouth, Dec 23, 3 A M. Last evening, some incendiary set fire to a barn, belonging to the est of the late Col Moses Woodward; fire swept & burned many hses, viz: Daniel Webster's, Joshua Haven's occupied by his bro Thos; hse of the est of the late Col Supply Clap, occupied by the widow Furness. Also the residence of Miss Eliz Hale, Beyson R Freeman, John O M Remick; Fisher Hse occupied by Dr Josiah Dwight; widow Adams' hse; Geo Wentworth's hse & store. Others who lost their shops: Geo J Gerrish, saddler; Sam'l Beck, painter; Abner Greenleaf, brass founder; Sam'l Barker, grocery store; Col Jas Sheafe; Jacob Sheafe; John Davenport; & Jacob Cutter. The fire was seen at Boston, a distance of 60 miles. No lives were lost; no vessels burnt.

Nicholas Warner, boot & shoe cleaner; business in the cellar of the hse next to McLeod's Tavern. Local ad.

—A—

Abbot, 266
Abbott, 123, 268, 291
Abell, 170
Abercrombie, 296
Abernathy, 234
Abert, 105, 314
Aborn, 36, 294
Achison, 194
Achman, 105
Achmann, 245
Achord, 261
Adair, 152
Adams, 2, 11, 20, 22, 25, 38, 49, 51, 56, 74, 76, 95, 97, 107, 119, 125, 151, 154, 158, 159, 160, 168, 171, 173, 175, 179, 185, 193, 194, 201, 220, 255, 260, 266, 274, 277, 281, 286, 299, 303, 324, 325
Adamson, 189
Addison, 61, 67, 73, 78, 84, 123, 202, 221, 236
Addition, 55
Addition to Prevention, 194
Addition to Sterling Park & Strife, 194
Addition to Turkey Thicket, 94
Adee, 160
Adelphi Mills, 45
Aderton, 165
Adlington, 3, 101
Adventure, 193
Afflick, 261
Afrew, 52
Ager, 113
Agnew, 35, 108
Aiken, 292
Aikin, 154
Aisquith, 170
Aitkin, 151, 183
Albertson, 52
Albinson, 58
Albright, 156, 255

Alden, 254
Alderson, 142
Aldrich, 148, 176
Aleson, 2
Alexander, 10, 44, 73, 75, 85, 89, 124, 126, 159, 168, 172, 179, 233, 245, 254, 267, 269, 279, 281
Alexander's Island, 85
Alford, 206, 244, 261, 290
Alger, 12, 125
Allein, 136
Allen, 26, 31, 89, 97, 112, 113, 130, 146, 147, 165, 166, 174, 188, 234, 235, 240, 258, 260, 264, 306, 307
Allen's Fresh, 313
Allender, 231
Alleson, 214, 250
Allison, 146, 205, 277
Allstan, 9
Allston, 70
Almond, 30
Alphonson, 209
Alshouse, 123, 220
Alston, 242, 251
Alwyn, 271
Alyed, 154
Amberson, 151
Amzeen, 102
Anan, 276
Anchong Hills, 194
Anders, 161
Anderson, 36, 42, 43, 68, 69, 76, 88, 93, 97, 117, 120, 128, 138, 143, 144, 146, 152, 168, 172, 173, 189, 197, 232, 234, 269, 270, 276, 282, 289, 300
Andesley, 31
Andrews, 9, 13, 34, 55, 63, 72, 88, 109, 208, 244, 254
Andrus, 130
Angel, 63, 293
Angell, 133, 166, 268

Angus, 240
Annin, 24, 92
Anthony, 146, 173
Antill, 135, 170
Antonie, 240
Anvil, 32
Apple Hills, 195
Applegarth, 271
Appler, 178, 213
Appleton, 199, 202
Aprice, 164, 206
Aquasco, 14
Archer, 75, 144, 190, 192
Archibald, 179, 239
Arel, 150
Armistead, 4, 6, 9, 17, 67, 68, 113, 223, 236, 243, 254, 264, 268
Armitingen, 201
Armroyd, 7, 14
Armstead, 66
Armstrong, 67, 88, 113, 144, 146, 151, 152, 158, 163, 168, 169, 172, 175, 207, 213, 273, 301, 308
Arnold, 130, 135, 142, 159
Arrel, 232
Arrington, 58
Arrowsmith, 154, 207
Arther, 206
Arundel, 234
Arundell, 4
Arvin, 111
Asabaird, 223
Asadean, 244
Asbury, 264
Ashcom's Green Field, 54
Ashe, 257
Ashely, 166
Ashford, 191
Ashley, 5, 10, 17, 90, 148
Ashmore, 274
Ashton, 65
Ashworth, 253
Askin, 183, 201
Aspinwall, 146

Astor, 160
Atchison, 303
Atherton, 260
Athon, 212
Atkinson, 103
Atlee, 52
Attaway, 238
Attwater, 208, 263
Attwood, 212
Atwater, 202
Atwood, 38, 111
Audrain, 14
Audrian, 14
Augan, 242
Austin, 6, 16, 49, 103, 184, 227, 260
Avery, 22, 69, 144, 244, 254
Avidths, 214, 250
Ayer, 135
Aylwin, 89, 191
Ayre, 268
Ayres, 59, 244, 283
Ayton, 45, 304

—B—

Babbit, 15
Babcock, 243
Bacchus, 197
Backhouse, 31
Backus, 68, 227, 289
Bacon, 12, 18, 25, 69, 102, 140, 207, 222, 228
Baddock, 67
Badger, 79
Badin, 107
Baen, 131
Baer, 135, 270
Bagley, 36, 267
Bailey, 16, 24, 36, 81, 101, 112, 143, 145, 148, 151, 166, 184, 213, 254, 255, 267, 277, 278, 304, 306
Baillard, 166
Baily, 2, 44, 175, 192, 202
Bain, 87
Bainbridge, 48, 131, 183, 260, 265
Bair, 176

Baird, 37, 123, 135, 159
Baker, 5, 7, 10, 20, 34, 53, 58, 70, 72, 88, 90, 121, 123, 128, 150, 158, 162, 180, 192, 205, 208, 220, 223, 229, 238, 245, 255, 258, 264, 272, 273, 279, 293, 307, 310
Balch, 19, 105, 123, 170, 180
Baldridge, 274
Baldwin, 22, 44, 111, 112, 131, 159, 166, 197, 261, 278, 308, 310
Baldwin's Tavern, 35
Baldy, 102, 151
Balfour, 111, 143, 256
Ball, 4, 42, 109, 127, 145, 155, 168, 178, 199, 215, 238, 247, 262, 272, 285, 290, 292, 310, 312
Ballard, 162, 236, 291
Ballinger, 115, 146
Ballthrope, 50
Baltzer, 199
Bamain, 323
Bambrick, 57
Bangs, 147
Banister, 146
Bankhead, 239, 249
Banks, 11, 15, 88, 112, 281
Bankson, 170
Bannister, 213
Bannon, 86
Banot, 304
Baptist's Hope, 54
Barbee, 202, 283
Barber, 31, 81, 103, 167
Barbour, 90, 100, 145, 197, 202, 240, 322
Barclay, 45, 49, 91
Barcley, 213, 290
Bard, 69, 232
Barker, 112, 147, 160, 186, 201, 224, 325
Barkesdale, 12

Barksdale, 203
Barlow, 14, 23, 33, 74, 101, 106, 159, 271, 274, 278
Barnaby, 306
Barnard, 150, 215
Barne, 129
Barnes, 56, 58, 101, 117, 129, 133, 134, 138, 139, 140, 172, 202, 209, 223, 231, 247, 255, 264, 269, 286, 301, 308
Barnett, 12, 151, 164, 205, 228, 230
Barnetts, 202
Barney, 143, 190, 207, 209, 305
Barnham, 179, 244
Barns, 48, 158, 310
Barnum, 31, 59, 171, 176
Baron, 11, 70
Barrell, 131
Barrendoe, 54
Barret, 43, 97
Barrett, 102, 199, 249, 301
Barrette, 177
Barron, 19, 44, 51, 96, 148, 246, 323
Barry, 22, 27, 39, 41, 50, 55, 78, 99, 121, 123, 129, 158, 198, 210, 237, 274, 275, 278, 287, 292, 302, 310
Barshdale, 158
Bartee, 12, 276
Barth, 177
Bartholemews, 95
Bartholomew, 90, 137
Bartle, 175, 301
Bartleman, 210
Bartlet, 44, 148, 150, 203
Bartlett, 24, 93, 145
Bartley, 267
Barton, 107, 126, 136, 151, 163, 166
Bartram, 16, 209
Bary, 125
Basey, 251

Bashford, 54
Basset, 199
Bassett, 70, 166
Bate, 321
Bates, 7, 51, 54, 99, 109, 119, 147, 183, 193, 260, 278, 280, 292, 313, 316
Batson, 16, 283
Battaile, 239, 249
Battersea, 195
Batterwitch, 192
Battey, 150
Bauhay, 215
Baum, 14, 144, 238
Bauman, 167
Bawn, 210
Baxter, 112
Bayard, 69, 167
Bayles, 242
Bayley, 228
Bayley's Risque, 54
Baylies, 228
Baylis, 166
Baylor, 152, 168
Bayly, 49, 225, 228
Baynard, 95
Bayne, 317
Baynes, 47, 48, 303
Baynes 1st & 2d lots, 195
Beach, 28, 159, 268
Beal, 83
Beal's Reserve, 195
Beale, 45, 74, 97, 101, 107, 120, 123, 135, 178, 223, 280
Beall, 4, 6, 7, 8, 13, 17, 18, 19, 36, 47, 50, 56, 65, 66, 74, 78, 88, 94, 96, 97, 105, 106, 116, 124, 128, 143, 157, 168, 170, 181, 186, 189, 190, 195, 197, 199, 202, 210, 224, 225, 250, 251, 257, 265, 270, 282, 293, 295, 303, 304, 308, 313, 317, 321, 323
Beall's Addition, 262
Beall's Gift, 222, 230
Beall's Addition, 96

Beall's Industry, 7
Bealle, 155
Beals, 319
Beam, 189
Bean, 50, 78, 95, 148, 202, 226, 299
Beanes, 28, 108, 132
Beans, 81, 108, 251
Beans's Landing, 194
Beard, 46, 163, 292
Beardsley, 13, 276
Beasley, 12, 199
Beatties, 183
Beatty, 43, 47, 61, 86, 126, 183, 262, 279, 281
Beatty & Hawkins Addition to Gtwn, 2
Beaumont, 90
Beaverdam, 55
Bebee, 299
Beck, 4, 9, 16, 70, 117, 121, 137, 181, 196, 252, 304, 319, 322, 325
Beckam, 185
Beckes, 98
Becket, 150
Beckett, 217, 282, 290
Beckford, 178
Beckham, 179
Beckley, 127
Beckman, 169
Beckwith, 43
Bedds, 6
Bedel, 148
Bedell, 181
Bedford, 129, 135, 208, 251
Bee, 118, 147
Beebe, 31, 142, 199
Beecher, 142
Beek, 117
Beekman, 149
Beeman, 148
Beggs, 94
Begley, 170
Beill, 170
Beitel, 52
Belcher, 71
Belding, 261
Belfield, 127, 169
Belknap, 133, 230

Bell, 48, 90, 98, 147, 160, 162, 225
Bellamy, 301
Belle Field, 311
Bellechasse, 124
Bellevieu, 207
Bellingham, 164
Bells, 273
Bellson, 274
Bellune, 301
Belmain, 28
Belt, 47, 62, 77, 104, 140, 196, 229, 267, 270, 275, 304, 308, 313
Belton, 162
Bement, 160
Benbow, 88
Bend, 82, 134, 182
Bender, 146, 147
Benedict, 67, 112, 267
Benezett, 162
Bennet, 63, 140, 148, 149, 150, 155, 159, 251
Bennett, 18, 26, 52, 93, 156, 271, 298, 308
Benson, 79, 111, 199, 250
Bentin, 146
Bentley, 30, 218, 223, 234
Benton, 84, 106, 115, 272
Beresford, 306
Bergen, 230
Berkeley, 4, 71
Bernard, 112, 125, 160, 210
Berry, 4, 29, 87, 88, 95, 106, 116, 121, 124, 143, 148, 161, 173, 181, 186, 195, 196, 199, 215, 251, 254, 259, 272, 291, 293, 303, 304, 308, 312
Berryman, 4, 253
Bester, 193
Bestor, 15, 140, 293
Beterman, 215
Betterton, 39
Betton, 38
Betts, 21, 273

Beverley, 7, 9, 105
Beverly, 27, 123
Bevis, 224
Bewley, 244
Beymer, 234
Biays, 136, 144
Bibb, 7, 69, 70, 228
Bicker, 167
Bickley, 113
Bicknell, 43, 130, 235
Biddle, 91, 151, 202, 236
Bidt, 103
Bier, 234
Bigelow, 69, 135, 147, 166, 182, 228, 242
Bigford, 205
Biggs, 108, 133
Bigham, 235
Bigspring Estate, 310
Billington, 38
Bing, 260
Bingham, 63, 128
Binns, 141, 144, 220
Biot, 23
Birch, 162, 226, 236
Bird, 57, 71, 89, 133, 148, 198, 254, 260, 261
Birdsail, 193
Birdsall, 185
Birge, 319
Birk, 57
Birkhead, 172
Birney, 92
Bisby, 159
Biscoe, 201, 220, 308, 311
Bishop, 21, 77, 130, 267
Bissel, 140, 296
Bissell, 162
Bitouzey, 136
Bixby, 138, 265, 289, 308
Black, 147
Black Ash, 196
Black Fox, 60
Blackburn, 32, 60, 134
Blackiston, 231
Blackledge, 70
Blackler, 138
Blackley, 102, 151

Blacklock, 64, 195, 303
Blacklock's Venture, 195
Blackman, 4
Blackney, 154
Blackstone, 113
Blackwell, 150
Blackwood, 52
Blagden, 19, 41, 118, 119, 129, 138, 156, 178, 248, 295, 296
Blagdon, 41
Blagge, 82, 110, 280
Blair, 97
Blaisdell, 88
Blake, 4, 14, 35, 37, 40, 41, 71, 125, 127, 136, 138, 178, 187, 188, 279, 288
Blakeway, 213
Blanchard, 52, 56, 59, 68, 156, 189, 234, 319
Blancy, 43
Bland, 144
Blanque, 124
Blauvelt, 163
Bledsoe, 254
Bleecker, 232
Bleeker, 69
Blidge, 213
Blinn, 273
Bliss, 17, 148
Blithe, 152
Blodget, 166, 221
Blodgett, 199
Blood, 107
Bloodgood, 130
Bloomfield, 80, 125, 144, 151, 167, 187, 213
Blount, 66, 70, 108, 113, 149, 169, 208, 256
Blyth, 306
Blythe, 37, 310
Boardley, 173
Boardman, 17, 38, 134
Boarm, 81
Boarman, 35, 88, 111, 131, 142, 194, 303
Bobbit, 290
Bobbitt, 93

Bobo, 21
Bodortha, 22
Boersiler, 198
Boerstler, 150, 205
Boges Increase, 54
Bohn, 143
Bohrer, 198
Boileau, 141
Boiman, 129
Bollman, 3
Bolman, 100
Bolsaubin, 17
Bonaparte, 106, 189
Bond, 11, 46, 54, 72, 79, 212, 226, 229, 282
Bonnet, 319
Bontz, 314
Booker, 152
Boon, 23, 149, 202, 298
Boone, 193
Boons, 153
Boos, 96, 170
Booth, 55, 133, 236, 302
Boothe, 293
Borrows, 288, 306
Boscawen, 46
Bosfort, 2
Boshard, 99
Bosley, 262
Bosque, 240
Bossier, 124
Boston 50 Weems, 54
Bostwick, 159
Botts, 97, 99, 110
Bouchard, 41
Boudon, 71, 259
Boughman, 124
Boughton, 312
Boulton, 89
Bourke, 208
Bousman, 97
Bouton, 176
Bowden, 40
Bowdoin, 79
Bowen, 274, 305, 312
Bower, 234
Bowers, 154, 209
Bowie, 3, 13, 36, 50, 60, 84, 111, 120, 126, 140, 184, 187, 193, 207, 220, 253,

270, 272, 279, 284,
294, 303, 321
Bowles, 283
Bowling, 194, 303
Bowling Green, 315
Bowman, 67, 102, 147,
157, 167, 179, 242,
261
Boyd, 3, 5, 24, 39, 56,
58, 62, 66, 69, 79,
92, 99, 100, 122,
125, 129, 130, 135,
140, 159, 177, 182,
184, 208, 213, 229,
230, 235, 243, 247,
258, 273, 275, 279,
285, 286, 288, 294,
304, 309, 319
Boyer, 13, 36, 260
Boyert, 99, 101, 109,
119
Bozman, 274
Bracken, 10
Bradbury, 242, 264
Braden, 251
Bradey, 65
Bradford, 21, 33, 133,
146, 152, 166, 185,
202, 267, 304
Bradhurst, 141
Bradley, 36, 53, 69, 90,
112, 115, 125, 138,
140, 148, 166, 174,
208, 227, 234, 248,
254, 260, 276
Bradly, 178
Brady, 20, 158
Bragg, 185
Brainard, 112
Branch, 17, 148
Brand, 90
Brandt, 194, 303
Branham, 102
Bransel, 138
Brantley, 133, 234
Brashears, 126, 156,
293, 312
Brawley, 133
Brawner, 173
Brawning, 147
Braxton, 97
Brearley, 145
Brearly, 150, 154

Breckenbridge, 40
Breckenridge, 34, 40,
70, 74, 80, 99, 100,
132, 181, 184, 207,
213, 224, 226, 280,
282, 305, 308, 323
Breneman, 251
Brent, 3, 6, 7, 9, 10, 14,
15, 27, 28, 32, 34,
35, 36, 41, 42, 45,
50, 53, 60, 64, 66,
68, 69, 70, 76, 80,
82, 86, 87, 89, 101,
106, 107, 108, 110,
116, 127, 128, 129,
131, 138, 139, 144,
153, 154, 161, 162,
164, 165, 172, 177,
179, 185, 186, 192,
198, 215, 219, 222,
227, 230, 232, 233,
237, 238, 239, 240,
245, 249, 250, 253,
256, 257, 259, 261,
264, 265, 266, 268,
269, 270, 271, 272,
274, 275, 278, 281,
285, 287, 288, 290,
291, 292, 293, 295,
302, 304, 305, 306,
308, 309, 312, 313,
319, 322
Brenton, 24
Brentwood Farm, 195
Brereton, 15
Bresland, 170
Brett, 20, 151
Brevoort, 252
Brewer, 4, 8, 16, 32,
42, 48, 51, 57, 59,
65, 72, 82, 91, 94,
96, 111, 128, 140,
154, 158, 170, 188,
219, 229, 251, 295,
317
Brewster, 141, 148
Brian, 25
Brice, 63, 202
Briceland, 235
Brickett, 113
Bricknall, 20
Brico, 64
Bridge, 71

Bridges, 39, 224, 276,
321
Bridget, 175
Bridgewater, 268
Briggs, 12, 37, 223, 268
Brighaam, 228
Brigham, 242
Bright, 20, 111, 143,
236
Brightwell, 193
Brink, 186
Brisco, 144
Briscoe, 3, 39, 41, 45,
65, 73, 115, 138,
153, 193, 209, 287,
318
Britcher, 84
Brittain, 147, 150
Britton, 159, 173
Broad Creek, 83
Broadbrooks, 80
Broaddus, 267
Broadhead, 167
Broadnax, 20, 238
Brobson, 300
Brock, 179, 189, 190,
224, 225
Brockenbrough, 42,
142, 197, 218
Brockway, 299
Brodeau, 210, 310
Brogden, 197, 199, 250
Broke, 291
Brokenbrough, 114
Broker, 137
Bromley, 26, 38, 153,
316
Bronaugh, 41, 53, 78,
148
Bronsal, 183
Brook, 36, 97, 132,
165, 190, 217, 302
Brookbank, 164
Brooke, 9, 18, 19, 36,
42, 50, 79, 86, 97,
109, 112, 114, 126,
134, 143, 159, 190,
239, 248, 298
Brooke Crt, 194
*Brooke Hill &
Cuckhold*, 193
Brooke's Addition, 1

Brookes, 189, 292, 311, 312
Brookfield, 39, 194
Brooks, 17, 64, 93, 112, 145, 163, 166, 168, 219, 274, 307
Broom, 218, 291, 292, 318
Broom Lawn, 40
Brother's Joint Iinterest Enlarged, 196
Brouwer, 237
Brower, 26, 101
Brown, 1, 2, 16, 25, 30, 31, 36, 42, 55, 57, 60, 62, 67, 68, 69, 70, 74, 75, 97, 99, 102, 124, 125, 129, 133, 135, 137, 141, 142, 143, 144, 147, 149, 150, 158, 164, 168, 172, 177, 180, 183, 187, 190, 191, 192, 197, 199, 202, 207, 209, 215, 219, 225, 228, 230, 232, 234, 236, 239, 246, 247, 251, 252, 254, 255, 258, 262, 267, 270, 273, 276, 277, 281, 283, 284, 288, 296, 301, 304, 306, 307, 316
Brown's Purchase, 32, 74
Browne, 154
Brownlow, 207
Brownson, 17, 165
Bruce, 22, 36, 68, 103, 149, 162, 186, 191, 192, 277, 304, 324
Bruen, 167
Bruff, 130, 310
Bruia, 167
Bruin, 169
Brumley, 24, 37, 44, 61, 74, 77, 119, 212, 215, 221, 250, 285
Brundige, 41
Brune, 42
Bruntlot, 192
Brush, 68, 72, 73, 190, 273, 319

Bruyn, 130
Bry, 124
Bryan, 21, 35, 137, 141, 223, 243, 251, 265, 273
Bryant, 52, 147, 277, 287, 292, 324
Bryson, 25, 151
Buchanan, 144, 182, 193
Buchannan, 97
Bucher, 222
Buck, 113, 135, 177
Buckland, 295
Buckley, 108, 217, 254
Bucklin, 146, 148
Buckner, 140, 159
Buckpart & Pomfret, 54
Budd, 206, 291
Buel, 256
Buell, 176
Buffington, 52
Buffum, 260
Buford, 22, 58, 168, 277
Bulkeley, 277
Bulkley, 160, 193
Bull, 309
Bullock, 54, 260
Bulman, 219
Bumley, 283
Bumpass, 112
Bunce, 185, 193
Bunyie, 316
Burband, 146
Burbeck, 68, 225
Burch, 60, 75, 130, 132, 161, 164, 204, 205, 271, 281, 291, 303
Burchan, 47
Burchstead, 17, 95, 107
Burd, 145, 222
Burdell, 5, 67
Burford, 187, 276, 283, 289
Burgess, 65, 164, 172, 182, 193, 304
Burk, 144
Burke, 16, 100, 240
Burkloe, 59
Burley, 67, 308
Burn, 145, 200

Burnet, 231
Burnett, 167, 183
Burnham, 158, 171, 283, 290
Burnhan, 84
Burns, 48, 139, 156, 221, 252, 262, 268
Burr, 115, 128, 130, 150, 172
Burrall, 157, 268
Burrill, 160
Burrow, 10
Burrowes, 99, 167
Burrows, 52, 289, 306, 316
Burt, 31, 115
Burton, 21, 57, 107, 236, 285
Burwell, 70, 133
Bury, 218
Bush, 15, 72, 191, 273
Bushby, 32
Bushel, 202
Bussard, 40, 117, 123, 183, 197, 227, 266, 270
Busson, 277
Butler, 3, 7, 17, 30, 33, 70, 108, 111, 125, 142, 145, 146, 160, 166, 167, 173, 206, 248, 249, 251, 267, 272, 283, 307, 310
Butterfield, 113
Butterwitch, 213
Butterworth, 184, 193
Buttingham, 194
Butts, 110, 160
Buzzard, 24, 262
Byad, 102
Byerly, 151
Byers, 24
Byrne, 243
Byron, 192, 198
Byus, 184

—C—

C__yton, 292
Cabell, 20, 23, 114, 168, 217
Caddotte, 183
Cadmune, 196

Cadwallader, 57
Cady, 10
Cahoone, 38
Cain, 20, 67
Calder, 60
Caldwell, 20, 29, 31, 41, 74, 81, 85, 119, 120, 125, 126, 149, 150, 185, 203, 207, 208, 245, 254, 258, 259, 261, 271, 295, 296, 302
Cale, 251
Calhoun, 17, 70, 182, 212, 233
Call, 43, 169, 171, 248, 288
Callaham, 210
Callan, 140
Caller, 146
Callier, 31, 32
Callis, 37, 149
Calson, 297
Calter, 31
Calvert, 43, 86, 143, 184, 199, 236, 253, 274
Cambell, 69
Cambray, 169
Cameron, 83
Camp, 22, 143, 148, 214, 250, 267
Campbell, 9, 15, 17, 38, 58, 69, 77, 79, 83, 88, 90, 92, 101, 125, 130, 146, 149, 152, 167, 172, 180, 191, 194, 197, 200, 203, 214, 231, 235, 241, 242, 251, 272, 287, 303, 313, 319, 324
Campher, 268
Campin, 16
Cana, 87, 296
Canby, 36, 104, 143
Candler, 37
Canfield, 58, 276
Canghran, 152
Cann, 256
Cannon, 19, 78, 306
Canoe Neck, 54
Canter, 15

Canton, 70
Cantrel, 124
Caperton, 284
Capon Springs, 48
Caprian, 49
Capron, 16
Capt John, 49
Carberry, 55, 57, 139, 173
Carbery, 284
Card, 38, 145, 269
Carden, 239, 241
Carderock, 280
Cardwell, 218, 290
Carey, 21, 111, 182, 232, 234
Carl, 130
Carle, 154
Carleton, 52, 67, 111, 219, 316
Carll, 141
Carlton, 138, 140, 158, 166, 176, 215
Carmac, 151
Carmack, 214, 250
Carmichael, 31, 306
Carnahan, 251
Carne, 115, 323
Carnes, 226
Carpenter, 35, 36, 53, 54, 96, 140, 141, 170, 276, 281
Carr, 8, 23, 68, 102, 133, 142, 147, 151, 165, 166, 206, 219, 228, 231, 234, 235, 249, 270, 287, 304
Carrick, 113, 197
Carrick's Industry, 197
Carrier, 279
Carrington, 168
Carrol, 4, 54, 203, 215
Carroll, 4, 6, 48, 55, 66, 82, 86, 96, 101, 106, 107, 125, 127, 138, 155, 182, 203, 216, 238, 270, 278, 279, 310
Carson, 147, 150, 209, 243, 306
Carswell, 171, 183, 189
Carter, 4, 12, 39, 43, 44, 111, 127, 137,
159, 175, 182, 198, 220, 230, 234, 240, 261, 292, 299
Carty, 147, 307
Caruth, 268
Casanave, 49, 270
Case, 68
Casenave, 91
Casey, 31, 47, 65
Cashell, 238, 302
Casman, 26
Cass, 139, 252
Cassady, 301
Cassanave, 183
Cassedy, 180
Cassell, 251
Cassidy, 143
Cassin, 23, 32, 41, 75, 89, 120, 144, 156, 181, 193, 206, 271, 286, 287, 296, 297
Casso, 8
Caston, 64
Caswell, 260
Catlett, 35, 57, 189
Catlin, 277
Catter, 315
Caulking, 103
Cavendish, 71
Cavet, 72
Cawood, 87
Cazanave, 210
Cazenove, 252
Cenas, 137
Chace, 227
Chadborn, 67
Chadburn, 176
Chalmers, 6, 161, 283
Chamberlaine, 133
Chamberlin, 228
Chambers, 167, 192, 251, 276
Champayne, 4, 127
Champfer, 323
Champion, 69, 225, 227
Champlin, 69, 82, 273
Champney, 19
Chance, 90, 196, 232
Chancellor, 111
Chancey, 67
Chancy, 294
Chandlear, 306

Chandler, 31, 37, 44, 46, 70, 147, 163, 203, 205, 230, 268, 312
Chapell, 233
Chapin, 47, 226
Chapman, 49, 102, 116, 146, 167, 195, 208, 236, 303
Chappel, 59, 299
Charies, 273
Charles, 6, 35, 212
Charles & Benjamin, 94
Charless, 82
Charlton, 148, 280
Chas Rest, 55
Chase, 42, 45, 144, 145, 156, 162, 178, 182, 197, 203, 278
Chatard, 172
Chauncey, 15, 85, 233, 234, 281, 287
Chauveau, 77
Chaveau, 88
Chaveaux, 260
Cheatham, 114, 217, 318
Cheeney, 304
Cheever, 323
Cheeves, 70
Cherry, 29, 185, 235
Chesheur, 282
Cheshire, 98, 180, 241
Chesley, 313
Chesnut Hill, 301
Chess, 251
Cheves, 5, 233, 260
Chew, 105, 123, 191, 206, 284
Cheyney, 165
Chichester, 33, 36
Chick, 306
Child, 142
Childers, 301
Childress, 7, 297
Childs, 36, 41, 52, 65, 107, 147, 316
Chiles, 268
Chilley, 109
Chilton, 262
Chinn, 4, 127
Chipman, 31, 149, 160
Chisholm, 80, 146, 191

Chison, 54
Chittendem, 319
Chittenden, 69
Choate, 64
Chosley, 89
Chouteau, 46
Christian, 113, 232
Christie, 150, 207, 224, 228, 252, 296
Christophe, 25
Christopher, 239
Chron, 30
Chrystie, 149, 154, 225, 246
Chunn, 146
Church, 59, 67, 151, 168, 209
Churchill, 145
Chusman, 192
Cilley, 148, 165
Cist, 200
Clagett, 28, 57, 66, 87, 195, 203, 220, 303
Clagget, 117, 293
Claiborne, 3, 45, 101, 182, 240
Clairborne, 197
Clap, 325
Clapp, 199
Clark, 4, 22, 37, 43, 51, 52, 59, 74, 78, 90, 92, 97, 101, 102, 106, 115, 125, 133, 146, 148, 150, 159, 168, 182, 184, 185, 186, 188, 207, 214, 215, 228, 235, 239, 250, 252, 283, 284, 287, 292, 308, 319
Clarke, 1, 8, 22, 25, 32, 36, 39, 40, 41, 50, 66, 78, 85, 86, 112, 119, 126, 140, 148, 149, 160, 169, 183, 185, 201, 205, 207, 213, 228, 236, 246, 247, 271, 289, 293, 296, 299, 300, 314
Clarkson, 166, 175
Claslin, 147
Clason, 160
Claude, 75, 158
Clawson, 83

Claxton, 131, 236, 311
Clay, 39, 61, 70, 95, 97, 99, 117, 185, 201, 208, 220, 246, 263, 265, 293
Clayborne, 274
Clayton, 179, 231, 276
Clear Drinking, 311
Clements, 272, 275, 281
Clendenen, 90
Clendinen, 35, 108, 121
Clephan, 27, 30, 95
Clerklee, 74, 195, 320
Clerklu, 303
Cleveland, 225, 234, 307
Cleves, 112
Clevinger, 44
Cliffden, 174
Clifford, 83
Clift, 167
Climson, 28
Clinch, 18, 46, 147
Clinton, 6, 21, 61, 95, 132, 139, 147, 167, 184, 245, 258
Cliver, 140
Cloakey, 290
Clopton, 70
Close, 130
Cloud, 147, 257, 297, 307
Cloyd, 154
Club, 268
Clubb, 302
Clure, 67
Clymer, 256
Coale, 35, 108, 265
Coalman, 306
Coalter, 36
Coates, 203, 244, 276, 290
Coats, 272
Cobb, 5, 17, 70, 139, 162, 166, 175, 183, 197, 230
Cobbett, 87
Cobourne, 135
Coburn, 76, 208, 264
Cochran, 7, 70, 91, 116, 167, 267

Cochrane, 22, 29, 278, 296
Cock, 96, 164, 178
Cocke, 3, 53, 121, 125, 144, 180, 190, 286, 296, 314, 319
Cocken, 60
Cocker, 138
Cockey, 187, 205
Cocking, 7, 22, 300, 319
Cocks, 17, 230
Coddington, 16, 130
Coe, 130
Coffee, 156
Coffie, 151, 317
Coffin, 53, 76, 209, 232, 273
Coggin, 93
Cogswell, 148, 166
Cohagen, 160
Cohen, 124, 184
Colberth, 111
Colbourn, 8
Colburn, 91, 112
Colby, 130, 276
Colcord, 67
Cole, 58, 71, 112, 130, 141, 192, 213, 302
Colebrook, 194
Coleman, 13, 31, 44, 107, 131, 146, 176, 182, 238, 244
Colerick, 25
Coles, 86, 145, 148, 238
Coley, 93
Colfax, 159
Collard, 37, 63, 98, 177
Collet, 96, 157, 221, 227, 293
Collett, 271
Collington, 176
Collins, 4, 35, 37, 62, 108, 115, 207, 230, 280, 302, 309
Colson, 146, 255
Colter, 29, 31
Colville, 154
Colvin, 53, 55, 268
Colwell, 133, 149
Cornb, 319
Cornegy, 103

Comegys, 121
Compton, 29, 66, 89, 193, 194
Compton Purchase, 54
Comstock, 130, 267, 321
Conant, 113
Conaway, 38
Conclusion on Seneca, 61
Condit, 69
Cone, 148, 238, 315, 316
Congdon, 225
Conkey, 292
Conlon, 266
Conn, 144, 207, 289
Connell, 65, 225
Connelly, 145, 209, 269
Conner, 146, 260
Conningham, 268
Connor, 153, 170, 173
Conover, 230
Conrad, 233
Constant, 18, 101
Contee, 39, 96, 193, 194, 207, 288
Converse, 270, 290
Convert, 97
Conway, 34, 126, 145, 159, 167, 203, 221, 234, 271
Conyers, 43, 97
Conyngham, 52, 210, 267, 301
Coody, 63
Cook, 6, 38, 39, 58, 67, 69, 93, 97, 101, 103, 107, 146, 154, 185, 186, 209, 213, 226, 232, 244, 249, 252, 254, 269, 274, 305, 309, 312
Cooke, 15, 134, 137, 182, 194, 218
Coolidge, 82, 129, 180, 190, 203, 272
Coolspring, 194
Coolspring Addition, 193, 194, 196
Coombe, 27, 129, 310
Coon, 77

Cooper, 51, 81, 82, 141, 192, 203, 215, 239, 245, 246, 251, 253, 293, 297
Cope, 9, 215
Copeland, 97, 147, 192, 324
Copsey, 93
Corbet, 170
Corbin, 55, 102
Corcoran, 65, 100, 105, 126, 174, 183, 233, 279
Cord, 13, 15, 65, 81
Corlass, 199
Corly, 28
Cormel, 251
Cormick, 307
Corning, 148
Cornwaleys, 274
Cornyn, 151
Corry, 38
Corse, 317
Cortlandt, 167
Coschang, 194
Coschargs, 194
Costegan, 57
Costigan, 190
Cotheall, 16
Cothran, 43
Cottle, 292
Cotton, 274
Cottrel, 151
Coulson, 25
Coulter, 172
Countess of Berkeley, 71
Courtney, 57, 142, 159, 172
Courts, 195, 303
Cousins, 39
Couther, 192
Coutts, 97, 99
Covel, 235
Covington, 319
Cowan, 145, 207, 238, 290
Cowie, 192
Cowles, 43
Cowlet, 154
Cowper, 9
Cox, 5, 111, 119, 123, 133, 143, 149, 167,

220, 260, 272, 280, 291, 295
Coxe, 89, 141
Coxen's Rest, 196
Coyle, 81, 82, 99, 109, 118, 119, 120, 140, 174, 182, 191, 286, 315
Cozens, 36
Cozzens, 70
Crabb, 19, 24, 150, 182
Crabbs Redoubt, 24
Crackburns Purchase, 54
Crackels, 119
Crafford, 182
Craig, 32, 59, 91, 97, 145, 152, 167, 168, 198, 199, 203, 234, 244, 250
Craige, 209, 242
Cram, 253
Crammond, 203
Cramphin, 41
Cranch, 5, 14, 32, 86, 88, 107, 116, 136, 173, 280
Crane, 145, 166
Cranston, 34, 307
Crary, 151
Craton, 258
Craufurd, 22
Craven, 75, 123, 172
Crawford, 69, 91, 121, 123, 134, 146, 148, 155, 172, 173, 175, 183, 189, 191, 198, 201, 214, 215, 223, 232, 237, 242, 250, 263, 265, 267, 271, 282, 285, 309
Crawley, 155
Cray, 267
Creagh, 29
Crease, 84, 313
Creeger, 308
Creighton, 7, 85
Cresholm, 170
Crew, 179, 244
Crismond, 102
Crittenden, 152
Croasdale, 185
Crockett, 169

Croes, 28
Crofoot, 149
Croghan, 152, 169
Croker, 63
Crolius, 36
Cromwel, 108
Cromwell, 5, 35, 172, 191
Crooked Lane, 194
Crooker, 146, 191
Crookes, 160
Crookshank, 2, 24, 41, 117, 227, 261
Crosby, 126, 130
Crosier, 302
Cross, 60, 187, 201, 276, 316, 322
Cross Roads, 88
Crossman, 185
Crostree, 313
Crouch, 123, 220
Crouse, 149
Crow, 234, 310
Crow's Mill, 315
Crowninshield, 239
Crummer, 176
Crump, 85, 301
Crutcher, 185
Culbertson, 150
Culbreth, 298
Cullison, 109
Culver, 16, 201
Cumberland, 46
Cumming, 224
Cummingham, 251
Cummings, 75, 150, 162, 167, 221, 226, 307
Cummins, 73
Cunningham, 147, 169, 205, 255, 313
Curran, 139
Current, 57
Currey, 43
Currier, 301
Curry, 90, 170, 210
Curtenius, 7
Curtis, 136, 151
Cushing, 12, 112, 171, 174, 213, 252, 301
Custis, 32, 42, 86, 136, 140, 210
Cutbush, 162, 209

Cuthbert, 144
Cutler, 18, 205, 260
Cutter, 232, 325
Cutting, 148
Cutts, 12, 69, 242, 274, 293
Cuyler, 223

—D—

Dabney, 182
<u>Dacres</u>, 63, 191, 213, 226
Dade, 93, 94, 98
Daffin, 226
Daft, 55
Daily, 38
Dakin, 112
Daking, 192
Dalany, 63
Dale, 18, 158
Dallam, 12
Dallas, 42, 173
Dalliba, 252
Dalton, 112, 317
Daltzell, 209
Dalvell, 58
Dam, 226
Dana, 21, 69, 71, 242
Dandridge, 197
Danford, 304
Dangerfield, 32, 36, 81, 86, 133, 136, 281
Daniel, 10, 34, 101, 197, 208, 230, 290, 312
Danielson, 152
Danner, 277
Danning, 220
Dantzlers, 53
Darby, 36, 133, 166, 230, 254
Dargen, 28, 89
Darke, 168
Darling, 30, 176, 283
Darlinton, 37
Darnall's Chance & Addition, 193
Darnell, 104, 310
Darnes, 161, 291
Darragh, 206
Darrow, 130
Daschkoff, 266

Dashiell, 28, 66
Dashwood, 206
Daugherty, 304
Daurman, 201
Daveiss, 66
Davenport, 69, 152, 205, 227, 230, 244, 325
Davey, 242
Davi, 251
David, 152
Davidge, 53, 121
Davidson, 10, 13, 14, 25, 36, 40, 90, 94, 102, 112, 118, 125, 128, 143, 156, 168, 169, 178, 193, 195, 214, 222, 228, 232, 237, 241, 250, 259, 275, 287, 295, 296, 299, 303, 319, 320
Davie, 43, 219, 262
Davies, 19, 90, 168
Daviess, 87, 91, 95, 107
Davis, 21, 23, 25, 43, 68, 69, 73, 86, 93, 97, 104, 106, 118, 119, 123, 126, 133, 140, 141, 145, 150, 151, 167, 173, 180, 188, 194, 197, 214, 220, 226, 230, 233, 235, 236, 240, 242, 249, 252, 257, 265, 281, 291, 299, 303, 304, 306, 307, 317, 323
Davy, 126
Dawes, 188
Dawner, 147
Dawny, 87
Dawson, 22, 51, 70, 138, 170, 178, 249, 273, 274
Day, 72, 276
Dayton, 167
De Blanc, 124
De Brahm, 169
De Butts, 53
De Camp, 177
De Carnap, 317
De Chaumont, 37

De Fienry, 169
De Forrest, 185
De Grand Pre, 207
De Krafft, 109
De Kraft, 220
de la Ronde, 124
De Lamotte, 144
De Leitensdorfer, 5
De Lord, 276
De Sheils, 178
De Stael, 1
De Witt, 230
De Zong, 277
Deakin, 196, 200, 203
Deakin's Hall, 61
Deakins, 90, 94, 117, 121, 210, 229, 280, 304
Deakins Hall Little Meadows, 196
Dean, 35, 110, 160, 205, 233, 279
Dearborn, 71, 104, 135, 144, 145, 165, 171, 208, 213
Dearing, 185
DeBerry, 22, 93
Deblock, 183
Deblois, 22, 206, 302
Debutts, 135, 141
Decatur, 85, 239, 240, 241, 287, 323
Decker, 95, 98
Dedier, 222
Dee, 319
Deering, 145
Deery, 296
Delameter, 12
Delamontagnie, 230
Delance, 130
Delano, 149
Delanot, 22
Delany, 240
Delaplaine, 91, 160
Delapline, 86
Delebrook Manor, 54
Delebrooke, 55
Delozier, 316
Delphy, 25
Dement, 99
Deming, 37, 112
Dempsey, 73
Dempsie, 129

Deneale, 32, 92, 110, 160, 273
Denew, 22
Denham, 48
Denison, 37, 85, 231
Denking, 18
Denmark, 238
Denning, 150
Dennis, 151, 225, 236
Dennison, 206, 210, 217, 231, 255, 301
Denniston, 185, 193
Denny, 110, 142, 157, 226, 296
Denoon, 49
Densley, 27
Dent, 52, 109, 173, 191, 195, 206, 303
Depeyster, 160
Deravere, 273
Derby, 25
Derey, 310
Derick, 251
Dermott, 69
Derr, 289
Derrow, 93
Derson, 67
Dervey, 36
Desart Party, 54
Desaussure, 70
Desha, 70, 146, 185, 201
Destrehar, 124
Deubell, 180
Deuse, 111
Devane, 148
Devereaux, 92, 254
Devise, 55
Devling, 28
Devol, 29
Devonshire, 54
Dew, 144
Dewel, 255
Dewitt, 179
Dewy, 145
Dexter, 166, 188
Deynard, 54
Dial, 273
Dibbell, 179
Dibble, 176, 179, 299
Dibblee, 13
Dibrell, 52

Dick, 147, 198, 203, 231, 233
Dickenson, 112
Dickerman, 225
Dickerson, 151
Dickey, 113, 135
Dickinson, 61, 268
Dickinson's Delight, 1
Dickson, 5, 79, 110, 148, 201, 254, 289
Dietrick, 290
Diffenderffer, 144
Digges, 6, 45, 47, 48, 57, 87, 88, 157, 203, 263, 275, 318
Diggs, 48
Digio, 49
Diguo, 34
Dill, 21, 52, 230
Dillen, 25
Dillicker, 103, 112
Dillon, 259
Dilrell, 21
Diman, 151
Dimmick, 124
Dimon, 276
Dines, 118, 129
Dingley, 20
Dinis, 49
Dinmore, 16, 29, 72, 74, 80, 222
Dinsmoor, 131
Dinsmore, 69
Diroff, 229
Dix, 148, 241, 249, 268
Dixon, 5, 43, 82, 97, 102, 118, 146, 157, 173, 229, 254, 260, 263, 291, 306, 319
Doake, 214
Dobbin, 90, 123, 126, 253, 262
Dobbyn, 41, 61, 128, 156, 284, 319
Docker, 25, 239
Dod, 141, 290
Dodds, 251
Dodge, 79, 158, 269, 319
Dodges, 300
Dodson, 303
Dogarthy, 38
Doherty, 169, 170

Dohrman, 271
Doin, 173
Dolphin, 269
Donahoe, 52
Donaldson, 144, 150, 209
Donation Lands, 153
Donlevy, 20, 112
Donnell, 288
Donnelly, 79, 149
Donnison, 183
Donohoe, 169
Dooling, 23
Dooly, 185
Dore, 57
Dorfeuill, 41
Dorman, 116, 139, 176
Dorrin, 290
Dorry, 51
Dorset, 257
Dorsett, 116
Dorsey, 7, 48, 65, 68, 77, 102, 116, 157, 170, 189, 208, 230, 294, 296
Dougherty, 170, 196
Doughty, 6, 180
Douglas, 14, 19, 72
Douglass, 39, 57, 74, 173, 254, 315
Douglass Hill, 314
Doulan, 232
Dounham, 55
Douthett, 234
Dove, 41, 229, 247
Dow, 37, 133, 159, 179, 256
Dowd, 63
Dowdney, 76
Dowl, 190
Dowl's Discovery, 280
Dowlin, 306
Downes Neglect, 194
Downing, 2
Downs, 30, 55, 68
Downy, 310
Dowson, 61
Dox, 149, 160, 240
Doxey, 44
Doyle, 113, 242
Doyne, 53, 222, 273
Drake, 58, 149, 159
Drane, 299

Draper, 12, 147
Drayton, 104, 147, 218, 257
Drew, 147, 166, 189
Driscol, 21
Drosey, 2
Droughon, 112, 255
Drum, 186
Drummend, 170
Drummond, 90, 265
Drury, 8
Duane, 18, 94, 209
Dublin, 195
Dubois, 163, 167, 193, 294
Duboise, 38
Dubose, 234, 276
Ducatel, 51, 262
Duckett, 3, 11, 36, 144, 164, 304, 324
Duckworth, 63
Dudley, 137, 208, 298
Duer, 214, 254
Dufeur, 79
Duffoy, 306
Duffy, 293
Dufief, 73
DuForest, 17
Dufossat, 162
Dufour, 296
Dugan, 43
Duggin, 292
Duke, 106, 117, 294
Duke of Baden, 59
Dulany, 15, 24, 34, 41, 135, 141, 195, 203, 271, 303
Duley, 8
Dulin, 315
Duly, 280
Dunba, 193
Dunbar, 213, 260
Duncan, 31, 144, 145, 148, 152, 223, 234
Duncanson, 2, 35, 110, 308
Dunham, 91, 142, 289
Dunlap, 124, 198, 237
Dunlevy, 186, 260
Dunlop, 20, 26, 110, 126, 142, 302
Dunlora, 68

337

Dunn, 21, 57, 63, 92, 121, 191, 261, 271
Dunscomb, 263
Duplessis, 208
Duponceau, 41
Duport, 214, 251
Duportail, 169
Duralde, 7
Durand, 175
Durant, 37, 234
Durke, 100
Durkee, 140, 171, 173
Durkey, 178
Dursley, 71
Dusenberry, 158
Dusenbury, 162
Dutcher, 221
Dutteroe, 2
Dutton, 188
Duval, 9, 48, 84, 86, 148, 178, 185, 201
Duvall, 5, 6, 13, 26, 47, 50, 65, 75, 77, 81, 82, 86, 121, 158, 193, 197, 226, 227, 238, 254, 267, 283, 295, 296, 304, 310
Dwight, 150, 159, 198, 325
Dwyer, 191
Dyer, 11, 27, 111, 142, 146, 148, 195, 249, 270, 272, 278, 303
Dyoe, 150
Dyott, 105

—E—

Eads, 245
Eakin, 86
Earl, 104
Earle, 70, 203, 233, 267
Earp, 2
Easterbrooks, 88
Eastman, 18, 148
Easton, 251
Eaton, 5, 44, 145, 158, 235, 276, 298
Ebert, 312
Ecclestion, 171
Eccleston, 13, 168
Echolls, 133, 185
Echols, 21

Eckel, 266
Eckfeldt, 209
Eddowes, 11
Eddy, 150
Edelen, 15, 303, 317
Edelen's Hogpen Enlarged, 195
Edelin, 1, 70, 237, 265
Eden, 54, 56, 203
Edene, 107
Edgar, 104, 160
Edgarley, 20
Edgerton, 301
Edmondson, 2
Edmons, 256
Edmonson, 221
Edmonston, 281, 285, 315
Edsail, 151
Edwards, 15, 18, 52, 70, 112, 152, 162, 168, 171, 202, 245, 251, 264, 274, 293
Eggerton, 148
Eggleston, 169
Eilkin, 130
Elbert, 169
Elby, 157
Elder, 175
Eldridge, 151, 307
Elgar, 132, 189, 286
Elickson, 76
Elio, 59
Eliot, 265, 319
Eliott, 139
Eliza Manor, 55
Elizabeth's Portion, 196
Elkins, 264
Ellerbeck, 53, 205
Ellery, 199
Ellicott, 77, 97, 257
Elliot, 25, 51, 124, 145, 152, 154, 226, 280, 283, 295
Elliott, 11, 123, 176, 197, 251, 320
Ellis, 74, 133, 173, 235, 272
Elliston, 132
Ellott, 297
Ellsworth, 103
Elmore, 147, 251, 276

Elson, 316
Elton, 15
Ely, 69, 130, 242
Elzy, 288
Emack, 287
Emerson, 112, 185, 254, 283
Emery, 210
Emmerson, 192
Emmet, 184
Emory, 222, 271
Emott, 69
Enault, 74
Endais, 109
Endicott, 17
Endley, 301
Engle, 123, 220
English, 73, 266
Ennalls, 75
Eno, 36, 100, 113, 125, 189, 262, 288
Enos, 135, 150, 264
Enslie, 191
Ensworth, 58
Entwisle, 110, 160
Eppes, 182, 273
Erkin, 209
Erskine, 104
Erving, 14, 138, 164
Erwin, 283
Esday, 292
Esenbeck, 65, 139
Esminard, 236
Espy, 151
Essex, 2
Essington, 197
Essom, 272
Estep, 226, 320, 321
Esterbrook, 17
Estes, 162, 282
Estill, 290
Etherington, 306
Etter, 266
Etting, 200, 290
Eustis, 17, 238
Ev, 223
Evan's Range, 197
Evans, 5, 12, 29, 31, 67, 77, 90, 93, 119, 133, 145, 146, 149, 159, 176, 178, 205, 206, 216, 223, 232, 233, 240, 244, 247,

249, 280, 281, 283, 292, 311
Eve, 92
Eveleth, 161, 225
Evelith, 293
Eversfield, 194, 303
Everson, 254
Everts, 299
Ewell, 15, 35, 77, 92, 103, 116, 134, 154, 164, 212, 249, 253, 266, 293
Ewing, 185, 223, 230
Exeter, 195
Eyers, 176

—**F**—

Fabian, 43
Faddell, 67
Fahrastock, 52
Fain, 251
Fairall, 250, 254
Fairchild, 300
Fairfax, 4, 32, 87, 127
Fairlie, 25
Fairman, 87
Fairsville, 261
Fake, 192
Falkirk, 54
Fallington, 319
Fallon, 284
Falls, 31
Fannin, 238
Fanning, 145, 175
Far, 25
Farewell, 148
Farley, 20, 145
Farm, The, 57
Farnham, 283
Farnow, 310
Farnsworth, 163
Farott, 146
Farrand, 45
Farrar, 147
Farrel, 295
Farrell, 25, 75, 140, 160, 255, 278
Farrington, 216, 302
Farris, 183
Farrow, 147, 233
Fasset, 319
Fauble, 313

Faust, 18
Faw, 126, 233
Fawkes, 21
Fawn, 264
Fay, 5, 130
Febiger, 168
Febney, 55
Federal Mills, 158
Fee, 88
Feely, 30
Feemster, 261
Fees, 22
Fell, 158
Fellow, 116
Felt, 88, 112
Felton, 147
Feltwell, 214
Fendal, 163
Fendall, 242
Fendell, 27
Fennell, 122
Fennimore, 125
Fenno, 229
Fenwick, 3, 13, 54, 55, 85, 86, 97, 102, 173, 186, 197, 200, 203, 224, 225, 228, 229, 233, 245, 247, 252, 270, 272, 274, 297, 311, 322
Fenwick Manor, 55
Fergus, 218, 283
Ferguson, 87, 140, 151, 190, 191, 196, 304
Fern, 63
Fernald, 166
Ferrall, 313
Ferred, 71
Ferrill, 99
Ferris, 61, 176
Ferry, 301
Ferry Landing, 280
Fetter, 151
Fiak, 69
Ficket, 34
Ficklin, 20
Fiddian, 213
Field, 17, 113, 114, 217, 261, 281
Fielding, 16, 223
Fields, 34, 106, 238, 290
Filschew, 129

Fin, 125
Finagan, 98
Finch, 93, 149, 228, 257
Find, 151
Findlay, 1, 90, 155, 158, 205, 274
Findley, 6, 69, 163, 218, 232, 252
Finget, 173
Fink, 228
Finley, 61, 153, 169, 202, 243, 307
Finly, 94
Finn, 170
Finney, 4, 149
Finnigan, 128
Fish, 167, 209
Fisher, 21, 49, 51, 72, 74, 92, 135, 147, 152, 179, 208, 210, 220, 231
Fishing Island, 196
Fisk, 248
Fislar, 90
Fitch, 21, 69
Fitler, 104
Fitzgerald, 91, 162, 181, 210, 281, 292
Fitzhugh, 11, 32, 59, 81, 84, 86, 137, 160, 270
Fitzimons, 126
Fitznurding, 71
Fitzsimons, 61
Flagg, 43
Flavitt, 213
Fleete, 274
Fleming, 45, 76, 80, 151, 152
Fletchall, 19
Fletcher, 20, 131, 133, 148, 170, 282, 323
Flick, 214, 250
Fling, 131
Flinn, 158
Flournoy, 171, 213
Flower, 93
Floyd, 18, 66, 175, 323
Fluker, 110
Fobes, 223
Foering, 9
Foilette, 205

Foley, 57
Follet, 148, 319
Follett, 158
Folson, 159
Fombell, 273
Fonerden, 170, 182
Fontaine, 145
Fontleroy, 168
Food, 43
Foot, 134
Foote, 36, 87
Forbes, 291, 318
Force Put, 196
Ford, 120, 135, 140, 147, 175, 199, 234, 238, 277
Fork, 164
Forman, 167
Forneau, 38
Forney, 149
Forrest, 5, 40, 41, 42, 58, 73, 78, 84, 97, 98, 101, 110, 120, 128, 135, 155, 168, 178, 183, 185, 186, 187, 190, 193, 194, 195, 223, 248, 259, 264, 272, 280, 297, 319
Forrest Enlarged, 194
Forrest of Dean & Abells Chance, 55
Forrest Sherwood, 194
Forrister, 307
Forsyth, 113, 228
Forsythe, 163
Fortes, 127
Fortier, 7
Forward, 208
Fosdick, 14
Foster, 25, 43, 47, 72, 88, 107, 112, 124, 146, 147, 148, 151, 158, 160, 163, 172, 179, 237, 267, 287
Fosure, 244
Fouche, 300
Foulk, 151
Fountain, 192, 277
Fournoy, 52
Fourth Addition, 54
Foushee, 197
Fowble, 25

Fowle, 147
Fowler, 92, 98, 159, 203, 212, 247, 281
Fox, 105, 112, 126, 147, 175, 177, 192, 267, 283
Foxall, 123, 264, 311
Foyles, 172
Frame, 143
Frances, 273
Francis, 5, 6, 9, 10, 90, 200
Frank, 140, 171, 196, 304
Frank's Adventure, 196
Franklin, 41, 63, 69, 70, 161, 240
Frankling, 272
Franks, 168, 201
Fravit, 192
Frayser, 302
Frazer, 47, 68, 151
Frazier, 97, 320
Frazize, 245, 247
Free, 304
Freear, 229
Freeland, 97, 126, 179
Freeman, 4, 7, 63, 68, 206, 225, 226, 261, 275, 325
Freeston, 94
French, 54, 105, 129, 130, 154, 159, 161, 210, 230
Freneau, 317
Friend, 23
Friendly Grove Factory, 44
Friendship, 54
Fromentin, 118
Frost, 10, 53, 58, 59, 80, 185, 203, 253
Frothingham, 249
Fry, 176, 209, 219, 269
Fryatt, 140
Frye, 124, 127, 216, 309
Fulcher, 212
Fuller, 38, 107, 147, 202, 216, 232, 276
Fullerton, 123, 220

Fulton, 23, 91, 123, 135, 143, 155, 170, 220, 227
Funk, 206, 239
Funston, 290
Furber, 158
Furness, 325

—G—

Gabos, 166
Gaches, 234
Gaden, 181
Gadsden, 201, 243
Gaffigon, 101
Gaillard, 69
Gaines, 33, 146, 237, 276
Gains, 296
Gainsey, 209
Gaither, 46, 49, 134, 182, 210, 256, 305
Galbraith, 67
Gale, 133, 141, 150, 160, 182
Gales, 41, 66, 107, 219, 279, 280, 319, 323
Galezio, 2
Gallagher, 261
Gallego, 97
Gallespie, 159
Galusha, 20
Galworth, 303
Gamble, 15, 67, 113, 145, 186, 198, 266, 309
Gamefield, 196
Gandall, 37
Gangaware, 214, 250
Gannett, 69
Gannon, 41
Gano, 139
Gansevocdt, 149
Gansevoort, 66, 167, 231, 242
Ganssevoort, 171
Gantt, 13, 23, 26, 27, 126, 183, 187, 194, 195, 196, 209, 216, 228, 260, 284, 303, 304, 315
Gantt's Enlargement Enlarged, 195

340

Garcia, 265
Garden Spot, 54
Gardiner, 9, 62, 88, 112, 116, 141, 151, 194, 200, 294, 303, 320
Gardiner's Meadows, 194
Gardner, 42, 45, 48, 111, 115, 144, 276, 307
Garetty, 301
Garland, 37
Garner, 176, 308
Garnett, 86, 93, 97, 183
Garnhart, 323
Garrard, 122, 164, 228, 251, 264
Garren, 305
Garret, 149, 152
Garretson, 206
Garrett, 155
Garrick, 21
Garrison, 103, 180
Garton, 192, 213
Garvi___., 161
Gary, 251, 257
Gascoigne, 164
Gaskins, 168
Gasley, 234
Gassaway, 42, 113, 135
Gatchel, 172
Gates, 21, 125, 150, 168, 194, 234, 277, 303
Gatewood, 97
Gatton, 321
Gaul, 231
Gavit, 223
Gayle, 147
Geddis, 92
Gee, 148
Geers, 322
Gegg, 190
Geiger, 87
Genet, 70
Genious, 173
Genners, 216
George, 133
Geouges, 214, 250
Gerald, 148
Gerard, 97
Gerer, 97

Gerles, 310
German, 69, 145
Germond, 277
Gerock, 21
Gerrard, 171
Gerret, 209
Gerrish, 325
Gerry, 139, 219, 258, 293
Gershom, 158
Getsendanner, 304
Gettings, 189
Getty, 3, 75, 157, 158, 256
Geyer, 139
Gheislin, 84
Ghiselin, 158
Gholson, 70, 103, 273
Gibbon, 97, 98, 194
Gibbons, 45, 303
Gibbs, 154
Gibson, 15, 17, 25, 30, 36, 46, 90, 97, 125, 137, 141, 148, 168, 172, 225, 228, 238, 247, 264, 301, 306
Gideon, 251
Gilbert, 57, 130, 149, 199
Gilchrist, 169, 205
Gilcrease, 198
Gilder, 150
Gilead, 196
Giles, 2, 69, 123, 126, 140, 168
Gill, 144, 164, 276
Gillam, 185
Gillead, 11
Gillespie, 31
Gilliam, 125
Gillies, 178
Gilliland, 151
Gillingham, 181
Gillis, 29, 140, 258, 279
Gilliss, 40, 41, 50, 64, 116, 178, 184, 188, 233, 274
Gillum, 238
Gilly, 295
Gilmam, 69
Gilman, 106, 276
Gilmor, 190

Gilmore, 90, 175
Gilmour, 10
Gilpin, 86, 143, 214, 233, 250
Gimot, 169
Girard, 122, 155
Girardin, 97
Giraud, 160
Gird, 110, 160
Gisfiden, 72
Gist, 150, 168, 185
Gittings, 7, 116, 285
Given, 255
Givens, 235
Glasco, 91, 173, 222
Glasgow, 123, 220, 233, 303
Glass, 30, 92
Glassell, 149
Glassgow, 195
Gleaning, 196
Glendy, 64
Glenn, 35, 102, 208
Glenson, 21
Gloninger, 222, 233
Glover, 2, 6, 53, 80, 83, 90, 108, 110, 116, 140, 165, 261, 262, 266, 275, 280, 287, 300, 309
Glynne, 147
Gobright, 10
Godard, 292
Godberry, 112
Goddard, 33, 76, 108, 153, 179, 230, 262, 281
Godfrey, 58, 199
Godwin, 114, 149, 150, 151, 260
Gody, 238
Goff, 97, 113, 267
Goforth, 124
Goil, 214, 250
Goir, 250
Gold, 69
Goldsborough, 3, 38, 41, 70, 80, 94, 118, 125, 238, 248, 253
Goldsmith, 54, 313
Good Luck, 194
Goodal, 104
Goodale, 149

Goodall, 111, 144
Goodday, 178
Goodhue, 133, 141, 290
Gooding, 18, 74, 95, 107
Goodlet, 113
Goodman, 112, 256
Goodrich, 38, 58, 69, 140, 148, 227
Goodrick, 251
Goodridge, 135
Goods, 44
Goodwill, 196
Goodwin, 31, 159, 160, 163, 202, 290
Goodwyn, 39, 70, 126, 149, 217, 273
Gookin, 145
Gorden, 304
Gordon, 2, 21, 31, 81, 99, 103, 148, 173, 196, 297, 309
Gore, 188
Gorham, 188
Goshen Mills, 305
Goslins Add, 54
Goss, 192
Goszler, 119
Gott, 214
Gould, 176, 192
Goulding, 214, 250, 296
Gourdine, 233
Gourdon, 170
Gouvion, 169
Grace, 86
Gradings, 21
Grady, 149, 299
Grafton, 146
Graham, 36, 41, 57, 61, 63, 86, 136, 143, 147, 167, 202, 203, 229, 240, 270, 277, 287, 292
Grammar, 140, 198, 199
Grammer, 259, 273, 293
Granberry, 9
Granger, 21, 52, 208, 235, 267
Grant, 10, 14, 191, 255
Grassin, 32

Grave's Chance, 54
Graves, 133, 152
Gray, 4, 34, 35, 43, 45, 50, 64, 70, 71, 110, 114, 138, 145, 146, 151, 152, 163, 166, 172, 173, 187, 209, 221, 226, 242, 256, 273, 277, 307
Graybill, 233
Grayson, 75, 101, 164, 189, 207
Greaton, 165
Greatwood, 66
Greaves, 63
Greeley, 135, 171
Green, 12, 17, 24, 42, 69, 74, 78, 89, 97, 98, 99, 135, 145, 159, 166, 168, 173, 189, 209, 220, 251, 253, 293, 294, 298
Green Hill, 45, 48, 88
Green's lot, 55
Greene, 148, 150, 206
Greenhow, 97, 99, 197
Greenleaf, 5, 15, 136, 138, 265, 325
Greenleaf's Point, 136, 202, 228, 265, 288, 311, 312, 318
Greenleaf's Point, 47
Greenough, 12, 18
Greenup, 66
Greenwell, 8, 129, 173, 195, 220
Greenwood, 149, 192, 213, 217, 306
Greer, 18, 49, 106, 122, 251
Greetham, 117
Gregg, 58, 62, 69, 240
Gregley, 2
Gregory, 5, 37, 67, 103
Greig, 309
Grey, 63, 76, 148
Grey Eagle Enlarged, 193
Grice, 9
Gridley, 87
Grier, 168, 283
Griffin, 97, 198, 203, 251

Griffith, 34, 75, 77, 170
Griffiths, 192
Griggs, 16
Grimes, 240
Grimke, 169
Grindage, 150
Grindall, 194, 303
Grinder, 143
Grinnell, 160
Griswell, 192, 213
Griswold, 91, 112, 134, 148, 227, 234, 255
Groce, 322
Groghegan, 298
Groome, 298
Groomes, 278
Gross, 141
Grout, 319
Grover, 177
Groverman, 62
Groves, 267, 322
Grundy, 66, 70, 218
Grymes, 208
Gues, 200
Guiger, 95
Guildersleive, 133
Guinea, 113, 164
Guise, 268
Gullidge, 155
Gummere, 267
Gun Powder Mills, 253
Gunby, 168
Gunning, 83
Gurley, 43
Gustin, 142, 244
Gutherie, 255, 261
Guthrie, 289
Guy, 152, 192, 213, 295
Guyant, 176
Guyon, 130
Guyton, 236, 247
Gwathmey, 97
Gwinn, 182
Gwinne, 152
Gwynn, 121, 182
Gyles, 38

—H—

Habersham, 7, 169
Hacker, 287
Hacket, 113

Hackett, 214, 250
Hackley, 152
Haddon, 320
Hadley, 290
Haerlem, 311
Haga, 214, 250
Hagan, 183
Hager, 55, 130
Hagerty, 104, 289
Hagner, 118
Hahn, 92
Haight, 130, 160
Haile, 15, 175
Hailman, 276
Hairston, 133, 227
Hait, 166
Hale, 69, 148, 218, 325
Halfehide, 274
Hall, 7, 56, 59, 69, 70, 75, 84, 93, 111, 113, 115, 124, 125, 130, 131, 132, 145, 147, 168, 182, 184, 192, 199, 203, 207, 208, 222, 223, 228, 250, 251, 254, 291, 292, 300, 302
Hallam, 164
Hallet, 160
Halley, 49
Halloway, 223
Hallowell, 20
Halsey, 131, 173, 206
Ham, 237
Haman, 123
Hamben, 276
Hambleton, 102, 206
Hamer, 53, 55, 126, 179, 255, 295
Hamilton, 29, 49, 56, 63, 74, 75, 92, 93, 99, 147, 153, 163, 168, 185, 226, 229, 233, 238, 246, 248, 267
Hamlin, 244
Hammock, 192, 213
Hammon, 8
Hammond, 4, 32, 43, 127, 142, 157, 254, 261

Hampton, 25, 31, 75, 167, 173, 213, 236, 262, 312
Hamsley, 62
Hamstead, 54
Hanchet, 135
Hancock, 31, 99, 254, 261
Hand, 167
Handey, 288
Handsdall, 68
Handy, 77, 195, 219
Hanes, 300
Hankins, 321
Hankinson, 133, 142
Hanks, 201
Hanley, 166
Hanna, 3, 51, 126, 207, 266
Hannah, 158, 256
Hanning, 283
Hansbrough, 202
Hanse, 132, 133
Hanson, 8, 82, 105, 116, 138, 182, 185, 243, 260, 266, 279
Hapan, 170
Haphazard, 54
Hara, 147
Harbaugh, 60, 105, 140
Harbeson, 175
Harcourt, 154
Hard Bargain, 61, 108
Hard Fortune, 55
Harden, 35, 108, 148, 238
Hardenburgh, 130
Hardey, 195
Hardin, 4, 185
Harding, 199, 304
Hardman, 168
Hardy, 61, 109, 183, 303, 307
Hare, 16, 67
Hargesheimer, 144
Hargraves, 32, 50
Hargrove, 255
Haring, 151
Harison, 150
Harland, 307
Harleston, 169
Harley, 98
Harlow, 98

Harman, 133, 276, 282
Harmar, 168
Harmer, 167
Harner, 90
Harney, 169
Harper, 59, 69, 96, 125, 148, 276
Harrell, 141
Harrington, 21
Harringtor, 191
Harris, 12, 28, 29, 43, 67, 69, 70, 86, 89, 138, 145, 148, 149, 170, 190, 197, 206, 207, 233, 235, 242, 251, 289, 291, 298, 300
Harrison, 2, 5, 12, 20, 30, 36, 39, 41, 51, 61, 62, 66, 68, 87, 95, 107, 110, 113, 114, 121, 122, 132, 134, 137, 146, 147, 149, 152, 156, 158, 168, 173, 183, 187, 188, 201, 203, 213, 217, 226, 228, 235, 238, 242, 243, 262, 264, 268, 281, 295, 301, 306, 310, 313, 314, 318, 324
Harriss, 267
Harrold, 63
Harryman, 155
Hart, 12, 16, 37, 43, 112, 145, 179, 216, 251, 252, 275, 292
Hartlove, 156
Hartly, 164
Hartman, 160
Hartshorne, 70, 89
Hartwell, 301, 323
Harver, 258
Harvey, 21, 102, 158
Harvie, 99
Harwood, 30, 36, 181, 225, 263
Hasett, 311
Haskell, 166
Haskins, 20, 307
Haslet, 290
Haslett, 312
Hastings, 217

Hatch, 20, 29, 148
Hatchet, 149
Hatchets, 194
Hatfield, 287
Hathaway, 225
Haven, 325
Havens, 158
Haw, 224, 246, 296
Hawes, 70, 169
Hawkes, 130
Hawkings, 147
Hawkins, 42, 54, 68, 94, 95, 107, 144, 152, 159, 174, 238, 240, 243, 251
Hawks, 312
Hawley, 176, 179, 244, 277
Haworth, 192
Hay, 167, 168, 197, 200, 259, 260
Hay Park, 280
Hayden, 151
Hayes, 102, 130, 197, 239, 293, 298
Haynes, 176, 273
Hayre, 302
Hays, 26, 112, 113, 146, 150, 169, 316
Haysler, 199
Hayward, 65, 179
Hazard, 15, 25, 54
Hazel, 262, 306
Hazen, 135, 170
Hazletine, 177
Hazleton, 151, 266
Hazzard, 54, 195
Head, 188
Headley, 20
Headlych, 99
Heald, 252
Healy, 272
Heard, 187
Hearn, 237
Hearsey, 208
Heath, 1, 165, 187, 198, 207, 246, 257, 292, 306, 318, 321, 322
Heaton, 148
Hebb, 60, 235, 258
Hebert, 124
Hebron, 102

Hedges, 20, 145, 251, 273, 286, 311
Heffnoman, 257
Heighe, 19
Heise, 50, 291
Helder, 154
Hellen, 1, 14, 44, 125, 199, 254
Helm, 58, 113, 185
Helmes, 304
Helms, 206, 256
Helorig, 149
Hemler, 29, 31
Hemmenway, 16
Hemmersly, 203
Henderson, 5, 71, 124, 148, 151, 169, 173, 187, 203, 244, 254, 306, 324
Hendrick, 135
Henerick, 136
Hening, 197
Henley, 296
Henning, 102, 246
Henrigues, 229
Henry, 53, 144, 145, 151, 184, 258, 299
Henworth, 213
Hepburn, 10, 78, 82, 98, 193, 195, 203, 302, 303
Hepworth, 54
Herbert, 19, 119, 136, 188
Herd, 202
Herefor, 97
Herford, 14, 41, 78, 81, 119, 140, 198, 205, 275
Heriot, 76
Herkimer, 142
Herman, 74
Heron, 97, 152
Herrick, 7
Herring, 160
Herriot, 38
Herriott, 18
Hersey, 35
Herty, 62
Hervey, 97, 154
Heston, 4, 127
Heth, 168
Heugh, 158, 230, 249

Hewett, 101
Hewitt, 14, 39, 40, 50, 56, 75, 110, 156, 188, 220, 245, 247, 282, 287, 319
Hews, 159
Heyer, 160
Hibbs, 192
Hichman, 251
Hickley, 179
Hickman, 152, 175, 185, 310
Hicks, 234, 239
Hid, 150
Higden, 41, 119, 286
Higdon, 41, 226
Higginbotham, 278
Higgins, 26, 60, 93, 180
High, 178
Hight, 124, 140, 153
Hightower, 152, 277
Highway, 307
Higinbotham, 164
Hilbus, 208
Hildreth, 184
Hill, 18, 22, 31, 53, 91, 113, 130, 169, 192, 203, 230, 260, 270, 289, 299, 302, 319
Hillary, 219
Hilleary, 44
Hillegas, 126
Hillen, 172
Hilliary, 174
Hilton, 123, 195, 303
Hinckley, 219
Hindman, 18, 262
Hindmand, 214
Hindsdall, 159
Hinkle, 41
Hinman, 296
Hinton, 137, 148, 224
Hiorns, 107
Hiriart, 124
Hitchcock, 43, 93, 223, 234, 263
Hite, 28, 148, 276
Hoan, 170
Hoard, 301
Hoban, 40, 128, 138, 140, 156, 158, 197
Hobart, 17, 141, 175
Hobbs, 31

Hobby, 166
Hockett, 157
Hodgden, 93
Hodge, 88, 272
Hodgers, 151
Hodges, 20, 34, 36, 47, 48, 63, 87, 109, 118, 132
Hodgkin, 64, 194
Hodgkins, 303
Hodgson, 61, 101, 229, 323
Hodnett, 53
Hoe, 210
Hoeckly, 144
Hoffman, 35, 108, 121, 182, 183, 206, 233, 236, 278, 307
Hog Pen Enlarged, 232
Hogan, 45, 109, 150, 276, 279
Hoge, 229
Hogeboom, 149, 230
Hogg, 169, 244
Hogpen, 196
Hogpen & Sasser's Green, 194
Hogpen Addition Enlarged, 194
Hogpen Enlarged & Knock, 90
Hoit, 146
Holbrook, 68
Holcomb, 241
Holden, 166
Holder, 152
Holdridge, 166
Holdship, 183
Holecroft, 251
Holforth, 217
Holgate, 144, 220
Holiday, 91
Holl, 4
Holland, 43, 125, 128, 145, 208, 209, 237, 285
Hollaway, 221
Holler, 72
Hollery, 195
Holley, 148, 303
Holliday, 43, 44, 55, 118, 170, 203, 265, 287

Hollin, 190
Hollingshead, 17, 243, 281
Hollingsworth, 68, 122, 127, 144, 186, 187
Hollins, 144
Hollinsworth, 4
Holliway, 147
Holly, 221
Holmead, 45, 316
Holmer, 169, 189
Holmes, 25, 31, 94, 114, 128, 130, 146, 165, 208, 217, 220, 243, 244, 245, 247, 261, 292, 322
Holstein, 250
Holstien, 214
Holt, 112, 152, 191, 218, 219, 223, 238, 261, 283
Hom, 156
Homans, 208
Hone, 160
Honyman, 218
Hood, 163
Hooe, 40
Hook, 145
Hooker, 4
Hoomes, 226
Hooper, 186, 242, 267, 272, 293, 322
Hoot, 249, 281
Hope, 33, 37, 51
Hopewell, 54, 186, 292
Hopkins, 43, 58, 89, 133, 136, 138, 145, 156, 169, 185, 191, 196, 198, 201, 208, 211, 251, 254
Hopkinson, 263
Hoppock, 150
Hopton Park, 54, 55
Hornell, 267
Horner, 4, 114, 172, 217
Hornketh, 209
Horsely, 266
Horsey, 69, 131, 140
Horwel, 151
Hosack, 133
Hosey, 192, 213
Hoskingson's Folly, 11

Hotchkiss, 179
Houghton, 308
House, 156
Houston, 23, 46, 146, 267
Houstoun, 18
How, 123, 234, 316
Howard, 11, 38, 54, 63, 92, 128, 133, 148, 153, 168, 216, 221, 222, 229, 233, 244, 254, 272, 283, 314
Howe, 20, 21, 111, 132, 169, 187, 232, 260, 277, 279
Howell, 41, 69, 151, 152, 230, 231, 264, 317
Howes, 132
Howland, 37, 130, 160
Howson, 149
Hoxton, 14, 190
Hoye, 36, 94, 260, 280
Hoyle, 217, 267
Hubbard, 30, 68, 124, 130, 135, 230, 242, 276, 277, 290
Hubbel, 103, 108
Hubbell, 134, 171
Huber, 267
Hubert, 244
Hubley, 167
Hucorn, 281
Huddleston, 55, 74
Hudson, 16, 183
Hufty, 69
Huger, 169
Huggins, 68
Hugh, 84
Hughes, 20, 23, 68, 96, 126, 137, 139, 143, 157, 170, 194, 198, 220, 242, 270, 281, 286, 303, 307
Hughs, 210
Huginin, 149, 231
Huginnin, 228
Hugmin, 228
Hugo, 150
Hugunin, 252
Hukill, 284, 324
Hulings, 168

Hull, 7, 31, 88, 129, 144, 166, 186, 189, 190, 191, 192, 197, 201, 205, 213, 214, 251, 252, 266, 323
Hulme, 155
Humbough, 235
Hume, 133, 156, 164
Humphrey, 130, 238
Humphreys, 4, 77, 118, 155, 166, 185, 301
Humphries, 146, 305
Hundley, 277
Hungerford, 30, 70, 81, 88, 273, 298
Hunsby, 237
Hunt, 3, 141, 151, 206
Hunte, 82
Hunter, 12, 31, 62, 74, 79, 93, 95, 97, 134, 147, 150, 152, 251, 281, 286, 319
Hunter's Fields, 196
Hunter's Folly, 196
Huntingdon, 18, 227
Huntington, 166, 230, 254
Hunton, 172
Huntoon, 177
Huntt, 63, 238
Hurd, 176
Hurdle, 293
Hurlbut, 130, 255
Hurley, 195
Hurst, 125, 266
Hurtbut, 186
Husband, 205
Huston, 151
Hutchenson, 209
Hutchings, 182
Hutchinson, 29, 52, 58, 90, 92, 112, 148, 178, 179, 264, 301
Hutchison, 91
Hutson, 155
Hutton, 144, 255
Huych, 150
Hyatt, 38, 59, 78, 100, 212, 226, 301, 312
Hyde, 65, 130, 207, 227, 276
Hyland, 94
Hylton, 8

Hyman, 133
Hyneman, 69, 223, 233
Hyrne, 169

—I—

Igleheart, 129, 304
Inclosure, 55
Indian Fields, 194
Indian Town, 50
Ingersol, 146, 150, 209, 219, 233
Ingersoll, 144, 243, 258
Ingham, 232
Ingle, 41, 64, 65, 66, 138, 235, 248, 270, 274, 295
Inglesby, 70
Inglis, 75
Ingraham, 216, 265
Ingram, 28, 310
Innes, 226
Insley's Discovery, 196
Ireland, 8, 209, 298
Irvin, 86
Irvine, 17, 150, 152, 167, 189
Irwin, 233, 261
Isaac, 182
Isaacs, 173, 274
Isaacs Park, 196
Isabel, 180
Isbell, 235
Isburn, 26
Israel, 34
Iter, 267
Ivanoff, 32
Iverson, 86
Ives, 63
Izard, 144

—J—

Jack, 146
Jacks, 241
Jackson, 2, 69, 72, 99, 112, 152, 157, 159, 160, 165, 166, 184, 186, 188, 207, 208, 225, 228, 229, 233, 284, 289, 308, 314, 317, 324
Jacob, 97

Jacobs, 92, 97, 175, 192, 213
Jaffray, 219
Jamamien, 39
James, 12, 14, 50, 90, 125, 156, 173, 188, 195, 226, 236, 239
Jameson, 140, 169, 192, 210, 281
Jamieson, 126
Jamison, 144, 268
Jannet, 89
Janney, 66, 131, 183, 300, 315
Janny, 78
Jansen, 130
Jarber, 61
Jarboe, 54, 64, 312
Jarrett, 141
Jarvis, 40
Jas' Park, 280
Jas Addition, 55
Jay, 195
Jayne, 231
Jeano, 324
Jeffers, 188
Jefferson, 15, 68, 180, 264
Jeffery, 220
Jeffrey, 312
Jeffries, 76
Jenkins, 34, 35, 79, 132, 145, 163, 170, 195, 230, 236, 238, 254, 303
Jennifer, 203
Jenning, 202
Jennings, 18, 34, 113, 172, 187, 202, 203
Jerrod, 97
Jervis, 159
Jessamin, 194
Jessamine, 195
Jessop, 52, 121, 158
Jett, 150, 267
Jewet, 148
Jewett, 290
Joaquin, 192, 213
John Geyer, 220
Johncherez, 20, 42
Johns, 111, 279, 280, 281, 294, 298

Johnson, 2, 6, 18, 23, 27, 29, 30, 37, 42, 46, 48, 58, 63, 64, 66, 70, 74, 84, 93, 97, 102, 110, 119, 124, 140, 142, 144, 146, 161, 164, 166, 167, 170, 173, 175, 176, 182, 185, 188, 190, 192, 196, 200, 201, 203, 205, 209, 225, 227, 236, 245, 247, 254, 255, 260, 263, 269, 273, 276, 280, 286, 287, 293, 301
Johnston, 2, 26, 54, 75, 94, 106, 133, 145, 146, 151, 152, 167, 183, 192, 199, 213, 235, 297
Joice, 221
Joncherez, 281
Jones, 4, 6, 7, 9, 13, 14, 18, 26, 34, 35, 38, 39, 52, 58, 59, 61, 67, 68, 73, 74, 75, 76, 77, 78, 84, 90, 102, 103, 104, 108, 114, 117, 127, 128, 133, 142, 144, 146, 149, 150, 151, 153, 160, 161, 173, 174, 184, 188, 192, 195, 196, 206, 208, 210, 217, 225, 227, 228, 235, 236, 242, 247, 250, 251, 253, 254, 261, 269, 273, 276, 278, 279, 281, 289, 290, 291, 292, 294, 298, 299, 303, 304, 305, 307, 308, 311, 314, 315, 320, 321, 322
Jonny, 243
Jordan, 54, 176, 267, 275, 323
Jordon, 63
Jos & Ann, 195
Josslyn, 125
Jotham, 176
Jourdan, 299
Joy, 266
Joyner, 7
Joynes, 168
Judah, 97
Judkins, 245
Judson, 185
Justice, 94

—K—

Kachlein, 151
Kain, 199, 250
Kaldenbach, 2
Kalderbach, 2
Kampmann, 267
Kane, 160
Kankey, 282
Katchem, 72
Kay, 218
Keadle, 35
Kealey, 47, 280
Kean, 239, 300
Kearney, 56, 140, 150, 151, 156, 158, 198, 228, 231
Kearsley, 145
Kedglie, 2
Keech, 27, 54, 106
Keefe, 60
Keefer, 133, 142
Keeler, 31, 102, 130, 158
Keerl, 51
Keese, 151
Keesly, 94
Kehr, 152
Keickley, 224
Keifer, 26
Keith, 78, 88, 147, 201, 267, 288
Keithly, 313
Kelham, 29
Kell, 182
Keller, 49, 207
Kellogg, 124, 207
Kelly, 8, 9, 90, 110, 134, 142, 170, 186, 191, 192, 278, 292, 301, 307, 318
Kelso, 142, 144, 244, 277, 283
Kemp, 1, 154, 170, 171, 186, 210, 241
Kemper, 31, 62
Kenan, 147, 302
Kendrick, 254
Kenna, 289
Kennedy, 15, 21, 58, 159, 182, 184, 256, 260, 300, 307
Kenner, 209, 262
Kennett, 12
Kenney, 149, 173
Kenny, 290
Kenon, 307
Kent, 36, 45, 70, 86, 132, 143, 150, 191, 209, 279, 282, 284, 318
Kercheval, 113
Kerr, 22, 38, 64, 144, 151, 163, 211, 218, 248, 283, 308
Kersey, 107
Kershaw, 233
Kershner, 65
Kesler, 211, 214, 250
Key, 40, 70, 79, 87, 89, 115, 123, 133, 138, 143, 149, 266, 269, 273, 289, 309, 318
Keyes, 149
Keyler, 102
Keys, 112, 138, 175, 197, 267
Kid, 91
Kidd, 179, 185
Kilbourn, 234, 245
Kilburn, 113
Kilgour, 27, 182
Kilham, 63
Killbee, 267
Killigan, 323
Kilty, 39, 42, 158
Kimball, 36, 92
Kimble, 255
Kimbol, 143
Kimmell, 142
Kimshaw, 211
Kincaid, 145, 255
King, 18, 32, 46, 57, 62, 65, 70, 74, 82, 83, 90, 96, 109, 112, 119, 126, 141, 145, 147, 149, 150, 151, 152, 171, 177, 178,

180, 181, 185, 192,
193, 195, 211, 216,
219, 227, 228, 229,
232, 236, 240, 242,
247, 252, 281, 283,
290, 298, 303, 313
King of Eng, 101
Kingsbury, 66, 125, 146, 234
Kingston, 254
Kinney, 158
Kip, 231
Kirby, 186, 230, 281
Kirk, 175, 179, 214, 308
Kirkby, 150
Kirkpatrick, 261, 307
Kirtland, 130
Kissuck, 26
Kitcham, 17
Kite, 235
Kitty Burns, 46
Klinger, 214, 250
Knapp, 16, 22, 101, 166, 256
Knauss, 283
Kneller, 60, 187, 227, 247
Knight, 20, 51, 109, 177, 236
Knock, 232
Knode, 143
Knott, 54, 187, 245
Knowles, 4, 178, 225, 307
Knox, 43, 147, 165
Koch, 171, 313
Koones, 4, 92
Koontz, 126
Korkight, 3
Korkright, 5
Kosciusko, 169
Krider, 323
Krout, 276
Kruger, 214
Krugh, 175
Krumbhaar, 177
Kuhn, 270
Kurtz, 294

—L—

L'hommedieu, 76

La Branche, 124
La Cassagne, 115
La Croix, 201
La Fayette, 169
La Neuville, 162
La Reuse, 273
Labbadie, 262
Labille, 47, 67
Lacock, 69, 233, 240
Lacour, 104
Ladd, 10, 53, 80, 106, 148, 244
LaForest, 97
Lagary, 238
Laight, 82, 110, 280
Laing, 225
Laird, 117, 204, 219
Lake, 56, 298
Laline, 53
Lamar, 43, 147, 161, 261
Lamater, 301
Lamb, 12, 169, 235, 283
Lambert, 36, 52, 69, 156, 221, 260, 283
Lambright, 64
Lamning, 5
Lamon, 77
<u>Lamotte</u>, 144
Lancaster, 117, 187
Lance, 245, 248
Land, 136, 260
Land Above, 196
Lander, 138
Landon, 4, 33, 127, 207
Lane, 21, 30, 58, 147, 150, 169, 178, 223, 255, 266, 283, 289, 303, 308
Langar, 57
Langdon, 109, 139
Langham, 152, 188
Langmaid, 290
Lanham, 196, 236, 303
Lanham's Delight, 196
Lanham,s Delight, 196
Lanier, 255
Lansdale, 1, 55, 168, 317
Lapham, 58
Lapsley, 265
Laraby, 265

Larkin, 126, 151
Larmont, 192
Larned, 146
Larrabee, 17, 252
Larwell, 145
Lassell, 255
Lately, 57
Latham, 12, 76, 244
Lathrop, 31, 112, 244
Latile, 198
Latimore, 88
Laton, 240
Latrobe, 46, 62, 120, 124, 227, 249, 309
Lattimore, 174
Laub, 134, 307
Laugelan, 175
Laumoy, 169
Laurence, 151
Laurie, 6, 14, 33, 50, 77, 90, 141, 161, 173, 274, 279, 295, 296, 301
Laury, 208
Laval, 163
Lavar, 174
Law, 14, 21, 41, 45, 69, 125, 129, 137, 156, 183, 225, 227, 271, 287, 310
Lawrance, 63
Lawrason, 83, 108, 205
Lawrence, 26, 37, 60, 151, 158, 159, 160, 183, 228, 270, 283, 291, 307, 309
Laws, 144
Lawson, 20, 148, 193, 203, 207, 217, 264
Lay, 186
Laymaster, 119
Le Baron, 253
Le Bone, 179
le Count, 299
Le hermite, 111
Le Roy, 126
Leach, 189, 218, 305
Leary, 175
Leatch, 67
Leath, 54
Leaver, 174
Leaverworth, 149
Leavitt, 176

Leawright, 86
Lecroix, 97, 99
Lee, 2, 3, 10, 11, 18, 27, 31, 32, 68, 93, 96, 111, 123, 131, 133, 136, 151, 152, 168, 173, 182, 186, 192, 194, 196, 227, 241, 251, 264, 275, 279, 288, 303, 310, 322, 323
Leech, 321
Leeds, 49, 276
Leek, 82, 303
Leeke, 82, 203
Lefavour, 108
Lefever, 19, 69, 161
Lefferts, 160
Leftwich, 182, 228
Legate, 145
Legel, 229
Legge, 146
Legget, 152
Lehmer, 88
Lehre, 300
Leib, 69, 144
Leidler, 203
Leigh, 148
Leiper, 9, 139, 144, 209
Leitch, 304
Leitensdorfer, 14
Leith, 193, 195
Lemmon, 260
Lemoine, 308
Lemon, 21, 244
Lenox, 122, 126, 140, 155, 156, 193, 222, 273, 278
Lent, 151, 228
Lenthall, 224, 246
Lenud, 17
Leonard, 6, 154, 175, 241, 274, 293, 321
Leonard's Lot, 195
Leps, 48
Lequex, 146
Lesley, 97
Lester, 209, 301
Letchworth, 194
Levake, 148
Levels Enlarged, 196
Levely, 232
Levenworth, 167

Levering, 35, 106, 108, 143, 206, 207
Levins, 307
Levitt, 174
Levy, 241
Lewellin, 9
Lewis, 9, 12, 13, 20, 32, 34, 44, 58, 70, 87, 104, 119, 121, 124, 128, 130, 136, 141, 143, 144, 147, 149, 164, 169, 176, 177, 188, 191, 192, 213, 221, 230, 233, 242, 243, 249, 253, 262, 274, 276, 292, 309, 317
Liancourt, 100
Libbey, 146
Libby, 115, 233
Liber, 83
Liggett, 224
Lightner, 141, 267
Lightser, 134
Lilly, 240, 325
Limpster, 195
Lincoln, 16, 165
Lindley, 12, 180
Lindo, 126, 181, 294
Lindsay, 40, 51, 64, 79, 86, 103, 144, 154, 221, 248
Lindsey, 21
Lindsley, 167, 234, 270, 281
Lingan, 26, 44, 87, 97, 196, 304, 311, 324
Linggan, 96
Link, 214, 250
Linkins, 221
Linn, 149
Linstead, 55
Linthicum, 194, 303
Lintner, 112
Linton, 41, 43, 208, 242
Linvill, 173
Lippincott, 83
Lister, 178
Litchworth, 303
Lithgou, 268
Lithgow, 314
Litle, 42, 51, 302

Little, 22, 70, 73, 182, 191
Little Belt, 42
Little Turtle, 188
Littlefield, 166
Littlejohn, 172
Littlepage, 97, 99
Littler, 44
Livandais, 124
Livermore, 188
Livers, 193, 302
Liversage, 63
Livingston, 48, 69, 91, 129, 130, 149, 155, 167, 201, 227, 263, 292
Lloyd, 68, 72, 143, 243, 323
Lockard, 67
Lockart, 20
Locke, 22, 236, 317
Lockerman, 183
Lockhart, 43
Lockwood, 21, 43
Lodge, 105
Loftis, 306
Loga, 81
Logan, 92, 147, 152, 167, 243, 299
Loggins, 65
Logue, 251
Lomax, 18
Londo Derry, 194
Londonderry, 194
Long, 16, 18, 63, 67, 99, 109, 119, 121, 150, 192, 205, 219, 221, 223, 234, 255, 277, 299
Long in Dispence & Farthing's Gift, 54
Long Meadows, 266
Longcoat Enlarged, 195
Longden, 73, 110, 160
Longlade, 183
Loomis, 17
Lorain, 255
Lorance, 173
Lord, 112
Loring, 52, 147
Lorman, 121, 200
Losey, 230

Loudon's Pleasure, 196
Louis, 22
Loundes, 70
Lousong, 251
Love, 2, 26, 51, 52, 77, 158, 185, 196, 223, 235, 267, 272, 274, 278
Lovell, 146, 208
Lovering, 23
Lovett, 160, 225
Loving, 307
Low, 95, 251
Lowden, 136
Lowe, 8, 74, 103, 106, 169, 178, 195, 196, 258, 303
Lowndes, 82, 200, 233, 253, 324
Lownds, 281
Lowrey, 26
Lowry, 2, 26, 74, 212
Lucas, 13, 26, 38, 67, 74, 78, 152, 173, 252
Luce, 164
Lucket, 150
Luckett, 66, 168, 207
Luckie, 67
Luddington, 44
Ludford's Gift, 194
Ludlow, 15, 130, 180, 206, 211, 260, 291
Lufborough, 262
Luff, 184
Luffborough, 174, 226, 286
Luminis, 12
Lush, 224
Lushwood, 192
Lutterloh, 147
Lux, 203
Lyde, 206
Lydner, 125
Lyle, 17, 69, 79, 233
Lyman, 76, 108, 146, 147, 167, 173, 188
Lynch, 168, 183, 200, 204, 212
Lynchfield, 56
Lynn, 110, 160, 164, 216, 279, 281
Lyon, 13, 37, 83, 149, 251, 272, 296, 301

Lyons, 2
Lysle, 265
Lythea, 310
Lytle, 169

—M—

M'Afee, 267
M'Alla, 150
M'Allister, 251
M'Arthur, 252
M'Bride, 267, 289
M'Call, 264, 305
M'Carman, 251
M'Caulay, 287
M'Clannahan, 264
M'Clelland, 290
M'Cloud, 306
M'Clure, 267
M'Concklin, 304
M'Connell, 290, 307
M'Cord, 277
M'Cormick, 248, 257, 259, 280, 281, 297, 304, 317
M'Coy, 254, 255
M'Crea, 213
M'Culloch, 279
M'Cullock, 277, 286
M'Cutchen, 277, 308
M'Dermott, 293
M'Donough, 303
M'Dormot, 251
M'Gahey, 261
M'Ginniss, 117
M'Glassin, 317
M'Gowan, 255, 268
M'Intosh, 264, 290, 300
M'Kenna, 312
M'Kenney, 288, 317
M'Kenny, 281
M'Kezy, 282
M'Kinney, 267
M'Laughlin, 297
M'Lean, 121
M'Leod, 294, 317
M'Mechen, 121
M'Murtry, 267
M'Neill, 254
M'Niel, 148
M'Pherson, 270
M'rae, 197

M'Ree, 169, 243
M'Stay, 221
M'Williams, 308
M Lingan, 170, 182, 205, 221
M'Candless, 28
M'Clary, 51
M'Cleary, 7
M'Clenachan, 32
M'Cormack, 24
M'Cormick, 9
M'Coy, 33
M'Creery, 32
M'Culloch, 6
M'Donald, 30
M'Dowell, 14
M'Elwee, 56
M'Kee, 49
M'Kelvey, 17
M'Pherson, 17, 129
Mabry, 260, 307
Mabson, 18
Mac Aray, 150
Macauley, 102
Maccubin, 181
MacDaniel, 2, 6, 24, 25, 27, 35, 41, 46, 62, 66, 119, 177, 188, 199, 201, 224, 250, 293, 315
MacDonald, 129, 130
Machen, 77, 85, 87, 156
Machesney, 97, 151, 228
Machin, 65
Mack, 244, 277, 283
Mackail, 132
Mackall, 14, 65, 98, 144, 272, 294, 298
MacKenzie, 172, 262, 300
Mackey, 15, 38, 204
Mackubin, 119
Maclay, 72
Macleod, 9, 160, 188, 286
Maclure, 9
MacNamara, 14, 17
Macomb, 17
Macon, 70
MacPherson, 70, 206, 234

350

Macrae, 150, 225, 227
Macubbin, 225
Maddox, 1, 153, 213, 243, 317
Maddux, 305
Madille, 49
Madison, 9, 10, 13, 62, 85, 95, 114, 115, 117, 120, 123, 127, 134, 135, 148, 153, 161, 164, 170, 173, 177, 218, 258, 263, 265, 292, 293
Maffet, 102
Maffit, 93, 206
Maffitt, 84
Magaw, 167
Magill, 44
Maginnis, 159
Magowen, 255
Magrath, 206
Magruder, 10, 30, 34, 39, 40, 57, 77, 81, 84, 87, 100, 105, 108, 109, 116, 118, 121, 124, 150, 157, 183, 189, 192, 193, 194, 220, 230, 231, 248, 250, 259, 265, 279, 281, 303, 308, 314, 319, 321, 322
Magruder's Choice, 195
Magruder's Plains, 196
Magruder's Farm, 94
Maguire, 96, 193, 303
Mahar, 239
Maiden's Dowry, 193
Maill, 154
Maillard, 126
Main, 126, 225
Maine, 316
Maitland, 46, 257
Major's Choice, 196
Malcolm, 149, 167
Malcomb, 20
Male, 150
Mallary, 4
Mallory, 197
Malony, 146
Malot, 206
Maloy, 74, 173, 220
Maltby, 216

Manager, 63
Mandeville, 34, 126, 148, 271
Manigault, 173
Mankins, 281
Manly, 155
Mann, 144, 148, 238
Manning, 147, 153, 232
Manro, 127
Mansfield, 17, 155, 196, 214, 264, 303, 307, 319
Mansker, 156
Mantz, 11, 22, 25, 26, 122, 137, 154, 188, 211, 270
Manz, 66
Maple Swamp, 196
Maquille, 124
Mara, 115, 173
Marbury, 36, 51, 86, 111, 127, 143, 239, 260
Marcadin, 126
March, 17, 277
Marcle, 251
Marcus, 132
Marcy, 67
Marigny, 124
Marinor, 292
Marion, 5, 169
Mark, 38
Market Overton, 194, 195
Markham, 298
Markle, 228
Marks, 97
Marley, 116
Marlon, 192
Marr, 211
Marriot, 77
Marriott, 158
Marrow, 101
Mars, 87
Marshall, 3, 4, 47, 87, 97, 150, 160, 166, 211, 235, 255, 259, 317
Marsteller, 50, 126, 258
Martin, 3, 12, 26, 28, 43, 47, 70, 76, 90, 102, 112, 124, 128, 130, 144, 146, 149, 150, 156, 158, 160, 163, 167, 172, 173, 175, 189, 200, 201, 211, 230, 270, 273, 276, 286, 292, 297, 298, 304
Marvin, 130, 152
Marye, 30
Maryman, 133, 134, 153, 243
Mason, 11, 24, 33, 36, 54, 86, 111, 118, 121, 123, 136, 143, 162, 186, 200, 204, 211, 252, 259, 260, 263, 270, 272, 279, 297, 310, 315
Massen, 236
Massey, 14, 41, 111, 143, 200, 290, 298
Massie, 316
Masterman, 112
Masters, 19, 163, 196, 303
Mastic, 16
Mathers, 63, 81
Mathews, 7, 107
Matlack, 209
Matot, 164
Mattes, 283
Matthews, 21, 27, 39, 52, 60, 76, 80, 85, 92, 103, 116, 157, 158, 168, 179, 197, 199, 200, 201, 228, 229, 277
Matthias, 250
Matticks, 25
Mattingley, 54, 55
Mattingly, 137, 289
Mattocks, 185
Mattox, 10
Maul, 64
Maull, 164
Maund, 4, 127
Mauro, 59, 182
Maury, 28, 89
Maxcey, 283
Maxey, 104
Maxwell, 26, 38, 61, 69, 93, 97, 152, 220, 248, 306, 323

May, 45, 119, 152, 173, 221, 232, 251, 310
Mayburry, 186
Mayhen, 194, 220
Mayhew, 303, 307
Maylan, 28
Maynadier, 86, 271
Maynard, 179, 244
Mayo, 24, 47, 97, 307
Mays, 307
Mc Afee, 33
Mc Clain, 51
Mc Cormick, 80
Mc Elduff, 16
Mc Ray, 20
Mc'Coy, 32
McAlister, 44
McArthur, 139, 156, 189, 245
McBee, 234
McBride, 70, 158
McCalister, 190
McCall, 84, 149, 163, 225
McCalla, 20
McCalley, 97
McCallister, 112
McCallough, 205
McCallum, 170
McCally, 228
McCartey, 228
McCarty, 44, 49, 78, 86, 88, 149, 175, 228, 232
McCarty's Island & Sugar Land Tract, 78
McCaskett, 63
McCatchon, 112
McCauley, 12, 226
McCaulley, 125, 159
McClain, 161
McClary, 22, 51, 71, 148
McClelland, 8, 113, 140
McClenachan, 205
McCleney, 106
McCloud, 83
McCluny, 151
McClure, 58, 240
McCobb, 135
McComb, 66, 104, 226

McConnell, 101
McCormick, 24, 27, 41, 60, 64, 66, 75, 81, 87, 100, 110, 127, 128, 136, 142, 156, 158, 160, 161, 170, 173, 178, 220, 221, 224, 268, 273, 274
McCoy, 32, 157, 161, 224
McCracken, 224
McCraw, 37
Mccreary, 234
McCreery, 68
McCue, 245
McCulloch, 72, 84, 144, 159, 190, 198
McCulloh, 144
McCutchen, 179
McDade, 215
McDaniel, 10, 123, 140
McDonald, 27, 35, 65, 95, 108, 144, 148, 150, 161, 172, 182, 191, 202, 232, 234
McDonough, 151, 183, 196
McDougal, 151
McDougall, 167
McDowell, 89, 144, 150, 158, 162, 202
McElderry, 273
McElroy, 151
McElwee, 48, 116, 216
McEvoy, 242
McEwen, 102, 151
McFadden, 170
McFadon, 117
McFarland, 146
McFarlane, 175
McFarlin, 151
McFeaden, 170
McFeeley, 241
McFeely, 151
McGahey, 235
McGaughay, 283
Mcgavock, 149
McGee, 88, 140, 151, 253
McGill, 192, 213
McGinley, 37
McGlassin, 151
McGlue, 228

McGowan, 75, 85, 105, 153, 177, 188, 248
McGrath, 36, 211
McGuigan, 201
McGuire, 22, 44, 82, 110, 160, 170, 212
McHenry, 168
McHolland, 57
McIlhenny, 120
McIllvaine, 180
McIllvein, 176
McIlvain, 150
McIntire, 170
McIntosh, 36, 169
McIntyre, 130, 230
McIvin, 126
McKay, 157
McKay's Bottom, 157
McKee, 65, 70, 126, 180, 185, 193, 201, 221
McKenney, 4, 19, 124, 183
McKenny, 264
McKenzie, 128, 259
McKeon, 145, 160, 241
McKim, 61, 70, 126, 212
McKin, 97, 231
McKinley, 114, 191, 217
McKinney, 146, 233
McKinnon, 207
McKnight, 34
McKoy, 70
McLane, 58, 140
McLaughlin, 52, 149, 151
McLean, 126, 156, 245
McLeed, 154
McLeod, 62, 110, 161, 212
McMahan, 90, 95
McMahon, 229
McMechen, 192
McMechin, 231
McMillan, 152
McMullen, 144, 158
McMurray, 257
McNair, 22
McNamara, 191
McNantz, 32, 126, 173, 187, 268

McNeal, 148
McNeale, 125
McNeall, 21
McNeil, 112
McNeill, 141
McNemar, 198
McPherson, 114, 168
McQuakin, 204
McQueen, 22, 43, 63, 74, 147, 158
Mcrae, 225
McWhorter, 112
McWilliams, 55, 66, 107
Mead, 17, 122, 123, 179
Meade, 36, 44, 46, 113, 148, 152, 220, 269
Means, 171, 248, 288
Mears, 16, 300
Meason, 265
Meather, 191
Mebane, 147, 234, 236
Mechlin, 49, 50, 285, 295, 296
Medford, 280
Medley, 286
Mee, 191
Meek, 113, 145
Meeks, 156
Meem, 316, 321
Meggs, 298, 317
Megrue, 58
Mehlin, 178
Meigs, 57, 60, 135, 139, 179, 197, 264
Melhado, 266
Mellan, 5
Mellon, 166
Meloy, 87
Melville, 51, 309
Melvin, 17, 118, 123, 229, 261
Melwood, 87
Mentges, 167
Mention, 2
Mercer, 87, 200, 218
Mercer's Bottom, 97
Merchant, 150
Meredith, 121
Merewether, 133
Meriam, 80
Meriweather, 146

Merky, 211
Meroney, 52
Merrian, 43
Merrikin, 13
Merrill, 12, 81, 257, 276
Merry, 151
Merryfield, 299
Merryman, 4, 127, 133, 134
Merryweather, 204
Merson, 200
Messenger, 20, 213
Messenget, 4
Messing, 152
Mestill, 71
Metcalf, 87, 130
Metcalfe, 69
Metinger, 152
Metoalf, 290
Mewbern, 194, 204, 303
Michael, 307
Michaels, 227, 264
Michell, 216
Michler, 123, 220
Middart, 215, 250
Middle Ground, 55
Middlebrook Mills & Estate, 324
Middleton, 77, 107, 144, 245, 287, 294
Middlton, 138
Midgley, 217
Miekle, 147
Miles, 2, 276
Mill, 10, 18, 71
Mill & Mill seat, 55
Millard, 55, 85
Millckin, 4
Milledge, 92, 161
Milleman, 144
Miller, 5, 16, 18, 23, 43, 52, 71, 90, 92, 103, 113, 125, 130, 141, 147, 152, 155, 172, 173, 183, 186, 190, 191, 192, 197, 199, 207, 208, 211, 238, 248, 252, 302, 310, 322
Millet, 52

Milligan, 23, 71, 121, 131, 152, 161, 260, 292
Millikin, 151
Millington, 191
Mills, 10, 67, 74, 77, 92, 115, 142, 149, 150, 206, 234, 289, 290, 305
Mills Marsh, 54
Milner, 69
Miltenberger, 51
Milton, 18
Milward, 213
Mims, 13
Minchen, 72
Minchin, 65, 73, 80, 129
Miner, 123
Mingo Bottom farm, 108
Minifie, 25, 38, 127, 128, 259, 269, 270, 309
Minnick, 108
Minor, 110, 159, 160, 177, 204, 220, 288
Miscalley, 43
Mistake, 94
Mitchel, 220
Mitchell, 4, 64, 84, 86, 90, 123, 127, 133, 138, 144, 147, 152, 168, 169, 195, 208, 209, 220, 224, 226, 233, 263, 280, 281, 285, 303, 304, 307
Mitchill, 121, 187
Mittwoft, 192, 213
Mix, 155
Mixer, 159
Moffat, 225
Moffatt, 268
Moffett, 298
Moffitt, 313
Molleston, 311
Mollowny, 209
Molton, 147
Molyneaux, 191
Monagan, 21
Moncrieffe, 42
Monroe, 71, 146, 185, 259, 286

Montague, 88, 112
Montegut, 207
Montgomery, 12, 32, 75, 113, 115, 126, 142, 143, 150, 152, 182, 185, 199, 201, 277
Monzey, 142
Mood, 179
Moody, 93, 292
Mooers, 149
Moon, 231, 232
Mooney, 130, 151, 180
Moony, 296
Moore, 3, 8, 14, 15, 18, 25, 30, 37, 39, 46, 49, 56, 62, 70, 72, 103, 112, 115, 123, 126, 130, 140, 146, 148, 151, 152, 158, 168, 174, 180, 182, 193, 196, 220, 238, 266, 267, 268, 277, 282, 287, 288, 293, 297, 298, 299, 302, 303, 307, 321
More, 248
Moreau, 33
Morel, 307
Moreland, 83
Morgan, 1, 57, 65, 69, 93, 110, 114, 124, 126, 135, 136, 145, 148, 152, 168, 217, 224, 240, 255, 266, 267, 300, 309, 317
Morgue, 38
Moriarty, 121
Morin, 40, 75, 80, 182, 226
Morphew, 229
Morrell, 4, 182, 299
Morrill, 165, 276
Morris, 5, 12, 28, 41, 44, 45, 52, 125, 129, 147, 150, 152, 160, 167, 191, 196, 207, 209, 211, 216, 228, 244, 254, 261, 299, 303, 304
Morrison, 135, 159, 267, 292
Morriss, 196

Morrissett, 2
Morrow, 8, 20, 70, 151, 179, 244, 251, 255
Morse, 88, 150, 276, 277, 283
Morsell, 61, 183, 256, 279, 284
Morson, 20
Mortimer, 74
Morton, 119, 193, 256, 259, 281
Moscrop, 38, 216
Moseley, 169, 207
Mosely, 227
Mosher, 29, 121, 172, 310
Mosley, 69
Moss, 50, 59, 97, 108, 126, 218, 250, 279
Mosser, 244
Mott, 130, 179
Moulton, 4, 112
Moultrie, 169
Mountain Prospect, 81
Mountfort, 145
Mountjoy, 152
Mountz, 230, 248
Mouzy, 133
Moxeley, 303
Moxley, 196
Moye, 37
Moyer, 211
Moylan, 32, 167, 204
Mrs Lee, 33
Mt Calvert Manor, 222, 230
Mt Pleasant, 280
Mt Washington, 312
Mt Welby, 141
Mudd, 46, 140, 184
Mudge, 71, 293
Mugg, 54
Muhlenberg, 168
Muhlenburg, 18
Muier, 93, 102
Muir, 19, 94, 109, 135, 164, 183, 206, 313
Mulany, 149
Mull, 85
Mullany, 137, 160, 223, 228
Mullen, 191, 276
Muller, 73, 130

Mullet, 179
Mullikin, 13, 121
Mullin, 292
Mulloney, 40
Mumford, 38, 114, 218, 230, 259, 260, 280
Munday, 179
Mundell, 47, 48
Mundy, 152
Munford, 197
Munro, 4, 125, 177
Munroe, 12, 14, 40, 67, 68, 123, 126, 292, 319
Munson, 103
Muntress, 292
Murdoch, 84, 110, 150, 211
Murdock, 148
Murfee, 169
Murfree, 236
Murfrey, 173
Murnan, 169
Murphey, 240
Murphy, 49, 57, 154, 191
Murray, 112, 123, 124, 168, 179, 182, 185, 196, 220, 235, 239, 244, 254, 260, 263, 304, 307
Murren, 321
Muse, 93, 102, 142, 220, 298
Musson, 209
Muter, 42
Myers, 9, 26, 40, 76, 97, 149, 151, 164, 178, 201, 241, 294

—N—

Naggs, 202
Nagle, 167
Nally, 243, 263, 294
Name unknown, 196
Nargin, 129
Nassert, 208
Nathans, 103
Natt, 183
Naylor, 185, 213
Neal, 34, 251, 253, 316

Neale, 49, 58, 103, 128, 139, 149, 186, 204
Needham, 57
Neeld, 143
Neely, 113
Neil, 238
Neilly, 254
Neilson, 102, 163, 183
Nelle, 58
Nellis, 130
Nelme, 12
Nelson, 30, 54, 60, 70, 77, 97, 114, 148, 150, 169, 182, 186, 193, 217, 228, 232, 260, 268, 272, 282, 290
Nesbitt, 268
Nevill, 145, 168, 274
Nevit, 181
Nevitt, 35, 194, 212, 260, 262, 281, 301, 303
New, 15, 70
New Bermingham Manor, 196
Newbold, 9, 69
Newby, 275
Newell, 58, 166, 175, 206
Newman, 57, 145, 192, 213, 267
Newnan, 238
Newton, 56, 70, 88, 109, 195, 273, 303, 313
Nexsen, 59, 265, 293
Ney, 124
Nicholas, 18, 26, 46, 72, 113, 145, 148, 151
Nicholas' Hunting Qrtr, 196
Nicholl, 114, 204, 304
Nicholls, 9, 52, 93, 245, 260, 277, 294
Nichols, 1, 86, 115, 291
Nicholson, 5, 28, 41, 49, 61, 74, 99, 140, 141, 143, 150, 167, 170, 200, 205, 206, 285

Nickhim in Deerrange & Meadows, 195
Nicklin, 121, 124, 184
Nicola, 167
Nicoll, 66
Nicols, 281
Niel, 144
Niles, 144, 183
Nixon, 166, 235, 294
No Name, 55, 193, 195
Noah, 17, 80
Noble, 223
Noel, 225, 288
Nolan, 115
Nolin, 183
Noon, 240
Norcum, 147
Norman, 37, 159, 192
Norris, 90, 95, 116, 146, 147, 241, 282, 324
North, 7, 52, 125, 168, 204, 283
Northorp, 322
Northrup, 178
Northup, 252
Northway, 319
Norton, 147, 290
Norvell, 64, 90, 152, 315, 316
Norwood, 28
Nourse, 53, 143, 145, 159, 192, 281, 322
Nowland, 12, 255
Noyes, 151
Nungesser, 141
Nutting, 21, 223
Nuttle, 97
Nyce, 142
Nye, 146

—O—

O'Bannon, 117, 171, 315
O'Brian, 165
O'Brien, 170, 208, 228, 299
O'Donel, 239
O'Donnell, 239
O'Hara, 154
O'Hare, 191
O'Neal, 132

O'Neale, 249, 322
O'Neil, 126, 307
O'Neill, 172, 282
O'Reilly, 233
O'Connell, 3
O'Conner, 34, 145, 153
O'Connor, 86, 160
O'Mara, 47
O'Neal, 41, 50, 101, 154
O'Neale, 6, 122, 190, 218
Oakes, 66
Oatts, 21
Ober, 26, 188, 317
Ockington, 122
Odam, 16
Odell, 149
Oden, 13, 35, 200, 203, 204, 220, 311
Odin, 246
Odivine, 244
Odlin, 256
Offutt, 37, 311
Ogden, 32, 37, 96, 126, 130, 145, 160, 167, 208, 227
Ogg, 314
Ogilevie, 231
Ogilvie, 150, 228, 252
Ogle, 32
Oglesby, 65
Oglivie, 160
Okill, 218
Okison, 31
Oliphant, 155
Oliver, 20, 28, 30, 124, 166, 190, 267, 281
Olmstead, 77, 319
Olney, 166
Ongrain, 260
Oofsbournby, 71
Oram, 184
Orange Mills, 44
Orgain, 113
Orm, 305
Orme, 24, 39, 74, 147, 282
Ormes, 102
Ormsby, 70, 185, 206, 284

Orr, 9, 89, 109, 120, 129, 156, 171, 255, 266, 271
Osborn, 17, 88, 133, 157, 220, 222
Osborne, 107, 288
Osgood, 23, 131, 299
Osler, 213
Oswold, 200
Otis, 24, 147, 160, 188, 244
Ott, 48, 51, 56, 116, 140, 174, 182, 198, 221, 233, 259, 266, 271, 272, 279, 286, 290, 320
Otterback, 172
Otwood, 37
Ouder, 78
Ould, 116, 117, 122
Outlet, 195
Overall, 235
Overstocks, 226
Overton, 18, 46, 62, 152, 219
Owen, 77, 87, 90, 314
Owens, 18, 95, 96, 111, 115, 315
Owings, 229
Owner, 91
Oxen Hill Manor, 196
Oxley, 217
Oxmantown & Maiden Bradley, 195

—P—

Padgett, 215, 303
Padgett's Rest, 193
Pagan, 147
Page, 15, 32, 97, 99, 105, 114, 125, 129, 141, 148, 173, 217, 273, 276, 279, 287
Paggett, 194
Paige, 149
Paine, 20, 88, 123, 142, 220
Paint Branch, 196
Painter, 126, 167
Pairo, 19, 117, 121, 171, 252
Paleskie, 200

Palfreyman, 218
Palmer, 36, 127, 147, 230, 283, 290
Pamar, 149
Pane, 129
Parcel, 72
Pardee, 68, 149
Pardoe, 63
Pardy, 12, 22
Park, 92
Parke, 98
Parker, 9, 12, 20, 37, 76, 91, 92, 101, 103, 112, 113, 148, 149, 155, 162, 180, 253, 266, 268, 274, 275, 282, 283, 323
Parkes, 218
Parkham, 22
Parkinson, 204
Parkman, 4, 188
Parks, 93, 204
Parley, 244
Parmale, 245
Parmely, 21
Parnham, 302
Parr, 168
Parrot, 36, 301
Parrott, 85, 87, 97, 216, 218, 233, 238
Parry, 184, 193, 215, 250
Parson, 1
Parsons, 73, 133, 140, 145, 166, 188, 207, 251, 260, 314, 315, 322
Parting Path, 54
Partridge, 17, 243
Pascum, 194
Pasteur, 18, 290, 309
Pate, 21, 206
Paton, 160, 190, 257
Patrick, 186, 299
Patten, 83, 103, 168, 169, 266
Pattersen, 97
Patterson, 28, 64, 67, 80, 99, 107, 144, 165, 173, 175, 178, 190, 212, 248, 262, 285, 309
Pattison, 94, 118, 238

Patton, 16, 108, 111, 183, 204, 307
Paul, 51, 164, 303
Paulding, 209
Paxson, 179
Paxton, 148
Payia, 13
Payne, 102, 148, 188, 207, 251, 309
Payson, 112, 182
Peabody, 123, 205
Peaches Meadows, 197
Peacock, 51
Peake, 323
Pearce, 82, 112, 234
Pearson, 52, 70, 89, 321
Pease, 14, 77, 134, 260, 307, 323
Pechio, 144
Peck, 4, 127, 146, 153, 166, 175
Peckham, 163
Pedersen, 160
Peebles, 147
Peed, 2
Peeling, 58
Pegau, 273
Pegram, 114, 217
Peirce, 251
Pelham, 147, 169
Peltier, 207
Pelton, 159
Peltz, 2, 128, 181, 223, 231, 285
Pelz, 140
Pendergrast, 144, 187
Penington, 306
Penn, 51, 57, 76, 114, 158, 217
Pennington, 306
Pennock, 9
Penrose, 91, 157, 170, 171
Pentland, 87, 151
Pentz, 205
Peoples, 94
Perceval, 164
Perin, 87
Perine, 230
Perkins, 26, 65, 67, 74, 87, 92, 166, 188, 200, 283, 292

356

Perks, 173
Perley, 146
Perrow, 20, 93, 103
Perry, 7, 12, 21, 26, 30, 57, 65, 80, 85, 138, 147, 198, 216, 227, 307, 311, 314, 315
Peru, 61
Peter, 32, 36, 52, 103, 107, 111, 115, 123, 136, 143, 174, 221, 233, 252, 257, 269, 270, 271, 279, 280, 281, 286, 301, 317
Peters, 92, 95, 133, 142, 166, 173, 205, 206, 225, 237, 277, 307
Peterson, 15, 21, 70, 154, 191, 192, 221, 287, 290
Petit, 126
Petterson, 97
Pettet, 91
Pettibone, 6, 30
Pettibones, 266
Pettingal, 44
Pettingell, 166
Pettit, 262
Petty, 183
Pettypool, 149
Peyster, 145
Peyton, 62, 145, 150, 162, 279, 281, 282, 318
Phelan, 57
Phelps, 31, 37, 43, 112, 142, 148, 149, 228, 256, 276, 290
Phenix, 310
Philbrick, 235
Philips, 51, 93, 136, 143, 155, 175
Phillips, 144, 150, 152, 204, 218, 292
Philpot, 72
Phinney, 149
Phoenix, 265, 293, 296
Piatt, 151, 207
Pickens, 70, 147, 159
Pickering, 228, 242
Picket, 58, 99
Pickett, 200, 289

Pickit, 97
Picton, 75, 154
Pierce, 12, 49, 100, 143, 145, 151, 176, 178, 183, 211, 228, 325
Piercey, 185
Pierson, 175, 180, 193
Pifer, 145
Pignald, 27
Pigott, 97
Pike, 46, 149, 225, 281, 285, 317
Pi-Ki, 227
Pile, 98
Piles, 193, 303
Pinckney, 104, 125, 144, 169, 213, 323
Pine, 287
Piney Grove, 196
Pinkney, 44, 47, 53, 68, 91, 92, 99, 170, 171
Piolett, 102, 158
Piper, 69, 93, 232, 234
Piscataway Manor, 194
Pise, 171
Pitkin, 69
Pitman, 12, 185
Pittman, 59, 267
Pitts, 50
Plains of Jerico, 54
Plaisted, 254
Plant, 60
Plate, 114
Plater, 117
Platt, 167, 217
Pleasant Hill, 194
Pleasant Hills, 280
Pleasant Spring Enlarged, 196
Pleasanton, 316, 318
Pleasants, 1, 9, 20, 25, 70, 97, 114, 197, 218, 273
Pleasenton, 287
Pleasonton, 297
Plowden, 35, 86
Pluck, 231
Plum, 187
Plumb Point, 19
Plume, 9
Plumer, 109, 114

Plummer, 21, 72, 84, 149, 236, 308
Plunket, 6, 89, 175
Plymouth, 195
Poe, 157, 175
Pohig, 307
Poindexter, 114, 217, 264
Pole, 33
Polk, 1, 28, 42, 62, 125, 144, 179, 220, 241, 255, 292
Pollard, 43, 70, 91, 97, 148, 200
Pollock, 44, 62, 101, 181, 183, 200, 256
Pollock's Bldgs, 38
Polock, 122
Pomfret Fields, 55
Pomroy, 43
Pond, 69
Ponsenby, 263
Ponsonby, 274
Pool, 42, 52
Poole, 317
Pope, 69, 157, 166, 300
Popen, 304
Popkin, 166
Poplar Hill, 91
Poplar Hills, 194
Porning, 49
Porter, 11, 21, 34, 35, 43, 56, 66, 69, 125, 136, 142, 146, 162, 167, 199, 204, 206, 220, 233, 246, 251, 256, 257, 258, 260, 261, 318, 321, 322
Porto Bello, 60
Posey, 156, 168, 220, 238, 264
Post, 150, 319
Postle, 158, 234
Poston, 52, 158
Pothier, 201
Potter, 12, 53, 69, 130, 173, 260, 276
Pottinger, 150, 206
Potts, 35, 212
Poulson, 169
Powell, 211, 233, 250
Power, 115, 133
Powers, 151, 174, 312

357

Poydras, 67, 124
Prather, 273, 275, 314
Pratt, 5, 6, 10, 37, 90, 145, 147, 192, 200, 229, 277
Pravote, 26
Preble, 205
Prendergast, 29
Prentiss, 15, 49, 292
Presbury, 51, 170
Prestman, 163, 226, 294
Preston, 24, 114, 148, 217
Prevention & Inclosure, 195
Prevote, 80, 269
Price, 5, 19, 38, 40, 42, 43, 53, 92, 111, 144, 152, 166, 231, 286, 301, 306, 320, 322
Priddy, 30
Pride, 320
Priestly, 162
Prigg, 194
Prigges, 303
Prime, 207
Prince, 20, 30, 37, 71, 102, 112, 208, 260
Prince Geo of Brunswick, 101
Pringle, 182, 190
Prinyear, 205
Prioleau, 271
Pritceard, 238
Pritchard, 14, 148, 186
Pritchett, 21
Probasco, 104
Procter, 168
Proctor, 145, 146, 313, 317
Prosser, 113, 163
Prout, 30, 41, 56, 204, 215, 216, 232, 248, 309
Provine, 268
Pryor, 103, 142, 167
Puckett, 307
Pugh, 307
Pullman, 192, 213
Pumphrey, 4, 127
Punchard, 20, 111
Purden, 51

Purdy, 37
Purkins, 220
Purnall, 65
Purnell, 121
Purrel, 310
Pusey, 244
Putman, 301
Putnam, 71, 93, 165, 166, 290
Putney, 146
Pye, 8, 57, 118, 121, 139
Pynnco, 112

—Q—

Quail, 90
Quantril, 105
Quarles, 101, 202
Queen, 1, 2, 8, 23, 24, 25, 27, 30, 33, 37, 42, 48, 49, 55, 57, 66, 67, 73, 75, 78, 80, 81, 84, 87, 90, 91, 98, 101, 103, 119, 128, 153, 156, 161, 164, 170, 172, 174, 177, 178, 180, 181, 187, 190, 191, 212, 217, 226, 251, 252, 265, 270, 271, 289
Queenfield, 105
Quereau, 178, 287
Query, 152
Quicksall, 193
Quigley, 56, 170
Quincy, 69, 222, 228
Quinlan, 4, 127
Quinto, 251
Quinton, 77

—R—

Rabbitt, 318
Raborg, 237
Raboy, 237
Raden, 160
Radford's Chance, 195
Rady, 176
Ragan, 21, 250
Railey, 43
Rain, 244

Rainey, 52, 186
Rakestraw, 67
Ralph, 141, 195, 284, 303
Ramble Hounslow & Strand, 55
Ramsay, 2, 6, 34, 290
Ramsey, 18, 168
Ramsford, 37
Randal, 150
Randall, 36, 37, 63, 299
Randle, 206
Randolph, 70, 87, 90, 93, 114, 136, 144, 148, 149, 217, 218, 228, 231, 271, 273, 307, 312
Rankin, 52, 195, 303
Ranney, 155, 163, 236
Ransom, 43
Raphael, 97
Rapine, 3, 23, 41, 138, 156, 173, 178, 220, 221, 233, 239, 269, 287, 295
Rapp, 236
Ratcliff, 12, 141, 215
Ratcliffe, 95, 320
Rathbon, 67
Rathbone, 158, 219, 231
Rattler, 287
Rauchner, 146
Rawlings, 58, 290
Ray, 130, 234, 242, 254, 306
Raymond, 176
Rayons, 43
Raysdon, 192
Rayseon, 213
Reab, 150, 228, 277
Read, 43, 92, 119, 121, 128, 142, 147, 161, 162, 191, 255, 277, 301
Reading, 167
Ready, 12, 192
Reagan, 15
Reap, 84, 175
Reardon, 191, 244
Reclimair, 215
Recover, 48
Recovery, 48

Reddick, 128
Redding, 152
Reddington, 130
Redfield, 263
Redman, 58, 95, 98, 185
Redmon, 92
Redmond, 98
Rednover, 211
Redout, 78
Reed, 9, 29, 63, 64, 69, 125, 151, 162, 165, 192, 205, 206, 215, 217, 228, 238, 242, 250, 251, 264, 269, 292, 313
Reed's Swamp, 194
Reeder, 20, 54, 55, 215, 250
Reeder's Purch, 54
Rees, 145, 152, 241
Reese, 238
Reeves, 152
Refuse, 195
Regen, 49
Reid, 67, 92, 114, 165, 168, 183, 223, 238, 247, 260
Reilly, 163
Reily, 25, 116, 220, 232
Reinhardt, 234
Reintzel, 126, 183
Reintzell, 75, 91
Reld, 262
Remick, 325
Remington, 112
Renner, 262, 318
Rennie, 51
Rennolds, 217
Rentch, 236
Resurvey, 94
Resurvey on Honesty, 280
Resurvey on Martin's Fancy, 196
Resurvey on Miller's Beginning, 196
Reynaud, 124
Reynolds, 16, 76, 93, 125, 135, 142, 147, 150, 154, 175, 191, 206
Rezin, 99

Rham, 152
Rhea, 66, 70, 167
Rhodes, 55, 86, 109, 147, 173, 213
Rice, 16, 30, 52, 53, 125, 139
Rich, 130, 150, 160
Richards, 16, 20, 42, 43, 44, 63, 75, 81, 144, 145, 146, 182, 233, 303
Richardson, 28, 36, 43, 56, 85, 104, 112, 113, 125, 163, 170, 198, 219, 242, 251, 260, 268, 301, 303
Richmond, 206
Richter, 252
Rickets, 19
Ricketts, 279
Riddeck, 244
Riddge, 126
Riddick, 133, 171
Riddle, 126, 151, 204, 206
Riddlesperger, 77
Rider, 5
Ridge, 194, 195
Ridgeley, 47, 117, 143, 185
Ridgely, 41, 55, 69, 85, 156, 157, 184, 226, 248, 257, 271
Ridgeway, 18, 193
Ridgley, 75, 82, 180, 226
Ridgway, 44, 102, 109, 305
Riding, 323
Ridley, 169
Ridout, 219
Ried, 281
Rigden, 10
Riggen, 297
Riggold, 248
Riggon, 307
Riggs, 6, 7, 41, 75, 77, 205, 273, 282
Rily, 55
Rimmer, 323
Rinch, 92
Rindge, 185, 267

Ringgold, 33, 57, 70, 86, 186, 204, 237, 246, 259, 270, 319
Ripley, 21, 146
Rippey, 152
Ritchey, 236, 247
Ritchie, 114, 144, 183, 197, 218, 225, 306, 320
Rivers, 21, 308
Rix, 52
Roach, 226, 232, 260, 283
Roads, 107
Roane, 18, 70, 114, 145, 147, 217
Robb, 52, 56, 286, 289
Robbins, 21, 264
Robert, 226
Roberts, 12, 15, 63, 69, 84, 85, 88, 146, 158, 160, 183, 192, 201, 207, 213, 232, 234, 236, 239, 277
Robertson, 9, 18, 20, 52, 69, 83, 84, 90, 93, 105, 137, 152, 197, 206, 221, 306
Robeson, 4, 147, 283
Robinson, 7, 21, 30, 31, 37, 66, 69, 90, 91, 142, 144, 149, 158, 160, 165, 168, 197, 205, 207, 215, 251, 272, 276, 301, 305
Robson, 192
Roby, 205
Roch, 105, 245
Roche, 184
Rochester, 92, 261
Rockey Point, 55
Rockhall Mill, 315
Rockwell, 254
Rocky Point Fortified, 316
Rocky-Point, 257
Roddy, 26
Rodger, 40
Rodgers, 34, 43, 63, 68, 72, 146, 192, 198, 223, 229, 236, 250, 315, 322
Rodman, 69

Rodney, 13, 15, 91
Roe, 89, 112, 191
Roger, 193
Rogers, 37, 38, 67, 72, 80, 93, 100, 101, 120, 130, 137, 175, 182, 189, 192, 226, 232, 262, 288, 303
Rogerson, 272
Rolfe, 290
Rolins, 91
Rollette, 201
Romark, 173
Romlinson, 231
Ronan, 17
Ronde, 124
Ronno, 170
Room, 213
Root, 37, 130, 145, 149, 159
Ropes, 146
Rose, 22, 59, 67, 68, 108, 113, 130, 180, 211, 214, 223, 260, 262, 307
Rosecranse, 167
Rosecrantz, 231
Rosegill, 105
Ross, 3, 20, 26, 65, 121, 130, 167, 172, 187, 192, 199, 204, 205, 256, 259, 284, 305
Rossell, 150
Round Bottom Farm, 108
Rounds, 310
Rouse, 130, 159, 162, 214, 260, 276
Roussin, 124
Rowan, 107
Rowe, 200, 268
Rowels, 173
Rowland, 301
Rowles, 65, 84, 129, 158, 230, 249
Rowlett, 97, 324
Roxbury, 168
Roy, 152
Royal, 232
Royster, 43
Royston, 77, 261
Rubeau, 212

Rudd, 196, 303
Rudgate, 202
Rudge, 154
Rueff, 185
Ruffin, 145
Ruggles, 67, 68, 228, 242
Ruhlon, 37
Ruland, 135
Runaways, 193
Runells, 30
Runk, 113
Runyon, 180, 186
Ruquhart, 193
Rush, 50, 86, 100, 187, 198, 266, 275, 300
Russ, 26
Russel, 21, 31, 70, 126, 157, 174, 217, 222, 225, 285
Russell, 37, 51, 52, 66, 67, 112, 114, 138, 144, 158, 168, 176, 204, 229, 289, 292, 299, 314
Rustin, 197, 304
Ruth, 192
Rutherford, 97, 110, 114, 217, 233
Rutledge, 72
Rutter, 151, 204, 264, 311
Ryan, 11, 192, 325
Ryckman, 237
Ryland, 212
Ryther, 277

—S—

Sackett, 162, 234
Sage, 260
Sager, 269
Sago, 191
Sailly, 108, 111
Salisbury, 242
Sallee, 142, 290
Salsbury, 251
Salter, 244
Samington, 42
Sammons, 149, 228, 231
Sampson, 129, 261
Samuel, 244, 302

Samuelsen, 229
Sanborne, 21
Sand, 158, 200
Sanderson, 110, 160
Sandford, 26, 74, 95, 97, 144, 161, 171, 173, 179
Sands, 204
Sanford, 3, 86, 180, 216, 274, 296, 297
Sanger, 223, 247
Sangster, 140
Sansbourg, 194
Sappington, 161
Sargent, 188
Sashworth, 246
Satterwhite, 206, 266, 296
Saulsberry, 298
Saunders, 17, 45, 55, 58, 90, 110, 150, 152, 160, 186, 205, 267, 272, 276
Saver, 204
Sawyer, 12, 49, 63, 70, 148, 299, 309
Sax, 125
Sayle, 211
Sayre, 130
Scannell, 34, 137, 153, 237
Schaeffer, 170
Schaney, 311
Schany, 13
Schee, 244, 283
Scheer, 29
Schell, 88, 277
Schener, 151
Schermerhorn, 160
Schley, 182
Schnebley, 211
Schnebly, 86
Schnroeder, 182
Schoch, 28
Scholfield, 11, 45, 59, 60, 106, 132, 252, 272
Schooly, 158
Schuyler, 149, 162
Scisson, 240
Scoffield, 149
Scolfield, 213
Scot, 160

Scotland, 54, 176
Scott, 9, 10, 29, 33, 36, 55, 59, 87, 108, 109, 118, 129, 135, 145, 146, 149, 150, 151, 154, 156, 160, 164, 165, 168, 169, 170, 184, 185, 186, 188, 190, 191, 193, 211, 213, 224, 225, 228, 234, 251, 252, 257, 264, 266, 269, 282, 290, 296, 298, 303, 315, 317
Scotti, 258
Scull, 95
Seabrook, 197
Seamans, 135
Searcy, 225
Searle, 249
Sears, 130, 188, 307
Seaton, 219
Seaver, 69, 228
Seay, 176
Sechler, 277
Secomb, 93, 111
Second Thought, 196
Seddon, 112, 254
Sedwich, 36
Sedwick, 57
See, 306
Seek, 193
Seering, 234
Segar, 49, 268
Selby, 193, 251, 270, 303
Selby Cliffs, 282
Selden, 32, 38, 145, 249
Seldon, 87
Sellers, 133
Sellman, 65
Semmes, 46, 49, 70, 73, 224, 253, 266, 283
Sengster, 150
Senseney, 244
Senter, 92, 145, 270
Sergeant, 209
Sernamont, 15
Serratt, 110
Serrurier, 23
Sessford, 46
Seth, 133

Sevier, 66, 70, 207, 222
Sewall, 153, 155, 157, 183, 302
Sewell, 233, 271
Sexton, 115, 157
Seybert, 69, 215, 232, 250
Seymour, 290
Shaaff, 211, 303, 305
Shaeff, 273
Shaffer, 72
Shaffner, 8, 24, 62, 76, 104, 169
Shafford, 322
Shanby, 303
Shanes, 282
Shanks, 2, 251, 258
Shanly, 80
Shannon, 135, 145, 299
Shannonhouse, 208
Shanon, 2
Sharer, 152
Sharlock, 26
Sharp, 135, 142, 158, 301
Sharpe, 145, 201
Sharps Island, 306
Shatfield, 292
Shattuck, 91
Shaumburg, 144
Shaver is Shaved, 7
Shaw, 52, 69, 106, 165, 175, 211, 215, 250, 267, 277, 293
Shawaker, 236
Shaylor, 148
Sheafe, 224, 325
Sheard, 217
Sheckles, 320
Shee, 150
Sheely, 126
Sheer, 178
Sheffey, 70, 105
Sheil, 16
Shelby, 185
Sheldon, 31, 130, 148, 166
Shelhamer, 310
Shell, 211
Shelton, 148
Shepard, 309
Shepherd, 94, 239

Sheppard, 25, 67, 125, 138, 166
Shepperd, 144
Sherburne, 166
Shercliff, 55
Sheredine, 298
Sherlock, 190
Sherman, 101, 244
Sherod, 245
Sherrill, 289
Sherrod, 261
Sherwood, 43, 227, 267, 299
Shields, 58, 206, 266
Shindle, 68
Ship, 152
Shipley, 108
Shippard, 63
Shippen, 201
Shippin, 215, 250
Shipwrights Maggot, 81
Shipwrights Wood Yd, 81
Shirley, 193
Shober, 67, 125
Shoemaker, 72, 123, 130, 220
Sholer, 192
Shommo, 149
Shore, 83, 102, 212
Short, 13, 218, 221
Short Hills, 263
Shorter, 25, 173, 220, 245, 248
Showalter, 21
Showell, 268
Shreeve, 74, 167
Shreve, 294
Shrim, 207
Shriver, 2, 162, 267
Shroad, 63
Shroder, 39
Shroeder, 35, 108, 208
Shrub, 51
Shubrick, 206
Shuck, 293
Shumate, 37, 61
Shumway, 22, 56, 62, 266
Shute, 37, 67
Shuter's Hill, 135
Sibley, 163
Sidebotham, 204

Sidney, 310
Sill, 166
Silliman, 168
Silly, 205
Silver, 37
Silver Hills, 195
Simerall, 228
Simimpson, 76
Simkins, 254, 310
Simmes, 98
Simmons, 14, 32, 78, 86, 149, 154, 202, 221
Simms, 119, 187, 208, 263, 276
Simonds, 292
Simons, 18, 83, 111
Simonton, 234
Simpkins, 147, 242, 282
Simpson, 51, 55, 155, 156, 177, 185, 201, 208, 221, 253, 265, 284, 291, 304
Simrall, 202
Sims, 112, 294
Sinclair, 77, 231, 293, 308
Singleton, 5, 44, 67, 103, 125, 208
Sinnott, 115
Siter, 158
Siverly, 58
Skeet, 176
Skiddy, 179
Skilly, 251
Skinner, 58, 142, 158, 205, 215, 223, 303, 307, 308
Skinners, 63
Skipwith, 3
Skyren, 181
Slacum, 45
Slader, 12
Slaght, 90
Slater, 30, 216
Slaughter, 36, 144, 185, 206, 301
Slaymaker, 222
Slidell, 160
Sloan, 226, 301
Slocum, 31
Sloo, 295, 296

Slosson, 160
Slowman, 72
Sluby, 211
Slye, 3
Small, 17, 30, 266, 270
Smalley, 130, 145
Smallwood, 35, 41, 62, 138, 144, 168, 173, 177, 219, 233, 246, 263, 296, 303, 319
Smead, 148
Smether, 246
Smiley, 102, 209
Smilie, 69, 233, 246, 247
Smith, 2, 4, 7, 8, 9, 14, 15, 17, 18, 19, 21, 30, 32, 34, 35, 36, 38, 39, 43, 44, 46, 47, 50, 55, 59, 60, 63, 66, 67, 69, 70, 72, 73, 74, 75, 79, 80, 83, 86, 90, 91, 93, 96, 97, 99, 100, 101, 106, 108, 109, 112, 121, 123, 124, 127, 132, 133, 135, 136, 137, 139, 140, 141, 142, 144, 145, 146, 147, 150, 151, 152, 155, 159, 160, 161, 162, 163, 165, 166, 167, 169, 173, 174, 176, 177, 179, 180, 181, 185, 189, 190, 191, 192, 194, 196, 198, 199, 200, 201, 202, 204, 205, 207, 208, 209, 211, 212, 213, 215, 216, 220, 221, 222, 223, 227, 229, 233, 242, 244, 245, 246, 248, 251, 254, 255, 260, 261, 262, 265, 267, 270, 273, 274, 276, 277, 279, 280, 283, 285, 286, 290, 294, 295, 301, 303, 307, 308, 311, 313, 319, 320, 324
Smith's Discovery, 55
Smithers, 129

Smithwick, 58
Smock, 234, 237
Smoot, 75, 113, 308
Smuthers, 2
Smyth, 13, 144, 171, 172, 213, 231, 240, 241
Snead, 145, 169
Sneethen, 47
Snell, 142
Snelling, 107, 117, 202, 252
Snoddy, 141
Snodgross, 113
Snow, 29, 69, 260
Snowden, 8, 23, 33, 78, 165, 211, 232, 309
Snowden's Manor Engaged, 165
Snowden's Third Addition to his Manor, 165
Snowden's Manor Enlarged, 23
Snowden's Second Additon to his Manor, 23
Snowhill, 28, 54
Snyder, 141, 163, 201, 231
Somers, 58, 191, 260, 276
Somervell, 301
Somervill, 186
Somerville, 188
Somis, 225
Sommerville, 132, 174, 177
Sonnini, 190
Soper, 47, 122, 157, 196, 303
Soper's Rest Enlarged, 196
Sotterley, 117
Southall, 144, 244
Southerland, 130
Southey, 39
Southgate, 97, 191, 211
Soward, 51
Soyars, 182
Spafford, 268

Spalding, 1, 8, 49, 56, 127, 133, 164, 269, 309
Spangler, 254
Spann, 18
Sparks, 31, 150, 296, 300
Sparrow, 20
Speake, 33, 65, 79, 95, 107, 109, 193, 281
Speare, 204
Speed, 103
Speeding, 51
Spence, 238, 247
Spencer, 77, 87, 93, 95, 102, 145, 167, 228, 298
Spengler, 157
Sperry, 9
Speyer, 208
Spier, 91
Spiller, 302
Spillman, 12, 20, 92
Spooner, 27, 212
Spotts, 113
Sprague, 4, 135
Spratley, 103
Sprigg, 1, 86, 104, 105, 107, 182, 193, 196, 200, 201, 208, 233, 258
Spriggs, 300, 303
Spring, 290
Spring Hill, 311
Springer, 244, 277
Sproat, 151
Sprogel, 151
Sproul, 150
Sproull, 240
Sprout, 166
Spry, 192
Spurk, 72
Spurr, 166
Spurrier, 32, 74
Spurrier's Interest, 32
Squire, 111, 246
Sroufe, 159
St Assard & Slingsbey, 81
St C'air, 251
St Clair, 81, 106, 167
St Clare, 243
St Clements Manor, 54

St Colombe, 300
St Geo, 262
St John, 67, 88, 92
St John's, 54
St Johns, 54
St Luke & Eliz, 195
St Medard, 162
St Thos' Manor, 98
St Wms, 55
Stacy, 166
Stade, 234
Stafford, 165, 173
Stagg, 149, 160
Staines, 294
Stake, 151
Staley, 13
Stall, 215, 250
Stallings, 225
Stanard, 159
Standford, 95
Stanfield, 186
Stanford, 70
Stanley, 130, 213, 231
Stanly, 312
Stannard, 150
Stans, 216
Stansbury, 82, 163, 205, 236
Staples, 259
Stark, 58, 148, 165
Starkweather, 130
Starns, 109
Starpley, 307
Starr, 166
Starrett, 158
Staunton, 103, 177
Stedman, 255
Steel, 209
Steele, 26, 84, 151
Steiner, 270
Stelle, 54, 180, 256, 274
Stem, 159
Stempstead, 191
Stenford, 298
Stephen, 7, 84, 158, 205, 236
Stephens, 6, 12, 103, 112, 176, 198, 204, 301, 306
Stephens Good Luck, 54
Stephens Venture, 54

Stephenson, 22, 92, 140, 169, 202, 260, 265
Stepp, 224
Steptoe, 85
Sterling, 21, 30, 279
Sterne, 207
Sterret, 182, 200
Sterrett, 190, 288, 294
Stetson, 71, 99
Stettenius, 310
Stettinius, 60, 78, 79, 140, 187, 297, 299
Steuart, 35, 108, 182, 256, 298
Steuben, 169
Steven, 52
Stevens, 4, 26, 167, 222, 266, 298
Stevenson, 61, 76, 92, 97, 114, 156, 160, 163, 170, 217, 218, 220
Steward, 20, 207, 300
Stewart, 5, 19, 40, 59, 70, 79, 85, 143, 145, 149, 151, 167, 168, 185, 187, 196, 204, 211, 233, 242, 251, 264, 268, 288, 297, 300, 304, 320
Stewert, 74
Stickney, 188
Stiles, 177
Stillwell, 21, 160, 277
Stimas, 287
Stinbergen, 86
Stinson, 157
Stith, 18, 43, 58, 186
Stities, 144
Stocker, 183
Stocking, 193
Stockton, 36
Stockwell, 41, 216
Stoddard, 284
Stoddart, 68, 177, 211, 229
Stoddert, 5, 9, 39, 66, 180, 181, 211, 230, 235, 236, 324
Stoddert's Mill, 77
Stoke, 93
Stoker, 215, 250

Stokes, 5, 20, 31, 36, 88, 112, 145, 236, 239
Stone, 21, 150, 159, 196, 211, 240, 261, 291, 303, 307, 308, 309
Stonestreet, 196
Stoney Harbor, 195
Storey, 21, 98
Storke, 267
Storm, 160
Storrs, 197
Story, 20, 84
Stothart, 43
Stott, 67
Stout, 37, 103, 153, 171, 180
Stoutenburgh, 134
Stovall, 159, 185
Stover, 157
Stow, 96
Stranahan, 224
Strangman, 34
Stratton, 20
Street, 147
Streshly, 153
Stretch, 14, 41, 105, 138, 153, 274, 285
Stricker, 6, 180, 190, 207
Strickland, 110, 132
Strife, 197
Strife & Boston, 195
Stringfield, 133
Strong, 15, 69, 138, 160, 207, 248, 300
Strother, 43, 147, 220, 244
Stuart, 44, 47, 48, 92, 109, 114, 118, 146, 203, 217, 304
Stull, 192, 270, 295
Sturges, 69, 146, 151, 222, 227
Sturgess, 4
Sturgus, 220
Sturtivant, 147
Sugartree Bottom, 45
Sullivan, 63, 69, 103, 121, 150, 188
Summerville, 87
Summey, 147

Sumner, 166, 169, 188, 223, 307
Sumprter, 245
Sumpter, 248
Sunsberry, 303
Suter, 284
Suters, 51
Sutherland, 257, 324
Sutphen, 151
Suttle, 37
Sutton, 23, 57, 124, 163, 185, 215
Swain, 8
Swan, 43, 141, 169, 190
Swann, 29, 66, 89, 194, 279, 303
Swarthy, 201
Swartwout, 240
Swayze, 158
Swearengen, 163
Swearingen, 17, 60, 181
Sweeney, 118, 270
Sweeny, 66, 107, 138, 140, 225, 249, 267, 296, 322
Sweet Air, 107
Sweitzer, 319
Swift, 66, 68, 130, 166, 186, 243
Swingle, 250
Sycebothom, 197
Syclebothom, 196
Sydebothem, 304
Sydebothom, 304
Sykes, 103, 231, 307
Symes, 273
Symmes, 23
Symms, 112
Synnott, 102
Synott, 255

—T—

Tabb, 72
Tabbs, 26, 68, 215, 250, 270
Taber, 130
Taggart, 69, 142, 242
Tait, 69, 140, 233
Take place, 94
Talbert, 24, 111

Talbot, 51, 86, 94, 166, 168, 173, 255, 317
Talburt, 303
Talburtt, 60
Talbut, 49
Talcott, 209
Taliaferro, 30, 81, 143, 146, 159, 239, 249, 273
Tallenet, 196
Talliaferro, 20, 93
Tallmadge, 34, 69, 133, 227
Tallmage, 167
Tallman, 69, 299
Talman, 299
Taney, 65
Tannehill, 28, 123, 220, 233
Tanner, 26, 100
Tanyard & Reed's Meadows, 193
Tan-Yard & Wiglel's Park, 194
Tapp, 16
Tappan, 150, 249
Tapscott, 58
Tarbison, 274
Tarrant, 244
Tasker, 127
Tate, 288
Tattnall, 226
Tayloe, 5, 38, 55, 64, 79, 86, 97, 125, 136, 226, 271, 312, 321
Taylor, 9, 14, 18, 20, 21, 36, 39, 43, 44, 50, 62, 69, 72, 76, 77, 83, 85, 90, 92, 94, 97, 111, 113, 114, 130, 135, 144, 146, 147, 148, 152, 160, 168, 169, 175, 182, 192, 196, 198, 215, 217, 226, 232, 239, 244, 249, 252, 257, 260, 267, 276, 288, 296, 304, 305, 317, 324
Taylor's Course, 194
Taylorton, 193
Teackle, 3
Tebbs, 20

Tecumseh, 314
Teeple, 130
Teisher, 287
Tekell, 127
Tellfair, 228
Temple, 168
Templeman, 44, 101, 211
Ten Eyck, 290
Tenant, 153
Tenley's Chance, 195
Tenny, 26, 318
Terbol, 229
Ternant, 169
Terpin, 2
Terra Excultabalus, 194
Terrel Green, 315
Terrell, 30
Terrell & Bowling Green, 194
Terrill, 276
Terry, 182
Terry Wills, 54
Tervin, 13
Thackston, 169
Tharp, 320
Thatcher, 134, 276
Thatham, 194
Thayer, 166
Thirley, 303
Thom, 24, 88, 247
Thomas, 20, 23, 40, 41, 49, 50, 65, 68, 98, 151, 162, 165, 191, 199, 204, 211, 214, 216, 220, 222, 241, 257, 272, 297, 301, 304, 308
Thompson, 2, 4, 22, 24, 27, 34, 41, 54, 55, 61, 73, 81, 85, 95, 98, 101, 113, 117, 119, 121, 124, 139, 146, 149, 150, 158, 161, 166, 171, 174, 182, 188, 190, 193, 199, 204, 209, 211, 216, 217, 220, 226, 233, 244, 250, 254, 267, 269, 281, 285, 289, 322

Thomson, 24, 123, 185, 227, 238
Thorn, 154, 186, 276, 277
Thorndike, 123, 299
Thornely, 219
Thornton, 7, 32, 79, 115, 143, 206, 233, 267, 271, 275, 282
Thoroughgood, 274
Thorpe, 127
Thos & Sarah, 195
Threlkeld, 32, 36, 86, 143, 174, 211, 233, 286, 310
Throckmorton, 44
Throop, 167
Thrustom, 91
Thruston, 53, 116, 136, 147
Thumlert, 33
Thurston, 30, 64
Thyer, 135
Tibbins, 184
Tier, 83
Tiernan, 35, 108, 144
Tiffany, 261
Tilden, 71
Tilghman, 65, 168, 205, 270
Tillard, 168, 303
Tilley, 173, 196, 304
Tillman, 298
Tilly, 2
Tilton, 7, 175
Timberlake, 125, 206, 255
Timberland, 197
Timms, 74, 184, 273
Tims, 116, 183
Tingey, 24, 86, 125, 129, 190, 238, 240, 253
Tippet, 62, 121, 174, 182, 184, 219, 288
Tippett, 6, 41, 48, 70, 79, 81, 89, 99, 104, 164, 258, 279, 304
Tisdale, 147
Titchle, 54
Titcomb, 165
Titus, 276
Tnfts, 31

Tobey, 146
Todd, 83, 113, 133, 148, 152, 170, 175, 239, 254, 255, 318
Tolbert, 24, 220
Tolburt, 26
Toler, 220
Toley, 30
Tomiton, 175
Tomlin, 305
Tomlinson, 112, 183, 265, 280, 281
Tomlison, 314
Tompkins, 76, 197, 204, 278
Tomplin, 261
Tompton, 215, 250
Tone, 100
Tonn, 127
Tontine, 199, 250
Tooke, 136
Toole, 202
Toomy, 146
Topham, 135
Torborn, 21
Torney, 145
Tortin, 146
Totten, 17, 58, 160, 228, 243
Toulmin, 93, 122
Tower, 299
Towles, 5, 149, 168
Town, 226
Town Creek, 61
Townley, 163
Towns, 290
Townsend, 17, 21, 57, 71, 130, 133, 160, 180
Townshend, 31, 277, 303
Towson, 144, 226
Tracy, 69, 145, 148, 206
Trail, 276
Travers, 34, 95, 140, 158, 243, 258, 285, 316
Trawbridge, 16
Treadwell, 38
Treanor, 292
Treat, 146, 185, 259
Tredway, 205

365

Tremble, 104
Trent, 99
Trescott, 152, 166
Tretcher, 312
Trevor, 267
Trimble, 157
Triplett, 74, 281
Trippe, 1, 146
Tripplett, 249
Trott, 277
Trotter, 38
Trouins, 97
Troup, 70, 228
Trowbridge, 130
Trueman, 194, 303
Trueman's Hills, 194
Trull, 149
Trumania, 54
Trumbull, 68, 166
Trussel, 299
Truxtun, 9
Tubbs, 166, 235
Tuck, 192
Tucker, 25, 37, 123, 182, 253
Tuckerman, 149
Tuckfield, 26, 42, 61, 164, 311
Tudor, 71, 168
Tuel, 28
Tufts, 59
Tunstall, 182
Tupper, 38, 166, 188, 197
Tureau, 13
Turnbull, 304
Turner, 43, 57, 62, 69, 92, 147, 149, 151, 154, 157, 159, 163, 183, 186, 204, 206, 217, 219, 228, 232, 239, 248, 249, 276, 287, 320
Turpin, 145
Turreau, 237
Tuthill, 37
Tutt, 92, 244
Tuttle, 4, 16, 146, 267
Tutwiler, 285
Tweedy, 140
Twigg, 233
Twiggs, 146
Twitten Ham, 54

Two Bros, 316
Twombly, 71
Tyfield, 21
Tyler, 69, 126, 127, 145, 147, 176, 186, 230, 251, 253, 268, 314, 321
Tyler's Discovery, 195

—U—

Ullery, 205
Ulry, 190, 198
Umbults, 215
Umstot, 234
Underhill, 277
Underwood, 80, 115, 178, 192, 220
Unthank, 67
Updegraff, 100
Upham, 84, 148
Upshaw, 73
Urquhart, 15, 124, 207, 303
Usher, 289

—V—

Vail, 113, 147, 261
Valeau, 228
Valentine, 37
Vallean, 151
Valleau, 228
Vallett, 140
Valley Tract, 263
Van Bibber, 4, 127
Van Cortlandt, 6, 69, 230
Van Dalsem, 150
Van Der Poel, 145
Van Deursen, 145
Van Dyke, 18
Van Horn, 10, 106, 120, 172, 205, 259
Van Mannick, 200
Van Ness, 25, 29, 32, 35, 82, 110, 125, 152, 214, 230, 249, 257, 264, 271, 272, 279, 280, 288
Van Neste, 133
Van Orden, 130
Van Ostade, 249, 253

Van Rensselaer, 224, 231
Van Schaick, 167
Van Syckle, 67
Van Vranken, 43
Van Zandt, 75, 129, 318
Vanbibber, 153, 215
Vanbibbers, 39
Vance, 52, 207, 267
Vandenburgh, 290
Vanderburg, 209
Vandercook, 230
Vanderhorf, 179
Vandevender, 201
Vandeventer, 162
Vandyke, 167
Vankirk, 260
Vanranst, 13
Vanusen, 209
Vanvleet, 130
Vanwey, 117
Vanzandt, 75, 105, 272
Vanzant, 64
Varden, 69, 73, 117, 140, 250, 251
Varnum, 10, 14, 69, 92, 134, 137, 140, 177, 197, 277, 280, 316
Varon, 284
Vashon, 148
Vassar, 72
Vasse, 162
Vaughan, 49, 168, 183
Vaughn, 158
Vawter, 300
Veazey, 298
Veazy, 236, 306
Veirs, 249
Veitch, 65, 110, 160
Venable, 43, 97, 99, 259
Verderie, 191
Vergennes, 91
Vermillion, 26, 316
Vernon, 9, 77, 167
Verplank, 61
Vesey, 290
Vest, 93
Vickars, 290
Vickroy, 93, 234
Viddler, 26
Viduler, 295

Viele, 34
Viers, 154, 249
Vietch, 61
Villard, 17, 228
Villfranche, 170
Vincent, 16, 170
Vineyard, 195
Vingen, 192
Vinson, 34
Vint, 1, 59, 129, 184
Vinton, 88, 290
Virgen, 213
Vogdes, 9
Von Kapff, 42
Voorhees, 126
Vose, 146, 166
Voss, 1, 39, 50, 62, 81, 243, 286

—W—

W Berry, 259
Waddell, 12
Waddle, 234
Wade, 18, 37, 97, 196, 230, 303
Wadleigh, 102
Wadsworth, 68, 83, 114, 163, 224, 228, 276
Wage, 147
Wagener, 5
Wager, 150, 323
Wagganian, 298
Waggener, 169
Waggoner, 267
Wagler, 50, 117
Wagner, 182
Waight, 133
Wainwright, 9, 118
Waite, 51, 52, 130
Wakefield, 258
Waldon, 97
Waldren, 230
Waldridge, 167
Wales, 12
Walker, 2, 24, 25, 26, 27, 29, 35, 40, 41, 43, 45, 48, 50, 51, 52, 58, 60, 69, 74, 82, 85, 93, 100, 109, 110, 116, 119, 121, 127, 141, 148, 154, 157, 159, 184, 185, 198, 199, 204, 215, 216, 217, 220, 229, 242, 243, 260, 269, 276, 280, 283, 309, 316
Walkers, 193
Wall, 149, 228, 313
Wallace, 169, 181, 183, 189, 266
Wallack, 263
Waller, 125
Wallis, 99, 269
Walls Refuse, 194
Walls Refuse Enlarged, 194
Waln, 155
Walpole, 15
Walraven, 262
Walsh, 57, 87, 278
Walter, 51, 251
Walters, 267
Walton, 133, 141, 142, 173
Walworth, 234, 264
Wane, 81
Waner, 91
Wannall, 305
Wannel, 140
Wannell, 67
Wanton, 97
Ward, 15, 44, 63, 71, 79, 115, 135, 147, 166, 170, 179, 188, 200, 204, 215, 216, 228, 230, 242, 250, 256, 259, 292, 306, 310
Warden, 32
Wardlow, 260
Ware, 88, 244
Warfied, 291
Warfield, 38, 121, 182
Waring, 35, 118, 132, 150, 181, 199, 211, 250, 259, 300, 315, 324
Waring's Grove, 284
Wark, 144
Warkfield, 257
Warley, 145, 146
Warner, 26, 27, 39, 51, 126, 144, 165, 167, 179, 209, 235, 325
Warnick, 320
Warnock, 90
Warr, 186
Warren, 52, 104, 146, 176, 188, 251, 274, 310
Warrick, 95
Warwick, 310
Washington, 7, 44, 46, 78, 79, 85, 111, 123, 127, 133, 141, 169, 204, 256, 259, 260, 261, 266, 271, 310
Wason, 215
Waterman, 197, 319
Waters, 26, 90, 122, 155, 188, 229, 248, 273, 280, 285, 316, 318, 322
Waterston, 59
Watkins, 6, 11, 124, 132, 147, 255, 260, 261
Watson, 4, 15, 40, 65, 108, 110, 141, 142, 145, 151, 152, 158, 164, 194, 207, 218, 278, 303
Watterson, 13
Watterston, 2, 80, 116
Watterstone, 96
Wattington, 251
Wattles, 149
Watts, 40, 85, 226, 240, 251, 283
Waugh, 1, 62, 94, 134, 215
Way, 40, 49, 65, 75, 125, 138, 140, 156, 269
Wayman, 215
Wayne, 3, 4, 14, 167, 300
Wead, 20
Weakley, 24
Weatherburn, 28, 29
Weaver, 35, 47, 113, 159, 291, 307
Weaver's Delight, 195

Webb, 18, 25, 26, 88, 95, 103, 112, 166, 169, 171, 192, 213
Webe, 139
Webet, 139
Webster, 3, 40, 86, 135, 156, 195, 223, 226, 251, 273, 277, 305, 325
Weday, 149
Wedderburn, 115
Wedgwood, 217
Weedon, 168
Week, 148
Weeks, 133
Weems, 92, 175, 211, 257, 324
Weighman, 216
Weight, 218
Weightman, 23, 34, 66, 94, 117, 125, 156, 271, 287, 294
Weigly, 151
Weir, 185
Weisenfelts, 167
Welch, 97, 126, 212, 287
Weld, 188
Welden, 234
Well Found & Wheatley's Content, 55
Wellborne, 147
Welles, 188
Wellford, 148
Wellington, 147
Wells, 5, 16, 95, 111, 115, 124, 130, 148, 152, 186, 188, 206, 230, 300
Welsh, 18, 74, 77, 232, 242
Weltner, 168
Wemberly, 173
Wendel, 242
Wentworth, 325
Wesiger, 244
Wesson, 166
West, 5, 14, 25, 47, 76, 100, 144, 151, 185, 189, 221, 235, 242, 251, 316, 321

West Qrtr Enlarged, 195
West River farm, 218
Westerfield, 112
Westfall, 223
Westfield, 54
Weston, 63, 64, 92, 132, 145
Westray, 290
Wetherill, 209
Wetmore, 267
Wever, 19, 110, 142
Whaling, 298
Whann, 65, 111, 206, 221, 272, 281, 284, 294, 313
Whartenby, 18
Wharton, 14, 66, 86, 124, 161, 177, 184, 204, 222, 304
What You Please, 195
Whatson, 21
Wheat, 37, 83, 98, 177, 196, 303, 311
Wheation, 115
Wheatley, 12
Wheatly, 109
Wheaton, 29, 65, 69, 100, 101, 193, 228, 237, 242, 265, 292, 319
Wheeler, 9, 77, 109, 133, 179, 201, 216, 244
Wheeler's Hope, 195
Wheelock, 113, 145
Whetcrofft, 200
Whetcroft, 22, 51
Whipple, 84, 95, 115, 123, 269
Whistler, 152, 225, 252
Whitaker, 154
Whitby, 178
Whitcomb, 125, 165, 235
White, 2, 22, 43, 57, 69, 81, 84, 87, 90, 112, 122, 128, 129, 130, 137, 141, 146, 147, 148, 150, 154, 160, 162, 168, 172, 179, 182, 184, 185, 189, 192, 208, 216,
221, 254, 256, 257, 272, 280, 281, 291, 292, 295, 299, 301, 302
White Acre, 55
Whitehead, 151, 273
Whitehill, 20, 123, 220, 222, 223, 232, 274
Whitehouse, 212
Whitelock, 58
Whiteside, 69
Whitesides, 74, 77
Whiting, 18, 113, 125, 149, 166, 261
Whitlock, 97, 99, 150
Whitman, 149
Whitmore, 103, 150
Whitnall, 31
Whitney, 95, 137, 158, 245
Whittaker, 307
Whittemore, 16
Whitten, 67, 164
Whittier, 283
Whittington, 223
Whittlsey, 207
Whodes, 155
Whyte, 261
Wicker, 81
Wicks, 102
Widgery, 69
Widow's Trouble, 195
Wiebert, 169
Wieland, 275
Wier, 92
Wiestling, 52
Wiggen, 290
Wiggin, 218
Wiggins, 102
Wight, 174
Wigton, 193
Wikoff, 124
Wilcocks, 264
Wilcox, 91, 112, 113, 149, 208, 260
Wilde, 146
Wilder, 79
Wilds, 146
Wiley, 15, 19, 36, 86, 123, 143, 166, 221, 265
Wilkes, 37, 312
Wilkins, 14, 176, 205

368

Wilkinson, 15, 27, 65, 66, 68, 110, 115, 132, 152, 173, 185, 213, 225, 232, 262, 290
Willard, 68, 92, 112, 159, 307, 314
Willcoxer, 299
Willett, 167, 172
William, 204
Williams, 2, 3, 15, 17, 26, 31, 33, 36, 41, 42, 43, 44, 56, 65, 66, 68, 70, 73, 77, 78, 86, 87, 88, 92, 93, 100, 102, 106, 110, 111, 123, 124, 134, 135, 144, 145, 148, 150, 157, 164, 168, 170, 176, 191, 205, 206, 209, 212, 219, 224, 225, 232, 234, 236, 238, 243, 244, 245, 247, 249, 253, 256, 260, 271, 273, 275, 277, 281, 285, 296, 298, 299, 301, 307, 308
Williamson, 94, 96, 105, 115, 119, 174, 190
Willingham, 55
Willink, 216
Willis, 17, 24, 58, 146, 148, 150, 166, 289, 298
Willock, 9
Willoughby, 42
Wills, 30
Willson, 32, 321
Wilmer, 172, 204, 205, 317
Wilmore, 282
Wilmot, 264
Wilson, 2, 9, 13, 31, 32, 34, 35, 37, 43, 48, 52, 56, 57, 58, 63, 65, 66, 67, 70, 76, 77, 80, 87, 90, 97, 102, 105, 106, 108, 109, 126, 141, 143, 144, 150, 164, 170, 171, 173, 177, 179, 180, 182, 185, 189, 193, 206, 212, 216, 235, 242, 243, 251, 260, 270, 272, 277, 284, 302, 303, 319
Wilwright, 149
Wimbish, 182
Wimple, 185
Wimsett, 2
Winchester, 121, 125, 134, 144, 182, 213, 224, 258, 262, 264, 276, 292
Winder, 150, 168, 170, 212, 221, 240, 241, 249, 251
Winemiller, 116
Winfree, 197, 301
Wing, 197
Wingart, 281
Wingate, 12, 125
Wingman, 83
Winlock, 92
Winn, 15, 40, 70, 145, 147, 192, 213, 315
Winslow, 112, 166
Winston, 5, 146, 236, 244, 316
Winter, 124, 324
Winters, 118, 135
Wirgman, 121
Wirt, 114, 218, 265
Wise, 151, 152, 206, 306
Wiseman, 273
Wiss, 306
Witherell, 58
Withers, 249
Withington, 218
Witt, 133
Wolcott, 157, 162
Wold, 164
Wolf, 113, 132, 239
Wood, 4, 86, 88, 95, 101, 126, 127, 161, 168, 181, 197, 218, 221, 233, 242, 244, 256, 272, 276, 283, 289, 290, 307, 319
Woodbridge, 31, 81, 92, 167
Woodbury, 12, 154
Woodcock, 92
Woodford, 145, 222, 223, 224
Wooding, 182
Woodruff, 16, 58, 267
Woods, 139, 148, 218
Woodson, 267
Woodward, 63, 186, 266, 282, 309, 325
Woodworth, 130, 176, 230, 242, 282, 283, 299
Woody's, 105
Woodyear, 35, 108, 144, 170
Wool, 149, 228, 231
Woolcott, 90
Woolfolk, 264
Woolford, 168
Woolley, 176
Wooten, 174
Wootten, 116
Wootton, 57, 189
Worcester, 75
Wormeley, 105
Wormley, 105, 216
Worrell, 123, 236
Worthington, 19, 39, 40, 60, 69, 73, 74, 96, 111, 121, 143, 156, 157, 179, 198, 209, 240, 260, 271, 287
Wotton, 126
Wren, 86
Wrens, 307
Wright, 21, 27, 29, 30, 41, 45, 59, 64, 67, 82, 83, 93, 100, 101, 116, 128, 129, 143, 152, 156, 167, 174, 189, 206, 222, 226, 251, 262, 273, 277, 282, 288, 308
Wright's Park, 194
Wyatt, 175
Wyer, 300
Wyeth, 276
Wyllis, 167, 169
Wyndham, 17, 162
Wynkoop, 160
Wynn, 4

Wynn's Chance, 194, 195
Wynn's Middle Lot, 195
Wynne, 148

—Y—

Yancey, 114, 217, 316
Yancy, 223
Yater, 263
Yates, 130, 230
Yeates, 207
Yeaton, 217
Yewell, 243
Yieldingbury, 54
Yoe, 132
York, 293
Yorke, 183
Yost, 220
Youman, 215
Young, 10, 19, 22, 26, 27, 33, 35, 43, 49, 50, 51, 52, 54, 62, 66, 88, 90, 93, 95, 102, 110, 111, 119, 120, 121, 129, 130, 140, 142, 158, 160, 170, 171, 173, 174, 179, 189, 190, 193, 196, 201, 203, 204, 207, 216, 217, 221, 232, 233, 239, 241, 248, 249, 251, 260, 271, 273, 274, 279, 280, 286, 295, 297, 303, 304, 310, 323
Young man's Venture, 54
Youngman, 92
Youngs, 29, 149, 150

—Z—

Zamas, 164
Zantzinger, 151
Zeigler, 77
Zeilin, 139
Zollinger, 186

Other Heritage Books by the author:

National Intelligencer *Newspaper Abstracts, Special Edition: The Civil War Years, 1861-1863*

National Intelligencer *Newspaper Abstracts 1846*
National Intelligencer *Newspaper Abstracts 1845*
National Intelligencer *Newspaper Abstracts 1844*
National Intelligencer *Newspaper Abstracts 1843*
National Intelligencer *Newspaper Abstracts 1842*
National Intelligencer *Newspaper Abstracts 1841*
National Intelligencer *Newspaper Abstracts 1840*
National Intelligencer *Newspaper Abstracts, 1838-1839*
National Intelligencer *Newspaper Abstracts, 1836-1837*
National Intelligencer *Newspaper Abstracts, 1834-1835*
National Intelligencer *Newspaper Abstracts, 1832-1833*
National Intelligencer *Newspaper Abstracts, 1830-1831*
National Intelligencer *Newspaper Abstracts, 1827-1829*
National Intelligencer *Newspaper Abstracts, 1824-1826*
National Intelligencer *Newspaper Abstracts, 1821-1823*
National Intelligencer *Newspaper Abstracts, 1818-1820*
National Intelligencer *Newspaper Abstracts, 1814-1817*
National Intelligencer *Newspaper Abstracts, 1811-1813*
National Intelligencer *Newspaper Abstracts, 1806-1810*
National Intelligencer *Newspaper Abstracts, 1800-1805*

www.ingramcontent.com/pod-product-compliance
Lightning Source LLC
Chambersburg PA
CBHW071951220426
43662CB00009B/1084